Legality and Legitimacy in Global Affairs

Legality and Legitimacy in Global Affairs

Edited by Richard Falk,
Mark Juergensmeyer, and Vesselin Popovski

Oxford University Press, Inc., publishes works that further
Oxford University's objective of excellence
in research, scholarship, and education.

Oxford New York
Auckland Cape Town Dar es Salaam Hong Kong Karachi
Kuala Lumpur Madrid Melbourne Mexico City Nairobi
New Delhi Shanghai Taipei Toronto

With offices in
Argentina Austria Brazil Chile Czech Republic France Greece
Guatemala Hungary Italy Japan Poland Portugal Singapore
South Korea Switzerland Thailand Turkey Ukraine Vietnam

Published by Oxford University Press, Inc.
198 Madison Avenue, New York, New York 10016

www.oup.com

Library of Congress Cataloging-in-Publication Data
Legality and legitimacy in global affairs / edited by Mark Juergensmeyer, Richard Falk, and Vesselin Popovski.
p. cm.
Includes bibliographical references and index.
ISBN 978-0-19-978157-7 (hardback) — ISBN 978-0-19-978158-4 (pbk.) 1. International law. I. Juergensmeyer, Mark.
II. Falk, Richard A. III. Popovski, Vesselin.
KZ3410.L44 2012
341—dc23 2011044667

This volume is sponsored by United Nations University and the Orfalea Center for Global and International Studies,
University of California, Santa Barbara.

1 3 5 7 9 8 6 4 2

Printed in the United States of America
on acid-free paper

CONTENTS

PREFACE

Can international actions be regarded as legitimate even if they are not legal? And are legal actions in the global arena sometimes deemed illegitimate? A multiplicity of transnational forces—from economic practices and environmental policies to sanctions and outright military interventions—interfere in the domestic affairs of states. Some of those intrusions are not legally sanctioned, but still could be tacitly approved by public opinion. Political leaders of countries have been overthrown and others tried for war crimes, sometimes through judicial proceedings that have no official legal precedent or sanction beyond the will of the victor—as in the case of the Nuremberg Military Tribunal that put on public trial the leaders of Hitler's Nazi regime for crimes against humanity, crimes against peace, and war crimes. Can we judge these once legally dubious undertakings to be legitimate? Can they serve as precedents for future legal developments and guiding examples for future actions?

Military intervention is a particularly vexing example of the problem. The army of one state is not supposed to invade another state. Yet cross-border military actions have been frequent in recent decades—on occasions approved by the UN Security Council, as in the case of Libya in 2011 and the Gulf War in 1991. Sometimes, as in the case of Kosovo in 1999, the intervention was not legally sanctioned, but claims were made that the humanitarian purposes, the urgency of the timing, the proportionality of the use of military force, and the end result of averting a humanitarian catastrophe were sufficient to encourage the international community to acquiesce to the legitimacy of the action post facto and even to exhibit approval. In these cases the actions may be regarded as morally and politically *legitimate*, even if they are not formally *legal.* Then there is the case of the US-led invasion in Iraq in 2003, which was regarded by many as blatantly illegal and illegitimate, although it was presented by officials in Washington and London as an action that was justified by its humanitarian purposes and its attempt to preemptively disrupt plans to conduct violence on a horrendous scale through weapons of mass destruction, claims that never gained international consensus.

This book investigates both the general theoretical nature of the relationship between legality and legitimacy and its particular characteristics in specific contexts. It goes beyond the task of simply debating whether certain regimes or intervening acts are legal or legitimate, but also deconstructs these concepts through their interplay in each case. In doing so, it seeks a deeper, more complete appreciation of the dynamic relationship between legality and legitimacy and how the distinction operates in practice, as well as in theory. Indeed, exploring these concepts in specific contexts demonstrates both the wide scope of issues and areas that could be affected, and the extent to which legality-legitimacy tensions pervade a range of substantive concerns. The volume attempts to answer questions about how legality is defined and how legitimacy is constituted and judged; and it explores the links between the concepts with regard to the actions of global powers and international institutions such as the United Nations. The chapters present the authors' interpretations of the relationship between legality and legitimacy, colored and shaped by their disciplinary background and by their specific expertise in various aspects of global politics.

This project is the result of a collaborative effort over several years. Reliance on the distinction between legality and legitimacy first achieved prominence in the report of the Independent International Commission on Kosovo, of which Richard Falk was a member. The idea for doing a project and a volume on the topic came from Vesselin Popovski at the United Nations University (UNU) in Tokyo, who approached the Orfalea Center for Global and International Studies at the University of California, Santa Barbara with a proposal for a joint study on the connection between legality and legitimacy, not only with respect to the use of force, but in a variety of other areas such as environmental protection, arms control, and international criminal justice. The Director of the Orfalea Center, Mark Juergensmeyer, enthusiastically accepted the idea, and Richard Falk agreed to provide the intellectual leadership and serve as project coordinator. A fruitful workshop in Santa Barbara in 2007 brought together a distinguished group of scholars who presented papers, responded to each others' ideas, and later revised their papers into book chapters.

This volume would have been impossible without the efforts of Victor Faessel, program director of the Orfalea Center, who served as the project's managing editor. He coordinated the workshop, corresponded regularly with the authors, and meticulously took control of all aspects of the volume's production from the beginning of the project to its completion. In preparing this manuscript for publication, we also wish to thank the administrative staffs of the Orfalea Center in Santa Barbara and UNU in Tokyo for their helpful support. At UNU, Nicholas Turner has been an extremely effective administrator of the project, and Yoshie Sawada handled perfectly all financial arrangements. At the Orfalea Center, Cori Montgomery has provided valuable administrative support. The editors are also grateful to David McBride and the editorial staff at Oxford University Press for their commitment and advice.

Richard Falk, Mark Juergensmeyer, and Vesselin Popovski

Legality and Legitimacy in Global Affairs

1

Introduction: Legality and Legitimacy

NECESSITIES AND PROBLEMATICS OF EXCEPTIONALISM

Richard Falk

I. Dilemmas of Action and Restraint in Twenty-First-Century World Politics

The policy and conceptual challenges associated with navigating the treacherous divide between freedom and restraint in world politics reflects the particular character of world order and global governance at this historical juncture. Jurisprudentially, the issue posed is related to the appropriate limits of conformity to international law in a variety of substantive circumstances where what is prescribed by law seems inconsistent with perceived urgencies associated with widely shared common interests and values. The concern possesses a distinct relevance to present-day circumstances because the institutional foundations of global governance are quite weak in a number of crucial policy areas where existing international law guidelines do not seem to come sufficiently to grips with the realities of globalization or the sticky political procedures relied upon to authorize effective action beyond strict legal limits that may in any event be rendered inoperative due to the intrusion of geopolitical forces. More concretely, the veto power of the five permanent members of the UN Security Council can be used on a purely discretionary basis to block decisions strongly supported by the great majority of the governments of member countries, by the overwhelming sentiments of world public opinion, and in defiance of the generally agreed ground rules of world order behavior even when these enjoy unquestioned status as norms of international law.[1]

That is, flexibility on an inter-governmental level, among sovereign states, to loosen the constraints of international law by way of either interpretation or evasion, depends on obtaining a relevant authorizing consensus. This consensus can be formally achieved in a number of ways, but most persuasively by the action of appropriate international institutions charged with overseeing a particular issue area of global concern (e.g., peace and security, environment, trade) or with regard to a geographical area (e.g., Europe, Africa). The role of the UN Security Council with respect to both authorizing uses of force, as in the Gulf War of 1991, or calling for or condemning a use of force, as in the Lebanon War of 2006 or the Gaza War of 2008–2009, is illustrative, as is the imposition of collective sanctions through a decision of the UN Security Council. In the chapters that comprise this book we are evaluating the pros and cons of moral/political decisions to undertake contested actions of various sorts that seem contrary to what most observers would regard to be the requirements of international law, and beyond this, of the second-order guidelines that both validate the unlawful acts in the first instance and put principled limits on whatever behavior is undertaken.

The shape of the fundamental dilemma of legality is enmeshed in the procedures and structures of global governance, although it pertains to some degree in every social order. There are always exceptional circumstances that appear morally and politically to call for a suspension or evasion of normal legality. On the one side, a major purpose of international law is to constrain and stabilize the exercise of power to the extent possible on the basis of a more reliable rule of law that gradually supersedes the law of the jungle. At the same time, international law struggles with the challenges of making international law effective and fair in the absence of world *government* and given the weakness, or even nonexistence, of a global *community* resting on shared values. It must meet this challenge in the face of the doctrine of sovereignty that is generally interpreted as limiting the obligations of states to undertakings to which they have given their consent. The realities of geopolitics are such that powerful states often disregard the sovereignty of weaker states and also ignore binding obligations of international law that have been accepted in principle by all states, but are only selectively implemented. The *spontaneous* or self-enforcing authority of law (as distinct from its *enforced* authority) needs to supplement procedures of enforcement and governmental oversight if the powerful as well as the weak are eventually to become law-abiding actors in their international behavior. Instilling worldwide respect for international law via patterns of socialization, inducing self-imposed restraint, is more necessary than ever given the challenges of multilayered globalization and of more dispersed weaponry of mass destruction. In essence, it is important to shift attention from enforcement to compliance. That is, the only feasible basis for extending the domain of *effective* international law is for the political cultures of the leading sovereign states to *internalize* the implementation of its most crucial norms, especially those dealing with national and human security; *external* enforcement procedures of the sort that exist within well-governed domestic societies are not available on a horizontal basis given the distribution of power in the world, coupled with the reluctance of major states to transfer police and peacekeeping capabilities to international institutions.[2] Such enforcement is also rendered more difficult by the persisting vitality of nationalistic claims based on sovereign rights and national security.[3]

Such a prospect of self-enforcement is not likely to materialize in the near future as it requires the elites in large states to grow convinced that their own wellbeing is better safeguarded by reliable horizontal regimes of law than by a continued reliance on discretionary geopolitics that privileges vital national interests over compliance with international legal obligations. To some extent, such attitudes supportive of essentially voluntary adherence to treaty regimes do already exist in such areas as world trade (via the World Trade Organization), diplomatic protocol, and the public order of the oceans (via the Law of the Sea Treaty). Because of this emphasis on the importance of voluntary respect for international law being the expression of enlightened self-interest for even the most powerful of states, it may seem especially imprudent to lend credibility to arguments validating unlawful conduct in exceptional circumstances.

The revival of interest in Carl Schmitt's theories of sovereignty as oriented around the state of exception serves as a signal that even with states possessing strong constitutional traditions, adherence to the rule of law in times of crisis is inherently tenuous. If this is the case for law in its domestic applications, it is even more the case when considering the reliability of international legal guidelines. It is Schmitt's influential view that once exceptions are granted, their tendency is to become the rule, and further that the nature of sovereignty is indistinguishable from the authority and power to create exceptions.[4] That is, since the right of exception inheres in sovereignty there is no prospect of stability for *any* legal regime whenever the political order is severely stressed. There is certainly no obligatory force that inheres in international law (aside from those few areas where incentives to violate are minimal: international postal service, maritime safety signals, diplomatic immunity) given the invocation of sovereign rights as an ever-present reality, which has frequently been relied upon to trump contrary legal claims whenever vital interests are perceived to be at stake.

For instance, advocates of harsh interrogation techniques after 9/11 in the United States pushed aside the constraints of the Geneva Convention and the anti-torture norm as commonly understood.[5] Despite the reassurances from leaders that "torture" was reserved for exceptional circumstances associated with ticking-bomb scenarios and the avoidance of future 9/11 attacks, reliance on torture became widespread in various prisons under American military command. It became routine with respect to persons detained on suspicion of terrorism, the majority of whom turned out to be entirely innocent.[6] This issue of bending the constraints of international law is particularly significant in relation to the United States, the only truly global state actor, and the only country that currently invokes in a self-justifying spirit a tradition of "American exceptionalism" that is treated as conferring an exemption from normal legal obligations.[7] For much of the rest of the world, this kind of overt unwillingness to accept the constraints of international law is seen as disruptive of world order. This perception of disruptiveness reached an extreme during the Bush presidency due to its strident endorsement of unilateralism and its explicit repudiation of the constraints of the United Nations Charter.[8]

There are reasons to view American exceptionalism as being less exceptional than it seems. To an important extent, in the vital settings of peace and security there is a multistate constitutional validation of geopolitical exceptionalism built into the authority of the United Nations. It takes the form of the veto power given to the five permanent members of the Security Council, who were deemed back in 1945 to be the most powerful among existing sovereign states. They were also the countries that prevailed in World War II and claimed the authority to shape the future global constitutional order. As the Cold War's diplomacy confirmed, global governance under UN auspices on most issues of transnational importance was paralyzed by this distribution of authority. The wartime alliance among the victors was superseded by an intense ideological rivalry between geopolitical actors that generated a distinctive global setting that was neither peace, nor war.

There is a contrary realization that in many circumstances where transnational problems of protection or enforcement are concerned, only powerful state actors have the will and capability to uphold global public interests, whether the context is humanitarian protection of vulnerable people, the prevention and eventual elimination of international piracy, as well as the safeguarding of the global commons against behavior harmful to the climate, to ocean quality, and to endangered species. In essence, tolerable levels of global governance depend on global leadership and engagement that may not always be able to find a convincing rationale in international law to vindicate action that seems morally desirable and politically necessary and feasible. The formation of new rules of international law depends heavily on gaining the consent of sovereign states, and this is often a slow and unsatisfactory process as states have differing priorities, capabilities, and circumstances. As a result, international law is not able to keep up with the rapidly changing practical and normative requirements of a viable and equitable world order.

The resulting dilemma can be expressed as one of a rigid insistence that no global undertaking is justifiable if it appears contrary to international law and the opposite claim that global leadership tends to be beholden to a geopolitical logic that often supersedes the guidelines provided by law. The perspective of this volume is to seek an accommodating perspective that acknowledges the importance of enhancing respect for international law by the powerful as well as the weak, but also realizes that given the complexity and fragility of world order, powerful actors cannot be usefully or reliably confined *unconditionally* to a legal straitjacket. It also insists that whenever the straitjacket is loosened in response to moral and functional imperatives, the resulting behavior continues to be constrained by secondary rules.

It is against this background that recourse is made to legitimacy as a potential *principled* source of meta-legal authority by political actors confronting a range of global challenges. The need to invoke legitimacy implies that existing international law is in some relevant sense deficient or nonresponsive to a perceived urgency. Such a deficiency should be corrected if at all possible as it erodes respect for the rule of law generally to acknowledge occasions where it may be both benevolent and practical to engage in unlawful behavior. This may not be possible if the existence of the gap between legality and legitimacy is expressive of a political cleavage between important states or groups of states. Such a political cleavage will also be exhibited by differing ideological and geostrategic interpretations of the meaning of "legitimacy" in a variety of situations where the authority of law is questioned. Such a divergence will lend weight to the impression that the invocation of legitimacy is highly subjective, operating essentially as an excuse to violate relevant rules of international law.

To the extent feasible, it is obviously important to adapt or reform international law to take account of a set of circumstances not adequately addressed by existing legal rules and principles. It is never desirable to have such a gap, but whenever such a gap exists, it is still necessary to have a principled way of justifying noncompliance with the law. Furthermore, the existence of the gap should be tolerated only as a temporary expedient. It is important to close the gap by means of legal reform to the extent possible and as rapidly as possible. If this is not done it undermines respect for international law and fosters an impression of chaos and expediency in world politics. The dynamic interaction of legality and legitimacy will be tested in this volume in a variety of substantive perspectives. The strengths and weaknesses of these interactions will be analyzed both by international law specialists and by those with primarily a social science background. In this sense, the orientation is both seeking a rich interpretative tapestry relating to the global policy agenda and a sophisticated methodological approach that appreciates the differing analytic styles of lawyers and social scientists.

One objective of the legality/legitimacy approach as opposed to reliance on the right of exception or some sort of analogy to civil disobedience is to avoid the law/no law contrast. If the alternative to respect for international law is to undertake "legitimate" action, then the resulting behavior is not situated in a no law domain, but in a setting where a secondary regime of rules is available and obligatory. In other words, the violation of an underlying norm of international law carries with it the responsibility to adhere to a framework of secondary norms.[9] If it involves recourse to force, for instance, the claim of legitimacy will only be upheld if the mission complies with international humanitarian law and post-conflict policies respectful of international human rights standards. That is, legality/legitimacy introduces flexibility in requirements of adherence to first-order legal constraints, but reintroduces the relevance of international law by recourse to second-order legal constraints. In the end, assuming that the basis for the initial recourse to legitimacy is convincing, the overall evaluation of legitimacy is a matter of degree associated with the extent of compliance with second-order legality, but also with an assessment of conformity with the justifying moral imperative that prompted action in the first place, and validation of the political rationale based on feasible costs relative to the goals achieved.

For instance, the 2003 Iraq invasion was oversold in the United States as "a cakewalk" to win public support for the undertaking via minimizing anticipated costs relative to the purported goals of dismantling Iraq's program relating to weapons of mass destruction and of replacing a brutal tyrant with a constitutional governing process. The shortcomings of political foresight in human affairs, together with the temptation to manipulate facts and justifications to provide a rationale for "'unlawful" action, tends to arouse suspicions about the wisdom of vindicating reliance on legitimacy as a means to circumvent the authority of law. Yet, is there an alternative given the inability of legal guidelines to both constrain and authorize in a manner that is sensitive to the range of future contingencies?

The dynamic of mobilizing support to rescue a vulnerable people or to overcome a dangerous threat to the global commons (ocean garbage dumping, piracy) is, first of all, a question of geopolitics or political will. The peoples of Darfur and occupied Palestine, especially Gaza, have discovered that the most vital precondition for securing protection is not the form of words used to describe the undertaking nearly so much as the presence and depth of political will on the part of those with the capabilities and resolve to take effective action. Intervention is particularly tricky as a terrain for policy and analysis, being overwhelmingly influenced by contextual factors and by a serious and growing reluctance of leading political actors to expend resources or risk the lives of their citizens unless *immediate strategic*, as well as humanitarian and long-range sustainability, concerns are perceived to be at stake.

The objective conditions in Darfur and Gaza would seem to make these ideal cases for protective action under UN auspices, but in the case of Darfur there is an insufficiently strong political will to support the costs and risks of mounting an effective protective mission, while in Gaza the geopolitical alignment of Israel with the United States effectively precludes protection for the Gazan population despite their widely documented desperate humanitarian plight. The frustrations associated with these disclosures of inconsistency (Why Kosovo? Why not Darfur, Gaza?), makes serious inquiry seem especially needed to gain an understanding of both the interconnectedness of political realities in the face of growing globalization and the unmet challenges associated with global governance in the early twenty-first century. In effect, the inquiry is into the role and limits of international law, and the usefulness of a second tier of normative guidelines that purport to give juridical shape to *principled* legitimacy.

It would also seem useful to assess the viability and utility of this two-tier normative framework in substantive settings other than those involving the use of force. It may be that a focus on the legality/legitimacy distinction in the context of contested uses of force offers a misleading understanding of a wider set of concerns about identifying and selectively overriding the limits of international law in the face of change and controversy. It has often been observed, most prominently by Hersh Lauterpacht, that the law governing the use of force is the worst criterion by which to judge the overall effectiveness and authority of international law, as it most directly contradicts and challenges the primacy of the sovereignty of states in relation to security and survival concerns. In this respect, there may be more productive roles for both first-order legality and second-order normativity (that is, legitimacy) in substantive areas other than the use of force. Such issue areas tend to be far more removed from the ravaging fires of geopolitics and the ultimate prerogatives of sovereign states, and hence more amenable to rule-governed approaches. After all, states have generally recognized their reciprocal interests in stability and even in fairness in the distribution of burdens, and at the same time sovereign states, due to their attachment to autonomy and their heavy bureaucracies, always have difficulty adapting international law to changing conditions. In this regard, it makes sense to consider invoking legitimacy as a residual reordering device to compensate for the absence of an available legislative initiative, thereby getting rid of anachronistic norms and enacting more satisfactory legal guidelines without waiting for cumbersome formal lawmaking procedures to provide an adjustment. Yet here too there are problems—the very availability of such second-tier guidelines of legitimacy for international behavior and policy can cause confusion about the nature of law, as well as weaken respect for first-tier guidelines of legality.

It is our editorial purpose to consider these issues in various substantive contexts, and by so doing to clarify both the constructive roles of the legality/legitimacy distinction, and the complications of either unconditionally affirming its utility or concluding that, on balance, the validating of action by reference to its character as "unlawful" yet "legitimate" is an unacceptable weakening of the authority of international law, and may in practice turn out to be one more geopolitically controlled instrument of primary benefit to the strong. As editors, we do not prejudge the outcome of this debate, but seek to enable the conflicting perspectives and assessments to be better understood.

II. Justifying Humanitarian Intervention in Kosovo

The purpose of this section is to argue more explicitly in favor of a legality/legitimacy discourse that is attuned to the deficiencies of "legality" as an unconditional source of authoritative guidance for the international behavior of governments representing sovereign states. The initial impetus is to explore circumstances in which compliance with international law might produce sufficiently adverse results as to create moral and political pressures to consider the option of breaking the law.[10] For reasons of conceptual clarity, the analysis is rooted in the debate about the Kosovo War of 1999, which was also the birthplace of reliance on the legality/legitimacy distinction and a clear encounter with opposed policy considerations. Other authors in this volume were encouraged to proceed on parallel lines so as to assess the Kosovo experience from various angles of perception. Reliance on a legality/legitimacy discourse turned out to be an effective way of finding a consensus on the Independent International Commission on Kosovo and is discussed in its report with respect to evaluating the core issue of the status of the legally controversial NATO military action taken in Kosovo in 1999.[11] Because of this background, there is a natural tendency to anchor discussions of the legality/legitimacy discourse in relation to the debate on Kosovo, and this is exhibited in the chapters that follow by what may seem to be a repetitive emphasis on Kosovo. But this seems excusable, and even useful, because it should help readers identify agreements and disagreements more clearly. At the same time, the editors recognize that the use of force in Kosovo-type situations raises a range of specific issues that are not necessarily present in other issue areas of global policy, and therefore we invited contributions on a range of additional problems where concerns about the limits of adherence to existing international law might arise. This broadening of the substantive scope of inquiry allows consideration of whether the legality/legitimacy distinction has utility beyond settings involving controversial uses of international force, as well as suggesting to what extent the distinction varies in its application depending on substantive context.

The paradigmatic example of Kosovo does address directly the general issue that strict canons of respect for international law are arguably inappropriate behavioral guidelines in some circumstances where strong moral factors seem to require unlawful action and political conditions exist that make such action likely to achieve goals by acceptable means and costs. This Kosovo debate that both preceded and followed the NATO War raises these issues in a generic form that seemed to pose the challenge of acting beyond the law in stark and urgent terms, but not in such an unambiguous manner as to satisfy those skeptical of NATO/US motivations and recourse to a war option or those critical of the means by which the military option was exercised and the subsequent occupation carried out.[12]

It is usually the case that the reform possibilities in these legality/legitimacy situations can be best addressed indirectly. For instance, the NATO War on Kosovo in 1999 provoked controversy that revealed two sets of tensions: a *political* divide between friends and enemies, on one side, the antagonists in Kosovo, Western Europe, and North America supporting the Kosovars while on the other side, Russia supporting Serbia. One aspect of this standoff meant that an authorization for the use of force could not be obtained in the UN Security Council due to the expectation of a Russian veto. In light of this situation, the United States and its NATO partners decided that it was preferable to intervene without seeking authorization from the Security Council because otherwise the alternatives were to forego efforts to protect the Kosovar population from threatened ethnic cleansing or intervening in manifest defiance of the UN Charter as force is there prohibited except in self-defense unless mandated by the Security Council. In light of this precedent, which provoked controversy at the time and after the event, a heated and unresolved policy debate ensued about the conditions suitable for humanitarian intervention.

A direct approach advocated by some would have been to establish informally or formally an agreement that the veto would not be used by the permanent members of the Security Council in contexts where humanitarian intervention was being proposed. An indirect approach, which turned out to be superficially more successful within diplomatic venues sensitive to the Pandora Box implications of endorsing "intervention," "involved circumventing part of the controversy by recasting the language of authorization. The language shift was to implement a "responsibility to protect" rather than undertake a "humanitarian intervention."[13] This approach seemed more acceptable to member states concerned about their sovereign rights, worried about weakening the nonintervention and prohibition of force norms, and seeking not to open the door to possible geopolitical abuse. Subsequent experience in concrete circumstances raises doubts as to whether this adjustment of language facilitates, and whether it should facilitate, UN authorization for uses of force to protect vulnerable peoples facing an imminent humanitarian catastrophe. As suggested, the exemplary failures to respond effectively to either Darfur or Gaza reinforces the impression that it is less the language of authorization that matters than the presence or absence of political will and the dictates of geopolitical logic. Of course, the related issue is whether it is desirable to exert pressure on the Security Council to erode the strict prohibitions on the use of force that animate an understanding of the charter as dedicated to achieving war prevention above all other goals.[14]

In Kosovo, there were present a combination of humanitarian and geopolitical circumstances and conditions that controversially prompted pressures to engage in protective action (and weaken the post-Bosnia stigma of inaction), opting for humanitarian intervention as it was then understood. International law, by most interpretations, would have disallowed outside military action in Kosovo to avert renewed ethnic cleansing associated with unresolved conflicts arising from the breakup of former Yugoslavia. When a military intervention did occur under NATO auspices in 1999, it presented a bewildering tension between the seeming prevention of a humanitarian catastrophe befalling the vulnerable Albanian Kosovar population and the international law norm prohibiting the use of force for purposes other than for self-defense unless authorized by the UN Security Council In effect, the claimed moral imperative justifying this particular intervention seemed to be achieved at the world order costs of having the most powerful country in the world leading a dominant strategic alliance with a European regional writ in violating the most fundamental rule of international law governing the international use of force.[15] Arguably, the Kosovo precedent made it easier for the United States (and its far thinner new "coalition of the willing") in 2003 to embark on an invasion of Iraq despite the absence of any credible claim of self-defense and in view of the refusal of the UN Security Council to provide authorization despite strenuous diplomatic maneuvering by the United States. The combined impact of the Kosovo and Iraq precedents seem to have eroded respect for the authority of international law and the UN Charter, at least for the time being.[16] These apparent negative effects are conjectural, almost impossible to assess, but disturbing nonetheless because of their seeming plausibility.

From a conceptual and policy standpoint, it seemed essential to find some way to overcome and understand this tension in a principled manner. As will be explained below, the idea of "legitimacy," although problematic in certain respects and contexts precisely because it diluted and adapted but did not eliminate the authority of law, seemed useful, if not necessary, to convey the sort of convergence of moral imperatives and political feasibility that seemed to vindicate a disregard of constraining rules of international law under emergency conditions. Exploring the proper relationship between legality and legitimacy is the concern of this inquiry. The Kosovo setting is a useful context for this exploration, but an inquiry to be most broadly valuable should not be confined even to the rather broad category of peace and security issues. What seems useful and desirable in one substantive or historical setting may turn out to be dysfunctional and harmful in another. In this respect, the comparison of Kosovo (1999) with Iraq (2003) is instructive. This Kosovo case for intervention was so persuasive in view of Serbia's repeated reliance on severe forms of ethnic cleansing in Bosnia a few years earlier, culminating in the genocidal massacre of as many as seven thousand Bosnian Muslim males in 1995 at Srebrenica. The choice in Kosovo a few years later thus seemed to involve passivity in the face of another phase of ethnic cleansing or stepping in to rescue the Kosovar Albanian population before the killing and coerced ethnic expulsions began, and thus proceeding without a legal mandate. The military operation commenced with the expectation that the desired results could be achieved within a few days of bombing from high altitudes, but Serbian resistance turned out to be more robust than anticipated, and the war was only brought to an end after eighty-two days of bombing that resulted in escalating attacks on civilian targets in Belgrade.

Even within this structure of assessment, there are several interpretative problems associated with disregard of the relevant rules of international law. The first of these concerns the construction of the facts. Some critics of the NATO intervention questioned the imminence of ethnic cleansing, others contended that the American-led military approach failed to pursue a diplomatic solution in good faith, and still others argued that anti-Serb armed resistance forces, known as Kosovo Liberation Army (KLA), deliberately created incidents that would produce a violent Serb response in Kosovo, with the objective of provoking intervention by foreign forces. These issues are more concerned with the *empirical* conditions that existed in Kosovo than with the *conceptual* focus emphasized here, but the two perspectives cannot be totally separated from one another as there will always be skepticism about the facts by those who view with disfavor the disregard of international law. Further, as the global system lacks authoritative means to resolve disputes about facts and intentions, there is an understandable anxiety that only dominant states will be in a position to take advantage of this slippery legitimacy option.

The second line of concern about evading legal duties relates to world order, contending that in a world of sovereign states, what may seem "legitimate" in one setting will serve as a precedent to justify illegal behavior in a quite different setting where the net effects are clearly dangerous and detrimental. It was, for instance, argued before the Iraq war that NATO's successful role in Kosovo without any prior UN mandate lent weight to the claim of the Bush presidency that an attack upon Iraq was legitimate even though it could neither be claimed to be undertaken in self-defense nor on the basis of Security Council authorization. In other words, diluting legal authority, even if it is persuasive in one set of circumstances, helps open the way to more dubious actions allegedly undertaken to achieve morally desirable results, but actually motivated by geostrategic ambition. In Iraq, these results were supposed to be the coupling of the removal of a brutal, dictatorial, and dangerous regime led by Saddam Hussein, and its replacement by a constitutional democracy that upheld the human rights of the Iraqi people. The fact that in each instance it was the United States, the dominant geopolitical actor in the current global setting, that led the effort to circumvent international law added to doubts about the net benefits of the Kosovo operation even if the majority historical judgment is accepted that it did almost certainly prevent a humanitarian catastrophe from befalling the Kosovars. Was this reliance on legitimacy to trump legality providing yet another instrument for the *geopolitical* subordination of international law in world politics? It is difficult to imagine any state that did not at least have the status of a regional hegemon daring to have recourse to unlawful force for the sake of achieving a legitimacy outcome.

Perhaps, also, this seeming difficulty with the Kosovo War as a precedent was less due to the primacy of geopolitics than to the extremism of the neoconservative approach to American foreign policy that gained ascendancy after the 9/11 attacks. In other words, without 9/11 and the neoconservative orientation, American political leadership would not likely have tarnished the Kosovo precedent by invading Iraq where no imminent humanitarian catastrophe existed. Instead, this precedent might have had a positive and necessary effect, encouraging more robust international action to prevent mass political killing in such places as Darfur and the Congo, and severe patterns of human rights abuse in Myanmar and Gaza.

Part of the evaluative complexity results from the convergence of strategic and humanitarian interests on the part of the principal intervening actors, as well as suspicions generated by the unavoidable subjectivity associated with assessing intentions as well as facts. For instance, Noam Chomsky grounds his sharp criticisms of Washington's supposed humanitarian concerns in Kosovo by highlighting the contradictions embedded in American foreign policy. Why, for instance, Chomsky asks, was the Kosovo response not matched by some comparable response to the oppressive approach adopted by the Turkish government toward its Kurdish minority? Chomsky insists that double standards in so-called humanitarian diplomacy discredits the Kosovo response.[17] There is no doubt that such double standards exist to taint the interventionary claim, but do such inconsistencies at the level of policy resolve the argument?

This presence of strategic interests could be seen in a more positive light as creating the motivation for engaging in an *effective* undertaking, unlike in Somalia (1993) or Rwanda (1994) where no significant strategic interests existed, and it proved to be politically impossible to mount effective protective action even under circumstances of a severe, imminent humanitarian catastrophe. The criticism of the Iraq war from these perspectives should not be primarily directed at the strategic motivations of the United States, but at the absence of an appropriate humanitarian rationale requiring a condition of imminent threat, as well as the absence in Iraq of political conditions enabling an effective military operation at feasible human and economic costs for both the intervening actor and the target society. Under the circumstances existing in Iraq before the invasion, an argument based on legitimacy should fail, and compliance with international law should prevail.

The main purpose of this chapter, and the overall project, is not limited to this core assessment of legality and legitimacy in the current world setting with respect to the use of force, although this may be the most critical subject-matter and the one that gave rise to this controversial jurisprudential move to trump legality by a reliance on legitimacy. The broader question is to think about the relations of legality and legitimacy in a variety of other substantive settings. Does legitimacy introduce a useful enrichment of the traditional discourse on authority in the global setting and world order provided by international law and international ethics? How should considerations of legitimacy impact upon debates about global policy in other substantive settings where there exists dissatisfaction with legality as an unconditional source of guidance for the behavior of governments and other actors? Does legitimacy introduce a necessary evaluative perspective that is respectful of legal claims to control behavior, yet also mindful of the limits of law in relation to concrete claims of justice, human dignity, global security, and environmental sustainability? It seems important to underscore the point, so often neglected, that recourse to a legitimacy rationale for contested action is not an abandonment of legal guidance, but a more subtle shift from a first-order legal framework to a second-order framework.

Because of the absence of legislative agency, international legality is particularly subject to modification and manipulation by the practice of powerful states.[18] Some commentators on international law, for instance, give persistent patterns of practice overriding priority in relation to prior legal expectations, thereby effectively blurring the distinction between violations and interpretations, treating "law" as a process of authoritative decision rather than a framework of rules.[19] The corrective of legitimacy has the potential to provide less power-driven criteria for changes in the obligatory character of legal rules, and greater control over the bending of existing legal norms to adapt to changing circumstances.

Within the scope of this restricted conception of legality and legitimacy, it seems obvious that legality is more directly situated in the domain of state action, subject to political and geopolitical forms of (de)construction, whereas legitimacy is more properly associated with the domain of civil society broadly conceived to include public morality and is more commonly influenced by patterns of social (de)construction. Such a contrast should not be exaggerated as there is a considerable societal impingement on legality, as well as on political, and especially geopolitical, impingement on the construction of arguments as to legitimacy in specific contexts. "Political" is used in world order settings to refer primarily to state action but also the essentially intergovernmental directives of the United Nations, while "geopolitical" calls attention to the role of contextually dominant states, and "social" encompasses the entirety of societal forces, including religious, labor, corporate, citizen activists and their organizations. The spread of democracy, and its validation as the only fully "legitimate" type of governance at the level of the state, gives added weight to the voices of these non-Westphalian actors, as do the limits on the capabilities of state actors to insulate their territorial space from adverse transnational impacts or to act collectively to protect and promote global public goods in addressing such widely shared concerns as terrorism, crime, climate change and pollution, disease, ethnic cleansing, genocide, crimes against humanity, and mass migration.

III. The More General Reliance on Legitimacy in World Politics

In recent writing about world politics, there is a definite upsurge of interest in "legitimacy" from a number of different angles, reflecting a variety of concerns that seem mainly to relate to the problematic and contested roles of soft and hard power under current conditions of world order.[20] Ian Clark interrogates this development by asking "why so much legitimacy talk?" In his words, "There might just as well be talk of international legality or morality, or justice—and to some degree this has been present as well. Nonetheless, the language of legitimacy has been dominant."[21] I think the primary explanation for this focus on "legitimacy" rather than these other related concepts is that legitimacy (and illegitimacy) more naturally encourages attention being given to questions of the *appropriate* authority to act coercively in a range of contested conditions without necessarily accepting or rejecting the primacy and relevance of law as the basis for assessment. In this regard, legitimacy talk exhibits the realist penchant to be liberated from legalism and moralism when evaluating the contested behavior of sovereign states, but in language that is sensitive to political considerations and does not leave morality out of the decision process. It loosens the constraints of legality, while being mindful of process constraints. Legitimacy does weaken the constraints of legality by giving restricted forms of permission to other *principled* ways to justify and regulate controversial policy.

More specifically and historically, legitimacy exhibits the widespread disagreement in international relations that is associated with several overlapping clusters of issues: norms and procedures authorizing recourse to force in the relations among states; the interplay of sovereign states and other actors under conditions of violent conflict and under conditions of unfolding humanitarian and natural disasters that cannot be adequately dealt with by territorial governmental authority; the nature of global leadership and hegemonic geopolitics as an element of world order; and the historical evolution of postwar arrangements designed to constitute "international society" in accordance with specified ordering principles.[22] There is a great deal of attention to the gain and loss of legitimacy on the part of the United States as a result of its response to 9/11, especially in relation to the Iraq war, its torture policies, and its overall discretionary recourse to force in the context of the "global war on terror."[23] One strand of this attention involves a debate among prominent realists as to whether the American loss of legitimacy reflects its disregard of international law or its failure to project its power prudently and effectively.[24] This debate does reflect a disagreement about the relations of legality and legitimacy by seeming to suggest that legitimacy is a matter either of the degree of conformity to international law, making a state actor achieve greater legitimacy by a more consistent compliance practice, or the extent to which the ascendancy of power ensures respect, which is equated with legitimacy. In the use here of legitimacy, the concept is tied to legality and provides a parallel track of authority constraints in the event that moral and political pressures encourage departures from the strictures of legality.

If addressing the broader agenda of global policy choices, the word "legitimate" is used as a modifier to denote "reasonable" and "rational" as in Anne-Marie Slaughter's use of "legitimate difference" as a way of denoting qualified respect for a pluralist world order.[25] In this respect, legitimate difference takes account of divergent views deriving from cultural orientation, form of government, and developmental priorities. This complements Slaughter's main emphasis on patterns of international cooperation based on what she calls the disaggregation of the state, relying on specific sub-bureaucracies to represent the interests of the state, and to handle more efficiently the growing complexity of international life with its manifold expressions of transnationalism.[26]

With a different set of concerns, I have used the phrase "legitimate grievances" as a qualified acknowledgement that political changes should be made to overcome conditions of perceived injustice. A particularly urgent context for such attention involves a response to the perception that the Islamic world has been wronged and wounded by certain aspects of American diplomacy, and that addressing these grievances would appear to be an effective, necessary, and justifiable way to diminish the wider appeal of religious and political extremism emanating from Muslim societies.[27] It should be noted that only "legitimate" grievances warrant this rectifying approach. The failure of the United States to deal fairly and impartially with the Palestinian struggle for self-determination or the future status of the city of Jerusalem are examples of legitimate grievances. In contrast, any demand that the United States abandon its support for the security of Israel would be an "illegitimate grievance," not deserving of action in response. To some extent, but not fully, the borderline between legitimate and illegitimate can be tracked by reference to the rules and principles of international law, making legitimacy serve here the function of reinforcing legality rather than validating limited departures under special circumstances.

There is also a recent related fascination with legitimacy that arises from the work of international law scholars who are preoccupied with explaining the distinctive role and character of law in world politics. The work of Thomas Franck, in particular, has exerted considerable influence by way of his highly conceptual argument that most governments are drawn toward compliance with international law because it enhances their reputation as respected actors on the global stage; from such a perspective, legitimacy partially compensates for the absence of enforcement mechanisms, thus justifying a positive reassessment of the effectiveness of international law as well as making sense of patterns of seemingly voluntary compliance with legal obligations in the absence of enforcement mechanisms.[28] This narrower, more traditional, juridical preoccupation with legitimacy is associated with patterns of denial and attainment of full membership in international society by governmental entities seeking full access to the arenas of global diplomacy as sovereign states.[29] The granting of diplomatic recognition to a government was treated in international law for centuries as a formal bestowal of entitlement to full membership as a state among states, while withholding recognition and refusing to engage in diplomatic relations operated as a denial of such a status, and arguably weakens the applicability of the norm of nonintervention, or more generally, deference to the prerogatives of the territorial sovereign. As international society became more complex, admission to international institutions began functioning as a form of collective legitimation, while denial of access, as well as expulsion or suspension of membership, gives rise to the stigma of illegitimacy, weakening deference to claims of territorial sovereignty. For instance, Afghanistan under Taliban rule in 2001 was diplomatically isolated, undermining its status as a sovereign state and its claim to exercise territorial sovereignty that should be respected by other states and by the United Nations.

Even this sampling should make evident that there exists a bewilderingly diverse, and even contradictory, set of uses of "legitimacy" in contemporary commentary on world order that marks the historical moment as one of contested conceptual and normative boundaries. Against this wider background, this chapter and project looks at a range of substantive and theoretical issues associated with this tension between "legality" and "legitimacy," and mainly sets aside other kinds of concerns about the role and relevance of legitimacy, although individual authors were given freedom to approach the legality/legitimacy divide in their own ways. This focus is quite different from the Franck undertaking to explain that most states generally seek to establish a reputation for legitimacy in the sense of being respected as a responsible international actor, and that this motivation tends to diminish the enforcement deficit that has afflicted jurisprudential and geopolitical thinking about the utility of international law. The interest of this project emphasizes whether international law should always have the last word with respect to identifying *acceptable* behavior by states, and other international actors, or whether additional criteria of acceptability derived from moral and political considerations should be brought to bear in *exceptional* circumstances. Using legitimacy to escape the first-order constraints of legality has costs and is risky, but its virtue is to bring into the open lines of justification for controversial and contested conduct, and not take refuge in cynical accounts of the primacy of power in international relations, or what amounts to the same thing, embrace a posture of legal nihilism. To reinforce a point earlier made, a shift to the legitimacy framework only frees a political actor from first-order legal constraints. It brings to bear a procedurally oriented second-order framework of behavioural guidelines.

Closely related to this consideration is the series of questions posed by any advocacy of such an opening. Does such an approach introduce a needed, yet restricted, flexibility into the operation of international law in a range of circumstances that cannot be adequately anticipated or in relation to which there exists an absence of consensus due to differing political motivations? Or, quite oppositely, does this approach invite geopolitical opportunism, providing powerful states with a generalized excuse for circumventing the carefully crafted constraints of international law? Although these questions apply to the whole of the global agenda, their most vivid application to date involves the use of force. Taking account of the arguments pro and con, it is possible to contend that the Kosovo War illustrates the constructive role of legitimacy talk, while the Iraq war exemplifies the dangers. The discussion that follows explores the reasoning behind this distinction in somewhat more depth.

From a jurisprudential perspective, the loosening of first-order legal constraints is posing a challenge to the authority of positivist orientations, and an implied move toward reliance on more normative and sociologically grounded conceptions of law that can better assimilate moral imperatives and political considerations. Whether a balance can be struck between conditioning departures from positive legal constraints and adherence to a principled framework of secondary constraints is certainly controversial. To determine whether or not such a balance can be struck is partly a call for empirical assessment and partly an inquiry into policy priorities (is it better to authorize reasonable departures from legality or to curtail geopolitical discretion to the extent possible?). Surely, the answer cannot be offered in the abstract, and calls to mind Robert Cox's cautionary admonition that all theorizing in international relations is self-interested.[30]

IV. Variations on the Theme of Legality and Legitimacy

My personal engagement with the distinction between legality and legitimacy goes back to my experience as a member of the Independent International Commission on Kosovo. In trying to respond to the events associated with the Kosovo

War of 1999, the members of the commission were somewhat confused about whether to acknowledge the violation of international law associated with recourse to non-defensive force without prior authorization from the UN Security Council.[31] Respected legal scholars had approached the issue in a number of different ways, with those inclined to follow legalist or positivist understandings of legal obligations condemning the recourse to force because it directly violated the core norm of the UN Charter prohibiting non-defensive force in the setting of international disputes. The harshest critics of American foreign policy generally went further, rejecting on the basis of extreme suspicion the alleged humanitarian motivations for the NATO military operation.[32] For instance, Michael Glennon endorsed the war by dismissing the UN Charter framework as essentially no longer authoritative, and being satisfied that a collective ad hoc undertaking dubbed "a coalition of the willing" provided sufficient justification.[33] But such a broad basis for acting beyond the charter seemed to move in a nihilistic direction, removing altogether the basic undertaking to promote war prevention goals after World War II by establishing a series of normative restrictions on recourse to force by sovereign states.

Arguing less structurally, Thomas Franck insisted that the factual grounds existed to respond to the humanitarian urgency of the situation on the ground in Kosovo, especially given the fresh memories of the massacre at Srebrenica, and that it was preferable to acknowledge openly a violation of the international law prohibition without challenging, as Glennon did, the viability of the entire charter framework governing the international use of force.[34] Yet Franck also creates a non-principled basis for violating first-order legal constraints without restricting the scope of violation by insisting on the relevance of second-order constraints.

Both Glennon and Franck refrained from offering legalistic arguments that could have formally reconciled the NATO war with international law. Such arguments relied on strained interpretations of prior UN Security Council resolutions that had described the situation in Kosovo as constituting a threat to international peace and security within the meaning of Chapter VII of the charter.[35] This classification paves the way for subsequent authorization of force by the Security Council in its role of enforcement, but to argue that an earlier identification of a threat to the peace validates a recourse to war by states or NATO without a subsequent explicit authorization of force is to erode badly the foundational identity of the United Nations as dedicated to war prevention. An aspect of this identity was the procedural requirement that in all circumstances of international dispute, recourse to force was "legal" only after all reasonable efforts had been made to reach a diplomatic solution.

The Kosovo Commission was aware of these various lines of response relating to the use of force, and accepted the contention that the apprehension of Serb "ethnic cleansing" in Kosovo was imminent and could and should be prevented by a timely NATO intervention. Further, that the seeming impact of the use of force, despite criticisms of the tactics employed, did have a net positive effect by securing de facto independence for Kosovo, by earning clear expressions of approval from the overwhelming majority of the Kosovar population, and by inducing almost all of the refugees who had left Kosovo, fearing both NATO bombing and Serb violence, to return. In other words, the commission was seeking a more acceptable way to explain its overall view that international law had been violated, but that, despite this, the outcome was definitely beneficial and to be affirmed from the perspective of global policy and should therefore not be condemned despite its evident illegality. Reinforcing this assessment were the related views, which were controversial even within the commission, that the NATO governments, especially the United States, had done their best to find a diplomatic solution, appropriately making recourse to war as a choice conform to the charter approach, thus as required a policy of last resort. In the background was the view that given the circumstances, the UN Security Council in the proper discharge of its duties should have authorized the use of force to protect the people of Kosovo, and that it was only the irresponsible geopolitics of Russia and China that made it appear to the pro-intervention side that it was worse than useless to seek Security Council approval because of the near certainty of a veto. Given this construction of the context, it seemed to the commission unreasonable to condemn the intervention because it was *technically* in violation of international law and the UN Charter.

With these considerations in mind the distinction between legality and legitimacy seemed helpful. In effect, by treating the Kosovo War as illegal, but nevertheless legitimate, the Commission was doing three things: it was acknowledging the incompatibility between the use of force and international law, but it was also affirming a beneficial outcome by pointing to the humanitarian results of military action, as constrained by a second-order legal framework that sought to regulate how force was used, taking particular account of international humanitarian law. In effect, the legitimacy of the use of force gave decisive weight to the claims of moral responsibility for protecting an imminently threatened and vulnerable Kosovar population that was believed to be at great collective risk as well as recognizing that NATO possessed the will and capabilities to carry out the mission successfully, and then follow through with a sufficient peacekeeping effort, as well as turn over the post-conflict reconstruction of Kosovo to the United Nations. When the UNSC failed to pass a resolution of censure, introduced by Russia and directed at the intervention, and later took over the political and civil administration of Kosovo, it could be argued that the United Nations was conferring a certain retrospective legal validity on the use of force. Of course, such conceptual acrobatics should not be allowed to hide the dark side of the precedent, namely, that leading members of the United Nations went to war under conditions that were neither self-defense nor based on Security Council authorization. The repudiation of first-order legal guidelines in deference to contradictory moral and political imperatives is problematic, given the existence and role of political actors of great inequality when it comes to power. It could be argued that in a world where already governments of sovereign states are dominated by "realists," this vindicating of a legitimacy meta-norm actually encourages power politics and disdain for the obligatory force of law.

The commission realized that it was on such a hazardous slippery slope and did its best to confine the authority of the precedent in three main ways: first, it urged the permanent members of the Security Council by formal action or informal agreement to suspend future uses of the veto in situations of humanitarian emergency; second, it made clear that the Kosovo case was a narrow exception to the seemingly unconditional prohibition in the UN Charter on non-defensive uses of force in international relations; and third, the commission set forth a framework of second-order guidelines that were supposed to ensure that any use of force in a future Kosovo-like situation would be humane in execution, humanitarian in motivation and effects, and law oriented in *implementation.*

In this regard, the report set forth no less than eleven principles that needed to be followed by the intervening side if it were to be allowed a claim of legitimacy, even assuming that the factual precondition of an imminent humanitarian emergency existed in the target country.[36] The three so-called "threshold principles" were attempts to confine the Kosovo precedent to a very special and specifed set of circumstances: first of all, there must be present severe violations of the international law of human rights or of international humanitarian law that subjected the population to "great suffering and risk" due to the unwillingness or incapacity of the territorial state to overcome the situation; second, the use of force must be exclusively concerned during all phases of an intervention with the protection of the victimized population, without the pursuit of such strategic goals as establishing military bases or access to resources; and third, the intervention must be reasonably calculated to achieve these goals quickly, minimizing collateral damage to civilians, and avoiding any retaliatory or punitive use of forces directed at the target government, their military or nonmilitary personnel, or their civilian supporters.

The other eight guidelines are described in the Kosovo Report as "contextual principles." They are supposed to ensure that the instrument of war is chosen as a last resort and that force is used in a manner consistent with the rules of international law and the humanitarian nature of the undertaking. For instance, principle ten asserts that "territorial or economic goals are illegitimate as justification for intervention and withdrawal of military forces should occur at the earliest point consistent with the humanitarian objectives."[37] That is, the commission adopted an approach to legitimacy that was multifaceted and designed to downplay, and if possible, to diminish the gap between legality and legitimacy as soon as possible subsequent to the intervention itself. In this respect, the legitimacy rationale as applied to Kosovo can be treated as a kind of anticipatory and provisional effort at charter reform, modifying the strict prohibition on the use of non-defensive force in the event of an unfolding humanitarian catastrophe that could not be addressed in a manner conforming to *existing* international law due to the absence of a political consensus among the permanent members of the Security Council.

The Kosovo experience engendered a wide-ranging debate about how to approach such issues in the future, as well as to whether the humanitarian rationale was the true story of the war, or a public relations mask. The action in Kosovo generated considerable distrust and hostility in Third World countries. Some of the criticism expressed strong postcolonial attachments to sovereignty that refused to grant validity to any interventionary uses of force regardless of accompanying humanitarian claims, being fearful of a cascade of claims invoking exceptional circumstances. This attitude also incorporated bad memories of colonial powers doing horrible things to dominated Third World peoples while claiming for themselves the high moral ground.[38] Whenever non-defensive force is made a policy option, it is empowering a country or countries in the North to act in an interventionary mode. It is difficult to contemplate the opposite pattern of a country or countries in the South intervening in the North.

At the same time, important voices in international society were advocating a middle ground that would encourage collective action under UN auspices in future situations where humanitarian catastrophes were underway or imminent. By far the most influential effort along these lines flowed from the recommendations of another commission set up by an initiative of the Canadian government, the International Commission on Intervention and State Sovereignty (ICISS). The brilliant stroke struck in the report of this commission was to seem responsive to the concerns of the postcolonial outlook in Asia, Africa, and Latin America by abandoning altogether the language of "humanitarian intervention," and substituting the normative words "responsibility to protect" (or simply, R2P).[39] As with the Kosovo Commission, the ICISS set forth a framework of constraining principles also derived from the long tradition of customary international law. Using the language of responsibility rather than intervention seemed to shift attention from the target country to the international community, weakening opposition by governments. The norm, R2P, worked its way through to the UN system, with some authoritative language being agreed upon at the High-level Plenary Meeting of the General Assembly in 2005, and later put into a resolution of the Security Council. The operative ideas combine an affirmation of the responsibility of "[e]ach individual state . . . to protect its population from genocide, war crimes, ethnic cleansing and crimes against humanity" with a parallel obligation of "[t]he international community to use appropriate diplomatic, humanitarian and other peaceful means . . . to help protect populations" from being victimized by these international crimes.[40] This commitment is extended to coercive action "in accordance with the Charter" should peaceful means prove insufficient to protect the relevant populations, as well as to work with regional organizations and to assist governments in developing their own capacity to protect populations from such criminality. What is left ambiguous is the key Kosovo issue of what happens when the United Nations fails or refuses to act despite the imminence of humanitarian catastrophe. To some extent, the issue of the veto is addressed by calling upon the General Assembly to implement R2P in the event that the Security Council is gridlocked or otherwise fails to take action. Is there a residual right or duty for states or a group of states or a regional organization to take forcible action? This is the essential proposal of the Kosovo Commission, as phrased in the terminology of legitimacy, but it could also be formulated by reference to R2P, which in a sense is already embodied in international law to some extent with respect to the duty to prevent and punish the crime of genocide. Whether this legal commitment overrides the charter's prohibition of non-defensive force is not indicated in the treaty or elsewhere. We are left with the haunting question of whether it is better to encourage a *principled* framework for exceptional uses of force in circumstances of humanitarian urgency or to leave the disposition of such situations to the play of contextual forces in each instance.[41]

V. Legality and Legitimacy with Respect to Afghanistan and Iraq

In the aftermath of the 9/11 attacks, the United States challenged the core conception of legality embedded in the UN Charter. Its initial challenge involved producing justifications for recourse to war against Afghanistan, which was providing sanctuary for al Qaeda's planning and training operations. There were two obvious difficulties with such a claim from the perspective of international law: the government of Afghanistan was not itself directly associated with the attacks, and the United States arguably did not exhaust diplomatic remedies, pushing aside as useless and not deserving of a response expressions by Taliban representatives of the willingness of their government in Kabul to negotiate both the arrest and transfer of al Qaeda leaders and operatives, and the assured removal from Afghan territory of all terrorists. The United States, in brief, attributed legal responsibility to the Afghan government, positing the rather novel doctrine that any government that "harbors" terrorists is fully responsible for their terrorist acts, whether complicit or not. On this basis, Washington was unwilling to consider a diplomatic solution and failed to put forth any reasons for the refusal. There was no articulation of a legal rationale by the US government, but there was also an absence of any serious legal critique at the United Nations or elsewhere of the proposed rush to war despite the seemingly unilateral expansion of the right of self-defense as it had been previously understood. In the inflamed aftermath of 9/11, the United Nations generally went along with US government's antiterrorist policies with few quibbles, acquiescing to the onset of war against Afghanistan.[42] This acquiescence was undoubtedly influenced by the dismal human rights record of the Afghan regime together with the almost universal refusal of foreign governments to enter normal diplomatic relations with the Taliban government.[43]

Such silence in the wake of war-making is precedent setting, and on the basis of the above discussion of the Kosovo debate, it expresses an *implicit* legitimacy claim. Here, the overriding of legality is premised on the *reasonableness*, given the surrounding circumstances, of using war as an instrument to respond to a prior devastating symbolic attack on US territory and to take steps to prevent future attacks. The legitimacy of war-making against Afghanistan was connected with the acceptance of the security of sovereign states as enjoying the highest priority from a world order perspective, a priority reinforced by the relative illegitimacy of the Afghan government and the real target of the war being a non-state extremist actor that posed a generalized threat to the security of all states and to world order generally, as well as to the United States in particular. There was no significant attempt at the time to validate the Afghan war under international law, as its occurrence did not occasion significant levels of criticism and controversy and the leadership of the US government did not acknowledge much need for collective formal approval. The claim to use force against Afghanistan is best conceived as an adaptation of prior conceptions of legality vis-á-vis war to new conditions of conflict and security that established, or rather extended, an earlier precedent expanding acceptable claims of self-defense beyond the textual language of the UN Charter. This expansion rested in this instance on the interpretation of the self-defense norm as subject to the rule of reason, expanding and contracting accordingly.

Recourse to war against Iraq in 2003 was an entirely different matter. The defensive rationale associated with the past behavior of the Baghdad regime, its supposed evasion of UN inspections with respect to the possession of weapons of mass destruction, and its failure to live up to the punitive conditions imposed by the Security Council in 1991 along with the ceasefire ending the Gulf War generated intense criticism and widespread controversy.[44] An acceptable recourse to war under these conditions would have to invoke legitimacy arguments, given the weakness of legality claims.[45] Anne-Marie Slaughter chose a seemingly pragmatic approach to these issues, arguing in advance of the invasion that although it would be illegal, it could still have become legitimate in the Kosovo sense if weapons of mass destruction were found, if Iraqis welcomed the American invaders as liberators, and if the United Nations presided over the economic and political reconstruction of governmental normalcy and restoration of Iraqi sovereignty.[46] Subsequent to the invasion, Slaughter acknowledged that none of these conditions had in fact been met, and that the Iraq war should in its unfolding be definitively considered as both illegal and illegitimate.[47] In general, it does not seem constructive to create an option of *provisional* legitimacy as that would weaken the prohibition on the use of force beyond claims of necessity and reasonableness. The actor seeking a dispensation from the duty to act lawfully should in all instances bear the burden of persuasion.

There are, of course, circumstances in which a course of action could be legal, yet highly illegitimate. Sticking to the general facts being discussed in this section, a flagrant example would be the imposition and maintenance of sanctions against Iraq during the period between the two wars waged against it, that is, between 1991 and 2003.[48] The UNSC clearly had the legal authority to authorize sanctions, but their punitive and indiscriminate impact on Iraqi civilian society, especially women and children, in the aftermath of a devastating war was abundantly demonstrated, and yet the sanctions were sustained for twelve years. From this perspective, although legal, the immorality and imprudent political effects of the sanctions were clearly illegitimate. Hypothetically, if in 2003 the UNSC had succumbed to American pressure and authorized an invasion of Iraq, most international law experts would have considered the recourse to war as legal, but it would have been no less illegitimate. Indeed, its illegitimacy would have been arguably even more damaging to the authority of both the United Nations and international law, reinforcing cynical arguments that geopolitics prevails within the organization even in relation to aggressive war-making. Under these circumstances, the attribute of "legality" would be nothing more than a fig leaf covering a contested policy, and relied upon by war-makers to obscure the primacy of power relations at the United Nations.

VI. Jurisprudential Implications

The focus on the use of force is one way of narrating the emergence of the legality/legitimacy discourse in policy debates. In a certain sense, as in the approach to the Iraq war taken by Wesley Clark, this discourse overlaps with a reliance on the just war framework as a way of evaluating a contested course of action.[49] One potential benefit of using the legality/legitimacy discourse is that it seems applicable to any policy domain of global interest as the range of presentations in this volume suggests. As such, it provides a flexible alternative to the sort of binary assessments that have no options other than "legal" or "illegal." This flexibility permits arguments about the comparative claims of law, morality, and politics to be put forth in any setting of decision or policy formation, and yet sustains the relevance of international law even in circumstances where the primary norm has been justifiably set aside.

Whether this discourse will prove durable and generalizable beyond the initial context of humanitarian intervention to other areas of contested policy is not evident at this point. One can imagine such debates in relation to preserving the rain forests or preventing ocean dumping of toxic wastes on the high seas. Because of the ill effects of the Iraq experience in particular, and the general opportunism of the Bush presidency with respect to the constraints of international law, there may be a jurisprudential backlash in the form of insisting on the unwavering authority of the legal text, and a suspicious response to claims of interpretative discretion to override the text due to allegedly exceptional circumstances. It may be more likely that there will be in the future a tendency to revert to law avoidance by acting inconsistently with primary legal norms, but without attempting to justify the action through legal argument. The status of US reliance in Afghanistan on drone aircraft to attack cross-border alleged Taliban or al Qaeda targets located on Pakistani territory is a current example that is not justified by an appeal to legal right, but the claim is merely asserted and defended.

But the pressure for flexibility under global conditions of rapid change in underlying conditions, combined with the sluggish capacity of law to adapt, is likely to give life to the legality/legitimacy discourse, although possibly in a different form than that which emerged after Kosovo. The domain of environmental policy, for instance, clearly appears to need some way of discouraging many forms of behavior that are currently legal, but responsible for severe harm. Similarly, the legality/legitimacy discourse seems useful with respect to the ongoing immigration debate in the United States and elsewhere. Multifaceted globalization by its nature blurs the boundaries between law as national, regional, and global, yet legal obligations remain spatially specified. Until global law robustly emerges, there will be a need to find ways to overcome the arbitrariness of legal categories unable to take account of the growing interdependence and fragility of life on planet earth.

In the past, the absence of legitimacy criteria allowed geopolitics to seize the legal high ground, as when Vietnam was condemned for its use of force in 1979 despite the clear effect of its intervention in ending the genocidal Khmer Rouge regime's governance of Cambodia. A rationale by way of legitimacy would have been supportive of Vietnam's recourse to force even if it could be shown that its action was also prompted by strategic goals, as was clearly the case for NATO with regard to Kosovo. The idea of illegitimacy can also contest immoral and imprudent claims of legality as suggested above with reference to the Iraq sanctions policy.

At the same time, it is true that if there were greater confidence in the processes by which legality was established, the case for a second level of assessment would be weakened, perhaps decisively. It is an acknowledged cost of relying on legitimacy as an escape clause that the authority of legality is weakened. Yet given the character of world order, especially the recent role of powerful yet irresponsible actors, in shaping and misshaping judgments of first-order legality, it seems on balance beneficial to retain and elaborate upon the principled flexibility associated with the legality/legitimacy discourse.

VII. The Volume Explicated

Against this background, we add chapter descriptions that highlight the contributions of each chapter, both as to substance and methodology. It is our hope that the cumulative impact of the volume becomes clearer, as well as giving a preliminary sense of the various approaches taken to the legality/legitimacy distinction by the authors with an eye to overall coherence despite considerable diversity of approach and assessment.

RAMESH THAKUR: LAW, LEGITIMACY, AND THE UNITED NATIONS

Ramesh Thakur's chapter examines the symbolic as well as the practical implications of what he sees as the gulf between lawful and legitimate behavior, both at and by the United Nations. This gap between legality and legitimacy is a serious challenge for the United Nations—indeed, Thakur argues that because it is evident in many different elements of the UN system, its cumulative implications have been underestimated.

Thakur cites the use of coercive economic sanctions, as a clear example of legal but illegitimate measures. Although they have solid legal basis in the UN Charter, they inflict harm mainly on civilians and are usually ineffective—if not actively counterproductive by strengthening repressive regimes. The illegitimacy of such discredited measures has directly eroded the legitimacy of the United Nations. Thakur goes on to question both the legitimacy and the legality of the global nuclear order, whereby the five permanent members of the UN Security Council are neglecting their own disarmament obligations while at the same time aggressively enforcing the non-proliferation elements of the Nonproliferation Treaty

Concerning the international use of force, the United Nations remains the only channel between legal authority and political legitimacy. Thakur notes that while the UN Security Council is the core enforcement mechanism for international law, its numerous legitimacy deficits have resulted in countries increasingly willing to defy its authority. The UN Security Council's authority is questioned due to a lack of legitimacy in its composition and procedures, and even in its outcomes. But the legitimacy failings of the United Nations are not limited to the Security Council—the creeping powers of the Security Council may be due at least in part to the shortcomings of an over-politicized General Assembly.

In order for the United Nations to effectively promote values such as accountability and good governance, it must exemplify those values in its own behavior. Thakur explores examples where such values have been lacking to various degrees, including those of the North-South divide evident within the United Nations, the selection process for the position of secretary-general, and the problem of abuses committed by UN peacekeepers.

Thakur's analysis demonstrates that legitimacy is about closing the gap between power and justice in international affairs, and highlights the dangers of impunity for violations of law by powerful states—such as that of the Iraq War of 2003. In particular, he draws attention to the dangers of the language of human rights being appropriated in the service of power and geopolitical interests, further exacerbating the divergence of legality and legitimacy.

ANDREW JOSEPH LOOMIS: LEGITIMACY NORMS AS CHANGE AGENTS: EXAMINING THE ROLE OF THE PUBLIC VOICE

The following chapter by Andrew Loomis explores the processes and means by which legitimacy considerations impact upon international politics, arguing that the existing literature has neglected the question of by whom legitimacy judgments are made. He casts the tension between legality and legitimacy as one between stability and transformation, which is ultimately resolved through the political process.

Loomis observes that the rigidity of legal structures normally impedes the capacity of norms to influence political outcomes; when norms evolve beyond law, the two are in tension. Legitimacy norms lead the way as a catalyst for incremental change in legal regimes. But if legitimacy is a subjective, perceptual concept, then who or what is the audience that issues legitimacy judgments? Referring to the erosion of the Westphalian state system, Loomis advances the case for the mass public as the constituency to initiate change in international politics, and therefore to take a central role in making legitimacy assessments.

But public demands for legitimacy involve different criteria than those of the political elites who design and implement policy. Such elites are accountable for policy success, and thus make judgments in mainly utilitarian terms, while the public is both more able and more inclined to evaluate policy in normative terms. Loomis distinguishes between feasibility and desirability, arguing that while the public may lack the knowledge and information to effectively judge feasibility, they can make judgments on desirability. While legal norms are vital in judgments by policy elites, moral and societal standards of legitimacy hold greater value to the wider public.

Loomis explores how political elites use norms strategically to gain support for their policies, citing US President George W. Bush's protracted efforts to legitimize the 2003 invasion of Iraq by seeking justifications that could satisfy societal expectations. Even in ridiculing international law, the United States remained bound to the need to justify its actions. Thus Loomis holds that the sensitivity of policy elites to public legitimacy claims, and their strategic use of legitimacy norms, are evidence that such norms constrain policy choices. Therefore, any comprehensive account of legitimacy in international politics must include a thorough examination of the public voice.

AMY BARTHOLOMEW: LEGALITY/LEGITIMACY: PROBLEMS AND PROSPECTS FOR LEGALITY UNDER AMERICAN EMPIRE

Amy Bartholomew's chapter offers a nuanced response to arguments rejecting international law. In recent years, such arguments have been evident both in the contempt in which it was held by the Bush administration, and in the reactionary urge to reject law as the "instrument of empire." While acknowledging the relationship between imperial power and international law, Bartholomew refutes the claim that international law should be rejected as it is so deeply contaminated by power that it perpetuates empire. She conducts a detailed exploration of this relationship, in order to better resist such arguments and reveal the potential within cosmopolitan law and human rights.

Bartholomew argues that contemporary American imperialism—most obvious with the Bush administration's recent contempt for human rights, democracy, and legality—has been inadequately described with such terms as "lawless." She asserts that American empire in fact depends on law, and more alarmingly, threatens to produce what she terms "empire's law." This is characterized by a state treating others as the addressees of law while exempting itself from legal obligation—seeing its own compliance with law as a matter of discretion. Bartholomew notes the parallels in the treatment of persons and the treatment of other nation-states by empire: rights are considered discretionary privileges, with others rendered rightless in a pervasive logic of prevention at all costs. In addition to this evasion of legal responsibilities, through empire's unilateral behavior it also attempts to act as the dominant author of law—as illustrated by the Bush Doctrine regarding the international use of force.

Bartholomew contrasts empire's law—law as the sovereign decision—with legitimate law, suggesting that the question of whether a certain law is legitimate or not depends both upon law's internal legitimacy and upon its relation to external democratic processes of legitimation. Drawing on arguments from Habermas, Bartholemew sees internal legitimation as depending on the processes and procedures provided by legality, and requiring anticipation of wider rational acceptability. Turning to the external legitimation of law, she again employs a Habermasian conception of deliberative democratic legitimation, maintaining that those addressed by law must be able to see themselves, to some extent, as authors of such law.

Bartholomew cautions that empire's law threatens both the internal legitimacy of law and the possibilities for its external democratic legitimation. In this sense, the Bush administration's policies regarding law were worse than merely acting lawlessly and had much more ominous implications. Thus Bartholomew emphasizes the importance of not only developing and defending legitimate legality, but of doing so as part of a wider politics that rejects the legitimacy of empire.

FRIEDRICH KRATOCHWIL: LEAVING SOVEREIGNTY BEHIND? AN INQUIRY INTO THE POLITICS OF POST-MODERNITY

In his chapter, Friedrich Kratochwil engages in a conceptual examination of the changing practice of sovereignty—as a concept established by, and central to, international law—which is being seriously challenged by the legitimacy debate. He suggests that in its dependence upon empirical methods, conventional analysis of the theory of sovereignty has been flawed. Kratochwil argues that the meaning of sovereignty is rather established by its use and by its connections with other concepts such as legitimacy that authorize or reject certain practices. In his casting of sovereignty, it serves to link decisions with the notion of legitimacy—that they should have authority and be respected by its subjects.

Sovereignty plays a crucial legitimizing role in domestic politics. But regarding the external dimension, Kratochwil traces the evolution of practices of international recognition of states to suggest that sovereignty has been transformed by the politics of nationalism and identity. Today, recognition is increasingly dependent upon participation in international organizations, revealing the communal character of such judgments. Kratochwil turns to the twin manifestations of this evolution in sovereignty—reformist multilateralism, on the one hand, and imperialist unilateralism, on the other—to suggest that both strategies neglect the role of history and local knowledge in creating a political order.

Kratochwil cautions that an obsession with generalizable models of best practices without consideration of context undermines the ability of local politics to find solutions by which different peoples author their own destinies. He criticizes the emphasis placed by the mantra of "good governance" on codified technical solutions to social problems, suggesting that both local knowledge and "the people" might matter more than expertise and imported best practices. Kratochwil's analysis suggests that real situations cannot be reduced to universalist principles; principles cannot prescribe their own application, and thus must always be interpreted. He questions the sustainability of the continued global emphasis on consumption and free trade, given the role the people have assumed as the source of law—and in doing so, presents sovereignty as vital for the political project of humanity.

YASUAKI ONUMA: INTERNATIONAL LAW AND POWER IN THE MULTIPOLAR AND MULTI-CIVILIZATIONAL WORLD OF THE TWENTY-FIRST CENTURY

In his chapter, Yasuaki Onuma focuses on the dynamic issues of law and power, and the problem of legitimacy in global society—strongly advocating trans-civilizational perspectives as a necessary corrective. Onuma argues for a far more nuanced casting of the relation between law and power than simply that of observance versus violation. He notes that law is needed by powerful states to legitimize their dominance, instrumentally decreasing the political costs of hegemony by securing voluntary submissions to their authority. But law also provides opportunities for the weak to challenge the powerful, and this is respected—if reluctantly—by the latter, in pragmatic recognition of the costs of ignoring law.

In order to glean a more nuanced understanding of the relationship between law and power, Onuma examines the constructive, constitutive function of international law. Because international law is a global normative system, it enters into the thoughts of human individuals through their daily affairs, whether in government, business, or as private citizens, constructing social realities and influencing behavior. Normative ideas can constitute power, even though they require power in order to be disseminated and influential. The power of international law depends upon its legitimacy, among other factors—if norms of international law are perceived as illegitimate, doubts will be raised as to whether they should be obeyed, reducing their effectiveness.

Onuma strongly advocates the trans-civilizational perspective on international legal affairs, supplementing and modifying the prevalent, West-centric perspectives of the international and the transnational. He notes that non-Western and female lawyers have been conspicuously absent, both in terms of constructing and of disseminating the idea of international law. He further suggests that existing international and transnational perspectives neglect the aspirations, expectations and frustrations of over 80% of the global population—and that we must rectify this imbalance, both for greater global legitimacy and for greater relevance to the expected realities of power in the twenty-first century.

Crucially, Onuma observes the common mistaken assumption that individuals belong exclusively to a certain civilization, suggesting that most people simultaneously behave and perceive the world according to a plurality of cultures and civilizations. The strengthening of international law's legitimacy that is vital for the global system in the twenty-first century will depend upon lawyers adopting the trans-civilizational perspective and paying much greater attention to culture, religion, and history.

GILES GUNN: THE TRANS-CIVILIZATIONAL, THE INTERCIVILIZATIONAL, AND THE HUMAN: THE QUEST FOR THE NORMATIVE IN THE LEGITIMACY DEBATE

Giles Gunn's chapter examines and further develops Onuma's argument regarding how the normative basis of legitimacy is constituted. Gunn suggests may be difficult to think in "trans-civilizational" terms in today's increasingly fragmented world—observing in particular a form of opposition between the global and the local. He goes on to highlight the difficulties involved in finding elements within various civilizations that could constitute common or shared values. The new forms of the "clash of civilizations" thesis—those of a clash *within* civilizations—are evident in terms of secularism and extremism, between various forms of geopolitical organization, and between integration and separatism. However, Gunn suggests that the divide between the global North and the global South constitutes the clash with the most powerful argument for an inter-civilizational perspective rather than a transnational one.

Gunn calls for a reconceptualization of being human, as a process rather than a condition—in that humans are dependent upon learning from their exposure to otherness. In this sense, all human experiences are potentially instructive, yielding insights not only for the individual, but also for cultures and civilizations. In advocating his conception of the inter-civilizational over Onuma's of the trans-civilizational, Gunn describes how it avoids the pitfalls of reductionism and totalism, while allowing us to see the other as a potential collaborator for our mutual benefit. He maintains that his conception of the inter-civilizational, supported by this re-conceived notion of the human, provides a better account of the normative basis of legitimacy. In conclusion, Gunn holds that it is through otherness that individuals, cultures, and civilizations become instruments for self-formation—and that if the normative can transform this otherness, it can indeed transcend the legal.

The chapters in Part 2 of the volume address more specific substantive settings wherein the legality/legitimacy distinction offers both clarifying opportunities for analysis and policy, but also presents problems. These chapters, to varying degrees, explore both the opportunities and the problems.

CHRISTINE CHINKIN: RETHINKING LEGALITY/LEGITIMACY AFTER THE IRAQ WAR

Christine Chinkin's chapter examines the legality and legitimacy of recent military interventions by Western powers, and specifically of the 2003 Iraq war. She traces the evolution of these issues from well before the Iraq war, and goes on to detail several post-Iraq cases. Since the end of the Cold War, the UNSC has understood—and applied—the notion of a threat to international peace and security in a wider range of situations than previously. But powerful states have also intervened without explicit UNSC approval, instead either claiming legality outside the charter, or asserting legitimacy in its absence (or indeed both). This has exacerbated the existing legitimacy deficits of the Security Council (also noted by Thakur and Falk in their chapters), including those of transparency, accountability, and membership.

Chinkin suggests that a central difficulty in assessing legality and legitimacy is the question of when such judgments should be made and examines the implications of this question through the various cases presented. Legality relies on compliance with binding rules, while legitimacy is based in subjective, changing perceptions. Indeed, legitimacy can expose gaps between such perceptions and law. Therefore actions seen as "illegal but legitimate" or "legal but illegitimate" raise serious questions regarding the legitimacy of law itself—and of the institutions and processes by which it is made.

Chinkin's analysis shows that the military interventions in Kosovo, Afghanistan, and Iraq have all contributed to such a legitimacy deficit of the international legal system in the post–Cold War period. She traces the evolution of two developing strands following Kosovo, which were to return to influence the debates leading up to the Iraq War—that of the responsibility to protect civilians at risk, and that of force employed absent of UNSC authorization. Chinkin suggests, similarly to Falk in this opening chapter, that the Kosovo precedent may have directly influenced further such unauthorized actions, including the Iraq War.

Following the invasion of Iraq, Chinkin observes that the coalition desperately sought the symbolic legitimacy of UNSC endorsement, while the United Nations tried to repair the damage the unauthorized action had done to its reputation. Neither of these aims was served by the weakly worded resolutions produced by the UNSC, which in fact led to deeply unpopular political and economic changes that undermined the domestic legitimacy of the occupation.

Chinkin concludes that the Iraq War was not an isolated case of international lawlessness, and with reference to several post-Iraq examples, argues that the UNSC continues to be instrumentalized by permanent members in furtherance of their national interests. While cautioning against the continuing displacement of international legality by powerful states' assertions of legitimacy,

Chinkin highlights the balancing effect of civil society, the media, activist lawyering, and scholarship.

ANNE ORFORD:LAWFUL AUTHORITY AND THE RESPONSIBILITY TO PROTECT

Anne Orford also tackles legality and legitimacy through the issue of intervention, but her chapter concentrates in particular on the shift from the concept of humanitarian intervention to that of R2P. Orford argues that the legitimacy arguments invoked in support of the Kosovo intervention were based in a metaphysical conception of law, whereby universal values—such as that of an ideal form of community—transcend particular laws. She suggests that humanitarian intervention's appeal to universal values shielded it from discussion and distanced it from politics and welcomes R2P as a shift away from such notions, bringing a more politicized conception of law.

The idea that the primary role of the state is protection is not new—Orford acknowledges its long history in Western political and legal thought. Indeed, there is nothing new in R2P's claim that every state has the responsibility to protect citizens against atrocity crimes, as these obligations already existed under international law. What R2P adds is the idea of an international duty to protect, and of attendant obligations for the international community. Orford suggests that as R2P brings not only the responsibility to react to crises, but also to prevent harm and to rebuild, the protection role for international governance is expanded—raising further questions such as how the international community's authority can be legal and legitimate. She asserts that the shift from humanitarian intervention to R2P reveals such questions to be fundamentally political, to be answered in political terms.

In conclusion, Orford observes that R2P provides a focus on how to guarantee security and protection for vulnerable people, which is much better suited to political analysis than are metaphysical questions such as how to ensure the universal values of humanity. She notes that much of the pro-humanitarian-intervention literature simply sees the international community as a benevolent actor and fails to acknowledge that intervention could create new exploitative relations and grievances. Such risks further underline the value of R2P in raising issues of legitimacy and political authority which should be central to any intervention.

MARK JUERGENSMEYER: THE LEGITIMACY OF INVADING RELIGIOUS REGIMES

In his chapter, Mark Juergensmeyer examines the legality and legitimacy of regime change, taking Afghanistan as his point of departure. Many arguments advocating the US attack in 2001 condemned the Taliban regime in a form of guilt by association, through its alleged connections to Osama bin Laden and the al Qaeda network. But forceful arguments were also put forward advocating its removal purely on the basis of its nature as an extreme religious regime, regardless of any link to al Qaeda. It is upon this controversial assertion that Juergensmeyer directs his analysis, examining the possibility for such moral justifications for toppling regimes that base their political legitimacy in religion.

Juergensmeyer begins his exploration by asking whether religious regimes are capable of internal change, as this would reduce or eliminate any claimed grounds for external intervention. He finds that it is possible for religious regimes to be relatively flexible and produce change from within, as evident in the diversity of political positions in the Islamic Republic of Iran. But religious positions—especially when supported by assertions of divine mandate—can also be rigid and authoritarian, particularly concerning matters of morality. While the same can be true of secular regimes, these have overwhelmingly progressed from systems of central authority to those of democracy, with elected representatives and independent judiciaries.

Juergensmeyer cautions that although many religious nationalists express remarkable enthusiasm for democracy, at least part of this is self-serving—for democracy would legitimize rule by the religious majority. Religions ultimately place greater value on the will of God than on the will of the people; and, indeed, religious figures often criticize democracy as a system of pandering to the self-interests of various groups. They instead argue for something akin to Plato's philosopher-king—a leader with the political insight to rise above self-interest and provide a broader vision.

Conversely, Juergensmeyer notes that almost every religious nationalist movement has rejected theocracy—rule by the clergy. He suggests that democratic principles are well established across the world, even within religious organizations. The difference is in the purpose that they see for the political system; while democratic theorists would argue that their system legitimates itself, religious politicians hold that the system must be put to higher purposes—and thereby achieve moral validity.

Juergensmeyer claims that while most religious regimes would not identify and protect *rights* as such, they mostly uphold some—usually fairly equivalent—conception of human dignity and personal security. Therefore, as long as the security and dignity of individuals is respected within society, the controversy over human rights is immaterial. While there remain fundamental cultural differences between individualistic and collectivistic societies, Juergensmeyer maintains that it is highly questionable whether these differences can justify the removal of religious regimes. He concludes that although the mere existence of radical religious regimes cannot usually justify invasion, there may be cases of widespread human rights abuses in which at least moral legitimacy, if not legal authority, for intervention exists.

ASLI BÂLI: LEGALITY AND LEGITIMACY IN THE INTERNATIONAL ORDER: THE CHANGING LANDSCAPE OF NUCLEAR NONPROLIFERATION

Aslı Bâli's chapter draws attention to the negative implications of undermining legality through legitimacy justifications, in the context of the arms control regime. She suggests that while humanitarian intervention is presented as a moral redress to the unjust constraints of international law, there may be greater humanitarian benefit in maintaining strict legal constraints against interventionism. As a legacy of the Kosovo debates, the reconceptualization of sovereignty as conditional on the performance of certain responsibilities has led to a weakening of the international prohibition on the use of force. Bâli asserts that in effect, a new exception has been created to the UN Charter's prohibition on the non-defensive use of force, albeit one restricted to the pursuit of humanitarian objectives.

Bâli warns that the logic underlying humanitarian intervention has recently been stretched to provide a new basis for interventionism involving unilateral preemptive and even preventive use of force; indeed, humanitarian and preemption-based arguments can be seen converging in the case of the Iraq War. This extension of intervention arguments, particularly on the basis of unilateral-threat determinations, undermines and destabilizes the collective security mechanism of the UN system.

This is particularly dangerous in the context of the nuclear nonproliferation regime, at a time when its core bargain is already under intense pressure. The regime relies upon providing incentives for non–nuclear weapon states to refrain from proliferation, including access to civilian nuclear technology, negative security assurances against nuclear attack, and commitments by nuclear weapon states to disarm. Bâli observes that these disarmament commitments have been ignored or disregarded by the nuclear weapon states—none more so than the United States—which have also restricted access to nuclear technologies. Of most concern is the emergence of a strong unilateral US counter-proliferation emphasis, raising the alarming possibility of preventive intervention in the name of nonproliferation.

Bâli cautions that these factors in their totality threaten to incentivize weak states to acquire new deterrent capabilities, and cautions that this distortion of the nuclear nonproliferation regime's incentive structure could even bring about a new nuclear age. Returning to the central question related to the norm of conditional sovereignty—whether to permit "legitimate" departures from legality or whether to maintain constraints on geopolitical discretion—Bâli argues that such constraints are vital to the stability of the international security order.

The chapters in Part 3 explore the relevance of the distinction between legality and legitimacy in substantive settings other than those involving the use of force. In this regard, the effort is to determine whether the distinction is useful as a general jurisprudential tool rather than limited to taking account of the tensions associated with applying the constraints of international law to controversial use of force.

LORRAINE ELLIOTT: LEGALITY AND LEGITIMACY: THE ENVIRONMENTAL CHALLENGE

In her chapter, Lorraine Elliot explores legality and legitimacy issues in the context of global environmental governance. Legitimacy concerns are relevant in this area primarily due to the widely acknowledged failure of political institutions to respond adequately to the ongoing deterioration of the global environment, as well as the exclusion of much of civil society from representation within such institutions.

Elliot suggests that the nature of environmental change, transcending national borders and demanding effective political responses that states alone cannot provide, questions the very relevance of sovereignty in international order. She criticizes the statist conception of international environmental law, which sees states as both the authors of the legal order and the subjects of law—and therefore those whose consent is required for legitimacy. This conflation of legality with legitimacy assumes states are responsible actors within the international society of states, and bearers of rights and responsibilities. Not all states are democratic, representative, or accountable to their citizens, and indeed authority in environmental governance is no longer held exclusively by states—private actors and forms of agency are increasingly taking on regulatory roles. Agencies such as the Intergovernmental Panel on Climate Change have come to function independently and derive legitimacy from their scientific credibility, rather than by being established by states.

In making assessments of legitimacy, Elliot maintains that we must consider whose beliefs count, as well as the criteria that we apply. Environmental challenges highlight a central problem in conceiving of legitimacy in international order as being constituted by a community of states—that this neglects any notion of global citizenship. Those directly affected by policies and their impacts have little say or consent in governance. Environmental harms, with their associated social, political, and economic implications, are inflicted transnationally, often with those most vulnerable most severely affected. Indeed in the long term, eventually all citizens will suffer from the effects of environmental change—and this global political community is therefore the constituency of global environmental governance.

Elliot concludes that legality is not sufficient for global environmental governance to be legitimate. Rather, this depends upon recognition of the global nature of its constituency and the duties arising from environmental injustices within this constituency. Furthermore, the institutions and rule-systems of environmental governance must be accountable to their constituents, and perform effectively to build trust. Elliot emphasizes the need for continual scrutiny of consent and legitimacy, not only that of specific rules and decisions, but that of the entire system of global environmental governance.

VESSELIN POPOVSKI: LEGALITY AND LEGITIMACY OF INTERNATIONAL CRIMINAL TRIBUNALS

Vesselin Popovski's chapter examines the evolution of international criminal justice, from the earliest known tribunal to the International Criminal Court (ICC). He traces arguments supporting and criticizing these tribunals, from both legality and legitimacy perspectives, and explores the implications for the relationship between the two concepts.

Popovski sees the Nuremberg and Tokyo trials as a strong example of legitimacy trumping legality, forcing international law to address the gaps they highlighted. The trials were exceptional, unprecedented measures, which were nevertheless seen as preferable to the two alternatives of amnesty or extrajudicial executions. They suffered from numerous legality failings related to their establishment and fundamental flaws in legal procedure, while their legitimacy was also lacking in terms of impartiality, objectivity, and hypocrisy. But despite these shortcomings, they gradually gained widespread legitimacy by contributing to sustained peace in Germany and Japan and implementing the concept of individual criminal accountability in international law.

This implementation progressed with the International Criminal Tribunals for the former Yugoslavia and for Rwanda (ICTY and ICTR). Their legality was also challenged by defense lawyers on several grounds, such as their establishment by a political organ—the UNSC—rather than by law. But in terms of process, ICTY and ICTR provided very robust guarantees of proof beyond reasonable doubt, which in fact were even higher than those of domestic courts. The ad hoc tribunals served to fill a gap in the international system, in the absence of an international criminal court or the necessary domestic capacity. The creation of the ICC aimed to address this shortcoming permanently, demonstrating the desire of the international community to enhance the enforcement of international humanitarian law and human rights law. Popovski suggests that despite opposition among powerful states, the ICC benefits from strong legality and legitimacy due to its complementarity to domestic jurisdiction, stringent legal procedures, and close relations with civil society. He notes that those legitimacy concerns that do exist are a direct result of those of the UNSC, including its unrepresentative composition.

Popovski concludes that assessments of legitimacy will naturally vary between victims seeking justice and compensation, and the needs of social reconciliation. In this sense, legitimacy is essential in considering the need to balance demands for justice with considerations of communal cohesiveness. To achieve greater legitimacy, he advocates a wider conception of justice that follows the spirit as well as the letter of the law and suggests that to close the gaps between law and justice, criminal justice must be complemented by social justice.

DANIELE ARCHIBUGI AND MARIANO CROCE: LEGALITY AND LEGITIMACY OF EXPORTING DEMOCRACY

The chapter by Daniele Archibugi and Mariano Croce provides an assessment of the concept of exporting democracy, informed by distinctions between legality and legitimacy. They suggest that previous accounts of the relationship between legality and legitimacy have neglected the notion of democratic participation—and assert that in fact it is this notion that constitutes the relationship by both constructing criteria for legitimacy and providing a rationale for the enforcement of laws. Indeed, when legitimacy is separated from democratic participation, it is vulnerable to manipulation and self-serving instrumentalization. While legality is a relatively fixed category, the process and outcome of assessing legitimacy is subjective and highly dependent upon the conception of legitimacy one holds.

Archibugi and Croce take issue with both the ends and the means of exporting democracy—a concept that has become evident through the aims explicitly expressed by leaders of some dominant Western powers to spread democracy with the use of military force. They see exporting democracy by any means as an inconsistent concept, paradoxically denying the affected people the opportunity to democratically decide on their form of government.

Using force as the means to promote democracy is both illegal and illegitimate, not least because democracy is a nonviolent regime. Using violence will inevitably harm the individuals who are supposed to benefit from—and be protected by—democracy. Indeed, even if the public in question express a desire for democracy, it does not automatically follow that they would accept regime change by an external power. Archibugi and Croce argue that exporting democracy militarily has also proved unsuccessful historically, only rarely succeeded in creating democratic regimes.

Using persuasive rather than coercive means to export democracy avoids many of these difficulties, by working to achieve change from within the state in question. Democracy can be promoted through a combination of top-down economic and political incentives offered by democratic states, as well as bottom-up progress with improved links and cooperation between citizens in democratic and authoritarian states. As far as peaceful means pursue an internal process of democracy, rather than an externally imposed change in the system, they can be seen as both legal and legitimate. However, Archibugi and Croce assert that questions of legality and legitimacy are irrelevant in evaluating peaceful attempts to export democracy—as such efforts cannot be neatly categorized and defined, but are better seen as an ongoing process of creating conditions conducive to the development of democratic ideals and practices.

Archibugi and Croce conclude that invoking democracy as a justification for acting illegally both weakens international legality and appropriates legitimacy. They suggest that this highlights a deficit of democratic participation in international legitimacy and advocate peacefully spreading democracy as a way forward.

This would enlarge the basis for legitimation of the international legal system and encourage cooperation for necessary reform of international regulations, by both modifying international legality and agreeing on criteria for corrective legitimacy.

Endnotes

1. There exists a complementary problem when the UN Security Council authorizes action that appears to violate the sovereign rights of member states. This Lockerbie decision of the International Court of Justice suggests that there is no judicial review of Security Council decisions. For instance, if the Security Council had authorized the invasion of Iraq in 2003, would that have overridden Iraq's rights under international law? Put differently, can the Security Council and the United Nations violate international law with impunity, or are their decisions "the law," creating a tension for the country that resists on the basis of its moral and political claims to being victimized by the manipulation of lawmaking procedures?

2. Compare this reluctance with the readiness of all states, regardless of size, to entrust vital interests to alliance relationships based on the existence of a common enemy. The twenty-first-century test is whether alliances, such as NATO, can be kept in being on the basis of shared positive interests, or whether the sustainability of alliance relationships will depend on the emergence of a new enemy. There have been efforts in the West to regard Islam or China or a resurgent Russia as such a new enemy, but so far with limited results.

3. Vertical procedures are available to the extent that a geopolitical actor reinforces an existing legal regime. To a certain extent, the United States has played this role in relation to the nuclear nonproliferation treaty regime.

4. See Carl Schmitt, *The Concept of the Political*, trans., expanded ed. (Chicago: University of Chicago Press, 2007); Schmitt, *Legality and Legitimacy* (Durham, N.C.: Duke University Press, 2004); Schmitt, *Political Theology: Four Chapters on Sovereignty* (Chicago: University of Chicago Press, 2005); Giorgio Agamben, *Homo Sacer: Sovereign Power and Bare Life* (Stanford, Calif.: Stanford University Press, 1998).

5. The disclosure of the so-called torture memos and the extensive discussion of the abandonment of the unconditional prohibition of torture is a textbook illustration of the ease with which even a constitutional democracy rooted in the rule of law is ready to put aside its most cherished norms when national security threats are perceived. For discussion of this atmosphere of threat after 9/11, see Jack Goldsmith, *The Terror Presidency: Law and Judgment inside the Bush Administration* (New York: Norton, 2007).

6. See Jane Mayer, *The Dark Side: The Inside Story of How the War on Terror Turned into a War on American Ideals* (New York: Doubleday, 2008).

7. For views on American exceptionalism, see Michael Ignatieff, ed., *American Exceptionalism and Human Rights* (Princeton, N.J.: Princeton University Press, 2005).

8. A strong indictment of the Bush presidency for its refusal to pursue a lawful foreign policy is depicted in Philippe Sands, *Lawless World: America and the Making and Breaking of Global Rules* (New York: Viking, 2005); also see Jordan Paust, *Beyond the Law: The Bush Administration's Unlawful Responses in the 'War' on Terror* (Cambridge: Cambridge University Press, 2007).

9. This is spelled out in the report of the Independent International Commission on Kosovo. See Independent International Commission on Kosovo, *Kosovo Report* (Oxford: Oxford University Press, 2000), 163–198. Henceforth cited as *Kosovo Report*.

10. A parallel cluster of concerns has arisen for individuals required to participate in wars or war policies that are contrary to their sense of the requirements of international law, personal morality, or prudent behavior. For a stimulating inquiry in an American setting see William F. Felice, *How Do I Save My Honor? War, Moral Integrity, and Principled Resignation* (Lanham, Md.: Rowman & Littlefield, 2009).

11. See *Kosovo Report*, Note 9, esp. 163–198. I should point out that I was a member of the commission and an advocate of the legality/legitimacy approach to acknowledging both the unlawfulness of the NATO military operation and the humanitarian approval of the undertaking and its results.

12. It is, of course, possible to endorse the first-order recourse to force to rescue the vulnerable Albanian Kosovars and yet be highly critical of the failure to abide by second-order constraints, such as taking maximum care to avoid civilian casualties or being mindful of restraints on legally dubious weaponry and tactics. I would also add in retrospect a critical attitude toward recourse to one-sided war as a means of resolving a political dispute, recalling that NATO suffered not a single combat casualty while inflicting hundreds. For a full exploration of this line of argument, see Richard Falk, "Torture, War, and the Limits of Liberal Legality," in *United States and Torture: interrogation, incarceration, and abuse*, ed. Marjorie Cohn (New York: NYU Press, 2011).

13. The responsibility to protect approach was articulated in an influential report presented by a Canadian-based international commission. See "Responsibility to Protect," Report of the International Commission on State Sovereignty and Intervention (December 2001).

14. Support for this interpretation of the UN Charter derives from a reading of the Preamble, as well as Articles 2(4) and 51.

15. Even here there exists normative ambiguity as the NATO alliance was formed to protect Western Europe from external attack, not to promote security or humanitarian goals within Europe.

16. For argument along these lines see Richard Falk, *The Costs of War: The UN, International Law and World Order after Iraq* (New York: Routledge, 2008).

17. See Noam Chomsky, *New Military Humanism: Lessons from Kosovo* (Monroe, Maine: Common Courage Press, 1999).

18. For an elaborate argument along these lines, see Jack L. Goldsmith and Eric Posner, *The Limits of International Law* (New York: Oxford University Press, 2005), esp. 23–78.

19. See Anthony C. Arendt and Robert J. Beck, *International Law and the Use of Force: Beyond the UN Charter Paradigm* (New York: Routledge, 1993); A. Mark Weisbrud, *Use of Force: The Practice of States since World War II* (1997) in relation to the use of force; this assessment is more jurisprudentially set forth by the New Haven School, Myres S. McDougal and Feliciano P. Feliciano, *The International Law of War: Transnational Coercion and World Public Order* (New Haven, Conn.: New Haven Press, 1994).

20. A helpful commentary on this development can be found in Marie Gillespie, "Security, Media, Legitimacy: Multi-ethnic Media Publics and the Iraq War 2003," *International Relations* 20, no. 4: 467–486 (2006); for a more comprehensive and theoretically sophisticated approach, see Ian Clark, *Legitimacy in International Society* (Oxford: Oxford University Press, 2005). For an illuminating discussion, with considerable scholarly documentation, of the distinction between hard and soft law, see Jack M. Beard, "The Shortcomings of

Indeterminacy in Arms Control Regimes: The Case of the Biological Weapons Convention," *American Journal of International Law* 101, no. 2 (2007): 271–321, esp. 273–275.

21. Clark, *Legitimacy*, note 4, p. 1.

22. On this fourth cluster, see John Ikenberry, *After Victory: Institutions, Strategic Restraint, and the Rebuilding of Order after Major Wars* (Princeton, N.J.: Princeton University Press, 2001).

23. The apparent abandonment of the language of a war on terror in the early phase of the Obama presidency seems to signal greater reliance on diplomacy and police methods to deal with threats of transnational terrorism. Arguably, the new approach has not yet been tested by large-scale terrorist incidents directed at an American target.

24. For the former view, see Robert W. Tucker and David Hendrickson, "The Sources of American Legitimacy," *Foreign Affairs* 83 (2004): 18–32; for the latter view, see Robert Kagan, "America's Crisis of Legitimacy," *Foreign Affairs* 83 (2004): 65–87.

25. Anne-Marie Slaughter, *A New World Order* (Princeton, N.J.: Princeton University Press, 2004), 29.

26. Slaughter, *A New World Order*, n. 26.

27. Richard Falk, *The Great Terror War* (Northampton, Mass.: Olive Branch Press, 2003).

28. Thomas Franck, *The Power of Legitimacy among Nations* (Oxford: Oxford University Press, 1990).

29. For comprehensive review, see Brad R. Roth, *Governmental Illegitimacy in International Law* (Oxford: Oxford University Press, 1999).

30. In the background here is the vast literature surrounding the approach taken by Carl Schmitt in the circumstances of action beyond the law by a sovereign state. For the essence of the Schmitt worldview, see his 1932 *The Concept of the Political* (Chicago: University of Chicago Press, 1996).

31. For discussion, see *Kosovo Report*, Note 9, esp. 163–198.

32. For example, Chomsky, *New Military Humanism*, n. 17.

33. Michael J. Glennon, "Why the Security Council Failed," *Foreign Affairs* 82, no. 3 (2003): 16–35; the argument is elaborated in Glennon, *Limits of Law, Prerogatives of Power: Interventionism after Kosovo* (New York, Palgrave, 2001).

34. Thomas M. Franck, "Break It, Don't Fake It," *Foreign Affairs* 78, no.4 (1999) 116–118.

35. Security Council resolutions on Chapter VII.

36. *Kosovo Report*, Note 9, 192–195.

37. *Kosovo Report*, Note 9, 195.

38. For a persuasive demonstration of why suspicions are well grounded, see Anne Orford, *Reading Humanitarian Intervention: Human Rights and the Use of Force in International Law* (Cambridge: Cambridge University Press, 2003); for a more typical presentation of the liberal internationalist case in support of intervention, see Tom Weiss in Julie Mertus and Jeffrey W. Helsing, eds., *Human Rights and Conflict: Exploring the Links between Rights, Law, and Peacebuilding* (Washington, D.C.: United States Institute of Peace, 2006).

39. "Responsibility to Protect," Report of the International Commission on State Sovereignty and Intervention (December 2001).

40. High Level Panel on the Responsibility to Protect norm.

41. For an elegant, detailed depiction of the practice and argumentation relating to humanitarian intervention, see Nicholas Wheeler, *Saving Strangers: Humanitarian Intervention in International Society* (Oxford: Oxford University Press, 2000).

42. For overall analysis written in the aftermath of the 9/11 attacks, without sufficient critical distance see Falk, *The Great Terror War* (Northampton, Mass.: Olive Branch Press, 2003).

43. At the time of 9/11, only three governments maintained full diplomatic relations with the Taliban government. After the attacks, two of these broke diplomatic relations with Afghanistan, leaving only Pakistan. The government of Pakistan officially explained that it was only maintaining diplomatic relations so that it could serve as a conduit for the intergovernmental communication of formal messages.

44. See principal UN Security Council Resolutions on Gulf War. UN Security Council Resolution 678, 29 November 1990 (authorizing use of force); 687, 2 March 1991 (imposing conditions on Iraq in relation to ceasefire).

45. Oddly and unconvincingly, Gen. Wesley Clark proposes the opposite argument, contending that the Iraq war was legal, enforcing prior Security Council decision, but illegitimate because it was imprudent, unsuccessful, and destructive of world order and America's reputation as global leader. Clark, "Just War Theory," public lecture, UCLA, January 22, 2007.

46. Anne-Marie Slaughter, "Good Reasons for Going around the UN," *New York Times*, March 18, 2007.

47. Slaughter, "The Use of Force in Iraq: Illegal and Illegitimate," *ASIL Proceedings 2004*, 262–263.

48. See Richard Falk, *The Costs of War: International Law, the United Nations and World Order After Iraq* (New York: Routledge, 2008).

49. See W. Clark, n. 45 above.

PART ONE

2

Law, Legitimacy and the United Nations

Ramesh Thakur

> The UN Security Council, the World Bank, the IMF and the World Trade Organisation make decisions that affect us all. They do so without our consent. . . . Global governance is a tyranny speaking the language of democracy. . . . The purpose of a world parliament is to hold international bodies to account. It is not a panacea. It will not turn the IMF or the UN Security Council into democratic bodies . . . But it does have the potential to impose a check on them.[1]

In 2007, Zimbabwe was elected as chair of the UN Commission on Sustainable Development. A more grotesque choice is hard to imagine. Founding President Robert Mugabe inherited a beautiful and prosperous country and has systematically ground it to ruins, the unbounded goodwill of the international community attending the euphoria of his country's birth notwithstanding. What then are we to make of the UN's unique legitimacy that Kofi Annan was so fond of invoking while he was Secretary-General (SG)? This came on top of the decades of imbalanced and obsessive focus by the old Human Rights Commission on alleged Israeli violations of human rights while turning a blind eye to so many other regimes. It became morally bankrupt and an embarrassment to the UN system. To reverse growing cynicism about the hypocrisy of existing institutions and practices, and noting that states often seek membership in the commission to shield themselves from scrutiny, Annan recommended the creation of a smaller Human Rights Council to facilitate more focused debate and discussions.[2] That "reform" has been implemented, but progress on substance is not yet obvious. While the Human Rights Commission found it difficult to indict any country other than Israel, the Security Council seems to require compliance from all countries but Israel. It would be interesting to learn which side in the Arab-Israeli conflict holds the organization in greater contempt because of perceived illegitimacy owing to bias.

The report of Annan's High-Level Panel on UN reforms had included an intriguing sentence: "The maintenance of world peace and security depends importantly on there being a common global understanding, and acceptance, of when the application of force is both legal and legitimate."[3] The gulf between law and legitimacy is applicable more generally than the panel suggested. Consider Annan's successor in office. On January 1, 2007, Ban Ki-moon took office as the United Nations SG. The basis of his "election" was a series of straw polls in the UN Security Council (UNSC) in which he received the most votes while escaping a single negative vote from any one of the five permanent members (P5). Shashi Tharoor, who consistently ranked second in the polls, attracted one P5 (US) "discouragement" and withdrew. Ban was then elected unanimously by the UNSC and the election was ratified by acclamation by the General Assembly (GA).

Two conclusions may be drawn from this. First, Ban is the legally elected SG: all proper procedures were followed and he was duly sworn in. Second, the choice between him and Tharoor was made effectively by Washington. While the United States cast an indicative veto against one candidate, 177 of the 192 members of the organization had neither voice nor vote on the ultimately successful candidate. The SG is meant to be the world's top diplomat and the embodiment of the international interest. In an age of democratic legitimacy, why should the bulk of the world's countries and people accept him as "their" representative when they had neither voice nor vote in his selection? That is, the antiquated and opaque selection procedures seriously compromise the legitimacy of the outcome even though it is perfectly legal. Perhaps the point can be grasped by noting that during his tour of the Middle East in April 2007, Ban pointedly did not meet the Palestinian prime minister Ismail Haniya of Hamas, even though he was the legally elected leader in a region rather short of elected leaders.[4] The reason? Israel and the United States regard Hamas as a terrorist organization, and therefore illegitimate.

In this chapter, I shall argue that the gulf between law and legitimacy is a more serious crisis-in-the-making for the United Nations than is commonly realized. The reason for the underestimation of the extent and gravity of the gap may be that separate segments of the international community have problems with disparate elements of the gap and fail to capture the different dimensions in their cumulatively devastating impact on the UN's self-proclaimed legitimacy. I draw attention to the risks of the growing gap with respect to UN sanctions, the challenge of nuclear weapons, the use of force, international criminal justice, the structure and procedures of the UNSC, and accountability deficits among UN officials. Even so, this is an illustrative list, not an exhaustive account. I conclude with a comment on the danger of replacing an objective rule of law with an inherently subjective interpretation of international legitimacy as the primary basis of international action. Because much of the legitimacy-privileging justification is grounded in the vocabulary of humanitarianism, I will pay particular attention to the contentious aspects of the human rights discourse.

1. Authority, Legitimacy, Power

The distinction between law and legitimacy is an old one for political philosophers and intersects with the equally familiar discourse on the grounds of political obedience. Power is the capacity simply to enforce a particular form of behavior. Authority signifies the capacity to create and enforce rights and obligations which are accepted as legitimate and binding by members of an all-inclusive society who are subject to the authority. Ian Hurd distinguishes between coercion, self-interest, and legitimacy as alternative grounds for rule obedience and argues that, precisely because there is no international government to enforce them, states' compliance with international rules is a function of the legitimacy of those rules *as perceived by the norm-conforming states*.[5] That is, they are regarded as proper or appropriate by the actors to whom they are addressed within a socially constructed system of values and beliefs. If the source of legitimacy is institutions (either formal organizations or recurring and stable patterns of behavior), then those institutions indicate the existence of an international authority even in the absence of world government. For "the international system clearly exhibits some kind of order in which patterns repeat, institutions accrete, and practices are stable."[6]

The United Nations is the only truly global institution of a general purpose which approximates universality. The size of UN voting majorities, the forcefulness of the language used, and the frequency with which particular resolutions and language are recited are important because of the political significance attached to its perception as the closest we are able to get to an authentic voice of humanity. The role of custodian of collective legitimacy enables the United Nations, through its resolutions, to articulate authoritative standards of state behavior. The United Nations was meant to be the framework within which members of the international system negotiated agreements on the rules of behavior and the legal norms of proper conduct in order to preserve the society of states. Thus, simultaneously the United Nations was to be the forum for mediating power relationships, accomplishing political change that is held to be just and desirable by the international community, promulgating new norms, and conferring the stamp of collective legitimacy.

The United Nations is the site where power is moderated by lawful authority as law and legitimacy come together; or at least they should, in terms of the core identity on which the international organization was constructed. A community denotes shared values and bonds of affinity. An international community exists to the extent that there is a shared understanding of what constitutes legitimate behavior by the various actors in world affairs. A gulf between lawful and legitimate international behavior at or by the United Nations is prima facie evidence of an erosion of the sense of international community.[7] The United Nations is the symbol of an imagined and constructed community of strangers who have banded together to tackle the world's problems collectively and to work together cooperatively in the pursuit of shared goals. In this sense, the organization is first and foremost the repository of international idealism, the belief that human beings belong to one family, inhabit the same planet, and have joint custodial responsibility to husband resources and protect the environment for all future generations of life on this planet.

Deriving from this, the core UN mandates are primarily normative: to preserve peace, promote development, and protect human rights. Operational plans are implementation strategies of these essentially normative mandates. This in turn means that ethics, principles, and values are central to the identity of the United Nations and must inform all its activities and operations. This also explains why allegations of financial fraud by UN officials or sexual misconduct by UN peacekeepers are so intensely damaging to the United Nations. This is why hints of South Korea having in part "bought" the post of SG for Ban,[8] strenuously denied by Seoul, were not helpful.

Yet another pertinent example might be the way in which Taiwan has been "banned" and made to disappear from the United Nations, just like undesirables were officially banned under South Africa's apartheid regime and therefore could not be covered by news reports. Taiwan is refused membership, is not granted observer status, and does not figure in the UN's statistical databases. "Yet the irony is that in recent generations Taiwan has been a world leader in embodying the ideals of the U.N.'s own charter"—it is prosperous and free-wheelingly democratic, "the world's first Chinese democracy."[9] Taiwan's exclusion is procedurally legal—but is it constitutional and legitimate, bearing in mind that Taiwan "is indisputably a sovereign state. . . . Free and democratic"?[10] In January 2006, Mukhtar Mai, the Pakistani woman whose defiant response to go public about her pack rape on the orders of a tribal court made her a worldwide symbol of courage in the face of official apathy and discouragement, was denied the opportunity to speak at the United Nations because Pakistan protested that its prime minister was visiting the organization that day.[11] So much for "We the people."

The bases of UN legitimacy include its credentials for representing the international community, agreed procedures for making decisions on behalf of international society and political impartiality.[12] But sometimes this elides into claims of legitimacy based on the technical identity of the Secretariat as an international civil service, which is quite problematic. When Iraq's interim leaders requested UN assistance for training Iraqi judges and prosecutors who would be trying Saddam Hussein and his senior associates, the response from Annan was that the organization would not assist national courts that can impose the death penalty.[13] In his report on transitional justice, Annan reaffirmed that the United Nations would neither establish nor participate "in any tribunal for which capital punishment is included among possible sanctions."[14] But whose preferred political morality is this? What proportion of the world's people live under governments that have capital punishment on their statutes, including China, India, Indonesia, Japan, the United States? Who sets the relevant international standards and benchmarks? Does the United Nations somehow have a state of grace above its member states?

If the UNSC is the geopolitical center of gravity in the UN system, the GA is its normative center of gravity. Thus the legal competence to authorize the international use of force vests in the UNSC, but the legitimacy of a GA resolution is the greater for being the only authentic voice of the mystical "international community." The GA-UNSC clash of corporate interests intersects with the sometimes bitter North-South divide at the United Nations that has found expression in recent times on such issues as "humanitarian intervention," the relative priority to be accorded to tackling terrorism and global poverty, and internal UN management reform.[15] The new Secretary-General soon encountered a backlash on the last count.[16] But it is broader than that, and goes to the heart of the debate between law versus legitimacy. International law was a product mainly of the European states system and international humanitarian law too has its roots essentially in Europe. In the age of colonialism, most Africans, Asians, and Latin Americans became the victims of Western superiority in the organization and weaponry of warfare. They continue to be the objects but not the authors of norms and laws that are supposedly international.[17]

A world order in which developing countries are norm-takers and law-takers while Westerners are the rule setters, interpreters, and enforcers will not be viable because the division of labor is based neither on comparative advantage nor on equity. The risk is under-appreciated because the international discourse in turn is dominated by Western, in particular Anglo-American, scholarship. The net result of this, in turn, is that the bulk of scholarly analyses and discourse "privilege the experience, interests, and contemporary dilemmas of a certain portion of the society of states at the expense of . . . the large majority of states."[18] That is, the very universality from which the United Nations draws its legitimacy is in some crucial respects more token than real.

2. Sanctions: Legal but Illegitimate?

If Kosovo was an illegal and yet legitimate intervention by NATO, as argued by the independent international commission,[19] the reverse might be said of many sanctions regimes. Attempts to enforce authority can only be made by the legitimate agents of that authority. What distinguishes rule enforcement by criminal thugs from that by police officers is the principle of legitimacy. Legitimacy is thus the conceptual rod connecting the exercise of authority to the recourse to power. Enforcement includes diplomatic and economic coercion. Coercive economic sanctions developed as a conceptual and policy bridge between diplomacy and force for ensuring compliance with UN demands. Recourse to sanctions increased dramatically in the 1990s.[20] Calls for effective sanctions continue to be made sporadically with respect to Iran, Myanmar, Sudan, and Zimbabwe.

The right of the UNSC to impose sanctions in response to "any threat to the peace, breach of the peace or act of aggression" (Article 39) is clearly spelt out in the UN Charter: measures "not involving the use of force" including (but not limited to) "the complete or partial interruption of economic relations" (Article 41). Support for sanctions rests in their image as a humane alternative, and perhaps a necessary prelude, to war, which is increasingly regarded as a tool of the very last resort. Yet in contrast to wars, sanctions shift the burden of harm solely to civilians, mainly women and children. They cause death and suffering through "structural violence" (starvation, malnutrition and disease) on a scale exceeding the "cleaner" alternative of war. Yet the track record of sanctions in ensuring compliance with UN resolutions is "uneven."[21] They inflict undeniable pain on ordinary citizens while imposing questionable costs on leaders who are often enriched and strengthened on the back of their impoverished and oppressed people by the law of perverse consequences. All too often, sanctions are a poor alternative to, not a sound supplement to, a good foreign policy.

All this has steadily undermined their legitimacy. Once seen as an attractive nonviolent alternative to war, sanctions became increasingly discredited for their harsh humanitarian consequences on the civilian population.[22] Instead of the authority of the United Nations legitimizing sanctions regimes, the baleful effects of sanctions began to erode the legitimacy of the United Nations.[23] This was exacerbated by the paucity of intellectual and institutional foundations for the organization's sanctions policy. In response, the international community has been trying to refine and improve the tool in both design and implementation. Interest shifted to incorporating carefully thought out humanitarian exemptions or looking for "smarter" alternatives to comprehensive sanctions that put pressure on regimes rather than peoples. But even when much improved from a moral, political, and technical point of view and conceptually compelling, smart sanctions remain unproven in actual practice.

3. Nuclear Weapons

One of the countries under threat of increasingly broad-ranging sanctions in 2007–9 was Iran. The reasons for this were concerns about a clandestine pursuit of nuclear weapons. But in this case, there was a real question mark about the nuclear legality of those who would impose sanctions; about the legality of the UNSC in imposing sanctions as a tool of geopolitical dominance rather than lawful enforcement; and about the legitimacy of the nuclear order as presently constituted.[24] That is, it is a good illustration of what Richard Falk in his framing chapter to this volume calls the geopolitical manipulation of normative idealism.[25] The issue of nuclear weapons is useful also in highlighting the behavior-regulating role of legitimacy in international relations. And the arguments over Iran in some respects merely reprised the legal-legitimate dichotomy passionately debated when India and Pakistan tested in 1998,[26] and also over the India-US civilian nuclear cooperation agreement of 2006.[27]

India had argued for decades that the most serious breaches of the anti-nuclear norm were being committed by the five nuclear powers (N5, who coincide with the P5) who simply disregarded their disarmament obligations under Article 6 of the Nuclear Nonproliferation Treaty (NPT). The imbalance of reporting, monitoring, and compliance mechanisms between the nonproliferation and disarmament clauses of the NPT, India insisted, had in effect created nuclear apartheid. Against this background, the UN response to the 1998 tests posed the question of moral equivalence. The N5 preach nonproliferation while engaged in consenting deterrence. Their nuclear stockpiles are in defiance of the World Court's 1996 advisory opinion of a legal obligation to nuclear disarmament; India and Pakistan breached no international treaty, convention, or law by testing. For the N5—who are also the P5—to impose sanctions on the nuclear gatecrashers was akin (on this issue) to outlaws sitting in judgment, passing sentence and imposing punishment on the law abiding.

The attacks of September 11, 2001, concentrated minds on the prospect of terrorists acquiring weapons of mass destruction (WMD). A conceptual Rubicon was crossed by UNSC Resolution 1540 (April 28, 2004) in directing sovereign states to enact and enforce laws to prohibit nonstate actors from developing, acquiring, transferring, or using WMD; and to take and enforce effective domestic control, physical protection, accounting, and border control measures to prevent proliferation.

The unprecedented intrusion into national law-making authority can be read as the toughened new determination of the international community to take effective action. But it was not without controversy. A former member of the UN/OAU Expert Group on the Denuclearization of Africa noted that "by arrogating to itself wider powers of legislation," the UNSC was departing from its charter-based mandate. Excessive recourse to Chapter 7 could signal a preference for coercion over cooperation, while framing the resolution within the global war against terrorism was meant to silence dissenting voices. And the council's effort to seek global adherence to its resolutions was undermined by its unrepresentative composition and the veto power of the P5.[28] Many nongovernmental organizations (NGOs) too criticized the resolution's silence on the role of disarmament in promoting nonproliferation, as well as the UNSC effort to transform itself into a world legislature.[29]

The biggest tension in the arms-control regimes remains that between nonproliferation and disarmament. Article 6 of the NPT is the only explicit multilateral disarmament commitment undertaken by all the N5. Implementing Article 6 of the NPT instead of dusting it off occasionally as a rhetorical concession would dramatically transform the NPT from a nonproliferation into a prohibition regime. The N5 regard Article 6 as a peripheral obligation. Yet, as argued by the Nobel Prize-winning director-general of the International Atomic Energy Agency (IAEA), "Without this linkage, there would have been no agreement on an NPT in 1968—and it is hard to envision any new international nonproliferation compact that would not inherently contain such a linkage."[30]

If any one country can justify nuclear weapons on grounds of national security, so can others. Tehran portrays its actions as consistent with its NPT right to acquire nuclear technology and materials for peaceful purposes. The NPT requirements reflect the technical and political world of 1968. The series of inflammatory statements and incendiary steps by Mahmoud Ahmadinejad since he became president may make his pursuit of the nuclear weapons option illegitimate, but they do not by themselves prove Iran's actions to date to be illegal.

The security deficits of Iran's geostrategic environment include three de facto nuclear powers (Israel, Pakistan, and India) in its own region to the west and east; aggression in recent memory by neighbor Iraq, including the use of chemical weapons delivered by Scud missiles, which was at least tolerated if not condoned by the same Western powers that later turned against the author of the aggression; two nuclear powers (China and Russia) in the Central Asian regional context; a history of Anglo-American aggression against Iran; and a circle of US bases and forces around it in the context of having been designated a member of the "axis of evil."

Confronted with such a strategic environment, a prudent national security planner could not reasonably be faulted for recommending an acceleration rather than an abandonment of the nuclear program. Tehran too could cloak its actions in arguments that legitimacy is different from and on a higher plane than legality. American advocates of robust national postures argue that global regimes are unreliable instruments of security, international law is a fiction, and the United Nations is an irrelevant nuisance. Countries have to rely on their own military might to avoid becoming the victims of others. The NPT was negotiated for another time and another world. In the harsh world of today's international jungle, the only reliable route to ensuring national security is through national military might, including nuclear weapons.

All of which might put the ball back in the UN's court. But its authority too has been diminished by the Iraq war.[31] What is to stop other leaders from mimicking the bumper-sticker argument about not needing a permission slip from the United Nations to defend one's country? In other words, repeated US assaults on UN-centered law governing the international use of force have undermined the norm of a world of laws, the efficacy of international law, and the legitimacy of the United Nations as the authoritative validator of international behavior.

A norm cannot control the behavior of those who reject its legitimacy. Norm compliance by those who reject the legitimacy of the existing order will be a function of their incapacity to break out, not of voluntary obedience. The de facto position of "nuclear might equals right" is an inducement to join the club of nuclear enforcers. It is curious, to say the least, that those who worship at the altar of nuclear weapons are the fiercest in denouncing as heretics anyone else wishing to join their sect. In order to enhance their credentials as critics and enforcers of the norm, the N5 need to move more rapidly from deterrence to disarmament. There were early signs that the Obama administration might well take a lead on this. The logic of nonproliferation is inseparable from that of disarmament. Hence the axiom of nonproliferation: as long as any one country has them, others, including terrorist groups, will try their best (or worst) to get them. If they did not exist, nuclear weapons could not proliferate. Because they do, they will. The pursuit of nuclear nonproliferation is doomed without an accompanying duty to disarm.

Paradoxically, counter-proliferation efforts may well be legitimate even if illegal. The reality of contemporary threats means that significant gaps exist in the legal and institutional framework to combat them. Within the constraints of the NPT, a non-nuclear country can build the necessary infrastructure to be but a screwdriver away from acquiring nuclear weapons. Nonstate actors are outside the jurisdiction and control of multilateral agreements. Recognizing this, a US-led group of like-minded countries launched the Proliferation Security Initiative (PSI) to interdict illicit air, sea, and land cargo linked to WMD. Its premise is that the proliferation of such weapons deserves to be criminalized by the civilized community of nations. The PSI signals a new determination to overcome an unsatisfactory state of affairs through a broad partnership of countries that, using their own national laws and resources, will coordinate actions to halt shipments of dangerous technologies and materiel.

4. Atrocity Crimes and International Interventions

The PSI involves a limited use of force by groups of countries acting outside the UN framework. The law-legitimacy distinction arose with particular cogency with respect to the legal system promulgated and enforced by the apartheid regime in South Africa. If the constitutional system itself was essentially a criminal regime, then could not opposition to it be held up as legitimate even if illegal? That debate had barely faded when the same dilemma flared up in the 1990s with the spate of humanitarian atrocities and the role of international indifference, inaction, or intervention with respect to them. Except this time, the roles of the global North and South were reversed. When NATO launched a "humanitarian war" without UN authorization in Kosovo, it raised a triple policy dilemma:

- To respect sovereignty all the time is to be complicit in humanitarian tragedies sometimes;
- To argue that the UNSC must give its consent to international intervention for humanitarian purposes is to risk policy paralysis by handing over the agenda either to the passivity and apathy of the council as a whole, or to the most obstructionist member of the council, including any one of P5 determined to use the veto clause;
- To use force without UN authorization is to violate international law and undermine world order.

The three propositions together highlight a critical law-legitimacy gap between the needs and distress felt in the real world and the codified instruments and modalities for managing world order. Faced with another Holocaust or Rwanda-type genocide, on the one hand, and a Security Council veto, on the other, what would we do? Doing nothing would progressively delegitimize the role and undermine the authority of the UNSC as the cornerstone of the international law-enforcement system. But action without UN authorization would be illegal and also undermine the lawful authority of the UNSC. The legality-legitimacy distinction was to resurface four years later over Iraq and leave many Westerners rather less comfortable than the Kosovo precedent.[32]

In making up the rules of intervention "on the fly" in Kosovo,[33] NATO countries put at peril the requirement for a lasting system of world order grounded in the rule of international law. The attempt "to limit the reach of the Kosovo precedent did not prevent the advocates of the Iraq war from invoking it to justify toppling Saddam."[34]

The Iraq war's legality and legitimacy will be debated for years to come. The belligerent countries insisted that the war was both legal and legitimate, based on a series of prior UN resolutions and the long and frustrating history of combative-cum-deceitful defiance of the United Nations by Saddam Hussein. Others conceded that it may have been illegal but, like Kosovo in 1999, it was nevertheless legitimate in its largely humanitarian outcome. For a third group, the war was both illegal and illegitimate.[35]

Similarly, there were three views on the significance of the war for the UN-US relationship: that it demonstrated the irrelevance, centrality, or potential complicity of the United Nations.[36] For the neoconservatives, because it exists, the United Nations should be disinvented.[37] The second point of view acknowledged the need to confront Saddam but ruled out acting without UN authorization. The third argument accepted UN authorization as necessary but not sufficient, preferring irrelevance to complicity. In the opinion of some, the United Nations is "now more than ever reduced to the servile function of after-sales service provider for the United States, on permanent call as the mop-up brigade."[38]

Humanitarianism provides us with a vocabulary and institutional machinery of emancipation. But "[f]ar from being a defense of the individual against the state, human rights has become a standard part of the justification for the external use of force by the state against other states and individuals."[39] The use of force may be lawful or unlawful; the decision to use force is a political act; almost the only channel between legal authority and political legitimacy with regard to the international use of force is the United Nations. Conceding to any regional organization the authority to decide when political legitimacy may override legal technicality would make a mockery of the entire basis of strictly limited, and in recent times increasingly constricted, recourse to force for settling international disputes. Conversely, restricting the right solely to NATO is "an open argument for law-making by an elite group of Western powers sitting in judgment over their own actions"[40]—as well as that of all others. In effect, the West's position vis-à-vis the rest is: we shall hold you to account for your use of force domestically while exempting our international use of force from any external accountability.

While the West wants to proscribe the unconstrained use of force to maintain domestic order, developing countries want to proscribe the use of force by outsiders to enforce justice within errant member states. There is also the moral hazard that outside intervention on behalf of groups resisting state authority by force encourages other recalcitrant groups in other places to resort to ever-more-violent challenges, since that is the trigger to internationalizing their power struggle.

The tension is both powerful and poignant with respect to moving the globally endorsed responsibility to protect from norm to action (or words to deeds, principle to practice). Here we enter the realm both of *normative inconsistency*, selective application and enforcement of global norms against friends and adversaries—downplaying the human rights abuses of Central Asian states and Israel while highlighting those of Iraq and Iran, for example—and *normative incoherence*, when different norms clash with each other, as between human rights requirements and prohibitions against the use of force. Is it permissible—legitimate—to violate some aspects of international law in order to enforce respect for human rights laws? Is it still legitimate if some states are more equal than others in facing international pressure and sanctions, including military intervention as the ultimate sanction? The French foreign minister advocated invoking the responsibility to protect to override the junta's recalcitrance about accepting international assistance after Cyclone Nargis in Myanmar in 2008, but was notably silent about possible Israeli war crimes in Gaza in 2009. Such selectivity will quickly delegitimize the new norm whose path to global endorsement was quite contentious.[41]

In a Security Council debate on the protection of civilians in armed conflict on December 4, 2006, Chinese ambassador Liu Zhemin warned that the 2005 Outcome Document was "a very cautious representation of the responsibility to protect populations from genocide, war crimes, ethnic cleansing and crimes against humanity . . . it is not appropriate to expand, willfully to interpret or even abuse this concept."[42] Yet that is precisely what was suggested in 2008 in the context of Cyclone Nargis and more recently by the London-based One World Trust.[43] Ban is surely right in warning that "it would be counterproductive, and possibly even destructive, to try to revisit the negotiations that led to the provisions of paragraphs 138 ad 139 of the Summit Outcome."[44] Nor is this an isolated phenomenon. A major reason for the failure of the 2005 Outcome Document to include a single reference to the nuclear-weapons challenge was the backlash to the unilateral reinterpretation by the five NPT-licit nuclear powers of the NPT that it was solely about nonproliferation obligations by the rest instead of a package bargain between nonproliferation and disarmament obligations.

5. International Criminal Justice

African and Asian countries achieved independence on the back of extensive and protracted nationalist struggles. The anticolonial impulse was instilled in their countries' foreign policies and survives as a powerful sentiment in the corporate memory of the elites. All too often, developing-country views either fail to get a respectful hearing at all in Western policy and scholarly discourse, or are patronizingly dismissed.[45] There has been something of a revival of the enterprise of liberal imperialism, which rests on nostalgia for the lost world of Western empires that kept the peace among warring natives and provided sustenance to their starving peoples. This is at variance with the developing countries' own memories and narratives of their encounter with the West. Typically, their communities were pillaged, their economies ravaged, and their political development stunted. Whether it was Britain in Kenya or Belgium in the Congo,[46] the colonial powers were brutal in dealing with dissent and rebellion.

The displacement and ethnic cleansing of indigenous populations was carried out with such ruthless efficiency that the place of settler societies like Australia, Canada, and the United States in contemporary international society is accepted as a given because, as Paul Keal notes, the "criteria fixed by the inner circle" of powerful states "articulate rules of legitimacy and norms of behaviour."[47] Presumably the same explanation holds for the failure of even a peep of protest by the United Nations for the alleged atrocities committed by the US military in Fallujah in April 2004, including the use of chemical weapons prohibited under international humanitarian law. As one commentator observed on the eve of the third anniversary of the siege, "The US has overthrown a regime while supposedly searching for phantom weapons of mass destruction, only to use such weapons on the newly 'liberated' civilian population."[48] He offers as explanation for the failure of any lasting international outcry an all-encompassing weariness, "a kind of fatigue, a sense that ethical action is just too troublesome in our complicated and distracted world"—unless, of course, the sense of ethical outrage can be mobilized by the powerful to launch all-out military assaults against troublesome upstarts who do not kowtow to the resplendent ruler of the new middle kingdom.

The actions of the former colonial powers are as free of international criminal accountability today as they ever were. Discarding diplomatic language in favor of some blunt talking, on March 17, 2009, US Secretary of State Hillary Clinton warned Sudan's President Omar Hassan al-Bashir that he and his government "will be held responsible for every single death that occurs" in Darfur's refugee camps.[49] She was speaking in response to the expulsion of thirteen international aid groups, who provided around half of all assistance delivered in Darfur, in retaliation against the arrest warrants for Bashir issued by the International Criminal Court (ICC) in The Hague. Left unsaid was that no American can be held internationally responsible for a single death that occurs anywhere in the world. An initiative of international criminal justice meant to protect vulnerable people from brutal national rulers has been subverted into an instrument of powerful against vulnerable countries.

All four ICC indictments to date have been against Africans: nationals of the Central African Republic, the Democratic Republic of the Congo, Uganda, and Sudan.[50] When a person under ICC indictment is welcomed to Egypt by the president himself and attends an Arab League summit at which even Ban Ki-moon was present, the net result is to bring the system of international criminal justice into disrepute. Unlike Bashir or the other Africans in the dock, whose alleged atrocities were limited to national jurisdictions, the Bush administration asserted and exercised the right to kidnap suspected enemies in the war on terror anywhere in the world and take them anywhere else, including countries known to torture suspects.[51] Many Western allies colluded in the distasteful practice of rendition. No Westerner has faced criminal trial for it. In a surreal twist worthy of Kafka, we send terror suspects to be tortured to countries which we then brand as human rights abusers.

What of charges of war crimes by Hamas and Israelis in Gaza earlier this year? There was a furor in Israel as some soldiers claimed they shot unarmed civilians, sometimes under orders from their officers.[52] And we are all aware of the Hamas tactic of hiding its fighters and weapons amidst civilians, knowing that that will risk the death of innocents as Israelis return fire. The deaths of fellow Palestinians is less consequential to them than the international censure of Israel for killing innocent civilians.

Which rights that Westerners hold dear would they be prepared to give up in the name of universalism? Or is the concept of universalism just a one-way street—what we Westerners have is ours, what you heathens have is open to negotiation? One hint of the answer lies in the following: "the diffusion of international norms in the human rights area crucially depends on the establishment and the sustainability of networks among domestic and transnational actors who manage to link up with international regimes, to alert Western [*sic*] public opinion and Western [*sic*] governments."[53] The philosophical antecedents of such beliefs lie in the eighteenth–nineteenth-century theory of evolutionary progress through diffusion and acculturation from the West to the rest. The implicit but clear assumption is that when Western and non-Western values diverge, the latter are in the wrong, and it is only a matter of working on them with persuasion and pressure for the problem to be resolved and progress achieved.[54] The cognitive rigidity is shown again in "Pressure by Western states and international organizations can greatly increase the vulnerability of norm-violating governments to external influences."[55] Self-evidently, only non-Western governments can be norm violators; Western governments can only be norm setters and enforcers.

The rejection of the ICC[56] by Washington highlights the irony that the United States "is prepared to bomb in the name of human rights but not to join institutions to enforce them."[57] Even if we agree on universal human rights, they still have to be constructed, articulated, and embedded in international conventions. The question remains of the agency and procedure for determining what they are, how they apply in specific circumstances and cases, what the proper remedies might be to breaches, and who decides, following what rules of procedure and evidence. Under present conditions of world realities, the political calculus—relations based on military might, economic power, and media and NGO dominance—cannot be taken out. The resilience of the opposition to the internationalization of the human conscience lies in the fear that the lofty rhetoric of universal human rights claims merely masks the more mundane and familiar pursuit of national interests by different means.

6. The United Nations Security Council (UNSC)

Almost all the above examples relate to the UNSC as the core of the international law-enforcement system. General Rupert Smith argues that in Bosnia, "The existence and actions of the Security Council negatively affected events . . . The consequence of this failing was the destruction of the credibility of the UN." He concludes that "If the Security Council . . . is to change so as to wield force for good, then structural and organizational changes are necessary."[58] An unreformed UNSC has been experiencing a steady erosion of international legitimacy, which helps to explain the growing willingness of many state and nonstate actors to openly defy its edicts. That is, the increasing divergence of UNSC-sourced law from legitimacy dramatically reduces the efficacy of the United Nations in regulating the international behavior of a growing number of actors. For legality and legitimacy to come together again in the UNSC, its composition and procedures must be changed urgently to reflect today's military and ideational realities.

The legitimacy of the UNSC as the authoritative validator of international security action suffers from a quadruple legitimacy deficit: performance, representational, procedural, and accountability. Its performance legitimacy suffers from two strikes: an uneven and a selective record. It is unrepresentative from almost any point of view.[59] Its procedural legitimacy is suspect on grounds of lack of democratization and transparency in decision making. And it is not answerable to either the General Assembly, the World Court, the nations, or the peoples of the world.

Western countries often fret at the ineffectual performance legitimacy of the Security Council. Their desire to resist the council's role as the sole validator of the international use of force is the product of this dissatisfaction at its perceived sorry record. But the moral authority of collective judgments does depend in part on the moral quality of the *process* of making those judgments.[60] "When democrats disagree on substance, they need to agree on process," writes Michael Ignatieff.[61] The collective nature of the decision-making process of the UNSC is suspect because of the skewed distribution of political power and resources among its members. If the UNSC were to become increasingly activist, interventionist, and effective, the erosion of representational and procedural legitimacy and the absence of any accountability mechanisms would lead many countries to question the authority of the council even more forcefully.

There is a logical slippage between normative idealism and *realpolitik* in picking and choosing which elements of the existing order are to be challenged and which retained. If ethical imperatives and calculations of justice are to inform, underpin, and justify international interventions, then there is a powerful case for reforming the composition of the UNSC and eliminating the veto clause with respect to humanitarian operations. To self-censor such calls for major reform on the grounds that they are unacceptable to the major powers and therefore unrealistic is to argue in effect that the motive for intervention is humanitarian, not strategic; but the agency and procedure for deciding on intervention must remain locked in the strategic logic of *realpolitik*.

The United Nations is usually attacked for doing too little, too late. Has the UNSC been doing too much and too soon? In recent times, the UNSC has been co-opting functions that belong properly to legislative and judicial spheres. It has taken on a legislative role in resolutions on terrorism and nonproliferation. This is intruding into the realm of state prerogatives as negotiated in international conferences and conventions. The decisions of the UNSC are binding, so 192 legislatures are denied their right of review over international treaties. The Security Council imposed sanctions on Libya for its failure to extradite two citizens accused of being the brains behind the Lockerbie bombing (Resolution 748, March 31, 1992). That is, without a trial and conviction, the council was bent on compelling one sovereign state to hand over its citizens to another sovereign state on the basis of allegations from the latter—which had itself, just a few years earlier, defied the World Court's verdict in a case brought against it by Nicaragua.

In August 2004, the council approved a US-backed resolution demanding the immediate withdrawal of all foreign forces from Lebanon—at a time when more than 100,000 US troops were occupying Iraq. No one held their breath over any possible UN investigation of the tens—or is it hundreds—of thousands killed in Iraq since 2003. On May 31, 2007, a sharply divided UNSC voted 10-0-5 to establish an international criminal tribunal to prosecute the perpetrators of the suicide-assassination of Lebanon's Prime Minister Rafiq Hariri and twenty-two others in February 2005, which put the organization "in the business of stigmatizing and punishing individuals for a political crime."[62] The five abstainers—China, Indonesia, Qatar, Russia, and South Africa—explained that the resolution bypassed the Lebanese Parliament's constitutional role in approving international agreements.[63] Hezbollah issued a statement denouncing the UNSC resolution as "illegal and illegitimate at the national and international level."[64]

It is easy to understand why Iranians might have come to the same conclusion about the UNSC after their bitter war with Iraq. For eight long years, despite clear evidence of aggression by Saddam Hussein (who during this time was the West's useful idiot) and his use of chemical weapons, the council's standard response was to suggest that "both belligerents were equally at fault."[65]

If and when the UN Charter is reformed, one item on the agenda should be curbs on untrammeled authority in the UNSC that is presently subject to no countervailing political check or judicial review.[66] The idea that the P5 should concentrate legislative, executive, and judicial powers to themselves violates elementary notions of due process. Imagine if abuser regimes, and only they, had permanent membership and veto powers in the new Human Rights Council.

Western commentators seem to point routinely to China and Russia as the veto-wielding problem members of the P5. In fact, since the end of the Cold War, the country to have cast the veto most frequently is the United States. Britain and the United States have been among the most heavily involved in warfare and armed conflict over the last century; if we limit the period to that starting after the Second World War, a third country in the list would be Israel. Not the least because of the veto power in the Security Council, there is no prospect of anyone from any of these three countries being placed in the ICC dock in the foreseeable future. Little wonder that the precedent-setting indictment of the president of Sudan by the ICC in March 2009 drew protests from the majority of the African Union, the Arab League, and the Nonaligned Movement (the world's most representative general-purpose body after the United Nations itself) about the selective justice being meted out by the ICC. Until such time as Washington (and London) are prepared to lead the campaign for the abolition of the veto clause, it is difficult to see how the expectation, threat, or use of veto by others can legitimize any US or British action that circumvents the veto. Those who live by the veto cannot rightfully complain about having to die by the veto.

7. The UN-US Dualism

The push for democratization in the world has been led by the three Western members of the P5 (Britain, France, and the United States). Yet the three have been the most fiercely resistant to bringing democracy and transparency to the workings of the council itself.

In some respects, it is more accurate to speak these days of the P1 rather than the P5. Authority is the right to make policy and rules, while power is the capacity to implement the policy and enforce the rules. The United Nations has global reach and authority but no power. It symbolizes global governance but lacks the attributes of international government. While lawful authority remains vested in the United Nations, power has become increasingly concentrated in the United States, which has global grasp and power but not international authority. The exercise of power is rendered less effective and generates its own resistance if divorced from authority. The latter in turn is corroded when challenges to it go unanswered by the necessary force. Lack of capacity to be the chief enforcer acting under Chapter 7 means that the United Nations remains an incomplete organization, one that practices only parts of its charter. That being the case, Ed Luck asks, "Is it tenable for the UN to say that it only wants to walk on the soft side of the street but nevertheless wants to have some degree of control over what happens on the other side as well?"[67]

Until the First World War, war was an accepted and normal part of the states system, with distinctive rules, norms, and etiquette. In that Hobbesian world, the only protection against aggression was countervailing power, which increased both the cost of victory and the risk of failure. Since 1945, the United Nations has spawned a corpus of law to stigmatize aggression and create a robust norm against it. The United Nations exists to check the predatory instincts of the powerful toward the weak—one of the most enduring but not endearing lessons of history. Since 9/11, an America that was already over-armed has militarized its foreign policy still more.

The implications of an American empire for law and legality in world affairs are discussed later in this volume by Amy Bartholomew. Might the US irritation at the United Nations owe as much to its effectiveness in constraining imperial US behavior as alleged UN ineffectiveness against others? The Bush administration rejected President Harry Truman's counsel that America must deny itself the license to do as it pleases, ignored President John F. Kennedy's wisdom that America is neither omnipotent nor omniscient, and rode roughshod over four decades of tradition of enlightened self-interest and liberal internationalism as the guiding normative template of US foreign policy.[68] Paul Heinbecker, Canada's former UN ambassador, comments that the distance from hubris to delusion is short; the Bush Administration covered it in a sprint.[69]

At the same time, most Western countries, including the United States, rightly point to the total dysfunctionality of the General Assembly. There is merit to the argument that at least one explanation for the creeping powers of the UNSC is the loss of focus and efficiency by the assembly. It is far more interested in finger pointing and point scoring than problem solving. Its fascination with procedural technicalities and square brackets fails to excite anyone outside. One of its low points surely was the equation of Zionism with racism, a resolution that mercifully has since been rescinded. Thus in many quarters, the chief cause of the steady erosion of UN legitimacy is the GA, not the UNSC.

8. Accountability, Integrity, and Legitimacy Deficit

International organizations that are perceived by their members as legitimate are governmental in the way in which they exercise social control through the promulgation of norms (standards of behavior) and laws (rules of behavior). The United Nations, not unlike national governments, represents a structure of authority that rests on institutionalized state practices and generally accepted norms. But "governmental bodies are expected to be accountable and open to opposition,"[70] otherwise they will suffer an erosion of their legitimacy. The UN's authority to preach the virtues of good governance and accountability to others will be gravely compromised by any departures from these values in its own behavior.

In recent times, the organization has been in turmoil, struggling to cope with a string of allegations of fraud and misconduct by foot soldiers and senior officials. I have remarked on the poisonous North–South divide at the United Nations, which has a corrosive effect on the organization's legitimacy to the extent that it derives from its identity as a universal organization and developing countries comprise the majority of its membership. Sometimes this is turned on its head by Western critics who blame management shortcomings on quota politics imposed by the third-world majority on UN recruitment and promotion policy and practice. Yet my own research showed the fallacy of such a charge. The senior ranks of the UN system are dominated by nationals of the rich and powerful countries.[71] The point was borne out by the senior appointments made by the new Secretary-General.[72] And in the case of the choice of his deputy, the general consensus is that Ban had available another African woman candidate who would have raised fewer initial questions about management and competence. That is, it is the individual exercise of judgment that may be flawed, not the general principle of equitable geographical and, increasingly, gender representation.

Another canard is about the oil-for-food scandal. Yes, the affair showed up lapses and weaknesses in the internal management culture and practices of the UN Secretariat. But, in the total sweep of the scandal, these were minor. The really important lessons were four. First, the United Nations simply does not have the capacity, in size and technical resources, to manage such a program and should firmly refuse any such task in the future. Besides, even the record of US authorities since 2003 is considerably worse.[73] Second, UN officials did in fact raise queries about potential shenanigans with the appropriate oversight committee of the UNSC, but their concerns were not taken up for serious investigation. The main players in the council had other priorities. If judgments are to be made, they should be about the council members, not UN officials.[74] Third, the real money was changing hands between business firms and executives and ministers and officials of member governments, not UN officials. After a $35 million inquiry, the Volcker committee found a risible $150,000 that one official could not satisfactorily account for: unaccounted, not even prima facie evidence of having received a bribe. By contrast, many non-UN politicians, officials, and business executives were implicated in serious sums of money. The biggest single questionable payment, some AUD300 million, concerned the originally government-owned and later government-backed Australian Wheat Board (and subsequently just AWB) dealings with Saddam Hussein.[75] Finally, for all these flaws, the program actually succeeded in its humanitarian goals, just as the UN inspection teams succeeded in disarming Saddam of WMD.

In a similar vein, who should be held accountable for the flawed judgment and actions of an SG—UN officials or those with the most say in (s)electing him?[76] When America's love affair with Annan soured and the right-wing commentators in particular decided to go after him, the United Nations as a corporate entity was just as liberally smeared, and some of us UN officials too had to bear barbs directed at the United Nations for its supposed lack of institutional ethics. Leaving aside the question of Annan's legacy and whether or not the attacks were merited or ill-intentioned,[77] the facts are fairly straightforward and uncontestable. In 1991, the African candidate with the widest support in the UNSC was Salim Ahmed Salim. He was much too radical for Washington's taste and was vetoed. Instead Boutros Boutros-Ghali was chosen SG. Five years later, he was out of favor in Washington and was replaced by Annan, who was then at American instigation reappointed unanimously for a second term. So if Annan turned out to be deficient, should critics direct their ire at the United Nations as an institution, at UN officials, or at the US government?

That said, the real UN scandal of the last dozen years or so has been with respect to predatory peacekeepers.[78] Fifteen years ago, Amnesty International argued that the time was overdue for the United Nations to build measures for human rights promotion and protection into its own peacekeeping activities.[79] If the United Nations is to maintain its human rights credibility, soldiers committing abuses in its name must face investigation and prosecution by effective international machinery. (The abuses are not confined to UN peacekeepers. Amnesty concluded that "the international community"—that is, NATO peacekeepers as well as UN civilian personnel—made up around 80 percent of the clientele of women trafficked into prostitution in Kosovo.[80])

Annan admitted to being "especially troubled by instances in which United Nations peacekeepers are alleged to have sexually exploited minors and other vulnerable people," repeated his policy of zero tolerance of such offences, and reaffirmed the UN's commitment "to respect, adhere to and implement international law, fundamental human rights and the basic standards of due process."[81] He appointed Prince Zeid al-Hussein, Jordan's ambassador to the United Nations who had personal civilian peacekeeping experience in Bosnia, to study the abuses and make recommendations on improving the accountability of UN peacekeeping missions. Prince Zeid's report concluded that sexual exploitation of women and girls by UN security and civilian personnel in Congo was significant, widespread, and ongoing.[82] Annan concurred with the analysis and recommendations with respect to the investigative processes; the organizational, managerial, and command responsibility; and individual disciplinary, financial, and criminal accountability. But, when the problem of peacekeepers as sexual predators has been known at least since the Namibia and Cambodia operations, why was no action taken earlier and who has been held accountable for the lapse?[83]

9. Conclusion: Objective Law vs. Subjective Legitimacy

International law, like all law, is an effort to align power to justice. Politics is about power: its location, bases, exercise, effects. Law seeks to tame power and convert it into authority through legitimizing principles (e.g., democracy, separation of powers), structures (e.g., legislature, executive, and judiciary) and procedures (e.g., elections). Law thereby mediates relations between the rich and the poor, the weak and the powerful, by acting as a constraint on capricious behavior and setting limits on the arbitrary exercise of power. Conversely, the greater the gap between power and authority, the closer we are to anarchy, to the law of the jungle where might equals right, and the greater is the legitimacy deficit. Equally, the greater the gap between power and justice in world affairs, the greater is the international legitimacy deficit. When the powerful subvert the proper relationship to make law subservient to their agenda for keeping others in line, as seems to be happening with the ICC, the many will reject, resist, and rebel against such a perversion of justice.

The *rule of law ideal* has been diffused from the West to become an international norm. It asserts the primacy of law over the arbitrary exercise of political power by using law to tame power; the protection of the citizen from the arbitrary actions of the government by making both, and their relationship to each other, subject to impersonal and impartial law; and the primacy of universalism over particularism through the principle of equal in law, whereby individuals coming before the law are treated as individuals, divorced from their social characteristics.

A normative commitment to the *rule of law* implies a commitment to the principle of relations being governed by law, not power. It also implies a willingness to accept the limitations and constraints of working within the law, in specific instances if necessary against individual notions of just or illegitimate outcome. Fidelity to international regimes, laws, and institutions must be required of and demonstrated by all countries. Trashing global institutions and cherry-picking norms and laws is incompatible with using them to compel compliance by others. To those who uphold the law themselves, and only to them, shall be given the right to enforce it on others.

In apartheid South Africa, in colonial India, and in any situation where conscience dictates that individuals resist laws that they regard as unjust—that is, illegitimate—citizens accept the resulting punishment meted out by the legal process as the necessary price for acting on the basis of their core beliefs. By contrast, in international affairs, the legitimacy–legality distinction is used in the effort to seek *escape* from any penalty for acting outside the law: yes, Kosovo may have been illegal, but because our intervention was legitimate, we deserve praise and reward, not blame and punishment.

The Kosovo and Iraq interventions underlined widespread perceptions that powerful countries can break the rules of the charter regime with impunity. This has widened the gulf between law and legitimacy. Susan Woodward makes the telling point that the Security Council still does not have "a policy on how to address and manage conflicts that threaten the territorial integrity of a country from within." This is a policy dilemma for Serbia that most developing countries could identify with and most Western countries did not. The result was "a cavalier invocation by the Security Council of Chapter VII authority without providing the mandate or resources necessary to stop the war."[84] She goes on to indict the council for bearing "the larger moral responsibility, for never having sought to craft a policy of its own independent of the actions of its members . . . either for the Yugoslav conflicts or for the generic problem which it will continue to face." It "failed to defend the territorial integrity of a member state, and it then failed to establish and enforce rules on the recognition of statehood and borders."[85]

As David Kennedy notes, war has always been with us, and so has humanitarianism: "an endless struggle to contain war in the name of civilization."[86] He argues that, by and large, the humanitarian community has failed to confront the reality of bad consequences flowing from good intentions. The central objective of traditional humanitarian policy making has been to reduce the frequency and violence of war. Now many humanitarians demand the use of violence and war in order to advance the humanitarian agenda.

But how can one "intervene" in Kosovo, East Timor, Iraq, or Darfur and pretend to be detached from and not responsible for the distributional consequences with respect to wealth, resources, power, status, and authority? This dilemma is inherent in the structure of interventions and has nothing to do with the false dichotomy between multilateral interventions in one context and unilateral in another. "The effort to intervene . . . without affecting the background distribution of power and wealth betrays this bizarre belief in the possibility of an international governance which does not govern."[87]

By virtue of their growing influence and power, humanitarian actors have effectively entered the realm of policy making, at the same time as their emancipatory vocabulary has been captured by governments and other power brokers. International humanitarians are participants in global governance as advocates, activists, and policy makers. Their critiques and policy prescriptions have demonstrable consequences in the governmental and intergovernmental allocation of resources and the exercise of political, military, and economic power. With influence over policy should come responsibility for the consequences of policy. When things go wrong or do not happen according to plan, the humanitarians share the responsibility for the suboptimal outcomes.

Human rights has become the universal vocabulary of political legitimacy and humanitarian law of military legitimacy. But rather than necessarily constraining the pursuit of national interests in the international arena by military means, human rights and humanitarian law provide the discourse of justification for the familiar traditional means of statecraft. Much as humanitarians might want to believe that they still hold up the virtue of truth to the vice of power, the truth is that the vocabulary of virtue has been appropriated in the service of power. Far from bridging, that increases the distance between law and legitimacy, particularly at the United Nations.

Endnotes

This paper was delivered as the Sir Ninian Stephen Annual Lecture in Melbourne, Australia, on December 7, 2009, and published in the *Melbourne Journal of International Law* 11, no. 1 (June 2010). It is reprinted with permission.

1. George Monbiot, "The Best Way to Give the Poor a Real Voice is through a World Parliament," *Guardian* (London), April 24, 2007.

2. Kofi A. Annan, *In Larger Freedom: Towards Development, Security and Human Rights for All.* Report of the Secretary-General (New York: United Nations, document A/59/2005, March 21, 2005), paras. 140, 182, and 183.

3. High-Level Panel on Threats, Challenges and Change, *A More Secure World: Our Shared Responsibility* (New York: United Nations, document A/59/565, December 2004), para. 184.

4. Warren Hoge, "UN Chief Starting to Wield Personal Authority in Mideast," *International Herald Tribune*, April 2, 2007. The title of the article notwithstanding, everything that Ban did on the trip as reported in it conformed to Washington's priorities and perceptions.

5. Ian Hurd, "Legitimacy and Authority in International Politics," *International Organization* 53:2 (Spring 1999): 379–408. For example, Hurd notes that many borders are undefended and indefensible, such as Canada's with the United States. Coercion or the fear of retribution is inadequate to explain US restraint in not taking over Canada. Nor does one find a continual calculation and recalculation by states of the costs and benefits of conquest as would be predicted by a rational self-interest model. Instead there is a "taken-for-grantedness" of borders as a whole. Revisionist actors are and are seen as dangerous "rogues" by others precisely because they approximate the self-interested model. Ibid., 395–398.

6. Ibid., 400.

7. Amitai Etzioni argues similarly that the greater threat to the European Union is not the so-called democratic deficit, but a "community deficit, the lack of shared values and bonds"; "The Community Deficit," *Journal of Common Market Studies* 45:1 (2007): 23.

8. Richard Beeston and James Bone, "Seoul Tries to Buy Top UN Job," *Australian*, September 29, 2006; "Ban Denies Influence-Peddling Charge," *Japan Times*, October 29, 2006.

9. Claudia Rosett, "Celebrating the Real Success Story," *Wall Street Journal Europe*, October 5, 2005.

10. Chen Shui-bian (President of Taiwan), "The Shunning of a State," *Washington Post*, May 11, 2007.

11. Warren Hoge, "Heeding Pakistani Protest, UN Blocks Talk by Rape Victim," *New York Times*, January 21, 2006.

12. See Robert O. Keohane, "The Contingent Legitimacy of Multilateralism," in *Multilateralism under Challenge? Power, International Order, and Structural Change*, ed. Edward Newman, Ramesh Thakur, and John Tirman (Tokyo: United Nations University Press, 2006), 56–76.

13. "U.N. Won't Train Iraqi Judges," *Daily Yomiuri*, October 24, 2004; Marlise Simons, "Iraqis Not Ready for Trials; UN to Withhold Training," *New York Times*, October 22, 2004.

14. Kofi A. Annan, *The Rule of Law and Transitional Justice in Conflict and Post-Conflict Societies*. Report of the Secretary-General. (New York: United Nations, document S/2004/616, August 23, 2004), para. 64(d).

15. "Poor Nations Block Key UN Reform," *BBC News*, April 29, 2006, downloaded from http://news.bbc.co.uk/go/pr/fr/-/2/hi/americas/4957140.stm on April 29, 2006.

16. Colum Lynch, "Secretary General Faces a Backlash," *Washington Post*, February 14, 2007; "G-77, NAM Oppose Deadline to Approve UN Restructuring Plan," *Doordarshan News* (India's state TV), February 2, 2007, downloaded from www.ddinews.gov.in/International/International+-+Headlines/nam.htm on February 2, 2007.

17. See Ramesh Thakur, "Global Norms and International Humanitarian Law: An Asian Perspective," *International Review of the Red Cross* 83, no. 841 (March 2001): 19–44.

18. Mohammed Ayoob, "Inequality and Theorizing in International Relations: The Case for Subaltern Realism," *International Studies Review* 4, no. 3 (Fall 2002): 29.

19. *Kosovo Report: Conflict, International Response, Lessons Learned* (Oxford: Oxford University Press for the Independent International Commission on Kosovo, 2000).

20. See David Cortright and George A. Lopez, *The Sanctions Decade: Assessing UN Strategies in the 1990s* (Boulder: Lynne Rienner, 2000).

21. Kofi A. Annan, *We the Peoples: The Role of the United Nations in the 21st Century* (The Millennium Report) (New York: UN Department of Public Information, 2000), 49.

22. See David Cortright, George A. Lopez, and Linda Gerber-Stellingwerf, "Sanctions," in *Oxford Handbook on the United Nations*, ed. Thomas G. Weiss and Sam Daws (Oxford: Oxford University Press, 2007), 349–369.

23. The United Nations has a particularly low image among Iraqis in large part because of the UN sanctions regime, which inflicted severe pain on the population without removing Saddam Hussein.

24. See Jane Boulden, Ramesh Thakur, and Thomas G. Weiss, eds., *The United Nations and Nuclear Orders* (Tokyo: United Nations University Press, 2009).

25. See also the chapter by Asli Bali in this volume.

26. See Ramesh Thakur, "The South Asian Nuclear Challenge," in John Baylis and Robert O'Neill, eds., *Alternative Nuclear Futures: The Role of Nuclear Weapons in the Post–Cold War World* (Oxford: Oxford University Press, 2000), 101–124.

27. See Jayantha Dhanapala and Daryl Kimball, "A Nonproliferation Disaster," *Proliferation Analysis* (Washington, D.C.: Carnegie Endowment for International Peace, 2008), downloaded from http://www.carnegieendowment.org/publications/index.cfm?fa=view&id=20292&prog=zgp&proj=znpp,zsa on July 26, 2008; Sumit Ganguly and Dinshaw Mistry, "The Case for the U.S.-India Nuclear Agreement," *World Policy Journal* (Summer 2006): 11–19; William C. Potter, "India and the New Look of U.S. Nonproliferation Policy," *Nonproliferation Review* 12:2 (July 2005): 343–354; and Ramesh Thakur, "U.S.-India Nuclear Accord a Win-Win Outcome for All," *Daily Yomiuri*, November 27, 2005, and "Don't Let the India-US Nuclear Deal Unravel," *Globe and Mail*, April 27, 2007.

28. Abdalmahmood Abdalhaleem Mohammad, "Security Council and Non-proliferation," *The Hindu* (Chennai), May 28, 2004.

29. Jim Wurst, "NGOs Criticize Nonproliferation Draft for Ignoring Disarmament," *U.N. Wire*, downloaded from www.unwire.org on April 1, 2004.

30. Mohamed ElBaradei, "Preserving the Non-Proliferation Treaty," *Disarmament Forum* 4 (2004): 3.

31. See Ramesh Thakur, *Fast Forward to the Past? The Line in the Sand from Iraq to Iran*, CIGI Working Paper No. 7 (Waterloo, Ontario: Centre for International Governance Innovation, August 2006).

32. See Ramesh Thakur, *War in Our Time: Reflections on Iraq, Terrorism and Weapons of Mass Destruction* (Tokyo: United Nations University Press, 2007).

33. Michael J. Glennon, "The New Interventionism: The Search for a Just International Law," *Foreign Affairs* 78, no. 3 (May/June 1999): 6.

34. Robert W. Tucker and David C. Hendrickson, "The Sources of American Legitimacy," *Foreign Affairs* 83, no. 6 (November/December 2004): 31.

35. For the three arguments, see David Kreiger, "The War in Iraq as Illegal and Illegitimate"; Charlotte Ku, "Legitimacy as an Assessment of Existing Legal Standards: The Case of the 2003 Iraq War"; and Ruth Wedgwood, "The Multinational Action in Iraq and International Law," all in Ramesh Thakur and Waheguru Pal Singh Sidhu, eds., *The Iraq Crisis and World Order: Structural, Institutional and Normative Challenges* (Tokyo: United Nations University Press, 2006), 381–425.

36. This is developed in Ramesh Thakur, "Iraq, UN and Changing Bases of World Order," *Economic and Political Weekly* 38, no. 23 (June 7–13, 2003): 2261–2266.

37. See Richard Perle, "Thank God for the Death of the UN," *Guardian*, March 21, 2003.

38. Alexander Cockburn, "It Should Be Late, It Was Never Great," *The Nation*, December 22, 2003, p. 9.

39. David Kennedy, *The Dark Sides of Virtue: Reassessing International Humanitarianism* (Princeton, N.J.: Princeton University Press, 2004), 25.

40. David Chandler, *From Kosovo to Kabul: Human Rights and International Intervention* (London: Pluto, 2002), 135.

41. That story is told in three books by three people closely associated with it: Gareth Evans (co-chair of the International Commission on Intervention and State Sovereignty), *The Responsibility to Protect: Ending Mass Atrocity Crimes Once and for All* (Washington, D.C.: Brookings, 2008); Ramesh Thakur (ICISS commissioner), *The United Nations, Peace and Security: From Collective Security to the Responsibility to Protect* (Cambridge: Cambridge University Press, 2006); and Thomas G. Weiss (ICISS research director), *Humanitarian Intervention* (Oxford: Polity, 2007).

42. S/PV.5577, "Security Council Open Debate on Protection of Civilians in Armed Conflict," UN Security Council Verbatim Record, December 4, 2006, p. 8; quoted in Sarah Teitt, "Assessing Polemics, Principles and Practices: China and the Responsibility to Protect," *Global Responsibility to Protect* 1, no. 2 (2009): 216.

43. Elodie Aba and Michael Hammer, *Yes We Can? Options and Barriers to Broadening the Scope of the Responsibility to Protect to Include Cases of Economic, Social and Cultural Rights Abuse* (London: One World Trust, Briefing Paper No. 116, March 2009).

44. Ban Ki-moon, *Implementing the Responsibility to Protect: Report of the Secretary-General* (New York: United Nations, document A/63/677, January 12, 2009), para. 67.

45. See Ramesh Thakur, *Towards a Less Imperfect State of the World: The Gulf between North and South* (Berlin: Friedrich Ebert Stiftung, Dialogue on Globalization Briefing Paper, April 4, 2008).

46. For two recent books that dramatically revise the severity and scale of British repression and what today would be termed atrocities, see David Anderson, *Histories of the Hanged: The Dirty War in Kenya and the End of Empire* (New York: W. W. Norton, 2005); and Caroline Elkins, *Imperial Reckoning: The Untold Story of Britain's Gulag in Kenya* (New York: Henry Holt, 2005). For an account of the scale of humanitarian atrocities committed by Belgium in its African colony, see Adam Hochschild, *King Leopold's Ghost* (Boston: Houghton Mifflin, 1999).

47. Paul Keal, *European Conquest and the Rights of Indigenous Peoples: The Moral Backwardness of International Society* (Cambridge: Cambridge University Press, 2003), 188.

48. Jonathan Holmes, "The Legacy of Fallujah," *Guardian*, April 4, 2007.

49. "U.S. Blames Sudan's President for Darfur 'Catastrophe'," CNN, March 17, 2009, http://edition.cnn.com/2009/WORLD/africa/03/17/us.sudan/index.html, accessed on March 18, 2009.

50. For a troubling account of the arbitrary and corner-cutting basis on which the ICC Prosecutor has operated, including in relation to Sudan's president, see Julie Flint and Alex de Waal, "Case Closed: A Prosecutor without Borders," *World Affairs* (Spring 2009), available at http://www.worldaffairsjournal.org/2009%20–20Spring/full-DeWaalFlint.html, accessed on April 1, 2009.

51. For details of the secret but leaked ICRC report on the Guantanamo detainees, see Mark Danner, "US Torture: Voices from the Dark Sites," *New York Review of Books* 56, no. 6 (April 9, 2009).

52. Ethan Bronner, "Soldiers' Accounts of Gaza Killings Raise Furor in Israel," *New York Times*, March 20, 2009, and Rory McCarthy, "Israeli Troops Describe Shooting Gaza Civilians," *Guardian*, March 20, 2009. The conquerors' arrogance can be seen also in Israeli sharpshooters ordering T-shirts showing a pregnant Arab woman with a bullseye superimposed on her belly, accompanied by the slogan "1 shot 2 kills"; Donald Macintyre, "Israel Military Condemns Soldiers' Shocking T-shirts," *Independent*, March 22, 2009.

53. Thomas Risse and Kathryn Sikkink, "The Socialization of International Human Rights Norms into Domestic Practices: Introduction," in Thomas Risse, Stephen C. Ropp, and Kathryn Sikkink, eds., *The Power of Human Rights: International Norms and Domestic Change* (Cambridge: Cambridge University Pres, 1999), 5.

54. Many in developing countries watched bemusedly from the sidelines when the same attitudinal divide opened up across the Atlantic in 2003 with respect to the US threat of war on Iraq and the stiff resistance from European citizens. The dominant view in Washington seemed once again to be that the European people could not possibly be right. The task was to show them the error of their ways or, failing that, to make sure that the European governments listened to the US administration rather than to their own people. That the administration could be wrong was a priori beyond the realm of possibility.

55. Thomas Risse and Stephen C. Ropp, "International Human Rights Norms and Domestic Change: Conclusions," in Risse, Ropp and Sikkink, eds., *Power of Human Rights*, 277.

56. The implications of this for law versus legitimacy debate are analyzed later in this volume by Vesselin Popovski.

57. Christine M. Chinkin, "Kosovo: A 'Good' or 'Bad' War?" *American Journal of International Law* 93, no. 4 (October 1999): 846.

58. Rupert Smith, "The Security Council and the Bosnian Conflict: A Practitioner's View," in *The United Nations Security Council and War: The Evolution of Thought and Practice since 1945*, ed. Vaughan Lowe, Adam Roberts, Jennifer Welsh, and Dominik Zaum (Oxford: Oxford University Press, 2008), 451.

59. See Ramesh Thakur, ed., *What Is Equitable Geographic Representation in the Twenty-first Century?* (Tokyo: United Nations University, 1999).

60. Amy Gutmann and Dennis Thompson, *Democracy and Disagreement* (Cambridge, Mass.: Harvard University Press, 1996), 4.

61. Michael Ignatieff, *The Lesser Evil: Political Ethics in an Age of Terror* (Princeton, N.J.: Princeton University Press, 2004), viii.

62. Gary J. Bass, "Does the UN Understand What It's Getting Itself Into?" *Washington Post*, October 30, 2005.

63. Colum Lynch, "UN Backs Hariri Murder Tribunal," *New York Times*, June 1, 2007.

64. "Hezbollah Condemns Hariri Court," *BBC News*, May 31, 2007, downloaded from http://news.bbc.co.uk/2/hi/middle_east/6707315.stm on May 31, 2007.

65. Charles Tripp, "The Security Council and the Iran-Iraq War," in Lowe et al., eds., *The United Nations Security Council and War*, 374.

66. In the *Namibia* and *Lockerbie* cases, the International Court of Justice cast doubts on the blanket immunity of the Security Council from judicial scrutiny but did not go so far as to enunciate a doctrine of judicial review. See Jose E. Alvarez, "Judging the Security Council," *American Journal of International Law* 90, no. 1 (January 1996): 1–39; and Thomas M. Franck, "The 'Powers of Appreciation': Who Is the Ultimate Guardian of UN Legality?" *American Journal of International Law* 86, no. 3 (July 1992): 519–523.

67. Edward C. Luck, "Another Reluctant Belligerent: The United Nations and the War on Terrorism," in *The United Nations and Global Security*, ed. Richard M. Price and Mark W. Zacher (New York: Palgrave Macmillan, 2004), 105.

68. See Tucker and Hendrickson, "Sources of American Legitimacy," 18–32.

69. Paul Heinbecker, "The Davey Lecture," Victoria College, University of Toronto, March 29, 2007.

70. Hurd, "Legitimacy and Authority in International Politics," 383.

71. Thakur, *United Nations, Peace and Security*, 310–314.

72. See Richard Beeston and James Bone, "Britain Names Price for UN Vote," *Australian*, October 6, 2006; Evelyn Leopold, "Mexican Biologist, British Diplomat Get UN Posts," *Reuters*, January 4, 2007 downloaded from www.alertnet.org/thenews.newsdesk/116789930341.htm on January 9, 2007; David Nason, "UN Chief 'Hits the Ground Stumbling,'" *Australian*, January 15, 2007; Tunku Abdul Aziz, "Ban Has Lost a Great Opportunity," *New Straits Times* (Kuala Lumpur), February 26, 2007.

73. See, for example, Philip Shenon, "Did Billions Sent by U.S. to Iraq Fund Insurgents?" *International Herald Tribune*, February 8, 2007, and the *New York Times* editorial on the same subject, "The Fog of Accountability," *International Herald Tribune*, February 9, 2007.

74. " . . . the one nation which shoved the inquiry forward from the beginning was most culpable—the United States"; Stephen Schlesinger, "Where Volcker Got It Wrong," *MaximsNews.Com*, downloaded from www.maximsnews.com/2005schlesinger1december.htm on December 2, 2005.

75. See the editorial in *The Australian*, March 29, 2006. See also David Leigh and Rob Evans, "Firms Accused of Bribing Saddam to be Investigated by Fraud Office," *Guardian*, February 14, 2007.

76. The lack of enthusiasm for Ban among UN officials was an open secret in New York; see Ewen MacAskill and Ed Pilkington, "Despair at UN over Selection of 'Faceless' Ban Ki-moon as General Secretary [*sic*]," *Guardian*, October 7, 2006.

77. For my views on his legacy, see Ramesh Thakur, "What Annan Has Contributed to World," *Daily Yomiuri*, December 26, 2006.

78. See Chiyuki Aoi, Cedric deConing and Ramesh Thakur, eds., *Unintended Consequences of Peacekeeping Operations* (Tokyo: United Nations University Press, 2007).

79. Amnesty International, *Peace-Keeping and Human Rights* (London: AI, 1994).

80. *Protecting the Human Rights of Women and Girls Trafficked for Forced Prostitution in Kosovo* (London: AI, document EUR 70/010/2004, 2004).

81. Annan, *In Larger Freedom*, para. 113.

82. Prince Zeid Ra'ad Zeid al-Hussein, *A Comprehensive Strategy to Eliminate Future Sexual Exploitation and Abuse in United Nations Peacekeeping Operations* (New York: United Nations, document A/59/710, March 24, 2005).

83. See, for example, Peter Dennis, "The UN, Preying on the Weak," *New York Times*, April 12, 2005.

84. Susan L. Woodward, "The Security Council and the Wars in Former Yugoslavia," in Lowe et al., eds., *United Nations Security Council and War*, 407.

85. Ibid., 440–441.

86. Kennedy, *Dark Sides of Virtue*, 323.

87. Ibid., 130.

3

Legitimacy Norms as Change Agents: Examining the Role of the Public Voice

Andrew Joseph Loomis

> *Law is a lot more than words you put in a book, or judges or lawyers or sheriffs you hire to carry it out. It's everything people ever have found out about justice and what's right and wrong. It's the very conscience of humanity. There can't be any such thing as civilization unless people have a conscience . . . .*
>
> —GIL CARTER, *READING A LETTER FROM A MAN CONDEMNED TO HANG AT THE HANDS OF A VIGILANTE GANG, "THE OX-BOW INCIDENT," 1943*

Structural theories in international relations have long been criticized for their inability to explain change in the international system. Defensive realism has been particularly susceptible to this charge, privileging relative power capabilities in causal explanations and grounding theory on the assumption that states prefer the status quo. States form balancing coalitions against other states' capabilities but do not seek to deconstruct the system by challenging for primacy.[1] The theoretical core of Realism omits an agent of change.

Although international relations scholarship often sets realism's focus on power in opposition to international legal theory's focus on institutions and legal norms, the theories share this key feature in their respective ontologies. Both theories fail to incorporate dynamic features into their theoretical constructions. Realism's logic that contributes to a status quo bias also applies to the constraining structural effects of legal institutions.

In both domestic and international contexts, codified law is the result of a belabored political dynamic that slows the deliberation process, insulates societal rules from the supposed volatility of public opinion, and impedes abrupt transitions in the character of the existing order. In consolidated liberal democracies, the courts share this function of acting as ballast against erratic change. Writing in the US context, Alexander Hamilton famously referred to the courts as the "least damaging" branch and the "weakest of the three departments of power," having "neither force nor will, but merely judgment."[2] The stabilizing effects of the law and legal institutions reinforce the soundness of the order. Legal rules do evolve, but rule-making procedures impede accelerated evolution.[3]

This is one desired effect of the law, felt most acutely by those benefiting from geopolitical order. Privileged parties resist a transition to some new form—powerful voices controlling the levers of economic influence in the Northern and Western countries, for example—and often seek refuge in the law to resist radical change. These beneficiaries of the status quo are understandably wary of alternative criteria for evaluating the soundness of the existing logic of the rules that perpetuate contemporary systems of control.[4]

And so the law displays a double edge. It offers itself as an impediment of change that services order and predictability. Concurrently, the inertia of the law inhibits progress by obstructing state behavior from being sensitive to and thus incorporating normative evolution. In either respect, relative to the volatility of public opinion, the structure of law alone is quasi-static and is an imperfect lens through which to analyze short-run political dynamics.

Yet legal principles do take new forms as time elapses and the *character* of legal structures evolves. It is in this investigation of normative change that the tension between *law* and the more subjective measure of *legitimacy* is revealed. The rationale for rejecting legitimacy as a qualifying criterion for state behavior is familiar. Claims of its subjective character, absence of clearly specified metrics to determine its standing, and lack of empirical record are deployed to discredit the language of legitimacy as a determinant of political behavior. Yet society is in constant motion, steadily tugging at the tethers that restrain both pro-social and regressive social developments. Where the law resists change, legitimacy is the progenitor of both progress and instability. At their core, norms of legitimacy are agents of change.

This chapter is a descriptive analysis of a normative concept and examines the extent to which legitimacy standards are at the leading edge of societal transformation. The central issue is not that legitimacy considerations *should* generate social change, but rather that they *do*. Legal structures are poorly equipped to generate short-term variation in international behavior, and comprehensive accounts of the dynamics of international politics demand the incorporation of the boundaries of normative legitimacy.

However, this chapter aims to take an additional step that makes a more provocative contribution to the dialogue on law and legitimacy. The claim that legitimacy considerations drive social change assumes that what is "legitimate" is processed by decision-makers who can meaningfully affect the policymaking process. Yet a precise examination of who, specifically, is making the legitimacy judgments to which policymakers are attentive is insufficiently conducted in the literature.[5] When legitimacy is accounted for in the literature, the concept consistently is presented as an elite judgment in which the public voice plays no part. This omission incapacitates researchers from understanding an important pathway by which legitimacy norms manifest themselves in the political process. Legitimacy is largely a public phenomenon that shapes the environment in which elites operate, creating a backdrop of acceptability that constrains elite behavior and affects political outcomes.

This chapter elevates the neglected role of the public voice in the standard explanation of how legitimacy standards exert themselves in world politics. Following an introduction of the concept of normative legitimacy, I will demonstrate how the tension between legal structures and normative shifts manifests itself in both international and domestic settings, illustrating how legitimacy norms are situated on the leading edge of societal transformation, shaping the legal structures that congeal in its wake. I will then demonstrate how it is the public that is largely responsible for shaping the normative landscape to which policy elites are sensitive, and describe how legitimacy considerations work their way through the political process.

Legitimacy Defined

Legitimacy recently has gained currency in both the academic and political communities. There is a presumption that exists in the popular press, for example, that perceived illegitimate US policies have depleted US authority levels. Simultaneously, old ontological debates have been rejoined in the international relations literature between structuralists and ideationalists over the extent to which perceived legitimacy is disruptive to expected international political outcomes.

Often missing from the published discussion, however, is a definition of legitimacy that facilitates a comprehensive evaluation of its effects on political outcomes. The popular literature does not even bother with the messiness of subjecting assumptions to empirical testing, and the political science literature—specifically within the constructivist research program—have largely restricted legitimacy to its role in identity formation.

Where the popular accounts of legitimacy set the bar too low for evaluating the role of legitimacy in international behavior, much of the international relations literature sets the bar too high. An accurate assessment of the function of legitimacy can only be made by relaxing the assumption that legitimacy norms are necessarily internalized into agent identity and observing its utility as a strategic resource.

The starting place in this discussion is accepting that legitimacy is a perceptual matter. Max Weber is culpable for generating extensive confusion within the social sciences over the concept of legitimacy by reducing it to its perceptual components. In essence, Weber suggests that legitimacy is that which people believe is legitimate. Yet, void of intrinsic content, such a definition fails to uncover the precise elements that render some policies acceptable and others abhorrent. Furthermore, such a conception confounds a thorough investigation of legitimacy's effects.[6]

The apparent subjectivity of the perceptual dimension of legitimacy expressed by Weber, however, does not render the concept unavailable for deeper theoretic treatment. For the purposes of this chapter, one strand of legitimation in particular is extracted from Weber's work. This is the dimension of legitimacy that relies on an assessment of the consistency of the state's behavior with societal beliefs. The basis of this judgment is the constellation of social norms that reinforce an assessment of the legitimacy of a state's policy. David Beetham writes that in determining the legitimacy of power arrangements, social scientists must make a judgment of "the normative standing . . . that the law validates . . . against those criteria of the right or the good . . . that pertain within the society in question."[7] The definition of "right" or "good," in other words, depends upon the social values that have been constructed and reinforced in a given setting. Beetham concludes, "Legitimacy for the social scientists is always legitimacy-in-context."[8] Legitimation claims are made in conformity with established rules that are justified according to shared beliefs and the existence of evidence of consent.[9]

The impact of societal norms on legitimation decisions is demonstrated by the 1999 NATO alliance's military intervention in Kosovo. The intervention was broadly supported in the West as a result of the objective to alleviate human suffering, ultimately the consequence of an evolving human rights norm, despite the fact that the absence of a UN Security Council mandate rendered the intervention illegal (by most accounts) under international law.[10]

Mark Suchman writes that legitimacy is "a generalized perception or assumption that the actions of an entity are desirable, proper, appropriate within some socially constructed system of norms, values, beliefs, and definitions."[11] Christian Reus-Smit picks up this definition, arguing that "legitimacy is inextricably dependent upon social perception and recognition."[12] Legitimacy is distinct from such values as rationality, justice, legality, and morality. Yet "the critical thing that differentiates legitimacy from these values is the necessity of social recognition. No action can be coherently described as legitimate if it is not recognized as rightful."[13]

Broadly accepted intersubjective societal norms form the outer boundary of legitimacy standards, reflected in the degree of public and elite receptivity.[14] Legitimacy denotes extensive public acceptance reflecting a symmetry of expectations. As Ian Clark has argued, legitimacy represents a resultant vector of competing legitimacy norms of morality, legality, and constitutionality. The public accounting of legitimacy reflects an assessment of the particular way these norms interact.[15] In the context of international politics, legitimacy is assessed as a measure of broad ideological receptivity of policy choice.

Law and Legitimacy, Stability and Social Change

The perceptual dimension of legitimacy provides the basis of conceiving of legitimacy as a change agent. This perimeter of acceptability forming the contours of legitimacy is continually adjusted through discourse that accompanies the shifting political landscape. Patrick Jackson calls this interaction a "socially significant process of negotiating and (re)drawing boundaries."[16]

Yet the capacity of legitimacy norms to affect political outcomes and drive social change is impeded by the relative rigidity of legal structures. A function of law is to establish a set of common expectations that enhances predictability in international behavior. As the following sections demonstrate, in both the international and domestic arenas, when societal norms have evolved beyond the confines of legal structures, legitimacy and law are in tension—one serving as a catalyst for change and the other lagging behind.

The International Scene

The international legal regime structures order and impedes erratic responsiveness to shifts in both material capabilities and public ideologies. Despite the contemporary international system being situated on the cusp of profound change, much of the international legal infrastructure—designed in another era to address a different set of geopolitical realities—continues to shape international outcomes.

In 1945, the destabilizing effects of two world wars and cross-border conflicts revealed that the principal threat to international order was aggressive war. To confront this danger, policymakers constructed a latticework of institutions that contracted states together and reinforced the notion of impermeable borders and the principle of territorial sovereignty. The UN Charter explicitly outlawed aggressive war, reifying the principle of territorial inviolability. Emblematic of the foundations of the postwar order, Article 2(4) of the Charter affirms, "All Members shall refrain in their international relations from the threat or use of force against the territorial integrity or political independence of any State."

Yet over the course of six decades, the factors perceived as destabilizing international order have been transformed. For contemporary policymakers and their publics, the incidence of aggressive war has receded. In its place has crystallized the dangers of weak states and the incapacity to manage internal threat dynamics. The mid-century concern of porous borders and inter-state war has gradually been replaced by the more immediate concern of hyper-nationalist violence, illiberal domestic institutions, transnational terrorism, and mass movements of displaced persons.

Three broad global trends have challenged the analytical purity of Westphalian sovereignty. First, relative to the cold war years, the emergence of sharp power asymmetries has undermined the validity and causal weight of the anarchy assumption.[17] Second, technological change has increased the lethality of weapons, mobility of people, and circulation of ideas, creating pressures on a state-centric system of rules and institutions. Third, and critical to this discussion, normative shifts have ushered in the era of human rights and an emerging consensus on the benefits of democratic forms of governance. Human rights concerns, a peripheral consideration in the immediate aftermath of the Second World War, later gave life to the UN Declaration of Human Rights, two conventions on social and political rights, and a raft of subsequent agreements defining new international crimes such as genocide, racial discrimination, torture, and arbitrary detention.[18] Alongside the explosion of political action on human rights is the rapid growth of democracy, doubling in less than thirty years, from 27% of all states in 1974 to 63% in 2001.[19]

As the source of perceived instability has shifted from permeable state borders to human insecurity, the strategy for reinforcing the geopolitical order necessarily required a direct challenge to the principle of state sovereignty. Together, the transformation of threat perception coupled with normative progress has deformed the borders that define the boundary of "legitimate" foreign policy.

Yet as the character of this new order has emerged, international legal structures characteristically have produced more incremental change. The ratification of new legal norms lags behind the currency of ideas and the acceptance of new legitimacy standards. Elements of the current legal structure were conceptualized at an earlier stage of normative evolution, when states and state-based threats dominated the conceptual landscape. International society exists today in an awkward transition from state-centric conceptions of security to preferred individual-centric solutions. The UN system has made impressive adjustments to keep pace with normative change, such as the 2004 report of the High-Level Panel on Threats, Challenges, and Change, which identified a set of threats that transcend traditional inter-state war. Yet as in all periods of abrupt change, static rules and institutions can be an insufficient remedy to account for evolving normative concerns and international threats. The High-Level Panel, for example, refused to endorse legitimate use-of-force measures to mitigate new and immediate threats beyond the UN Security Council, despite evidence that the Security Council can be excessively cumbersome to address the most acute contemporary dangers, such as the acquisition of weapons of mass destruction by nihilistic non-state actors.

The most pernicious effect of the failure of the current legal regime to keep pace with ideational progress is the law's restraining effects on the political system's capacity to correct the most destructive aspects of international politics. Due to the effects of structural inertia, responses to large-scale atrocities of human suffering continue to be held captive to state-based tools and narrowly conceived great power interests, justified through precise legal reasoning.

The prototypical case of the legitimacy-legality tension is that of humanitarian intervention and the prolonged inability of the international community to effectively protect vulnerable populations with anachronistic state-centric mechanisms. The awakening of consciousness of human rights has driven this conversation. After the decolonization movement of the 1950s and immigration of repressed Jewish populations out of the Soviet Union in the 1950s, international reporting on tragedies of oppression further helped to prick the public consciousness in the 1970s. As many as half a million people were murdered during Idi

Amin's dictatorial rule of Uganda between 1971 and 1979. Nearly two million people died after the Khmer Rouge seized power in Cambodia in 1975. Vietnamese refugees and victims of state-sponsored political violence in Central and South America were among those marginalized populations that received increasing levels of international attention. Reflecting the growing public focus on human rights, Amnesty International received the Nobel Peace Prize in 1977. Human Rights Watch was launched in 1978. Both non-governmental organizations and increasing numbers of citizens, groups quickly became powerful voices sounding the alarm on human rights concerns.

Equipped with material preponderance and wielding an asymmetric level of influence in channeling normative trends for productive purposes, the United States provided critical leadership in the construction of institutional remedies. The US Congress, reflecting constituent sentiment, began to seriously tackle human rights violations in the 1970s, establishing a human rights bureau in the US State Department. President Jimmy Carter identified the protection of human rights as a prominent feature of US foreign policy. The Reagan administration, publicly skeptical of the Carter administration's focus on human rights, adopted the language of human rights in efforts to build support for democratic freedoms in the Philippines, Haiti, Central America, and South Africa. A logical outgrowth of this normative development is that as the consideration of rights and freedoms took root, officials' liability for ignoring violations of human rights increased.

Yet this emerging human rights standard increasingly undermined the principle of territorial sovereignty, a conceptual pillar of international politics. Stanley Hoffmann has argued that a "triple evolution of the idea of human rights"—elementary civil and political freedoms, minority rights, and access to democratic governance—have pressed strongly against the norm of nonintervention.[20] Elites, charged with providing national security, are forced to balance the implications that the erosion of Westphalian sovereignty has for geopolitical stability with the pressure for progress demanded by the domestic base in the protection of human rights. National leaders increasingly contend with the dilemma that both the violation of another state's internal affairs and the passive observance of humanitarian catastrophe undermine the stability of the existing order.

This tension between stability and transformation—between law and legitimacy—ultimately is resolved through a political process. And while international legal instruments grind slowly, they do grind forward under the force of an advancing perception of legitimacy. Over time, the transition of concern from state to human security has correspondingly served to nudge international legal instruments from their state-centered orientation to greater attention to protecting vulnerable populations, giving cover to political elites attempting to reconcile legal rules with legitimacy norms when they diverge.

The Independent International Commission on Kosovo, issuing in 2000 its report on the 1999 NATO war in Kosovo, found that the war was "illegal but legitimate."[21] The finding held that, despite circumventing the legal requirement of acquiring consent from the UN Security Council, NATO answered a growing humanitarian disaster and served a function that the UN Security Council was unable to fulfill. "The intervention was justified," the commission found, "because all diplomatic avenues had been exhausted and because the intervention had the effect of liberating the majority population of Kosovo from a long period of oppression under Serbian rule."[22] According to the commission, NATO violated the letter of the law, but acted in accordance with the spirit of the UN Charter.[23]

The International Commission on Intervention and State Sovereignty, convened in 2000, picked up where the Kosovo Commission left off, responding to a Secretary-General Kofi Annan's challenge to the international community to develop a legal framework authorizing the use of force to alleviate humanitarian crises. The commission's report, "The Responsibility to Protect," shifted the burden of proof in the determination of the right to intervene, effectively easing the prohibition against intervention on behalf of a vulnerable population and further eroding the rigid notion of sovereign inviolability for the purpose of preserving human security.

As discussed above, a further contribution was issued in December 2004 in the final report of the UN High-Level Panel on global security threats and reform of the international system. The High-Level Panel's objective was to recommend measures to the secretariat to ensure effective collective action. In essence, the panel was building on the norm reinforced by the Kosovo Commission and the Commission on State Sovereignty in favor of protecting human welfare over strict recognition of rigid state borders. To this end, the panel identified six clusters of international threats, only one of which was that of interstate war, the threat that had dominated policymaking rationale inside the UN system since 1945. The other five threats were all internal dysfunctions or contagions that made no distinction between territorial units or recognition of state borders.[24]

As threats to the geopolitical order shifted from cross-border aggression and national security to extraterritorial dangers and human security, and as the global consciousness swelled in support of individual rights and freedoms, legal norms began to reflect this normative shift. Concurrently, the proposed solutions have evolved from the reinforcement of state borders to safeguarding human beings and a responsibility to protect. This transition is far from complete and legal rules continue to lag social norms of legitimacy. Nonetheless, the example of humanitarian intervention demonstrates how normative changes challenged the status quo and triggered necessary legal adjustments.

The US Domestic Scene

Shifting societal norms lead to legal changes over time. Yet in the short run, the inertia of the legal infrastructure resists the change that social norms are poised to initiate. Whereas the case of humanitarian intervention showcases normative developments triggering adjustments in legal concepts at the international level, a brief anecdote in the US national context demonstrates this point of the restraining effects of legal structures.

While this anecdote focuses on the American context, the resistance of courts to progressive (or regressive) change is not uniquely an American phenomenon. Although developments in the US domestic political scene continue to have a disproportionate influence on the tempo of international politics—a principal reason for the focus here on the US case—courts in advanced liberal democracies all exhibit this characteristic of muting the potential of an erratic political reaction to societal pressures during episodes of volatile public opinion.

During the summer months of 2006, public disenchantment and political agitation stirred in the American polity. In June, 33% of the public approved of President Bush, a drop in 17 points from the previous year. Just 23% approved of the Republican-majority Congress. Seventy percent of voters indicated they thought the country was on the "wrong track."[25] These numbers foretold a steady shift away from support for the political party in control, foreboding for Republican candidates heading into the November midterm elections.

Indicating an erosion of perceived legitimacy, acute public disenchantment over the weakness of the economy, corruption charges of prominent Republicans, and mismanagement of the war in Iraq persuaded large numbers of moderate nonideological voters to defect from their support of Republican candidates.[26] This domestic political unrest culminated in the 2006 November midterm elections, in which thirty seats in the House of Representatives and six seats in the Senate changed political parties, shifting control of both chambers to the Democratic Party for the first time since 1994. Eight months later, this trend in public opinion had continued. By July 2007, reflecting a surge in public support, the national Democratic Party had nearly four times the amount of money than the Republican Party. Senator Charles Schumer of New York reflected, "The contributions reflect the broad pendulum in America, which is that things are swinging to the Democratic side."[27]

The president also faced public approval levels at historic lows in the modern presidency, dropping below 30% in mid-2007.[28] At the same time, prominent Republicans in steadily increasing numbers were reevaluating their allegiance to the president's policy priorities. President Bush failed to persuade sufficient numbers of Republican senators to support his goal of immigration reform. His other three top domestic priorities—partial privation of Social Security, a restructured tax code including additional tax cuts, and additional restraints on litigation—all failed.[29]

This represents a sharp reversal from opinion levels in 2005 at the outset of the president's second term, when he spoke of the political capital he had earned from the election and was poised to disburse. This decisive shift in political winds, driven by public dissent with the results and the character of US policy, transformed the nature of politics in Washington.

This shift in the public mood stands in contrast with the decidedly conservative tilt the Supreme Court has taken in recent years. While the winds of change blow in one direction, the Court's decisions in the 2006–2007 term are qualitatively more conservative than the previous term, largely the result of the appointments by President Bush of Justices Samuel Alito and John Roberts. President Bush's reelection and political empowerment to nominate and have confirmed two conservative justices occurred at a time when conservatism was in the ascendancy rather than in retreat, as now appears to be the case. In the closing weeks of the 2006–2007 term, the Court issued four 5–4 decisions on school integration, abortion rights, campaign finance, and pay discrimination by employers, all of which reflect a strikingly more conservative Court than the one vacated by Justice Sandra Day O'Conner in 2006. A July 2007 poll found that 31% of the public believe the Supreme Court is too conservative, compared to 19% who felt that way in July 2005.[30]

This US domestic example illustrates how shifts in public opinion can be out of phase with the lethargy of the law and its institutions, and how the public push for change can be impeded by the recalcitrant legal structure. The same dynamic resisted abrupt political change when President Franklin Roosevelt battled with the Supreme Court under conservative Chief Justice Charles Hughes over New Deal programs, and when Richard Nixon struggled with a liberal Warren Burger Court and President Clinton contended with a conservative William Rehnquist Court. While cycles of history may be driven by ideologies of expansion and retrenchment, the court obstructs short-term change fueled by the public will.[31]

A substantial body of academic research finds that domestic courts indeed are a poor instrument to transform society. In his work on the US courts and social change, for example, Gerald Rosenberg presents evidence that the limited nature of constitutional rights, the lack of judicial independence, and the lack of power to implement policies all conspire to relegate the Supreme Court to a secondary role relative to the public will in transforming society.[32] On the 1954 decision *Brown v. Board of Education*, the case most commonly cited as evidence of the transformative role of the Court, Rosenberg writes, "The combination of . . . growing civil rights pressure from the 1930s, economic changes, the Cold War, population shifts, electoral concerns, the increase in mass communication—created the pressure that led to civil rights. The Court reflected that pressure; it did not create it."[33]

Thus the stabilizing effects of law both reinforce the order and impede rapid progress. As in other advanced democracies, as volatile shifts in the US public mood tug society in one direction through the institutions of Congress and the executive, the US courts diminish the prospects of radical change.

In both the international and domestic contexts, notions of legitimacy and the public will reside at the cutting edge of policy change. Legal structures impede change. Due to the utility of legitimacy considerations in updating legal instruments to meet the challenge of addressing contemporary threats, the increased academic treatment of legitimacy should be welcomed. Yet the *public* dimension of legitimacy considerations has been sorely neglected. Due to the legacy of public perceptions of legitimacy provoking legal change by constraining policymaking and shaping the environment in which elites operate, the study of legitimacy require a determined focus on the public voice.

The Essence of Public Perception

Despite this essential feature of legitimacy as conformity with societal expectations, legitimacy talk too often commits the fallacy of assuming a finding of "legitimacy" without explicitly identifying who is issuing the legitimacy judgment. As discussed above, legitimacy is a perceptual concept, and acknowledging its subjectivity or intersubjectivity still demands that a claim of legitimacy be paired with a claimant for it to have meaning. Christian Reus-Smit refers to this audience as "the social constituency of legitimation," defined as "the actual social grouping in which legitimacy is sought, ordained, or both."[34]

A declaration that the NATO military intervention in Kosovo was legitimate but the 2003 US invasion of Iraq was illegitimate, for example, rests on the implicit assumption that a certain audience rendered this finding. But what is this assumed audience? Public statements confirm that US administration officials advanced the claim that both interventions were legitimate. Russian and Chinese officials argued that neither was legitimate. How do we resolve the questions of whether the policy was legitimate and how this determination impacts foreign policy behavior? Specifically, where should one look to locate the source of legitimacy claims that has consequences for the trajectory of international politics, in particular its role in driving broad social change?

In short, the constituency that is most poised to initiate change in international politics is the mass public, a constituency that also is underrepresented in the legitimacy literature. The claim that the public plays an assertive role in legitimacy assessments and thus the course of international behavior is premised in part on the observation that the same geopolitical forces that have undermined the state-centric orientation to world politics have opened the space for the public to operate. Power asymmetry, technological revolution, and normative progress have all eroded the ideal form of Westphalian sovereignty. Contrary to the structural-rationalist conception of the international environment of billiard balls and black-boxed states, the public has greater capacity to influence policy in the twenty-first century. As one close observer of international trends recently noted, "foreign policy is no longer a rarefied game of elites: public opinion shapes the world within which policy makers operate."[35] As a result, the significance of the public's evaluation of a policy's legitimacy correspondingly has increased.

Given the divergent forces pressing upon the executive branch in the construction of foreign policy, policy elites seek broad social acceptability of policy to increase their prospects for success. Public support for executive policies helps build support of the mass public, Congress, as well as administrators in the executive branch. B. Thomas Trout first identified the acceptability sought by executives as "policy legitimacy," writing "the acquisition of legitimacy is acknowledged to be a fundamental requirement of any political regime . . . It is the continuing effort to provide the necessary quality of 'oughtness' to a society's presiding political institutions and to their actions."[36]

Alexander George builds upon the concept of policy legitimacy, suggesting that it serves as an invaluable asset in supplementing a president's ability to pursue a foreign policy consistent with his preferences. For George, policy legitimacy is constructed on the basis of a policy's *feasibility* and its *desirability*.[37] George identifies feasibility of a policy as the "cognitive" component, which convincingly relates means to ends and requires demonstrated competency on the part of executive leadership. The desirability of a policy is the "normative" component, and relates to the degree to which a policy "is consistent with fundamental national values and contributes to their enhancement."[38]

This distinction between feasibility and desirability in generating legitimacy is important to this discussion of the public voice, since those judging the legitimacy of a given policy will select from criteria according to the respective positions they occupy. This process highlights the differences between the elite and the mass public perceptions of legitimacy. It is logical that policy elites who are responsible for foreign policy success are more likely to conceive of policies that effectively connect means with ends, whereas agents less accountable for policy success are freer to make judgments premised on a policy's consistency with national values. Thus, seeking to measure the independent impact of normative constraints on decision making as distinct from value-neutral utilitarian calculations requires a focus on the public voice, where normative judgments likely are more active. It is reasonable to assume that the mass public is less cognizant than elites of highly sophisticated cause–effect relationships, but more likely to privilege policies perceived to be based on principles that coincide with widely accepted societal values derived from the national experience.

George does not explicitly match the cognitive and normative components exclusively with the elite and public spheres, respectively. He does argue, however, that the requirements for each aspect of policy legitimacy are affected by the "marked differences in level of interest and sophistication" among the actors involved, from the president and top advisors to the broader public. As one moves vertically downward from the policymaking elite to the mass public, "one expects to find a considerable simplification of the set of assertions and beliefs that lend support to the legitimacy of foreign policy."[39]

The tension between appealing to the mass public and elite in comprising a legitimation strategy is demonstrated by George's discussion of US President Franklin Roosevelt's fashioning of his postwar strategy. Roosevelt blurred a realist approach with an idealist approach in order to successfully balance efficacy with public support. His realist approach included his "four policemen" model, in which the United States, Great Britain, the Soviet Union, and China would coordinate their overwhelming power to keep the peace. Yet given the appearance that this strategy had with spheres of influence or balance of power—a model associated with centuries of European warfare and rejected by an idealist leaning American public—Roosevelt was cautious in publicly advancing his plan. To mollify the idealist strains in American thought, Roosevelt transformed the "four policemen" model into the United Nations Security Council, a deliberative body in which weaker powers would have a voice. Roosevelt also pleaded with Stalin to show restraint so as to avoid enflaming anti-Soviet sentiment in the United States. In the end, Soviet aggression eroded the public's tolerance for peaceful coexistence with the Soviet Union, enabling President Truman to engage in a containment strategy that had the realist characteristics of balance-of-power and spheres-of-influence approaches.[40]

It is instructive that Roosevelt did not merely pacify the public by espousing idealist rhetoric and pursue a divergent realist strategy consistent with his four policemen model. He adjusted the substance of US postwar strategy so as to conform to elements of the public's perception of a legitimate set of policies of engaging the Soviet Union and war-torn Europe.

The essential point raised by this differentiation between spheres in establishing policy legitimacy is that separate criteria exist for elite and mass public legitimation. Much of the public opinion literature argues that the public is ill-equipped to make sophisticated judgments on the efficacy of competing foreign policy approaches (the cognitive criterion). Yet while the public may lack the tools and information necessary to judge the feasibility of a set of strategies in achieving policy objectives, it does make judgments on the desirability of policy, a judgment that carries weight in the policymaking process.

Identification of the policy elites' cognitive criterion and public's normative criterion returns this analysis to the legality–legitimacy distinction. Policymakers access different standards in constructing, rationalizing, or supporting foreign policies than the broader public. Legal norms are an important justification of policy elites, in part due to the substantial contribution that legal conduct makes to functional reciprocity.

The public is not charged with guaranteeing national security, less equipped to construct or comprehend nuanced goal-oriented policy prescriptions, and less captive to the cognitive requirements of effective ends–means combinations. The wider public is more sensitive to sweeping conceptions of the national character and more persuaded by moral and societal standards of legitimacy, thus more insistent on their incorporation into a state's foreign policy.

This difference in legitimation standards also is a source of friction between elite policymaking and the public will that contains the mechanism of change. The dissonance that exists between the cognitive and normative components of legitimacy—and between the judgments of the policy elite and the public—require elites to reevaluate policy formulations in the search for political support. Reus-Smit suggests, "It is this disjuncture between its social constituency of legitimation and its chosen realm of political action that underlies the administration's current international crisis of legitimacy."[41]

As discussed, over time normative legitimacy redefines the contours of legality. Relative to the static character of rule-governed behavior and the stabilizing aspect of international law, the dynamic feature of legitimacy standards, directed by shifts in public notions of appropriateness, adjust conceptions of acceptable behavior. Over time, those norms influence the content of legal rules. Given their responsibility for societal change, shifting normative standards generated by the public voice have a profound impact on international behavior.

The Strategic Use of Norms

As exemplified above, the international and domestic contexts both exhibit at times a fundamental disjuncture between law and legitimacy. Legitimacy norms expressed by the broad public often outpace the law and can serve as a catalyst for change. Legal structures can serve to resist this change. A remaining task is to explain how public legitimacy norms inject themselves into the political process. One way of demonstrating the effect on political behavior is exploring how norms are used strategically by the political elite.

In addition to the inductive reasoning presented here of the sensitivity of policy elites to legitimacy norms, further evidence of the presence of legitimacy considerations in the policymaking process is the way in which policy elites leverage norms to achieve support for their policies. The language of legitimacy and the rhetoric of justification are reminders of how policymakers take seriously the potential constraining effects of normative aberrance, including the costs of failed legitimating efforts and the foreclosure of certain policy options. This is true for all states, including the materially dominant United States. Hurd reminds us, "Because states seem incapable of acting without a normative justification for their behavior, even highly revisionist states remain embedded in a society of international norms, ideas, and resources."[42]

Much of the literature, however, restricts legitimacy to its role in agent identity, suggesting that *habituation* is required for a norm to be regarded as legitimate. James March and Johan Olsen's "logic of appropriateness"—frequently cited as representative of legitimacy concerns and juxtaposed against a consequences logic—reduces the concept of legitimacy to automatic behavior. Legal scholar Thomas Franck suggests that the nature of legitimacy could be revealed by studying "rules which are *habitually* obeyed in international relations" (emphasis in original).[43] According to this construct, decisions over legitimate behavior exist subrationally and the wisdom of illegitimate policies is not actively considered. Changes in identity have incorporated legitimate behavior into habitual patterns and excised illegitimate acts from conscious thought.

The principal deficiency with restricting legitimacy to the realm of identity politics in this way is that it does not square with the empirical evidence. Agents do use normative arguments strategically to build support and secure vital interests.

Furthermore, such a conception of legitimacy risks the tautological definition that norms are legitimate when they are followed, and norms that are followed are defined as legitimate. Lastly, such a rendering obscures the costs of perceived policy illegitimacy, since by definition aberrance disqualifies the norm in question from holding the status of a legitimacy norm. While some legitimacy norms unquestionably are reflected in an agent's self-conception in the long run, they also can serve as a resource by profit-maximizing actors.

In his work on ideational influences in grand strategy formulations, Jeffrey Legro draws on both the strategic interaction and constructivist literatures and rejects the tendency in the literature to place cultural analysis associated with ideational variables in a mutually exclusive category from the study of rationality. "To focus on collective ideas . . . is not to deny strategy. Typically states will instrumentally pursue their interests and in a reasoned way connect means to goals."[44]

Ian Hurd's discussion of Libya's use of the norm of "liberal internationalism" in the UN sanctions case demonstrates the conception of legitimacy utilized as a strategic tool.[45] In Hurd's rendering, the Libyan government publicly defended the norm of liberal internationalism in an attempt to delegitimize the UN sanctions that remained in place following a finding of Libya's involvement in the 1988 airline bombing over Lockerbie, Scotland. Through Libya's presentation of a reinterpretation of liberal internationalism, the sanctions risked losing both legitimacy and efficacy as participating states began to defect from the sanctions regime. Furthermore, the weakened UN sanctions compromised the legitimacy of the Security Council itself. Powerful Western states—in particular the United States and the United Kingdom, unwilling to permit a sustained weakening of an institution that served to reinforce the liberal order—ultimately acquiesced and negotiated a compromise solution with Libya. The norm of liberal internationalism was not infused into the identity of the Libyan regime—in fact the appeal to the norm very likely was insincere. Yet the case demonstrates how norms can be utilized by states in achieving national objectives.

The shifting rationale employed by the United States for the 2003 invasion of Iraq similarly revealed that the US administration under President George W. Bush was engaged in a legitimation process of casting about for justification congruent with societal expectations in order to strengthen support for US policy. Yet the very fact that the United States, with all its material predominance, was engaged in such a process is evidence of political elites' sensitivity to societal norms of legitimacy. Hurd writes, "Even while undermining the legitimacy of some international rules, the US remains embedded in the process of justifying itself with the intersubjective structures of international society."[46] This society of states limits the number of cost-free policy options available to the United States.

There are other examples in the current legitimacy literature of how policymakers, cognizant of their constituencies, strategically invoke norms to pursue policy objectives. In the context of postwar European integration, Frank Schimmelfennig writes of the strategic use of normative arguments in the form of public claims to support their goal of expansion (on the part of some Western European state leaders) or inclusion (by Eastern European state leaders). Schimmelfennig finds that the effectiveness of European leaders' appeals for regional consolidation depended on the degree to which the public affirmed the norms that formed the sinews of those institutional structures.[47]

Patrick Jackson argues that the postwar reconstruction of Germany and ultimately the creation of a Western identity was primarily a public strategy of legitimation, deliberately conducted by European and American policymakers. The "rhetorical commonplace" of "Western Civilization" became a powerful hook whereby European policymakers generated support for the reconstruction of Germany.[48] It is worth noting that it was the *public* pronouncements, not the private ones commonly sought for evidence of causation, which enabled this particular legitimacy norm to exert itself in the public appeal for German rehabilitation.[49]

Judith Kelley presents evidence in a recent study that a statistically significant number of states that were signatories to the International Criminal Court statute refused to sign non-surrender agreements with the United States because they valued the rule of law more generally and the principle of *pacta sunt servanda*, which obligates states to abide by treaty commitments.[50] The key point here is that this preference for abiding by the rule of law and respecting treaty commitments is a public as much as an elite phenomenon, triggered by the public's self-conception of what constitutes their country's character. This is, at its core, an evaluation of a policy's consistency with standards of normative legitimacy. Kelley writes, "Efforts to justify violations of international law may . . . create 'cognitive dissonance' such that citizens, and therefore their states, have 'distaste for breaking the law.'"[51] In essence, societal pressures raise the costs for European leaders who fail to follow societies' lead in evaluating US foreign policy in normative terms, specifically for the policy's consistency with the dictates of constitutional constraints.

While norms of legitimacy may in fact become embedded into the psyches of key decision makers, norms are used by decision makers with their publics in pursuit of the national interest. Such an investigation requires importing normative factors into utility-based decision-making processes, collapsing neo-utilitarian theories (without the focus on material factors) and constructivist theories (placing the focus on choice rather than identity) into a single space. The degree to which policymaking elite are sensitive to public legitimacy claims and responsive to its constraints is evidence that legitimacy norms impact the course of international politics.

Conclusion

Two ironies are embedded in this chapter. The first is found in the observation that a tension exists between legality and legitimacy, and that between the two it is law that can serve as an impediment to social progress. Legal instruments are so frequently conceived of as curtailing illegitimate behavior that it is disorienting to consider law as a bulwark to the development of legitimacy norms. In fact, legal rules and normative legitimacy are coincident in most cases and rule following is generally perceived to be the hallmark of legitimate behavior. Yet when evolving societal beliefs outpace the content of legal structures, as in the case of human rights concerns and anachronistic international remedies, legality and legitimacy pull in opposite directions.

As in the domestic realm, legal regimes and law's institutional constraints enhance stability and predictability in the international system and protect society from the dangers associated with erratic change. Yet the law also obstructs rapid pro-social advancement, impeding near-term political action from addressing contemporary challenges that are incompatible with the solutions proffered by outdated law.

To fully understand how legitimacy norms function to affect change in international politics, however, the full range of participating actors must be accounted for. Therein resides the second irony of this chapter. In the contemporary era in which democratic regimes are widely regarded to be the mark of legitimate governance, it is striking the extent to which accounts of legitimacy in international politics dismiss the role of the public voice. Yet focusing exclusively on the policymaking elite will only produce a partial story. Elites are charged with safeguarding the nation's interests and thus develop rational policies that, unless pressed by their domestic publics, would exclude normative influences. The public, on the other hand, demands that policy be consistent with conceptions of the national character, requiring policymakers to balance legal considerations with public perceptions of legitimacy. Without this payoff for normative consistency that the public provides, normative legitimacy would rank low in the hierarchy of decision-making criteria.

This should not be a surprising finding. Why should we be surprised that *democratic* elites respond to the public's role in serving as a corrective for policy that is bankrupt of normative legitimacy? In fact, the public does demand fidelity to normative standards. Elite sensitivity to public evaluations of legitimacy, their evocation of legitimacy standards, and the strategic use of norms are all evidence of legitimacy's constraining effects, including perceived restrictions on the range of options available to policymakers. Given the public's proclivity to evaluate the legitimacy of policy in normative terms and due to the dynamic character of normative legitimacy, a full accounting of international outcomes—in particular, international change—is dependent upon a thorough examination of the role of the public voice.

Legitimacy norms and beliefs about the acceptability of behavior evolve according to a different schedule than the law, percolating from the collective conscience of the body politic. And because the public encourages conduct that conforms to the boundaries of societal legitimacy and extracts costs in cases of perceived illegitimacy, the public voice elevates normative legitimacy to operate as an agent of change.

Legal rules and legitimacy standards serve divergent functions in international politics. Legitimacy norms premised on societal beliefs are at the leading edge of social dynamism, providing the backdrop of appropriateness that shapes political behavior. Legal structures form the ballast that enhances stability and obstructs rapid change. Given the presence of the public voice in the determination of legitimacy standards, and due to the influence of legitimacy perceptions on political behavior, inclusion of the public and normative legitimacy in the calculus of international outcomes is the most effective means of accounting for this critical ideational feature that pervades the international experience.

Endnotes

1. For one account of the "status quo bias" in the international relations literature, see Randall Schweller, "Neorealism's Status Quo Bias: What Security Dilemma?" *Security Studies* 5 (Spring 1996): 90–121.

2. Alexander Hamilton's *Federalist 78*. See Alexander Hamilton, James Madison, and John Jay, *The Federalist Papers*, 393–394.

3. It is not the intention of the author to suggest that legal rules exclusively play a static role in international political dynamics. International legal regimes contain a variety of procedures that enable political dynamics to influence the character of the law, and for the law to adjust accordingly. Legal rules are presented in this chapter, however, as an ideal type, providing structural form relative to the volatility of public opinion.

4. On victors of war consolidating their power and securing their positions of privilege through international law and institutions, see G. John Ikenberry, *After Victory*, Princeton University Press, 2001: 50–79.

5. A comprehensive account of the legitimacy debate is presented in Ian Hurd, *After Anarchy: Legitimacy and Power in the United Nations Security Council*, Princeton University Press, 2007.

6. Ian Clark writes that since Weber, theorists "have found themselves unable to live comfortably either with, or wholly without, this concept." Clark, *Legitimacy in International Society*, Oxford University Press, 2007:18. David Beetham goes so far as to suggest that Weber's influence across a range of social science disciplines on the subject of legitimacy "as been an almost unqualified disaster." Beetham, *The Legitimation of Power*, Macmillan, 1991: 8.

7. Beetham, *Legitimation of Power*: 13.

8. Beetham, *Legitimation of Power*: 14.

9. Beetham, *Legitimation of Power*: 15–25.

10. The fact that there was universal NATO member country support for military operations in Kosovo is evidence that, at minimum, policymaking elites perceived the intervention to be legitimate. For an ex post facto evaluation of the legitimacy of military strikes in Kosovo, see the Independent International Commission on Kosovo, *Kosovo Report*, Oxford University Press, 2000; and the International Commission on Intervention and State Sovereignty, *Responsibility to Protect*, International Development Research Centre, 2001.

11. Mark Suchman, "Managing Legitimacy: Strategic and Institutional Approaches," *Academic Research Review* 10 (1995): 574.

12. Christian Reus-Smit, "International Crisis of Legitimacy," *International Politics* 44 (2007): 159.

13. Reus-Smit, "International Crises of Legitimacy:" 160.

14. For a more comprehensive treatment of the intersubjectivity (as distinct from objective or subjective notions) of legitimacy, see Friedrich Kratochwil in this volume.

15. Clark, *Legitimacy in International Society*: 207–210.

16. Patrick Jackson, *Civilizing the Enemy: German Reconstruction and the Invention of the West*, University of Michigan Press, 2006: 41.

17. For a comprehensive treatment of the erosion of the sovereignty norm, see Stephen Krasner, *Sovereignty: Organized Hypocrisy*, Princeton University Press, 1999. See also Samuel Barkin and Bruce Cronin, "The State and the Nation: Changing norms and the rules of sovereignty in international relations," *International Organization* 48 (Winter 1994): 107–130; Hendrik Spruyt, *The Sovereign State and its Competitors*, Princeton University Press, 1996: 3–58, 183–194; and David Lake, "The New Sovereignty in International Relations," *International Studies Review* 5 (2003): 303–323.

18. Susan Rice and Andrew Loomis, "The Evolution of Humanitarian Intervention and the Responsibility to Protect," in Ivo Daalder, *Beyond Preemption: Force and legitimacy in a changing world*, Brookings Institution Press, 2007: 59–95.

19. US Agency for International Development, *Foreign Aid in the National Interest*, 35. Data from Freedom House, *Freedom in the World 2001–2002*.

20. Stanley Hoffmann, *The Ethics and Politics of Humanitarian Intervention*, University of Notre Dame Press, 1996: 16.

21. Independent International Commission on Kosovo, *Kosovo Report*: 4.

22. Independent International Commission on Kosovo, *Kosovo Report*: 4.

23. Independent International Commission on Kosovo, *Kosovo Report*: 169.

24. These threats identified by the panel were intra-state war (civil wars, large-scale human rights abuses, and genocide), poverty, weapons of mass destruction, terrorism, and transnational organized crime. See the Secretary-General's High-Level Panel on Threats, Challenges, and Change, *A More Secure World: Our Shared Responsibility*, Crown, 2005.

25. Gwen Ifill interview with Andrew Kohut and Amy Walter, "PBS Newshour," June 6, 2006, http://www.pbs.org/newshour/bb/politics/jan-june06/midterm_06-06.html.

26. Andrew Kohut, "The Real Message of the Midterms," *New York Times*, November 13, 2006, http://midtermmadness.blogs.nytimes.com/?p=44.

27. Jeff Zeleny, "Congressional Democrats Pull Way Ahead in Money Race," *Washington Post*, July 15, 2007: A16.

28. Maura Reynolds and Noam Levey, "The Conflict in Iraq: Some Breathing Room; Progress Assessed," *Los Angeles Times*, July 13, 2007: A1.

29. Peter Baker, "Bush May Be Out of Chances for a Lasting Domestic Victory," *Washington Post*, June 29, 2007: A1.

30. Washington Post–ABC News poll results discussed in Robert Barnes and Jon Cohen, "Fewer See Balance in Court's Decisions", *Washington Post*, July 29, 2007: A3.

31. See Arthur Schlesinger, *The Cycles of American History*, First Mariner Books, 1999.

32. Gerald Rosenberg, *The Hollow Hope: Can Courts Bring About Social Change?* University of Chicago Press, 2008: 10–21.

33. Rosenberg, *Hollow Hope*: 169.

34. Reus-Smit, "International Crises of Legitimacy:" 157–174.

35. James Traub, "Islamic Democrats?" *New York Times Magazine*, April 29, 2007: 49.

36. B. Thomas Trout, "Rhetoric Revisited: Political Legitimation and the Cold War," *International Studies Quarterly* 19 (September 1975): 251–284, esp. 252–253.

37. Alexander George, *On Foreign Policy: Unfinished Business,* Paradigm Publishers, 2006: 17–19; published in an earlier version as "Domestic Constraints on Regime Change in U.S. Foreign Policy: The Need for Policy Legitimacy," in Ole Holsti, Randolph Siverson, and Alexander George, *Change in the International System*, Westview Press, 1980: 233–262.

38. George, *On Foreign Policy*: 17.

39. George, *On Foreign Policy*: 19.

40. George, *On Foreign Policy*: 30–42.

41. Reus-Smit, "International Crises of Legitimacy:" 164

42. Hurd, *After Anarchy*: 206.

43. Thomas Franck, *Power of Legitimacy Among Nations*, Oxford University Press, 1990.

44. Jeffrey Legro, *Rethinking the World: Great Power Strategies and International Order*, Cornell University Press, 2005: 183.

45. Ian Hurd, "The Strategic Use of Liberal Internationalism," *International Organization* 59 (2005): 495–526.

46. Hurd, "Strategic Use of Liberal Internationalism:" 201.

47. Frank Schimmelfennig, *The EU, NATO, and the Integration of Europe: Rules and Rhetoric*, Cambridge University Press, 2003: 286.

48. Jackson, *Civilizing the Enemy*: 72–111.

49. Jackson, *Civilizing the Enemy*: 32.

50. Judith Kelley, "Who Keeps International Commitments and Why? The International Criminal Court and Bilateral Nonsurrender Agreements," *American Political Science Review* 101 (2007): 586.

51. Kelley, "Who Keeps International Commitments and Why?" 577. Kelley cites Kenneth Abbot and Duncan Snidal, "Hard and Soft Law in International Governance," *International Organization* 54 (2000): 428.

4

Defending Legality in the Age of Empire's Law

Amy Bartholomew

Human rights, democracy, and legality have all been threatened with the US-led "global war on terror" and the Bush Doctrine, even while human rights and democracy were mobilized to justify them.[1] It is not news that the Bush administration held all three of these—human rights, democracy, and legality—in contempt. But its relationship to legality is, perhaps, the least well analyzed. While its stance toward international law is just one aspect of its treatment of legality, its contempt for international law was so profound that we might do well to concentrate on it.

It is important to note at the outset, however, that it is not just the neoconservatives of American empire that have treated legality, perhaps particularly, but certainly not exclusively, international law, and its institutions dismissively. So have some on the political Left (with which I identify), while of course they have done so for different reasons than the ideologues and power brokers of American empire and with different consequences. For example, in an essay in *New Left Review*, Perry Anderson argued that the support for international and cosmopolitan law provided by scholars like John Rawls and Jürgen Habermas functions as a "license for the American empire as placeholder for human progress."[2] A similar approach is found in China Mieville's Marxist critique of international law[3] which, premised on a commodity form version of Marxist theory, can find nothing of redeeming value in international law and a similarly "radical" (although not Marxist), I would say rejectionist, position is found in James Tully's anti-imperialist argument that international law and informal imperialism are so deeply imbricated and international law is so thoroughly contaminated by power that we should not struggle against empire on the basis of international law, for to do so is wrongly to contest it precisely on empire's own terms rather than "outside" of empire.[4] And Fleur Johns, writing on the war on terror and law, seems to align herself with this sort of orientation when she argues (as I will show in more detail below) that the most cogent response to the ongoing catastrophe at Guantanamo Bay is not a call for respect for or development of the rule of law, domestic and international, not a "return to the normative," but rather a Left Schmittian conception of ethical responsibility in which the functionary who implements programs at Guantanamo (and elsewhere) might embrace "vertiginous" "exceptional decisionism" as a mode of resistance.[5]

Juxtapose these sorts of critical positions that one finds today with the one adopted by the German jurist and political theorist, Franz Neumann. In *Behemoth*, first published in 1942, Neumann said the following about international law:

> Hardly any other ideological element is held in such profound contempt in our civilization as international law. Every generation has seen it break down as an instrument for organizing peace, and a theory that disposes of its universalist claims has the obvious advantage of appearing to be realistic. The fallacy should be equally obvious, however. To abandon universalism because of its failures is like rejecting civil rights because they help legitimize and veil class exploitation, or democracy because it conceals boss control. . . . Faced with a corrupt administration of justice, the reasonable person does not demand a return to the war of each against all, but fights for an honest system. Likewise, when we have shown that international law has been misused for imperialistic aims, our task has begun, not ended. We must fight against imperialism.[6]

I will suggest that we should take our cue from Neumann's approach to international law and legitimacy today. These contemporary positions on the broadly defined Left, on the other hand, mirror those that Neumann criticized and come perilously close to rejecting international legality and to abandoning its universalist claims. And, insofar as this is the case, their position does not simply mirror but threatens to abet the neoconservative one of contempt for international law. The imperial project of the United States that is afoot no less under Barack Obama than it was under George W. Bush may seem to provide one more argument in favor of a rejectionist stance by the Left toward international law, international institutions, and human rights, if we view them as necessarily the merely compliant instruments of empire, as critical positions too often do.[7] I think, however, that, on the contrary, in the context of an American empire that has issued a neoconservative threat to legality we need to replace the urge toward contempt and rejectionism with the aim of protecting the defensive, and expanding the emancipatory, potential within human rights, international and cosmopolitan law, and at least some international and transnational institutions, all of which are (although in unequal measure) better conceptualized as fields of contestation[8] than as simply compliant instruments of empire. But this sort of position requires a more serious engagement with law, legality, and legitimacy than the critics, to say nothing of the neoconservatives, have provided—the sort of engagement toward which Neumann points us.[9]

There is obviously merit in the view of international law as tightly imbricated with and contaminated by power and, as critical international law scholarship has amply demonstrated, the relationship between imperial power and international law is a complex and contested one, to be sure, indicating at the very best what

Upendra Baxi has called the "uncertain promise of international law."[10] No critical analyst can doubt, for example, that the Security Council functions by and large to legitimate the actions of the most powerful nations which, today, means preeminently the United States. But under conditions of American empire, while we must avoid an unconvincingly romantic view of international law as itself *sufficient* to contest empire, a more nuanced analysis of law—international, transnational, and domestic—than the sort which is on offer by the critics cited above is necessary: one that is capable of distinguishing between law as merely the reflex, instrument, or *decision* of the imperial power, international law as the global "sovereign decision," as mere will or empire's law, as I want to call it, on the one hand, and legitimate law or legality, on the other hand.[11] Such conceptualization is important, not just fodder for academic debate, precisely because human rights and democracy, and the legality with which they are necessarily linked, have all been deeply threatened under the terms of the Bush Doctrine[12] and the broader "global war on terror."

I will also argue that the contempt for legality and the set of practices with which it has been associated, preeminently the Bush administration's attempt to render others rightless, is inadequately captured in the many slogans that have come to characterize the actions and ideological position of American empire: that the United States has acted "lawlessly," producing "legal black holes," no man's lands of lawlessness and the like. While evocative, such terms seem inadequate to diagnose what is at stake besides human rights and human lives: legality itself has been threatened, and the negative image of a "lawless world" and its rhetorical brethren is insufficient to describe and analyze the ways in which the American empire's machinations have both *depended* on forms of law and threatened to *produce* empire's law.

This political constellation raises at the international level the need to rethink a critical position in relation to international legality. While claims of legitimacy have contributed to the crisis of international law, as we see in the arguments around humanitarian intervention as they have been mobilized to justify the invasion and occupation of Iraq and Afghanistan and, more generally, to circumvent legality, international law's legitimacy must more carefully be considered. The debate has often taken the form of legality versus legitimacy, a result that is unsurprising in the face of the difficulties posed by humanitarian crises when we still have an international law that is insufficiently responsive to the need for rescue.[13] But when both the neoconservative supporters of American empire and its radical critics are dismissive of legality and when the former have been, as I will argue, engaged in a project of threatening international legality—including the substantive norms, processes, and institutions with which it is associated—with a tactical and instrumental use of law, another set of considerations is at least equally relevant. That is the set of questions surrounding the legitimacy of international law itself. It is law's internal legitimacy and its relation to external processes of legitimation that indicate whether what is presented as law is legitimate law. To sketch this argument, I draw broadly on the work of Jürgen Habermas as my jurisprudential inspiration. In contrast to the claims of critics (of whom there are many) that

Habermas now functions merely as an "establishment philosopher,"[14] I argue that with respect to conceptualizing legitimate legality, his work provides an essential critical resource. In light of American empire,[15] and its turn to rule through empire's law, we need to recuperate the sort of attitude of *critical appreciation* for international legality that both Habermas and Neumann before him recommend (no matter how "liberal" that may seem) while we also need further to develop an analysis of its own imbrication with empire, the better to resist empire partly on the basis of international law that does, admittedly, in its current form at least, also constitute its "legal hegemony."[16] As Neumann stressed, the "the fight for an honest system" of international law, including the defense of international law's universality and diagnosis of the possibilities of developing the conditions for its further constitutionalization, must be coupled with the "fight against imperialism." Neither law nor politics is sufficient to this task; both are required.

1. Empire's Law

Empire's law, *Lex Americana*, is a form of rule that, as Ulrich Preuss has put it, has aimed at "the creation of a new world order whose law is not yet visible."[17] It is clear, however, that it is deeply at odds with the post–World War II project of globalizing its obverse which, borrowing Ronald Dworkin's phrase (coined to convey a different idea), we might call "law's empire."[18] With respect to international relations, law's empire refers to the post–World War II development of regimes of human rights and international law that foreshadowed (however imperfectly) a future order of legitimate international and cosmopolitan law. Empire's law, on the other hand, has threatened to derail that project and has sought to do so unilaterally and brutally with the projection of military as well as economic, cultural, and political power across the globe.[19] In order to map this territory that I am trying to reach with the idea of empire's law, let me outline several dimensions of it.

With both the Bush Doctrine and the so-called "war on terror," compliance with long-standing norms of law and legality itself have been treated in instrumentalist and consequentialist fashion as merely discretionary policy decisions by the United States rather than as binding legal commitments for itself. John Yoo, one of the principle architects of the torture memos in the Bush administration, may most clearly if bone-chillingly illustrate this point. When asked why the Bush administration was at pains to avoid the application of the Geneva Conventions to the interrogation of detainees, Yoo responded: "Think about what you want to do when you have captured people from the Taliban and Al Qaeda. You want to interrogate them.... [I]t seems to me that if something is necessary for self-defense, it's permissible to deviate from the principles of Geneva. . . ."[20] The selectivity and double standards of the United States' treatment of legal commitments in the "war on terror" have been widely commented on, of course,[21] and selectivity and double standards are nothing new.[22] But both the philosophical basis for this position as articulated by the "new Sovereigntists" associated with the Bush administration and its radical position toward international law (at least as it relates to human rights, international humanitarian law, and the use of force)[23] proceeded so far that many are coming to agree with Jordan J. Paust's early recognition (in 2005) that, with respect to the Geneva Conventions and the treatment of fundamental international human rights, the "inner circle" of the Bush administration formulated a common plan to violate and deny the protections of international law, which may amount to war crimes.[24]

With respect to the Bush Doctrine and the invasion of Iraq, Jürgen Habermas has argued that the United States "rejected" international legality as a medium for international governance. On the one hand, American empire has attempted to avoid the universalistic characteristics of legitimate legality.[25] It has sought to "reject" international law as a medium of regulation (insofar as it has) precisely because core features of internally legitimate law—inclusion of all affected, impartiality, "egalitarian universalism,"[26] reciprocity, reflexivity, publicity, and respect for basic rights—defend the principle of sovereign equality, whether the sovereign equality of nation-states or of individual persons,[27] and this is an egalitarian principle that empire will not lightly abide. On the other hand, Habermas has also suggested that in doing so it made "a revolutionary claim: if the regime of international law fails, then the hegemonic imposition of global liberal order is justified, even by means that are hostile" to it.[28] While important, Habermas's claim here is potentially misleading in two respects. It is potentially misleading, first, because the Bush administration treated law as a binding obligation for and on others treating them, at least, as addressees of legal obligation. When applied as a standard to be followed by others, particularly "the enemy," law became "ferocious and uncompromising."[29] This seems to suggest something rather different from the "rejection" of law that Habermas posits. Second, and as this already implies, that the aim or the consequence was the imposition of a "global *liberal* order," as Habermas suggests, is at least open to question—a point to which I will return.

If the first feature that characterizes empire's law is the treatment of legal obligation as merely a matter of empire's discretion involving instrumentalization, double standards, and selectivity, a second characteristic feature that follows closely from this is that others are rendered rightless. This seems obviously so in the case of the detainees whether at Abu Ghraib, Guantanamo, Bagram, or in the black sites or "secret" prisons scattered across the world,[30] as well as in the case of "extraordinary renditions." In these spaces and with these practices, persons have been stripped of their rights and also of their legal personality, which forms the basis for rights[31]—a move that has aimed, at least, at dissolving the legal limit.[32] Legal guarantees of rights were eschewed, with rights treated, rather, as merely discretionary privileges that may be revoked at will.[33] This also seems to be the case with international law on the use of force, where sovereign equality has similarly been treated as a mere privilege that may be withdrawn by empire, thus threatening to render other states "rightless," as well. As Preuss has put the point, "[a]ccording to the laws of empire, it is entirely legitimate to force regime change in a country falling within the empire's sphere of interest and influence. In the UN Charter, such action is categorically ruled out. The logic of empire accordingly implies that the UN requirements of *legality* do not hold a special place in the considerations of the United States."[34] There is another parallel, as well, between the treatment of persons and the treatment of other nation-states by empire, and this is that the logic of prevention has pervaded all legal levels—international, transnational, and domestic. As the Bush Doctrine articulated a logic of prevention in terms of international (anticipatory) "self-defense," the "global war on terror" pursues this logic perhaps even more deeply, with its effects dispersed transnationally, for example, with preventive detention of "terrorists" as "unlawful enemy combatants."[35]

Third, not only has empire attempted to render others rightless and sought, at least, to treat them as merely the addressees of law while exempting itself from legal obligation, it has also, simultaneously, attempted to position itself as, and often acted as if it is, the sole (or at the very least dominant) author of law.[36] This, in fact, may be taken to be the core meaning of "hegemonic" unilateralism.[37] Consider the example of the Bush Doctrine on the unilateral *decision* to use and the unilateral *use* of force and preventive war. With the Bush Doctrine, the United States rejected international law's prohibitions on the unilateral use of force and attempted virtually unilaterally to establish a new norm of preventive war which would be available, in its view, only to itself—an arrogation of the right to decide upon and wage aggressive war "as an instrument of national policy."[38] From the point of view of international law, however, this stance could become a universalized norm recognized as available to all in the global legal order.[39] It seems clear that *either* of these results would be deeply threatening to humanity, in general, and to weaker states and their populations—those "rogue," "outlaw," and "failed" states that imperial power seeks to police—in particular.[40] However, as deeply worrisome as either result would be, perhaps an even more disturbing aspect of the Bush Doctrine and the broader "global war on terror" is the United States' self-proclaimed right unilaterally to define and to state law—to (re)constitute rule/law unilaterally and "monologically."

Not all of this has occurred under the glare of publicity, as the United States was forced to proceed in the case of the Bush Doctrine, articulated as it was in the National Security Strategy of the United States, and the invasion of Iraq, for which the United States sought Security Council approval before acting on its own, but also through subterranean and (once) secret means with practices like torture and detention in "secret prisons," all with their "ghosts," developed and deployed on the basis of classified legal memos and the extensive use of instruments like presidential signing statements and executive orders. Hence, it is not just the substantive results (including rightlessness and the unilateral attempt to transform prevailing norms) that are threatening. The processes through which these results were secured have also been significantly "unilateral," exceptional, discretionary and, perhaps especially from the perspective of others—particularly their addressees—arbitrary. Former insiders, like Jack Goldsmith (a Republican supporter of Bush who has insisted on the "dangers" of international law and the director of the Office of Legal Counsel in the Justice Department for nine months before he resigned in disgust in June 2004), have maintained that a "self-styled 'war council'" in the Bush administration proceeded with "minimal deliberation, unilateral action and legalistic defense," to undermine the rule of law.[41] Such accounts are all the more disturbing when bolstered in the post-Bush era with statements like those made by Condoleezza Rice when, in April 2009, she claimed that if practices like waterboarding were authorized by the president, "by definition" the practice would not violate the United States' obligations under the Convention Against Torture.[42]

Despite the characteristic "decisionistic" nature of such actions and justifications, the threat we have been faced with is fundamentally *not* that of a "lawless world."[43] That commonly heard expression, and associated ones such as "legal black holes," too often imply a negation, a lack, a literal law-less-ness. The Bush administration posed a more profound challenge than mere *illegality* or *unlawfulness* (violating particular, fundamental laws such as torture prohibitions and the law against aggressive war), mere *avoidance* of laws (attempting to evade the enforcement of law as in the Bush administration's rejection of the International Criminal Court, and the bilateral treaties it demanded, among others) or even the *suspension* of law (as when Bush claimed to have the authority to "'suspend Geneva as between the US and Afghanistan'"[44]). The United States' stance has issued in a threat to legality as a legitimate "mode of political regulation" and this has carried with it the threat of the crystallization of a form of rule/law that is divorced from legitimate legality but is dependent on and beholden to the idea of law: empire's law. To be sure, in one sense, "lawlessness" is a condition that does unarguably lie at the heart of the Bush Doctrine and the "global war on terror," but neither the physics of power nor the threat that has been posed is adequately captured with such phrases and this is for at least two reasons.

First, it is because these processes are themselves *indebted to law* rather than lying beyond or entirely outside of it.[45] They are indebted to law because, as has become clear, the "spaces of exception" like Guantanamo[46] and the "exceptional" legal rules like the Justice Department torture memos depend on law, lawyers,[47] legal institutions, and legal discourses themselves for their formulation and effectivity.[48] For example, Fleur Johns has detailed how Guantanamo is precisely *not* a "legal black hole" in the sense of being law-*less* or, she argues, even shot through with discretionary power, but is, rather, a place where law operates "in excess." It has been characterized by "elaborate regulatory efforts by a range of legal authorities,"[49] the details of which have become all too familiar to the literate reading public—"unlawful enemy combatant" status, military tribunals, Combatant Status Review Boards, the Military Commissions Act, and so on. Guantanamo is an intricate "legal regime";[50] its minute, technical governance functions through forms that are at least closely associated with, and claimed to be, law. Yet, this is in a territory with a long history under imperial America's rule, Guantanamo Bay,[51] that was deliberately chosen, with a status, "unlawful enemy combatant,"—and a tribunal system that were concocted precisely in order to lie outside the existing international legal regime governing war, longstanding American military law, and the American constitutional regime of rights. In this attempt to evade the constraints of basic norms in international, military and constitutional law Guantanamo has been, even before the US Supreme Court decisions, the "focus of painstaking work of legal classification."[52]

The creation of the category of "unlawful enemy combatant" may be taken as a stunning, if by now well-known, example that lies at the heart of the processes described here—a status not known to international law[53] and of dubious domestic lineage. Peter Jan Honigsburg may put the point best when he says of "enemy combatant" status:

> The creation of the term enemy combatant was not an accident. What could be more convenient for the administration than to create a new term that avoids international law scrutiny; a new term that could be used to sidestep the application of international law, thereby shielding the administration's behavior and treatment of the detainees; a new term where government officials may bestow or withdraw the rights or protections of the detainees at whim; a new term that deliberately confuses issues and facilitates sound-bites and hair-splitting, rather than legal-reasoning; a new term that the administration alone has defined; and a new term that provides legal cover from unlawful behavior and, as former Attorney General John Ashcroft and White House Counsel Alberto Gonzales articulated, shelters the individual members of the administration from being charged with war crimes?[54]

Despite important US Supreme Court decisions extending habeas corpus and the protections in Common Article 3 of the Geneva Conventions to the detainees at Guantanamo, the Supreme Court has not seriously questioned or challenged the status of "unlawful enemy combatant"[55] that lies at the centre of US claims to be able to pick up suspects anywhere in the world, interrogate them "harshly," and detain them until the end—if there is an end—of the "global war on terror." By accepting the term quite uncritically, the Supreme Court has given it legal standing, a standing which follows empire across the world.

In fact, then, the "exception *to* the law is *of* the law," as Peter Fitzpatrick and Richard Joyce cogently put the matter, and imperial power's rule (and "the exception's attendant sovereign rule") is "[re]constituted by law."[56] Virtually every attempt to evade the constraints of legal norms, to place itself outside the ruling legal regime, has relied on the discourses, practices, and institutions of law itself. This relies on law as a tactic,[57] a strategy of exceptionalism. In important respects, this has become pervasive for, as William Scheuerman says, "once the cancer of *normlessness* is allowed into the legal system, it is only a matter of time before it infects healthy legal organs as well."[58] And this has not just been a matter of the "cancer of normlessness" at the international level, but at every level—international, transnational, and domestic—as nation-states and regional regimes have been rewarded and coerced into following suit by the United States.[59]

But what is the character of this law that has constituted the exception? This brings me to my second argument for why it is important not to conceive of all of this as a "lawless world." It is important to emphasize that it is not mere lawlessness or the suspension of law that lies at the core of the Bush Doctrine and the US-led "war on terror," but something even more threatening, because it is potentially more *constitutive* than the ideas of suspension of law and "lawlessness" imply.[60] While much of this may accurately be described as it is by an outraged Jordan J. Paust, Law Foundation Professor at University of Houston and former faculty member of the Judge Advocate General's School, as an "unprincipled plan to evade the reach of the law,"[61] I want to suggest that the possible consequences of all of this go well beyond even evasion and violation. The United States has also used "paralegal" tactics[62] which may shift or transform the norms of international (and domestic) law. The potential for this global state of exception to become normalized is clear when the most powerful empire in history has attempted to rewrite the rules, perhaps only for itself but with foreseeable potential consequences for international law, degrading long-held fundamental norms, encouraging, coercing, and pressuring other, less powerful states to follow along, thus not just evading law or even just eroding an international political culture that is critically important to the sustainability of international legal norms, but also threatening the erosion of the post–World War II international law regime pertaining to the use of force, international humanitarian law, and human rights norms across the world.[63] And, this has opened up the possibility, of course, of the emergence of new "norms" and possibly new tolerances for practices that not long ago were prohibited by sacrosanct norms, many of which have (had?) *jus cogens* status.

The torture debate is instructive here in part because a "debate" over its justifiability was virtually unimaginable in the United States as recently as September 10, 2001. Furthermore, torture and "coercive interrogation" have not just been practiced and spread by the imperial state and its subordinates but have been parsed and *virtually justified* by the Bush administration (with reversals and denials of course), thus threatening to move torture from the despicable, subterranean, illegal actions to which a state responding to crises might illegitimately and illegally resort to a regime that *seeks legal standing* with terrible implications for human rights and legitimate legality and the sort of political culture that sustains them. This argument has been made particularly well by Jeremy Waldron, who emphasizes the importance of the distinction between torture as a practice of states and torture treated as a legal policy.[64] In Waldron's words, the various torture memos were written in an effort to "see whether something like torture can be accommodated within the very legal framework that purports to prohibit it. . . . An effort is being made to see whether the law can be stretched or deformed to actually permit and authorize this sort of thing."[65] And this has not simply been a matter of "fine tuning" the law; rather, it poses a fundamental threat to a basic norm.[66] Furthermore, Waldron argues the rule against torture is an archetype of the rule of law, and (relying on Judith N. Shklar) he associates the rule of law with the "repudiation of brutality; the promise of the rule of law is that it sets its face against brutality."[67] The Bush administration's parsing and justification of torture is, therefore, even more consequential than threatening a crucial, longstanding universal norm: it attacks legitimate legality in terms of the threat it poses to basic human rights, it asserts that commitment to international legal norms is a discretionary matter,[68] and it asserts imperial presidential authority. Waldron concludes that it does not just (as terrible as even this would be) "assault" the entire legal regime concerning torture;[69] rather, it may have a "systemic corrupting effect" on law more generally[70] insofar as it attacks an archetype, an icon that expresses the entire spirit of law. One might say simply, without (I hope) doing violence to Waldron's nuanced argument, that such moves threaten the future of legitimate law because, violating the fundamental premise of human dignity, they violate and threaten to erode basic human rights commitments, commitments that are a necessary aspect of the integrity of legitimate legality.[71]

It is important, of course, not to present a complicated, tension-filled, possibly contradictory and contested set of American state practices, justifications, and machinations in simplified terms as leading to a telos of iron-clad propositions (not even the Bush administration was that simple, as heated debates between the inner circle of the White House, Justice, State, and Defense Departments indicate, not to mention the disputes between the administration and the US Supreme Court and within the Supreme Court itself).[72] Neither should one assume certainty of the result. Certainly, the United States Supreme Court has played a not inconsiderable role in developing a jurisprudence that might constrain the state especially with its decisions in *Hamdan*, where the Court held that Common Article 3 of the Geneva Conventions applies to the detainees, and in *Boumediene*, in which a majority of the Court extended constitutional habeas corpus to them.[73] Yet not only, but also not least, because the Supreme Court has not rejected the status of "unlawful enemy combatant" itself, one can see that the threat lies in an uneven but discernible movement toward performing a *constitutive undoing* of the post–World War II regime of international legality with the threat of a consolidation of a much more draconian regime of "law" and rule. The struggle has been waged by American empire to impose, but also to gain popular legitimacy for, this law. Fear, anxiety, security, the racialized other, the "enemy" threatening the "homeland," patriotism, and attachment to a purportedly "exceptional imperium" have all been mobilized by neoconservative hawks in order to elicit support for and popular legitimation of such transformations.

It is not the normal operation of legitimate legality ("the norm") that is in play here, or where legitimate legality is in play what we see is a complicated patchwork of legitimate legality and something else that parades under the name of "law," a mere pretender to the status of legality.[74] In this respect Fleur Johns's analysis of Guantanamo, for example, is misleading when she suggests that the proliferation of laws, procedures, and legal discourses at and around Guantanamo undermines claims that it has functioned apart from "normalcy,"[75] when in demonstrating the "excess" of law at Guantanamo she explicitly conflates that "law" with "liberal proceduralism"[76] and the rule of law,[77] and when she criticizes those who view it as a "'decisive departure from the legal status quo.'"[78] Contrary to analyses like this, the rule *by* law at Guantanamo—the proliferation of governmental tactics that provide the appearance of legality—remains at its heart both highly arbitrary and an attempt to produce certain results precisely in line with the administration's view of its needs and its demands.[79] While one might suggest that the "law" on the ground at Guantanamo has aimed to manage first-level discretion by virtue of minute regulation, the crux of the matter is the denial of accountability and the instantiation of executive arbitrariness dressed up in legal veneer.[80] The discretion of those on the ground is entirely dependent on the sovereign decision. How else can the stunningly arrogant move to construct a "legal" regime at Guantanamo that is unfettered from international law and constitutional norms—from fundamental norms that are crucial to legality—be characterized but as "exceptional"? This decisionism has both emanated from and sought to reinvigorate the imperial presidency as it aimed to disarticulate its rule from the constraints of legitimate legality with its processes of "liberal proceduralism" and the "normal" demands of both international law and domestic constitutional law[81] and sought to emplace another law.

We might draw on Neumann again and his critique of Schmittian decisionism that undergirded National Socialism: "Law is now a technical means for the achievement of specific political aims. . . . Law is merely an *arcanum dominationis*, a means for the stabilization of power."[82] Whether the transformation to a much more draconian regime of "law"—or *arcanum dominationis*—will be successful in our time remains an open question that depends not just on the US Supreme Court as well as the Obama presidency and Congress but also on the international legal apparatuses and the capacity and willingness of the political and legal public spheres to contest and influence them. If it were to be successful, it would mean that the law that would rule the globe would be empire's law—an attempt unilaterally to author and constitute and to impose and enforce an illegitimate and unaccountable form of rule that shares little with legitimate legality, by a global power that has sought to arrogate to itself the role of global sovereign by declaring the exception (and hence declaring itself exceptional).[83] This form of global rule has threatened international, transnational, and domestic legality—and it has threatened domestic legality not just within the United States as one can readily see in numerous examples, but perhaps most obviously with the participation of certain European governments as well as Canada in "extraordinary renditions"[84]—while it has eroded advances in international legality and the democratic protection and development of sovereign equality and human rights, all of which are crucial to defending against the excesses of empire.[85] The threat, then, from the point of view of international legality, lies in the United States' treatment of law merely as a "derivative of the will of the sovereign"[86]—that is, derivative of its own will as something like the global sovereign.

We might do well to attempt to capture this, though, in less Schmittian terms. One threat that has emanated from American empire with the war on terror has been the possible production or constitution of a different form of rule from the global liberal legal order that has reigned at least in principle since World War II. The aim, it seems, has not been that of reconstituting a "liberal global order" as Habermas, for one, suggests. Rather, the aim has been something more like establishing globally, transnationally, and domestically a neoconservative order of rule which, referring to domestic contexts, Nicos Poulantzas aptly called "authoritarian statism" (and about which Stuart Hall claimed, in 1980: "We are in the middle of a deep and decisive movement toward a more disciplinary, authoritarian kind of society,"[87] referring to the tutelage of the likes of Margaret Thatcher and Ronald Reagan). It has been about arming neoliberal capitalist globalization with a neoconservative political order of global rule. The possibility of global neoconservatism has been raised by the critical scholars of capitalist globalization and American imperium, and much attention has been paid to the neoconservatives like Wolfowitz and company,[88] but the formation of global neoconservatism requires more analysis, particularly as it pertains to transformations in forms of law at all levels. Addressing domestic politics, David Harvey describes neoconservative rule as making "the anti-democratic tendencies of neoliberalism explicit through a turn into authoritarian, hierarchical, and even militaristic means of maintaining law and order."[89] And, with respect to neoconservative imperialism, he recognizes that American empire has been oriented toward coercive forms of global domination through the pursuit of a neoconservative form of global governance.[90] Similarly, Panitch and Gindin outline the ways in which American empire has borne the "burden" of policing the world, not just militarily but also by setting the template for smashing dissent transnationally.[91]

Habermas is right, I think, that what is at stake here is a "hegemonic imposition" of rule, but what I believe he missed is the fact that that rule may not be aimed at establishing a "global *liberal* order."[92] Rather, under the Bush administration, American empire sought a form of law/rule that is *in principle*, not just in practice, hierarchical and asymmetrical, rather than egalitarian; *in principle*, not just in practice, biased; and *in principle*, not just in practice, asserted the hyper-sovereignty of the United States—rendering other nation-states *in principle*, not just in practice, less than sovereign equals while it has sought to render individual subjects rightless—reduced to mere objects of disciplinary rule with a vengeance. These are characteristic features not of liberalism but, rather, of a neoconservatism that renders neoliberalism's "antidemocratic tendencies" "explicit," precisely as Harvey suggests. This is the project American empire pursued transnationally and globally under the Bush administration through the penetration of other states with its "law," empire's law, and by dominating international institutions.[93]

Hannah Arendt's insight that the "unilateral power of the lone ruler will in the end consist of nothing more than the non-communicative violence of the military"[94] may exaggerate military power, in general, and may be insufficient to capture the multipronged character of global neoconservatism with its "imperial policing"[95] of dissent, violations of human rights (both international and constitutional), worldwide system of gulags, and so on, all of which are means of securing its order, in addition to its military occupations, but surely it does not exaggerate the threat that "non-communicative violence" poses. Empire's law may be viewed as a form of such non-communicative violence that has attempted to marginalize others—whether individuals or nation-states—treating them as mere objects or addressees of law/rule, neither as equal subjects nor as authors of law, while writing raw brutality into law/rule. In these ways, the Bush administration threatened to take legality, not just its detainees and its myriad other imperial subjects, "to the waterboards."[96] Thus was a new phase in the ongoing American imperial project struggling to be born. Under such conditions we must not abandon international law. Rather, following Neumann, we should "fight for an honest system" and must count the defense and development of legitimate legality as a part of the project of both constraining and contesting American empire.

2. Rethinking/Revaluing Legality—Dimensions of Legitimacy and Legitimation

The threat to legality has also been fostered in some important respects by reliance on the notion of legitimacy itself. Here I might either respectfully disagree with Richard Falk, or at least argue that we need to tease out different valences or consequences of claims around "legitimacy." In a discussion of humanitarian intervention and the use of force, Falk suggests that "[l]egality clarifies the core obligations relating to force, while legitimacy tries to identify *and delimit* a zone of exception that takes account of supposedly special circumstances."[97] But I think we can now see that the notion of "legitimacy" at play in debates about humanitarian intervention has constituted a "zone" that is not "delimited" at all. Rather, reliance on "legitimacy" in this context has contributed to the expansion of "zones of exception" that threaten legality. But, what do we mean by legitimacy here? We can trace this back at least to the mobilization of morality and the demands of cosmopolitan solidarity as providing the legitimacy that humanitarian actions may claim as contributing to both the excessive *moralization* of international politics and the *demotion* of legality within them. The moralization of politics associated with such claims to legitimacy gained a new lease on life with the impending invasion of Iraq—the physical expression of the Bush Doctrine—which was supported not just by neoconservatives in the Bush administration but also by liberal hawks like Michael Ignatieff and even by Marxist human rights fundamentalists such as Norman Geras.[98] The argument developed during the post-Cold War era regarding the moral right to humanitarian intervention got played out, too, with respect to Iraq with claims supported by an unholy union of neoconservative, Marxist, and liberal hawks that the supposedly benevolent empire bears both the right and the duty—the "burden"—to save strangers as well as to guard ("our") security by whatever means necessary. It now seems obvious that this sort of moralistic reliance on humanity/humanitarianism fuelled one of the chief opponents of human rights—imperialism—and has threatened the legal structures that are necessary to their realization.[99] In these ways, we can see how claims of legitimacy may function as license for demoting, or even undermining, legality.

As Richard Falk has also put it, however, "under conditions of unipolarity, international law assumes a more important role than within global settings where countervailing centers of state power exist."[100] Under these conditions, we need to consider the relationship between law and legitimacy in somewhat different terms. And, here, in trying to think through the idea of legality—legitimate law—we might benefit from drawing on Jürgen Habermas's work, despite the fact that Habermas provides a too friendly and too "realistic" acceptance of what he views as a possibly "benign" American imperial state[101] to lead the way and also a sometimes too optimistic faith in the institutions of international legality—in the "matrix of law"[102]—as perhaps *sufficient* to constrain it. In fact, the description and diagnosis of empire's law that I have sketched draws loosely on the conception of legitimate law, or what I am calling legality, that Habermas develops. So, let me now reverse procedure, in a sense, and attempt to unpack some of the elements of legitimate international law. I will do so primarily by drawing on Habermas's defense and description of legality as the form in which "egalitarian universalism"[103] can be institutionalized in a way that holds the promise—a promise that will never be fully realized—of addressing many of the problems diagnosed above. Of course, neither politics nor legitimacy can be reduced to legality[104] but Habermas's work can help us attend (albeit in unequal and uneven measure), to both the internal legitimacy of international law and the external democratic legitimation of it. This sort of orientation to the relationship between law and legitimacy seems to me to provide a necessary (although not sufficient) defense of international legality (and projects of legalization) against threats of moralization and empire's law and it at least raises the question of how international law's external legitimation may be furthered.

From his discourse-theoretic view of justice and morality, Habermas has produced his discourse theory of law and democratic legitimacy in his magnum opus in legal and political theory, *Between Facts and Norms*, a central claim of which is that "the democratic process bears the entire burden of legitimation" as the "only postmetaphysical source of legitimacy."[105] Habermas notes that much political theory suggests that the "legitimacy of any democratic order requires a broad agreement that goes beyond mere compliance."[106] Yet modern societies are shot through with difference and disagreement, so how should we understand the requirement of "broad agreement"? It is the anticipation of rational acceptability that a proceduralist conception of legitimation like his requires. Developing a discourse theory of democracy and deliberative politics has been at the heart of Habermas's work for many years now, although his work has been developed primarily at the level of the nation-state and domestic law, and only recently has he begun seriously to address questions of international, cosmopolitan, and transnational law and legitimacy. In this recent work, Habermas has sought to develop conceptions of cosmopolitanism, post-nationalism, and multilevel governance that spans international, transnational, and nation-state levels in ways that constitutionalize international relations while avoiding the implication of the development of a world state or global republic.[107]

Turning first, and very briefly, to the external legitimation of international law, the key insight of a Habermasian conception of deliberative democratic legitimacy is that those who are the addressees of law must also be able to understand themselves, in some sense, as its authors. And, yet, there is a widely recognized but still very ineptly conceptualized and addressed "legitimation deficit" in current forms of global governance.[108] Despite recognizing this legitimation gap, in my view Habermas has not so far (along with so many others) convincingly conceptualized how we might actually meet the demands of deliberative democratic legitimation at the international level.[109]

Nevertheless, it is significant that in the aftermath of the violence that spawned September 11, 2001, the violence that marked that date in our psyche and the violence that has been unleashed in response, Habermas does not retreat from a commitment to a proceduralist conception of deliberative democratic politics. Rather, he stresses anew the importance of cross-cultural deliberation to address what Arendt called "non-communicative violence." Far from abandoning the project of deliberative democracy in the face of such violence, he argues, "the spiral of violence begins as a spiral of distorted communication that leads through the spiral of uncontrolled reciprocal mistrust, to the breakdown of communication. If violence thus begins with a distortion in communication, after it has erupted it is possible to know what has gone wrong and what needs to be repaired."[110]

Under these conditions, the importance of "*mutual* perspective-taking" aimed at mutual understanding becomes all the more clear.[111] This is only possible under "symmetrical conditions" where the aim is neither conversion nor imposition, but rather the pursuit of "*intersubjectively* shared" understandings.[112]

Habermas provides, here, an important critical orientation that offers the promise of responding to the mistrust that is unleashed anew with each bomb delivered in the name of human rights, each dictate handed down by the United States as it has instrumentalized the language of human rights and freedom for imperial purposes, and each neoconservative threat to legality. And it is primarily in terms of the "medium" of law that Habermas argues we should seek the practical conditions to establish the necessary "symmetrical conditions of mutual perspective taking."[113] The still underdeveloped character of Habermas's work so far on the deliberative democratic (external) legitimation of international law—a weakness that is matched, of course, by international law itself—is amply compensated for by his astute observations and conceptualization of the internal legitimacy of the legal medium.

Contrary to both those critics who would dismiss international legality under conditions of empire and those human rights fundamentalists who would emphasize morality or legitimacy at the expense of legality, Habermas's conceptualization and defense of international and cosmopolitan law reveals legality's "gift," the gift of its "egalitarian universalism" which comprises an anti-imperial core.[114]

The discourse theory of law shows that the unilateralist or "monological" position adopted by the neoconservatives of American empire has failed in at least five respects: it has failed to protect the most basic rights and norms that are, themselves, necessary to legitimate legality[115]; it has failed to include the perspectives of *everyone affected*; it has failed to respect the requirements of *impartiality* that justice requires; it has been incapable of dealing with the *epistemic demands* that are so weighty in matters as complicated and fraught as war; and it has ignored the basis for developing *insight* which can only be gained through argumentation and the confrontation of views that is implicit in the "public redemption of validity claims."[116] Habermas emphasizes the central importance of "inclusive legal procedures" that may address these deficits to the judgment of such matters adequate to ground coercive political action.[117] One might suggest that Habermas has emphasized "law's empire" as an antidote to the threat of the emergence of what I am calling empire's law.[118] At the heart of this is Habermas's claim that legitimate legality's "inclusive legal procedures" institutionalize the demands of "egalitarian universalism" in a manner that respects a commitment to impartiality *in principle*, which is grounded in reflexivity and reciprocity, is based on public reasoning, a confrontation of alternate points of view and claims, and which has the capacity to render *accountable* claims that one actor is acting for the good of all or "in the equal interests of all." Habermas has put the matter as follows. Even (I insist counterfactually) the

> best case scenario of the *benevolent hegemon* meets, for cognitive reasons, insurmountable obstacles in identifying those courses of action and those kinds of initiative that accord with shared interests of the international community. The most circumspect state that decides only in [*sic*] its own authority on humanitarian interventions, on cases of self-defense, on international tribunals etc. can never be sure whether or not it actually disentangles its national interests from the shared and generalizable ones. This is not a question of good will or bad intention but an issue of the *epistemology of practical deliberation*. Any anticipation from one side, of what should be acceptable for all sides, cannot be checked but by subjecting a supposedly impartial proposal to an inclusive process of deliberation, by the rules of which all parties involved

> are equally required to take into consideration the perspectives of the other participants, too. This is the cognitive purpose of impartial judgment that legal procedures are expected to serve, in the global as well as in the domestic arena.
>
> Benevolent unilateralism is deficient in terms of a lack of legal provisions for impartiality and legitimacy.[119]

While in *Between Facts and Norms* Habermas emphasizes the importance of the democratic genesis of legitimate law at the domestic level—or external legitimation—reflecting on international law he has illuminated the internal legitimacy of legality itself, the processes and procedures that legality provides which "ensure" (in principle) the equal standing of parties and the impartiality (in principle) of the process. Conceptualized in relation to American empire, he states: "Without inclusive legal procedures there is nothing compelling the predominant party to give up the central perspective of a great empire, or to engage in the de-centering of meaning-perspectives that an equal consideration for the cognitive point of view of all interests requires." It is only through the "matrix of law" that the "ever controversial elements of 'justice' translated into the verifiable category of 'legality'" can legitimately be sorted out. The "whole point of inclusive legal procedures" at the international level is to avoid the false universalism of empire's or others' particular claims and to ascertain through the confrontation of "different points of view and consideration of reciprocal interests" that they can impartially be judged.[120]

Here, Habermas's political work seems carefully grounded in his theoretical work in *Between Facts and Norms* where he argues that morality, which is "specialized for questions of justice," is a system of knowledge, but even deliberative morality has no contact with "the institutions that ensure that justified moral expectations are actually fulfilled." Morality, Habermas argues, requires an "institutionalized legal system that supplements" it "in a manner effective for action."[121] The legal code establishes a "procedural rationality" inducing "timely, unambiguous and binding decisions." Therefore, it provides a "procedural rationality of its own that compensates for the weaknesses of its complement, the procedural rationality inherent in the process of argumentation."[122]

This line of analysis, which reveals international legality's "gift"[123] of an anti-imperial core, is far from revolutionary, of course. It is also ambivalent in its implications in the way, for example, that it privileges states over other actors.[124] On its own, it asserts "norms" in the face of compelling "facts" that raise very serious questions about its possible actuality. But it is here that we might follow Neumann: "when we have shown that international law has been misused for imperialist aims, our task has begun, not ended." The project implied by this task is enormously important as part of contesting empire's law. And Habermas is, of course, not alone in making such an argument: authors as diverse as Slavoj Žižek, Peter Fitzpatrick, and Martti Koskenniemi have all argued similarly that legitimate international law is crucial for reasons of sovereign equality, impartiality, adequate judgment based on public reason-giving, self-restraint, the development of insight, *and* as a means of resistance and "democratic hope."[125] Both the force of Habermas's argument and this happy meeting of progressive minds across theoretical perspectives should persuade us, I think, that the conceptualization, defense and expansion of legitimate legality at the international level is a properly "radical" exercise and a better response than is provided by either the neoconservatives or the radical critics of international law whom I cited at the beginning of this chapter. Of course, if it is the case that the defense of international law is to be conducted as much in terms of its procedural qualities in principle as in the defense of its substantive, fundamental norms, then we are drawn back to the necessity of both diagnosing the ways in which those procedures relate to "legal imperialism"[126] or "imperial law"[127] and the difficult task of conceptualizing radical reforms that might actually have traction and be effective. Taking international law seriously as an arena of contestation against all forms of empire implies the necessity of a very serious agenda of struggles around reform of those institutions in order to develop the promise of the internal legitimacy of international law and to address its currently exceedingly thin external legitimation.

A SUMMARY AND A CAVEAT

Both international law *and* empire's law have been and are to some great extent determined by American imperial (and other) power, as critical analyses of international law have long shown at least with respect to the former.[128] The *difference* between them, however, is as important to identify as their similarity. A critical account of legality should emphasize its relationship to power and approach the political as complex with legality conceptualized as a site of contestation, rather than as an "instrument" either of empire or of cosmopolitan desire. Conceived in this way, legality constitutes an arena of struggle and international and cosmopolitan law are viewed as sites of unequal contests which, however, depend in principle on the universality and impartiality, on the internal legitimacy, of law. As such, even the powerful are enveloped within legality's egalitarian universalism such that they must sometimes submit to the internal logic of international and cosmopolitan law[129] and may, perhaps even more powerfully, be criticized for engaging in contradictions—failing to adhere to the very legal logic, processes, and fundamental norms that they have themselves authored and, more importantly, to which they typically claim to be committed.[130] This is the message we can take from both Habermas's and Neumann's defense of the universalism within legitimate international law.

Empire's law, on the other hand, seeks exceptions, evasions, and legal arrangements that accommodate empire's needs and desires while *in principle* marginalizing others—treating them as law's mere objects, not rights-holders, equal subjects, or equal authors. American empire has threatened to reconstitute and refound the law virtually by unilateral fiat, with enormous pressure placed on its "coalition" and "allies," to say nothing of its enemies, threatening both the internal legitimacy of law and future possibilities for its external democratic legitimation. It is for these reasons that it is inadequate to assume or argue that the Bush administration's position in relation to law was one merely of acting "lawlessly" or to assume that it was, legally speaking, law/rule as usual. Its implications were and are much more threatening than either of these positions reveals.[131] The question remains how much precedential weight eight years of neoconservative global rule under Bush and the US-led "global war on terror" will have, how much they have become imbricated in the workings and global political culture of empire and thus how difficult it will be for progressive forces in global and local civil societies to reverse this constitutive undoing.

While an adequate evaluation of the likelihood of the Obama administration reversing the American "ship of state" and guiding it back to law's empire is beyond the bounds of this chapter, it is clear that there is more continuity than discontinuity between the Bush and the Obama years with respect to empire's law. There is growing evidence that, despite his more internationalist orientation (especially in word but sometime even in deed as we see in relation to gaining a Security Council resolution to intervene in Libya), it has proved to be difficult to unravel all of what Bush has wrought. But the Obama administration has also been increasingly tempted *not* to try to reverse the constitutive undoing of empire's law. While specific instances of this may have been due to Congress, the Obama administration's position in this area cannot convincingly be blamed on anything other than its own decisions to reproduce, and in some cases even expand, key Bush era policies as necessary for the continuation of American empire.

The Obama administration has also used law tactically to avoid its obligations, to pursue, detain and kill its enemies, and to cover its tracks. For example, in an early sign of its intentions and echoing the Bush administration's treatment of fundamental international norms as merely discretionary policy choices, the Obama Justice Department argued in an extraordinary rendition court case that the *case* should be dismissed because to go forward would reveal "state secrets."[132] It now seems clear that this legal argument was made not just to shield the office of the president with past crimes in mind but also with the future in mind. The Executive Director of Human Rights Watch has observed that with Obama's refusal to prosecute key players who have engaged in or justified torture, "President Obama has treated torture as an unfortunate policy choice rather than a crime. His decision to end abusive interrogation practices will remain easily reversible unless the legal prohibition against torture is clearly reestablished."[133] Yet, it very well might not be a matter of "reversing" a decision to end torture. There is strong evidence that extraordinary renditions, secret detentions and torture continue to be practiced today. The treatment of Bradley Manning stands as a high profile example of a continuation, perhaps even an escalation, of the brazen use of torture, in this case against an American whistleblower.[134] Furthermore, the Obama administration has accepted the substance of "unlawful enemy combatant" status even while it publically rejects the term[135] and it has, of course, revamped the Military Tribunals at Guantanamo instead of putting accused terrorists held there on trial in criminal courts,[136] thereby "legalizing the very procedures and abuses of power that earned the Bush administration fierce condemnation."[137] But, it has gone further yet, with Obama signing an executive order in March 2011 that formalizes the indefinite detention of dozens of the remaining Guantanamo detainees.[138] Also telling is the pressure it placed on the United Kingdom not to release information about a tortured detainee who was in US custody.[139] When the United Kingdom refused to release the information, it was thanked by the Obama administration.[140] All of this has proved to be part and parcel of the expansion of the war on terror on the ground in Afghanistan, Pakistan, Yemen, and Somalia, including targeted killings and the explosive growth of the use of drone attacks which those around the administration have busily been defending as both necessary and legal.[141] Even with the Libyan intervention that was rendered formally legal with a Security Council resolution, we see that NATO has gone far beyond what most experts think it in fact authorized[142] and, significantly, Obama seems to have used the Security Council to avoid dealing with the American Congress in a move that has been described as "moving onto ground that even Bush did not occupy" in the "construction of an imperial presidency" unbound by Congress.[143] Just on the basis of this brief snapshot, we can see there is considerable evidence of continuity between the Bush and the Obama versions of neoconservative empire.

We can be certain of two things, today. First, without serious contestation by international, transnational, and national civil societies to defend fundamental human rights and legitimate international law, the United States is unlikely to change course. In this case, empire's law can be expected to metastasize. Second, so long as the United States remains an empire, any progressive change of course with respect to legality will mean, at best, that the United States may revert from a neoconservative model of global rule to a more liberal or "benevolent" one. This in itself may limit but does not negate the possibility for developing legitimate international law that may contribute to global justice.

CONCLUSION

Having introduced this chapter with Franz Neumann and pursued my argument through categories provided by Jürgen Habermas (as well as Hannah Arendt for good measure) let me end, with intentional intellectual promiscuity, with some comments made by Jean-Paul Sartre. In an interview he gave to *New Left Review* in 1967 on the question of why he was so centrally involved in the Bertrand Russell Tribunal during the Vietnam War he countered the criticism that the tribunal was dependent on "petit bourgeois legalism." Sartre argued that giving a "juridical dimension to acts of international politics" was crucial not just to "combat the tendency of the majority of people only to judge the conduct of a social group or of a government in expedient or in moral terms."[144] It was also necessary to appeal to those very forces "which must today be aroused and shaken" by legalism and to be able to judge whether imperial power is exceeding "the limits that it set for *itself*."[145] In the context of an analysis that speaks of the "durable American hegemony" (which he did not fool himself meant in the 1960s bipolar power[146]) Sartre thus emphasized the importance of legality, by which he meant legitimate law, as a way of imposing limits upon empire. Not one to fall prey to an idealist conception of law or rule or morality, Sartre grasped then, as I suggest we should now and as Habermas emphasizes, the importance of defending, deploying, and further developing legitimate legality at the international (and every other) level. But he also went beyond Habermas to emphasize, as I think we must today, that this project must be *an integral part of a broader politics that rejects the legitimacy of empire*[147]—whether neoconservative, "liberal," "benign," or otherwise. Legitimate legality may help contest the neoconservative, authoritarian variety of American empire, a struggle that remains crucial in which to engage since in the absence of contestation we should expect empire's law to linger in, perhaps even burrow into, even a more "liberal" American empire. American empire requires political contestation no less grand and no less "polyvocal" than itself. And this will have to go far beyond a defense, or even a radical reform, of international law and its institutions. As Neumann recognized, it is only when social and economic equality is achieved that general law will be fully meaningful.[148] This is perhaps especially so in the international realm. This is why he rightly argued "we must fight against imperialism."

Endnotes

1. See Amy Bartholomew, "Empire's Law and the Contradictory Politics of Human Rights," in Amy Bartholomew, ed., *Empire's Law: The American Imperial Project and the "War to Remake the World"* (London: Pluto, 2006), 161–192; and Amy Bartholomew and Jennifer Breakspear, "Human Rights as Swords of Empire," in Leo Panitch and Colin Leys, eds., *The New Imperial Challenge* (London: Merlin Press, 2003), 125–145. Also see Upendra Baxi, "The 'War *on* Terror' and the 'War *of* Terror': Nomadic Multitudes, Aggressive Incumbents, and the 'New International Law,'" *Osgoode Hall Law Journal* 43 (2005): 7–43, where he argues: "Enactments of the 'war on terror' stand super-justified in terms of the protection and promotion of human rights and fundamental freedoms, the international or global rules of law, and, most comprehensively, as a worldwide installation of market-friendly democracy and freedom" (9).

2. Perry Anderson, "Arms and Rights: Rawls, Habermas and Bobbio in an Age of War," *New Left Review* 31 (2005): 5–40, here 31. Also see, Perry Anderson, "Casuistries of Peace and War," *London Review of Books*, March 6, 2003, http://www.lrb.co.uk/v25/n05/ande01_.html, where, in the course of an argument against those who criticized the impending invasion of Iraq on the grounds of unilateralism, preemption, and the human costs of war—that is, at least in part, those who criticized it as a violation of, and challenge

to, international law—he argues the world would be better off without the Security Council. Also, Perry Anderson, "Force and Consent," *New Left Review* 17 (September–October 2002): 5–30.

3. China Mieville, *Between Equal Rights: A Marxist Theory of International Law* (Chicago: Haymarket Books, 2005). Mieville's critique is premised on commodity form theory and a theory of imperialism. He concludes: "I am a denier in the sense that I see no prospect of a systematic progressive political project or emancipatory dynamic coming out of international law" (316).

4. James Tully, *Public Philosophy in a New Key Volume II: Imperialism and Civic Freedom* (Cambridge, Cambridge University Press, 2008). Tully treats international law as "entangled" within imperialism and therefore as incapable of providing any alternative to imperial power. For example, Tully considers a wide range of critical literature on US imperialism and contends that the "allegedly non-imperial languages and practices on which their [the critics'] criticism and alternatives are based are neither outside of contemporary imperialism nor the means of liberating us from imperialism." This includes both international law and democracy. Instead, in every instance "both the languages and the practices they presume to be external to imperialism (non-imperial) turn out on closer examination to be internal to, or play a role in, contemporary imperialism." What is presented as an alternative to imperialism is, in fact, just "another aspect of imperialism" (130).

5. Fleur Johns, "Guantanamo Bay and the Annihilation of the Exception," *European Journal of International Law* 16, no.4 (2005): 613–635, here 631–632. For a similar analysis, see Nasser Hussain, "Beyond Norm and Exception: Guantanamo," *Critical Inquiry* 33, no. 4 (2007): 734–753. It might be noticed that Johns's suggestion echoes Agamben's description of "the camps" where he says "[t]he normal order is de facto suspended and in which whether or not atrocities are committed depends not on law but on the civility and ethical sense of the police who temporarily act as sovereign. . . ." Giorgio Agamben, *Homo Sacer: Sovereign Power and Bare Life*, trans. Daniel Heller-Roazen (Stanford, Calif.: Stanford University Press, 1995), 174.

6. Franz Neumann, *Behemoth: The Structure and Practice of National Socialism, 1933–1944* (New York: Harper and Row, 1966 [1944/1942]), 158–159. There is a delicious irony here: while in exile from Nazi Germany in the United States, Neumann became central to American war strategy when *Behemoth* was a key text guiding the Research and Analysis Bureau in Washington, D.C. As William Scheuerman tells the story: "In what is undoubtedly one of the most curious moments in the otherwise sordid history of the American Secret Service, not only was a group of exiled socialists responsible for much of the OSS's research, but a study with clear Marxist features was contributing, however indirectly, to American war policy." William E. Scheuerman, *Between the Norm and Exception: The Frankfurt School and the Rule of Law* (Boston: MIT Press, 1997), 123–124.

7. In addition to the positions mentioned above, see, for example, Anderson, "Force and Consent"; Anderson, "Casuistries of Peace and War"; Tariq Ali, "Re-colonizing Iraq," *New Left Review* 21 (May–June 2003): 5–19; Tariq Ali, *Bush in Babylon: The Recolonisation of Iraq* (London: Verso, 2003); Danilo Zolo, *Invoking Humanity: War, Law and Global Order* (London: Continuum, 2002); and Costas Douzinas, "Humanity, Military Humanism and the New Moral Order," *Economy and Society* 32, no. 2 (2003): 159–183.

For an alternative view see, Peter Fitzpatrick, "'Gods Would Be Needed. . .': American Empire and the Rule of (International) Law," *Leiden Journal of International Law* 16 (2003): 429–466, who says: "a deficient law seems inexorably to come to power. There remains a tangential force of international law which some would discern in its ability to lay down processual paths along which power passes in taking effect, or at least some of its effects, but even that consolation is being diminished of late by the perceived ability of power now to transform the processes constituting international law itself" (447).

8. For the roots of this analysis see Nicos Poulantzas, *State, Power, Socialism* (London: New Left Books, 1978), esp. 31.

9. I agree, for example, with Balakrishnan Rajagopal's demand that we analyze the role of resistance from below, around, and within international law and with Sundhya Pahuja when she seeks to appreciate international law's simultaneously "imperializing effect and its anti-imperial tendency." Sundhya Pahuja, "The Postcoloniality of International Law," *Harvard International Law Journal* 46 (2005): 459–469, here 460, and Balakrishnan Rajagopal, *International Law from Below: Development, Social Movements, and Third World Resistance* (New York: Cambridge University Press, 2003).

10. Upendra Baxi, "What May the Third World Expect of International Law?" *Third World Quarterly* 27 (2006): 713–725, here 557. It seems significant that the authors of recent texts on law and imperialism, like Antony Anghie, Upendra Baxi, and Balakrishnan Rajagopal, argue for viewing international law as a site of resistance and contestation. For example, according to Baxi's reading of Anghie, "he insists on the potential for endless negotiation, rather than flat rejection, of international law on behalf, and even at the behest, of the continually oppressed subjects." Upendra Baxi, "New Approaches to the History of International Law," *Leiden Journal of International Law* 19 (2006): 555–566, here 562. Also see Samir Amin, "Whither the United Nations," in Bartholomew, ed., *Empire's Law*, 340–366.

11. As Peter Fitzpatrick has put it: if "international law is merely or ultimately the receptacle and instrument of power," we should conclude that American empire can wield it unproblematically. But, if this is so, "[i]f international law is so abject, so thoroughly receptive to power, and if, as its history richly reveals, it has been particularly accommodating of *imperium*, why should the assertion of American empire ever go beyond or be contrary to international law? Then it could be asked whether it might be that there is 'in' law, in international law, a life that in some identifiable way counters and resists *imperium*? And might we not be able to identify this identifiable way at those points where law counters and resists imperium?" Fitzpatrick, "Gods Would Be Needed," 457–458. Also see Terry Nardin, "International Pluralism and the Rule of Law," *Review of International Studies* 26 (2000): 95–110, here 102–103.

12. Perhaps the best short description of the Bush Doctrine comes from Jonathan Schell, "The Empire Backfires," *Znet* (March 11, 2004), %3ca href=www.zmag.org/content/showarticle.cfm?SectionID=11&;ItemID = 5129, who describes it as follows:

> Its aim, which many have properly called imperial, is to establish lasting American hegemony over the entire globe, and its ultimate means is to overthrow regimes of which the United States disapproves, preemptively if necessary. The Bush Doctrine indeed represents more than a revolution in American policy; if successful, it would amount to an overturn of the existing international order. In the new, imperial order, the United States would be first among nations, and force would be first among its means of domination. Other, weaker nations would be invited to take their place in shifting coalitions to support goals of America's choosing. The United States would be so strong, the President has suggested, that other countries would simply drop out of

the business of military competition, "thereby making the destabilizing arms races of other eras pointless, and limiting rivalries to trade and other pursuits of peace." Much as in the early modern period, when nation-states were being born, absolutist kings, the masters of overwhelming military force within their countries, in effect said, "There is now a new thing called a nation; a nation must be orderly; we kings, we sovereigns, will assert a monopoly over the use of force, and thus supply that order," so now the United States seemed to be saying, "here now is a thing called globalization; the global sphere must be orderly; we, the sole superpower, will monopolize force throughout the globe, and thus supply international order."

13. See the discussions in Richard Falk, "Legality and Legitimacy: The Quest for Principled Flexibility and Restraint," *Review of International Studies* 31 (2005): 33–50; and Jürgen Habermas, "Bestiality and Humanity: A War on the Border between Law and Morality," *Constellations* 6, no. 3 (1999): 263–272. This chapter was written long before NATO's intervention in Libya and this is not the place to explore that complex and somewhat different situation.

14. Gopal Balakrishnan, "Overcoming Emancipation," *New Left Review* 19 (January–February 2003): 115–128, here 123–124.

15. For the sort of interpretation I give to American empire, see Leo Panitch and Sam Gindin, "Theorizing American Empire," in Bartholomew, ed., *Empire's Law*, 21–43; and David Harvey, *The New Imperialism* (Oxford: Oxford University Press, 2003). In the context of international law, see Jean L. Cohen, "Whose Sovereignty? Empire Versus International Law," *Ethics and International Affairs* 18 (2004) 1–24.

16. Gerry J. Simpson, *Great Powers and Outlaw States: Unequal Sovereigns in the International Legal Order* (New York: Cambridge University Press, 2004).

17. Ulrich K. Preuss, "The Iraq War: Critical Reflections from 'Old Europe,'" in Bartholomew, ed., *Empire's Law*, 52–70, here 66.

18. Ronald Dworkin, *Law's Empire* (Cambridge, Mass.: Harvard University Press, 2004).

19. Baxi, for one, seems to agree with the contours of this analysis: "Certainly, from a TWAIL [Third World Approaches to International Law] perspective, these [sort of] features . . . present an immense reversal of the historic third-world contribution to the making of the post–Second World War international law normativity." "War *on* Terror," 36.

20. Cited in Jordan J. Paust, "Above the Law: Unlawful Executive Authorizations Regarding Detainee Treatment, Secret Renditions, Domestic Spying, and Claims to Unchecked Executive Power," *Utah Law Review* 2 (2007): 345–419, here 356.

21. For example, see Christiane Wilke, "War v. Justice: Terrorism Cases, Enemy Combatants, and Political Justice in U.S. Courts," *Politics and Society* 33 (2005): 637–669, here 660, where she says the reliance on the discourses of war in places like Guantanamo implies that "enemies" are "beyond the law, and that any legal process they are accorded is a matter of policy or grace, but not of rights." Also see Reg Whitaker, "Drifting Away from the Edge of Empire: Canada in the Era of George W. Bush," in Bartholomew, ed., *Empire's Law*, 265–281. Whitaker points to the United States' "'Hague Invasion' Act that gives the President the power to rescue any American held for war crimes" (270). Although the United States does not deny the "relevance of the [International Criminal] Court to other, lesser nations" and it has not refrained from "delivering war crimes suspects from elsewhere to the Hague," it "claims for itself the right of exemption from the rule of international law." Jean L. Cohen

("Whose Sovereignty?") argues that with the invasion of Iraq, the United States made its "move against international law explicit" (18).

22. See Jean Allain, "Orientalism and International Law: The Middle East as the Underclass of the International Legal Order," *Leiden Journal of International Law* 17 (2004): 391–404.

23. Peter J. Spiro, "The New Sovereigntists: American Exceptionalism and Its False Prophets," *Foreign Affairs* (November/December 2000), http://www.foreignaffairs.org/20001101facomment932/peter-j-spiro/the-new-sovereigntists-american-exceptionalism-and-its-false-prophets.html.

24. Jordan J. Paust, "Executive Plans and Authorizations to Violate International Law Concerning Treatment and Interrogation of Detainees," *Columbia Journal of Transnational Law* 43 (2005): 811–863. Also see Philippe Sands, *The Torture Team: Rumsfeld's Memo and the Betrayal of American Values* (New York: Palgrave Macmillan, 2008).

25. Jürgen Habermas, "Interpreting the Fall of a Monument," in Bartholomew, ed., *Empire's Law*, 44–51.

26. Habermas, "Interpreting the Fall of a Monument," 51.

27. Nico Krisch, "International Law in Times of Hegemony: Unequal Power and the Shaping of the International Legal Order," *European Journal of International Law* 16 (2005): 369–408, shows that these sorts of moves are not historically unprecedented. For example, he argues that in "the scramble for Africa in the 19th century, most territorial acquisitions by Europeans were accompanied by treaties with native rulers." (396). Dispute over the status of treaties/territories "only highlights how Europeans sought to circumvent the egalitarian implications of international law: how they moved into another legality that allowed them to deny the sovereign equality of their counterparts and to introduce hierarchies into the international order" (397).

28. Habermas, "Interpreting the Fall of a Monument," 45.

29. Nehal Bhuta argues, for example, in "A Global State of Exception? The United States and World Order," *Constellations* 10, no. 3 (2003): 371–391, here 380:

> The statements and posture of the Bush administration imply a vision of international order where 'law' is merely one policy consideration among others, not a binding obligation—except when applied to the enemy, with respect to whose illegal acts the notion of 'legality' adopts a ferocious and uncompromising polemical content. The restraints of legality to which an enemy is subject have no application to the United States, whose power permits—*and can be shown to permit*—it to arrogate to itself the entitlement to determine the boundary between law as principle and law as coercion. The affinities here with Schmitt are obvious: the sovereign is that which determines (by virtues of its actual or potential defeat of any who would challenge it) the exception. Order is not a matter of authority, but a matter of will, and legality is derivative of the will of the sovereign.

30. See, for example, Alan Freeman, "EU Eyes Alleged CIA Jails," *The Globe and Mail*, November 4, 2005, Toronto edition.

31. Wilke, "War v. Justice," 656.

32. Klaus Gunther, "World Citizens: Between Freedom and Security," *Constellations* 12, no. 3 (2005): 379–391, here 383.

33. William E. Scheuerman, "Carl Schmitt and the Road to Abu Ghraib," *Constellations* 13, no.1 (2006): 108–124, here 119.

34. Preuss, "Iraq War," 65–66. Emphasis added.

35. So much does this discourse and practice of prevention cut across levels of governance that we may suggest that the emphasis on prevention/preemption is now the "central statement of the new transnational security law." Gunther, "World Citizens," 390. And see Wilke, "War v. Justice," where, at 659, she argues with respect to Guantanamo: "The 'enemy combatant' cases highlight another crucial element of the designation of persons as 'enemies' as distinct from criminals. Criminals are judged on what they could be shown to have done. 'Enemies,' in contrast, are judged by their stipulated hostile commitment that constitutes them as an abstract threat. For dealing with enemies, prevention rather than punishment is the rule. The introduction of the 'preventive strike' doctrine into criminal and administrative law is based on the logically prior designation of the detainees as dangerous and unpredictable public enemies by the president."

For a compelling account of the role of the transnational effects of international law in the war on terror and the transformation of the Security Council, see Kim Lane-Scheppele, "The Empire's New Laws: The International State of Emergency After 9/11." Unpublished paper on file with the author, 2008.

36. Gunther, "World Citizens," 390: "the Western world influences the implementation of international legal norms without at the same time being considered as their addressees" and Bartholomew, "Empire's Law and Contradictory Politics," 161–192.

37. Habermas, "Interpreting the Fall of a Monument," 47. In "Does the Constitutionalization of International Law Still Have a Chance?" (in Jürgen Habermas, *The Divided West*, ed. and trans. Ciaran Cronin [Cambridge: Polity, 2006]), Habermas characterizes "hegemonic unilateralism" as a state seeking to justify "momentous decisions by appeal to its own national values rather than in terms of established procedures" (149).

38. Outlawed in the Kellogg-Briand Pact of 1928, reiterated in the Nuremberg Charter. For the former, see http://www.yale.edu/lawweb/avalon/imt/kbpact.htm. For the latter, see http://www.derechos.org/nizkor/nuremberg/judgment/cap5.html. Also see Ian Hurd, "Breaking and Making Norms: American Revisionism and Crises of Legitimacy," *International Politics* 44 (2007): 194–213. At 199, Hurd argues that the Bush Doctrine "was profoundly revisionist; it was expressly designed to delegitimate the existing practices around preemption and institutionalize a new norm based on a different understanding of immanence." He continues, at 200: "The American innovation, which ignited the controversy, was to attempt to unilaterally redefine the criteria for assessing what is an 'imminent' threat and so to rewrite the customary law understanding of the terms of imminence." And see Antony Anghie, "The War on Terror and Iraq in Historical Perspective," *Osgoode Hall Law Journal* 43 (2005): 35–66, where, at 49, he argues that "pre-emptive self-defence is a right that the United States intends to be confined only to itself and its allies" and Upendra Baxi, "War *on* Terror": "the invention of the doctrine of 'preemptive' self-defence" is a "unique, but wholly dubious, innovation in international law" (36); "Both the 'wars'—the war *of* and the war *on* terror—prefigure a 'new' international law now in the making within the 'circuits of nihilism.' Some new forms of political nostalgia for a regime of unrestrained and unsanctioned use of force by states now stand presented" (42).

39. So, for example, Anghie suggests that, since international law is premised on the notion that all sovereigns are equal and "self-defence is arguably the central and most fundamental right of the sovereign, it would follow that the right of pre-emptive self-defence will be enjoyed by all states. Such a doctrine would surely contribute to enormous

instability" (in "War on Terror and Iraq in Historical Perspective," 49). Also see Nehal Bhuta, "Global State of Exception?" and Lori Fisler Damrosch and Bernard H. Oxman, "Agora: Future Implication of the Iraq Conflict: Editors' Introduction," *American Journal of International Law* 97 (2004): 553.

40. For a serendipitous exposition, see Baxi, "War *on* Terror," esp. 34.

41. Quoted in Jeffrey Rosen, "Conscience of a Conservative," *New York Times Magazine*, September 9, 2007, www.nytimes.com/2007/2009/2009/magazine/2009rosen.html.

42. Quoted in "Historian Alfred McCoy: Obama Reluctance on Bush Prosecutions Affirms Culture of Impunity," *Democracy Now*, May 1, 2009, available at http://www.democracynow.org/2009/5/1/torture_expert_alfred_mccoy_obama_reluctance. Of course, this only echoes Bush's own words when, defending Donald Rumsfeld, he said "I'm the decider." "Bush: 'I'm the Decider' on Rumsfeld," CNN.com, April 18, 2006, http://www.cnn.com/2006/POLITICS/04/18/rumsfeld/.

43. Philippe Sands, *Lawless World: America and the Breaking of Global Rules* (London: Allen Lane [Penguin], 2005).

44. Quoted in Peter Jan Honigsburg, "Chasing 'Enemy Combatants' and Circumventing International Law: A License for Sanctioned Abuse," *UCLA Journal of International Law and Foreign Affairs* 12, no. 1 (Spring 2007): 1–74, here 27.

45. Cf. Bartholomew, "Empire's Law and Contradictory Politics."

46. See, for example, Derek Gregory, "Vanishing Points: Law, Violence and Exception in the Global War Prison," in Derek Gregory and Allan Pred, eds., *Violent Geographies: Fear, Terror and Political Violence* (New York: Routledge, 2007), 205–236. But also see Peter Fitzpatrick and Richard Joyce's argument that we should consider Guantanamo "the paradigm for our time of the state of exception" only if we realize that the exception is "not *to* but within law" (Peter Fitzpatrick and Richard Joyce, "The Normality of the Exception in Democracy's Empire," *Journal of Law and Society* 34 [2007]: 65–76, here 76). For another argument that Guantanamo functions within "detailed rules and norms" and is thus part of a transformed law, see Claudia Aradau, "Law Transformed: Guantanamo and the 'Other' Exception," *Third World Quarterly* 28, no. 3 (2007): 489–501, here 491.

47. On the role of lawyers, see the extraordinary abstract to the essay written by Jordan J. Paust. Paust's abstract reads in part: "Not since the Nazi era have so many lawyers been so clearly involved in international crimes concerning the treatment and interrogation of persons detained during war." "Executive Plans," 811.

48. Even the National Security Strategy relied on claims about law: "For centuries international law recognized that nations need not suffer an attack before they can lawfully take action to defend themselves against forces that present an imminent danger of attack. Legal scholars and international jurists often condition the legitimacy of preemption on the existence of an imminent threat—most often a visible mobilization of armies, navies and air forces preparing to attack. We must adapt the concept of imminent threat to the capabilities and objectives of today's adversaries." President George W. Bush, The White House, *The National Security Strategy of the United States of America Part V* (September 17, 2002), www.whitehouse.gov/nsc/nssall.html.

49. Johns, "Guantanamo Bay," 614.

50. As Justice Department lawyers recognize. See Simon Reid-Henry, "Exceptional Sovereignty? Guantanamo Bay and the Re-Colonial Present," *Antipode* (2007): 627–648, at 630 where he recounts that Philbin and Yoo describe it as "part of a whole new legal 'system.'"

51. Amy Kaplan, "Where is Guantanamo?" *American Quarterly* 57 (2005): 831–858.

52. Johns, "Guantanamo Bay," 617. Also see Susan Marks, "State-Centrism, International Law and the Anxieties of Influence," *Leiden Journal of International Law* 19 (2006): 339–347. Marks says, "Guantanamo is certainly a place in which people have few rights, but it is no legal vacuum or mystery" (347).

53. Daniel Moeckli, "The US Supreme Court's 'Enemy Combatant' Decisions: A 'Major Victory for the Rule of Law'?" *Journal of Conflict and Security Law* 10 (2005): 75–99; and Mark David "Max" Maxwell and Sean M. Watts, "'Unlawful Enemy Combatant': Status, Theory of Culpability, or Neither?" *Journal of International Criminal Justice* 5 (2007): 19–25. Maxwell and Watts (military lawyers) argue that the MCA codified the term "unlawful enemy combatants" but, despite the USSC's use of the term "unlawful combatant" in the 1942 case of *Quirin*, "the label has had little formal currency as a term of art in the law of war" (20). They continue (21–22):

> Although *Quirin* relied on the notion of "unlawful combatant [cy]" as a basis of criminal liability, the term's meaning is blurred by its failure to appear in the positive law of war existing at the time of the case as well as in the current, treaty-based law of war. This is not to say that the law of war has been ignorant of civilian participation in hostilities. Indeed, the 1949 Geneva Conventions, though generally silent on the conduct of actual hostilities, deal squarely with civilians who engage in "activities hostile to the security of the State" or even sabotage. Years later, 1977 Additional Protocol I, dealing more directly with the conduct of hostilities, also anticipated hostile civilians, providing for the suspension of their protection from international targeting "for such time as they take direct part in hostilities." Importantly, however, each of these major law of war treaties following *Quirin* declined to exclude hostile civilians from the class of civilians generally. Neither treaty, although clearly presented the opportunity, elected to create a third status or class of persons known as "unlawful combatants." Instead, both instruments reject divesting civilian status in favour of permitting temporary derogation of the protections associated with the civilian class.

54. Honigsburg, "Chasing 'Enemy Combatants,'" 6.

55. *Hamdan v. Rumsfeld* 548 U.S. 557 (2006); *Boumediene v. Bush*. 553 U. S. 723 (2008).

56. Fitzpatrick and Joyce, "Normality of the Exception," 65, emphasis added.

57. See, preeminently, Giorgio Agamben on the state of exception, which he describes as characterized by the following constellation: "the separation of 'force of law' from the law. It defines a 'state of the law' in which, on the one hand, the norm is in force [*vige*] but is not applied (it has no 'force' [forza]), and, on the other, acts that do not have the value [valore] of law acquire it's 'force.'" Giorgio Agamben, *State of Exception*, trans. Kevin Attell (Chicago: University of Chicago Press, 2005), 38.

58. Scheuerman, "Carl Schmitt and the Road," 122.

59. Of course, other states have welcomed the opportunity the "war on terror" has provided them for their own reasons, as well.

60. On "suspension of law," see Judith Butler, "Indefinite Detention," in Judith Butler, *Precarious Life: The Power of Mourning and Violence* (London: Verso, 2004): 50–100, here 51. Also see Aradau, "Law Transformed," 491.

61. Jordan J. Paust, "Executive Plans," 825.

62. As Judith Butler has called them in "Indefinite Detention."

63. Similarly, see Habermas, "Does the Constitutionalization of International Law Still Have a Chance?" 181–182 on "replacing" norms and procedures.

64. See Jeremy Waldron, "Torture and Positive Law: Jurisprudence for the White House," *Columbia Law Review* 105 (2005): 1681–1750.

65. Waldron, "Torture and Positive Law," 1741.

66. Waldron, "Torture and Positive Law," 1709.

67. Waldron, "Torture and Positive Law," 1743. Also see Amnesty International for one report among many others. Amnesty says:

> the US government has gone to great lengths to restrict the application of the Geneva Conventions and to *"re-define" torture.* It has sought to justify the use of coercive interrogation techniques, the practice of holding "ghost detainees" (people in unacknowledged incommunicado detention) and the "rendering" or handing over of prisoners to third countries known to practice torture. The detention facility at Guantanamo Bay has become the gulag of our times, entrenching the practice of arbitrary and indefinite detention in violation of international law. Trials by military commissions have made mockery of justice and due process.

Amnesty International (Irene Khan), "Report 2005—Forward," (May 25, 2005), http://www.amnesty.org/en/alfresco_asset/8393105b-a3ba-11dc-9d08-f145a8145d2b/pol100052005en.pdf.

And see Alfred McCoy, "Tomdispatch: Alfred McCoy on How Not to Ban Torture in Congress," *TomDispatch.com*, February 8, 2006, http://www.tomdispatch.com/post/57336/tomdispatch_alfred_mccoy_on_how_not_to_ban_torture_in_congress: "This country may, in fact, be undergoing an historic shift with profound implications for America's international standing. It seems to be moving from the wide-ranging but highly secretive tortures wielded by the CIA during the Cold War decades to an open, even proud use of coercive interrogation as a formal weapon . . . acceptable both to U.S. courts and the American people."

68. Waldron suggests that Yoo's memo asserts that the United States need not consider itself bound by customary international law or even *jus cogens* principles. With respect to those, the United States has carte blanche. Only specific treaty obligations could bind it. Waldron, "Torture and Positive Law," 1694.

69. Waldron, "Torture and Positive Law," 1709.

70. Waldron, "Torture and Positive Law," 1718, also see 1737.

71. At 1735, Waldron ("Torture and Positive Law") suggests: "Starting at the bottom of the so-called slippery slope, I am arguing that if we mess with the prohibition on torture, we may find it harder to defend some arguably less important requirements that in the conventional mode of argument are perched above torture on the slippery slope. The idea is that our confidence that what lies at the bottom of the slope (torture) is wrong informs and supports our confidence that the lesser evils that lie above torture are wrong too."

For a discussion of the conceptual relationship between basic rights and democracy see Jürgen Habermas, *Between Facts and Norms: Contributions to a Discourse Theory of Law and Democracy*, trans. William Rehg (Cambridge, Mass: MIT Press, 1998).

72. For one account of the struggles within the state, see Jack Goldsmith, *The Terror Presidency: Law and Judgment Inside the Bush Administration* (New York: W.W. Norton, 2007).

73. *Hamdan* and Ronald Dworkin, "Why It Was A Great Victory," *New York Review of Books* 55, Issue 13, 2008.

74. The otherwise extremely interesting work of Gregory ("Vanishing Points") and Aradau ("Law Transformed") misses this. For an illuminating discussion of this as a "legal grey hole," see David Dyzenhaus, "*Schmitt v. Dicey*: Are States of Emergency Inside or Outside the Legal Order?" *Cardozo Law Review* 27 (2007): 2005–2040.

75. Johns, "Guantanamo Bay," 623.

76. Johns, "Guantanamo Bay," 614.

77. Johns, "Guantanamo Bay," 618–619.

78. Johns, "Guantanamo Bay," 619–620. Like Johns, Aradau objects to conceptualizing Guantanamo as a "space of exception" because this leads to the "endorsement and fortification of the legal space of the norm." Aradau, "Law Transformed," 491. She concludes, "This paper has questioned the endorsement of the 'rule of law' by human rights lawyers" (498). But this is precisely what is required.

79. On the idea of rule *by* law, see R. Rueban Balasubramaniam, "Indefinite Detention: Rule by Law or Rule of Law?" in Victor J. Ramraj, ed., *Emergencies and the Limits of Legality* (Cambridge: Cambridge University Press, 2008), 118–142. Also see, for example, Gabor Rona's statement that military tribunals "would only be necessary if the administration wanted to assure convictions that might not otherwise be certain" in criticizing Obama's [then] possible [now achieved] resurrection of the tribunal system at Guantanamo. Quoted in William Glaberson, "US May Revive Guantanamo Military Courts," *New York Times*, May 1, 2009, http://www.nytimes.com/2009/05/02/us/politics/02gitmo.html

80. Cf. Dyzenhaus, "*Schmitt v. Dicey*."

81. On discretion, see Scheuerman, "Carl Schmitt and the Road." For this reason, I disagree with Johns that Guantanamo is a "profoundly anti-exceptional legal artifact" ("Guantanamo Bay," 615).

82. Neumann, *Behemoth*, 448.

83. Bartholomew, "Empire's Law and Contradictory Politics," 163. Also see Antony Anghie, *Imperialism, Sovereignty and the Making of International Law* (Cambridge: Cambridge University Press, 2005), 300–301:

> The WAT [war on terror], if it is to be accommodated within international law, has such far-reaching consequences that it can be seen, in effect, as creating a new international jurisprudence, of "national security," that recreates the sort of Hobbesian universe whose defining character is fear, and which will be based on the right of the world's one super-power, the United States, to wage unilateral, preemptive war, rather than the system of the United Nations.
>
> . . . These basic characteristics of the WAT suggest, I would argue, why we could be seen as living in what might be termed a "Vitorian moment"—that is, a moment when the conceptualization of "the other"—the terrorist, the barbarian—invokes a response that combines doctrines of violation, self-defence, intervention, transformation and tutelage that threaten the existing law and could result in a dramatic shift in the character of law. . . . The measures taken in the WAT have tested, if not undermined, international human rights law, international humanitarian law and most significantly, the law relating to the UN Charter and the use of force.

Also see 305.

84. See, for example, Amnesty International, "Partners in Crime: Europe's Role in US Renditions," Amnesty International, June 14, 2006, http://web.amnesty.org/library/Index/ENGEUR010082006.

85. See Bartholomew, "Empire's Law and Contradictory Politics." Also see Michael Byers, "Terror and the Future of International Law," in *Worlds in Collision: Terror and the Future of Global Order*, ed. Ken Booth and Tim Dunne (London: Palgrave Macmillan, 2002), 118–127. For a penetrating discussion of the relationship between sovereignty and human rights, see Cohen, "Whose Sovereignty?"

86. Bhuta, "Global State of Exception?" 380.

87. Poulantzas, *State, Power, Socialism*, and Stuart Hall, *Drifting into a Law and Order Society* (London: Cobden Trust, 1980).

88. For the latter, see especially Anne Norton, *Leo Strauss and the Politics of American Empire* (New Haven, Conn.: Yale University Press, 2004) and Shadia B. Drury, *The Political Ideas of Leo Strauss* (New York: Palgrave Macmillan, 2005).

89. David Harvey, *A Brief History of Neoliberalism* (Oxford: Oxford University Press, 2005), 195. Also see Harvey, *New Imperialism*.

90. Harvey, *New Imperialism*.

91. Panitch and Gindin, "Theorizing American Empire."

92. See Habermas, "Does the Constitutionalization of International Law Still Have a Chance?"179–184. The closest Habermas comes to recognizing this as neoconservatism is p. 186. For an interesting analysis, see Kanishka Jayasuriya, *Reconstituting the Global Liberal Order* (London: Routledge, 2005). Jayasuriya argues: "The most significant dimension of this transformation is the privileging of legitimacy as against legality within the new global order" (22). "What is being transformed [post–Cold War] is not US hegemony but the post-war *liberal* hegemony of the United States" (24); this "assertion of the right to act outside the normal processes of legality is made in the name of legitimacy," a shift towards "culturalism" and values. Increasingly, legitimacy is argued rather than legality.

93. For important analyses of "hegemonic international law" or "imperial law" developed through the structural infirmities of the Security Council that offer imperial power a formal way of solidifying sovereign *in*equality, see Richard Falk, "The Power of Rights and the Rights of Power: What Future for Human Rights?" *Ethics and Global Politics* 1 (2008):81–96 and Habermas,"Does the Constitutionalization of International Law Still Have a Chance?" For analyses of the post-9/11 era in terms of law and legality that emphasize the changing role of the Security Council in relation to counterterrorism and how its new "legislative" role threatens human rights and the rule of law transnationally, see Scheppele, "Empire's New Laws," and Jean L. Cohen, "A Global State of Emergency or the Further Constitutionalization of International Law: A Pluralist Approach," *Constellations*. 15, no.4 (2008): 456–484.

94. Preuss, "Iraq War,"66.

95. Panitch and Gindin, "Theorizing American Empire."

96. Waldron, "Torture and Positive Law," 1741.

97. Falk, "Legality and Legitimacy," 35.

98. Cf. Michael Ignatieff, "The Burden," *New York Times Magazine*, January 5, 2003, 22; and Norman Geras, "A Moral Failure," *Wall Street Journal.com Opinion Journal*, August 4, 2003, http://www.opinionjournal.com/forms/printThis.html?id+110003834 (accessed May 22, 2004). A controversy erupted over the "Euston Manifesto," of which Geras is a primary author

but which also included Michael Walzer, Nick Cohen, Paul Berman and others. It set out a politics for a new, new Left that stresses the importance of the "responsibility to protect" and a "new internationalism" that includes respect for and reform of international law. However, it seems to continue in the tradition of the human rights hawks' virtual disregard for legality as the means by which decisions about intervention should be decided. See Norman Geras, Nick Cohen, et al., "The Euston Manifesto," March 29, 2006, http://eustonmanifesto.org/joomla/index.php?option=com_content&task=view&id=12&Itemid=41.

99. See Cohen, "Whose Sovereignty?"

100. Falk, "Legality and Legitimacy," 47.

101. See Jürgen Habermas (interview with Eduardo Mendieta), "America and the World: A Conversation with Jürgen Habermas," *Logos* 3.3 (2004): np and Habermas, "Does the Constitutionalization of International Law Still Have a Chance?" 115–193.

102. Habermas with Mendieta, "America and the World." Although he is not as "idealistic" or blinded as many assume: see, for example, his comments on the "monstrous selectivity" of Security Council treatments of humanitarian crises. Jürgen Habermas, "Dispute on the Past and Future of International Law: Transition from a National to a Postnational Constellation" (unpublished presentation at the World Congress of Philosophy, Istanbul, Turkey, 10 August 2003).

103. The idea of "egalitarian universalism" is prominent in Habermas's writings around the Iraq War. See "Interpreting the Fall of a Monument."

104. Andreas Kalyvas, "Popular Sovereignty, Democracy, and the Constituent Power," *Constellations* 12, no.2 (2005): 223–244, here 230: "politics cannot be reduced to abstract, mechanical legality."

105. Habermas, *Between Facts and Norms*, 450, 448.

106. Jürgen Habermas, "On Law and Disagreement: Some Comments on Interpretive Pluralism," *Ratio Juris* 16 (2003): 187–194, here 187.

107. See, for example, Jürgen Habermas, "The Kantian Project of Cosmopolitan Law," public lecture at Purdue University, October 15, 2004, on-line video-stream of the lecture at http://www.cla.purdue.edu/phil-lit/events/habermas.html; Jürgen Habermas, "A Political Constitution for the Pluralist World Society?" in *Between Naturalism and Religion: Philosophical Essays*, trans. Ciaran Cronin (Cambridge, UK: Polity Press, 2008), 312–353; Habermas, "Does the Constitutionalization of International Law Still Have a Chance?" and Jürgen Habermas, *The Postnational Constellation: Political Essays*, ed. and trans. Max Pensky (Cambridge, Mass.: MIT Press, 2001).

108. Habermas, "Political Constitution for the World Pluralist Society?"

109. See Jürgen Habermas, "The Constitutionalization of International Law and the Legitimation Problems of a Constitution for World Society," *Constellations* 15, no.4 (2008): 444–455; Habermas, "A Political Constitution for the World Pluralist Society?"; and Habermas, "Does the Constitutionalization of International Law Still Have a Chance?" For a discussion, see Amy Bartholomew, *Justice Without Guarantees* (New York: Columbia University Press, forthcoming 2012). Also see William E. Scheuerman, "Global Governance without Global Government? Habermas on Postnational Democracy," *Political Theory* 36, no. 1 (2008): 133–151 and William E. Scheuerman, "All Power to the (State-less?) General Assembly!" *Constellations*, 15, no. 4 (2008): 485–492.

110. Jürgen Habermas, "Fundamentalism and Terror: A Dialogue with Jürgen Habermas," in Giovanna Borradori, *Philosophy in a Time of Terror: Dialogues with Jürgen Habermas and Jacques Derrida* (Chicago: University of Chicago Press, 2003), 25–43, here 35.

111. Habermas, "Fundamentalism and Terror," 37. He argues, the "critical power to put a stop to violence, without reproducing it in circles of new violence, can only dwell in the telos of mutual understanding and in our orientation toward this goal."

112. Habermas, "Fundamentalism and Terror," 37. This sort of orientation is also adopted by some leading figures in Islam. Mark Lynch quotes Abd al-Qadir Bajmal as saying, post-9/11, "'the essence of the crisis of our world today is at its core the loss of the bases of mutual understanding between those . . . who live in intellectual and political isolation.'" Mark Lynch, "Transnational Dialogue in an Age of Terror," *Global Society* 19 (2005): 5–28, here 8. Also see Raja Bahlul, "Toward an Islamic Conception of Democracy: Islam and the Notion of Public Reason," *Critique: Critical Middle Eastern Studies* 12 (2003): 43–60.

113. Habermas with Mendieta, "America and the World."

114. The idea of a "gift" is indebted to Anne Orford, "The Gift of Formalism," *European Journal of International Law* 15, no. 1 (2004): 179–195.

115. Speaking directly about the domestic context, Habermas famously argues in *Between Facts and Norms* that human rights or the rule of law and democracy or popular sovereignty presuppose one another. In his recent work on the constitutionalization of international law, he views the international or supranational level (as distinct from the transnational and domestic/nation-state levels) to be properly *restricted* to the enforcement of peace and human rights. While he is not explicit here, I assume that the commitment to human rights at the international level, like that at the domestic, is necessary to human dignity which is itself connected to both private and public autonomy. See Habermas, "Does the Constitutionalization of International Law Still Have a Chance?"

116. Jürgen Habermas, "A Genealogical Analysis of the Cognitive Content of Morality," in *The Inclusion of the Other: Studies in Political Theory*, ed. and trans. Ciaran Cronin and Pablo De Greiff (Cambridge, Mass.: MIT Press, 1998), 3–48, here 37.

117. Habermas with Mendieta, "America and the World," np.

118. Dworkin, *Law's Empire*.

119. Habermas, "Dispute on the Past and Future of International Law," 8, second emphasis added. See Habermas, "Does the Constitutionalization of International Law Still Have a Chance?" 184–185 for a very similar statement.

120. Habermas with Mendieta, "America and the World," np.

121. Habermas, *Between Facts and Norms*, 113.

122. Habermas, *Between Facts and Norms*, 178–179.

123. Orford, "Gift of Formalism."

124. See, for example, Pahuja, "Postcoloniality of International Law."

125. Martti Koskenniemi, "'The Lady Doth Protest Too Much': Kosovo, and the Turn to Ethics in International Law," *Modern Law Review* 65 (2002): 159–175, here 174; Slavoj Žižek, *Iraq: The Broken Kettle* (New York: Verso, 2004); and Fitzpatrick, "Gods Would Be Needed."

126. Simpson, *Great Powers and Outlaw States*.

127. Habermas, "Does The Constitutionalization of International Law Still Have a Chance?"

128. Preeminent here is TWAIL. And, in the context of the Middle East, see Jean Allain, "Orientalism and International Law," 391.

129. See Habermas, "Fundamentalism and Terror," 42. Also see Andrew Arato, "Empire's Democracy, Ours and Theirs," and Trevor Purvis, "Looking for Life Signs in an International Rule of Law," both in Bartholomew, ed., *Empire's Law*, 217–244 and 110–136, respectively.

130. On this, see Bhuta, "A Global State of Exception?" 385 who suggests (relying on Koskenniemi's account) that Wolfgang Friedmann argued his is not just a

> defence of a culture of formalism, but an implicit view that forcing states to account for their conduct in terms of existing legal standards amounts to an insistence on "accountability, openness and equality whose status cannot be reduced to the political positions of any one of the parties whose claims are treated within it." In other words, it forces states to run the risk of committing a performative contradiction by ensnaring them within the idealizing presuppositions of a legal discourse: this, in turn, provides a toehold for criticism.

And this amounts to "an essential principle of democratic politics."

Also see the Neumann quotation that introduces this chapter and Habermas:

> Discourses inspired by [universalism] are distinguished from all other discourses by two essential features. On the one hand, the universalistic discourses of law and morality can be *abused* as a particularly insidious form of legitimation since particular interests can hide behind the glimmering facade of reasonable universality. This ideological function, which had already been denounced by the young Marx, forms the basis of Carl Schmitt's resentment when he throws "humanity"—the insistence on standards of egalitarian individualism—together with "bestiality" in one pot. What fascists like Schmitt seem to overlook, and what Marx clearly saw, is the *other* characteristic of this discourse: the peculiar self-reference that makes it the vehicle for self-correcting learning processes. Just as every objection raised against the selective or one-eyed application of universalistic standards must already presuppose these same standards in the same manner, any deconstructive unmasking of the ideologically concealing use of universalistic discourse actually presupposes the critical viewpoints advanced by these same discourses. Moral and legal universalism is, thus, self-reflexively closed in the sense that its imperfect practices can only be criticized on the basis of its own standards.

Habermas, "Fundamentalism and Terror," 42. Also see Andrew Arato, "Empire's Democracy, Ours and Theirs," 223 for an instructive discussion of how the discourse of democratization instrumentalized by imperial power in fact "lands the bearers of the discourse in an international legal field that does not allow democracy to be openly replaced by its opposite. The democratic justification to an extent binds, at least to some extent, even those who use it in bad faith." And see Amy Bartholomew, "Should a Marxist Believe in Marx on Rights?" in *The Socialist Register*, eds. Ralph Miliband and Leo Panitch (London: Merlin Press, 1990), 244–264, on the tradition of Marxism and human rights for a similar proposition. Finally, see Martti Koskenniemi, *The Gentle Civilizer of Nations: The Rise and Fall of International Law, 1870–1960* (Cambridge: Cambridge University Press: 2002), 502–505.

131. Andreas Fischer-Lescano, "Torture in Abu Ghraib: The Complaint against Donald Rumsfeld under the German Code of Crimes against International Law," *German Law Journal* 6, no. 3 (2005), 689–724, here 690–691. The previous two paragraphs are taken from Bartholomew, "The Contradictory Politics of Human Rights," although the last line, in response to Fleur Johns, is added.

132. See Glenn Greenwald, "Major Defeat for Bush/Obama Position on Secrecy," *Salon.com*, May 28, 2009, http://www.salon.com/news/opinion/glenn_greenwald/2009/04/28/secrecy.

133. Human Rights Watch, "United States: Investigate Bush, Other Top Officials for Torture," 11 July 2011, http://www.hrw.org/news/2011/07/11/united-states-investigate-bush-other-top-officials-torture.

134. The Editors, "Obama's 'War on Terror,'" *The Nation*, 10 March 2011, http://www.thenation.com/print/article/159168/obamas-war-terror. The *Nation* editorial concludes (echoing Scheuerman's comment that "once the cancer of *normlessness* is allowed into the legal system, it is only a matter of time before it infects healthy legal organs as well," "Carl Schmitt and the Road," 122) that with this we "now see clearly a kind of social cancer: the exercise of inhumane and abusive power simply because it is the state's prerogative."

135. William Fisher, "Obama Loses Phrase 'Enemy Combatants,' But Detention System Remains the Same," *Alternet*, March 18, 2009, http://www.alternet.org/story/132153/obama_loses_phrase_%22enemy_combatants,%22_but_detention_system_remains_the_same/?page=1; William Douglass and Carol Rosenberg, "Obama's New Detainee Policy: Break from Bush or the Same?" *McClatchy*, March 13, 2009, http://www.mcclatchydc.com/2009/03/13/63963/obamas-new-detainee-policy-break.html.

136. William Glaberson, "U.S. May Revive Guantanamo Military Courts," *New York Times*, May 2, 2009.

137. The Editors, "Obama's 'War on Terror.'"

138. The Editors, "Obama's 'War on Terror.'"

139. See, for example, Marc Ambinder, "US Threatens Independent British Judicial System," *The Atlantic*, May 12, 2009, http://politics.theatlantic.com/2009/05/us_threatens_independent_british_judicial_system.php.

140. See Charlie Savage, "Obama's War on Terror May Resemble Bush's in Some Areas," *New York Times*, February 18, 2009. So much has Obama's war on terror resembled Bush's that Savage reports that an editorial in the *Wall Street Journal* suggested that "it seems that the Bush administration's antiterror architecture is gaining new legitimacy."

141. See John Cella, "Obama Administration Offers Legal Defense of Drone Attacks, Targeted Killing," *Harvard National Security Journal* March 28, 2010, http://harvardnsj.com/2010/03/obama-administration-offers-legal-defense-of-drone-attacks-targeted-killing/. For a critical evaluation, see Susan Breau, Marie Aronsson, and Rachel Joyce (for The Oxford Research Group), "Discussion Paper 2: Drone Attacks, International Law, and the Recording of Civilian Casualties of Armed Conflict," June 2011, http://www.oxfordresearchgroup.org.uk/publications/briefing_papers_and_reports/discussion_paper_2.

142. See Richard Falk, "Can Humanitarian Intervention Ever Be Humanitarian?" Citizen Pilgrimage blog, 4 August 2011, http://richardfalk.wordpress.com/.

143. Bruce Ackerman, "Obama's Unconstitutional War," *Foreign Policy* 24 March 2011. http://www.foreignpolicy.com/articles/2011/03/24/obama_s_unconstitutional_war?print=yes&hidecomments=yes&page=full.

144. Jean-Paul Sartre, "Imperialist Morality: Interview with Jean-Paul Sartre on the War Crimes Tribunal," *New Left Review* 1, no. 41 (1967): 3–10, here 5.

145. Sartre, "Imperialist Morality," 6.

146. Sartre, "Imperialist Morality," 9.

147. In this, of course, he is much more radical than Habermas.

148. Duncan Kelly, "Rethinking Franz Neumann's Route to Behemoth," *History of Political Thought* 23 (2002): 458–496.

5

Leaving Sovereignty Behind?

AN INQUIRY INTO THE POLITICS OF POST-MODERNITY

Friedrich Kratochwil

Introduction

To say that we live in a post-sovereign world seems to belabor the obvious. Nobody who observes the amount and speed of transborder transactions, migration flows, or appeals to human rights will fail to notice that the present hardly resembles the past for which "Westphalia" and the principle of "sovereignty"[1]—or "international anarchy" for that matter—has become the convenient shorthand. However, three particular puzzles arise.

One puzzle concerns historical issues, such as whether Westphalia was indeed a "new beginning" establishing a "state system" instead of continuing the personal relations characteristic of feudal politics[2] and representing at best a halfway house along the way to the modern state system. The second, connected puzzle concerns the appropriateness of our conceptual maps. If, for example, "balancing" is not a natural outcome of a multiplicity of actors[3] and if the issue of "exclusion" badly captures the nature of the sovereignty game—vide for example the rapid extension of laws with extraterritorial reach at the height of claims to unfettered sovereignty—then taking most of our conventional theories as road maps for political practice is like looking at a map of Kansas while we are trying to find our way on the Tuscan hills.

This raises a third "epistemological" puzzle of "how we know" what is the case and how long we shall trust guides that no longer seem to function. Of course, we want an adequate representation, but maps that try to represent "the world" on a "one to one" scale are useless. Many "scientists" insist, therefore, on simplicity and parsimony as criteria, no matter how complicated reality is. After all, abstraction, universal applicability, and transhistorical validity all seem to work hand in glove to provide us with secure knowledge and orientation. The real problem, of course, is that in getting from a concrete "here" to a specific "there" we are not much helped by what the general landscape rather than the specific configuration looks like, quite aside from the fact that the metaphor of a map is misleading. After all, social reality is not a ready-made ahistorical world but one that is continuously being "made" through the actions and practices of the actors. Thus, a more apt analogy would be a rule book, rather than a map that represents a preexisting topology. This rule book would contain the inventory of the dos and don'ts, but also exceptions, excuses, violations, amendments, and so on.

These initial puzzles have several corollaries. One concerns the realization that all these problems are connected, and that therefore we cannot hope that in answering one of them as, for example, finding a more exact "indicator" for sovereignty, such as "exclusion" along the lines of Krasner's argument,[4] we will be able to proceed. It seems that we have to solve all puzzles simultaneously rather than sequentially or by privileging one over the others.

This leads us to the second corollary. We must realize that accepting or rejecting our "maps" or "rule books" has more to do with our purposes and political projects than with their presumed accuracy of representation. It is, therefore, not surprising that for those like Tesón, who postulate an international order built on morally justifiable principles, unmediated by history, law and politics, the ridding the world of "tyrants,"[5] will always trump the prohibition of intervention derived from sovereignty. Similarly, practitioners and scholars dedicated to international organizations, particularly the United Nations, have argued for a shift in the meaning of sovereignty. Sovereignty has changed, from a right accruing to "persons of sovereign authority" in their original liberty, to a notion of a "right" that is some type of "trust" bestowed upon states by mankind and/or the international community in order to enable them to meet their purposes and obligations.[6] Far from being an inalienable, or a "natural," antecedent to any social contract or convention, the possession of this right, particularly in its "defensive" role of defeating claims to intervention, is now made dependent on the *right use* of sovereign powers. Although all rights are, of course, socially recognized claims, and thus the notion of a "natural right" in an asocial state of nature is a somewhat misconceived construction (despite its popularity since the seventeenth century), such a change in meaning is significant.

Some scholars, particularly those focusing on the European project, will claim that talking in terms of sovereignty is simply missing the mark, as modern politics both within states and increasingly between states is the politics of multilevel governance among networks.[7] The latter has little to do with the old conception of hierarchical and vertical ordering that classical sovereignty implied by its division of the "inside" and the "outside."[8] The emergence of new organizational forms bridging the internal and external as well as the public–private divide are certainly an important new phenomenon.[9] But the fact that virtually none of the classical states possessed a clear hierarchy—vide the separation of powers in constitutional thought—should alert us to the fact that both historical reality and conceptualizations of sovereignty were always somewhat at odds with the simplistic template of hierarchical versus horizontal ordering.[10]

Here a third corollary comes to the fore. In investigating sovereignty, we have to examine the *use* of the term in different contexts. This is different from "defining" the concept according to taxonomic criteria and relating it to phenomena in the "outer world." In focusing on *use* rather than *representation*, we have to note how this concept functions by its links with (to?) other concepts, such as the "state," "legitimacy," the "people," and the "use of force," and by its acknowledgment which practices are thereby authorized or delegitimized. In other words, we have to examine the semantic field within which this concept is embedded as well as the changes in practices it entails.

Similarly, we cannot simply assume that the concept has no effect, if it is not explicitly used. Thus, while the US Constitution does not mention sovereignty, it does not mean that political practice could circumvent the issues to which sovereignty purportedly provides the solution. As the tragedy of the Civil War showed, the political processes in the "compound republic" had been increasingly at odds with the original institutional settlement. Questions of membership, the legitimacy of political "compromises," and issues of representation proved increasingly divisive.[11] Thus, as in a therapeutic discourse, noticing and investigating the *silences* might be as important as the explicit terms by which the conversation is conducted.

In this chapter, I follow the route of a conceptual analysis and show, first, why the notion of a representational language interferes with understanding how institutions function, and why the use of spatial metaphors, suggesting that sovereignty can be analogized to location or to the possession of palpable resources, is not very helpful. Instead, I propose to treat sovereignty as a *status* constituted by institutional rules. My second task is to inquire into the "silences" of the sovereignty *problematique.*

From these initial remarks the plan of the article can be derived. In the next section, I outline some of the conceptual puzzles that arise when we treat "sovereignty" like a natural fact and attempt to get the right match between the concept and the "world out there." Here the "descriptivist fallacy," as well as spatial representations, serves as my foil. Section three is devoted to the "constitutional debates" that derived from the perception of the fragmentation of the international legal order.[12] More recently, the debate postulated the "responsibility to protect" as being part of "sovereignty," which is shared by state(s) and international institutions alike. In section four, I examine a more imperial conception of international order emerging from the discussion of the new internationalists and the even further-reaching assertions of unilateral measures for the protection of human rights and the sovereign constitutional order of the United States. Section five, the conclusion, briefly returns to the issue of the silences created by arguments about governance and of the postmodern form of politics that left sovereignty "behind."

Getting It Right: The Puzzles of Sovereignty

According to the standards of positivist social science, the meaning of a concept consists in its reference. Thus, concepts need a clear definition and proper operationalizations—in other words, we have to apply the concepts to the empirical world and measure whether a concept and the reality "out there" match. Although widely accepted, there are several flaws in this account. First, even in some purely "descriptive" contexts, such as when we ascribe terms such as "big" or "little" to a phenomenon, the application of concepts is not a simple matching operation. For instance, what is a "big" deviation will differ if I repair a watch or computer, or if I build a 60-story office tower. A deviation of 2 millimeters in the first two cases is extremely "big" while it is so "little" in the case of the building that mentioning it seems ridiculous. There is simply no "fact of the matter" as the philosopher would say. Consequently, the meaning of a term is constituted by the practices and purposes of the "field" (e.g., watch-making, computer technology, or architecture) rather than by a "property" of the object.

Second, concept formation, as cognitive psychology has shown,[13] does not take place via the traditional modes of abstraction and taxonomic measures. It starts with a "best exemplar" instantiating the concept. Here the studies on color concepts—which seem as "objective" as one can think of—are highly instructive. These exemplars are then used in expanding the scope through analogies, until the instantiations become problematic. This procedure inevitably makes for fuzzy boundaries as conceptual development does not occur via generalization and abstraction but rather through the construction of *types* and their *comparison*.

Third, since the social world is not natural but one of artifice, the concepts we use are not some indices for a preexisting reality but are constitutive for this world as Aristotle noted.[14] Modern ordinary-language philosophy has further shown what role rules and shared normative understandings play in this context. The argument is that meaning cannot be derived from reference to the "things out there" but derives from the *use of concepts* according to shared criteria. It has liberated social analysis from the bane of the Humean fork, according to which only referential statements are meaningful and ascriptions of values are beyond rational assessment since "tastes" are beyond discussion. Yet, this means that politics based on common understandings and on non-idiosyncratic validity claims would be impossible. Indeed, it would be the end of politics if an argument was nothing more than the indication of personal likes and dislikes.

Furthermore, using value-laden concepts is quite different from stating personal preferences. Thus, the grammar of "good" is far from arbitrary even though no participation in the "idea" of goodness or some ontological order is necessary. The use of the word is governed by two criteria, one of which signals that we recommend something (on non-idiosyncratic grounds), and the second, field-dependent criteria, provide the intersubjective reasons in virtue of which we invoke the recommendation. What makes a car, a fountain pen, or even an action "good" is not some reference to an intrinsic property of the objects, but the use of the term in a language community. Thus, if someone claims that X is a good car and I ask for reasons (i.e., the articulation of the field-dependent criteria), I might expect answers as to the beautiful design, the efficiency or power of the engine, and so on. In contrast, if someone answers: "Because it is blue," then we know that he is either joking or does not know what the term means.[15] Of course, the application of the criteria might be contested, but even such contestations must follow certain rules in order to be understandable.

Similarly, when we want to know what sovereignty means, we have to know how the word functions in our discourses and which rules govern its use. Here the notion of a rule as a device for "letting you go on"—rather than as a summary concept of observed regularities—becomes important.[16] Precisely because rules do not function like efficient causes, their action-guiding function will not result in identical repetitions or exemplars. Instead, the patterned behavior will always show a good deal of "deviations," not only through exceptions and exemptions but even in the reproduction of the standard patterns instantiating the concept. In this way, the reproduction of the social world always entails changes as well as the production of "structures." The changes are sometimes only interstitial, making it appear that they can be neglected in favor of the more permanent features. Sometimes the changes are more significant, as when, for example, certain problems are "brought under" an existing set of institutional rules, such as when "services" are treated like "goods." Sometimes the implications of a change are downright revolutionary, as when sovereignty is no longer ascribed to rulers but to "the people" or a nation. Other times we have difficulties in assessing the nature of the changes. Thus, the new term of *sovereign equality* introduced at the San Francisco Conference could be taken as a momentous change, since sovereignty became here a mere modifier of equality, but the subsequent practice of states hardly justifies such an assessment.[17] Nevertheless, recent developments, such as the World Summit in 2005, might endow these antecedents with new significance.[18]

Consequently, the investigation of the sovereignty *problematique* must be more than anti-essentialist. It necessarily has to be *historical*, requiring a contextual scanning of the semantic field to which it belongs. Precisely because such an investigation is historical, we must also be aware that we can no longer subscribe to a narrative of "progress." Thus, neither the shift of sovereignty from the prince to the state, nor the silencing or overcoming of sovereignty through a global governance discourse, can be taken without further ado as an indicator of human emancipation.[19] Indeed, it is easy to show that the silencing of sovereignty claims by human rights discourses has more to do with the presuppositions of this discourse—in other words, with abstracting from any particularity and mediation of historically contingent institutions—than with the empirical proof of an "evolution" brought about either by conscious design or working itself out behind the backs of the actors.[20]

With these caveats in mind, we can now see why studies relying on simple "definitions" of sovereignty as "supreme will" or "exclusion" are essentially misleading, as are notions that sovereignty can be determined in terms of a certain percentage of "power" that an independent actor possesses, that it has been "transferred" (to Brussels), or that it has been "lost" due to the new interdependencies and the "internationalization of the state."[21] The common mistake here is to assume that sovereignty is a "thing" that is susceptible to the treatment of natural facts, such as counting and measuring. In committing this fallacy, everything becomes a matter of degree, and sovereignty is either the "amount" of independence left, or in the more pessimistic interpretation, it becomes a case of "organized hypocrisy."

It is, however, a descriptive fallacy, as H. L. A. Hart pointed out,[22] to believe that there has to be something out there "corresponding" to my terms when I, for example, speak of property or of a legal person. Thus, contrary to our naïve understanding, many uses of speech have no constative function. When I say "I hereby appoint you," I am not describing anything, as when I say for example "I fish" or "I listen." In the former case, instead, I am *doing* something, and the "speech act" has meaning through the shared conventions underlying this practice, despite the fact that there is inevitably a self-referential element involved in such an utterance.[23] In this way, we can see that "sovereignty" is also an institutional practice, in which speech acts figure prominently by claiming decision-making authority on the basis of this exercise of a right that has been conferred to the claimant, and by the institutional rules that established her actor status.

This move from "things" and their description to a process in which claims and counterclaims are made and "trumps"—such as rights—are used has important implications. It allows us understand better the "sovereignty game" in its historical and analytical dimensions. Historically, it has been noted that sovereignty is not rooted in the classical political vocabulary. Sovereignty originally merely meant a relationship of superiority, without necessarily implying supreme authority. Thus, in accordance with the feudal roots of this concept, an actor could have several "sovereigns" depending on the issue and the feudal contract. Questions of "sovereignty," in the sense of claims to supreme authority, were first voiced in terms of *imperium*. Already in the time of Frederick II, territorial power holders maintained that in his kingdom a ruler was like an "emperor," since no other power was recognized. The transformation of this notion of supreme legitimate power into the modern concept of "sovereignty" occurred in the writings of Bodin and Hobbes. Even here, though, the concept is exemplified originally by terms like *majestas* (Bodin)[24] rather than by the classical legal vocabulary of *imperium* or *potestas*, or by reference to the "mortal God, the biblical Leviathan" (Hobbes).[25]

Unfortunately, I cannot follow up on references to the "sacred" by explicating the new meaning of sovereignty; a few remarks will have to suffice. In both cases, the implication of the "sacred" provides important clues as to the underlying political imagination animating this new concept of sovereignty. For one, it casts doubt on the idea that sovereignty is an entirely secular notion that emerges out of religious struggles and becomes the harbinger of modernity (even if the resulting international system became a secular construct). Moreover, it also shows that the classical categories of "law" and, in particular, of inventing a social order on the basis of institutional arrangements created by speech acts perhaps could be expressed only in terms of an analogy to the creation *ex nihilo* ascribed to God.

Finally, it lets us understand the dynamic of the concept which retains an aura of the sacred, by putting the enabling condition beyond reach, as the "source" is beyond "law" itself. This sacred touch is not lost when sovereignty is later ascribed to "the people" rather than to the traditional sovereign. It is therefore no accident that writers like Carl Schmitt[26] have noticed the religious roots of many supposedly "modern" secular concepts, including sovereignty. However, despite these "sacred" and imperial traits, the emerging sovereignty game disabled at the same time any imperial pretensions by establishing the "inside" of a sovereign regime as an arena off-limits, and by delegitimizing any politics made in the name of a particular orthodoxy.

The focus on institutions and on speech acts also explains another manifestation of the inherent tension of the concept of sovereignty. On the one hand it links, through the nearly unfathomable and *ex ante* not specifiable speech act, that something is the case with the notion of legitimacy—in other words, to a demand that this determination should stand and should command assent from the "subjects." This part is most clearly articulated by Hobbes, where the authoritative decision of the sovereign can never be subject to further discussion. On the other hand, it also links the institutional enabling conditions—to the notion that certain acts of the sovereign might be *ultra vires* thus allowing for contestation. It also becomes clear why the dynamics of the first strand is usually elaborated in terms of the "will" problematic—whereby at best "self-limitation" of the sovereign can set some limits—while the second strand issues an institutional analysis and the "constitutionalization" of the concept.

Recognizing the crucial role "sovereignty" played for the legitimization of "domestic" politics, we can resolve some conceptual confusion about its external dimension. Again, a "historical" approach is useful. As Werner and de Wilde correctly point out:

> The Westphalian system is easily misunderstood as resting on a belief in the de facto isolation and autarky of resulting entities, most of which were territorially defined, and called states. In fact, however the Westphalian system is quite the opposite. It takes as its starting point the inevitable permeability of borders and the inevitable international interdependence of states, including both their governments and their societies. The only reason to sit down in Munster and Osnabrueck for more than four years of negotiations (1644–48) is that 150 years of warfare had shown the difficulty of establishing sovereign power by brute force only . . . Subsequently attempts were made to provide for

> a normative structure to deal with this permeability of territories and the interdependence of rulers and societies in an orderly way.
>
> Given the relatedness of the Westphalian principles—mutual recognition among sovereigns, territoriality of sovereign entities and the "exclusion of external actors from domestic authority structures" (Krasner, *Sovereignty*, 1999, p. 20)—it is unfortunate that Krasner's typology of sovereignty restricts the term . . . to the "exclusion of external actors" principle. The essence of Westphalian sovereignty is its negotiated nature. This discursive characteristic sets it apart from a more imperial image of sovereignty in which locally accumulated power expands and fades away in concentric circles. The endurance of the Westphalian sovereignty rests in the resilience of the discourse it gave birth to.[27]

There are several corollaries that follow from this argument. The first is that sovereignty is not a "fact" resulting simply from the interactions of a plurality of actors, as some structural theories want to have it. It is the *ascription of a status* to an actor based on mutual recognition. To that extent it can be possessed, but like the concept of property, it is easily misunderstood when, for example, a property title *in rem* is construed as an attribute of the "thing" owned instead of as a socially respected claim made by the owner of having exclusive authority to decide on its use.

Second, it should be obvious that both theories got only half of the things right. While facts and norms obviously interact, nothing follows from facts or from norms alone since for practices and speech acts both are necessary. Third, understanding sovereignty as an ascription of status rather than a possession resulting from certain palpable capabilities explains also why "recognition" might be continued even though regimes are no longer in effective command of their states. Such is the case when a "government" in exile rather than the domestically existing de facto regime is recognized. Similarly, even severe limitations of an actor's liberties, such as imposing on him the duty to stay neutral, does not mean that he has thereby lost his status as a sovereign, even though he has to forgo certain policy options. Thus, "status" and capacity to act are loosely coupled and belong to different orders, and this circumstance explains for example the emergence of "quasi-states" in the aftermath of colonization, as Jackson has pointed out.[28]

Finally, practices of recognition have shifted over time. While possession of land[29] and noble lineage were originally necessary criteria, the state- and nation-building processes of the nineteenth century stipulated that effectiveness of rule in an area over a distinct population provided the criteria for recognition. Later, the paramount importance of "the people" as the ultimate source of legitimacy gave rise to the practices of withholding recognition, if the power was wielded by regimes that were not considered representative, by not having gained power by constitutional means or because they were not considered part of "the people" as "foreigners" and colonial overlords. It is not difficult to fathom that here the politics of nationalism and identity have left their mark and transfigured "sovereignty."

As more recent state practice indicates, recognition today is increasingly connected to participation in international organizations, devaluing the singular judgments by individual sovereigns and stressing the "communal" character of such status attributions. It is to those practices that I want to turn in the next section, where both the changing practices and their doctrinal elaboration within the United Nations and the US public are addressed.

Changing the Rules of the Sovereignty Game: Governance and the "Responsibility to Protect"

The thesis that we have entered a period in which our political concerns have to be global, and for which the concerns of sovereignty are either irrelevant or more a hindrance than a help for understanding, is not new. Meanwhile, it comes in two versions. One is reformist, largely elaborated within the United Nations and within a changing guard of multilateralists. The other is "imperial," exemplified not only by some proposals of the former US administration, but by a much wider American public advocating more or less explicitly a "going alone" strategy.[30] Here the reverberations of September 11 as well as the frustrations experienced with the failures of multilateral diplomacy have left their mark.

Thus, while the analyses of the threats and challenges of the post-Cold War and post-September 11 world are surprisingly similar, the strategies for coping with them differ quite markedly. Perhaps the new concept of the "responsibility to protect" shows both the commonality and the divergence between the new internationalists and the advocates of empire. Both use the concept of protection as their legitimizing principle. The former emphasizes international supervision and "good governance," the latter relies on proactive US policies or on a "coalition of the willing." Thus, the difference seems to concern largely the *means* and not the goals. However, since in both politics and law the distinction between goals and means is often difficult—because what would be effective or efficient might have unpredictable consequences and risks or be "illegal"—putting the issues as involving only differences in strategies (i.e., the means) might be too simple. True, an "imperial" strategy has demonstrable dangers from which a more circumspect and reformed multilateralism might save us. There are, nevertheless, good reasons to doubt that the specific reforms lumped together under the catch-all concept of "good governance" to be implemented by multilateral institutions such as the United Nations, World Bank, and so on are benign and likely to work.

What one misses badly in both strategies is a conception of politics and the realization that history and local knowledge matter for creating a political order. Here notions of autonomy and the belief in being the author of one's own actions are necessary before they can become self-sustaining. While the imperial strategy thwarts such efforts by simple fiat, the capillary controls of new forms of governmentality are not that innocent either. They are prone to stifle allegedly "unproductive" opposition and displace politics by "objective" expertise and "neutral" administration.[31]

Since these issues are of central importance for the sovereignty *problematique*, I want to examine first the practices and doctrinal developments as they were observable within multilateral fora, especially the United Nations, for which the New York Summit (September 14–16, 2005) provides a good example. While, of course, in New York many more issues were on the agenda including the reform of the United Nations' structure itself, I want to focus here only on the part of the "responsibility to protect" and its history. The analysis of the imperial response in the next section will largely focus on declaratory statements of the US government and some of the more influential contributions to the public debate on the meaning of US sovereignty and its role in international politics.

As to the doctrinal development of the responsibility to protect: when former Secretary-General Kofi Annan formulated his proposals, his report titled *In Larger Freedom*,[32] incorporated the suggestions of several earlier reports, development studies (sustainable development), and public debates (democratic peace) that had been occasioned by the end of the Cold War and September 11. Annan's report attempted not only to provide a synthesis of an emerging consensus on how security and development were connected—via democratization and new forms of transparency and accountability—but it also tried to give doctrinal coherence to the practices of complex peace-keeping and peace-making missions that had involved the world organization in domestic affairs and had given rise to policies often far removed from the United Nations' original mandate. This new role had been controversial, and the multilateral interventions involving the use of force to quell conflicts within state borders had therefore to be interpreted as "exceptional" initiatives, explicitly denying their capacity to serve as precedents. An example in this regard is the original justifications of the intervention in Haiti in order to restore to power the elected president ousted by a military coup d'état. The Security Council described it as an "exceptional response" that was justified by a new kind of "complex and extraordinary" threat, and by its abnormality as "une mission de type nouveau," motivated more by the restoration of democracy than by response to a threat to regional stability.[33] As subsequent practice demonstrated, however, international interventions with important democratization components became the norm.[34]

Two further developments need to be mentioned. One is the adoption of "good governance" as a framework for UN activities in 1997, and the second is the expansion of the notion of "security"[35] that emerged from the High-Level Panel Report of 2004, *A More Secure World: Our Shared Responsibility*.[36] Here the conceptual shift occurred, from a notion that "sovereignty" was virtually the sole legitimizing principle of international politics to one that stressed "responsibility," in other words, that the exercise of sovereign rights was dependent on the duty of states to protect their people from both man-made and natural disasters. The crucial point is that Kofi Annan links back to the aspirational part of the UN Charter in which the *peoples* are named and that he expands on the idea that states have responsibilities not only vis-à-vis each other but above all to their own people. The idea that populations and not states are the ultimate beneficiary of international action is now fully developed in the principle of "responsibility to protect," which is shared by governments and international organizations in humanitarian emergencies.

The inclusion of this principle not only fundamentally alters the dynamics inherent in the Westphalian order, but it also makes human rights and public accountability an intrinsic part of state responsibility. Thus, the exercise of sovereign prerogatives is conditional upon reasonable, responsible, and law-abiding behavior toward citizens and other states. In this new framework, the international arena is patterned by the interaction of states functioning under the rule of law internally as well as externally. Such a constitutionalization of sovereignty, which accrues to states no longer as part of natural liberty, but as "trust" by the people, is of course likely to engender fears as it also authorizes new reasons for intervention that were originally categorically barred by Article 2.7 of the UN Charter.

Such concerns were not only on the minds of some "dissenters" like the Venezuelan and Jamaican presidents,[37] who saw in this conceptual revolution a new enabling condition for the strong to intervene in weak states, the presumed "community authorization" notwithstanding. That such fears were not imaginary was evidenced by President Bush's statement at the New York summit. Bush's interpretation of the "shared responsibility" for securing peace had a distinctly unilateral ring. Instead of being the outcome of multilateralism, coordination, international rules, and regulations under UN lead, international peace is the result of individual states' commitment to it: "Peace is the responsibility of every nation and every generation." Moreover, even though the United States engages in unilateral initiatives, she is working for the "accomplishment of the UN ideals," in particular the "responsibility to protect": "With courage and conscience, we will meet our responsibilities to protect the lives and the rights of others. And when we do, we will help fulfil the promise of the United Nations."[38] This was a not-too-distant echo of the self-serving arguments of Britain and France during the Suez crisis that using force was not in violation of the UN Charter, since the mission was in accordance with the "purposes" of the world organization.

Not surprisingly, the Outcome document, while agreeing on the "universality, indivisibility and interrelatedness of human rights,"[39] restated the principle of state sovereignty, leaving unresolved the conundrum between noninterference and international responsibility of protecting populations from gross violations of human rights.[40] In its paragraph 5, the member states committed themselves to "support all efforts to uphold the sovereign equality of all States, respect for their territorial integrity and political independence . . . To non-interference in the internal affairs of States, and respect human rights and fundamental freedoms."[41]

What attracted less attention but should have been debated more extensively were some proposals for dealing with the new threats and of implementing the shared responsibilities. In keeping with the experiences of organization theory[42] that signaling interest and accepting the legitimacy of certain concerns usually translates into the creation of a new organization or bureau—even if this further impairs the workings of existing structures—a new Peace-Building Commission and Human Rights Council plus a High Commissioner for Human Rights was proposed. After all, creating new structures generates bureaucratic fights about missions and competences, and increases "red tape" and coordination costs. It also results in multiple principal/agent problems and thus encourages irresponsible behavior on both the side of the bureaucracy and on the "user side," which might play one agency against the other.

Thus, a remarkable shortcoming of these "multilateral solutions" is the heavy emphasis on technical solutions, not only with regard to organizational but also to social problems. While this phenomenon is the result of "good governance" doctrines that dominated the debates over the last decade, this emphasis is somewhat odd given the state of the art in management and public administration. Increasingly, the *best practice* is not to rely on code books and standardized rules but on discretion, teamwork, and *ex post* accountability. The ideas that best practices are readily codifiable *ex ante*, that they are context independent, and that they do not require "local knowledge" fly in the face of all experience and managerial theory.

Additional difficulties that make the idea of technical solutions of political issues problematic concern the following. First, even the clearest rule has to be interpreted, and since virtually all situations are ambiguous, *judgment* is required for deciding which rule should be applied. This judgment call, however, cannot be defined by another rule *ex ante* because this would involve us in an infinite regress. Finally, since "what works" depends crucially not only on the intention and knowledge of the administrator, but also on the reactions of others, who are rooted in their traditions, "local knowledge" is important. Particularly when the goal is not simply the delivery of services, where the "others" have only to stand in line, but where processes of conflict resolution and of political decision making are at issue, holding on to the codified wisdom of best practices, based on Western experiences, will not do.

Even economists, who possess probably the most advanced expertise in the social sciences, had to realize in the aftermath of the Asian crisis that imposing "conditionality" tailored in accordance with traditional orthodoxies will not induce economic growth and might actually make matters worse. The fact that the most successful countries in achieving economic growth have done so largely in defiance of the expert advice delivered by international financial institutions should provide us with much food for thought as it demonstrates that both local knowledge and "the people" might matter more than expertise and imported best practices.

A New Internationalism: The Law's Empire or the Law of the Empire?

In short, the above discussion suggests that the flaws of such strategies lie not in implementation but rather in their underlying assumptions. Here the belief in progress is matched by an equally problematic notion of social analysis that has a distinctive Hegelian ring to it. What exists is reasonable, and therefore further questions as to whether we should continue on this path can be brushed aside. The legitimacy of a decision, be it a legal or a political one, is no longer a function of how it was made (i.e., either through an authorizing act of the sovereign[43] or through the application of formal rules to a case at hand), but it becomes now solely a question of whether the "output" is accepted. In law, this orientation gives rise to hostility toward "formalism" and in politics to an attitude that all that is necessary is to be on the side of "universalism." As Jean B. Elshtain so aptly put it: "The United States is itself premised on a set of universal propositions concerning human dignity and equality. There is no conflict in principle between our national identity and universal claims and commitments."[44] Apparently, all further questions can then be reduced to instrumental considerations. Instead of debating the "why" and "how" of, for example, interventions, the crucial issues are now only the "where" and "when," since "humanity" itself provides the goals and determines the strategies of those able and willing to shoulder that task.

Nowhere does this bane of shoddy thinking become more visible than in the attempts of construing anything desirable as a "human right." Thus, while we can all agree that a democratic form of government is desirable, construing popular sovereignty—which is one essential feature of democracy—as an individual "human right"[45] betokens considerable conceptual befuddlement. It not only commits a category mistake by reducing political categories into moral ones, but it also mistakenly identifies a regulative principle for legitimating joint political action for a "right" that someone qua "human person" possesses. There is a distinction worth pondering between the "good citizen" and the "good person," as Aristotle suggested.[46] There is also the more general problem of whether we can apply moral categories developed for dealing with problems individuals encounter in their private life, without much ado, to other more "political" contexts. Here appeals to universalism are hardly serving any purpose except ruling out claims which are too self-serving. The political realm is always one of the contingent and particular, and not of the universal and atemporally valid. Thus, even if the universal and "eternal" might be linked to our choices, it is *historical mediations* that deserve particular attention.

For example, to call the toppling of Saddam Hussein's regime a "humanitarian intervention" and to justify it on the basis of the democratic peace argument is not only making nonsense of our political vocabulary, but it also hopelessly muddies the waters at a time when conceptual clarity is the precondition for dealing effectively with complex situations. After all, the classical meaning of humanitarian intervention was to thwart specific crimes against humanity and to rescue actual and potential victims of an ongoing massacre. It was not designed to overthrow "tyranny" or to spread democracy in the hope that such regimes might be more peaceful and cooperative in the future. The fact that this latter goal is then justified further in terms of the security requirements of the United States—suddenly the people of Iraq matter only incidentally—suggests how untenable such universalist justifications are. They are not only cynical with regard to the rights and interests of the victims, they are—and one suspects *they have to be*—self-serving and "irresponsible." Actual political "responsibility," namely the "need to answer" for one's decisions, cannot be to an abstract "universal humanity," but it has to be to a concrete "people" that bears this burden.

Traditional realists have therefore warned that dressing up one's particular historical experience in universalist garb and trying to impose it on others is likely to ruin politics, which inevitably has to assume the plurality of visions and voices. The resulting crusading spirit makes compromises, the virtue of traditional diplomacy, impossible, as Hans Morgenthau suggested:

> Thus carrying their idols before them the nationalistic masses of our time meet in the international arena each group convinced that it executes the mandate of history, that it does for humanity what it seems to do for itself, and that it fulfils a sacred mission ordained by Providence, however defined. Little do they know that they meet under an empty sky from which the Gods have departed.[47]

It took Mogadishu, Iraq, Kosovo, and Darfur to show an equally disturbing disjuncture between aspirations and praxis. The actual problems requiring action are managed by oversight, selectivity, some half-hearted responses, and by the counterproductive nature of force for the "pacification" of a population. The frequent visceral response to the difficulties encountered is, however, not to recognize the impossibility of the goal—that is to say, of making some other people democratic "by force." Rather, the tendency is to blame the insufficiency of means. Interventions are called "virtual wars," and they later produce only virtual victories, as Michael Ignatieff reminds us:

> Since the means employed are limited the ends achieved are equally constrained: not unconditititional surrender, regime change or destruction of the war-making capacity of the other side, only an ambiguous end state. Why do virtual wars end so ambiguously?
>
> Liberal democracies that are unwilling to repair collapsed states, to create democracy where none existed and to remain on guard until the institutions are self-sustaining and self-reproducing, must inevitably discover that virtual victory is a poor substitute for the real thing.[48]

This is certainly a remarkable statement. The near-exclusive focus on means that has frequently been the bane of military analysis recalls blaming the "loss of Vietnam" on "political interference" and bombing restrictions, even though there were hardly any targets left on the military's wish list. Both historical experience and political reflection demonstrate that outcomes delivering "the real thing" have been the exception. Consequently, the flaw in this argument is not the limited engagement of means but the postulation[49] of goals, which are far beyond what military power or even skillful diplomacy can deliver. The noted ambiguity of the "end state" is thus not an anomaly but an elemental fact of political life. Here contingencies matter, and compromises and less-than-perfect solutions cannot be made to disappear by the universalist rhetoric of human rights or by some eschatological fantasy about the "end of history" when all accounts are finally settled and the new eon begins.[50]

Finally, it is not quite clear how such a theory, which shifts the focus from the state and the sovereignty of a people to the individual and to a principle of "civilian inviolability," as Slaughter proposes,[51] is able to make good on its claims. Short of transforming the international game into an empire, where the plurality of political projects is silenced by fiat, no such expectation seems realistic. True, such an imperial solution might not involve actual territorial possession as more subtle but effective means of disciplining and of exercising the "capillary control" of governmentality have been developed. Here Foucault[52] and the Marxists from Wallerstein[53] to Hardt and Negri[54] provide ample food for thought. Nevertheless, the idea that such a shift to universalism and "best practices," unmediated by any of the particularities of politics, historically embedded institutions, and local knowledge, is able to bring about a cosmopolitan millennium is hardly convincing. Most of our experiences in peace-keeping and of "reforming" failed or "rogue" states point in the other direction.[55]

Remember that the tragedy of Yugoslavia was at least partially brought about by the "advice" of the IMF to make the country ripe for a free market and democracy. It consisted in having the central government reclaim control over significant aspects of economic policy, a move that upset the delicate balance between the republics and opened the doors for the subsequent disintegration and ethnic irredentist politics.[56] When the United States and NATO finally intervened, they did so by invoking human rights and civilian protection, but the bitter truth was that even if we believed in the sincerity of such claims—hardly unproblematic in the face of President Clinton's steadfast refusal to stop the killing by committing ground troops—we had become participants in a series of disputes about sovereignty among warring groups, and we had chosen sides. The abstract principles of humanitarianism and universal rights provided preciously little guidance for determining which political claims, and of which group, should be recognized.[57]

This example provides a useful reminder that in any halfway realistic situation the assessments of what is the case, and what are the options, can never be reduced to the clarification of "principles," as universalist as they might be. The reason for this is that principles cannot prescribe their own application and are thus in need of interpretation. Similarly, the "fact pattern" of a case might be susceptible to different readings involving different principles and value trade-offs. It requires indeed a leap of faith—and considerable obsessiveness in the face of contrary experience—that stating a universalist norm somehow can resolve our practical and moral dilemmas.

Those of us who have had the privilege of being around a bit longer will remember in this context the arguments of the New Haven school and its hostility to both legal formalism and traditional institutions. Instead, the shining supreme value of "human dignity," and a "process" of claims and counterclaims, were supposed to deliver solutions embodying this universalist commitment.[58] On closer inspection, however, the results nearly always justified US policies during the Cold War. That such derailments are pure coincidence seems rather unlikely. They are rather part and parcel of a fundamental failure in understanding the links between law, politics, and problems of justification, all of which cannot be reduced to waving the magic wand of a supreme value, or to playing all types of alleged human rights as trumps in debates or deliberations about policies.[59]

Recognizing this predicament does not mean that we have to "return" to the verities of yesteryear or to decisionism beyond any rational appeal. It does mean, however, that we have to take seriously the contingency of our historical institutions and the plurality of visions that makes politics, paying attention to the "particular" necessary. If we want to avoid the obvious dangers of a slippery slope, then we have to defend the "statist" notion that humanitarian intervention is based on clearly demarcated exceptions to the rule of nonintervention rather than on a general principle issuing from the universality of human rights. We also have to counteract the tendency that the identification of threats carries with it also automatically the legitimization of certain acts. Such a presumption of the legitimacy of preventive action gives rise to a policy of suspicion and ascribes rights only to those who carry our briefs. Ultimately, such a policy involves us in political projects that are beyond anyone's capacity and that have to result ultimately in cynicism and frustration. In short, humanitarian intervention is not a one-size-fits-all policy for all types of dangers threatening humanity. As Terry Nardin aptly remarks: "[Humanitarian intervention] belongs to the world of inter-state relations, as a modification of that world. One state can 'intervene' in the internal affairs of another if there are rules that distinguish internal from external."[60]

In a world that did not recognize sovereignty as a constitutive principle, we could not have "interventions," as we would only have encountered more or less effective policies including those involving acts of force lacking legitimacy—very similar to war of all against all. The other possibility is illustrated by the Chinese empire, where a claim to authority over all mankind had to meet any resistance with "punishment." After all, individual lawbreakers as well as the "barbarians in outer darkness" *had to be* criminals. The parallels to some of the more recent writings in international law, where sovereignty is defended on constitutional grounds,[61] while at the same time claims of other states to the same privilege are disregarded, are striking. They raise serious doubts that this "constitutional moment" is one in which the values that we connect with the notion of a constitution are safeguarded.

Conclusion

This inquiry into the changing practice of sovereignty approached the problem from a conceptual perspective. Instead of taking the burgeoning literature of global governance and cosmopolitan democracy as my point of departure, I argued that much of the analysis concerning the "death of sovereignty" is seriously flawed by attempting to solve the puzzles of sovereignty through empirical analysis and/or through some normative understandings that are frequently amiss in appraising the historical developments. In order to avoid these shortcomings, I further argued that sovereignty cannot be analyzed like a natural fact and be subjected to observation, measurement, or "causal inference." In criticizing this descriptive fallacy, I maintained that the meaning of the concept is not established by reference but by its *use* and its connections to other concepts within the semantic field. Here issues of legitimacy, of authorizing, and of preventing certain actions figure prominently and show how attempts at determining the "degree" of sovereignty are bound to fail. In short, sovereignty has to be understood as a status ascription bounded by institutional rules rather than as a possession of certain palpable capabilities. Furthermore, I maintained also that the "silences" with respect to sovereignty in both the examples of the United States' compound republic and the European Union provide important clues as to the function of this concept.

As these considerations provided the background for the subsequent analysis, I approached two discourses dominating the present sovereignty *problematique*: one more doctrinally oriented and conducted within the multilateral framework of the United Nations in the aftermath of the Cold War and September 11; the other, often characterized by more imperial claims and assertions of entitlements and privileges accruing to the United States in virtue of its position within the international system and as the defender of universalist values. While both discourses hinge on the (non-)intervention presumption as a crucial part of the sovereignty game, the first focuses more on the institutional implications of shifting the center of attention from the "state" to the people and making thus the exercise of sovereignty dependent upon the implementation of human rights. Here the "responsibility to protect" figures prominently. The US discourse on the other hand unites a variety of interpretations of the "new internationalism" ranging from traditional Great Power notions subject to "Concert," that is, UN approval, to blatant assertions of the preventive use of force against rogue states and of the right of unilateral action in pursuit of democracy and human rights.

The purpose of these two inquiries was not only to sketch briefly some prominent positions and assess their impact on contemporary practice but to also show some commonalities among them. In this context, I tried to demonstrate how the conjuncture of reasoning with universal principles and the social scientific aspirations of finding social laws and causal mechanisms provide a particularly volatile mix of ideas that prevents us from understanding politics and is likely to lead to disastrous choices and unachievable commitments. If historical conjunctures are translated into causal mechanisms, repeatable anywhere and anytime, then the obsession with context-free "best practices" and the establishment of technocratic regimes—be they in the form of subnational networks or as "responsible" disaggregated states—are the "relevant utopias." Such attempts are likely to result in fantasy systems—be they multilaterally tempered or unilaterally imposed—that foreclose finding solutions based on local knowledge and the particular circumstances which are the domain of politics.

There were of course periods in which a conception of participatory politics requiring civic commitment was foreign to "the people." They were subject to imperial rule, perhaps even reasonably well protected by law, as in the later Roman Empire, or largely irrelevant to the exercise of public power, as in the Middle Ages. Today we are reminded that politics has changed again, becoming a politics of lifestyles[62] rather than one of existential questions. What unites us is more that which interests us *singly and privately* than that which binds us *together* and creates a "common thing," the *res publica* of old. The reduction of politics to the "commodious life" encouraging more and more consumption might be available to us in the more privileged regions of the world. The rest of mankind seems to steadily sink into servitude and irrelevance, as was the lot in large segments of the early Middle Ages.

The prophets of such a secular change in the understanding of politics are already offering their version of what is to come. We are told to understand politics as an appendix to the right of "free trade"[63] where we possess the status of "consumers," somewhat enhanced by human rights. Whether such visions contain desirable political projects, or are even possible, given that the "sovereign"—the "people"—is the main "source" of law, can seriously be doubted. In any case, such derailments serve as a useful reminder of the enduring importance of sovereignty, and that leaving sovereignty behind might also entail leaving behind much of the project of people as political animals.

Endnotes

1. For an early assessment of the changing international order, see Cyril Edwin Black and Richard A. Falk, eds., *The Future of the International Legal Order*, 4 vols. (Princeton, N.J.: Princeton University Press, 1969–1972).

2. The *locus classicus* for this assessment that was widely accepted despite its questionable historical accuracy is Leo Gross, "The Peace of Westphalia, 1648–1948," *American Journal of International Law* 42, no. 1 (1948): 20–41.

3. See Kenneth Neal Waltz, *Theory of International Politics* (Reading, Mass.: Addison-Wesley, 1979).

4. Stephen D. Krasner, *Sovereignty: Organized Hypocrisy* (Princeton, N.J.: Princeton University Press, 1999), 3.

5. Fernando R. Tesón, "Ending Tyranny in Iraq," *Ethics and International Affairs* 19, no. 2 (2005): 1–20, at 19.

6. See International Commission on Intervention and State Sovereignty, "The Responsibility to Protect" (Ottawa: International Development Research Centre, 2001).

7. See Ian Bache and Matthew Flinders, eds., *Multi-Level Governance* (Oxford: Oxford University Press, 2004).

8. See R. B. J. Walker, *Inside/Outside: International Relations as Political Theory* (Cambridge: Cambridge University Press, 1993).

9. On the new global compact involving industry in novel public private partnerships, see John Gerard Ruggie, "Reconstituting the Global Public Domain: Issues, Actors, and Practices," *European Journal of International Relations* 10, no. 4 (2004): 499–531.

10. See in this context Jack Donnelly, "Sovereign Inequalities and Hierarchy in Anarchy: American Power and International Society," *European Journal of International Relations* 12, no. 2 (2006): 139–170; Friedrich Kratochwil, "Of Systems, Boundaries, and Territoriality: An Inquiry into the Formation of the State System," *World Politics* 39, no. 1 (1986): 27–52.

11. See the discussion of Daniel H. Deudney, *Bounding Power: Republican Security Theory from the Polis to the Global Village* (Princeton, N.J.: Princeton University Press, 2007).

12. See, e.g., Pierre-Marie Dupuy, "The Constitutional Dimension of the Charter of the United Nations Revisited," *Max Planck Yearbook of United Nations Law* 1 (1997); Bardo Fassbender, "The United Nations Charter as Constitution of the International Community," *Columbia Journal of Transnational Law* 36, no. 3 (1998): 529–620.

13. See George Lakoff, *Women, Fire, and Dangerous Things: What Categories Reveal About the Mind* (Chicago: University of Chicago Press, 1987).

14. Aristotle, *Politics*, translated by T,A Sinclair (Harmondsworth, Engl: Penguin, 1962), Bk. 1, Chap. 2.

15. See R. M. Hare, *The Language of Morals* (Oxford: Clarendon Press, 1972).

16. See Ludwig Wittgenstein, *Philosophical Investigations*, trans. G. E. M. Anscombe (New York: Macmillan, 1953).

17. The term made its appearance apparently for the first time in the Moscow Declaration of October 30, 1943, in which the Allied powers agreed on the a future establishment of a "general international organization" (the later UNO). For a historical account, see Ruth B. Russell, *A History of the United Nations Charter; the Role of the United States, 1940–1945* (Washington, D.C.: Brookings Institution, 1958), 111ff.

18. See Bardo Fassbender, "Sovereignty and Constitutionalism in International Law," in *Sovereignty in Transition*, ed. Neil Walker (Oxford: Hart, 2005).

19. For a critical assessment of such claims, see Friedrich Kratochwil, "Global Governance and the Emergence of 'World Society,'" in *Varieties of World-Making: Beyond Globalization*, ed. Nathalie Karagannis and Peter Wagner (Liverpool: University of Liverpool Press, 2007): 266–83.

20. See, e.g., Alexander Wendt, "Why a World State Is Inevitable," *European Journal of International Relations* 9, no. 4 (2003): 491–542.

21. See Robert W. Cox, "Social Forces, States and World Orders: Beyond International Relations Theory," *Millennium* 10, no. 2 (1981): 126–155.

22. H. L. A. Hart, *Essays in Jurisprudence and Philosophy* (Oxford: Oxford University Press, 1983), 23f.

23. See John Searle, *Speech Acts: An Essay in the Philosophy of Language* (Cambridge: Cambridge University Press, 1969); John Searle, *Rationality in Action* (Cambridge, Mass.: MIT Press, 2003).

24. Jean Bodin, *The Six Books of the Commonwealth*, ed. Kenneth D. McRae (Cambridge, Mass.: Harvard University Press, 1962).

25. Thomas Hobbes, *Leviathan*, ed. C. B. MacPherson (Baltimore: Penguin Books, 1968).

26. Carl Schmitt, *Political Theology: Four Chapters on the Concept of Sovereignty*, ed. by George Schwab (Chicago: University of Chicago Press, 2005).

27. Wouter G. Werner and Jaap H. de Wilde, "The Endurance of Sovereignty," *European Journal of International Relations* 7, no. 3 (2001): 283–313, here 288.

28. Robert H. Jackson, *Quasi-States: Sovereignty, International Relations, and the Third World* (Cambridge: Cambridge University Press, 2000).

29. For an interesting, Marxist-inspired discussion calling attention to importance of the changing modes of production and their impact on social formations and their politics, see Justin Rosenberg, *The Empire of Civil Society: A Critique of the Realist Theory of International Relations* (London: Verso, 1994).

30. See, e.g., the conclusions of the high-profile task force convened by the US Institute of Peace, which was chaired by George Mitchell and Newt Gingrich, and which argued for the legitimacy of unilateral action outside of the UN framework in cases of dire emergencies. Task Force on the United Nations (2005), "American Interests and U.N. Reform" (Washington, DC: United States Institute of Peace), esp. 20–32.

31. For an extensive critique of the politics of expertise (or rather the displacement of politics), see Friedrich Kratochwil, "The Genealogy of Multilateralism: Reflections on an Organizational Form and Its Crisis," in *Multilateralism under Challenge? Power, International Order and Structual Change*, ed. Edward Newman, Ramesh Thakur, and John Tirman (Tokyo: United Nations Press, 2006): 139–59.

32. UN Secretary-General Kofi Annan, *In Larger Freedom: Towards Security, Development and Human Rights for All* (New York: United Nations, 2005).

33. United Nations, *Les Nations Unies et Haïti, 1990–1996. Avec une introduction de Boutros Boutros-Ghali, Secrétaire Général de l'organisation des Nations Unies*, Livres Bleus Des Nations Unies 11 (New York: Département de l'Information des Nations Unies, 1996), 3.

34. It must be noted that before the 1990s, the few UN interventions with an institution-building or democratization component (such as for example the Namibia transition) were conducted within the framework of "decolonization" processes, and not because of a connection between democracy and international security.

35. The distinction of man-made and natural disasters is, e.g., given up—allowing thus ecological concerns such as global warming to become a matter of shared domestic and international responsibility as a "threat" is now generically defined as: "Any event or process that leads to large-scale death or lessening of life chances and undermines States as the basic unit of the international system is a threat to international security."

UN Secretary-General's High Level Panel on Threats, Challenges and Change (2004), A More Secure World: Our Shared Responsibility (New York: United Nations, 2004).

36. Ibid.

37. See, e.g., "Statement by H. E. Hugo Chavez Frias, President of the Bolivarian Republic of Venezuela," available at: http://www.un.org/webcast/summit2005/statements.html; "Statement by the Most Honourable P. J. Patterson, Prime Minister of Jamaica on Behalf of the Group of 77 and China in the Financing for Development Session United

Nations General Assembly," available at http://www.un.org/webcast/summit2005/statements.html.

38. See "Statement of H. E. Mr. George Bush, President of the United States of America," *2005 World Summit, High Level Plenary Meeting*, available at http://www.un.org/webcast/summit2005/statements.html. Quotation at p. 5 of President Bush's statement.

39. General Assembly (2005), "Outcome Document, 60th Session" (UN Doc. A Res 60/1), para.13 and 121. [Cited as "Outcome Document."]

40. For an assessment, see, e.g., Alex J. Bellamy, "Whither the Responsibility to Protect? Humanitarian Intervention and the 2005 World Summit," *Ethics and International Affairs* 20, no. 2 (2006): 143–169.

41. "Outcome Document," para. 5.

42. John W. Meyer and Brian Rowan, "Institutionalized Organizations: Formal Structure as Myth and Ceremony," *American Journal of Sociology* 83, no. 2 (1977): 340–363.

43. Anne-Marie Slaughter, *A New World Order* (Princeton, N.J.: Princeton University Press, 2004).

44. Jean Bethke Elshtain, "International Justice as Equal Regard and the Use of Force," *Ethics and International Affairs* 17, no. 2 (2003): 63–75, at 67.

45. To name just one product of this cottage industry: W. Michael Reisman, "Sovereignty and Human Rights in Contemporary International Law," *American Journal of International Law* 84, no. 4 (1990): 866–876.

46. Aristotle, *Politics*, above note 14.

47. Hans J. Morgenthau, *Politics among Nations: The Struggle for Power and Peace*, 4th ed. (New York: Knopf, 1967), 249.

48. Michael Ignatieff, *Virtual War: Kosovo and Beyond* (New York: Henry Holt, 2000), 208ff.

49. For a good discussion, see Anthony Burke, "Against the New Internationalism," *Ethics and International Affairs* 19, no. 2 (2005): 73–89.

50. Francis Fukuyama, *The End of History and the Last Man* (New York: Free Press, 1992).

51. See Anne-Marie Slaughter and William Burke-White, "An International Constitutional Moment," *Harvard International Law Journal* 43, no. 1 (2002): 1–22, at 8.

52. See Michel Foucault, *The History of Sexuality*, vol. 1, trans. Robert Hurley (New York: Pantheon Books, 1978).

53. Immanuel Maurice Wallerstein, *The Modern World System: Capitalist Agriculture and the Origins of the European World Economy in the Sixteenth Century* (New York: Academic Press, 1976).

54. Michael Hardt and Antonio Negri, *Empire* (Cambridge, Mass.: Harvard University Press, 2000).

55. See, e.g., Dennis C. Jett, *Why Peacekeeping Fails* (New York: St. Martin's Press, 2000).

56. See Susan L. Woodward, *Balkan Tragedy: Chaos and Dissolution after the Cold War* (Washington, D.C.: Brookings Institution, 1995).

57. For a discussion of the Yugoslavian case and its implications for "external sovereignty," see Helen Thompson, "The Case for External Sovereignty," *European Journal of International Relations* 12, no. 2 (2006): 251–274.

58. See Myres McDougal, "Some Basic Concepts About International Law: A Policy Oriented Framework," in *The Strategy of World Order*, ed. Richard A. Falk and Saul H. Mendlovitz, vol. 2, *International Law* (New York: World Law Fund, 1966).

59. For a thoughtful analysis of these points, see Jean L. Cohen, "Whose Sovereignty? Empire Versus International Law," *Ethics and International Affairs* 18, no. 3 (2004): 1–24.

60. Terry Nardin, "Humanitarian Imperialism," *Ethics and International Affairs* 19, no. 2 (2005): 21–26, here 23.

61. See, e.g., Jack Goldsmith and Eric A. Posner, *The Limits of International Law* (Oxford: Oxford University Press, 2006).

62. See Ulrich Beck, *Die Erfindung Des Politischen: Zu Einer Theorie Reflexiver Modernisierung* (Frankfurt am Main: Suhrkamp, 1993).

63. See, e.g., the proposal by Ernst-Ulrich Petersmann, "Time for a United Nations 'Global Compact' for Integrating Human Rights into the Law of Worldwide Organizations: Lessons from European Integration," *European Journal of International Law* 13, no. 3 (2002): 621–650.

6

International Law and Power in the Multipolar and Multicivilizational World of the Twenty-first Century

Yasuaki Onuma

Introduction

What "era" are we going to have in the twenty-first century? Many have raised this question since around the turn of the century. More than a few of them have answered as follows: while the nineteenth century was a century of Europe and the twentieth century was that of America, the twenty-first century will be a century of Asia.

The matter should not be regarded as quite so simple. Each of the two candidates for Asian superpowers, China and India, has its own problems. In the case of China, huge economic gaps in terms of regions and societal groups as well as the problem of authoritarian and corrupted governmental power will likely persist for some time. Similar huge gaps between the rich and the poor as well as glaring linguistic, religious, and ethnic diversity, and tensions arising from it, will likely remain in India. Further, Asia does not have such common features and cohesiveness as Europe.

Still, it is most likely that the power of Asia will substantially increase and the predominant power that the United States and Europe enjoyed throughout the twentieth century will diminish in relative terms. How will major powers such as the United States and major Western European nations react to such a changing power constellation? China and India had once enjoyed the status of the Middle Kingdom or the center of civilization. Both had regarded themselves as the center of the world and tended to act unilaterally, assuming their own rule as international. Yet both were humiliated in the nineteenth and twentieth centuries under colonial or semi-colonial rule. Judging from these historical experiences, it is reasonable to assume that both countries will behave in a more aggressive and assertive manner, and challenge Western hegemony on a global scale. How will existing powers, especially the United States, react to such challenges? Can they grow old wisely and adapt to this new reality?

Seen from a more general perspective, it is likely that we will witness major tensions and conflicts destabilizing the global order in the twenty-first century: (1) tensions between "transnationalization" of economics and information, on the one hand, and the territorially constructed sovereign states system on the other; (2) tensions between the global pursuit of human dignity, as typically advocated by the "civil society" of developed countries, and revulsion toward "intervention" from the outside based on the sense of humiliation shared by people in developing countries; (3) tensions between the increasing economic power held by Asian nations and the ideational/intellectual power held by Western nations.[1]

Law, which contributes to grounding, organizing, prescribing, and coordinating the behavior of social actors, does not exist in a power vacuum. It is produced, sustained, and realized by power. Law is a reflection of power. On the other hand, it prescribes, controls, directs, and constructs power. Law cannot be dissociated from power. With a change of the agents of various types of power who have different perceptions and perspectives of the world and of history, law—which accompanies power—changes as well. But how will law and power change? And how should they change? How should we see the change and how should we act in order to bring about desirable change?

Law should, and usually does, represent legitimacy. Here legitimacy is generally understood in terms of justice, fairness, legitimate representation of societal members, equality, accountability, and other normative values as recognized by societal members. Both substantive and procedural aspects of legitimacy are important.[2] Legitimacy includes legality or lawfulness, but it is a wider concept than that of legality or lawfulness. On the other hand, law is also a tool of power. This is another predominant understanding of law. This feature can hurt the legitimacy of law. Further, law itself is a power inasmuch as it can be enforced. Law is a power also in the sense that law as an idea constructs the world, including power itself.

In this chapter, I will seek to examine complex aspects and dimensions present in the relations between law and power, taking into consideration the problem of legitimacy in the global society of the twenty-first century. I will deal with the problem not only from international and transnational perspectives, which are prevalent perspectives dealing with trans-boundary, international, or global affairs, but also from a trans-civilizational perspective.[3] The task is so enormous that I can show only an extremely simplified sketch of the whole picture. Still, I hope, this sketch can contribute to discerning some of the complex aspects and dimensions of the problem on law, power, and legitimacy in global society.

I Complexities of Law and Power in Global Society

1 CAN INTERNATIONAL LAW CONTROL THE POWER OF STATES?

(1) International Order and Power Constellation in the Twentieth Century

The United States played the most important role in establishing and managing a number of international institutions, including the United Nations and international law, during the twentieth century. It utilized them as instruments to justify its hegemony by providing prevalent interpretations of international law and other international institutions. It often pursued and actually realized its national interests by claiming that it enforced or implemented international law. On the other hand, the United States did not hesitate to violate international law when it was deemed necessary to realize its vital interests, although it seldom admitted that it acted in violation of international law. The tendency to act unilaterally and to resort to force in violation of international law became more evident after the end of the Cold War, as exemplified by the invasion of Iraq in 2003. The United States thus invited not only harsh reactions and violence from extremist Muslims and Arabs, but also severe criticism from its own allies all over the world.

In contrast, Western European nations succeeded in establishing societies that can generally be characterized as more humane, more respectful of law, and less violent than the United States. In the European system, the protection of human rights, rigid and progressive environmental protection policies, and the pursuit of the prevention of crimes by establishing the ICC, are some examples of such humane endeavors. Law is an important instrument to ground these undertakings. The law embodying such features also constitutes power in the sense that no one can resist or rebut its ideational force, and in that it is actually being realized in the EU system. The claim of the Western European leaders appeals to people beyond Europe's borders because it embodies an idealistic pursuit of human well-being.[4] On the other hand, it may be characterized as utopian or hypocritical, ignoring the harsh realities of contemporary international society. Robert Kagan's cynical criticism of Europe[5] was a typical example of this view.[6]

Japan, which was sometimes characterized as one of the Western world's three polar powers in the latter half of the twentieth century, could transform its enormous economic power into neither political nor ideational power. It remained a "silent partner" of the Western powers, especially the United States. International law, for Japan, was not something it created with others. It was a given, established by the Western powers, to be followed and complied with. The attitude of Japan toward international law typically demonstrated its attitude toward international order or global society as a whole.

A far more vocal and conspicuous player in the latter half of the twentieth-century world was the developing countries as a group. They pursued a strategy of changing existing rules which were favorable to Western powers and establishing new rules of international law to their advantage by using the "power of the majority" in various international forums. The UN General Assembly is a typical arena for such struggles. Through this strategy, developing nations sought to resist Western hegemony and to realize their interests in the global arena. This strategy has encountered a serious setback with the failure of their economic and financial policies since the 1980s. But they still seek to transform the current North Atlantic-centric or Euro-America-centric[7] international order into one which is less disadvantageous to themselves.

Among developing countries, China and India have maintained leadership and have held a certain reputational power in the latter half of the twentieth century. China has been a permanent member of the UN Security Council since its creation. India has been a leader of the Third World nations and the nonaligned movement. Yet both of them were underdeveloped nations for more than a century. They were far behind the major Western nations in terms of military and economic power. However, since around the end of the twentieth century, the increase of their substantive power has been conspicuous. A number of experts tend to assume that they will become superpowers rivaling the United States and the European Union in the twenty-first century. The map of the twenty-first century will be very different from that of the twentieth century in terms of power constellation.

(2) Complex Relations between Law and Power in Global Society[8]

In order to manage societies, humans usually need, and actually use, law. In today's world, where a huge portion of humanity lives in a highly developed scientific and technological civilization, humanity needs similarly highly developed laws and coordination between such laws. An international society where noncompliance with international law is normal would be a world where the daily life of human beings would be impossible. This is because such activities as global trade, transportation, finance, and communications, on which people's daily lives depend, are managed in accordance with international law. The world without international law would also be a world where nations seek to manipulate and annihilate each other. It would be a world of struggle by all against all, leading each one to perish with the others. To avoid such consequences, humanity utilizes international law, which contributes to the coexistence of nations, together with other global institutions such as diplomacy, global media checking the power of states, global trade, financial institutions, and the like.[9]

Even the most powerful state cannot be a global empire, literally dominating all other states. This being the case, great powers need law and other ideational instruments to legitimize their dominance. It is profitable for these powers on the one hand to articulate, and on the other hand to camouflage, their hegemony with such refined instruments as law. Law contributes to decreasing the political cost of rule or hegemony because it can secure more voluntary submission from those who are ruled, by providing an image of the legitimacy of the rule. Every ruler in human society and history has thus used law as an instrument of their governing power.

Yet it is also true that law is more favorable to those who are ruled than the naked power of the ruler. Some of the current norms of international law have been made by the supremacy of the majority of smaller nations over the power of the powerful states. The latter, however reluctant they may be, seek to comply with those norms. Why? Because they know well that the image of legality on the part of the powerful is important in world and domestic politics. Policies ignoring law generally encounter resistance and criticism both domestically and internationally, and are more costly than policies respecting law.

In this way, relations between law and power are complicated, multidimensional, and sometimes contradictory. Law controls power, but power violates law. Power produces law, and law grounds power. Law is an instrument of communication, mediating relations between powers. Law is an ideational instrument for socially constructed and shared knowledge, understandings, and interpretations of various kinds of people, even including those warring with each other. The notion of law has various aspects and dimensions; so does the notion of power. The status and function of law in international society is defined and characterized by its relative relations with power. We cannot see the figure of law by examining law alone. Nor can we understand power by examining power alone.

International society is a society where humans are engaged in mutual and common affairs mainly through the institution of states. Humans have utilized law in order to realize various values and interests in various societies. Based on this experience, humanity created law in international society, and has managed affairs in international society through the institution of law.[10] Like many other laws, international law primarily functions as norms of conduct among international actors, mainly states. International law has generally been perceived as weak norms of conduct, because it has often been violated in such conspicuous cases as massive human rights violations and military invasions of smaller nations by powerful states. In actuality, however, international law, including norms regulating daily global communication, trade, and transportation, has been well observed, or at least not violated, in most cases. The relations between international law and power are far more complex and nuanced than a simple dichotomy between observance and violation.

(3) Actual Scenes Where International Law Is Invoked

International law, perceived primarily as norms of conduct addressed to states, has been observed, violated, referred to, invoked, discussed, applied, and realized or implemented mainly by states. The states actually appear and act through state agents or organs such as governments, military forces, parliaments, and courts. How then, are these agents actually involved in international law? What are the concrete scenes or contexts where international law is observed, referred to, invoked, discussed, utilized, applied, implemented, violated, and vindicated?

When state organs such as parliaments, governments, or courts enact laws, carry out policies, or review cases judicially, they examine these acts from various perspectives. These examinations include the review of the legality of their acts in terms of domestic law, including the constitutionality of the act. They also include the examination of whether these acts are in conformity with international law. For example, when a Japanese court reviews a certain act of government when the government is sued on account of a violation of gender equality, it will certainly examine the International Covenant on Civil and Political Rights as an important standard of the judgment. Likewise, when the US government seeks to protect US industry by temporarily prohibiting the import of some foreign product, it will no doubt examine relevant articles of the WTO Agreements.

As explained later, state organs generally choose to act in conformity with international law. However, in some cases, they choose to act contrary to international law. For example, when a state does not have sufficient financial and/or institutional infrastructure to implement its international obligations, the state is compelled to choose a course of action contrary to such international legal obligations. Likewise, when some provision of the constitution of a state requires its state organ to act contrary to a particular norm of international law, the state organ will most likely choose to act in accordance with the constitutional requirement, thus violating international law. Further, when a state organ considers that some vital interest of the state requires action contrary to international law, it will most likely choose to carry out such action.

When a state acts in a manner that is considered to be doubtful in terms of adherence to a certain norm of international law, the interpretation of the obligation that this norm imposes on the state becomes an object of controversy in various forms. For example, if the government of state A interprets some act of state B as violating a right of A under international law, it may protest B's action. If an individual X considers a certain act of the government of state B as violating his or her right protected by a human rights treaty to which state B is a party, X may sue state B in a court that has jurisdiction over the actions of state B.

In this case, the action of the government of state B becomes an object of scrutiny under international law. In the former case, diplomatic negotiation between state A and state B is one of the forums or arenas where the act of state B is examined. Other forums include organs of various international organizations such as the UN General Assembly, the UN Security Council, the UN Human Rights Council, and the ICJ. Here, the issue of international law can typically be seen from the traditional state-centric, that is, international, perspective.

The act of the government of state B also becomes an object of controversy for political parties, media institutions, and pressure groups or NGOs in state B itself. It further becomes an object of controversy for various international NGOs, third-party states, and global media institutions. Especially in the aforementioned latter case where the right of individuals is claimed to be violated by state B, the major forums or arenas are domestic legislatures, domestic courts, domestic and international media, and various international organizations, rather than inter-governmental negotiations or the ICJ.

As these examples suggest, actual scenes where international law comes to be discussed and disputed include various forums or processes. They are (1) diplomatic negotiations between conflicting states; (2) discussions, debates, and negotiations in international organizations; (3) adversarial processes between persons who claim their rights have been violated by the acts of a certain government of a state and the government that denies the claim; (4) discursive forums in local media of the state parties concerned; and (5) discursive forums in regional and global media such as CNN, the BBC, the *New York Times*, media organs of major world religions such as Catholic, Protestant, Muslim, and Buddhist organizations, as well as various media run by and covering diverse groups such as minorities, indigenous peoples, associations of influential corporations, and labor unions, which seek to cover any issues they regard as important.

In all these cases, the interpretation of a specific obligation imposed by an international legal norm becomes a crucial issue. Through these processes, international law either legitimizes or delegitimizes the acts of states as a consequence of legal judgment given by those various participants of the international legal process. International law functions as the norm of evaluation in the whole process, the result of which is that the state act in question is either legitimized or delegitimized, either globally, regionally, nationally, or locally.

In this way, international law is related to the actual behavior of states primarily as norms of conduct that enjoin states to take or refrain from taking a certain specific act. Based on this primordial function, international law evaluates the acts of states, and legitimizes or delegitimizes these acts. It is therefore natural that the first question people most often ask regarding international law is: "Can international law control the power of states? If so, in which fields, under what conditions, and to what extent?"

(4) Can International Law Control the Power of States?

A large number of experts have dealt with this subject.[11] Some experts have argued that states violate the most fundamental rule of international law, that is, the prohibition of the use of force in international relations, when they deem it necessary to do so. This being the case, they argue, international law essentially cannot control the power of states. Others have argued that this kind of argument is based on a limited number of conspicuous cases in which international law is manifestly violated by the naked power of the state. However, these experts assert, such an argument is impressionistic and states almost always observe almost all international legal rules. This can be demonstrated if one pays attention to the relationship between a large proportion of state behavior and international legal rules, including those covering international trade, communications, and transportation.

It is true that the acts arrived at by state organs usually *coincide with* international law. In many cases they do so unconsciously. The major task of state organs is to manage affairs that are needed to support the life of their people. The ordinary life of people all over the world would be impossible if states did not act in accordance with international law in such areas as global trade, communications, and transportation. Like domestic law, international law has become a part of our daily lives in the twenty-first century. State organs must usually act in accordance with international law in order to fulfill their duties as state organs. Law-abiding behavior, whether the law is domestic or international, is the rule rather than the exception for state organs.

Moreover, if a state government acts contrary to international law, it will usually be criticized by a number of actors. These criticisms are a consequence of the evaluative functions of international law as described above. The agents of these criticisms include: (1) the government of the state whose right or interest is violated by the illegal act of the state concerned; (2) a large number of states that have a general interest in the maintenance of the legal norm that is violated by the state concerned; (3) international organizations whose mandate includes maintenance and/or implementation of the norm concerned; (4) the national court whose mandate includes the guarantee of the legality of the actions of state organs; (5) opposition groups in the governing party or the opposition parties in the state concerned that are ready to criticize any failure of the government, including illegality under international law; (6) domestic pressure groups whose interest is protected by the norm concerned; (7) media institutions and NGOs that believe the norm concerned should be observed on normative and/or substantive grounds, and the like. These criticisms have a high cost for governments in political terms. They generally seek to avoid paying such a high cost.

In some cases, however, state organs act contrary to international law. I already provided these cases at p. 154. Still, state organs, which are fully aware of the disadvantages they would have to face, usually seek to avoid these disadvantages by trying to abide by the norm concerned as much as possible. Or, at least, they try to give the impression that they acted in accordance with international law. They seek to legitimize their actions by interpreting the norm in question to their advantage.

On the other hand, we must admit that it is difficult to *demonstrate empirically* that a state behaves in accordance with international law *because* international law prescribes it to do so. We may reasonably be able to assume that a state organ is aware of the rules of international law and regards compliance with it as a guiding principle in adopting a certain policy if the behavior of the state coincides or agrees with the rule of international law in many areas for a long period of time. However, even in such a case, it is difficult to demonstrate that the will to comply with the legal rule constitutes the *primary cause* of that state's behavior. Moreover, a large number of states do violate various kinds of international legal norms of human rights on a daily basis. Further, it cannot be denied that most governments will violate international law if they consider that the vital interests of their nation require them to do so.

Yet, the failure of international law to control the power of states in the aforementioned cases is not the failure of international law alone. The failure is a consequence of the malfunctioning of the entire system of the current global society. A critical decision, for example, of a certain government to resort to the use of force to settle an international conflict, in violation of a rule prohibiting the use of force in international law, may be a result of the combination of a number of factors such as: (1) a failure of diplomacy; (2) a heavy economic blow dealt to the people of the state concerned by the merciless global market; (3) frustrations held by domestic constituencies in terms of economic, financial and trade policies; (4) a sense of victimization and humiliation shared broadly by the population of the state concerned in regard to past wars, massacres, and massive-scale human rights violations; (5) a negative attitude held by major powers and influential mass media institutions toward the religion, beliefs, or value systems of the majority in the nation concerned, and various other factors.

International law, together with prudent diplomacy, wise economic and financial policies taken by major powers and financial international organizations, appropriate news reporting and criticisms by influential media institutions and NGOs, wise behavior with a sense of social responsibility by multinational corporations, and other relevant factors, can exert *some influence* on the decision making of governments. But on its own it cannot "prevent" a government from resorting to the use of force. When a government does so in violation of international law, this is indeed a failure of international law, which enjoins states to refrain from the use of force. But again, it is not only a failure of international law; it is a *failure of the entire global system,* which includes international law.

Moreover, even when states resort to force, international law still continues to function. Completely arbitrary use of violence disregarding any legal constraints invites desperate resistance from an enemy and can cause unbearable damage to the nation. Further, a war cannot last indefinitely. At some stage, belligerent parties must make peace. This requires them to make use of international law, which can provide a means of communication between belligerents (international law as a "common language") and practical instruments for a peaceful settlement.

As the above argument demonstrates, international law certainly controls the power of a state either directly or indirectly, and in various forms. The form and the degree of such control differ according to a number of factors and must be analyzed on an empirical basis. Solely arguing that international law can or cannot control the power of states is theoretically futile. A more qualified and nuanced argument must be sought. This task must be conducted in concrete fields such as human rights, environment, trade, and security.

2 DOES MIGHT MAKE RIGHT?

(1) Power in the Creation of International Law

The idea or perception of law and power that contrasts sharply with the prevalent notion that law controls power is the idea that power makes law. "Might makes right" is a typical expression of this idea. It is held by "realists" and is closely associated with the idea of law as a means of serving the interests of the powerful. It cannot be denied that this idea reflects certain realities between law and power in human society. But, in what sense and to what extent does this idea reflect the reality? Also, how and where can this relation between law and power be recognized in global society?

Some of the most conspicuous cases in which the relation is perceived as "power makes law" are where the power relations between two nations are asymmetrical, as reflected in the provisions of bilateral treaties between nations. Such examples are numerous; one of the most famous cases is the one of "unequal treaties" concluded between Western powers and Afro-Asian nations during the period of Western imperialism. Provisions granting Europeans consular jurisdiction in Afro-Asian nations are well known.

Bilateral investment treaties agreements (BITs) concluded mainly after the 1980s between developed countries and developing countries are more recent examples. After attaining independence from colonial rule, developing countries took a highly critical attitude toward the traditional norms of international law on foreign investment. They claimed that relations between enterprises engaged in exploiting natural resources and the countries where these activities are undertaken must be regulated by the sovereignty of recipient nations. From the 1960s to the early '80s, they succeeded in having the UN General Assembly adopt resolutions favorable to them by the power of majority in the General Assembly. The Resolution on the Permanent Sovereignty over Natural Resources of 1974 and the Resolution on the Charter of Economic Rights and Duties of States of 1974 are leading examples. They sought to change the rules and principles of international law regulating transnational investment by repeatedly adopting these resolutions and by menacing foreign investors through actions such as nationalization or expropriation of foreign assets.

After the 1980s, however, those aggressive policies of the developing countries suffered serious setbacks. Most of them could not respond to the merciless global market economy of the '80s and '90s. The aggressive policies represented by nationalization of foreign assets alienated foreign investors. Many developing countries suffered from the shortage of foreign investment and were forced to change their policies. They gradually came to conclude BITs, which were aggressively "proposed" by developed countries. These BITs include provisions which prescribe, among other things, (1) prohibition of local requirements, (2) compensation by market price in cases of expropriation, and (3) referral to international arbitration in case of disputes between the parties. These provisions basically reflect the demands of developed countries and their firms investing in the developing countries.[12]

As these examples demonstrate, bilateral treaties tend to directly reflect the power relations between contracting parties. In the case of multilateral treaties, this is not always the case. In addition to the power of individual states, the power of numbers—in other words, the power of the majority in the treaty-making process—plays an important role. There are a number of cases where smaller nations have succeeded in inserting provisions favorable to them by resorting to this power of the majority. The widening of the territorial sea and the creation of the huge area of the Exclusive Economic Zone in the UN Convention on the Law of the Sea of 1982 are leading examples. The principle of "common but differentiated responsibilities" in the UN Framework Convention on Climate Change of 1992[13] and the more specified norm that imposes a concrete obligation to reduce greenhouse gas only on developed countries and "countries with economies in transition" in the Kyoto Protocol of 1997[14] are further examples.

However, even in the conclusion of multilateral treaties, the substantive military, economic, and the "soft" power of a small number of the powerful states such as the US and Western European nations is at work. During treaty-making negotiations, they can menace smaller nations by alluding to the possibility of terminating their economic and technical aid, of taking economic and financial measures disadvantageous to them, or even of resorting to some military or paramilitary measures directed against some of them. These major powers also have far more equipped delegations in terms of knowledge and information, as well as the ability to disseminate their ideas in an effective manner. Global enterprises, media institutions, and NGOs are overwhelmingly West-centric, and can exert much influence on the process of multilateral treaty-making.

Therefore, in the case of multilateral treaties, the balance of power between the "power of the majority" held by weaker nations, that is, basically developing countries, and the combined "hard" and "soft" power held by a smaller number of the powerful nations produces the final outcome. The two International Covenants on Human Rights of 1966 and the UN Convention on the Law of the Sea of 1982 are leading examples. One can see in them some provisions that reflect the demands upheld by the power of major developed nations.[15] Some other provisions reflect the demands of smaller nations supported by their power in the form of the majority in the treaty-making process.[16]

(2) Primacy of Western Power in the Creation of "Customary" International Law[17]

According to the prevalent theory of international law, general international law, which is valid for every state in international society, exists only in the form of customary international law. However, as Robert Jennings wrote already in 1982, "most of the non-treaty international law of today is not custom at all, and never was."[18] This "customary" international law is very different from customary law in the general sense of the term. The latter generally signifies law that is recognized as law by most members of a society after long, repeated, and widespread practice among societal members. While some rules and principles of "customary" international law share this characteristic feature, most of the traditional "customary" norms of international law do not. Rather, the notion of "customary" international law was a product of power in two critical senses.

First, these "customary" norms were characterized as international law by a small number of Western Great Powers, based on the practice of these states. As Oscar Schachter frankly admitted, "[a]s a historical fact, the great body of customary international law was made by remarkably few States."[19] The norms characterized as "customary" were based on the limited practices and *opinio juris* of a small number of the Western Great Powers. The domestic laws, domestic court decisions, and diplomatic practices of smaller nations, especially those of today's developing countries, were hardly taken into consideration at all, although their population occupies the overwhelming majority of humanity.

Second, it is generally leading international lawyers of these Western powers who formulated domestic laws, domestic court decisions, diplomatic practices pursued by these Western powers, and arbitral awards between nations as "general" state practice and *opinio juris*. Theories and doctrines cited and referred to as authorities for strengthening their arguments were also those of a small number of Western European and North American lawyers. Few theories of non-Western international lawyers were cited or referred to. The intellectual/ideational power of the Western powers, whose major agents were their international lawyers, dominated the process of the creation and application of customary international law as general international law in international society.

When a large number of Afro-Asian nations attained independence and came to form a majority in international society after World War II, they severely criticized such power-based "customary" international law. Since then, the situation has changed to a certain extent. The tendency to identify customary international law *qua* general international law based on the judgments of the ICJ became more prevalent. The ICJ, on its part, became more inclined to rely on multilateral treaties and resolutions of the UN General Assembly as cognitive bases for identifying a certain norm as customary international law *qua* general international law. These tendencies, however, have been criticized by some positivist international lawyers as blurring the line between customary law and treaties. Reliance on UN General Assembly resolutions has also been criticized as disregarding state practice and/or as relying on non-legally-binding norms.

However, from the viewpoint of global legitimacy, identifying general international law by relying on multilateral treaties and UN General Assembly resolutions is far more legitimate than identifying general international law through a mystical process of traditional "customary" international lawmaking. In the latter case, participation in the lawmaking process was limited to an extremely small number of Western Great Powers. The fact that a large number of nations are parties to a multilateral treaty or that a resolution is adopted by consensus in the

UN General Assembly suggests that the requirement of representative and participatory legitimacy for global lawmaking is, prima facie, satisfied.[20]

As to the requirement of legitimacy with respect to democratic representation, however, some governments do not necessarily satisfy it. Therefore, it is not sufficient to end discussion by arguing that a treaty is ratified by a large number of state parties or that a UN General Assembly resolution is adopted by consensus. We need to see whether such a treaty or resolution actually represent the voices and aspiration of people on a global scale. That is why we need "transnational" perspectives and "trans-civilizational" perspectives to supplement and modify the international perspective.

When we see trans-boundary or global phenomena through an international perspective, we tend to pay attention only to inter-state or inter-governmental relations. However, in order to identify the voices of the global society in a more substantially legitimate manner, we must also pay attention to global public opinion as expressed through various media institutions and NGOs. These institutions and NGOs should include not only the dominant Western ones but also less conspicuous non-Western institutions and groups. These institutions and groups represent the views, voices, aspirations, frustrations, and even the desperations, of various religious groups, indigenous peoples, ethnic minorities, and other cultural or civilizational groups. The deficits of democratic representation and "multicivilizationality" often found in inter-governmental agreement or consensus can be rectified through these multicultural, multicivilizational, and multilayered perspectives.

As far as the legally binding nature of UN General Assembly resolutions is concerned, one may be able to respond to the criticism that UN resolutions lack legally binding force, and therefore cannot be a "source" of international law, in the following way.

According to the traditional theory and practice of "customary" international law, not all acts of a state should be construed as constituting "state practice." Only a limited number of the acts of a state which are characterized as constituting "state practice" and reflecting the *opinio juris* of the states concerned have been selected from numerous state acts. We should view a vote by the representative of a state in the UN General Assembly from the same perspective as described above.

Thus, we should construe that a certain limited number of instances of voting constitute "state practice" and reflect the *opinio juris* of the states concerned. It is a matter of course that not all UN General Assembly resolutions should be construed as "state practice" or as reflecting the *opinio juris*. Only a very limited number of provisions in a resolution that express the legal consciousness of the voting states can, and should, become cognitive bases through which one could identify "state practice" and *opinio juris*. Once this common feature is attained, we can, and should, recognize that the reliance on multilateral treaties and UN General Assembly resolutions is far more legitimate and reasonable for purposes of identifying norms of general international law, compared to reliance on the mystical process of traditional "customary" lawmaking.[21]

In this way, as far as the question of legitimacy is concerned, identifying general international law through multilateral treaties and UN General Assembly resolutions is far more legitimate than identifying general international law through the traditional theory of "customary" international law. On the other hand, norms of general international law created in the manner described above may not necessarily enjoy sufficient support from major powers. In such a case, their effectiveness may be doubted. For example, the United States is not a party to a number of multilateral treaties embodying the public values or interest of international society as a whole; examples include the UN Convention on the Law of the Sea, the Kyoto Protocol, and the ICC Statute. Although the United States ratified the ICCPR as late as 1992, it severely restricted its domestic effect by attaching reservations, understandings, and declarations to it. The United States has been explicitly refusing to ratify the ICESCR, one of the most important and universal of human rights treaties, as well as the Convention on the Rights of the Child. Under such circumstances, the effectiveness of some norms of these treaties may be seriously undermined in cases where the United States is involved in the implementation of these norms.

From the perspective of a fair, legitimate, and stable international order, as well as one that requires the responsibility of the leading state vis-à-vis this order, the US attitude just discussed must be severely criticized. Both the policymakers and citizens of the United States need to understand that such refusals to ratify important multilateral treaties, which should be taken as representing the common will, value, and interest of global society, both weakens the international order and hurts the prestige of the United States as a reliable, legitimate, and respected leader of international society. Self-righteousness is the worst enemy of legitimate and stable international order. We should expect that the power of enlightened public opinion led by concerned experts journalists, media institution and NGOs and encouraged by the transnational action sharing the concern will gradually change the attitude of the United States as a whole.

(3) Law and the Power of (and in) the United Nations

The United Nations is the organization that enjoys the highest degree of legitimacy in international society. This is based on the fact that it is an official organization whose authority, mandate, and legitimacy are explicitly recognized by almost all nations, including the major powers. It has been managed on the basis of such recognition and has often acted in the name of the international community for more than sixty years. National governments, firms, media institutions, and NGOs usually recognize or acquiesce in such UN authority and deem its actions as the most legitimate in global society. At least in relative terms, the perception and image of the United Nations as the most legitimate organization representing the common values and interests of global society is one that is most widely shared by, and deeply rooted in, the peoples of the world. Herein lies the power of the United Nations.[22]

The General Assembly, composed of all member states, enjoys the highest representative legitimacy among all organs of the United Nations. Among the numerous resolutions it adopts, some have significant political meaning in global society. However, this organ is weak as an independent agent acting in a powerful, speedy, and effective manner. Because the General Assembly is composed of some 200 member states, the "power of the majority" applies in the adopting of resolutions. Yet for the resolutions to be effective in important political and economic areas, the power of the majority is not enough. It needs explicit agreement or at least acquiescence on the part of major powers, especially that of the United States. Lack of such agreement or acquiescence can result in a resolution that may appear normatively appealing but substantially hardly effective. The Charter of the Rights and Duties of the States, adopted in 1974 with strong resistance from major Western powers (especially the United States), is such an example.

Resolutions adopted in the Security Council include decisions with legally binding force. Resolutions adopted under Chapter VII, which "decide" certain enforcement measures, are typical examples. The provisions of such decisions, particularly those addressed toward states in general or all member states of the United Nations, can be an important cognitive basis for identifying norms of (general) international law. Moreover, because the resolutions of the Security Council are adopted with the agreement of permanent members, they enjoy a high degree of effectiveness in their implementation. If the power of the General Assembly lies in its representative and democratic legitimacy, the power of the Security Council lies in its effectiveness.

On the other hand, whether the Security Council behaves in accordance with international law constitutes an important problem in the judgment of the legitimacy of its behavior. The Security Council is to take measures from the perspective of whether an act of a state breaches or threatens "international peace and security" (Article 39 of the UN Charter). Whether the act in question is legal or not under international law does not matter to the Security Council when it identifies breaches or threats of the "international peace and security" and takes concrete measures. Further, measures taken by the Security Council to maintain or restore international peace and security might not be in accord with some international legal norms. In such cases, the relation between the power of the Security Council and the norms of international law becomes an issue of controversy. This raises the problem of whether such an act of the Security Council should be reviewed and, if found illegal, be rectified or annulled by other organs of the United Nations. In more concrete terms, the question is raised of whether the ICJ, the main judicial organ of the United Nations, is or should be entitled to review the legality of the acts of the Security Council.

Some international lawyers claim that the ICJ should have the power to review the legality of Security Council actions. However, if the ICJ actually uses such power and judges some acts of the Security Council as illegal, this would raise the serious problem of whether such a judgment should, and can, be implemented.

In the *Lockerbie* case of 1992, the ICJ, knowing too well of the disastrous consequences had it judged the resolution taken by the Security Council as illegal under international law, evaded confronting this difficult problem. It did not dare to judge the legality of the measures taken by the Security Council, even though their legality was highly dubious.

The Security Council is an organ based on the UN Charter. The charter is a multilateral treaty with universal validity, and occupies an almost constitutional status in international society. As such, one could reasonably assume that the Security Council has an inherent obligation to act in accordance with international law. Further, the Security Council knows well that the legality of its action will enhance its legitimacy and make it easier to obtain voluntary cooperation from member states in implementing the resolutions it adopts. It thus generally seeks to base its resolutions on international law in order to secure their legitimacy so that they will be accepted and implemented as voluntarily as possible by the UN members.

The Security Council thus takes legally doubtful measures only in exceptional cases. In most cases, it acts in accordance with international law and in such a way as to implement norms of international law. Further, although the competence to interpret international law is subject to the review of international courts such as the ICJ, cases where the rules or principles of international law are actually judged by the judiciary are exceptional. In most cases, interpretations of the norms of international law by competent international organs such as the UN Security Council, the UN General Assembly, and the UN Human Right Council are critical, having higher legitimacy and authority than those taken by individual states. In particular, Security Council resolutions, which are characterized as legally binding upon member states, can be enforced by such interpretations.

3 POWER THAT UPHOLDS AND REALIZES LAW

(1) Law as Compulsory Norms: Law as Adjudicative Norms and Power to Realize Law

Law is generally perceived to be a coercive norm. People share the perception that law can and should be coerced by authoritative power against the will of lawbreakers. This feature, many people would assume, differentiates law from other norms such as religious or ethical ones. This shared perception, together with other perceptions of law including law as representing justice, ultimately supports the effectiveness or efficacy of law. In the case of domestic law, this perception is institutionalized in the state enforcement mechanism of law. Law is thus accompanied by power as its enforcer. However, not all kinds of power as a whole can be a companion of law. Only such power as is perceived and recognized as legitimate by the addressee can be such a companion. If the power sustaining and realizing law is perceived as illegitimate, the law itself is regarded as illegitimate and resisted by the addressee.

International law, like any other law, is subject to various interpretations. The content of the norm is to be realized with a specific interpretation. Reflecting the decentralized structure of international law, the power and competence to interpret international law primarily rests with the government of each sovereign state. If an interpretation of a norm by a certain government is disputed by some other participants in international law, such as other governments or agents of international organizations, NGOs, or firms, this interpretation may be scrutinized in various forums or processes: diplomatic negotiations between the governments of the states concerned, various forums of international organizations such as the UN General Assembly or the Security Council, domestic or international courts, and the like. If conflicting parties reach an agreement as to the interpretation of the norm, there should be no problem. But, if they cannot reach agreement, how can international law as a compulsory norm be realized?

A state claiming that its right is violated by another state can, under international law, resort to countermeasures. However, the countermeasures of a state can generally be effective only against a less powerful state or at best a state with similar power. Although reciprocity has been regarded as a basic principle for securing the implementation of international law, reciprocity alone cannot secure international legal norms. "Just war" was once characterized as an enforcement measure under European international law. This just war was not merely a theory; European nations actually resorted to war for securing their rights and interests under international law, and justified their acts by the just war doctrine.[23] However, it is difficult to accept the just war doctrine—whose agents were individual states or even private persons[24]—under current international law, which generally prohibits the use of force by states and other subjects of international law.

When law is generally referred to as compulsory norms, the reference is made on the assumption that law can be coerced by the monopoly of the power of the state and the enforceability of the judgment of the court. If a party disagrees with a conflicting party in the interpretation or application of a certain legal norm, it can sue the other party without the latter's consent. If it wins in court, it can forcefully realize its right through the enforcement mechanism of the judiciary. International law lacks such institutionalized mechanisms. The ICJ does not have compulsory jurisdiction. A state cannot sue another state without the latter's consent. Moreover, the ICJ lacks an institutionalized mechanism for enforcing of its judgments. There have been a number of cases in which the losing party did not comply with the judgment of the ICJ. The Iranian hostage case of 1980 and the Nicaragua case of 1986 are leading examples.

Therefore, in international law, it is difficult to assume the enforceability of law by the judiciary mechanism. Although international law sometimes functions as adjudicative norms and is applied by international courts and arbitral tribunals, it lacks enforceability through adjudication. This marks a sharp contrast with domestic law, especially that of developed countries, where one can assume such enforceability. Here, even when people seek to settle their conflicts by non-judicial means such as negotiations, they behave under the "shadow of the court." A party whose factual evidence and legal claim is more solid can send a message to the other party to the effect that "you had better give in to the condition I claim in this negotiation. Otherwise, I will sue you and you will lose the case in the court." However, in international society, parties generally cannot resort to such tactics due to the lack of compulsory jurisdiction and enforceability mechanisms of the ICJ and other international courts.[25] We must locate the enforceability of international law elsewhere than in the mechanism of enforcement through adjudication.

(2) Collective Security, Unilateralism, and the Balance of Power in International Law

A collective security system may be characterized as an alternative to such a mechanism. It certainly has some features to be characterized as an enforcement mechanism of international law. Especially in the field of restraining the use of force by states, the UN enforcement actions under Chapter VII generally realize the universal norm of the prohibition of the use of force by states. The very existence of such a system plays a preventive role with respect to inter-state war and contributes to sustaining and guaranteeing the norm on the prohibition of the use of force.

From a strictly juridical perspective, however, there are problems with characterizing the collective security system as the enforcement mechanism of international law. First, it covers only the field of international peace and security—it does not cover all areas of international law. Further, even in this limited field, the collective security system cannot simplistically be characterized as an institutionalized enforcement mechanism of international law. Technically speaking, a collective security arrangement does not necessarily respond to violations of international law. The Security Council is to take measures when a state breaches or threatens "international peace and security." There may be a number of cases where the Security Council does not determine a certain act of a state to be a threat to international peace and security, although this act constitutes a violation of international law.

The UN collective security system is certainly an important mechanism for regulating and controlling armed conflicts and for sustaining and realizing the international legal norm of the prohibition of the use of force. Acts that are determined by the Security Council to be a threat to or breach of peace usually overlap with violations of international law on the prohibition of the use of force. Thus it is a valuable institution that is backed by its global legitimacy and the substantive power of the permanent members of the UN Security Council. The UN collective security system must definitely be improved and strengthened. Yet, this is not enough. The power and conditions that sustain and realize international law must be found not only in the collective security system, but also elsewhere.

Some regard the power of the United States as the power to sustain and realize international law. A kind of universalistic idealism, deeply rooted in the spirit of the people of the United States, supports such an understanding of international law. The United States has enacted a number of domestic laws, which, according to their interpretation, implement or realize norms of international law. We can see many such examples in the field of trade, antitrust, environment, and human rights, among others.

However, to characterize a unilateral interpretation and realization of international law as ultimately authoritative and legitimate means the negation of the very concept of international law. International law is a common code of conduct of all states in international society. Any enforcement measures taken by a single state or a group of states can be characterized as a realization of international law *only when such measures are endorsed, or at least acquiesced to, by the overwhelming majority of states*. If such measures are actually enforced without this endorsement or acquiescence, such "enforcement" action should be characterized as the use of naked power under the disguise of law enforcement. Self-righteousness, not justice, is at work.

Some international lawyers have argued that a balance of power is a prerequisite for the existence or well functioning of international law. Lassa Oppenheim is one such international lawyer.[26] It is often said that nineteenth-century Europe was a stable period of classical international law, when European diplomacy was carried out under a balance of power. International law functioned within this framework of diplomacy based on the balance of power. On the other hand, the fact that a number of international legal norms have been violated by the United States, a contemporary version of an empire,[27] also seems to suggest the need for a balance of power for international law to be realized in a legitimate manner.

However, the balance of power is not enough for international law to be realized in a fair and egalitarian manner. Under the balance of power between the Great Powers in nineteenth-century Europe, the rights and interests of smaller nations were often violated for the sake of the common interests of these European Great Powers. When a certain balance of power existed between the United States and the Soviet Union during the Cold War period, the members of the international society acquiesced in the violation of the rights and interests of smaller nations within the spheres of influence of the two superpowers in order to avoid total war between them. The Soviet interventions in the Hungarian Rising of 1956 and in the Prague Spring of 1968, as well as the repeated US military interventions in the Caribbean as well as Central American nations such as Nicaragua and Panama are leading examples.

As described above, neither the international judiciary, counter-measures, collective security, nor the balance of power alone supports and secures the realization of international law. On the other hand, it cannot be denied that states generally abide by international legal norms and realize them in almost all cases. Violations of international law, especially those involving the use of force, are certainly conspicuous, but they are exceptions rather than a rule. This general compliance with international law by states is not necessarily the result of the consideration by states of the possibility of sanctions or counter-measures against their illegal behavior taken by other states or international organizations.

"Horizontal sanctions," expressed in terms of reciprocity, counter-measures, reprisals, and other negative sanctions between states are generally assumed by international lawyers as a major mechanism to uphold international norms. However, they constitute only a part of the entire mechanism to uphold and realize international law.

As suggested earlier,[28] the fact that there exist a number of domestic actors—such as opposition parties, influential media institutions, courts, and NGOs, as well as various other actors—carefully monitoring the international legality of their government's actions, has an important meaning in terms of securing the lawful behavior of state organs. Also, the fact that the psychological framework unconsciously inviting lawful behavior is established in the minds of those who are in charge of decision making involving international law is of significant importance. In order to fully understand these mechanisms, we must also study the power of international law from the perspective of ideational or intellectual power.

II Ideational Power and International Law

1 INTERNATIONAL LAW AS SEEN FROM THE PERSPECTIVE OF IDEATIONAL POWER

(1) The Power of Ideas

When people consider the problem of law and power in global society, they tend to think of them in opposing or mutually contrasting terms. They tend to consider law as a normative idea, and power as military and economic power. "Realists" tend to emphasize the significance of military (and at most economic) power in the international arena, disregarding other types of power. They regard law as being irrelevant in global affairs, or merely as a tool of power, at most. This view is more or less accepted by the general public.

However, power is not limited to military and economic power. When we refer to the power of a small number of Western nations in the creation of international law, this power is not limited to their military and economic prowess. It also includes the intellectual and informational capability that can set the agenda in international conferences and draft the articles of treaties or resolutions. It also includes the capability to disseminate such draft articles over other alternatives, and the capability to influence and persuade international public opinion by means of influential international lawyers and various kinds of media, including influential law journals, TV programs, and newspapers.

So-called *opinio juris* in the creation of international law is basically a conscious or unconscious social construct that was shared, formulated, and disseminated by political, legal, military and intellectual leaders in the leading Western nations. It became prevalent through a combination of various factors: (1) the publication of books by major Western publishers such as Oxford University Press and of articles in leading law journals such as the *American Journal of International*

Law; (2) the predominant status of English and French languages in international society; (3) the strength of Western higher education and research institutions such as Harvard or Cambridge University; and (4) the widely shared high reputation of court decisions in Western nations, and the like.

Law is certainly a normative idea. It has an aspect of expressing normative goals or ideals in human endeavors. However, an idea by itself constitutes power. It appeals to the mind of people and invites people to act in a certain direction. Law as a normative idea thus has a power to induce people to realize the values and interests that law prescribes. The power of the ideas of human rights and democracy in domestic and international political arenas are typical examples. Both ideas have exerted a strong influence in decreasing the normative power of the nonintervention principle in international law. They have compelled a number of states to change their policies in the fields on human rights and democracy.

However, in order for law as an idea to become a power, it also needs a power outside of itself that can disseminate the idea of the law and help it become widely shared and accepted. Even the best idea cannot be a power if it lacks the linguistic, informational, educational, and economic means to be disseminated and widely shared. If one is a famous columnist for the *New York Times*, one has a good chance to have one's idea become widely known. It can be globally shared and finally realized. But if one is an unknown student of international law in a small country, one's idea will hardly be globally known even if it is a better idea for humanity than the one advocated by the columnist. It will virtually have no chance to be realized on a global scale. In the process of the formation of ideas, notions, and norms, certain kinds of power are at work in an implicit and unconscious manner. Even the most valuable normative idea cannot be realized if it is not disseminated, widely known, and shared by a large number of people who, as a whole, could influence global decision making.

In this way, when we consider the problem of international law from the viewpoint of ideational power, we have to consider the problem of how the idea can be disseminated, shared, and realized on a global scale as an ideational power. Here, however, we should be aware that today's global structures of information are overwhelmingly West-centric. We can watch the television programming of CNN and the BBC almost everywhere, but few view programs by Japanese, Brazilian, Tanzanian, Indian, or other TV stations except in those respective countries. The world that global decision makers, influential opinion leaders, and even ordinary citizens see today is the world that is more or less construed and constructed by CNN, the BBC, Google, the *Wall Street Journal* and the *New York Times*.

(2) So-called "Realism" in International Relations Theory and the Reality of Global Legalism

The widely perceived juxtaposition of law as norm and power as reality tends to invite people to question the relevance of international law. Many international relations experts and to a certain extent ordinary citizens have tended to believe that international law is unrealistic or irrelevant. This prevalent image or perception seems to originate in various factors, among which the following are important.

(i) During the interwar period, Edward Hallet Carr severely criticized Hersh Lauterpacht as utopian.[29] Since then, except for the English School, international relations experts have tended to ignore the raison d'être of international law. Further, many international relations scholars—especially a great number of those in the United States—ignore the importance of the history of international society, which has been characterized by legalism. This has strengthened the tendency among international relations experts to be ignorant of international law.

(ii) During the post-war period, "realism" was predominant in the United States. Such prominent figures as Hans Morgenthau, George Kennan, and Kenneth Waltz exerted great influence on the awareness of Americans in regard to international and global affairs, including both experts and ordinary citizens. These scholars all emphasized the importance of substantive or "hard" power, represented by military power, and were critical of legalism in international affairs. Their view has been globally shared, ironically, due to the predominant "soft power"—that is to say, the ideational rather than substantive or "hard" power—of the United States in the field of international affairs.

(iii) As referred to earlier,[30] people generally pay attention only to conspicuous cases of the flagrant violation of significant norms of international law. The violation of the principle of the prohibition of the use of force in international law is a typical example. Most people, even experts on international affairs, do not know that numerous norms of international law are at work and one's life itself is possible due to this constant work of international law. Like the air, which is essential for human life but usually goes unnoticed, international law is not generally noticed. Hence the prevalent image of international law as irrelevant.

(iv) Those who hold international law to be irrelevant regard it only as a regulative norm whose function is to control power. They ignore the fact that international law has many other functions, such as the communicative and constructive, the embodying of the shared understanding of international society, and the justificatory and legitimating. Because they concentrate on the regulatory power of international law, once one of its norms is not obeyed in a conspicuous manner they argue that international law is not relevant in international society.

A brief response to these four critical points is in order. I address each of them below.

First, it is true that Lauterpacht was severely criticized by Carr, and that he could not rebut Carr.[31] And this "utopian" Lauterpacht has been vaguely understood as the representative of international lawyers. The image of international law has also been associated with the notion of law as adjudicative norms to be applied and enforced by judicial mechanisms. This image has been particularly strong in countries with an Anglo-American legal system, where the idea of law is closely associated with the judiciary.[32] The fact that the United States and the United Kingdom have been most influential in the field of international law and international relations has contributed to the prevalence of the negative image of international law as irrelevant or unrealistic in international society.

However, Lauterpacht was not representative of international lawyers during the interwar period. In particular, his theory of settling all disputes through the international judiciary was severely criticized not only by Carr, but by numerous other international lawyers as well. Criticizing Lauterpacht's theory regarding international law only as adjudicative norms as unrealistic and irrelevant does not mean that international law or international lawyers in general are unrealistic or irrelevant. International law fulfils its societal functions not only as adjudicative norms to be applied and enforced by the judiciary; it carries out a number of other functions which, though not necessarily adjudicative, are nevertheless socially important as demonstrated below. Carr himself, who severely criticized Lauterpacht, fully appreciated the raison d'être of international law.

Second, it is also true that Hans Morgenthau recognized only a minor role for international law and Waltz ignored international law. George Kennan's criticism toward the moralistic and legalistic approach in US diplomacy was certainly most successful and well received. However, their criticism or denial of international law did not erase all features of legalism in international affairs. Legalism has been, and still is, predominant in European and American societies as well as in international society.

The international system tends to reflect predominant ideas and institutions of the major powers in the system.[33] Today's international system is a product of the expansion of Europe on a global scale during the modern period and the subsequent hegemony of the United States in the twentieth century. Therefore, today's international system is strongly characterized and influenced by the ideas and institutions of leading European nations and the United States. The European nations have shared and maintained a highly legalistic culture for a long period of time. The United States inherited this legalistic culture and has even strengthened it. These facts contributed to the imprinting of highly legalistic features on the modern international system. International law, as an important component of this system, thus has played, and is playing, a number of important societal functions in international society. To criticize the excessive legalistic approach, once prevalent in US diplomacy, is one thing. To deny the raison d'être and the reality of law in international society is quite another. Even if the former is correct, the latter assertion is clearly mistaken.

Third, as long as state organs act in conformity with international law, no problem relating to international law will occur. As suggested earlier,[34] this is the normality of international law in that the content of international legal norms is realized on a daily basis. State agents generally act in accordance with frameworks of both domestic and international law when they conduct affairs of states and negotiate with agents of other states. They make full use of domestic and international law as an instrument for realizing the values and interests they pursue. They also use law to settle various problems arising from these political and administrative processes. International law is also constantly referred to and utilized as a tool of communication by non-state actors such as NGOs, private companies, media institutions, ethnic minorities, indigenous peoples, religious groups, and other participants in global political, economic, and societal processes. It is also used as normative ideas to ground their claims and as means to realize their interests and values.

International law is not just letters on paper or merely ideas existing in theoreticians' or lawyers' minds. It is a normative idea which has actually been referred to, utilized, invoked, and applied by state agents as well as non-state actors all over the world for more than a century. It is an essential element of the sovereign states system, which has constituted, and still constitutes, the most fundamental principle of today's world. During the modern period, international law has played various important societal functions in legitimating and justifying state behaviors, providing a common language for inter-state negotiations, the settlements of disputes, and the like. When we consider the status and role of international law in global society, we must consider these actual roles and functions that international law has played and is playing in various contexts.

Fourth, as already suggested above, the function of international law is not limited to regulating or controlling the behavior of states as norms of conduct. Even those "realists" who regard international law as unrealistic and irrelevant admit that international law functions as an ideology to justify power. In fact, national governments, including the US government, often utilize notions of international law either to justify acts of their own or to criticize or blame acts of other hostile states. In this sense, international law is an important tool for realizing the national interest of any country. This aspect of international law was amply demonstrated in section I.2 above.

Moreover, when international law justifies the power of a certain state or group, it does not play its role merely as a tool of power. In justifying a certain act of a state, the government of the state must utilize international law in such a way as to persuade those who have different views on international law and/or who doubt the legality or legitimacy of the act. Further, the government must satisfy the requirement of consistency in its act because it bases its argument on law. In this way, the argument in international law to which a government resorts must satisfy various requirements of law. If the government takes an arbitrary interpretation of a rule or a double standard in justifying its act, international law as a justificatory tool will lose its persuasive power. It cannot play its role to legitimize power. In this way, international law qualifies, or poses a certain restriction on, the power of a state, precisely because it is utilized as a tool to justify acts of a state.

I have demonstrated elsewhere[35] that international law has played, is playing, and will continue to play a number of societal functions in international and domestic societies. These are its binding, communicative, value-declaratory, and justifying and legitimating functions. Here I will deal with another important function of international law, that is, the constructive or constitutive function, on which I have not deliberated to date. By expanding the research area of the functions of international law, I hope this chapter can contribute to analyzing and evaluating the status and role of international law in relation to power in a slightly more nuanced and elaborate manner.[36]

(3) The Constructive Function of International Law

The Power of International Law to Construct Social Realities

International law, at its birth and when it regulated international relations among European nations between the seventeenth to the nineteenth centuries, was merely one among many regional normative systems that existed in East Asia, South Asia, Central Asia, and other regions.[37] However, with the expansion of European dominance, hegemony, and influence over other parts of the world, it became a global normative system. Throughout the twentieth century, people all over the world regarded international law as the law of international society, which covers the entire globe. Humanity carried out a huge number of tasks in the fields of security, trade, health, transportation, and others, and managed a number of affairs on the shared assumption that international law is the law of global international society. Because of these accumulated facts—the ideas and behavior of humanity lasting over a century—all based on this assumption, international law has continued to define and influence thoughts and behavior among people all over the world. It is still defining and influencing us today.

Humans, whether they are members of private companies or governments, either in business or as citizens, are involved in trade, human rights, the global environment, and other international, transnational, or trans-civilizational matters. In such cases, they consciously, or more often than not unconsciously, adopt concepts or frameworks of international law such as territorial sovereignty, self-defense, and nationality. Seen from the perspective of international law, it enters the mind of these people without necessarily being recognized, and defines or influences their thoughts. Through such an unconscious process of influence, it induces the thoughts and behavior of people to move in particular directions. In this way, international law helps to construct and reconstruct, through such thoughts and behavior, certain social realities of the world, including the identity, consciousness, understanding, interpretation, and behavior of relevant actors in global society.

Based on these socially constructive functions, international law helps people, including those in conflict with each other, to mutually understand the identity of various actors, to communicate with each other in a common language, and to share common understandings in and of the global society. Through these functions, social institutions of mutual understanding which articulate and realize common values on a global scale are constructed and reconstructed on a daily basis. Together with diplomacy, the market economy, global networks of media institutions and NGOs, and the like, international law is one of the many institutions in global society managing a huge number of matters that are necessary for nations and other international, transnational, or trans-civilizational actors to coexist and cooperate with each other.

When these institutions are functioning well and life goes on in a routine manner, the ideas and institutions of international law, such as norms regulating trade activities or those guaranteeing the sovereignty of nations, remain unnoticed. When things go wrong, however, the existence of international law becomes more conspicuous. Together with other institutions such as diplomacy, mediation, and conciliation, international law functions to settle such problems as the use of force, massive violations of human rights, trade wars, and the like. This is one of the reasons why international law tends to be perceived as a means of settling disputes rather than as ideas tacitly construing and constructing realities.

When these problems do occur, not only those who are in charge of settling them but also certain ordinary citizens either consciously or unconsciously perceive these problems as "problems." When they do so, they consciously or unconsciously resort to a number of concepts and frameworks of international law, and understand these affairs through such concepts and frameworks. Here, international law contributes not only to settling conflicts by providing dispute-settlement mechanisms like international arbitration and judicial settlements. Even if the problem is not actually solved in accordance with international law, *it can help people to identify what the problem is* and also *to understand how it should have been, and how it should be solved, if ever this problem is to be solved in a normatively legitimate and authoritative manner by states*. This will help people to consider further the nature of the problem and the *possibility, desirability, and limits of its settlement either by legal, political, administrative, economic, or some other means.*

The Power to Make Ideas of International Law Become Known, Disseminated and Shared

On the other hand, various kinds of ideational power are at work in constructing, construing, and disseminating the idea of international law itself. Major notions and cognitive frameworks of international law—such as territories, nationality, sovereignty, human rights, self-defense—that people use today are those that have been constructed and construed by major Western, male, international lawyers represented by Lassa Oppenheim. Very few non-Western or female lawyers have played a significant role in constructing and construing major concepts and frameworks of international law.

It is doubtful, however, whether these predominant concepts or frameworks can claim global legitimacy if they have been constructed and construed by such a small circle of people. They may have certain legitimacy—technical or professional—as products of highly esteemed experts. However, even in terms of expertise, these experts had insufficient knowledge of law, politics, economy, culture, history, and other aspects of non-Western civilizations, which should have a bearing on international law. In terms of representative legitimacy, most traditional concepts of international law lack global legitimacy in that they were not created and disseminated in a manner representing humanity as a whole. More than 80% of the world population was not represented in the process where predominant notions and frameworks of international law were created and formulated. Rather, they became predominant through the power of Western states.

Nor can they represent realities of power constellation in the twenty-first-century world. Although Western nations have been predominant in their economic, military, informational, and cultural power since the nineteenth century, it is unlikely that they can maintain such a preponderant status in the twenty-first-century world. These West-centric notions and frameworks do not respond to the realities of the multipolar and multicivilizational world that is emerging in the twenty-first century. Such a discrepancy between the actual power constellation and the predominant cognitive framework is dangerous, because the discrepancy will easily lead to a misunderstanding of problems between major powers. In order to satisfy the requirements for representative global legitimacy and relevance to global power constellation of the twenty-first century, we must overcome excessive West-centrism in the conception of international law and global society.

The ideas, concepts, and perceptions of human rights in international law and in global discourse are leading examples. They have generally been created, claimed, and formulated by male Western lawyers, and have been disseminated by Western publishers, universities, and media institutions. When people think of human rights, they tend to associate them with "freedom from torture" or "freedom of expression," and other liberties or civil rights. They seldom associate with human rights the "freedom from hunger" or the "freedom to enjoy health," and other socio-economic rights. This fact suggests the predominance of a liberty-centric and West-centric cognitive framework on issues of human rights in general.[38]

The Vienna Declaration of 1993 adopted a more comprehensive notion of human rights by providing that "[a]ll human rights are universal, indivisible and interdependent and interrelated. The international community must treat human rights globally in a fair and equal manner, on the same footing, and with the same emphasis."[39] However, because of the West-centric dominance over the human rights discourse on a global scale, the liberty-centric notion of human rights is still predominant. International lawyers, other experts, government officials, journalists, and activists refer far more to the Universal Declaration of Human Rights, which was adopted in 1948 and reflects the traditional liberty-centric notion of human rights, than to the Vienna Declaration.

Rectifying the excessively liberty-centric notion of human rights, which has been and still remains globally predominant, is an important theoretical and practical task for international lawyers, human rights experts, and other intellectuals. Disseminating the comprehensive notion of human rights, which is exemplified in the Vienna Declaration, expresses the most globally legitimate notion of human rights, and yet is not sufficiently known by ordinary citizens, is another important task for those experts. Their responsibility lies not only in teaching and research in universities or research institutions. It also lies in disseminating correct ideas by various media such as newspapers, TVs, journals, and the internet, to ordinary citizens, whose normative consciousness constitutes the basis of a sound international legal order.

2 IN PURSUIT OF GLOBALLY LEGITIMATE PERSPECTIVES IN GLOBAL DISCURSIVE SPACE

(1) Problematization of West-centrism in International Law

Various Critiques of West-centrism and their Problems

As to the various problems of the West-centrism in international law and the attempts to overcome such problems, I have already dealt with them elsewhere. One major area of research has been the history of international law. In "Eurocentrism in the History of International Law,"[40] I analyzed the theory of Francisco de Vitoria and its function to justify Spanish colonization of America as a prototype of the theory and function of European international law. In "When Was the Law of International Society Born,"[41] I tried to re-construe and reconstruct the history of international law by comparing three regional normative systems—Eurocentric, Islamo-centric and Sino-centric ones—and by analyzing the process in which the European system overwhelmed other competing systems.

The other field is human rights. In a number of writings, I have sought to ground the universal validity of human rights by introducing a trans-civilizational ("inter-civilizational" in the earlier writings) perspective in addition to international and transnational perspectives, which tend to be West-centric.[42] The field of human rights is probably the richest field of international law where similar effort have been made. The cross-cultural perspectives on human rights advocated by Abdullahi Ahmed An-Na'im are leading examples.[43] Rather than reiterating these earlier arguments, I will briefly sketch the history of overcoming West-centrism in international law based on my earlier studies and my own experiences and observations.

There is already a long history of voices dissenting against West-centrism in the wider sense of the term. In the nineteenth century, with the attainment of independence by the Latin American nations, a number of their governments along with international lawyers and intellectuals began criticizing Euro-centric or North Atlantic-centric features of international law. National liberation movements by Afro-Asians struggling against the West-centric international order were active from the nineteenth to the twentieth century. In the early twentieth century, numerous political and intellectual leaders of Japan, the only non-Western Great Power at the time, were critical of Anglo-America-centric features of international order.

However, these dissenting voices could not bring about concrete changes in the international legal order. Claims by Latin American international lawyers were, on the whole, not accepted by Western powers and mainstream international lawyers of the time. Although some of their claims were accepted as special customary international law, they were valid only to Latin American nations, thus lacking universal validity. The national liberation movements were brutally suppressed by the Western powers (and Japan) up to the middle of the twentieth century. The Japanese proposal to insert a racial equality clause in the League of Nations Covenant was rejected at the Versailles Conference of 1919.

It was during the period of decolonization from the 1960s to the early 1980s that the criticism of West-centric features of international law was most energetically raised. Actual claims and moves for revising such features were actively developed mainly in the UN General Assembly but in other forums as well. Political and intellectual leaders of the newly independent nations of Asia and Africa severely criticized existing rules and principles of international law as a tool of Western colonialism and imperialism. They sought to establish the New International Economic Order and New International Information Order, which should be fairer and more equitable.

These movements brought about certain concrete notions and institutions. However, these movements were closely associated with the state policies of developing countries. Heavily influenced by Marxist-oriented, state-planned economy, they took radical economic policies and based them on the notion of sovereignty over natural resources. With the malfunctioning and decline of such radical economic policies after the mid-1980s, the theoretical movements to overcome the West-centric nature of international law claimed mainly by Third World international lawyers gradually lost their power and influence. This decline is not only due to the decline of the substantive power of the developing countries; their claims had theoretical problems as well.

The first problem was that the arguments made by Third World intellectuals were mainly concerned with economic aspects of humanity. As far as economic conditions are concerned, however, it became more and more difficult to talk about the Third World as a single group.[44] In the multinational treaty-making process, such as that of the UN Convention on Climate Change and multilateral negotiations involving economic interests of various governments, producers, and consumers, like those taking place at WTO conferences, the Third World nations no longer acted as a single group.[45] More fundamentally, although many problems have their causes in economic poverty and inequality, humans are not driven solely by economic factors.

Terrorism is a good example. Terrorism may have some causal relations to poverty or economic inequality, but it does not originate from these alone. It has political, social, religious, cultural, and historical dimensions. The extremist interpretation of an influential religion, coupled with political resentment associated with ethnic tensions or conflicts, may produce terrorism. Also the memory of past wars and massacres of an ethnic group committed by other ethnic groups may be a cause of terrorism. Thus, we need a comprehensive perspective that pays attention not only to economic factors and dimensions, but also to political, social, cultural, religious, and historical ones.

The second problem was that, although Third World intellectuals were critical of existing international law for being unfairly favorable to Western nations, they tended to follow the prevalent cognitive framework of international law. Many of these international lawyers claimed that Asian and African nations had contributed to the development of international law, or that international law had also existed in Asia or in Africa. These claims, like those that democracy or human rights had existed in Asia or in Africa, were based on the criticism of the West-centric attitude of monopolizing anything good as a creation of Europe or North America. This criticism was understandable given the hidden West-centric tendency in any discourse dealing with historical products that are valuable for humanity. However, from a theoretical perspective, such claims as those arguing for the existence of democracy, human rights, or international law in Asia or in Africa tend to ignore the historicity of these ideas and institutions, and are highly questionable.[46] A similar problem was in their assertion that some of the UN General Assembly resolutions are legally binding. Many of their arguments were within the traditional framework of positive law versus natural law, and the traditional concept regarding law as a norm of adjudication. They could not overcome the positivistic and judiciary-centric construction of international law.

Thirdly, although they were critical of the self-righteousness, double standards, and aggressive nature of Western nations, they kept silent about their own problems. This double standard on the part of the developing countries became more and more apparent as the serious human rights conditions in many Asian and African nations became evident from the 1980s onward. Everything wrong, everything judged negatively was, more than a few political leaders and intellectuals of the developing countries argued, a result of the colonialism and imperialism of the West. Corruption, authoritarian and repressive regimes, and persisting inhumane, discriminatory, and cruel social practices in the Third World tended to be overlooked by non-Western leaders and intellectuals, including international lawyers. Such a claim tends to absolve the responsibility of the newly independent nations themselves and to indulge both the leaders and the ordinary citizens of these nations.

These problematic features were most conspicuous from the 1960s through to the 1980s and still linger today. They can be seen even in such nations as China and India, the candidates for superpowers in the twenty-first century. Because Western colonial rule and hegemony in international society seriously hurt their pride, they share a strong sense of victimization and humiliation. Thus, they tend to emphasize only the negative aspects of West-centric features of the existing global society and close their eyes to their own problems.

The Need for "Inter-civilizational" or "Trans-civilizational" Perspectives

In 1981, I was invited to give a paper as a member of the panel on the education of international law at the 75th annual meeting of the American Society of International Law. At that time, I was shocked by the fact that major international law casebooks and course books used in US law schools and universities were incredibly egocentric, tacitly equating what is American with what is international. These casebooks and textbooks were composed of a huge number of US domestic laws and jurisprudence, and incredibly few international and foreign materials. Also, by far the majority of the writings excerpted in these books were authored by US lawyers. In three texts that I dealt with, the percentage of excerpted writings by US writers ranged from more than 75% to 98%.[47] To one who had been accustomed to textbooks of international law that pay far more attention to materials from treaties and international jurisprudence, these did not appear to be course books for students of international law at all. Rather, they seemed like textbooks on US domestic law.

We must admit that each country tends to have its own preferences for selecting writings and laws or jurisprudence for textbooks on international law. Japanese textbooks include more Japanese materials than do textbooks of other nations. The same is basically true with any textbooks. This is understandable and to a certain extent justifiable because they are basically addressed to the readers of their own countries. However, even considering this common tendency, the course texts and casebooks used in the United States were too egocentric, even parochial. They paid excessive attention to their own laws, jurisprudence, and writings, ignoring foreign and international ones. They simply lacked a notion that *the United States is one of many sovereign states*, which constitutes a fundamental basis for any study of international law.

In 1981, criticism of Euro-centrism or West-centrism was already visible in a number of disciplines such as anthropology, history, and sociology. Edward Wadie Saïd's *Orientalism* was extremely popular among US and European intellectuals. Yet, the situation of US international legal education was as I described above. This fact suggests that international legal education in the United States was mainly concerned with producing future domestic lawyers, who were interested in international law as interpreted and applied by the US courts. They did not seem to be interested in the functioning of international law in international society. Seen from the other side, they reflected the prevalent psychology of the American people (including international lawyers) to equate what is American with what is universal. On the other hand, these casebooks or course books reflected the power, that is, the intellectual power, of the United States that was prevalent in international society. As long as the students understood what US laws prescribe, what US courts rule, and what US lawyers interpret or claim, they were supposed to understand international law as then functioning in international society.[48]

It is a matter of course, however, that one cannot understand international law only by reading materials produced by US lawyers and institutions, as international law is and should be universal, to be applied to people all over the world. In this sense, the attitude exemplified by the international legal education in the United States must definitely be rectified; about this there should be no doubt. On the other hand, merely criticizing the US-centrism or West-centrism and tacitly absolving corrupted and authoritarian non-Western leaders of responsibility are not enough. Such one-sided criticism, flawed with a double standard, could not be persuasive and constructive as a public discourse. In order to overcome West-centrism in a more constructive manner, we need a theoretical tool to see international legal phenomena from a fairer and more comprehensive perspective, taking into consideration political, economic, social, cultural, and historical dimensions.

This is why we need the "inter-civilizational" or "trans-civilizational" perspective, in addition to international and transnational perspectives, when we see international legal affairs. For any education, research, discussion, and dialogue to become legitimate on a global scale, they must be conducted in such a way as to listen to the voices of people all over the world, and to understand the values, virtues, assumptions, and views embraced by these people. However, although perspectives paying attention to cultures and civilizations have long been adopted, previous arguments involving cultures and civilizations have often led people to interpret trans-boundary or global phenomena as conflicts between antagonistic cultures, religions, and civilizations as understood in a substantive, monolithic, and mutually exclusive manner. In order to overcome such a conception and to establish the trans-civilizational perspective as a third perspective to supplement the prevailing international and transnational ones, we have to conceptualize the trans-civilizational perspective as a functional, rather than a substantive and monolithic notion.

(2) The Need for Changes of Perspective in Responding to the Multipolarization of the Globe

Although criticism of Euro-centrism or West-centrism has become common among intellectuals, the West-centric nature of the world has been persistent. The United States, the most influential nation in global discursive space, has generally been ignorant of "others" in the outside world and has remained self-righteous. The admirable nature of the United States as a nation, that is, a keen interest in and concern for justice in universal terms, frequently finds expression as self-righteousness because it often lacks proper understanding of cultures, religions, histories, and civilizations in the outside world. The people of the United States, including intellectuals, have tended to equate what is "American (in fact "of the US")" with what is universal.

Although Western European intellectuals have been slightly better in understanding different cultures and civilizations, their fundamental lack of interest in non-European civilizations and cultures is basically the same as that of their US counterparts. For them too, the history of ideas or thought begins with Greek philosophy, moves to medieval theology and natural law doctrines, then to the Enlightenment and social contract theory, and on to Hegel, Marx, and Nietzsche, to Jaspers, Heidegger, and Foucault, and often including other Western thinkers of the twentieth century. Confucianism, Islam, Hinduism, and any other great ideas or thoughts of the non-Western world have been virtually ignored.

To make matters worse, the influence of Afro-Asian and Latin American nations in terms of intellectual/ideational power declined toward the end of the twentieth century. This tendency became even more conspicuous after the end of the Cold War. A counter-ideology to liberal/capitalist democracy has virtually disappeared. The emergence of the aggressive advocacy of democracy, market economy, human rights, and rule of law, as defined and understood in a West-centric manner, demonstrates this tendency. This is regrettable because it has contributed to the unipolarity of the world in terms of intellectual/ideational power.[49]

As I referred to at the beginning of this chapter, the world of the twenty-first century will be a world of multipolarity in terms of economic power, and to a certain extent, military power as well. Yet, most people are not fully aware of the civilizational implications of what this radical change is going to bring about. This is because despite these changes in substantive power, the informational/intellectual/ideational framework is still overwhelmingly West-centric. Since ideationally influential people are still caught in this West-centric cognitive and normative framework, and because people all over the world are heavily influenced by these privileged few, most of humanity cannot recognize that a critical change is occurring in the actual world.

This can have dangerous consequences. If the predominant perception of the world does not conform to the actuality of the world, there will be serious misunderstandings, miscalculations, and failures in assessing realities, including those of power constellation. This is why I have repeatedly emphasized, and am emphasizing, the need for and importance of a trans-civilizational perspective. By deliberately adopting it, we can supplement and modify the existing two prevalent West-centric perspectives, the international and the transnational.

I cannot be very optimistic of the overall situation. However, we might be able to see some positive signs of gradual change in the field of international law.[50] At the inaugural meeting of the European Society of International Law in 2004, Martti Koskenniemi gave a paper drawing attention to the ideological functions of European international lawyers in justifying the imperialistic policies of the Western Great Powers.[51] Although this paper was severely criticized by Pierre-Marie Dupuy,[52] the very fact that such a paper was presented as a keynote address at the inaugural meeting of the European Society of International Law is significant.

In April 2007, the Asian Society of International Law [53] was established. Thus far, it is the American Society of International Law that has been the most active academic and professional society of international law. It has produced a number of important academic and practical papers, attracted international lawyers from all over the world, and has given opportunities to exchange views and opinions. Yet, in order to enrich the study and overall understanding of international law, we need a plurality of active academic societies that can compete with each other.

The very fact that both the European and the Asian societies of international law were born at the beginning of the twenty-first century might carry a symbolic meaning: that international legal study based on multipolarity and "multicivilizationality" began to be visible, responding to the emerging realities of the multipolar and multicivilizational global society. To me, speaking as one who argued in 1981 the need for an inter-civilizational perspective, it has taken a little too long for these activities to get started. However, I perfectly understand that the ideational/intellectual power remains long after the substantive power of predominant nations declines or decreases.[54] Even with the emergence of China and India as superpowers rivaling the United States and the European Union—countries that may bring about a decline of the substantive power of the major Western nations in relative terms—the ideational/intellectual power of the latter group will persist. In the field of international law, the ideational/intellectual power of Afro-Asian nations or any other non-Western agents will continue to be much lesser than that of the United States and Western European nations and their agents.

On the other hand, both European nations and the United States recognize the value of cultural and civilizational diversity. The global significance of bio- and cultural diversity is firmly recognized in the twenty-first-century world. From a normative perspective, strengthening "multi-culturality" or "multicivilizationality" is now recognized as one of the common public policies of humanity. Moreover, with the increasing economic power of Asian nations, their ideational/intellectual infrastructures—such as universities, libraries, research institutes, publishers, and media institutions—will be strengthened. Thus, it is likely that their ideational/intellectual power will steadily increase over the twenty-first century.

When I argued the need for an inter-civilizational perspective in the twentieth century, it was basically a normative or moralistic argument that such a perspective is needed from the viewpoint of global justice: voices of the weaker, peripheral, and powerless must be heard. In the twenty-first century, however, it is no longer a merely moralistic argument. It is also a realistic argument based on the changing realities of power constellation in global society. In order to minimize the danger arising from the huge gap between the actual world of the power constellation and the predominant perception of the world, it is necessary to accommodate the cognitive framework to those emerging actualities of the twenty-first century. Those who are engaged in managing global affairs must behave based on shrewd calculation of the actual power constellation in the world. To accommodate diverse perspectives on the world is a prerequisite for the coexistence and co-prosperity of humanity in the multipolar and multicivilizational world of the twenty-first century.

(3) The Powers of Legitimate International Law

The Power of Shared Normative Consciousness in Upholding Law

As I noted in II.1.(1), a normative idea can constitute power. It appeals to the minds of people, and urges people to strive in the direction that these ideas prescribe. They have the power to make people realize what these ideas define as socially desirable or undesirable, even prohibited. On the other hand, in order for any idea to be disseminated, widely shared, and potent enough to construct social realities, it also needs power. Some ideas are effectively disseminated and widely shared as international or transnational ideas, but others are not. Only an idea with the infrastructure to support and disseminate it in terms of global reputation, powerful media institutions, particular cultural or civilizational preferences, and financial resources can become one with the strong ideational capability to construct social realities on a global scale. The power of international law as an idea and institution can be either strong or weak, depending on various factors and contexts. The legitimacy of international law is one of the most important of such factors.

Whether a certain act addressed to societal members by a political authority can be accepted as legitimate ultimately depends on the shared perception of the addressee of the act. This is the case even with a nation where the supreme court or constitutional court enjoys the power to review the constitutionality of state acts, including legislation. Even if the court judges a certain act of administration or a certain law as unconstitutional, this judgment cannot be realized without the accumulated and widely shared normative consciousness that the judgment must be respected and obeyed by state organs. Only with such deeply rooted and widely shared normative consciousness of the societal members underlying the judicial system, does an administration—which, with its actual power of police, military forces, and financial policies, could well ignore such a judgment—actually obey it.[55]

This is all the more the case with a global society, where no institutionalized enforcement mechanism exists. It is ultimately the globally shared normative consciousness that international law must be legitimate, and therefore be obeyed by states, that upholds and helps realize the norms of international law. If the creation, invocation, or application of international law is perceived as unjust, unfair, selective, or inconsistent by people throughout the world, its legitimacy will be doubted and undermined. This perception of illegitimacy raises doubts as to whether this norm of international law should be obeyed and realized, although from an institutional perspective it is claimed to be lawful by the political authority. If this perception of illegitimacy is serious, the effectiveness of the norm becomes problematic. The addressee of a legal norm may resist its implementation by means of tacit or open criticism, sabotage, or defiance.

The formalistic and procedural legitimacy of international law has been based on the shared understanding that international law is made by states and implemented by states, which have been considered to be the major legitimate actors in international society. Because nation-states have been considered to be the legitimate agents or organs to conduct affairs on behalf of aggregates of citizens who belong to them, their products and forms of management, including international law, have generally been perceived as legitimate. Also, states have had the actual power to create and realize international law and to effectively manage affairs transcending national boundaries. These perceptions and realities have supported the prevalent state-centric understanding of the legitimacy of international law.

However, toward the end of the twentieth century, this assumption became problematic. The legitimacy of states, and especially that of undemocratic states or states seriously violating human rights, came to be doubted and contested. Moreover, states came to find it difficult to effectively control various kinds of trans-boundary phenomena. Trans-boundary economic, financial, and informational activities conducted mainly by non-state actors such as multinational enterprises became too huge to be controlled by states. Thus, the significance of a transnational perspective, which pays attention to these non-state actors and their ideas and activities, was vocally claimed and came to be widely accepted.

A number of intellectuals, especially those in developed countries, argued for the significance of transnational economic and informational activities. They advocated a global civil society, the decline or retreat of states, and the like. The role of NGOs as public advocacy agencies influencing various phases of the creation and realization of international law came to be highly valued by influential Western experts and media institutions. The term "civil society" became fashionable and was often utilized as trumping governmental or inter-governmental initiatives, decisions, and policies, as well as their implementation. Ordinary citizens in developed countries came to share these views and to accept criticisms of state-centrism. Even if some legal norm was enacted by inter-governmental negotiations, its legitimacy came to be questioned if some of the governments involved are considered to lack legitimacy in terms of democracy, human rights, good governance, and the like.

In this way, many people began to think that in order to understand and evaluate trans-boundary or global affairs, they would need to take into consideration not only inter-state or inter-governmental activities or ideas but also activities and ideas which originate from, and are claimed, disseminated, carried out, and realized by, non-state actors. The importance of "transnationalism" thus came to be emphasized more and more. This transnationalism came to be particularly triumphant after the end of the Cold War. Today, even government officials understand that they have to adopt not only an international perspective but also a transnational one to understand, assess, and respond to the complex issues in global society.

Problems of International and Transnational Perspectives

By adopting the transnational perspective in addition to the international perspective, our ability to appreciate complex realities of today's world has certainly been enhanced. The once-prevalent approach, of considering global or trans-boundary affairs in terms of, or in association with, monolithically assumed nations or nation-states, as exemplified in "national cultures" or "national character," came to be questioned. Interpreting such affairs unconsciously in association with existing nation-states has come to be qualified in various respects.

Yet, even this qualification of the international perspective by the transnational perspectives is not sufficient to see, understand, and attempt to solve global or trans-boundary problems in the twenty-first century. Even by adopting the two prevalent perspectives (i.e., international and transnational) we cannot fully address the issues of the multipolar and multicivilizational world, which is increasingly revealing its complex aspects and dimensions. Even with the combination of international and transnational perspectives, we can hardly recognize and respond to various forms of the aspirations, expectations, frustrations and resentments held by the overwhelming majority of humanity: the people in the non-Western world, who comprise more than 80% of the human species.

By consciously or unconsciously adopting the international perspective, we tend to pay attention to the ideas and phenomena that are produced, referred to, appear or occur in relation to, or in association with, the ideas, activities, and phenomena between states, or more concretely, between governments. Ideas, activities, and phenomena associated with ordinary citizens, private corporations, and other groups are excluded, in most cases unconsciously. Moreover, we are inclined to pay attention to more conspicuous inter-state relations, that is, those involving major Western states such as the United States, the United Kingdom, and France, represented by their governments. Almost all media institutions over the globe tend to report diplomatic problems between the United States and other countries that are related with the United States. People seldom pay attention to the overwhelming number of smaller countries, whose population, if combined, far exceeds that of the United States. In short, by adopting the international perspective, which is state-centric, we unconsciously exclude two factors from our vision: (1) views, claims, aspirations, expectations, frustrations, and resentments held by ordinary citizens, private corporations, and various kinds of human groups; and (2) views, claims, aspirations, expectations, frustrations, and resentments held by governments and a far larger number of people in non-Western nations.

By consciously or unconsciously adopting the transnational perspective, we tend to pay attention to the ideas and phenomena which are produced, referred to, appear, or occur in relation to, or in association with, the ideas, activities, and phenomena mainly produced by, referred to, appear or occur in relation to conspicuous non-state actors. They are basically powerful multinational enterprises and leading NGOs, most of which are Western. Microsoft, Citibank, Amnesty International, and Greenpeace, whose ideas and activities are most actively reported and disseminated by powerful Western media institutions, are leading examples.

How should we assess these non-state actors in terms of reflecting the voices of humanity, especially those excluded by adopting the international perspective? In other words, can we characterize these non-state actors as representatives that can supplement the global legitimacy that may be lacking if we adopt only the international perspective? Viewed from the perspective of the representative legitimacy of global democracy, it is difficult to characterize multinational corporations as such representatives. They are agents of the world capitalist economy. Although massive populations in the non-Western world desperately want economic development, these multinational corporations cannot be their representatives. Some of the more influential NGOs, on the other hand, seek to work for the people of the global South in a spirit of solidarity. In a number of cases, NGOs advocate and act as if they represent voices of peoples in the developing countries, which are mostly non-Western nations. In the areas of economic development, global finance, and the environment, this tendency is particularly strong. In functional terms, some of them thus enjoy representative legitimacy within global society, even among people in the non-Western world.

However, it cannot be denied that the basic assumptions, ways of thinking, and cultural propensities of many influential NGOs are evidently West-centric.[56] Most of the globally influential NGOs are based in the West; NGOs in Asia and Africa are far less influential. To make matters worse, some of the non-Western NGOs are even more West-centric than their Western counterparts, because of their members' educational backgrounds in the West, their inferiority complex toward Western society, and their elitist status in their own societies.

In this way, although we can supplement and modify our state-centric way of thinking and patterns of behavior by adopting a transnational perspective, it is difficult for us to rectify our deeply rooted West-centric perspective. On the contrary, because Western corporations, NGOs, and media institutions are major agents of transnational activities, we might unconsciously tend even more strongly to see trans-boundary and global affairs from a West-centric perspective by emphasizing the importance of the transnational perspective. However good-willed many of the NGOs may be, however important their functions have been in rectifying the state-centric global policies, this negative aspect of "transnationalism" should not be overlooked. If influential NGOs truly want to be public agents that can legitimately represent the voices of non-Western peoples that are not heard in major global discursive processes, they have to deliberately adopt trans-civilizational perspectives.

(4) The Trans-civilizational Perspective: A Way to Fill the Legitimacy Deficit in Global Discursive Space

Significance of the Trans-civilizational Perspective

In order to rectify problematic features of the international and transnational perspectives, we need a third perspective from which we can see, sense, and interpret neglected aspects in global discursive space and thus supplement the two predominant perspectives in understanding the multipolar and multicivilizational world of the twenty-first century. A trans-civilizational perspective is such a perspective. It is a perspective from which we see, recognize, interpret, assess, and seek to propose solutions to problems transcending national boundaries by developing a cognitive and evaluative framework based on the recognition of the plurality of civilizations that has long existed in human history.[57]

As mentioned earlier, I first argued the need for an "inter-civilizational" perspective in 1981.[58] Since then, the importance of seeing various trans-boundary or global phenomena in terms of civilizations and cultures has grown enormously. On the other hand, I have received various kinds of criticism, which are often based on the misunderstanding of my argument. Particularly, criticisms associated with the famous claim of a "clash of civilizations" by Samuel Phillips Huntington have been persistent. Since 2001, I have been arguing for a "trans-civilizational" rather than an "inter-civilizational" perspective to respond to these criticisms and to minimize misunderstandings. My argument for the trans-civilizational perspective is basically a general and rudimentary way of seeing things in a different manner from prevalent international and transnational perspectives, which are often unconsciously taken. It is not proposing some alternate theory or methodology. Rather, it proposes that such a way of seeing the world is needed in addition to international and transnational perspectives. A minimal clarification is in order.

Cultural, religious, and civilizational diversities were once preserved and protected in the sovereign states system by the principle of nonintervention, which had been one of its most fundamental principles. However, toward the end of the twentieth century, this principle gradually deteriorated. The tremendous power of the global market economy and the global flow of information undermined the nonintervention principle. In the fields of trade, foreign exchange, and transboundary investment, the power of the global market economy has penetrated the territorial sovereignty of most countries. Substantive bases underlying the nonintervention principle came to be seriously undermined. The United States, the largest beneficiary of private transnational activities, has enacted extraterritorial laws that are often in conflict with the traditional principle of nonintervention. It has gradually transformed the sovereign states system to its own liking.

Furthermore, the power of new ideas has weakened the nonintervention principle's power as an idea. Problems relating to human rights and the global environment have caused concern among a large number of people in developed countries, where media institutions and NGOs exert great influence on the decision-making process of public affairs. These problems, once characterized as matters falling within the domestic jurisdiction of a state, came to be characterized as matters of international concern under the strong pressure of "global"—more precisely, Western led and disseminated—public opinion. Diverse civilizational factors, which had been preserved within national boundaries under the nonintervention principle, came to be taken up and criticized from outside. Various religions, social practices, customs, or cultures in non-Western societies came to be characterized as violating human rights norms. And they came to be severely criticized by Western governments, media institutions, and NGOs.[59] The nonintervention principle no longer provides an effective shield for such criticism.

Some of the reactions from non-Western societies to such criticism assumed the character of repercussions in terms of religions, cultures, and civilizations. Thus, the conflicts between the West-centric globalizing forces undermining the nonintervention principle and the repercussions from various non-Western nations have given the impression of a series of "clash of civilizations." "Asian values" or "Asian human rights," which were vocally asserted by some East Asian leaders to criticize West-centric discourses and policies of human rights in the early 1990s, are some examples.[60] Terrorist attacks by nationals of some Muslim nations are another example. In actuality, there were various causes and aspects of these conflicts. However, people have tended to understand them in terms of cultural, religious, and civilizational conflict. The prevalent understanding of the September 11 terrorist attacks reveals this tendency.

Many Western governments and commentators were aware of the danger of such an understanding. They argued that the "war against terrorism" should not be construed as a conflict between civilizations. However, they could hardly dissuade those who dare to resort to terrorism or the larger number of people who support or acquiesce in it. For example, some of the Muslims who characterize attacks against Israel and the United States as jihad believe that their civilization *has already been attacked by the Western civilizations*, whether they are Judeo-Christian or modern, secular, and capitalist. According to this perception, their religion, cultures, values, customs, and social practices have been threatened by various means, including military, economic, and ideological, by the West. They thus justify their acts of violence as jihad, characterizing them as defensive acts or counter-attacks against an aggressive Western civilization, regarding the latter as the civilization of power.[61]

Here, we can see a strong inclination to understand civilizations as substantive entities to which humans belong in an exclusive manner. Also, we must take into consideration that the very space or arena where ideas, claims, and arguments are exchanged is overwhelmingly West-centric. There is little space for non-Western discourses. However loudly they shout, however sophisticatedly they argue, their voices and arguments are hardly heard by Western elites who can exert influence on the global decision-making process. They have been in desperation that their arguments cannot be understood or even heard by those who control affairs in Israel, the "Middle East"—a typical example of the predominance of Eurocentric way of seeing the world—and other regions of the world. If their voices are not heard there is no other course but to resort to violence. Whether one likes such reasoning or not, this is the way they tend to think.

The Need to Minimize Conflicts between Egocentric, Unilateral Universalism

Another phenomenon which requires the trans-civilizational perspective, as suggested in the introduction, is the resurgence of Asian powers, represented by China and India as candidates for the status of superpowers in the twenty-first century. As demonstrated earlier, these two powers had experienced being an empire or a center of civilization in their regions for a long period of time. They were thus accustomed to their egocentric universalism since the very early days of history.[62] Yet, they suffered humiliation in their recent history. A strong sense of humiliation and victimization based on these historical experiences characterizes the way they see today's world. They tend to interpret the behavior and claims of the former colonial and imperial powers, most of which are today's leading Western nations (and, in case of China, Japan), through the eyes of these historical experiences.

It is thus no wonder that both nations feel today's West-centric construct of global society is uncomfortable and unnatural. Today's prevailing system does not necessarily represent the consciousness or understanding of the world that underlies their ways of thinking, their patterns of behavior, or their foreign policies. Greenwich, not Beijing or Delhi, is the base point of the world. China is in the "Far East," not Europe in the Far West. The Christian calendar is the common calendar of the world. For those who once regarded themselves as being at the center of the world, all these West-centric constructs of the world can appear unnatural. It is likely that this sense of unnaturalness and discomfort will increase and become more conspicuous with the increase of their substantive power and self-confidence through the twenty-first century. They may feel more and more frustrated with the West-centric organization and construction of global society, which does not fit their understanding and their sense of the world in terms of cultures, religions, and civilizations. When they become more powerful and find that they can more aggressively assert their understanding of the world toward others—including the United States and major Western European nations—they will likely do so.

It is true that both China and India have lived in the modern sovereign states system, which originated in Europe, for more than a century. They have behaved, like the United States, the United Kingdom, and many other Western nations, on the basis of the calculation of their self-interest within this system. Like Western major powers, they have thus far behaved basically in accordance with international law, although they sometimes violated particular norms. However, when they think about "self" and "others," when they consider "interests," the way that they understand them—the cognitive framework through which they recognize and interpret them—is embedded in their cultural, historical, and civilizational underpinnings. Even if they appear to interpret the world in the same way as their Western counterparts, there may remain a number of differences due to these factors.

The United States, on the other hand, has been totally accustomed to seeing the world from its position as a superpower, and in many cases the only superpower, with its idealistic, self-righteous universalism. Unless it deliberately pays more attention to cultural, religious, and civilizational aspects of other nations and peoples, the United States will find it difficult to understand why these new superpowers behave in such an aggressive and different manner. Even Western European nations, which are relatively less self-righteous yet ignorant of other civilizations, will also be embarrassed by such new confrontational situations. In order to avoid, or at least minimize, such serious consequences, we need to adopt a perspective through which we can better understand the cognitive frameworks tacitly, and often unconsciously, adopted by the resurging superpowers. The trans-civilizational perspective provides such a cognitive and normative framework.

The Functional Trans-civilizational Perspective to Enhance the Ideational Power of International Law

I am not claiming a cultural or civilizational determinism. On the contrary, the trans-civilizational perspective should oppose any substantiation or absolutization of the notions of civilizations or cultures. It should not presuppose the monolithic entity of culture or civilization. Humans do not belong exclusively to a particular culture or civilization. In most cases, human beings simultaneously sense, think, and behave according to plural civilizations and cultures.[63]

For example, contemporary Western European people think, see, feel, and act according to modern European civilization, which is basically secular, scientifically, and technologically oriented. However, albeit unconsciously and implicitly, most of them also think, see, feel, and act according to the Christian civilization or culture, which originated in the premodern period. Many of the words they use, ways they eat and work, and other patterns of behavior they adopt are characterized by the teachings and norms of Christianity. They have further adopted a lifestyle of mass production, mass consumption, and mass disposal. This is often associated with the "American way of life," and has been accepted by most people in developed societies. Further, most European children grow up watching Japanese animation films on TV, and thus unconsciously adopt some aspects of Japanese culture.

In this way, Western European people simultaneously see, think, feel, and act according to a plurality of cultures and civilizations. They do not exclusively "belong to" a particular national culture, modern European civilization or Christian civilization. For other people, whether they are Koreans, Nigerians, or Cubans, the situation is basically the same. Even if a nation takes an anti-United States policy, its people usually enjoy Hollywood movies and MacDonald's. Even if an East Asian nation takes a typically world capitalist economic way of life, it may maintain some Confucian ways of thinking or patterns of behavior in their ordinary life. We should therefore define the concepts of civilization and culture in functional terms that allow humans to behave according to the plurality of civilizations and/or cultures simultaneously.

Moreover, when I refer to the term "trans-civilizational perspective," this "civilization" is to be defined as a common way of thinking and patterns of behavior that geographically extend beyond a single nation, and historically last for a considerable period of time.[64] However rigidly an expert tries to "define" culture or civilization, he or she has to admit that these terms continue to be used equivocally according to countries, times, generations, disciplines, contexts, and other factors. Such equivocal usage of the term cannot be avoided, because both "civilization" and "culture" are words that are used not only in various disciplines but also in ordinary life as nontechnical terms.[65] Their polysemy should be understood as a sign of the fruitfulness, rather than the weakness, of these terms.

As I argued in section II.2.(1), although the term "trans-civilizational" sounds new, trans-civilizational perspectives have actually been adopted by policymakers, experts, and ordinary citizens for years. Trans-boundary phenomena have been seen and interpreted from various trans-civilizational or inter-civilizational perspectives tacitly and often unconsciously. The important task for us is to make explicit this actual adoption of trans-civilizational perspectives by people in general and to liberate them from an exclusive and substantive notion of civilization.

We must *re-characterize* it as a functional notion, in order to avoid reasoning and conclusions associated with the "clash of civilizations" and conflicts of cultures. These conclusions are often brought about by arguments that pay attention to diverse cultures and civilizations understood in a substantive, monolithic, and mutually exclusive manner. Appreciating trans-boundary phenomena in terms of culture and civilization certainly contributes to a multidimensional understanding of the complex realities of the world. Yet, appreciating cultures and civilizations *as a substantive, monolithic, and mutually exclusive notion* of does not.

With these points in mind, it is important to enhance and strengthen the legitimacy of international law so that it can contribute to the smooth functioning of the changing global system—the multipolar and multicivilizational world of the twenty-first century. In order to carry out this crucial task, international lawyers and other experts must understand that seeing the global society in terms of national interest or civic normative values is not enough. They must deliberately adopt the trans-civilizational perspective, understood in functional terms, to modify and supplement the prevalent international and transnational perspectives. They must make serious efforts to see and understand trans-boundary and global affairs by paying attention to their cultural, religious, and historical aspects and backgrounds. They must pay special attention to cultures and civilizations of non-Western regions, which tend to be overlooked and excluded in the present West-centric discursive space—without, however, substantiating the notions of culture or civilization.

These efforts are especially required of leading Western international lawyers. They have been indulged by the fact that it is mainly people of the United States and Western European nations who have constructed today's world. They still tacitly assume that what is Western is universal, when dealing with history, law, politics, international society, philosophy, or any other human endeavors. They need to be aware of their privileged position in dealing with any trans-boundary or global affairs in global discursive space that involve international law, which is a powerful institution in their favor, yet one that is disadvantageous to the others. They need to learn the teachings of Islam, Buddhism, and Confucianism in addition to Christian theology. They need to read the *Mahabharata*, works by Ibn Khaldun and Mencius, in addition to Plato, Jean-Jacques Rousseau, Lev Nikorajevich Tolstoj, and Max Weber.

On the other hand, non-Western international lawyers should not pamper themselves by simply criticizing West-centrism in international law. Non-Westerners can be spoiled because when dealing with the issue of West-centrism, they are automatically situated in a morally advantageous position. Moreover, a number of non-Western intellectuals are often more West-centric than the Westerners themselves. They must liberate themselves from this kind of enslavement of the soul. Only by encouraging and building on such deliberate and conscious efforts to change our own perspectives, whose West-centric features are unconsciously and deeply rooted in the minds of contemporary people, including non-Western intellectuals, can we gradually change the perspectives of people at large, and thus contribute to a less violent, less destructive, and less biased construction of the world.

Endnotes

In this article, I seek to express the order of the name given according to the proper way respective of culture. For example, Chinese, Japanese, Korean, and Vietnamese names generally appear with family name preceding given name. To avoid confusion, those family names are written in capital letters.

1. ONUMA Yasuaki, "Towards an Intercivilizational Approach to Human Rights," *Asian Yearbook of International Law* 7 (2001): 21–27.

2. International legal studies have always dealt with the problem of legitimacy in various forms and in various ways, but the pioneering work dealing with the problem of legitimacy characterizing it as a core question is Thomas Franck, *The Power of Legitimacy among Nations* (New York: Oxford University Press, 1990). However, the definition of legitimacy adopted in this book is so narrow that Franck himself changed his position in his following work, *Fairness in International Law and Institutions* (New York: Oxford University Press, 1995). See also Ian Clark, *Legitimacy in International Society* (New York: Oxford University Press, 2005); and Clark, *International Legitimacy in World Society* (New York: Oxford University Press, 2007).

3. I will elaborate the notions of international, transnational and trans-civilizational perspectives through this chapter as a whole, but particularly in section II.2. See also Onuma, "Toward an Intercivilizational Approach" (n. 1 above), 28–31.

4. Western European leaders and intellectuals gradually came to be self-confident about their ideals and accomplishments, and came to be more and more critical of the United States, toward the end of the twentieth century. In their eyes, the United States appears as an uncivilized nation, which internationally often resorts to violence, and domestically suffers from a huge number of serious crimes and maintains a savage system of death penalty.

5. Robert Kagan, *Paradise and Power: America and Europe in the New World Order* (London: Atlantic Books, 2003), 53–76.

6. I do not necessarily share this view. Kagan's view itself, like those of other "neoconservatives," has a utopian feature in that it argues that the United States should, and can, change undemocratic nations into democracies even by resorting to force. On the other hand, the idealistic universalism held by Western European intellectuals often shares self-righteous features and may be characterized as hypocritical in that it criticizes a more conspicuous self-righteousness of the United States without sufficient reflection on their own. See ONUMA Yasuaki, "Comment," in *European and US Constitutionalism*, ed. G. Nolte (Cambridge: Cambridge University Press, 2005), 301–304.

7. The terms "Eurocentrism" and "Eurocentric" have been generally used to express the way of viewing the world from a European, or European and North American, perspective, with an implicit belief, either consciously or subconsciously, in the preeminence of European or Western cultures, values and civilizations at the expense of non-Europeans or non-Westerners. In actuality, it has been a way of thinking centered on the United States and Western Europe that has been referred to under the term of Eurocentrism. In this sense, it may be more appropriate to express this view as "North Atlantic–centrism," or

"(West-)Euro-North-America-centrism." However, for the sake of convenience, I will basically use the term "West-centrism," although I fully understand that this term has a problem as to "from whose perspective the term refers to 'West.'"

8. For more details, see ONUMA Yasuaki, "International Law in and with International Politics: The Functions of International Law in International Society," *European Journal of International Law* 14, no. 1 (2003): 105–139.

9. On the other hand, lawyers should understand that legality is not an absolute value. There are a number of values and virtues more important than legality in human society. This is also the case with global society. *Fiat jus et pereat mundus* cannot be the maxim of the global society. Avoiding a nuclear war between the US and the USSR (Russia), for example, has been, and still is, far more important than observing numerous rules of international law.

10. In addition to public international law, private international law, domestic laws, laws of international organizations, EU law, and other kinds of law have been and are functioning in international society as well. However, (public) international law coordinates and controls these various laws, and provides a certain degree of harmony to these laws. Thus in international society, it is (public) international law that is most conspicuous and important among all laws.

11. I myself dealt with this subject in Onuma, "International Law in and with International Politics" (n. 8 above). The argument I present here is basically the one that I demonstrated in this article. There are, however, a few arguments that are different from those I made earlier, reflecting the subsequent development of my ideas.

12. In some developing countries, governments have used these requirements as a tool or lever to reform the economic structure and psychology of traditionally state-owned, inefficient firms. In such cases, there has been a tacit agreement between the governments of developed and developing countries, as well as with the investing firms of the former. Simply characterizing BITs as reflecting asymmetrical power relationship between the developed and developing countries overlooks these complex aspects of the BITs.

13. Preamble and Art. 3 of the United Nations Framework Convention on Climate Change, *U.N. Treaty Series* 1771 (1992): 166–168, 169–170.

14. Art. 3 of the Kyoto Protocol to the United Nations Framework Convention on Climate Change, UN Doc. FCCC/CP/1997/7/Add.1, December 10, 1997.

15. Arts. 37–44 of the United Nations Convention on the Law of the Sea, *U.N. Treaty Series* 1833 (1982), 411–413 and a number of provisions stipulating rigid civil and political rights in the International Covenant on Civil and Political Rights.

16. Arts. 133– 191 of the United Nations Convention on the Law of the Sea (n. 15 above), 445–477; Art. 1 of the International Covenant on Economic, Social and Cultural Rights, *U.N. Treaty Series* 993 (1966), 5; Art. 1 of the International Covenant on Civil and Political Rights, *U.N. Treaty Series* 999 (1966), 173.

17. Arguments provided here are based on ONUMA Yasuaki, "The ICJ: An Emperor without Clothes?" in *Liber Amicorum Judge Shigeru Oda*, ed. ANDO Nisuke and others (The Hague: Kluwer Law International, 2002), 203–212, and ONUMA Yasuaki, "A Transcivilizational Perspective on Global Legal Order in the Twenty-First Century," in *Towards World Constitutionalism*, ed. R. St. J. Macdonald and D. M. Johnston (Leiden: Martinus Nijhoff Publishers, 2005), 176–181.

18. Robert Jennings, "The Identification of International Law," in *International Law*, ed. B. Cheng (London: Stevens, 1982), 6.

19. Oscar Schachter, "New Custom," in *Theory of International Law at the Threshold of the 21st century*, ed. J. Makarczyk (The Hague: Kluwer Law International, 1996), 531. See also Charles de Visscher, *Théories et réalités en droit international public*, 4th ed. (Paris: A. Pedone, 1970), 170; Brigitte Stern, "La coutume au coeur du droit international," in *Mélanges offerts à Paul Reuter*, ed. D. Bardonnet and others (Paris: A. Pedone, 1981), 492–494; A. Roberts, "Traditional and Modern Approaches to Customary International Law," *American Journal of International Law* 95 (2001): 767–768.

20. The behavior of governments could generally be construed as representing the will of those nations' peoples, provided that this assumption is not rebutted by some factual evidence.

21. Onuma, "ICJ: An Emperor without Clothes?" (n. 17 above).

22. On the other hand, the United Nations as an entity enjoying the status of an independent subject in international society is severely limited. In dealing with the problems involving international peace and security, the most important act of the United Nations is that of the Security Council, which is composed of fifteen member states. In most cases, the will of the permanent member states—the United States, the United Kingdom, France, Russia, and China—and not the Security Council per se, is crucial.

23. ONUMA Yasuaki, "War," in *A Normative Approach to War: Peace, War, and Justice in Hugo Grotius*, ed. Onuma (Oxford: Clarendon Press, 1993), 57–121.

24. Onuma, "War" (n. 23 above).

25. When Hersch Lauterpacht claimed that all inter-state disputes can, and should, be settled by the judiciary, E. H. Carr severely criticized him as utopian; E. H. Carr, *The Twenty Years' Crisis, 1919–1939* (London: Macmillian, 1946), 193–207. Lauterpacht could not rebut Carr. Although the number of international courts and the cases which the ICJ deals with have increased since then, the situation has basically not changed since then either. There is neither universal compulsory jurisdiction of the international courts nor an enforcement mechanism of these courts. States, or people at large, are not ready to accept such mechanisms in international society.

26. Lassa Oppenheim, *International Law, Peace,* vol. 1 (London: Longmans, Green and Co., 1905), 73–74, 185.

27. ONUMA Yasuaki, "When Was the Law of International Society Born?" *Journal of the History of International Law* 2, no. 2 (2000): 18 n. 38; Karl Zemanek, "Is the Nature of International Law Changing?" *Austrian Review of International and European Law* 8 (2003): 3.

28. See text at 154–156.

29. See n. 25 above.

30. See text at 155.

31. Lauterpacht did criticize the realists in his writing (H. Lauterpacht, "On Realism, Especially in International Relations," in *International Law Being the Collected Papers of Hersch Lauterpacht,* vol. 2, ed. E. Lauterpacht [Cambridge: Cambridge University Press, 1975], 53.). But it was not a logical, coherent, academic, and professional criticism. It was rather an emotional and fragmented one, which lacks persuasive power.

32. Lauterpacht is typical of scholars who understood law in terms of adjudicative norms. His book *The Function of Law in International Community* (Oxford: Clarendon Press, 1933) dealt exclusively with international law as adjudicative norms. No other function

of international law than the adjudicative function is dealt with in this book of some 500 pages, although it is titled *"The Function of Law,"* not *"The Adjudicative Function of Law" in International Community.*

33. In East Asia, Chinese characters and literature, ways of negotiation, ceremonials, Confucianism (originating from China), and other Chinese ideas and institutions were generally adopted by political entities in the region. They functioned as common cognitive and normative frameworks in East Asia. In Europe, French, later followed by English—which were the languages of the leading powers—became the common language of diplomacy and economic activities. A number of ideas and institutions that are characterized today as European originated in either England, France, Italy, or Germany, which have been major powers in European history.

34. See 154, 170 of the text.

35. Onuma, "International Law in and with International Politics" (n. 8 above).

36. From the 1990s on, we see an increasing interest in international law among international relations experts, including those in the United States, where such interest was scarce. Although this interest is thus far shared mainly by institutionalists and constructivists, I believe that realists must admit these important functions of international law if they are ever to be realistic in their observation of the actual world.

37. Onuma, "When Was the Law of International Society Born?" (n. 27 above).

38. Onuma, "Towards an Intercivilizational Approach" (n. 1 above) and references cited therein.

39. Art. 5 of the Vienna Declaration and Programme of Action, U.N. Doc. A/CONF.157/23.

40. Onuma, "Eurocentrism in the History of International Law" (n. 23 above), 371–386.

41. Onuma, "When was the Law of International Society Born?" (n. 27 above).

42. Onuma, "Towards an Intercivilizational Approach" (n. 1 above); ONUMA Yasuaki, "In Quest of Intercivilizational Human Rights: Universal vs. Relative Human Rights Viewed from an Asian Perspective," in *Human Rights and Humanitarian Law*, ed. D. Warner (The Hague: Kluwer Law International, 1997), 43–78.

43. A. A. An-Na'im, *Human Rights in Cross-Cultural Perspectives* (Philadelphia: University of Pennsylvania Press, 1992).

44. A small number of countries such as Singapore, South Korea, Malaysia, and Thailand underwent significant economic development, but a far larger number of countries in Africa became even more miserable in economic terms than they had previously been.

45. Moreover, the end of the Cold War meant the disappearance of the major part of the Second World, the Soviet bloc. It would be difficult to talk about the First, Second, and Third Worlds in the twenty-first century.

46. For example, although every civilization had its own mechanisms to pursue the spiritual and material well-being of humanity, these mechanisms were not characterized as human rights. According to an excellent characterization by Raimundo Panikkar, they were the *existential functional equivalent* of human rights (R. Pannikar, "Is the Notion of Human Rights a Western Concept?" *Diogenes* 120 [1982]: 77, 78.). For more detailed analyses, see Onuma, "Towards an Intercivilizational Approach to Human Rights" (n. 1 above), 35–37; Onuma, "In Quest of Intercivilizational Human Rights" (n. 42 above), 65–67.

47. See my remarks in "Promoting Training and Awareness—The Tasks of Education in International Law," *Proceedings of the American Society of International Law* 75 (1981): 163–167.

48. Did they reflect the intellectual and ideational power of the time correctly? Probably not. At least the ideational power of French-speaking international lawyers and Soviet international lawyers was stronger than that suggested by these US course books. And given the emerging power of majority and aggressiveness of the developing countries in the 1970s, their ideational power was also stronger than what was suggested by these course books. The US course books contributed to strengthening the status quo in favor of the United States by tacitly underestimating the writings of non-US international lawyers.

49. The combined intellectual/ideational power of the United States and the Western Europeans has been substantially enhanced. In recent years, one can see a number of trans-Atlantic dialogues in various fields including that of international law. This is a desirable development in that it can enrich the perspectives of US people—including international lawyers—and other experts by introducing to them some non-US perspectives. As referred to earlier, the US people, due to their dominant position that allows them to live without understanding "others" in international settings, are generally more parochial in their comprehension of the outside world than other peoples. In this sense, the increase of trans-Atlantic dialogue should be appreciated and encouraged. Naturally, however, this is not enough. We cannot enact, interpret, and realize international law in a globally legitimate manner by merely relying on trans-Atlantic dialogues and agreements. The West-centric advocacy of democracy, market economy, human rights, and rule of law is based not only on the intellectual/ideational power of the United States. It is based on the power of expertise, information, culture, and capital available for the dissemination of ideas held by the leaders, intellectuals, higher research and educational institutions, and media institutions of the North Atlantic region including Western European nations. They share common cognitive frameworks for understanding, interpreting, and constructing the world, which they have inherited from the West-centric twentieth century itself. Therefore, the vitalization of trans-Atlantic dialogues tends to strengthen, rather than to weaken, this West-centric framing of the world.

50. In 2000, I published an article on the history of international law as seen from a trans-civilizational perspective in the *Journal of the History of International Law*. This article was well received. In 2003, the *Austrian Review of International and European Law* published a volume that contained an agora organized by Karl Zemanek, who started his introductory article by referring to this article. In 2004, the *Journal of the History of International Law* 6, no. 1 featured a symposium on this article and thus dedicated its pages to six reviews. The authors were Ram Prakash Anand of India, Antony Anghie of the United States, Emmanuelle Jouannnet of France, Jörg Fisch of Switzerland, LI Zhaojie of China and Nicholas Onuf of the United States. They are all leading international lawyers, historians of international law, and international relations scholars.

51. Martti Koskenniemi, "International Law in Europe: Between Tradition and Renewal," *European Journal of International Law* 16, no. 1 (2005): 115–117.

52. Pierre-Marie Dupuy, "Some Reflections on Contemporary International Law and the Appeal to Universal Values: A Response to Martti Koskenniemi," *European Journal of International Law* 16, no. 1 (2005): 131–137.

53. http://www.asiansil.org/ (accessed November 12, 2011).

54. Even after the Roman Empire declined, Roman law and the Latin language continued to be influential in Europe for a long period of time. A number of Chinese features can still be found in today's Korea, Vietnam, Taiwan, and Japan, although the Sino-centric East Asian regional system collapsed more than a century ago.

55. Hans Kelsen, in his pure theory of law, resorts to the concept of "Grundnorm," which ultimately upholds the entire legal system. Herbert Lionel Adolphus Hart, in his *The Concept of Law* (Oxford: Clarendon Press, 1994), resorts to the notion of "rule of recognition" to ultimately uphold the legal system. Both, it seems to me, tacitly rely on this normative consciousness on the part of the addressee, the societal members as a whole, as the ultimate guarantor of the entire legal system. In some countries, especially in developing countries, where such accumulated common normative consciousness is lacking, the judgments of the supreme court are sometimes ignored or denied by the powerful administration. In these countries, the normative consciousness that the judgment must be respected and obeyed by state organs is not sufficiently accumulated and widely shared.

56. As to the problematic features of West-centrism in the major human rights NGOs, see Onuma, "Towards an Intercivilizational Approach to Human Rights" (n. 1 above), 38–46.

57. See generally ONUMA Yasuaki, *Jinken, kokka, bunmei* (Tokyo: Chikuma Shobo, 1998), 13–36, 332–337, 345–347. See also Onuma, "Towards an Intercivilizational Approach to Human Rights" (n. 1 above), 22–31.

58. Onuma, "Remarks" (n. 47 above).

59. Major Western states, which find it necessary to respond to mounting pressures from human rights NGOs, have taken a far harsher attitude toward those countries whose record of human rights violation is conspicuous. International organizations whose mandates are directly or indirectly related to the promotion or protection of human rights have also come to take a more severe attitude toward human rights violations in developing countries. The UN Human Rights Commission (now "upgraded" to the Human Rights Council) and its Subcommittee, as well as monitoring bodies of major human rights treaties, have become an arena where human rights violations in developing countries are heatedly discussed. Major developed countries and international financial institutions such as the World Bank and the IMF have come to impose conditions relating to human rights on the recipient nations when they lend money or provide economic assistance to them.

60. Onuma, "Towards an Intercivilizational Approach" (n. 1 above), 47–52. See also INOUE Tatsuo, "Liberal Democracy and Asian Orientalism," in *The East Asian Challenge for Human Rights*, ed. Joanne Bauer and Daniel Bell (Cambridge: Cambridge University Press, 1999), 27–59.

61. See ONUMA Yasuaki, "Bunmei wa shototsu shite inainoka?" *Asahi Newspaper*, November 30, 2001, 17.

62. See Onuma, "When Was the Law of International Society Born?" (n. 27 above), 11–18.

63. Onuma, "Towards an Intercivilizational Approach to Human Rights" (n. 1 above), 30–31.

64. Onuma, "Towards an Intercivilizational Approach to Human Rights" (n. 1 above), 29–31; Onuma, "Trans-civilizational Perspective on Global Order in the Twenty-First Century" (n. 17 above), 162–163.

65. In some cases the term "civilization" is understood as centering on material aspects of human life, whereas the term "culture" is understood as centering on the spiritual aspects of life. In Germany, this tends to be the case. In other cases, the term civilization is understood as synonymous with culture and is used to denote national characteristic features as well. In France, for example, when one refers to French culture, one tends to use the term "la civilisation française" rather than "la culture française." As to the equivocal usage of the terms of civilization and culture, see the classical works of L. Febre and others, *Civilisation: Le mot et l'idee* (Paris: La renaissance du livre, 1930); A. Kroeber and C. Kluckhorn, *Culture: A Critical Review of Concepts and Definitions* (Cambridge, Mass.: Harvard University Press, 1952).

7

The Trans-civilizational, the Inter-civilizational, and the Human

THE QUEST FOR THE NORMATIVE IN THE LEGITIMACY DEBATE

Giles Gunn

In a world where traditional international rules have sometimes proved inadequate, recent interest in the notion of "legitimacy" as a complementary source of legal authority has raised a number of issues—legal, moral, and what some would call "ontological."[1] These issues came to the fore most dramatically, though not for the first time, during the Kosovo War of 1999, when in the face of grave and intolerable human rights abuses it became necessary to override legal protections against intervention into the activities of sovereign states. These questions were soon to become still more urgent and vexed when "legitimacy" was employed by the administration of George W. Bush as an alternative, extra-legal criteria for rationalizing the invasion of Iraq. In both cases—and there have been more—reliance on "legitimacy" in favor of "legality" has permitted more than the circumvention of the law; it has supported the violation of the law. But breaking the law by finding a moral/legal rationale to transcend it may merely reflect the fact that contemporary forms of globalization have not only challenged the legal structures of the international order but the rules of politics as such. The crux of the matter, says one astute commentator on such matters, is "who or what decides on the legitimacy to change the rules." Politics at every level, from the subnational to the supranational, is undergoing radical change that is transforming state-based forms of legal authority.

Quite apart from how such alterations have occurred and are occurring, there are a number of questions embedded here. On one side are those raised by the nature of intervention itself: how egregious or heinous must the human rights violations be to trigger such action? Who makes this determination? What does it mean to substitute "legitimacy" for "legality" as a basis for international order under any circumstances? What political body or bodies has, or have, the right to make and enforce such substitutions? On the other side are those questions related to the problematics of the term "legitimacy" itself. Where does its authority come from? Who gets to decide what does and does not fall within its authority? Is there any principled normative basis outside the law for deciding such matters? And how, and on what, is such a normative basis to be grounded?[2] The argument of this chapter presupposes that legitimacy functions in an arbitrary manner, generally as deference to asymmetries of power, unless it is grounded on a discernable foundation provided by the delineation of "the human." Otherwise, important efforts at conditioning and constraining the behavior of states by bringing to bear the discipline of international law is weakened, if not discredited, without compensatory justification. The idea of legitimacy, and even more so, of the human, is that quest for a compensatory justification that is sensitive to the ever dangerous tightrope that connects the pole of order to the pole of change and flexibility as these tensions are actualized in a world order still shaped primarily by sovereign states struggling for dominance and autonomy.

My own concerns parallel those of Yasuaki Onuma, whose work is highly relevant to the investigations that follow.[3] Onuma has been arguing for more than a quarter of a century that global conflicts cannot be addressed and reduced, or world order preserved, so long as political thinking is based on perspectives that are merely "international" or even "transnational." International perspectives are subject to the Westphalian system's reliance on regimes of law within and between states to adjudicate and resolve humanitarian crises, and they eventually fall victim to the iron rule of self-interest. Transnational perspectives hold out better prospects for escaping the hold of the national imaginary, but while their chief non-state expressions, such as multinational corporations and international NGOs, have global pretensions, they still reflect a West-centric bias. So long as the "national" remains the default term to be utilized in confronting outrages to our sense of the human, state-based notions of sovereignty, and the hegemonic interests that trail in their wake, will inevitably trump all others.

The alternative is to develop a perspective that encompasses the international and transnational but goes beyond them by refusing to restrict itself to boundaries that are national, social, cultural, or even civilizational. Onuma calls this perspective "trans-civilizational" because it is based on a recognition of the plurality of civilizations that have existed over time, and is therefore responsive to the "various ways of thinking of diverse peoples and . . . [able] to identify values and virtues that are perceived as legitimate by as many people as possible."[4] This is a theoretical and evaluative construct premised on the assumption that human beings are not products of only one civilization, any more than all civilizations are products only of themselves. And just as civilizations are not fated or predestined to develop in only one direction, neither are the human beings whose convictions, identities, and solidarities are formed and experienced within their frames of meaning. As an instrument for engaging all trans-boundary problems in an increasingly global world, the trans-civilizational perspective offers itself, Onuma believes, as ultimately the only ethically and politically viable source of normative authority in a world marked by humanitarian catastrophes of intolerable violence, cruelty, and devastation.

My specific intent in this chapter is to examine this proposition further before putting it under some degree of critical pressure. I propose to do so by exploring the link, at once necessary but somewhat unacknowledged, between the trans-civilizational and the human. I assume that these two conceptual orientations are connected by way of the idea of rights, which is now routinely invoked to designate that which transcends the nation and also that which defines the human. I will begin by assessing how well the notion of the "trans-civilizational" holds up in its own terms, so to speak, as a necessary complement, if not supplement, to the ideas of the "international" and "transnational." This will lead me to propose that the better term for the kind of perspective Onuma is looking for may be instead "inter-civilizational," the one he began with, but I will go on to argue that the "inter-civilizational," as I understand it, may provide inadequate grounds to suggest or support any concept of "legitimacy" if it is not backed up with an acceptable concept of the human. It is no coincidence that the idea of the human is again being rethought as a result of the international failure to extend human rights to all. Rehabilitating this notion may thus hold the key to developing a nonsectarian, and convincingly universal, framework for normative thinking beyond the law. Before developing this argument, I will circle back to retrieve further elements of Onuma's conception of the "trans-civilizational" itself and place them in perspective.

Onuma's brief against perspectival constructs that are less than trans-civilizational, and employed to regulate global order and render it legitimate, is that because of their West-centric origins and usual bias they dismiss, overlook, or neglect the traditions, norms, and customs of up to 80% of humanity. Rather than aiding inter- and cross-cultural understanding, they delimit and frequently over-shape it. But the difficulty with invoking—as a corrective to such blindness—a still politically and intellectually broader, and historically deeper, perspective than the international or the transnational is that it implies for many people, as Onuma fully appreciates, the indefensible assumption that civilizations are self-contained, stable, and unified. If opinions like these derive from historical and cultural ignorance, as Onuma believes, they have nonetheless enabled Samuel P. Huntington and others like him to claim that civilizations are so different from one another as to, in effect, be incommensurable as well as incompatible. Such views, to which the clash of civilizations thesis is allied, are at a minimum essentialist and at a maximum absolutist and incipiently racist. Civilizations are clearly more fluid, fractured, diverse, inconsistent, and, above all, porous within themselves, not to say between themselves, than the "clash thesis" allows, but these same totalizing prejudices about civilizations resurface in a more benign but still simplistic and offensive form in all talk about "Asian values," "Muslim practices," "Latino beliefs," or "African problems."

What gives the lie to these prejudices is that a great majority of the world's people belong to more than one so-called civilization, and often by choice; that most civilizations are deeply influenced by, and thus the creatures of, contributions from other civilizations; that all civilizations are in processes of rapid change and of even more rapid re-description; that the structures of relation and tension between and among civilizations are arranged at all sorts of oblique angles and cross-hatched with diverse lines of pressure, fracture, hierarchy, and power.[5] Indeed, it is precisely because of this historicity, mobility, and adaptability that even in times of crisis, when their back, as it were, is up against the wall, civilizations can be repositories of ideas and values that are capable—at least potentially—of being widely shared even when variously expressed. Onuma's purpose in elaborating what might be called the conditions of possibility for such a trans-civilizational perspective, then, center around the hope that we can either extrapolate or fashion from it (I am not quite sure which) certain norms based on mutual goals and needs that can more constructively inform the work of law as it addresses humanitarian and other problems in the global sphere. For Onuma, this seems all the more plausible because the work of law, as he usefully points out, is not confined to responsibilities of control and adjudication but extends also to the guidance of life out of court.

Despite the appeal of such an argument—what perspective can provide a normative basis for the notion of "legitimacy" except one that takes account of the situation of all humankind?—I am troubled about what it may gloss. Talk of the trans-civilizational possesses its own legitimacy problem in an age when so many unities and large coherences have already been shattered, and we are now compelled to root some of our thinking, as even the "clash thesis" reminds us, in what Clifford Geertz refers to as "the world in pieces."[6] Even as civilizational differences make themselves available for explaining, and also for justifying or rationalizing redistributions of power and reconceptualizations of ideas of order and governance, there is abundant evidence of as much de-centering going on in the global sphere as of recentering, of deconstruction as of reconstruction, of de-territorialization as of re-territorialization. The civilizational, as we are calling it, is continually being threatened on the one hand by the so-called global or worldwide and on the other by the so-called local or regional, and while both the local and the global are in fact relative terms, the opposition between them is not so much between the "local" and the "worldwide" or "global" as between one kind of "local" that is more regional and specific and another kind of "local" that is more global and dispersed.

But this leads to a second issue that Onuma's notion of the trans-civilizational may gloss, or at least underestimate, which has to do with just how difficult it is to acquire or achieve such a perspective and what might be seen because of or through it.[7] As no one needs to be reminded, cultures are by themselves—forget about civilizations—extraordinarily complex organisms whose components at any given point or moment are difficult to disassemble and whose internal logic and power can not to be reduced to, or simply identified with, any one of them. As a vast ensemble of complex, interrelated, interactive forms in which parts inform wholes and wholes inform parts without managing to subsume or be subsumed by the other, culture has been likened to a game and its interpretation, as Geertz once pointed out in a famous series of comparisons, to the process of getting a joke, grasping a pun, fathoming a proverb, reading a poem, or even comprehending baseball. To follow a baseball game, Geertz observed, one must not only understand what a bat, a hit, an inning, a left fielder, a squeeze play, a hanging curve, and a tightened infield are but also, and most crucially, "what the game in which these 'things' are elements is all about."[8] To get the game, then, requires knowing what is at stake when the play conforms to an accepted structure of rules. The principle or point of the game, and the structure of rules defining it, go together: the principle or point at stake in the play exhibits some of the "truth" or "insight" embodied in the structure, while the structure grounds the meaning and significance embodied in the principle.

As I have pointed out elsewhere, this comparison is true as far as it goes but it falls short exactly where the thing to be known and the character of the knowable change in those games, whether cultural or civilizational, that are not completely rule-governed.[9] Cultures, not to say civilizations, are rife with such forms, and they, rather than the games whose rules are clear and discreet, often give both to cultures and to civilizations their distinctive styles and signatures. One set of such forms would be those considered aesthetic, another, those that are deemed religious, and still a third those, perhaps, viewed as legal. In figurative formations like these that are not, like rule-driven games, necessarily formulaic, and which make up a not inconsiderable amount of the content of any culture or civilization, complete knowledge—understanding "what the game in which these 'things' are elements is all about"—is inherently unattainable. Here the point of interpretation, indeed much of the purpose of the play, is to learn how to use the structure of rules to change or, at any rate, to complicate the game by exploiting what is not actually fully knowable or predictable and can frequently only be inferred. These are the meanings and significances that are not fully represented by the structure, or by any of its elements, but are simply potential to it. To be sure, such meanings are not easily defined or categorized in any given culture or civilization, but they are nonetheless indispensable to the kind of work that cultures and civilizations perform by constituting the horizon of possibility within which the relations between the known, the unknown, and unknowable are cast. Representing elements in any culture or civilization that are indefinite, even undecidable, but still determinative and consequential, they point to yet another dimension in their composition that makes them so difficult to disassemble or reconfigure.

Thus, by suggesting that it may be more difficult than it looks to extract from various cultures or civilizations elements that can be rearranged and recombined on some meta level into a pattern of shared values and beliefs, I do not mean to imply that such extrapolations never go on—they are of course going on all the time—but merely to point out that the hermeneutical processes by which the wisdom of one cultural or civilizational tradition can be rendered correspondent with those of another entails several discrete and rather arduous steps. The first involves an act of deciphering, of reading, of interpretation itself, which depends less on the identification of one mind or culture with another than on the determination by one mind or culture of what the other's is up to or seeks. The problem is that such determinations often depend on more than just the ability to solve a puzzle, get a joke, or figure out a poem. To fathom representative forms, elements, practices of cultures or civilizations other than one's own on the pulses, in what William Butler Yeats once called "the fury and mire of human veins," is like entering another *lebenswelt*, or felt world, in which one must learn to breathe in a different atmosphere or calculate in an alien mathematics.

The second step in the process that leads to cross-cultural understanding entails an act of translation in which we must convert the practices, performances, or purposes of one mind, culture, or civilization back into the purported idioms of our own. This step actually holds out more possibilities for misreading than the first, but we can only grasp what to some degree we can analogize, even if that operation only succeeds in de-familiarizing what we think we already know. What we cannot know, unless through some Barthian act of radical divine revelation, is the *totaliter aliter*;[10] all we can ever know, Emmanuel Levinas notwithstanding, is that which is not completely and absolutely different.[11]

Yet the fullest possible understanding of whatever it is that we seek to comprehend from across cultural or civilizational divides remains incomplete without a third and final step. This is the interpretive step known as appropriation where one attempts, with the techniques at one's disposal, to gauge the difference such translations make to one's previous self-understanding and the internal adjustments they exact as a consequence. Without this final step, interpretation is left hanging and the possibility of achieving new understanding permanently thwarted.

The third issue I wish to raise with regard to Onuma's attempt to delineate a perspective that would complement or supplement the international and the transnational, has to do with whether it is more useful to think in trans-civilizational terms or rather, to return his earlier description of his project, in inter-civilizational terms. Whatever Onuma may have meant by this term in his previous work, the aforementioned question begs to be raised due to one of the critiques that Huntington's clash thesis has consistently attracted. Edward Said may have only been the best known of Huntington's doubters when he described the latter's thesis as a "clash of ignorance" and reminded us that warring civilizations often share more affinities than we would like to believe and experience many of the same inner divisions.[12] This point has recently been made in a different way by Martha Nussbaum, who argues that most civilizations are now roiled by a similar struggle in which those who demand certainty and uniformity of belief are pitted against those who prefer a world of variety and change. In all modern nations, she writes, the real clash is to be found "within—between people who are prepared to live with others who are different, on terms of equal respect, and those who seek the . . . domination of a single religious and ethnic tradition."[13]

There is nevertheless a risk to conceiving the conflict in these terms because it may make it sound as though the clash within civilizations is essentially a replay of the battle between religious and ethnic absolutism and secular modernism. What is misleading about this is that the religious and the secular do not define a simple binary, much less designate different ends of a historical timeline, so much as represent different reflections and inflections of what we have come to recognize as the long *duree* of the modern. This is the period that began at least in the West, once the Westphalian system was more or less in place, with the rise of nationalism. Moreover, the so-called secular has often been created in no small measure out of elements of the religious that emerged as much from a relaxation of its constraints as from an outright repudiation of them. Hence what appears in historical processes of secularization to be a dismissal or negation of religion—according to conventional wisdom, the secular refers to a realm of thought and experience from which all traces of the supernatural or the transcendental have been rejected in favor of embracing more pragmatic solutions to perennial problems—is more often than not a reconstruction of the world out of many of those same interpretive and imaginative activities that religion itself has set free and that must now again be brought into play if some other form of confidence in the world is to take its place.

Arjun Appadurai defines the clash within civilizations in still other terms as a struggle between geopolitical systems that are vertebrate and those that are cellular. Vertebrate systems are organized around a large body of institutions, treaties, agreements, and protocols, and are symbolized by global bodies like the United Nations and the World Trade Organization that attempt to "ensure that all nations operate on symmetrical principles in relation to their conduct with one another, whatever their hierarchies of power and wealth."[14] Cellular systems are associated with non-state actors and epitomized by al Qaeda and its many imitators, operating outside the official international network of organizations and bureaucracies and organized less hierarchically through semi-independent units that rely on secrecy, loose coordination, offshore havens, and stealth. Appadurai is convinced that the post-9/11 conflict between these two systems has deeply threatened the Westphalian model of world order, producing a "crisis of circulation" that may only be resolved through the development of a new global civil society that operates altogether outside the control of nation states.

Yet another formulation of the clash thesis within rather than between civilizations has been offered by the *New York Times* columnist David Brooks, who has drawn attention to the quarrel between those who in America (and elsewhere) favor integration and those who prefer separatism.[15] The civil rights movement, women's liberation, demographic shifts in population, the communications revolution, and the end of the cold war, even globalization itself, all spoke to the possibility, indeed the hope, that people were coming together, even if only slowly and fitfully, across divides of all kinds. But now just as recent Supreme Court decisions serve to remind Americans that racial integration may be beyond achievement, so the threat of terror, the globalization of trade and commerce, and the self-interest at play in the geopolitical sphere may attest that in the long run people find it possible to trust only their own kind.

However, as much as this version of the clash within may, under some circumstances, bring those who wish to give credence and space to others into conflict with those who wish to force everyone to live within the shelter or, as the case may be, the prison of a single identity or outlook, the clash within civilizations that provides the best argument for an inter-civilizational rather than a trans-civilizational perspective is no doubt the one epitomized by the divide between the global South from the global North since it can also be found in virtually every civilization in the world. Here the greatest challenge is to bring people together who occupy vastly unequal economic, social, and political positions on the global scale, but this cannot be accomplished unless we can develop theoretical and axiological perspectives that not only recognize their differences but seek to combat the oppression, violence, and suffering their differences generate. Such initiatives have little to do with boiling down different civilizational values and synthesizing them in some encompassing formulation but rather with acknowledging, as Ashis Nandy contends, "that while each civilization must find its own authentic vision of the future and its own authenticity in [the] future . . . , neither is conceivable without admitting the experience of co-suffering which has now brought some of the major civilizations closer together."[16]

Nandy's specific concern is the problem of humanmade suffering: how to assess responsibility for it and help guide the struggle against it by reshaping social consciousness with the assistance of allegories of the future. This possibility, already reflected, perhaps, in the creation of the World Social Forum, and capable of being extended by what Richard Falk calls a "Global Peoples Parliament" and Ulrich Beck describes as a "global (citizens') parliament,"[17] is premised on the necessity of creating what Nandy terms a form of "intercultural communion."[18] This communion between and within rather than across civilizations possesses two fundamental coordinates. The first entails recognition, often overlooked in an era of more diversity than real pluralism, that the core values of a variety of civilizational complexes are already congruent enough to enable us to rise above many of the barriers of exclusivist consciousness. A recognition particularly difficult for people on the Left to achieve, it is essential if we are to move beyond the soporifics of typical clash thinking. The second is an acknowledgement that the search for the authenticity of any civilization is always a search for its "other face" either as hope or as caution to its neighbors. To discover the "other face" of any civilization depends, for Nandy, on the ability both to interpret one's own traditions for oneself and to incorporate the often recessive aspects of other civilizations as allies in one's own struggles for cultural self-discovery and development. The object of both recognitions is to create an inter-civilizational discourse that permits different parts of the world to learn from the experience of one another without pretending that norms can be derived that are similarly applicable in every situation to all. What is needed is not an agreement on norms per se, as though such an accord would allow them to be applied uniformly across the board, but on which norms will encourage us to learn and assimilate what other civilizations can teach us. The goal is not a new normative consensus, cosmopolitan or trans-civilizational, but, if I may put it this way, an "other" humanism that transforms the wisdom of different civilizations and cultures into allies in the self-realization of each.

One place where it would be fair to say that an inter-civilizational as opposed to trans-civilizational humanism has been evolving is in the international human rights movement, but despite real successes over the years, no one would deny that the movement has fallen far short of its goals. Such failures have convinced Judith Butler that part of the task of the international human rights movement is now "to reconceive the human."[19] Butler means by this that the failure to extend to all human beings the rights that are held to be inherent or intrinsic to every human being has obliged us to ask what, then, being human really means. Talad Asad would reply—and here is where one problem emerges—that the answer lies in considerable measure not so much in the idea that the human subject is constituted by certain inalienable rights, an idea deriving from natural law theory and influenced by early Christianity and Roman law, but in how those rights are recognized and adjudicated both by and in the world's various civil orders.[20] Even as *The Universal Declaration of Human Rights* refers to "the inherent dignity" and "the equal and inalienable rights of all members of the human family," it tacitly recognizes "that the universal character of the rights-bearing person is made the responsibility of sovereign states, each of which has exclusive jurisdiction of a limited group within the human family."[21] Given the scope of that jurisdiction, the universality of the rights that human beings are supposed to possess suffers a disturbing contraction. Suddenly "the self-owning, sovereign individual of the philosophers," who was always already a kind of socially and politically disembodied fiction, now becomes further de-realized. In a world where the global market decides who is human and what it means to realize its promise, "human rights become floating signifiers that can be attached to or detached from various subjects and classes constituted by the market principle and designated by the most powerful nation-states."[22]

But the situation is even more complex than Asad claims because neoliberalism has created a "new capitalism," as Richard Sennett prefers to call it, which has produced a culture whose features cannot simply be thought of as a replication, on the level of individual experience, of the operations of the market itself.[23] The culture produced by the market's neoliberal emphasis on deregulation, privatization, liberation, and freedom is by no means identical with those values. Moreover, the institution of these values at the global level has seriously destabilized social life by dismantling so many of the formerly fixed state and corporate practices that once lent structure to individual experience. Government, it will be remembered, has long established a compact with many of its citizens; corporations stood by their employees and became recipients, as a result, of their trust and loyalty. But now things are clearly different. The individual idealized by the new economy currently faces daunting challenges caused by the implementation of these values that are in fact almost their reverse image. For one thing, time becomes hazardous as almost never before because the disruption of careers and the increased mobility of business life demands constant movement from job to job and task to task, and this threatens the possibility of developing any consistent or sustainable life narrative, or even a recognizable sense of self. For a second, the acquisition of skills and the management of talent have become far more problematic because the velocity of technological and other changes has shifted almost all emphasis from past achievement to future potential. For a third, the pace of change erodes the illusion of permanence, encouraging the individual modeling her- or himself on the consumer eager to make new purchases and discard still serviceable ones, to forget the past and simply move on.

The world this evokes is the one inhabited by the figure of the consultant whose virtues are bankable only as long as they stay ahead of the downsizing and resizing and outsourcing and reinventing of jobs. Yet like all but a small minority of very successful players in the neoliberal economy, the consultant is also, like most everyone else, threatened by "the specter of uselessness."[24] This is the specter that haunts and frightens so many people in the new capitalism precisely because, as Sennett observes, "people are not like this": "they need a sustaining life narrative, they take pride in being good at something specific, and they value the experiences they've lived through."[25] Hence it is not merely that the cultural ideal associated with the new neoliberal institutions damage so many of the people forced to live in them; they damage them in some rather particular, and not always recognized, ways that radically diminish rather than augment their so-called autonomy and agency. The ideological hegemony of American neoliberalism thus leaves us in a peculiar intellectual position where, as Ignacio Ramonet, the chief editor of *Le Monde Diplomatique*, correctly lamented, "we have to formulate the problems it invents in the words it offers."[26]

One of those invented problems, to return to our earlier discussion, has to do with whether rights language has been so corrupted by the neoliberal framework of discourse within which it operates at the global as well as national level that, as Asad implies, we can no longer employ it to identify the human at all? The second, somewhat in contradistinction with the first, is whether at this late date we can ever any longer think about the human without recourse to the language of rights? This contradiction has from time to time elicited several different answers, which circle around the issue of whether we can reverse the usual procedure by deriving a sense of rights from a conception of the human rather than a sense of the human from a conception of rights. Suspending for the moment the actual history of these deliberations, which are in any case beyond the scope of this chapter, we can discern at least several different, though often related, arguments.

The first might be called the sustainability argument, which is organized around the attempt to define what is needed in the most minimal terms to live a recognizably human life. The nineteenth-century American writer Henry David Thoreau called such essentials "the grossest groceries" and came up with a list that was far from trivial, including food, shelter, clothing, and fuel, but to such basics like these have usually been added other elements such as security of person, recognition before the law—and the list goes on.[27] The second argument, recently reprised by Martha Nussbaum and Amartya Sen, might be called the capabilities argument and stresses what is absolutely indispensable to make a recognizably human life functional.[28] This argument focuses on the capacities that all human beings presumably possess by virtue of their innate endowments, and include the ability to feel, think, reason, and imagine in ways that, through adequate education, permit self-expression and a measure of free choice. Then there is the ethical argument, often linked to the sustainability argument, which takes up the definition of the human from the point of view of what all members of the human community deserve by way of recognition and response from their peers.[29]

A plea for equal moral consideration for all human beings, this argument is often reinforced by two others: first, a pragmatic claim that treating people with equal moral consideration has beneficial effects in reducing cruelty and relieving suffering;[30] second, an economic claim that the basic nature of the human is revealed most starkly in those systematic processes of dehumanization where it is most at risk of being lost. Such "crimes against humanity," as they have come to be termed,[31] are for good reason usually identified with the Holocaust and Nazi practices more generally, as well as other genocidal atrocities of the century just past. But thinking more historically, the provenance of such practices reaches back much farther, particularly the various forms of human slavery and severe incidents of collective punishment inflicted on enemies. It was Orlando Patterson who first defined slavery so famously as social death—"the permanent, violent and personal domination of natally alienated and generally dishonored persons"[32] —but David Brion Davis has gone on more recently to argue that in its New World incarnations, where it was most vicious, slavery deserves to be called "inhuman bondage" because its intention was literally to negate the human.[33]

Each of these arguments seeks at its purest to identify the human without necessary recourse to the language of rights, though in the process all of them have implied a basis for defining the human from which a notion of rights might be derived. In addition, it could be said that none of these arguments would have proved so durable had it not been for the creation of the international rights regime, despite the fact that all of them remain susceptible to cooptation by the neoliberal language of exchange and advantage. This is a language that has obviously grown more grotesque and discordant in a world where, conversely, loss and aggression seem to reign and "the powers of mourning and violence," as Judith Butler calls them, vie for the control of political life at the expense of human rights. If loss and aggression, which seem to feed off each other, can no more be accepted as norms for political life than commerce and leverage, are there any other grounds on which to found a new global political community that is at once protective and supportive of the human?

Butler's cautious answer is that there are inasmuch as we are all constituted in part—this is as close as she comes to any form of universalism—by the vulnerability of our own bodies. But how is that vulnerability—what she at other times calls our "injurability"[34]—to be converted into the basis of a new ethics capable of confronting and absorbing the aggression that is so frequently provoked and shadowed by it? Her answer is through the work of mourning, work that can open us to the similar vulnerability of others. Adopting some of the language of Levinas, she describes the realization of the other's violability as the recognition that ethically calls each of us into being. Finding ourselves confronted in ways we cannot deny or dismiss by the vulnerability of others, we come to exist in a new manner: "this impingement by the other's address constitutes us first and foremost against our will, or, perhaps put more appropriately, prior to the formation of our will." Moral identity has little do with taking a stand and everything to do with "the demand that comes from elsewhere, sometimes a nameless elsewhere, by which our obligations are articulated and pressed upon us."[35]

Butler's human is therefore no mere agent; something both active and acted upon, it is constituted instead by the linkage between the two, which provides the grounds of its responsibility and the possibility of creating an ethics that is nonviolent. A nonviolent ethics would not be an ethics purged of violence but rather an ethics capable of providing an appropriate motivation for opposing it. Nonetheless, just how this is to be accomplished is less clear than by what. Butler locates the source of this moral motivation in Levinas's well-known evocation of the face of the other. The face of the other reveals to us both the fragility and instability of the other's life and the conditions of our engagement with it. It is this latter point with which I have the greatest difficulty. That face, mediating to us what is sanctified about human vulnerability and fragility, is at the same time supposed to dispose us to be prepared to disrupt all the dominant forms of representation that seek to obscure or erase it anywhere that it is presumably in peril. But what, beyond self-interest, motivates us to do this? If we ask how this occurs, Butler returns to the subject of mourning, which, though not a substitute for politics, is nonetheless presumed to enable us to recognize in the face of the other both the precariousness that constitutes our own humanity and the reason to resist all that threatens to violate it worldwide.

There is much to admire in this argument along with a few things to question. Before noting several difficulties that attend her use of Levinas, I want to examine more closely, from the point of view of its normative implications, Butler's view of loss and her association of loss primarily with the body. As Freud (whom Butler often follows) said correctly about melancholy—it took him a while to get this straight about mourning—the experience of loss to which melancholy and mourning are both responses (the one Freud thought of as pathological, the second as curative) is ordinarily associated with far more than the loss of the body. What is grievable—and in a global register often as, or more, grievous—are losses that are not only physical but also symbolic, material but equally ideological, axiological, spiritual, losses, in other words, not just of other selves but of any object of value, from traditions and institutions to narratives and meanings. To many people in the world, the loss of individual life is far less unacceptable than the loss of status, or of authority, or of recognition, or of dignity, or of agency.

Butler knows all this, of course, but still fails to make enough of it, and this lapse in an otherwise very perceptive discussion of grief and mourning helps explain why she misses, or at least downplays, the element that so fatefully links the occurrence of loss with the outbreak of anger. What the anthropologist Renato Rosaldo has described as "the rage in grief"[36] that leads Ilongot men in the Philippines to want to cut off human heads as a response to loss emboldens and compels, and often inspires, other mourners to take up paramilitarism, espionage, and terrorism. Far from being a mere byproduct of grief, rage is an integral aspect of it that derives, as Freud observed, from the inability of the ego or self to represent loss as anything other than an impoverishment of itself, an impoverishment that frequently, and understandably, turns the ego or self vengeful. The only way to manage such feelings, much less assuage them, is through the intervention of symbolic forms that can draw off some of the anger in grief while at the same time providing a structure for redescribing it, and this is what the process of mourning, whether individual or collective, seeks to accomplish. Its purpose is to translate the loss suffered *by* and *to* the self, and in very significant part, as Butler says so beautifully, *of* the self, into an opportunity to acknowledge and memorialize, by working through memories initially too painful to recall or even bear, what the passage through the mourner's own world of the life that was lost could now possibly mean. What the mourner must give up is the consolation provided by fixation on the experience of her or his own loss, often through the violence it releases; what the mourner may receive in compensation, as a potentially acceptable substitute for the missing object, is the possibility of being able to comprehend and even celebrate what Lacan called "the unique value/valor of the dead's being."[37]

Mourning therefore involves a special kind of grieving and also, as Paul Ricoeur was among the first to comprehend, a special kind of remembering.[38] It is intended to enable victims of loss to come to terms with the pain of the past by recreating their image of it and redefining their relation to it. In this sense, though Butler doesn't put it this way, mourning may be thought of, both individually and collectively, as a crisis of representation and a technique for resolving it.[39] The crisis is precipitated by the initial movement of mourning itself, which involves two distinct elements: first, the abjection of a self that has suffered the loss of something felt to be essential to its own existence, and, second, the consequent negation of that self's ability to compensate for such loss except through the creation and then valorization and defense, often aggressive and vehement, of a representation of its own anguish. This crisis can be resolved only if the self can relinquish its introjection of a symbolic representation that memorializes, and possibly fetishizes, only its own experience of that loss and can reconstruct in its place a representation that valorizes instead whatever occasioned that initial, and initially unacceptable, sense of loss—but now in a form that can eventually be contemplated and enjoyed rather than simply lamented, endured, and possibly avenged.

But what role, to return to Levinas, does the face of the other play in enabling this shift of focus that comprises the act of mourning? And who exactly is that other to whose face we are called to respond? Is it, as can be inferred from the way

Butler uses Levinas, some aspect of ourselves associated with our own elemental precariousness, or is it something radically different and unlike ourselves, especially if we both share very different conditions? This is in part a rehearsal of the old argument that Levinas had with Derrida about whether the Other who summons us into ethical being is radically and irreducibly Different or part of the Same? Derrida won that argument, it seems to me, by insisting that if the other weren't part of the Same, we would not be capable of recognizing it and thus could not become answerable to it.[40]

But this, then, leads us back to the fundamental question about how we know ourselves as human, and what that process has to do with mourning and the possibility of developing a new basis for a global political community, as I have put it, beyond solidarity. The initial answer, on which I agree with Butler and with Levinas, and which goes back to Bakhtin, is that we begin to know ourselves "exotopically": by imaginatively constructing, as we feel ourselves to some extent confronted, as opposed to more personally addressed, by someone or some thing outside ourselves. Epistemologically and morally, this amounts to saying no more than that selves, like cultures and civilizations, develop only in relation to other selves, other cultures, other civilizations, or, more exactly, in relation to the symbolic materials by which those others (selves, cultures, civilizations) represent themselves both to themselves and to us. In this formulation, self and other are not conceived either as fundamental opposites of one another (here is one of the places where I differ with Levinas) or as complements, counterparts, or corollaries of one another (here is where I differ with Butler) but as components, however varied their circumstances, theoretically integral to each other's construction. They are, even if they fail to acknowledge this, potential allies, as Nandy calls them, in each other's composition, but what they stand to gain from this relationship, as he goes on to point out, is not so much the call to be ethical as the terms in which that form of accountability might make sense. If neither self nor other is, in Wallace Stevens's great line, "the single artificer of the world in which she sang . . . and, singing, made,"[41] so neither one is constituted merely by their reference to or address by the other. What each offers the other is what their own other face hides or obscures or denies, a knowledge that can only begin to be liberated and actualized through exchanges, interactions, and communions that at the individual level are inter- as opposed to trans-personal and at the cultural level and beyond are inter- as opposed to trans-civilizational.

Being human, then, refers to a particular kind of process, of action, rather than to a specific condition or state. While Butler is correct that the human is often found where we least expect to discover it, "in its frailty and at the limits of its capacity to make sense,"[42] what is disclosed at such boundaries is not simply that it is precious because it is vulnerable, frail, and perishable, but that, despite these limitations, the human, as with no other creature on the planet, is dependent on learning, even at the cost of its own existence, from its exposure to what is often as recessive in others as it is in itself. What is learned from exposure to the otherness in, as well as the otherness of, others is not how human experience is ultimately and everywhere the same or yields similar lessons but rather how, in its difference, it can nonetheless yield insights that are indispensable to cultural and civilizational, not to say individual, self-development and self-realization.

In sum, the human is that creature for whom all experience, including that of the other face of another civilization, is potentially instructive. This not only sets the terms of its dependency but suggests the terms of its accountability. Its accountability, however, is not to a set of values, beliefs, or perspectives that may or could exist at some supra-civilizational level but rather to how the impingement of the other's life on its own at whatever level, local or global, renders it, to use several of John Dewey's favorite words, both educable and responsible. In a more ancient vocabulary, this is to agree with Levinas that the self is rendered ethically significant by the neighbor rather than vice versa. Moreover, this is not the neighbor we are enjoined to become, as in the Christian tradition,[43] but the neighbor we are already bounded by, as in the Jewish.[44] In Christian texts, the neighbor is a "a category of being into which we may enter"; St. Paul goes even further by shifting the focus from the state of being a neighbor to and for others to the love that supports such a state or condition and thus fulfils the law by in effect replacing it.[45] In Jewish sacred texts, the neighbor is that which one already is by virtue of being encompassed by others who, like her- or himself, are similarly strangers to themselves and to everyone else.

The ethical commandment to love the neighbor as oneself thus works very differently in these two distinct traditions. In the Christian tradition, the relationship of neighbor to oneself is interpreted as a challenge to recognize, despite obvious and inevitable differences, one's similarity with others, whether selves or civilizations, and thus create by means of this empathetic identification a more universal human community. In the Jewish tradition, the relationship of neighbor to oneself is construed instead as a challenge to recognize, despite potential or obvious affinities with another, whether self or civilization, that "our foreignness to ourselves," as Butler puts it, "is the basis of our ethical connection with others." Hence the community of the human in the Christian tradition is composed of those who are regarded and treated as neighbors and opens toward perspectives that are shared or sharable by all but those excluded from this category. The community of the human in the Jewish tradition, on the other hand, is composed of those already neighbored by others and opens toward perspectives that in their strangeness to themselves are, like one's own, experienced as potential allies rather than enemies in the effort to further understanding and dialogue.

To bring this discussion back to the normative basis of the notion of legitimacy, I have argued that reliance on a conception of the trans-civilizational is less clarifying, and useful, than is the concept of the inter-civilizational when it is supported by a reconceived notion of the human. In addition to avoiding the hazards of either reductionism or totalism, the idea of the inter-civilizational allows us to perceive others as potential partners or collaborators in our own self-actualization. To view others, whether personal or civilizational, in this light is to see them as neighbors whom one is ethically called upon, in the two great Western religious traditions, to love. But it makes a world of difference whether that neighbor is viewed as, in Christianity, the self whose foreignness can be subsumed within one's own ethical universality or is viewed as the self whose foreignness constitutes the ethical basis of our recognition of ourselves. The normative transcends the legal only insofar as it transforms the otherness by which, as individuals, cultures, and civilizations, we are all bound into an instrument for self-formation rather than self-destruction. And it is only this transcendence of the normative that provides a satisfactory justification for introducing the idea of legitimacy to overcome the shortcomings of the legal in certain exceptional circumstances.

Endnotes

1. Renewed interest in ontological dimensions of international dilemmas and disputes has been shown by, among a number of others, James Rosenau and Stephen Gill. See James Rosenau, "Imposing Global Orders: a Synthesized Ontology for a Turbulent Era," in *Innovation and Transformation in International Studies*, ed. Stephen Gill and James H. Mittleman (Cambridge: Cambridge University Press, 1977), 221, and Stephen Gill, "Introduction," in *Innovation and Transformation in International Studies*, ed. Gill and Mittleman.

2. See Falk chapter in this volume for some answers.

3. See Onuma chapter in this volume.

4. Yasuaka Onuma, "A Trans-civilizational Perspective on Global Legal Order in the Twenty-First Century—A Way to Overcome West-centric and Judiciary-Centric Deficits in International Legal Thoughts," unpublished paper, 3.

5. These facts have been widely noted in arguments criticizing Huntington's claims, but they have probably been most usefully assembled in Amartya Sen's *Identity and Violence: The Illusion of Destiny* (New York: W. W. Norton, 2006).

6. Clifford Geertz, *Available Light: Anthropological Reflections on Philosophical Topics* (Princeton, N.J.: Princeton University Press, 2000), 218.

7. Onuma considers the term "trans-civilizational" to be a neologism and only later substituted it for the term "intercivilizational" to define a perspective more universal than the "international" and the "transnational." See his "Remarks," *Proceedings of ASIL* [American Society of International Law] 77 (1983): 163–170. As will become clear later in the paper, I do not see these terms as interchangeable but rather insist that the distinction between them is crucial.

8. Clifford Geertz, "On the Nature of Anthropological Understanding," *American Scientist* (January–February 1975): 14.

9. The next several paragraphs follow very closely my argument in Giles Gunn, *The Culture of Criticism and the Criticism of Culture* (New York: Oxford University Press, 1987), 111–112.

10. This is Karl Barth's description of God in the radical Reformed tradition of Protestantism.

11. See my rephrasing of the argument between Levinas and Jacques Derrida in *Beyond Solidarity: Pragmatism and Difference in a Globalized World* (Chicago: University of Chicago Press, 2001), 29.

12. Edward Said, "The Clash of Ignorance," *The Nation*, October 22, 2001.

13. Quoted, Panjak Mishra, "Impasse in India," *New York Review of Books* 54/11, June 28, 2007, 48.

14. Arjun Appadurai, *Fear of Small Numbers: An Essay on the Geography of Anger* (Durham, N.C.: Duke University Press, 2006), 25.

15. David Brooks, "The End of Integration," *New York Times*, Op Ed Page, July 6, 2007.

16. Ashis Nandy, *Traditions, Tyranny and Utopias: Essay in the Politics of Awareness* (Delhi: Oxford University Press), 54.

17. Richard Falk, "Toward the Revival of Principled Politics in America," *Tikkun: A Critique of Politics, Culture, and Society* (September/October 2004), 39; Ulrich Beck, *Power in the Global Age* (Cambridge, U.K.: Polity Press, 2006), 308.

18. Nandy, *Traditions, Tyranny and Utopias*, 54.

19. Judith Butler, *Precarious Life: The Powers of Mourning and Violence* (London: Verso, 2004), 91.

20. Talal Asad, *Formations of the Secular: Christianity, Islam, Modernity* (Stanford, Calif.: Stanford University Press, 2003), 135.

21. *The Universal Declaration of Human Rights*, quoted, Asad, *Formations of the Secular*, 137.

22. Asad, *Formations of the Secular*, 158.

23. Richard Sennett, *The Culture of the New Capitalism* (New Haven, Conn.: Yale University Press, 2006).

24. Sennett, *Culture of the New Capitalism*, 86 (spelling standardized to American English).

25. Sennett, *Culture of the New Capitalism*, 5.

26. Ignacio Ramonet, "The Control of Pleasure," *Le monde diplomatique*, May 2000.

27. Henry David Thoreau, *Walden*, ed. J. Lyndon Shanley (Princeton, N.J.: Princeton University Press, 1971), 12.

28. Martha Nussbaum, *Women and Human Development: The Capabilities Approach* (Cambridge: Cambridge University Press, 2000).

29. Charles Taylor, *Multiculturalism: Examining the Politics of Recognition* (Princeton,N.J.: Princeton University Press, 1994).

30. Richard Rorty, *Contingency, Irony, Solidarity* (Cambridge: Cambridge University Press, 1989), 141–188.

31. Originally employed to denounce the Turkish massacre of Armenians in 1915, the phrase was eventually developed by the international legal scholar Hersch Lauterpacht and applied by the Allied powers at the Nuremberg trials in 1945 as a charge against Nazi defendants.

32. Orlando Patterson, quoted, David Brion Davis, *Inhuman Bondage: The Rise and Fall of Slavery in the New World* (New York: Oxford University Press, 2006), 30.

33. David Brion Davis, *Inhuman Bondage*, 2–3.

34. Butler, *Precarious Life*, xii.

35. Butler, *Precarious Life*, 130.

36. Rosaldo, *Culture and Truth: The Remaking of Social Analysis* (Boston: Beacon Press, 1989), 2–7.

37. Jacques Lacan, quoted in Mitchell Breitwiesser, *American Puritanism and the Defense of Mourning* (Madison: University of Wisconsin Press, 1990), 41.

38. Paul *Ricoeur, Freud and Philosophy: An Essay on Interpretation* (New Haven, Conn.: Yale University Press, 1970).

39. This passage follows very closely an argument more fully developed in Giles Gunn, *Beyond Solidarity*, 18–19.

40. See Gunn, *Beyond Solidarity*, 29.

41. Wallace Stevens, "The Idea of Order at Key West," *The Collected Poems of Wallace Stevens* (New York: Alfred A. Knopf, 1954), 129–130.

42. Butler, *Precarious Life*, 151.

43. See Mark 12:28–33.

44. See Leviticus 19:17–18, 35.

45. Kenneth Reinhard, "Freud, My Neighbor," *American Imago* 54.2 (1997): 169.

PART TWO

8

Rethinking Legality/Legitimacy after the Iraq War

Christine Chinkin

"When *I* use a word," Humpty Dumpty said in rather a scornful tone, "it means just what I choose it to mean—neither more nor less."

"The question is," said Alice, "whether you *can* make words mean so many different things."

"The question is," said Humpty Dumpty, "which is to be master—that's all."

—LEWIS CARROLL, *THROUGH THE LOOKING GLASS, CHAPTER 6*

1. Introduction

My topic is legality and legitimacy after the Iraq war. I will start by problematizing the question. First, it is too limited. Why should the question be defined in terms of "after the Iraq war," not after some other event such as the war in the Democratic Republic of the Congo where some four million people have died and where the health consequences of HIV/AIDS will continue for generations? Events, even catastrophic events, from which powerful actors have remained aloof, have little visibility as key incidents[1] in the evolution of international law. They are not deemed the "moments of crisis"[2] of which our discipline is so fond and which shape the debates and mould state practice. Yet the war in the DRC has at least been subject to international legal adjudication,[3] a scrutiny that more powerful states have resisted with respect to their interventions. Second, why is Iraq cast as a definitive moment for assessing legality and legitimacy rather than being seen in conjunction with other events—Darfur, the Middle East, nuclear proliferation, the "war on terror," the US-backed use of force by Ethiopia in Somalia—which along with many others intersect and interact in complex ways with the Iraqi situation? Third is the import of the word "after": what constitutes "after the war" in Iraq? After the end of "major combat operations" declared by President Bush from the deck of the *USS Abraham Lincoln* on May 1, 2003; or after the formal occupation; or after the time when the ongoing violence and attacks finally come to a halt?

One of the problems of evaluating legality and legitimacy is determining at what point any such assessment should be made: looking back with hindsight or contemporaneously as events unfold? An individual's,[4] a population's[5] or a government's assessment can change as it must be contingent on external criteria, on emergent or revealed facts, on the success or failure of the enterprise, or on political standpoint. Inherent in these questions is the sense that questions of legitimacy and legality in the contemporary era cannot be divorced from the role of the United States as the major player, as a permanent member of the UN Security Council (SC), and as a hegemonic power[6] that attempts to use and manipulate international law to sustain its interests. The words of Hannah Arendt are pertinent:

> Power needs no justification, being inherent in the very existence of political communities; what it does need is legitimacy. The common treatment of these two words as synonyms is no less misleading and confusing than the current equation of obedience and support. Power springs up whenever people get together and act in concert, but it derives its legitimacy from the initial getting together rather than from any action that then may follow. Legitimacy, when challenged, bases itself on an appeal to the past, while justification relates to an end that lies in the future. Violence can be justifiable, but it will never be legitimate. Its justification loses plausibility the farther its intended end recedes into the future. No one questions the use of violence in self-defense, because the danger is not only clear but present, and the end justifying the means is immediate.[7]

2. Legality and Legitimacy

Legality denotes compliance with the binding rules (substantive and procedural) of the political entity, while legitimacy denotes the normative belief by other members of the community that a rule or institution ought to be obeyed. This perception "may come from the substance of the rule or from the procedure or source by which it was constituted."[8] There are four options: an activity may be deemed legal and legitimate; legal and illegitimate; illegal and legitimate; or illegal and illegitimate.[9] In determining legality, decision makers (and the audience) are likely to start from some common notion of what constitutes "the law." Nevertheless, conclusions as to the legality of certain actions may differ depending on such factors as the weight the decision-maker accords to different sources of law, diverse meanings given to acts or statements, which facts he or she deems relevant, and the preferred interpretative techniques.

A perception of legitimacy is subjective and culturally, socially, and historically contingent. The criteria for legitimacy in international affairs have been the subject of much debate,[10] especially in the context of action that has not been explicitly authorized by the appropriate body—in the case of the use of force that charged with the primary responsibility for the maintenance of international peace and security, the UN Security Council.[11] Divergent views on both legality and legitimacy are expressed between and across societies including those that generally share common values, as for example between the US and UK governments and those in Europe that opposed the 2003 invasion of Iraq.

Since the end of the Cold War, the SC has both authorized new "measures" under UN Charter Articles 39, 41, and 42, and given a wider meaning to the triggering concept of threats to international peace and security.[12] This extended activity has raised questions about whether there are limits to the SC's power, what those limits might be, and who has the competence to determine them. For example, is prolonged detention of an individual "legal" because the SC has decided it is necessary for "the maintenance of security and stability in Iraq,"[13] and is legality to be determined by international law, regional human rights law, or national law?[14] And by whom and with what consequence? The wider ambit of SC-authorized measures has been mirrored by unauthorized responses to perceived threats where SC approval has not been sought, has been sought but not been forthcoming, or the attempt to muster support abandoned as apparently unlikely to succeed. In such instances, claims of legality must be based on rules of international law that exist outside the charter, and arguments may be bolstered by assertions of moral or political legitimacy. Intervening governments have an obvious stake in attempting to legitimize their actions to their electorates, to their military forces, and to other states, generating responses from those with an interest in delegitimizing those same actions—often using the same language and rhetoric.

Legitimacy can be seen as a substitute for legality, thereby exposing a gap between law and international community values. An assessment of "illegal but legitimate" poses questions about the legitimacy of the law itself when it is perceived as being out of touch with the moral demands of international society, and about the role of the five permanent SC members as arbiters of such issues. Of course an apparent gap between legality and legitimacy is likely to be based on the moral and political subjectivities of those who claim an action to be illegal but legitimate (or legal but illegitimate). For those who identify such a gap, it also challenges the legitimacy of the international institutions that have failed to act in accordance with the supposed values and needs of the international community. Thus, in the view of President Bush in mid-March 2003, the United Nations had "not lived up to its responsibilities" by failing to authorize "all necessary measures against Iraq." In language echoing that of Hannah Arendt, he had told the General Assembly (GA) six months earlier that "a regime that has lost its legitimacy will also lose its power."[15]

The SC faces other challenges to its legitimacy,[16] such as its lack of transparent decision making and accountability, its unrepresentative composition, and its entrenchment of the privileges of power.[17] While George Bush was (rightly) concerned that the SC would not adopt the resolutions he sought with respect to the 2003 invasion of Iraq, others fear that it has become the instrument of its permanent members, in particular the United States, manipulated by it when it can do so and ignored when it cannot.[18] Ian Hurd has warned that "[l]egitimacy is easily lost if the audience comes to believe that the institution is in the end only a stand-in for one of its members. The myth of collectivity is essential for the legitimacy of the institution."[19] Thus SC legitimacy is challenged from opposing perspectives: by those who fear its control by the United States, and by the United States when it is unable to secure that control. Proposals for its reform have been made,[20] inter alia by the High-Level Panel on Threats, Challenges, and Change;[21] the former secretary-general;[22] and the UN General Assembly (GA), which in its Millennium Declaration resolved to intensify efforts "to achieve a comprehensive reform of the Security Council."[23] At the 2005 Outcome Summit, there was insufficient political will to affirm any proposals for UN Charter amendment with respect to SC membership and only a general expression of support for early reform.[24]

Against this backdrop, I consider three exercises of Western power over the past decade that have framed thinking about the legality and legitimacy of military intervention:[25] Kosovo, Afghanistan, and Iraq.[26] In none of these cases was there unambiguous SC authorization. Nor did the GA—a more representative body of world opinion than the SC—offer much assistance in determining the legality or legitimacy of these incidents of coercive action. Various legal arguments have been offered in support of the military action in each case, including intervention on humanitarian grounds, legal responses to terrorist acts, self-defense, and the right to remove an undemocratic regime that commits human rights abuses against its own people ("regime change"). Although different weight has been given to the various legal arguments (and by different protagonists), the justifications have become merged, especially in the context of Iraq.[27]

The three cases have supposedly contributed to a crisis of confidence about the legitimacy of the international legal system as it has moved further away from the long, post–Cold War decade when the West's clarion call of commitment to democracy, the rule of law, and human rights was reaffirmed as its preferred basis for political and economic (re)ordering of society.[28] In none of the cases has the formula been made fully effective, and its thinness has been exposed by double standards and bias in application. Nathaniel Berman has described that post–Cold War decade as "an era of the more or less steadily growing legitimacy of an activist internationalism":[29] a golden era—more imagined than real in light of failures of international response in Somalia, Rwanda, and Bosnia—that seems to internationalists as one when international law had status and coherence through upholding the humanitarian instincts of the so-called international community.[30] The exposure of the fragility of this status and coherence highlights concerns about the threats to collective security in an interdependent world.[31]

3. Military Intervention in Kosovo: Legal? Legitimate?

The first of the three military actions was the NATO campaign against Serbia in 1999.[32] A number of commentators[33] (and SC member states[34]) concluded that in the absence of SC authorization, the military action was in violation of articles 2 (4) and 53 of the UN Charter and as such was illegal. Other commentators and governments (notably the United Kingdom) argued that international law had evolved: there was sufficient state practice and *opinio juris* to sustain a principle of customary international law upholding a right of humanitarian intervention as a further exception to the charter prohibition on the use of force.[35] Although argued on the basis of traditional sources of law, this view is clearly motivated by a concern that the foundational principles of international law should uphold a moral position, that the case for legality is supported by the legitimacy of the coercive response. After all "an interpretation of international law which would forbid intervention to prevent something as terrible as the holocaust . . . would be contrary to the principles upon which modern international law is based."[36] A corollary of this argument is the need to agree fixed legal criteria to determine when intervention on humanitarian grounds might be undertaken so as to limit the potential of abuse of a precedent based on exceptional circumstances.

It was not only those who argued for the legality of the action who considered it legitimate. Among those who considered the action illegal the view was also expressed that it was in some sense legitimate: military action had been carried out to put an end to violations of human rights committed by the Serbs against the Kosovar Albanians rather than out of any self-interest of the NATO states. The SC's implicit endorsement of the agreement that ended the military campaign and established UNMIK (civil presence) and KFOR (security presence)[37] arguably supported this view,[38] as did the failure of the Russian attempt to have a resolution adopted condemning the action.[39] Only a "thin red line" separated the NATO action from formal legality;[40] if customary international law had not yet evolved a principle of humanitarian intervention, it was at least moving in that direction.[41] An expressed attitude was that an international legal system that stood back while people were being massacred because of a "deference to the UN or . . . outmoded or overly rigid restrictions on the use of force"[42] that upheld the supremacy of state sovereignty was not morally acceptable.

Nevertheless such assertions of legitimacy have their troubling aspects.[43] Could we be sure of the facts upon which the military action was based? How do we factor into the equation the mass movements of displaced persons that intensified with the commencement of the bombing? What is the legitimacy of bombing from 15,000 feet after the departure of OSCE verification monitors and without providing ground troops as protection for the population? What is the legitimacy of excluding human rights obligations from the actions of those bombing missions?[44] How are the criteria of reasonableness and proportionality to be applied to the *jus ad bellum* and *jus in bello* where the military objective is not to acquire territory or secure some strategic objective but to protect human rights? How do we assess the willingness to intervene in Kosovo against unwillingness in the Congo or Sudan, and the insistence on an Indonesian "request" to military intervention in East Timor some six months later?[45] Moving forward to 2011, the limited number of States that have recognized the Republic of Kosovo as an independent state and the International Court of Justice's narrow focus on the "legality" of Kosovo's unilateral declaration of independence in 2008 suggest that the tension between legitimacy and legality has not abated.[46]

Two merging lines of development can be discerned following the Kosovo moment that bear upon similar debates after the Iraq war. The first is relatively well evidenced, that is the growing interest in the concept of human security. Unlike national security, which focuses upon the state and the sanctity of state borders, human security puts the security of people at the center of international policy-making: "their physical safety, their economic and social well being, respect for their dignity and worth as human beings, and the protection of their human rights and fundamental freedoms."[47] The so-called "responsibility to protect" is vested primarily in states with respect to their own citizens but ultimately in the international community if states are unwilling or unable to give it effect. This language was used by the secretary-general in his report, *In Larger Freedom*,[48] spelled out as a commitment by the GA in its Outcome Document, 2005,[49] and generally endorsed by the SC in its Resolution 1674.[50] In express terms, on 17 March 17, 2011, the SC reiterated in Resolution 1973 the "responsibility of the Libyan authorities to protect the Libyan population" and authorized the "use of all necessary measures" to protect civilians.

The second is more nebulous. Kosovo represented a significant use of force without SC authorization, albeit under the auspices of a regional defense organization that had previously been called upon by the council to act on its behalf.[51] That its intervention was regarded as legitimate in at least some influential quarters may have been a factor in encouraging further unauthorized action, including that in Iraq in 2003. Although the circumstances were different, some features were similar, including the presence of a repressive regime with a history of human rights abuses. It is impossible to know the weight to be given to the different influences that motivated the US and UK leaders in Iraq. However while the neoconservative agenda appears to have been a considerable factor for President Bush, Tony Blair has expressed himself forcefully in terms of the need to uphold international community values. He has said that Kosovo cannot be seen in isolation because: "[It] is a just war, based not on any territorial ambitions but on values. We cannot let the evil of ethnic cleansing stand. We must not rest until it is reversed. We have learned twice before in this century that appeasement does not work. If we let an evil dictator range unchallenged, we will have to spill infinitely more blood and treasure to stop him later."[52] The strength of this opinion—and his own sense of "rightness" in having championed a "legitimate" conflict—may have strengthened his resolve four years later.[53]

4. Military Intervention in Afghanistan: Legal? Legitimate?

If there was at least some support for a verdict of "illegal but legitimate" in Kosovo, exercise of military power by the United States and its allies against Afghanistan in October 2001 was widely perceived as "legal and legitimate." The coalition of the willing had resounding support in the aftermath of the atrocities of September 11, 2001,[54] and the legitimacy of the US response was widely assumed,[55] except by those who were not "with us" in the "war on terror." The claim that the United States was acting in self-defense[56] rather than in illegal reprisal[57] was not seriously challenged.

Yet the legal argument might perhaps not be as strong as is often supposed. Security Council Resolution 1373, September 28, 2003, acknowledged the right to self-defense within its preamble but not in the body of its text. Nor did the SC explicitly state the right to apply following the September 11 attacks, as it did for instance with respect to Kuwait's right to self-defense after Iraq's 1990 invasion.[58] Resolution 1373 refers to "terrorist acts" not "armed attack," which is the trigger for UN Charter Article 51. The resolution provides numerous steps that states must undertake to undermine the financing of terrorism but does not use the now well-established formula of authorizing "all necessary means" to achieve its objectives. An explicit authorization of force is unnecessary for the inherent right of self-defense to arise, but this requires identifying the September 11 attacks as an armed attack, or as an act of aggression, of which an armed attack is a subcategory.

While flying civilian planes into the World Trade Center and Pentagon indisputably constituted attacks, they were carried out by non-state actors. Does this have legal import? The UN Charter regulates relations between sovereign states and is predicated upon that basis. This starting point is explicit in the GA definition of aggression which states that "aggression is the use of armed force by a State . . . ."[59] International law on the use of force was not developed for application to contemporary forms of violence operating outside the inter-state paradigm,[60] although this did not inhibit the NATO states from invoking Article 5 of the North Atlantic Treaty on September 12, 2001.[61] The ICJ has been more cautious. Its decision in *Armed Activities on the Territory of the Congo*, reiterates a generally narrow understanding of self-defense. The Court did not determine "whether and under what conditions contemporary international law provides for a right of self-defense against attacks by irregular forces."[62] Judges Simma and Kooijmans directly addressed the issue: Judge Simma considered that SC resolutions 1368 and 1373 "cannot but be read as affirmations . . . that large scale attacks can qualify as 'armed attacks'" within the terms of Article 51, and both he and Judge Kooijmans considered that armed attacks by non-state actors should be subject to the same tests as those committed by states.[63]

State practice is also unhelpful in elucidating whether there is a right to self-defense against terrorist acts. The only states with consistent practice on this are the United States and Israel, states that have suffered repeated terrorist attacks from outside their territory, and which have the military and intelligence capabilities to respond. The helpfulness of responses by other states in gauging the lawfulness of US and Israeli actions is limited because they are typically fashioned by political alliances rather than through legal evaluation.[64]

Some tests have been proposed for resolving this interpretative dilemma. One is that a military response to terrorist attacks is lawful when the acts are on a scale equivalent to what would be an armed attack if conducted by government forces—a test recognizing that in the twenty-first century, states do not have a monopoly on the ability to use force or commit horrendous acts—but which equates the scale of destruction to that associated with the exercise of state powers. A second is that self-defense is more likely to be accepted as legal when it is in response to terrorist acts on a state's own territory rather than those committed against its nationals abroad. A third is a twofold test requiring "a very serious attack on the territory of the injured state or on its agents or citizens while at home or abroad" and that these acts form part of a consistent pattern of violent terrorist actions rather than isolated or sporadic attacks.[65]

The issue of whether an armed attack emanating from non-state actors gives rise to the right to self-defense is connected to the questions of legal targets for defensive action, the objectives of that action and proportionality. Given that terrorist cells operate transnationally and constitute ill-defined targets, the crucial question is whether a state that provides a safe haven for alleged terrorists is an appropriate target. Was Afghanistan, at the time under an unrecognized and undemocratic regime with a record of human rights violations, responsible under international law for harboring those who planned and instigated terrorist attacks, and did such harboring constitute an armed attack giving rise to the right of self-defense? The US response equated the Taliban and the al Qaeda network by seeking (unsuccessfully) to destroy the latter through overthrowing the former. Such actions, which amount to assisting one party in a civil war, go well beyond the accepted use of force in self-defense,[66] which must be exclusively directed to repel the armed attack of the aggressor.

Despite the levels of destruction of civilian life and what might be characterized as legal niceties about whether the UN Charter is applicable to armed attacks committed by non-state actors, the international institutions upheld the legality of the 2001 military campaign against Afghanistan. The GA condemned the use of Afghan territory for terrorist activities and the export of terrorism from Afghanistan.[67] In an outstanding feat of misrepresentation it welcomed "the successful efforts of the Afghan people to remove the Taliban regime and the terrorist organizations it hosted" and urged a political settlement for a broad-based, gender-sensitive, multi-ethnic, and fully representative government—factors that would also retrospectively enhance the legitimacy of regime change. The assumption that domestic legitimacy is assured through conformity with democracy, the rule of law, and human rights bolsters that of international legitimacy. These factors—the need to deter further terrorist attacks, a repressive regime, and gross human rights violations—became merged and developed the context in which arguments for the legality and legitimacy of the war in Iraq would subsequently be put forward.

The United States and its allies sought other ways to bolster the legitimacy of its bombing of Afghanistan (at least to its domestic audience), for example through assertion of women's human rights. Before commencing military action against Afghanistan (but not until after September 11) there were concerted efforts to emphasize the nature of the Taliban's violations of women's human rights,[68] a strategy directed at depicting the Taliban as barbaric and deserving of destruction for reasons additional to their sheltering of terrorists. Afghan women were presented as the passive victims of an uncivilized regime to justify punitive action by the civilized, who would bring human rights and democracy in their wake. In ways reminiscent of colonial "civilizing" missions, this also serves to legitimize the violence that was committed against the persons and property of civilians in Afghanistan: "Once the depiction of the 'savage other' as an unruly horde is completed, the civilized self justifies its brutalization of the former as a heaven-ordained task of pacification and civilization. This mission, often backed with tremendous violence, is uniquely construed as an unavoidable task of creating order from the chaotic environment of the savage."[69] However, these attempts at constructing legitimacy have been undermined by the inconsistent approach to women's human rights in the reconstruction efforts in Afghanistan.[70] Some formal advances have been made, for example Afghanistan's accession to the Convention on the Elimination of All Forms of Discrimination against Women on 5 March 2003 and a constitutional guarantee of equality.[71] However, violations of women's human rights have been ignored or discounted by the United States when other imperatives have prevailed, including forming alliances with the Northern Alliance, Pakistan, and Saudi Arabia and in 2011 open discussion of negotiation with the Taliban. Military intervention has failed to deliver equality and security for many of Afghanistan's women.[72] The blatant appeal to women's human rights in the case of Afghanistan contrasts with the silence in this respect in both Kosovo[73] and Iraq and highlights the instrumentality of any reference to gender relations in assessing the legitimacy of military action. The likely positive effect of focus on advancement of women's human rights on domestic audiences in intervening states is typically subordinated to other political imperatives. Meanwhile, a legitimacy audit of foreign military intervention should take into account its possible consequences for women, such as the popular appeal of extremist movements, reduced physical security in public and private spaces, lessened ability freely to access employment, education, health, and other facilities, the feminization of poverty, and women's vulnerability to begging, prostitution, and being trafficked, and thus to gender-based violence. The general acceptance of the legality and legitimacy of the military intervention in 2001 has not continued. By 2011, it has become common-place to talk of a "legitimacy crisis" in Afghanistan fostered by the high financial and human costs (primarily to Afghan civilians but also to military forces), political instability, insecurity, and the resurgence of the Taliban. Nevertheless, the withdrawal of most foreign troops is envisaged by 2014. The long military action without achievement of its goals has contributed to this shift in perception and indicates the contingency of evaluations of legitimacy.

5. The Occupation of Iraq: Legal? Legitimate?

Kosovo and Afghanistan provide legal and political backdrops to the US- and UK-led invasion of Iraq in March 2003, following the various coercive actions that had continued since the 1991 ceasefire.[74] Strong opinions that the action against Iraq was illegal, including from other SC permanent members and numerous academic commentators, have been aired.[75] Many of the contextual factors deemed relevant in Kosovo or Afghanistan have been reiterated, either singly or in conjunction with each other, in attempts to cloak dubious legality with some legitimacy. The arguments for both legality and legitimacy have shifted and been given different emphasis at different times in response to factual and political changes, in particular the failure to find weapons of mass destruction in Iraq. Depending upon one's perspective, this either allows for a cumulative strength to develop or undermines the weight of all such arguments: one of the justifications must be valid, or at least taken together they must constitute a sound basis for the military action, or alternatively, none of the arguments can stand up alone and a multiplicity of arguments provides no greater credence.

The international institutions have given little assistance as they have remained largely silent. Unlike SC Resolution 1244, which "welcomed" the political solution to the Kosovo crisis, SC Resolution 1483, May 22, 2003, merely noted the letters recording the establishment of the Coalition Provisional Authority (CPA) in Iraq. The GA abdicated responsibility for bestowing either international approval or condemnation of the invasion and its aftermath. The former secretary-general did at last assert the illegality of the war in September 2004.[76] The ICJ has not been seised of the war in Iraq. However in the *Armed Activities on the Territory of the Congo* case it reaffirmed its earlier jurisprudence that UN Charter

Article 51 creates "strict confines" to the application of force in self-defense and that a state cannot use its "perceived security interests" to use force beyond those parameters.[77]

In contrast to its silence about the invasion, the SC "called upon" the CPA to promote the welfare of Iraqis "through the effective administration of the territory" thereby rendering the occupation (until June 28, 2004)[78] ostensibly legal. However it "goes without saying that the outcome of an unlawful act is tainted with illegality."[79] Moreover, the SC's endorsement of the CPA does not necessarily uphold either the legality or legitimacy of specific actions undertaken (or omitted) by it. The following sections examine some of the factors contributing to, or detracting from, the legality and legitimacy of US and UK actions as occupying powers in Iraq.

5.1 SYMBOLIC LEGITIMACY

After the contested invasion, the coalition powers needed the help of other members of the international community in Iraq's reconstruction, which would not be forthcoming if that period was widely perceived as an illegal and illegitimate occupation rather than as the "liberation" proclaimed by the United States. They therefore sought the symbolic legitimacy that would be accorded by SC endorsement, thus espousing behavior different from that they would otherwise have adopted because "they believe[d] the institution require[d] them to."[80] The United States and United Kingdom realized the inevitability of hard negotiation. Although they were willing to return to the SC to seek an acceptable resolution, their problem was twofold: they had to convince SC members to allow them to go beyond the restraints imposed by occupation law while not ceding primary authority to the United Nations through a post-conflict international administration, as in Kosovo.[81] Other SC members would not endorse the military action (as had arguably been achieved in Resolution 1244 on Kosovo) but did seek some status in Iraq. From their perspective there was the possibility of regaining some of the authority that had been eroded by the coalition's unauthorized recourse to force. As Ian Hurd has described it: "there is power in being seen as the legitimate author of . . . changes."[82] The post-conflict SC resolutions on Iraq were therefore hard-fought compromises with ambiguous and imprecise language.[83]

As they wanted to be thought of as "liberators"[84] of Iraq, the joint letter of May 8, 2003, from the US and UK permanent representatives to the president of the SC did not use the word "occupation" and asserted only that the two states were exercising "powers of government temporarily." In contrast, Resolution 1483 described the United States and United Kingdom by the less legitimate (but more factually accurate) designation of "occupying powers" acting through the CPA. This had implications for the relevant legal regime and the resolution spelled out the applicability of occupation law, "including" the Fourth Geneva Convention and the

Hague Regulations. The implication that other, unspecified principles of international law were also applicable allowed both for wider powers through SC authorization and further constraints through, for example, the applicability of human rights law. Paragraph 8 provided for the appointment of a Special Representative of the Secretary-General (SRSG) in Iraq and listed his "independent responsibilities," although the mandate was ill-defined and essentially limited to reporting to the council and coordinating various activities. The SRSG was required to work intensively with the Authority, which in contrast was not obliged to report to the SC. The "vital role"[85] of the United Nations in reconstruction was in fact little more than a face-saver for the organization and a weak legitimizing device for the United States and United Kingdom. The SC thus did not bestow either the sought-after legitimacy on the coalition, nor any clearly defined authority on the United Nations.

Security Council Resolution 1483 did provide the needed façade of legality after the divisiveness within the council caused by the invasion. But the symbolic power of the United Nations had been severely dented both by the United States' and United Kingdom's unauthorized recourse to force and by the United Nations' failure to make them accountable for it.[86] Within Iraq, the United Nations' previous history, including the long sanctions regime with its resultant hardships, and the manipulation by Saddam Hussein of the oil-for-food program with the connivance of the SC, undermined the institution's legitimacy. The unwillingness of other states "that are not occupying powers"[87] to work with or under the CPA, or to contribute to the multinational force, suggests that they did not consider the United Nations to have legitimated the enterprise.[88] The deadly attack on UN headquarters on August 19, 2003, shows the extent to which the institution's legitimacy had been damaged within Iraq.[89]

Particular points of contestation between the occupying powers, Iraqis, and the United Nations were the process for the transfer of power, the mode of selection of appropriate Iraqi representatives, and the powers they could exercise. In order to give credence to their self-designation as "liberators," the United States and United Kingdom emphasized from the outset their facilitation of "the efforts of the Iraqi people to take the first steps towards forming a representative government based on the rule of law."[90] The SC maintained the fiction of the continued "sovereignty and territorial integrity" of Iraq and expressed encouragement for the Iraqi people to restore and establish emblematic institutions for representative governance. The first step was the establishment of the Iraqi Governing Council (IGC) in July 2003. Although its members were appointed by the CPA,[91] the SC welcomed the broadly representative IGC "as an important step towards the formation by the people of Iraq of an internationally recognized, representative government"[92] and subsequently upheld it as "embodying the sovereignty of the State of Iraq."[93]

As attacks on the occupiers mounted after the summer of 2003, the United States increasingly needed the symbolic legitimacy the United Nations could bestow with respect to the modality and timing of the transfer of power and the constitutional basis for an Iraqi government. Paul Bremer, the CPA administrator, had favored the Iraqis drafting a constitution and elections being held during the occupation, but this became increasingly unlikely in face of opposition from within the IGC and the rising insurgency. In November 2003, the Bush administration changed its direction and agreed to a timetable for drafting a Transitional Administrative Law (TAL) and for local caucuses within the Iraqi governorates to elect delegates to a Transitional National Assembly, which in turn would elect an interim Iraqi government to assume power on June 30, 2004, when the CPA would terminate.[94] Direct elections would take place in 2005. These plans proved divisive among Iraqis, and the United States was unable to move forward, in part at least because Shi'a Grand Ayatollah Ali al-Sistani (who was demanding immediate direct elections) refused to meet with Paul Bremer. Bremer went "hat in hand"[95] to ask the United Nations to act as "an impartial third-party broker"[96] in assessing the feasibility of elections. The UN team, headed by Lakhdar Brahimi, met with all the key players and made influential recommendations. By "engaging with Iraqi society," Brahimi sought to "cultivate legitimacy for a step-by-step political process."[97] The non-elected interim government replaced the IGC on June 1, 2004, and remained until the implementation of the January 2005 elections. The interim government however was subject to SC Resolution 1546, and the TAL, which was adopted by the IGC after a process involving the CPA, the United Nations, and other groups. Security Council Resolution 1546 endorsed the interim government but did not refer to the TAL and imposed its own restrictions, notably that it was to refrain from any actions affecting Iraq's destiny beyond the interim period. This was at odds both with the reaffirmation of Iraqi sovereignty and the sweeping reordering of Iraqi society undertaken by the CPA. The United Nations thus secured some legitimacy for the transition of power without assuming responsibility for security in Iraq (and thus also avoiding blame for its failure). Security remained the task of the coalition forces, transformed after Resolution 1511 into a SC-authorized multinational force (MNF) and formally sustained after June 28, 2004, by "the request of the incoming Interim Government of Iraq."[98]

Symbolism suggests representations and imagery in place of reality. In many ways, this was the situation in "post-conflict" Iraq. The CPA was constructed by the United States and United Kingdom as a front behind which they could shelter, denying responsibility for their actions by claiming the CPA to be the responsible actor.[99] Similarly, the United States and United Kingdom maintained the fiction of the proactive role of the IGC, despite the CPA's "ability to ignore Governing Council objections to its decisions or to by-pass consultation in the first place."[100] This reality highlighted the symbolism of Iraqi defeat invoked by the language and indicators of empire, for example, the establishment of the heavily fortified, self-sufficient and Americanized Green Zone in Saddam Hussein's main palaces[101] and the tagging of Paul Bremer by Brahimi as the "dictator of Iraq,"[102] or "viceroy."[103] These characterizations are supported by the starting point of CPA Regulations and Orders—that they are promulgated pursuant to Bremer's authority "as administrator of the Coalition Provisional Authority." In Iraq, the administration became the preferred legal order of the invader and occupier.

5.2 "LEGITIMACY OF COHERENCE"[104]

Operating within the context of a coherent legal system that provides for consistency and certainty is another hallmark of legitimacy. Mark Suchman defined *legitimacy* as "a generalized perception or assumption that the actions of an entity are desirable, proper, or appropriate within some socially constructed system of norms, values, beliefs, and definitions."[105] This is especially apt as a yardstick against which to assess the CPA. Belligerent occupation is just such a socially constructed system: military power regulated and constrained by law. The United States and United Kingdom went beyond the restrictions imposed upon occupying powers by the Hague Regulations and Fourth Geneva Convention that require the occupier to "take all the measures in his power to restore, and ensure, as far as possible, public order and safety, while respecting, unless absolutely prevented, the laws in force in the country."[106] In its Regulation No. 1, the CPA vested in itself all legislative, executive, and judicial authority necessary to achieve its (not the SC's) objectives, six days before the adoption of SC Resolution 1483, thereby exposing the fiction of SC decision making. This authority was to be exercised by the CPA administrator. The Coalition Provisional Authority's Order 1 endorsed the disestablishment of the Baathist party and Order 2 dissolved many Iraqi entities, including the armed forces. These "transformative" actions could only be legally justified if authorized by the SC.

The extent to which SC Resolution 1483 (and subsequent resolutions), in conjunction with other principles of international law, for example human rights law, authorized the extensive reordering of Iraqi political and economic[107] structures is arguable.[108] What is unarguable is the impact of such changes in undermining the legitimacy of the occupation in the eyes of Iraqis who did not perceive them as "desirable, proper or appropriate."[109] The disbanding of the army created large-scale unemployment,[110] while the de-Baathification process tainted all former party members with the illegitimacy of the Saddam Hussein regime, regardless of the individual's own history and record. In addition to these legislative acts, numerous other factual aspects of the occupation militate against a conclusion of legitimacy with respect to Iraqis (and external actors) including inadequate preparations for the aftermath of military intervention,[111] failure to prevent looting, widespread detentions, coercive interrogatory techniques, and apparent disregard for civilian deaths as evidenced by the lack of records of their numbers or investigations of fatal incidents. Many failings stemmed from political factors such as the relationship between the United

Nations and the occupying powers, the reliance on Iraqi exiles, the Pentagon's post-conflict role, and the initial unwillingness of the CPA to allow states that had not supported the coalition to bid for contracts.[112] Other factors were rooted in the conduct of the civilian and military authorities in occupation Iraq that undermined the rule of law. The following are illustrative of many other examples that could have been discussed.[113]

First, the CPA by Order 17 accorded extensive immunities from the Iraqi legal process to the occupiers and their civilian contractors. Order 17 was renewed on June 27, 2004 (the day before the "handover" to the interim Iraqi government) to provide for continued immunity after the demise of the CPA. The legality of the occupiers' actions was not to be tested in Iraq. Second, these extensive powers and privileges might have been less damaging to the legitimacy of the occupation if the occupiers had themselves complied with human rights standards. This was conspicuously not the case as in the use of torture at Abu Ghraib and the death in British custody in Iraq of Baha Mousa, whose "dead body . . . was covered in blood and bruises."[114] Human rights abuses committed by the Saddam Hussein regime do not excuse those committed by the occupiers. Both the United States and United Kingdom have denied the applicability of their international human rights obligations to the actions of their forces in Iraq, insisting on the territorial application of the relevant instruments and preferring any assessments of legality to be made against the less demanding standards of the laws of war. This stance has been rejected by the UN human rights treaty bodies[115] and (in the case of the United Kingdom) the European Court of Human Rights.[116] No independent human rights monitor was mandated in Iraq such as the ombudsperson in Kosovo.[117] This culture of impunity is furthered by the failure of the prosecutor of the International Criminal Court to investigate allegations of war crimes and violations of the Geneva Conventions in Iraq.[118]

Failure to act within the principles asserted as the basis for regime change plays into the hands of radical opponents who can proclaim the justness of their cause while highlighting the dissonance between the occupiers' asserted values and those revealed by their behavior. In Hurd's words: "Sociologists and anthropologists report that resistance works best when presented in terms borrowed from the language of the authority and where the point is not to challenge the existing authority head-on but to argue that the existing authority is not being true to its own professed values."[119]

Third, the occupiers sought to enhance the legality and legitimacy of their actions through extensive use of SC powers under UN Charter Chapter VII while changing established laws (for example occupation law) in conjunction with a formalist legal regime promulgated by the CPA. That body was a hyperactive legislative body, creating a detailed legal regime that obscured the reality of rule by imperial decree (and the impossibility of delivery). In just over thirteen months, it adopted twelve Regulations (defining the CPA's institutions and authorities), one hundred Orders (binding instructions to Iraqis, including changes to Iraqi law), seventeen Memoranda (documents adjusting procedures applicable to a Regulation or Order) and twelve Public Notices (conveying the administrator's intentions to the public). The CPA's Regulation 1 asserted that "Regulations and Orders issued by the [CPA] administrator shall take precedence over all other laws."

Where explicit SC authorization was lacking for specific actions it was implied, for example through letters annexed to the relevant resolution and interpretative techniques that had been crafted to fit the argument. John Bellinger III, legal adviser to the US State Department, has explained that this was a deliberately adopted strategy. He has told how lawyers for the coalition partners analyzed the law of occupation and found that they "faced some difficult tasks in reconciling the legal rules."[120] Security Council resolutions were negotiated to "set forth specific rules to govern particular aspects of the occupation" irrespective of existing treaty obligations. Bellinger referred to the *Al Jedda* litigation in the UK courts to illustrate the effectiveness of this legal manipulation.[121] Mr. Al Jedda is an Iraqi/UK dual national who was detained between 10 October 2004 and 30 December 2007 without charge in a UK facility in Iraq. The secretary of state claimed that his detention was authorized by SC Resolution 1546, which decided inter alia that the MNF "shall have all the authority to take all necessary measures to contribute to the maintenance of security and stability in Iraq in accordance with the letters annexed to this resolution." The letters referred to were from the prime minister of the interim Iraqi government and then US secretary of state, Colin Powell. The latter stated that "[u]nder the agreed arrangement, the MNF stands ready to continue to undertake a broad range of tasks to contribute to the maintenance of security and to ensure forces protection. . . . This will include . . . internment where this is necessary for imperative reasons of security in Iraq. . . ." This language echoes that of the Fourth Geneva Convention, Article 78, applicable to occupation, but has no counterpart in human rights law. The UK courts determined that the resolution displaces the human rights guarantees accorded by the European Convention on Human Rights. Bellinger described this as "a good illustration of the Security Council's increasing willingness to address threats to international peace and security by invoking its Chapter VII authorities to create mechanisms to ensure accountability for specialized bodies of law, and to tailor those bodies of law when specialized legal frameworks are needed to effectively address the problem."[122] An alternative view is that it undermines the commitment of the international legal system to the rule of law by allowing the institutional hierarchy[123] to trump other values and legal obligations. In July 2011, the Grand Chamber of the European Court of Human Rights preferred this second view and held the UK to be in violation of Article 5 of the European Convention on Human Rights, determining that the language of the SC Resolution did not unambiguously indicate 'that the Security Council intended to place Member States within the Multi-National Force under an obligation to use measures of indefinite internment without charge and without judicial guarantees, in breach of their undertakings under international human rights instruments including the Convention.'[124]

The extension of the powers of Iraq's occupiers beyond those set out in the Hague Regulations and the Fourth Geneva Convention was a blatant illustration of what David Malone has called the geostrategic use of the SC by its permanent members, in particular the United States and United Kingdom, as a resource for their own purposes.[125] They ensure appropriate language within a resolution when it supports their interests while bypassing the council when it does not do so. Such "defiance legitimacy"[126] challenges the international community by flouting stable legal requirements and requiring acceptance that these are irrelevant and not suited to contemporary demands. Further, focus on the flouting of occupation law obscured the normalization, and thus legitimization, of the occupation in accordance with US (imperial) ideologies and objectives.[127] What was dimmed was that the "biggest mistake of the occupation . . . was the occupation itself."[128]

Language too was distorted, or came to mean the opposite of its normal meaning. The SC "reaffirm[ed] the sovereignty and territorial integrity of Iraq" (resolutions 1483 and 1511) in disregard of the empirical reality that sovereignty was made permeable and territorial integrity violated. Security Council Resolution 1546 (setting out the terms of the transfer of power from the CPA) imposed limitations on the "fully sovereign and independent" interim Iraqi government that supposedly "assumed full responsibility and authority." In *Al Jedda*, the UK courts upheld that the "maintenance of security and stability in Iraq"[129] justified detention without charge or trial for many years: "incommunicado detention in Iraq [became] a measure to protect human rights."[130] Expressions such as "implied Security Council authorization," "creeping unilateralism,"[131] "unreasonable veto,"[132] and "pre-emptive self-defense"[133] entered the international law lexicon as euphemisms for illegal action under existing law. The term "war on terror" legitimized the violence of the United States and its coalition partners: "[c]alling it a war legitimizes what is often a very one-sided violence—like calling bull-fighting a sport."[134] Language was used to shame those who resisted, as in "our boys" or the "Patriot Act." Thucydides put it rather more eruditely than Humpty Dumpty in his *History of the Peloponnesian Wars*: "Words had to change their ordinary meanings and to take that which was now given to them."[135]

6. Legitimacy: The View of Civil Society

Military intervention in Iraq was challenged by civil society within the West prior to March 2003 when huge public demonstrations against the war took place throughout the world.[136] The legality and legitimacy of the invasion and occupation were examined by a Peoples' Tribunal, the World Tribunal on Iraq (WTI). The WTI was a response to the frustration caused by the failure of state institutions to address these issues. It held over twenty sessions in different parts of the world to hear testimony and to evaluate the actions of especially (but not exclusively) the United States and United Kingdom against legal and moral criteria.

The WTI culminated in a final session in Istanbul in June 2005, where the findings of the preceding sessions on the legal, political, social, and ethical wrongs committed against the people of Iraq were summarized, analysis of specific crimes and violations was carried out, and statements made. The prestigious Jury of Conscience heard extensive victim and witness testimony, expert statements, and legal advocacy. It asserted its legitimacy to be "located in the collective conscience of humanity"[137] and speaking in this name made a series of findings, named those who should be subject to investigation, and made recommendations.[138] In the words of Justice Kirby of the High Court of Australia: "The growth of the activities of Peoples Tribunals is, in one sense, a response to the inadequacy of the institutions of the International Community. In another sense, it is an assertion of the rights of peoples themselves which are different from the rights of states and of international organizations."[139]The organizers of the tribunal sought to preempt accusations of its own illegitimacy[140] by invoking symbols of legitimacy, such as ensuring worldwide participation, including especially the global South, evoking the formal rituals of advocacy and the symbolism of a Jury of Conscience. Civil society resistance has been discounted by the coalition partners and in the state-centered international legal system does not constitute protest militating against acceptance of state practice.

A Peoples' Tribunal is one mechanism through which the voices of civil society may be heard, albeit in an unofficial (or non-state) setting. Others have been suggested. For example, the 1995 Commission on Global Governance proposed an International Assembly of People and a Forum of Civil Society with direct access to the UN system.[141] In 2000, the UN secretary-general proposed a NGO Millennium Forum, to be held in conjunction with the Millennium Assembly.[142] Richard Falk and Andrew Strauss have argued for a standing Global Peoples Assembly, organized and represented by civil society. Their vision is for a "globally democratic institutional structure that would enable the peoples of the world to have a meaningful and effective voice."[143] A less radical suggestion might be allowing participation of civil society representatives at meetings of the SC.[144]

7. Conclusions

In their use of military interventions in recent years, Western powers, notably the United States and United Kingdom, have attempted to shift the boundaries of legitimate behavior by claiming exceptions to the UN Charter based on a broad mix of values, human rights, democracy, and national security. Where possible, they have also sought legality within the terms of the charter, seeking the support of the Security Council to authorize "all necessary measures" in response to ever-widening understandings of what constitutes a threat to international peace and security, especially under the guise of the "war on terror." Where there is procedural legality it may be hoped that legitimacy will be assumed. However, while the cases of Kosovo and Afghanistan showed some readiness to admit the legitimacy of actions undertaken to further human rights and democracy or in pursuit of terrorists, this may have changed, and the legitimacy of the façade of legality through SC authorization may be also questioned. Events following the military interventions in Afghanistan and Iraq have demonstrated the ineffectiveness of force that lacks, or fails to sustain, international or national legitimacy, and SC authorization for the deployment of KFOR in Kosovo did not prevent the eruption of violence in March 2004. Examples of post-Iraq intervention illustrate how the SC continues to be used in the furtherance of the hegemonic mission of international law and how language, national laws, and supposed international values continue to be made contingent.

First, SC Resolution 1725, December 6, 2006, authorized an African Union (AU) protection mission to Somalia with an endorsement that border states should not deploy troops there. Later in December, in blatant disregard of this endorsement, Ethiopia deployed troops in Somalia, not as part of the AU mission but instead to fight against the Union of Islamic Courts in support of the Transitional Federal Government. It is also worth noting that "every independent account"[145] deemed the Union of Islamic Courts to have brought the first peace and stability to Somalia since 1991. Abuses were committed against civilians by all sides in this round of violence in Somalia, but it was "the Ethiopians with their superior weapons who are doing much of the harm in Mogadishu." Ethiopia also engaged "in a regional program of arbitrary detentions and unlawful renditions of individuals of interest to Addis Ababa and their allies in Washington."[146] Far from any recourse to the "responsibility to protect," the destruction of civilian life and property accompanying this military intervention caused little international outrage or condemnation. Ethiopia's contempt for Resolution 1725 was not condemned by the SC, which did not demand withdrawal of Ethiopian troops or impose sanctions against Ethiopia; it only "welcomed" Ethiopia's decision to withdraw its troops but without setting down any timetable or monitoring mechanism of progress toward this objective. Illegality was effectively legitimated because, as was said at the time, "Ethiopia and its Somali proxies, including a large number of warlords with notorious records of abuse from earlier conflicts, are perceived by the EU and US government as key allies in the 'war on terror' and are doing the west's dirty work against Somalia's Islamists. Behind the scenes the United States has been helping the Ethiopian military effort and interrogating suspects in Ethiopian detention."[147] The European Union apparently warned that "war crimes might have been committed," and that if this was the case it "would be complicit."[148]

Second, John Bellinger III has cited the US support for a Special Tribunal for Lebanon as evidence of that country's commitment to international law.[149] The tribunal "of an international character" was negotiated between the UN secretary-general and the Lebanese government pursuant to SC Resolution 1664, March 29, 2006. The council approved the statute and it was signed by the United Nations. However, under the Lebanese constitution, a treaty must be ratified by parliament, which was not done because of internal political disagreement. Security Council

Resolution 1757, May 30, 2007, overrode this requirement and brought the treaty into force. Some states spoke against "forceful interference" in the national constitutional process.[150] Such interference is of course not new. In 1992, Libya asserted that it was acting in compliance with the Montreal Convention, Article 8, by taking steps to submit the persons accused of bombing Pan Am flight 103 to its competent prosecution authorities because Libyan law prevents extradition of its own nationals. The ICJ would not review the SC resolution imposing sanctions for Libya's failure to comply with the US and UK demands,[151] although the council was superseding national law. The Special Tribunal for Lebanon can be viewed as an innovative and legitimate use of UN Charter, Chapter VII that will protect the Lebanese people and enhance their political freedom, or alternatively as an illegitimate and unwarranted intervention that constitutes misuse of SC powers.

The third example does not involve new SC resolutions but the continued flouting of old ones. Hamas, the government of Palestine elected in January 2006, was shunned by the international community and subjected to a political and economic embargo by the European Union and United States. Israel froze VAT monies belonging to the Palestinian Authority amounting to US $50–60 million per month, effectively imposing a collective punishment on Palestinian voters and creating—not responding to—a humanitarian crisis.[152] In the words of the UN special rapporteur, John Dugard: "This is difficult to understand." Israel, which is in breach of SC and GA resolutions, escapes economic sanctions while the people living under occupation were made subject to "possibly the most rigorous form of international sanctions" of modern times.[153] After Hamas gained control in Gaza in June 2007, the Palestinian president installed the unelected Salam Fayyad as prime minister, and the embargo was terminated. This too undermined any commitment to a "responsibility to protect" or democracy.

These three examples perhaps answer the question posed at the outset as to why the focus is on legality and legitimacy "after the Iraq War." They show that the Iraq war was not a single "one-off" experience of disrespect for the international rule of law in the contemporary world order. Rather it is part of a sequence of events commencing well before the 2003 invasion and continuing apparently unabated. Language and legal concepts have been hijacked and international legality claimed regardless of their compliance with formal legal requirements.[154] When adopted, some SC resolutions are discounted with impunity while others are imposed with disregard for other national, regional, or international legal orders. Bias and double standards permeate the mantra of democracy, human rights, and the rule of law, making assessments of legitimacy ever more conditional. At times it appears that we are sleepwalking our way to an international regime where legality has been displaced by the assertions of legitimacy by the powerful. However, there are also strenuous efforts made to resist this through the media, through civil society action, through activist lawyering, and through scholarship and analysis of what is occurring and its consequences. Although such efforts may be denied the force of state action, they offer a vital counterbalance to determinations of legality and legitimacy.

Endnotes

I would like to thank the Joseph Rowntree Charitable Trust for its support for a project by Phil Shiner of Public Interest Lawyers, Andrew Williams, University of Warwick, and myself on the International Law of Peace, which has been drawn upon in this article.

1. M. Reisman and A. Willard, eds., *International Incidents: The Law that Counts in World Politics* (Princeton, N.J.: Princeton University Press, 1988).

2. H. Charlesworth, "A Discipline of Crisis," *Modern Law Review* 65 (2002): 377.

3. *Armed Activities on the Territory of the Congo* (DRC v Uganda) 2005 ICJ Reports (Judgment of December 19, 2005).

4. E.g., in 2003 Anne-Marie Slaughter concluded the war in Iraq was illegal but *potentially* legitimate, whereas in 2004 she found it illegal and illegitimate, primarily because of the failure to find weapons of mass destruction in Iraq; Slaughter, "The Use of Force in Iraq: Illegal and Illegitimate," *American Society of International Law Proceedings* (2004): 262.

5. In the United Kingdom, the legitimacy of the Iraq war was severely undermined by the failure to make public the Attorney General's memorandum on the legality of the war and subsequent revelations as to changes in the opinion. P. Sands, *Lawless World: America and the Making and Breaking of Global Rules* (London: Allen Lane, 2005), 194–200.

6. D. Vagts, "Hegemonic International Law," *American Journal of International Law* 95 (2001): 843; M. Byers and G. Nolte, *United States Hegemony and the Foundations of International Law* (Cambridge: Cambridge University Press, 2003); N. Krisch, "International Law in Times of Hegemony: Unequal Power and the Shaping of the International Legal Order," *European Journal of International Law* 16 (2005): 369.

7. Hannah Arendt, *On Violence* (New York: Harcourt, Brace, 1970), 52.

8. I. Hurd, "Legitimacy and Authority in International Politics," *International Organization* 53 (1999): 379, 381.

9. A-M. Slaughter, "An American Vision of International Law," *ASIL Proceedings* (2003): 125.

10. T. Franck, *The Power of Legitimacy among Nations* (Oxford: Oxford University Press, 1990), was a significant contribution to this debate in international law; see also J. Brunnée and S. Toope, *Legitimacy and Legality in International Law* (Cambridge: Cambridge University Press, 2010).

11. Issues of legitimacy have arisen in other international law contexts such as law-making, and actions of non-state actors; A. Boyle and C. Chinkin, *The Making of International Law* (Oxford: Oxford University Press, 2007), 24–35; 99–103; 300–310.

12. E.g., the imposition of targeted sanctions regimes and listing individuals subject to such sanctions; establishing ad hoc international criminal tribunals in former Yugoslavia and Rwanda and a hybrid tribunal in Sierra Leone; actions against the financing of terrorism and the non-proliferation of nuclear weapons.

13. UNSCR 1546, June 8, 2004, § 10.

14. *R (On the Application of Hilal Abdul-Razzaq Ali Al Jedda) v Secretary of State for Defence* [EWCA]; [2006] 3 WLR 954; [2008] 1 AC 332 (HL). Lord Bingham considered that while "imperative reasons of security" may allow the UK to lawfully exercise the power to detain under UNSCR 1546, it "must ensure that the detainee's rights under article 5 are not infringed to any greater extent than is inherent in such detention."; ibid. § 39.

Baroness Hale considered the European Convention on Human Rights to be "qualified" but not displaced; ibid. §§125–126.

15. President's Remarks at the UN General Assembly, September 12, 2002, available at http://www.whitehouse.gov/news/releases/2002/09/20020912-1.html.

16. Security Council legitimacy is undermined by its actions in other contexts, for example its focus on Iran's nuclear program despite its traditionally low profile in nonproliferation and disarmament issues and the fact that the five permanent members are the original nuclear states; J. Simpson in UNA-UK, *New World* (January–March 2007): 14.

17. S. Murphy, "The Security Council, Legitimacy, and the Concept of Collective Security after the Cold War," *Columbia Journal of Transnational Law* 32 (1994–1995): 201.

18. E.g., J. Alvarez, "Hegemonic International Law Revisited," *AJIL* 97 (2003): 874.

19. I. Hurd, "Legitimacy, Power and the Symbolic Life of the UN Security Council," *Global Governance* 8 (2002): 35, 48.

20. The UN Commission on Human Rights was abolished in 2006 because it was perceived to have lost legitimacy and was replaced by the Human Rights Council; UNGAR 60/251, April 3, 2006.

21. *A More Secure World: Our Shared Responsibility,* Report of the High-Level Panel on Threats, Challenges, and Change, UN Doc. A/59/565, December 2, 2004, § 250.

22. *In Larger Freedom: Towards Development, Security and Human Rights for All*, UN Doc. A/59/2005, March 21, 2005, § 169.

23. UNGAR 55/2, September 8, 2000, § 30.

24. 2005 World Summit Outcome, UNGAR 60/1, October 24, 2005, § 153.

25. Focus on military activity is a limited concept of intervention; A. Orford, "Muscular Humanitarianism: Reading the Narratives of the New Interventionism," *EJIL* 10 (1999): 679. On economic liberalization as international intervention, see A. Orford, *Reading Humanitarian Intervention* (Cambridge: Cambridge University Press, 2003), 110–125.

26. In so doing, I recognize my own selectivity and accept that there are a number of other examples that could have been chosen.

27. E.g., in his September 12, 2002, speech to the GA, President George W. Bush brought together Iraq's 1990 aggression in Kuwait, Saddam Hussein's human rights abuses, terrorism (including that al Qaeda terrorists "are known" to be in Iraq), Iraq's possession of diverse weapons of mass destruction, violation of SC resolutions, and lack of cooperation with UN inspectors.

28. C. Chinkin and K. Paradine, "Vision and Reality: Democracy and Citizenship of Women in the Dayton Peace Accords," *Yale Journal of International Law* 26 (2001): 103.

29. N. Berman, "Intervention in a Divided World: Axes of Legitimacy," *EJIL* 17 (2006): 743, 744.

30. Ibid.

31. *In Larger Freedom*, §§ 76–86.

32. This instance of an institutional regional intervention without SC authorization has attracted much greater academic attention than the actions of ECOWAS through its military arm ECOMOG in Liberia and Sierra Leone and to which no SC member objected. For SC endorsement and commendation of these actions see UNSCR 788, November 19, 1992 (Liberia); UNSCR 1181, July 13, 1998; and UNSCR 1270, October 22, 1999 (Sierra Leone); T. Franck, *Recourse to Force* (Cambridge: Cambridge University Press, 2002), 155–162.

33. E.g., B. Simma, "NATO, the UN and the Use of Force: Legal Aspects," *EJIL* 10 (1999): 1; I. Brownlie, "Kosovo Crisis Inquiry: Memorandum on the International Law Aspects," *International and Comparative Law Quarterly* 49 (1999): 878.

34. Notably Russia and China; Franck, *Recourse to Force* (above n. 32) 168.

35. UK Ministers of the Crown stated that where there was "overwhelming humanitarian necessity, . . . in light of all the circumstances, a limited use of force is justifiable as the only way to avert a humanitarian catastrophe." House of Commons, Foreign Affairs Committee, *Fourth Report, Kosovo* (Session 1999–2000), Vol. 1, § 124.

36. C. Greenwood, ibid., § 129.

37. UNSCR 1244, June 10, 1999, "decides" that the political solution will be based on the general principles adopted by the G8 foreign ministers, but nowhere explicitly endorsed the NATO action.

38. The GA affirmed the mission costs as expenses of the organization but did not otherwise indicate any opinion as to the legality or legitimacy of the military action; UNGAR 54/245 B, July 21, 2000.

39. R. Wedgewood, "Unilateral Action in the UN System," *EJIL* 11 (2000): 349, 358.

40. B. Simma, "NATO, the UN and the Use of Force: Legal Aspects," *EJIL* 10 (1999): 1, 22.

41. A. Cassesse, "Ex iniuria ius oritur: Are We Moving towards International Legitimation of Forcible Humanitarian Countermeasures in the World Community?" *EJIL* 10 (1999): 23.

42. Independent Commission on Kosovo, *The Kosovo Report* (Oxford: Oxford University Press, 2000), 170; *Fourth Report, Kosovo* (above n. 35), § 138: "NATO's military action, if of dubious legality in the current state of international law, was justified on moral grounds."

43. C. Chinkin, "Kosovo: A Good or Bad War?" *AJIL* 93 (1999): 841.

44. *Bankovic v Belgium and Others*, 11 Butterworths Human Rights Cases 435 (E Ct HR, GC December 12, 2001).

45. In September 1999, the SC was "appalled" at the humanitarian situation in East Timor but still sought an Indonesian "request" before authorizing intervention; UNSCR 1264, September 15, 1999.

46. *Accordance with international law of the unilateral declaration of independence in respect of Kosovo* (Adv. Op.) 2010 ICJ Reports (Opinion of 22 July, 2010). Considering the question put to it the ICJ saw no reason to consider the validity (legitimacy) of recognition; ibid § 51. In July 2011 78 states have recognized Kosovo.

47. Report of the International Commission on Intervention and State Sovereignty, *The Responsibility to Protect* (Ottawa: International Development Research Centre, 2001), 15.

48. *In Larger Freedom*, §§ 132, 135.

49. World Summit Outcome, §§ 138–139.

50. April 28, 2006, § 4.

51. E.g., UNSCR 1031, December 15, 1995.

52. T. Blair, "Doctrine of the International Community," speech to the Economic Club of Chicago, Hilton Hotel, Chicago, USA, April 22, 1999, available at http://www.globalpolicy.org/globaliz/politics/blair.htm.

53. D. Keen, *Endless War? Hidden Functions of the "War on Terror"* (London: Pluto Press, 2006), 209.

54. The GA "strongly condemned" the September 11 "heinous" attacks; UNGAR 56/1, September 12, 2001.

55. "The unprecedented unity following the September 11 attacks translated into open or tacit support for military action in Afghanistan." H. Duffy, *The "War on Terror" and the Framework of International Law* (Cambridge: Cambridge University Press, 2005), 187.

56. Before commencing its bombing campaign, the United States asserted in a letter to the SC that its action was an exercise of its inherent right to self-defense. It provided little legal analysis of this position; ibid., 186.

57. The Declaration on the Principles of Friendly Relations, UNGAR 2625 (XXV), October 24, 1970, proclaimed that "states have a duty to refrain from acts of reprisal involving the use of force."

58. UNSCR 661, August 6, 1990.

59. UNGAR 3314 (XXIX), December 14, 1974.

60. However, the exchange of notes after the *Caroline* incident, which is accepted as specifying the criteria under customary international law for self-defense, concerned the acts of non-state actors.

61. NATO Press Release (2001), 124, Statement by the North Atlantic Council, http://www.nato.int/docu/pr/2001/p01-124e.htm.

62. *Armed Activities on the Territory of the Congo* (Democratic Republic of the Congo v Uganda) 2005 ICJ Reports § 147.

63. 2005 ICJ Reports, sep op Judge Simma, § 11–14; sep op Judge Kooijmans § 28–32.

64. This is not always the case. France and Spain refused permission for use of their airspace to the United States for its 1986 attack on Libya in response to terrorist attacks in West Berlin; M. Byers, *War Law* (London: Atlantic Books, 2005), 62. This instance of state practice militates against the development of a rule of customary international law allowing for military response to terrorist attacks outside a state's own territory.

65. A. Cassese, *International Law* (Oxford: Oxford University Press, 2nd ed. 2005), 469–472.

66. *Oil Platforms* (Islamic Republic of Iran v United States of America), 2003 ICJ Reports § 57–72.

67. UNGAR. 56/220 A and B, December 21, 2001; 56/176, February 7, 2002.

68. E.g., by Laura Bush and Cherie Blair. Previously attacks on the Taliban's treatment of women had emanated primarily from women's NGOs; H. Charlesworth and C. Chinkin, "Sex, Gender and September 11," *AJIL* 96 (2002): 600, 602.

69. I. Mgbeoji, "The Civilised Self and the Barbaric Other: Imperial Delusions of Order and the Challenges of Human Security," *Third World Quarterly* 27 (2006): 855, 858 (footnotes omitted).

70. The point applies more broadly to neglect and under-funding of reconstruction in Afghanistan; Keen, *Endless War* (above n. 53), 107–109.

71. Afghanistan Constitution, 2004, article 22. However article 2 enshrines Islam as the religion of the Islamic Republic of Afghanistan.

72. E.g., Amnesty International, "Afghanistan: Women Still Under Attack—A Systematic Failure to Protect," ASA 11/007/2005, May 30, 2005; Human Rights Watch, "The 'Ten-Dollar Talib' and Women's Rights: Afghan Women and the Risks of Reintegration and Reconciliation," July 2010.

73. Kvinna Till Kvinna, *Getting it Right: A Gender Approach to UNMIK Administration in Kosovo* (Stockholm: Kvinna till Kvinna Foundation. 2001).

74. Iraq had been regularly subjected to military action since the 1991 ceasefire, notably Operation Desert Fox, December 1998, when some 650 air strikes were launched. This violence had become sufficiently normalized for it to become widely asserted that the use of force commenced in March 2003.

75. A good overview is "Debate: Adjudicating Operation Iraqi Freedom," *ASIL Proceedings* (2006).

76. "Iraq War Illegal, Says Annan," BBC News, Thursday, September 16, 2004, http://news.bbc.co.uk/1/hi/world/middle_east/3661134.stm.

77. 2005 ICJ Reports § 148. Judge Simma refers explicitly to the Bush Doctrine of preemptive self-defense; sep op Judge Simma, § 11.

78. UNSCR 1546, June 8, 2004. The envisaged date for these changes was June 30, 2004, but they took place on June 28, 2004.

79. 2005 ICJ Reports, sep op Judge Kooijmans, § 60.

80. Hurd, "Legitimacy, Power" (above n. 19), 38.

81. In Afghanistan, the Northern Alliance forces had been part of the victorious coalition. The Agreement on Provisional Arrangements in Afghanistan Pending the Re-Establishment of Permanent Government Institutions (Bonn Agreement), 2001, provided for the Afghan Interim Authority with a mandate for six months, followed by a two-year Transitional Authority (TA) and elections.

82. The SC has "'discursive power,' that is the ability to 'promote and impose concepts as the basis of preferred policies.'" I. Hurd, "Legitimacy, Power" (above n. 19), 35, 37 (citing P. Chilton, *Security Metaphors: Cold War Discourse from Containment to Common House* [New York: Peter Lang. 1996], 6.)

83. Jack Straw, UK foreign secretary, told the House of Commons that "Of course, the resolution was indeed a compromise . . . Resolution 1483 was passed unanimously, after much negotiation"; Hansard, HC Debates, vol. 4, June 2003, column 189–190.

84. E.g., "The liberation of Iraq has cleared the path for today's action" [the adoption of UNSCR 1483]; Mr. Negroponte, Permanent Representative, USA, 4761 Meeting of the SC, May 22, 2003, UN Doc. S/PV.4761.

85. UNSCR, 1511, October 16, 2003, § 8.

86. Any attempt by the SC to condemn the invasion would have been vetoed by the United States and United Kingdom, but the GA could have been active in this regard; D. Krieger, "The War in Iraq as Illegal and Illegitimate," in *The Iraq Crisis and World Order*, ed. R. Thakur and W. Pal Singh Sidhu (Tokyo: UN University Press, 2006), 381, 389.

87. UNSCR 1483, Preamble.

88. Hurd notes that "*whether other centers of power come to the aid of an institution under threat*" is an indicator of legitimacy; Hurd, "Legitimacy and Authority" (above n. 8), 391.

89. Malone comments that UN officials were chastened by the realization that the organization's "legitimacy had been repeatedly tarnished in Iraq." D. Malone, *The International Struggle over Iraq* (Oxford: Oxford University Press, 2006), 227.

90. Joint letter, May 8, 2003 from the US and UK permanent representatives to the president of the SC, annexed to UNSCR, 1483.

91. The CPA website states that "The Governing Council was appointed by Coalition Provisional Authority Administrator L. Paul Bremer on July 13 2003." http://www.cpa-iraq.org/government/governing_council.html.

92. UNSCR 1500, August 14, 2003.

93. UNSCR 1511, § 4.

94. Malone, *International Struggle over Iraq* (above n. 89), 224.

95. Christian Science Monitor, February 12, 2004; http://www.csmonitor.com/2004/0212/dailyUpdate.html?s=mes.

96. Malone, *International Struggle over Iraq* (above n. 89), 224.

97. Ibid., 225.

98. SC Resolution 1546, June 8, 2004. Security Council authorization of the MNF has been reaffirmed by SC Resolution 1637, November 11, 2005, and SC Resolution 1723, November 28, 2006, until December 31, 2007.

99. The UK secretary of state for defense stated: "Governing authority in Iraq during occupation was, in accordance with UNSCR 1483 (2003) exercised by the CPA . . . the CPA was not a subordinate authority of the UK . . . Iraq remained a sovereign state"; respondents printed case, House of Lords in *R (Al Skeini) v Secretary of State for Defence* [2007] UKHL 26, June 13, 2007. The European Court of Human Rights rejected this analysis concluding that "the United Kingdom (together with the United States) assumed in Iraq the exercise of some of the public powers normally to be exercised by a sovereign government. In particular, the United Kingdom assumed authority and responsibility for the maintenance of security in South East Iraq." *Al Skeini and Others v United Kingdom* (Appl. No. 55721/07) (GC), July 7, 2011, § 149.

100. G. Fox. "The Occupation of Iraq," *Georgetown Journal of International Law* 36 (2005): 195, 205.

101. The title of a journalist's account of occupied Iraq symbolizes both the elements of empire and the failure to take account of reality during the period of the CPA: R. Chandrasekaran, *Imperial Life in the Emerald City* (London: Bloomsbury Publishing, 2007). Iraq was of course administered by the British Empire after World War I until 1932.

102. Malone, *International Struggle over Iraq* (above n. 89), 226; N. Berman, "Intervention in a Divided World" (above n. 29), 761 describes the adverse impact on third world states of colonial labels like "proconsul" in Kosovo.

103. The term favored by Chandrasekaran, *Imperial Life* (above note 101). Chandrasekaran notes that "[p]ublic questioning of his edicts was verboten" and that he micromanaged the CPA; ibid., 72.

104. Berman, "Intervention in a Divided World" (above n. 29), 757.

105. Cited in Hurd, "Legitimacy and Authority" (above n. 8) at 387.

106. Convention (IV) respecting the Laws and Customs of War on Land and Annex: Regulations Concerning the Laws and Customs of War on Land. The Hague, October 18, 1907, article 43. See also Geneva Convention (IV) relative to the Protection of Civilian Persons in Time of War. Geneva, 12 August 1949, article 64.

107. E.g., CPA Order 39 (amended by Order 46) on Foreign Investment gave foreign investors unrestricted rights to buy Iraqi companies.

108. A. Roberts, "Transformative Military Occupation," *AJIL* 100 (2006): 580, 613; D. Scheffer, "Beyond Occupation Law," *AJIL* 97 (2003): 842.

109. Of course, Iraqis are not homogenous as is clear from the different histories of the Kurds, Shiites, and Sunnis. Other distinctions are based on sex, class, wealth, urban, and rural inhabitants, and so on.

110. "Abruptly terminating the livelihoods of these men created a vast pool of humiliated, antagonized and politicized men." T. Ricks, *Fiasco: The American Military Adventure in Iraq* (London: Penguin Books, 2007), 162.

111. Amnesty International pointed out that although "[m]uch planning and resources seem to have been devoted to securing Iraqi oil fields . . . there is scarce evidence of similar levels of planning and allocation of resources for securing public and other institutions essential for the survival and well-being of the population. The response to disorder has been shockingly inadequate." Cited in UK Select Committee on Foreign Affairs, Tenth Report 2002–3, July 15, 2003, § 118.

112. Malone, *International Struggle over Iraq* (above n. 89), 206.

113. This section does not consider the many other actions of dubious legality that have undermined the legitimacy of the US claim to be upholding human rights and democracy, for example detentions in Guantánamo Bay, Bagram, and elsewhere, denial of prisoner of war status to detainees, and extraordinary renditions.

114. *R (Al Skeini) v Secretary of State for Defence* [EWCA]; [2006] 3 WLR 508, § 28–29 per Brooke LJ.

115. In its Third Periodic Report to the Human Rights Committee, the United States rejected the applicability of the International Covenant on Civil and Political Rights to its forces in Iraq; UN Doc. CCPR/C/USA/3, November 28, 2005, Annex. The Committee noted "with concern" the restrictive interpretation of the "position that the Covenant does not apply with respect to individuals under [US] jurisdiction but outside its territory," UN Doc. CCPR/C/USA/CO/3/Rev. 1, December 18, 2006.

116. *Al Skeini and Others v United Kingdom* (above n. 99).

117. UN Doc. UNMIK/REG/2000/38, June 30, 2000. The ombudsperson was replaced in 2005 with a Human Rights Advisory Panel; UNMIK Regulation No. 2006/12 of 23 March 2006 on the Establishment of the Human Rights Advisory Panel.

118. Although the United States is not a party to the Rome Statute of the International Criminal Court, 1998 the United Kingdom ratified the Statute on October 4, 2001.

119. Hurd, "Legitimacy, Power" (above n. 19), 46–47.

120. J. Bellinger III, "United Nations Security Council Resolutions and the Application of International Humanitarian Law, Human Rights and Refugee Law," International Conference, San Remo, *AJIL* 99 (2005): 891.

121. *R (On the Application of Hilal Abdul-Razzaq Ali Al Jedda) v Secretary of State for Defence* [EWCA]; [2006] 3 WLR 954; [2008] 1 AC 332 (HL).

122. J. Bellinger III, "United Nations Security Council Resolutions and the Application of International Humanitarian Law, Human Rights and Refugee Law," Address at International Conference, San Remo, September 9, 2005, available at : http://www.state.gov/s/l/2005/87240.htm.

123. The hierarchy is established by UN Charter, Article 103 which states that "In the event of a conflict between the obligations of the Members of the United Nations under the present Charter and their obligations under any other international agreement, their obligations under the present Charter shall prevail." See C. Chinkin, "Jus Cogens, Article 103 of

the UN Charter and Other Hierarchical Techniques of Conflict Solution," *Finnish Yearbook of International Law* 27 (2006): 63.

124. *Al Jedda v United Kingdom* (Appl. No. 27021/08) (GC), July 7 2011, § 105.

125. Malone, *International Struggle over Iraq* (above n. 89), 103.

126. N. Berman, "Intervention in a Divided World" (above n. 29), 743.

127. "Far from being 'legitimate, relevant and meaningful' . . . international law maybe becoming obsolete in the face of . . . 'imperial justice,'" V. Nesiah, "Resistance in the Age of Empire: Occupied Discourse Pending Investigation," *Third World Quarterly* 27 (2006): 903, 916.

128. Adel Abdel-Mahdi, member IGC, cited in Chandrasekaran, *Imperial Life* (above note 101), 323.

129. UNSCR 1546.

130. M. Koskenniemi, "International Law: Between Fragmentation and Constitutionalism," lecture delivered at Australian National University, Canberra, November 27, 2006.

131. Malone, *International Struggle over Iraq* (above n. 89), 84–113.

132. This concept was used by both the White House and then British prime minister Tony Blair in referring to the possible French veto of a resolution authorizing the use of force in Iraq.

133. The argument for a doctrine of preemptive self defense as explained in the US National Security Doctrine, 2002 was not pursued and has received a "chilly" reception; H. Duffy, "*War on Terror*" (above n. 55), 211.

134. Keen, *Endless War* (above n. 53), 214. F. Mégret, "War? Legal Semantics and the Move to Violence," *EJIL* 13 (2002): 361 also describes how the use of the word "war" contributed to the escape from the constraints of international law.

135. C. Gearty, "Is the Idea of Human Rights Now Doing More Harm than Good?" London School of Economics, October 2004, available at http://www2.lse.ac.uk/humanRights/articlesAndTranscripts/121004_CG.pdf

136. "Millions Join Global Anti-war Protests," BBC News, February 17, 2003, at http://news.bbc.co.uk/1/hi/world/europe/2765215.stm.

137. World Tribunal on Iraq at http://en.wikipedia.org/wiki/World_Tribunal_on_Iraq. The author attended the sessions of the Tribunal in London (2003); Stockholm (2004) and the final session in Istanbul (2005).

138. Ibid.

139. Justice Michael Kirby, "Peoples Tribunals and Due Process," First International Conference of People's Tribunal, Colombo, Sri Lanka, December 1994, available at http://www.lawfoundation.net.au/resources/kirby/papers/19941216_peoples.html.

140. C. Chinkin, "Peoples' Tribunals: Legitimate or Rough Justice?" *Windsor Yearbook of Access to Justice* 24 (2006): 201.

141. *Our Global Neighbourhood: Report of the Commission on Global Governance* (Oxford: Oxford University Press, 1995), 259.

142. UN Doc. A/52/850, March 31, 1998.

143. R. Falk and A. Strauss, "On the Creation of a Global Peoples Assembly: Legitimacy and the Power of Popular Sovereignty," *Stanford Journal of International Law* 36 (2000): 191, 195, n. 16 (citing the Perugia Assembly of the United Nations of Peoples).

144. The Aria formula allows for informal meetings between non-governmental organizations and members of the Security Council, and mandate holders such as special rapporteurs of the UN Human Rights Council also occasionally appear.

145. S. Lone, "Inside Africa's Guantánamo," *The Guardian*, April 28, 2007.

146. T. Porteous, "Somalia: A Failing Counter-Terrorism Strategy," *Human Rights Watch*, May 17, 2007.

147. Ibid.

148. UK Home Office, Border and Immigration Agency, Report of Information Gathering Mission, April 27–30, 2007, Somalia, May 17, 2007, para. 5.10

149. J. Bellinger III, "The United States and International Law," Remarks at The Hague, June 6, 2007.

150. E.g., South Africa thought it inappropriate for the SC to impose the tribunal on Lebanon; China believed the action would create a precedent for interference in a state's domestic affairs that could undermine the council's authority; Russia did not believe the establishment of the tribunal under chapter VII to be warranted; UN Doc. S/PV/5685, May 30, 2007.

151. *Questions of Interpretation and Application of the 1971 Montreal Convention arising from the Aerial Incident at Lockerbie* (Libyan Arab Jamahiriya *v* United States of America) Request for the Indication of Provisional Measures 1992 ICJ Reports 3 (Order of April 14, 1992).

152. Report of the special rapporteur on the situation of human rights in the Palestinian Territories occupied since 1967, UN Doc. A/HRC/4/17, January 29, 2007, § 51–53.

153. Ibid., § 54.

154. M. Koskenniemi, "'The Lady Doth Protest Too Much': Kosovo and the Turn to Ethics in International Law," *Modern Law Review* 65 (2002): 159.

9

Lawful Authority and the Responsibility to Protect

Anne Orford

Introduction

This chapter explores the implications of the shift in internationalist debates from the concept of humanitarian intervention to the concept of the responsibility to protect.[1] While the legality of humanitarian intervention dominated discussions about the use of force during the 1990s, the responsibility to protect concept has gradually colonized the international agenda since its development by the International Commission on Intervention and State Sovereignty (ICISS) in 2001.[2] The responsibility to protect concept is premised on the notion that "the primary raison d'être and duty" of every state is to protect its population.[3] If a state "manifestly" fails to protect its population, the responsibility and authority to do so shifts to the international community. The responsibility to protect concept came of age with its adoption by the General Assembly in its World Summit Outcome of 2005.[4] The General Assembly there endorsed the notion that the international community had a responsibility to protect populations from genocide, war crimes, ethnic cleansing, and crimes against humanity. The responsibility to protect concept has since garnered the enthusiastic support of states, international organizations, and civil society, and has shaped processes of institutional transformation and systemic integration at and around the United Nations (UN).

The shift from humanitarian intervention to the responsibility to protect significantly alters the ways in which authority is represented. The responsibility to protect concept grounds the legitimacy of authority—both of states and of the international community—on the capacity to provide effective protection to populations at risk. In a sense, this is not new—international law has long treated effective control over territory as an important criterion of statehood.[5] Yet the creation of the United Nations in 1945 saw the emergence of an international regime in which the principles of self-determination, sovereign equality, protection of fundamental human rights, and the prohibition against acquisition of territory through the use of force were also treated as central to determining the lawfulness of particular claimants to authority.[6] Those principles shaped the process of decolonization and delegitimized alien rule. Under the UN Charter, the lawfulness of authority over a given territory thus became a matter both of fact and of right. Where occupation by foreign states or administration by international organizations was permitted, it was conceived of as temporary, authorized for limited periods and for restricted ends. Humanitarian intervention in turn was understood as an exceptional measure that properly did little "to threaten the traditional rights of sovereigns."[7]

In contrast, advocates of the responsibility to protect seek to make an argument for the legitimacy of authority without reference to self-determination, popular sovereignty or to other *de jure* bases for determining who should have the power to govern in a particular territory. Rather, the legitimacy of authority is determinable by reference to the *fact* of protection. This factual grounding of authority marginalizes the more familiar claims to authority grounded on right, whether that right be understood in historical, universal or democratic terms. Indeed, this has been the effect of the turn to protection throughout modern history. While I have suggested that the turn to protection represents something novel in modern discussions about international authority and its proper role, the linking of *state* authority with the office of protection is as old as the modern European state itself. The appeal to protection has often emerged at times of civil war or revolution, and has been used to explain how to distinguish between competing claimants to authority. If we turn to that history, we can see that the invocation of *de facto* authority based on the capacity to protect can lead to dramatically different political projects justified in the name of protection. I will suggest that attending to the implications of that history is useful for thinking about the possibilities and dangers inherent in the linking of statehood, authority and protection.

Part 1 one of the chapter sets out a number of key changes in theory and practice involved in the emergence and institutional adoption of the responsibility to protect concept. It focuses in particular on the invocation of "protection" as central to the authority of states and the international community. Part 2 of the chapter seeks to analyze the nature of the account of legitimacy and legality that is suggested by those changes. I there relate key themes from the responsibility to protect literature to the work of two political and legal theorists who came to see protection as the basic responsibility and role of the state—Thomas Hobbes and Carl Schmitt. Part 3 concludes by suggesting that the shift from humanitarianism to protection as a justification for intervention raises new questions about the legality and legitimacy of international authority. The claim to be intervening on behalf of the universal values of a common humanity was represented as operating outside politics and transcending particular legal orders. In contrast, I will suggest that claims about what must be done to secure the protection of individuals and populations are much more readily understood as political claims. The overt politicization of international law and international authority by the adoption of the responsibility to protect concept may prove to be of value, both theoretically and practically.

1. From Humanitarianism to Protection: A Brief History of the Responsibility to Protect

The responsibility to protect concept was developed by ICISS in its report of 2001.[8] The event that posed the immediate catalyst to the work of ICISS was the Kosovo intervention conducted by NATO without Security Council authorization, although interventions without Security Council authorization had also been conducted by the Economic Community of West African States in Liberia and Sierra Leone during the 1990s.[9] The response to the Kosovo intervention by international lawyers and others was almost uniformly framed in terms of a tension between legality and legitimacy. The decision to intervene in Kosovo "signalled a new era in which the ground for intervention became more fertile while concerns about its legitimacy became increasingly intense."[10]

Perhaps the dominant legal argument in support of the Kosovo intervention was that made by commentators such as Bruno Simma or Antonio Cassese, who saw the Kosovo intervention as illegal but legitimate.[11] For such commentators, the question of the positive legality of the Kosovo intervention was quickly answered—it was illegal as it did not conform to any of the authorized grounds upon which states could have recourse to force under the UN Charter. However, they argued that a commitment to justice required the international community to support the NATO intervention in Kosovo, despite its illegality. The question of legitimacy did not depend upon positive legality—determining whether the intervention was legitimate involved asking whether it was in conformity with the universal values that transcended any given legal order. This was spelt out strongly by Michael Reisman, who argued that while lawyers knew that respect for formal authority and legal procedures was important, they also knew that "sometimes decisions have to be taken" without regard for such matters of form.[12] For Reisman, the intervention in Kosovo should be understood as coming under "the *exceptio* for that very small group of events that warrant or even require unilateral action when the legally designated institution or procedure proves unable to operate."[13] At the "moment of decision," the "legal requirement" calls for action "to save lives, however one can and as quickly as one can."[14] Such interpretations of the legitimacy of the NATO intervention supported the position put by political leaders such as British Prime Minister Tony Blair. Blair portrayed the NATO intervention in Kosovo as a "just war, based not on territorial ambitions, but on values."[15] According to Blair, the war in Kosovo was fought precisely to defend such values: "This war was not fought for Albanians against Serbs. It was not fought for territory. . . . It was fought for a fundamental principle necessary for humanity's progress: that every human being, regardless of race, religion or birth, has the inalienable right to live free from persecution."[16] Those accounts are based upon a conception of law that distinguishes particular laws of positive legal systems from universal values that transcend the rules of any existing legal system. Such a conception of the legitimacy of humanitarian intervention is based on the notion of an ideal form of community, of which actually existing states and their laws represent only imperfect copies. Jennifer Beard has argued compellingly that the impetus for the development of this metaphysical vision of law has been the encounters between the Old World and the New, or in contemporary language, the developed and the developing worlds.[17] In this vision, the developed world is the embodiment on earth of "an infinitely distant reality" and a "potential state of fulfillment," the promise of which will be fulfilled once the peoples of the New World are redeemed.[18] Legitimacy derives not from conformity to positive law, but from actions taken to realize universal values on earth.

The responsibility to protect concept represents a shift away from the appeal to universal values and ideal forms of community as justifications for intervention, and from the conception of a formal law with only a marginal relationship to politics. It replaces the exceptional claims of humanitarian intervention with an account of protection as a core component of the contemporary international normative order. The text that inaugurates this movement is the report of the Independent International Commission on Kosovo, appointed by the Swedish government in consultation with the UN Secretary-General to evaluate the precedent created by the NATO intervention.[19] This report concluded that the NATO intervention was illegal but legitimate, and sought to close that gap between legality and legitimacy. The commission noted that the legitimacy of the intervention "was and remains questionable in non-Western eyes. In the majority of countries of the world there is a much stronger commitment to the protection of their sovereignty than currently exists in the West," due to "the dual history of colonialism and the Cold War." For this audience, the NATO intervention was illegitimate because it violated the UN Charter obligations to respect the territorial integrity of member states and the prohibition against the unauthorized use of force. Yet the commission suggested that international law and the UN Charter regime was itself seen to lack legitimacy from the perspective of those who saw "armed humanitarian intervention as justified when populations are at risk of their lives." Legitimacy thus pulled in two directions. The report of the Kosovo Commission concluded: "Sometimes, and Kosovo is such an instance, the use of military force may become necessary to defend human rights. But the grounds for its use in international law urgently need clarification, and the tactics and rules of engagement for its use need to be improved." The establishment of ICISS was a second international initiative designed to respond to the perceived tension between state sovereignty and humanitarian intervention in the aftermath of the NATO action. The ICISS report introduced the responsibility to protect concept into the mainstream debate. According to Gareth Evans, who was the co-chair with Mohamed Sahnoun of ICISS, the inspiration for the responsibility to protect concept came from the work of Francis Deng on conflict management in Africa.[20] In *Sovereignty as Responsibility*, Deng and his coauthors had argued that responsibility rather than control should be seen as the essence of sovereignty, and that in African states, the government was often a "partisan" and thus acted as a "barrier," "preventing the international community from providing protection and assistance to the needy."[21] *Sovereignty as Responsibility* explicitly raised the question of the lawfulness of authority, arguing that if a government could no longer guarantee the security and welfare of the population, it may no longer be recognizable as the lawful authority over a territory. The responsibility to protect the population had become a function that was pooled between the state and the international community—if local claimants to authority could not fulfill that responsibility, they could not legitimately complain if the international community intervened to do so. Following Deng's lead, the ICISS report sought to articulate "a new way of talking about sovereignty" and "to invent a new way of talking about humanitarian intervention."[22] The new way of talking about sovereignty was to argue that "its essence should now be seen not as control but as responsibility."[23] If a state is unwilling or unable to meet this responsibility to protect its population, it then falls upon the international community to do so. The new way of talking about humanitarian intervention involved re-characterizing the debate "not as an argument about any right at all but rather about a responsibility—one to protect people at grave risk."[24] The people at grave risk were those "[m]illions of human beings" who "remain at the mercy of civil wars, insurgencies, state repression and state collapse."[25]

The concept of the responsibility to protect was taken up in the 2004 Report of the UN High-Level Panel on Threats, Challenges, and Change,[26] and in the subsequent report of the UN Secretary-General to the 2005 World Summit session of the General Assembly. The Secretary-General stressed the need to "embrace the responsibility to protect."[27] The responsibility to protect "lies, first and foremost, with each individual State, whose primary raison d'être and duty is to protect its population."[28] If "national authorities," however, are unable to "protect their citizens," the responsibility to do so "shifts to the international community."[29] The General Assembly in its 2005 World Summit Outcome accepted this notion of both an individual and an international responsibility to protect. It affirmed that "each individual state has the responsibility to protect its populations from genocide, war crimes, ethnic cleansing and crimes against humanity," and agreed that the "international community" also "has the responsibility to use appropriate diplomatic, humanitarian and other peaceful means . . . to help protect populations from genocide, war crimes, ethnic cleansing and crimes against humanity."[30] The World Summit Outcome stated that should a state "manifestly fail" to protect its populations, the international community was prepared to take collective action through the Security Council.

Since 2005, the responsibility to protect concept has been incorporated into UN operations in a way that humanitarian intervention never was. Ramesh Thakur has argued that the responsibility to protect concept "is directed primarily at the UN policy community in New York."[31] If so, the strategy appears to have met with success. Moves to institutionalize the responsibility to protect have led to a coordinated project of integration and rationalisation of UN activity. After his appointment as

Secretary-General, Ban Ki-moon promised he would "spare no effort to operationalize the responsibility to protect,"[32] and in January 2009 delivered a report to the General Assembly on plans for implementing the responsibility to protect.[33] Two senior positions to oversee the implementation of the responsibility to protect were created at the United Nations. Francis Deng was appointed to the newly styled position of UN Special Adviser on the Prevention of Genocide in 2007 and Edward Luck was appointed to the new position of Special Adviser to the Secretary-General on the Responsibility to Protect in 2008. The two advisers "share an office on genocide prevention and RtoP, helping the United Nations to speak and act as one."[34] According to Luck, institutionalizing the responsibility to protect concept will require "interagency cooperation," "a common policy and operational strategy," and an "integrated framework" for activities in areas including conflict prevention, capacity-building, humanitarian assistance, peace-keeping and security sector reform.[35] The responsibility to protect concept has been reaffirmed by both the General Assembly and the Security Council,[36] and states have also embraced the concept, apparently with greater willingness than was the case with humanitarian intervention.[37] In addition, regional organizations such as the African Union and the European Union have endorsed the responsibility to protect concept.[38] A range of actors, from US Naval Academy counterinsurgency specialists, through UN officials, to human rights activists and Christian aid workers, have now begun enthusiastically to redescribe and reconceptualize their missions in terms of protection.

States, international organizations, and civil society groups all treat the implementation of the responsibility to protect concept as requiring much more than responding to conflicts through force. According to ICISS, the responsibility to protect encompasses a responsibility to prevent conflict, to react to conflict, and to rebuild after conflict. The ICISS report outlines groups of techniques related to each of these aspects of the responsibility to protect—techniques for prevention such as surveillance, techniques for reaction such as the use of force, and techniques for rebuilding such as development assistance, administration, and punishment. The General Assembly accepted the broad vision developed by ICISS of the techniques that could be authorized as an exercise of the responsibility to protect. United Nations members undertook to help states build "capacity to protect their populations," assist "those which are under stress before crises and conflicts break out," establish "an early warning capability," and take "collective action, in a timely and decisive manner, through the Security Council . . . should peaceful means prove inadequate" to protect populations.[39] The UN Secretary-General's 2009 Report on "Implementing the Responsibility to Protect" focused upon prevention, capacity-building and assistance to states as the bases for implementing the responsibility to protect concept,[40] while his 2010 report on "Early Warning, Assessment and the Responsibility to Protect" stressed that the "expansion of the United Nations capabilities for early warning and assessment of possible genocide, war crimes, ethnic cleansing and crimes against humanity" would be central to the "effective, credible and sustainable implementation of the responsibility to protect."[41] The responsibility to protect concept is therefore an extremely ambitious one. Although its "scope is narrow," being limited to "the four crimes and violations agreed by the world leaders in 2005," the techniques for its implementation are broad.[42] According to Secretary-General Ban Ki-moon, those techniques involve "utilizing the whole prevention and protection tool kit available to the United Nations system, to its regional and subregional and civil society partners, and not least to the Member States themselves," with the aim of "integrating the system's multiple channels of information and assessment."[43]

The responsibility to protect concept thus treats protection as central to the authority of state and the international community. In that sense, those advocating this concept are part of a long tradition of Western political thought that links protection and authority. However, it is also important to note that the responsibility to protect concept develops that tradition in its suggestion that there is an *international* responsibility to protect, which provides the normative foundation for the protective authority exercised by the international community.[44] This matters because, as noted above, the responsibility to protect involves a responsibility to prevent genocide, ethnic cleansing, war crimes, and crimes against humanity, a responsibility to react if there is a risk of those crimes being committed, and a responsibility to rebuild after military intervention. In this sense, the responsibility to protect securitizes states in Africa, Asia, the Middle East, and Eastern Europe before, during, and after civil war or conflict breaks out. As a result, the potential presence of international actors as protectors is justified on a semi-permanent basis. It thus becomes important to reflect upon how the legality and legitimacy of international authority is conceptualized, and what the effects of that conceptualization might be. In order to explore this question, the next part of the chapter turns to the work of Thomas Hobbes and Carl Schmitt, two theorists of the state who sought to argue that the responsibility to protect lies at the heart of legitimate authority.

2. Protection, Legitimacy, and Spatial Order

This part considers three key ideas that inform the concept of the responsibility to protect. The first is the idea that the lawfulness of authority—both of the state and of the international community—is determinable by reference to the capacity to guarantee protection. The second is the focus upon the need to secure the legitimacy of legal and political authority through the decisive acts of a sovereign. The third is that statehood is a condition that is distinct from lawlessness, and that this distinction between modern states governed by the rule of law and failed states marked by the absence of law can be mapped onto a "spatial order of the earth."[45] As suggested above, this set of ideas can be usefully traced through the work of two political and legal theorists, Thomas Hobbes and Carl Schmitt.

PROTECTION AND OBEDIENCE

To invoke protection as the "raison d'être" of the state is to be in a complicated relation to a long tradition of absolutist theories of statehood. The English "prophet of the Leviathan,"[46] Thomas Hobbes, is often treated as the originator of this tradition. The treatment of protection as central to the relation between state and subject is given detailed elaboration in Hobbes's *Leviathan*, published in London in 1651.[47] This was just three years after the Peace of Westphalia brought the devastation of the Thirty Years' War in Europe to an end, two years after the execution of Charles I "in the name of the people of England" had shaken the established political order of Europe and led many countries to cut off diplomatic relations with the English republic,[48] and not long before the final defeat of the Royalists in the English civil wars would see the first Commonwealth of England replaced with a Protectorate led by the Puritan Oliver Cromwell. Hobbes was thus writing in a context in which the wars of religion had undermined appeals to a universal and shared set of values that could ground authority. Appeals to the truth of competing religious beliefs and the post-skeptical spirit of the new sciences were everywhere shaking the foundations of established political orders.[49] At the time Hobbes was writing *Leviathan*, it was still uncertain how the fundamental divisions between political and religious groups within European states, and particularly within England, would ever be bridged, or which if any values and political forms would emerge triumphant.

It was under such conditions that Hobbes developed his model for grounding authority on the capacity of the commonwealth to secure peace and protect its subjects. According to Hobbes, "during the time men live without a common power to keep them all in awe, they are in that condition which is called war; and such a war, as is of every man, against every man."[50] In this state of nature, there is no *civil* law, because such law "depends for its existence upon a 'common power.'"[51] It is important to note, however, that this did not mean that for Hobbes the state of nature was a lawless space. According to Hobbes, men in the state of nature were governed by the laws of nature, that is, by divine law.[52] The laws of nature existed to ensure the realization of each man's natural right to self-preservation.[53] According to Hobbes, the right to self-preservation could not reliably be realized in the state of nature.[54] In part this was because the laws of nature had no settled meaning. The unwritten laws of nature were not reliably available to men—men differed in their interpretation of Scripture or claimed to have received divine inspiration that could not be verified. The wars of religion had taught Hobbes that the lack of a reliable and agreed earthly judge of what the laws of nature required or meant in any given situation was dangerous. There could also be no security in the state of nature because there was no common power to enforce the law.[55] Men in such a condition lived in "continual fear, and danger of violent death."[56] For these reasons, Hobbes argued that the creation of political order depended upon the establishment of a common power—a commonwealth. The creation of such an earthly power was required by the "first and fundamental law of nature"—"*to seek peace, and follow it.*"[57] According to Hobbes, men covenanted as equals to create a commonwealth in order to bring about a condition in which the right to self-preservation could be realized.[58] The authority of the commonwealth would be grounded on its capacity to guarantee protection, understood as the realization and fulfillment of the laws of nature on earth.

Hobbes argued that how such an earthly power came into existence was immaterial to the question of its legitimacy. According to Hobbes, "the imperfect generation" of any given commonwealth was irrelevant to the rightful authority of the civil sovereign. The right of the sovereign did not depend on the means by which its "power was at first gotten," but on its possession.[59] After all, Hobbes comments, "there is scarce a commonwealth in the world, whose beginnings can in conscience be justified."[60] Hobbes's approach was thus very different to that of the revolutionaries of his age. For Hobbes, *nothing of importance* turns on the nature of the link between ruler and ruled, or on whether the territory of the commonwealth was acquired through conquest or otherwise unlawfully. Instead, Hobbes based his defense of power on its present efficacy rather than the validity of its origins. His was a theory that spoke to conditions of conquest and of civil war. Hobbes argued that the continual debate about the legitimacy of the conditions under which authority was first constituted was radically destabilizing and ultimately irresolvable. By refusing to ground the legitimacy of the commonwealth on ancient texts, historical claims, or popular sovereignty, Hobbes "pulled the rug out" from under arguments based on the nation as a "platform for resistance" to tyranny or misrule.[61] His approach was thus profoundly conservative.

If such moves were conservative in Hobbes's time, they are in many ways even more conservative to a twenty-first-century audience who are used to thinking about questions of legitimacy in terms of a romantic or nationalist notion of self-determination. Yet something similar is being staged with the turn to protection as the basis of international authority today. The linking of authority and protection is presented as a solution to the problem of creating political order in situations where such order is nonexistent or under threat due to "internal war, insurgency, repression or state failure." The lawful authority is the one capable of protecting populations at risk. The responsibility to protect concept thus does not conceptualize the legitimacy of authority in relation to a third term, whether that be the people, the nation, or the *Volk*. So whether or not the representatives of the international community should, say, be present in Iraq, Kosovo, or Darfur, will not be answerable in terms of the legitimacy of the initial acquisition of control over the territory in question or in terms of whether international authority was constituted in accordance with the will of the people. By focusing upon de facto authority, the responsibility to protect concept implicitly asserts not only that an international community exists, but that its authority to govern is, at least in situations of civil war and repression, superior to that of the state.

Yet despite the conservative effects of linking authority and protection, the way in which Hobbes conceived of the ends or goals of the commonwealth in part mediated that conservatism. Hobbes argued that men covenanted with each other as equals to bring into being the commonwealth. Through that act of covenanting, the commonwealth was entrusted with sovereign power for a particular end, "the procuration of *the safety of the people*."[62] For Hobbes, lawful authority was recognizable as such only to the extent that it governed in accordance with the terms of the covenant by which it was created.[63] The actions of those who represented lawful authority were constrained or limited by the terms on which their power to protect was authorized. What makes a person recognizable as the representative of a sovereign to be obeyed, rather than an enemy to be resisted, was a live question in Hobbes's England—let alone Ireland or Scotland. The answer was not altogether obvious if we think about the competing claims to authority at play in the English civil wars or the Irish rebellion. The civil wars had made a pressing issue of "the subject's duty when two or more legitimate authorities were competing to claim his allegiances at the sword's point."[64] Hobbes was addressing an audience who were repeatedly confronted with the open question of how to distinguish the representative of a lawful sovereign from an enemy or a usurper. *Leviathan* treats this question of public authority as a question of knowledge—how can we know that which is not available to us? Or as Hobbes put it: "this authority of man . . . how can it be known?"[65]

For Hobbes, "sovereignty is artificial and owes its existence to an authorization that each individual has to make to each other."[66] The sovereign thus created is recognizable as such, that is, *only successfully created*, to the extent that this artificial creature has certain attributes and is thus recognizable to its subjects and to other sovereigns.[67] The most important of these attributes is that the sovereign fulfils the terms of the covenant. While for Hobbes, "covenants, without the sword, are but words,"[68] it is still the case that "they would not be covenants were they not words (as opposed, say, simply to being force)."[69] Authors do not authorize absolutely anything. Rather, they authorize to certain ends. According to Hobbes:

> The office of the sovereign, (be it a monarch or an assembly,) consisteth in the end, for which he was trusted with the sovereign power, namely the procuration of *the safety of the people*, to which he is obliged by the law of nature . . . [B]y safety here, is not meant a bare preservation, but also all other contentments of life, which every man by lawful industry, without danger, or hurt to the commonwealth, shall acquire to himself.[70]

The sovereign is thus the one procuring the safety of the people and the right to self-preservation of the individual, as obliged by natural law and in conformity with the terms of the covenant.[71] The sovereign represents the unified will of the people, but that will is constrained by the ends for which the sovereign was created. The representatives of the sovereign cannot use their office to further their private interests or declare war against the people. Nonetheless, the power of the sovereign is absolute, and the subject has no right to resist that which he has covenanted to create—"in the act of our *submission*, consisteth both our *obligation*, and our *liberty*."[72] It is through the claim to represent a general interest or a common wealth that the state will continue to confront the individual "as a priority and as a *demand*," in particular, as a demand for obedience.[73] Hobbes makes very clear the tension between authority and freedom that is embodied in the form of the state.[74] By doing so, and by linking the legitimacy of authority with the ends for which it is created, Hobbes prefigured at least three traditions that emerged in the centuries to follow, and that are potentially directions in which the responsibility to protect concept might be taken today. First, he prefigured an individualist or liberal tradition, in which the authority of the commonwealth "was meant at least in theory to fulfill the values and needs of individuals."[75] Second, he prefigured a revolutionary tradition that would politicize the tension between the interest of the people (properly conceived), and the interest of the ruling class that could masquerade as the general interest as long as it controlled the state. Third, he prefigured a long line of counterrevolutionary theorists who would move away from the position "that the state originates from the 'material' interests and needs of individuals."[76] Those theorists would instead elevate the state as representative of the will of a unified people above the interests and needs of individuals. It was that latter move that was performed when Carl Schmitt, in developing his state law theory, returned to Hobbes and to the idea of a link between authority and protection.

THE MOMENT OF DECISION

In order to begin to analyze the political effects of relating authority and protection, I want now to turn to the writings of Carl Schmitt. Schmitt was writing at a time when Germany, and indeed Europe more generally, was struggling to come to terms with the devastation of World War 1 and with "the swell of revolutions and class-based civil wars that ran all across the continent from 1918 to 1923" in the aftermath of the Russian revolutions.[77] In this climate, the Weimar government was confronted with serious challenges to its authority. The communist revolutionaries of Russia and Germany had politicized the claim that the state existed to further the general interest of the collective.[78] The rise of the German Communist Party saw a wave of mass strikes and armed struggles for "possession of the streets and factories,"[79] while the creation of the SS, the right-wing paramilitary force loyal to Hitler in 1925, tested the capacity of the new republic to maintain a monopoly on the legitimate use of force. Tensions were further exacerbated by the mass unemployment and banking collapse that accompanied the global financial crisis of 1929.[80] The legitimacy of authority—whether the public authority of the state or the private authority of the employer—was under sustained challenge in both theory and practice.

It was in the context of these ongoing political and economic upheavals that Schmitt would turn to the work of Hobbes in order to fashion an account of authority that he saw as capable of responding effectively to the challenges facing the German state. The link between protection and authority articulated by Hobbes was at the heart of the state law theory developed by Schmitt during the 1920s and 1930s. Schmitt applauded Hobbes's efforts "to restore the natural unity" of the state.[81] He spoke approvingly of the image of the state as protector, in terms reminiscent of the language of the responsibility to protect.

> [I]t must be taken into consideration that the totality of this kind of state power always accords with the total responsibility for protecting and securing the safety of citizens and that obedience as well as the renunciation of every right of resistance that can be demanded by this god is only the correlate of the true protection that he guarantees.[82]

For Schmitt, this meant that if a political movement was capable of challenging the capacity of the state to guarantee protection and exercise force, the citizen would no longer owe an obligation of obedience to the state. "If protection ceases, every obligation to obey also ceases, and the individual once more regains his natural freedom."[83]

Thus for Schmitt, the capacity to guarantee protection was the basis of the legality and the legitimacy of authority. "No form of order, no reasonable legitimacy or legality can exist without protection and obedience."[84] Yet while Schmitt agreed with Hobbes that "the factual, current accomplishment of genuine protection is what the state is all about," he argued that this protection could be not guaranteed if the state was conceived of as a soulless security machine.[85] More was needed than a bargain based on the mutual relation between protection and obedience. The machine would not be able to function effectively if it had no claims to legitimacy other than its capacity to provide protection. Civil society would continually regroup to challenge a state imagined as purely mechanical and a law imagined as purely formal.

Schmitt responded to what he saw as the failure of Hobbes's theory in ways that strengthened its authoritarian tendencies. In particular, Schmitt argued that for the law and governance of a state to be legitimate, that state must be able to defend the will of the homogenous and unified people. In order for the state to survive, there must exist a sovereign capable of properly distinguishing between friend and enemy and thus preserving the national homogeneity that was for Schmitt the necessary condition of effective government. This had implications for Schmitt's conception of the relationship between legality and legitimacy. Schmitt argued that an individual could only submit to "a purely formal concept of law, independent of all content" where certain political conditions were in place.[86] In particular, there must be only one lawmaker, and that lawmaker must be "the final guardian of all law, ultimate guarantor of the existing order, conclusive source of all legality, and the last security and protection against injustice."[87] For a "'formal' concept of law" to be "conceivable and acceptable" in a parliamentary system, there must be "congruence between the parliamentary majority and the will of the homogenous people."[88] Underpinning this conception was the assumption that "every democracy rests on the presupposition of the indivisibly similar, entire, unified people."[89] If parliament did not represent the will of a unified people, respect for legislation would descend into sterile formalism. Schmitt argued that it made no sense to obey statutes passed by a (socialist) parliament simply on the grounds that as a matter of formal process they had been passed by a representative assembly. If the parliament had ceased to represent the will of an "indivisibly similar, entire, unified people," then the sovereign lawmaker who could act as guarantor of the legal order would have to be found elsewhere.

It was in this context that Schmitt wrote perhaps his most famous sentence: "Sovereign is he who decides on the exception."[90] For Schmitt, the essence of the legal form "lies in the concrete decision, one that emanates from a particular authority."[91] And every decision in turn "contains a constitutive element."[92] The law "cannot realize itself," this realization occurs through the decision, and yet the law does not prescribe "who should decide."[93] This is the constitutive element contained within each decision, and indeed secreted within every legal order. According to this conception of law, whenever "the legally highest authority does not have the actual capacity to make a decision and impose it according to the established procedures," the legal order comes under pressure.[94] Schmitt argued that in times of emergency, such as is experienced by people caught up in civil war, the preservation of the legal and political order depends upon the existence of a sovereign who can restore the legal form. The essence of the legal form in this conception is the decision. For a legal order to remain legitimate and command the loyalty of its subjects, it must allow for this sovereign decision to be taken if the existing order is under threat. The existence of a sovereign capable of taking such a decision, and properly distinguishing between friend and enemy, is the necessary condition of the existence and preservation of the state. Where for Hobbes the sovereign was brought into being so that men could escape the "miserable and hateful state" of war,[95] for Schmitt the sovereign was the name given to the "decisive entity" that was essential to the existence of the state in a world oriented "toward the possible extreme case of an actual battle against a real enemy."[96] Indeed, this propensity to do battle defined "the concept of the political" for Schmitt.

> If a people is afraid of the trials and risks implied by existing in the sphere of politics, then another people will appear which will assume those trials by protecting it against foreign enemies and thereby taking over political rule. The protector then decides who the enemy is by virtue of the eternal relation of protection and obedience.[97]

This decisionist conception of the relation between law and authority emerges in many arguments for humanitarian intervention and the responsibility to protect. This literature assumes that where existing order threatens to break down, a sovereign must be found who can in fact take the decision that a state of emergency exists. As Michael Reisman argued in relation to Kosovo, at the "moment of decision," the "legal requirement" calls for action "to save lives, however one can."[98] Much of the responsibility to protect literature continues to focus on the need for a decision to be made in times of emergency. As the ICISS report states: "The most compelling task now is to work to ensure that when the call goes out to the community of states for action, that call will be answered."[99] Advocates for the use of the responsibility to protect concept have to date focused most of their energy on arguing for military intervention, calling for decisions about the use of force to be made quickly and for the largest degree of force possible to be deployed.[100] To this degree, the responsibility to protect literature adopts Schmitt's solution to the dilemmas of legitimacy—the role to be played by the exceptional guarantor of the values of the legal order. The one who decides on the exception—the Security Council, the United State, NATO, the coalition of the willing—is the sovereign guarantor in this sense. This prioritizing of the role of the executive as guarantor of the legal order also manifests itself in the aftermath of military intervention, when international administrations exercise executive power in a manner which is almost unrestrained. These administrators function structurally as the sovereigns whose decision will guarantee that order is restored.[101] The ICISS report continues in this vein, suggesting that the responsibility to rebuild "may mean staying in the country for some period of time after the initial purposes of the intervention have been accomplished."[102] It treats certain goals as given, including the creation of "public safety and order," the "pursuit of war criminals," and pursuit of "economic growth and the recreation of markets."[103] There is little discussion to date of the legal limits to the actions that international administrators might take in the name of protecting populations at risk. The legitimacy of such an expansive presence of the international community is justified because it is represented as the guarantor of protection. In order to explore the implications of this further, I want now to turn to a third aspect of the responsibility to protect literature—its adoption of a spatial organization of the globe.

STATES OF NATURE/ZONES OF PROTECTION

Discussions about the responsibility to protect concept, like humanitarian intervention before it, are informed by the "consciousness" that they are "taking place in a global system."[104] A particular vision of a global spatial order underpins work on the responsibility to protect. The broader literature dealing with the responsibility to protect focuses on the challenge of achieving political order in particular places—Sri Lanka, Burma, Somalia, Kenya, Zimbabwe, the Democratic Republic of Congo, Darfur. Of particular relevance is the focus upon creating political order in Africa. Such is the concern about Africa as a space lacking political order that the Security Council passed a special resolution dealing with the Security Council's role in conflict prevention in Africa at the same time as the General Assembly adopted the World Summit Statement endorsing the responsibility to protect.[105] The responsibility to protect aspects of the World Summit Statement have been endorsed by Security Council resolutions on Darfur,[106] and in the report of the High-Level Mission on the situation of human rights in Darfur appointed by the UN Human Rights Council.[107] The latter report suggests that "in a region where impunity prevails and feeds upon itself, there is a vital need for accountability in Darfur."[108]

This reference to Africa as a region in which impunity prevails is a common one at conferences and in discussions about international humanitarian law and human rights law. It is worth stressing that such commentators do not mean that Africa is a place in which corporations seem able to violate international human rights law with impunity, nor are they referring to the normalization of immunities for peace-keepers deployed to Africa through the combined effect of status of forces agreements and Security Council resolutions.[109] Rather, these commentators mean that Africa is a region in which there is a local culture of impunity and an absence of the rule of law. The report of a day-long debate in the Security Council on the role of international law in fostering stability and order reflects a similar discourse, in which many participants discussed the challenge facing international law in terms of the "problem of the rule of law in a vacuum."[110]

The conceptualization of the challenge to which the responsibility to protect concept is said to respond is thus the creation of order where none exists, in what Hobbes called the *state of nature* and what might today be called the *zones of protection*.[111] This sense of a spatial dimension to the theory of the state was present in the work of Hobbes. The relation of Europe to the New World emerges in chapter 13 of *Leviathan*. Hobbes there famously asserted that "during the time men live without a common power to keep them all in awe, they are in that condition which is called war; and such a war, as if of every man, against every man."[112] Hobbes recognized that his audience may think that "there was never such a time, nor condition of war as this."[113] His answer to the skeptics who may not believe there was ever such a condition of war is that this state of nature or condition of war has a location:

> It may peradventure be thought, there was never such a time, nor condition of war as this; and I believe it was never generally so, over all the world: but there are many places, where they live so now. For the savage people in many places of America, except the government of small families, the concord whereof dependeth on natural lust, have no government at all; and live at this day in that brutish manner, as I have said before.[114]

The New World (America) stands for the condition into which European man may descend "were there no common power to fear," for example "in a civil war."[115] This reference to America is a warning to the readers of *Leviathan* that they may yet fall into this state of nature if they do not understand that it is in their interest to submit to a common power that can guarantee their security and protection.

The spatial order of the globe plays an even more central role in the theory of Schmitt. In *The* Nomos *of the Earth*, Schmitt argued that the spatial organization of the globe was the key to the development of the modern state system of Europe.[116] Schmitt argued that when Hobbes referred to the state of nature, he was influenced not only by the religious wars of Europe but also by the discovery of the New World.

> [Hobbes] speaks of the "state of nature," but not at all in the sense of a spaceless utopia. His state of nature is a *no man's land*, but this does not mean it exists *nowhere*. It can be located, and Hobbes locates it, among other places, in the New World.[117]

Schmitt argued that Hobbes had been influenced by the concretization of the state of nature through the creation of amity lines during the sixteenth and seventeenth century. These amity lines allowed Christian European governments to designate "great areas of freedom" as "conflict zones in the struggle over the distribution of a new world order."[118] The area beyond the line was "outside the law and open to the use of force."[119] For Schmitt, the designation of the space beyond the line as a conflict zone served to create a "sphere of peace and order ruled by European public law on the European side of the line."[120] Schmitt argued that this type of thinking was preserved in English political and legal thought while it became "increasingly foreign to the state-centered legal thinking of continental European nations."[121] In the seventeenth century, English lawyers such as Sir Edward Coke, Lord Ellesmere, and Sir Matthew Hale had argued that there were no legal limits to the exercise of royal power in the New World. According to such commentators, the imperial territories outside England, including Ireland, Scotland, Normandy, Jersey, and later acquisitions in North America and the West Indies, were subject to quite different legal regimes from those of England. Those territories that formed part of the "composite monarchy" were "ruled by the king alone through his royal prerogatives."[122] During the following centuries, British rule in Africa and India was characterized by ongoing martial law and emergency rule by the executive. While the British parliament had only a limited role to play in colonial territories, the executive arm of government "was not territorially defined" and was central to the project of governing the colonies.[123] Maintenance of the British imperial rule of law was dependent upon systematic recourse to martial law and emergency rule by the executive.[124] The British thus organized their empire in terms of a system of spatial differentiation. This history offers some support for Schmitt's argument that English legal thought has a well-developed sense for "specific spatial orders and variations of territorial status."[125]

To the extent that the theory of the state underpinning the responsibility to protect legitimizes increased intervention by the international community and ongoing emergency rule by the executive in designated zones of protection, it borrows greatly from the spatial ordering and forms of law underpinning colonial legal thought. To continue to represent the New World as a legal vacuum is to be working within this old European paradigm, in which the New World is imagined as a space without law, a "free and empty space."[126] Yet Schmitt's account of the *nomos* of the earth recognized that the purity of this spatial organization of the globe had not survived the era of revolution and decolonization. Schmitt bemoaned the fact that by the end of the nineteenth century, international law was no longer based upon the presupposition that "the soil of colonies outside Europe has a distinctive and characteristic status in international law."[127] For Schmitt, the "dissolution into general universality" had served to destroy "the traditional global order of the earth."[128] The richness of the concrete order of Europe was replaced by "an empty normativism of allegedly recognized rules."[129] However, for those who inhabit the legal spaces outside Europe, it is here that we begin to see the potential significance of bringing the responsibility to protect within the normative framework of international law.

3. The Responsibility to Protect and the Politics of International Law

The responsibility to protect doctrine introduces a new way of conceptualizing governance on a global scale. In some ways, as the previous section suggests, there is nothing new in linking protection and state authority. This has a long heritage in Western political and legal thought. It may be politically controversial and dangerous to say that protection is the central duty of the state, if this then leads to an authoritarian system where policing and security are privileged above all other ends of the state and where wars on terror or defending society are treated as justifications for abuse and the deployment of violence against internal enemies. Nonetheless, there is a long history of thinking about the state in these terms. What is different about the deployment of the language of protection in the current situation is its explicit relationship to international governance. The effect of the responsibility to protect concept is to constitute the zones of protection as spaces in which exceptional measures and actions may be authorized by a global guarantor of the law. Third World states are likely to prefer forms of international intervention short of military action, and thus to accept the presence of international actors on a semipermanent basis. We have already seen this phenomenon in the aftermath of the humanitarian interventions of the 1990s, where states accepted increased international governance rather than risk military intervention.[130] How the authority of the international community to govern these zones of protection will be justified, represented, and limited is thus extremely important.

The legacies of Hobbes and Schmitt are sobering here. Authoritarian theories of the state were taken up in a fascist Europe which saw law's function as being to further social goals on behalf of the will of a unified people. The authoritarian state diminished parliamentary participation and expanded executive governance in the name of achieving social and economic integration.[131] I have argued elsewhere that this has been the nature and effect of international administration in the aftermath of military interventions in Bosnia-Herzegovina and Timor-Leste.[132] International administrators adopt an authoritarian model of governance in which democratic participation is suspended until political order and economic integration are secured. International administrators function structurally as the sovereigns whose decision will guarantee that order is restored. They oversee the implementation of a model in which the economy is liberalized and priority is given to protecting the rights and investments of corporations. The focus upon increasing protective capacity, when accompanied by the empowerment of the executive, the privileging of the interests of private economic actors, and the expansion of policing and surveillance activities threatens the security of individuals and populations.

Hobbes and Schmitt thus stand for the dangerous potential posed by the reliance upon protection as a basis for the legitimacy of authority and of law. Yet it is not easy to dismiss the challenge that Schmitt posed to those who tried to rely on formalism to reject his authoritarian politics of law. Schmitt argued that the validity of law and the authority of those who govern cannot be established in purely formal or technical terms. Whether law is valid or authority is legitimate are political questions. Schmitt answered these political questions in ways that provided a legal language for the authoritarian politics of his age. He argued that in order for the state to secure its legitimacy, and for law to be politically valid, both legality and legitimacy must be derived from the values of a unified and homogenous community. Schmitt sought to limit politics to the act of distinguishing between friend and enemy, an act which generated the values of the homogenous community of friends. Those who rejected his vision were faced with the challenge of defending a politics of law that was not an apology for authoritarianism and unaccountable rule by executive fiat.

The international situation today poses similar challenges. How can the continued presence of the international community in Africa, the Middle East, South America, and Eastern Europe be justified? On what bases can the expanded authority of the international community in the zones of protection be represented as lawful and legitimate? These are political questions. It is in making the political nature of these questions visible that I find the value of the shift from the language of humanitarian intervention to that of the responsibility to protect. This shift reveals that the validity of international law and international authority are political questions and must be answered in those terms. The claim to be intervening on behalf of the universal values of a common humanity was so deeply embedded within a Christian metaphysics of action that it was difficult for those who believed that the Third World needed saving to experience humanitarian intervention as a politics. This made it difficult to take responsibility for the practices that were authorized in the name of universal values and the desire to bring into being a global civil society.

For example, while much of the human rights movement has been properly appalled by the abuses carried out by US military and security forces in the war on terror, advocates of humanitarian intervention in Africa and the Middle East do not ask whether increased intervention by the US military under its current rules of engagement offers the best strategy for the protection of individuals in the decolonized world. While much human rights activism has focused on the exploitative practices of multinational corporations in their operations in Africa and Asia, advocates of humanitarian intervention do not ask whether enabling an increased presence by foreign contractors in the aftermath of military intervention offers the best strategy for ending exploitation and suffering in the Third World. These concerns were forgotten in the support for increased resort to military action and increased multinational corporate presence implicit in the call for greater international intervention. Too little attention was paid to whether humanitarian intervention was in fact a good thing for the people it was designed to save.

In part, the lack of attention to the political effects of intervention follows from the idealization of the international community that was present in the work of many advocates for humanitarian intervention. By this I mean that much of the pro-humanitarian intervention literature tended to treat the international community as a benevolent actor, selflessly engaged in bringing human rights, democracy, and emancipation to a world in need of saving. This vision depends upon projecting the "inevitable political predicaments of sovereignty and representation" onto the state,[133] and away from the international community. The international community and international law are represented as if they are apolitical and unified,[134] and as if acts of intervention do not themselves set up new relations of domination and exploitation, clashes of interest, and unresolved grievances. Yet such political problems are as much a part of the constitution of the international community as they are of any state (or indeed any other body politic).[135] As a result, there has been inadequate attention paid in the theory and practice of humanitarian intervention to the ongoing work involved in legitimating (or delegitimating) the "transformation of power into authority of different kinds."[136]

In contrast, protection cannot be invoked today without also invoking the politics of representation that is incorporated within the Hobbesian vision. What counts as a threat? Whose sense of insecurity can be articulated within politics? How do the actions of this or that actor in fact guarantee protection or security, and at what cost? Invoking protection as the grounds of authority also invokes the long history of other attempts to legitimize authority through appeals to protection—the violent excesses of Cromwell's Puritan armies, the creation of protectorates as a colonial technique of rule, the return to protection by the counterrevolutionary state theorists of fascist Germany. After Hobbes and Schmitt, it is this movement between the ideal of protection and its implementation that has been thoroughly politicized. It is in this way that the responsibility to protect concept might in turn lead to a valuable politicization of the law relating to international intervention. Here the question raised by the responsibility to protect—how might subjects be guaranteed security and protection—has the potential to offer a sharper focus for political analysis than the much more metaphysical question—how can we bring into being a civil society to ensure that universal values are guaranteed to all of humanity?

The responsibility to protect literature thus implicitly raises the question of the lawfulness, in a strongly political sense, of the myriad decisions authorized by the notion that the responsibility to protect involves not just a responsibility to react, but also a responsibility to prevent and to rebuild. For example, how will those making decisions about intervention submit those decisions to public judgment and debate? What protocols will determine the processes that shape decisions about, say, resource ownership, contract allocation, and economic restructuring in the wake of military intervention? According to what laws are relations between the (international) executive and the (local) parliamentary government to be structured? Will international law respect the laws that predate the arrival of the new sovereign guarantor of protection, or will it continue to represent the zones of protection as if they are a legal vacuum? The way in which such questions are addressed will shape the political orders—both national and international—brought into being through these ongoing acts of intervention.

Those who have framed the responsibility to protect have done so in a way that allows for its foundational claims to be debated within politics to a much greater degree than was possible with the concept of humanitarian intervention. The appeal to universal values or to the interests of a common humanity served to shield arguments about humanitarian intervention from evaluation or to lift them above politics. At its best, the focus on protection works to "stake out a position that can be advanced within a political debate."[137] Bringing international intervention within a politicized account of international law offers some possibility that the ongoing encounter between Old World and New may yet lead to justice for those who inhabit the zones of protection.

Endnotes

1. This chapter was finalized in April 2009 and it has only been possible to make limited changes to take account of developments since that time. The arguments made in this chapter have been drawn upon and further elaborated in Anne Orford, *International Authority and the Responsibility to Protect* (Cambridge: Cambridge University Press, 2011).

2. International Commission on Intervention and State Sovereignty, *The Responsibility to Protect* (Ottawa: International Development Research Centre, 2001).

3. UN Secretary-General, "In Larger Freedom: Towards Development, Security and Human Rights for All," A/59/2005, March 21, 2005.

4. 2005 World Summit Outcome, A/RES/60/1, October 24, 2005, para. 139.

5. James Crawford, *The Creation of States in International Law*, 2nd ed. (Oxford: Oxford University Press, 2006), 37–89.

6. Crawford, *Creation of States in International Law*, 96–173.

7. José Alvarez, "The Schizophrenias of R2P," *American Society of International Law Newsletter* 23, no. 3 (2007): 1.

8. ICISS, *Responsibility to Protect*.

9. For a detailed analysis of the broader genealogy of the responsibility to protect concept, and its relation to the forms of protective authority exercised by the international

community in the decolonized world since the 1950s, see Anne Orford, *International Authority and the Responsibility to Protect* (Cambridge: Cambridge University Press, 2011).

10. Vasuki Nesiah, "From Berlin to Bonn to Baghdad: A Space for Infinite Justice," *Harvard Human Rights Journal* 17 (2004): 75, 77.

11. Bruno Simma, "NATO, the UN and the Use of Force: Legal Aspects," *European Journal of International Law* 10 (1999): 1; Antonio Cassese, "*Ex iniuria ius oritur:* Are We Moving towards International Legitimation of Forcible Humanitarian Countermeasures in the World Community?" *European Journal of International Law* 10 (1999): 23.

12. W. Michael Reisman, "Kosovo's Antinomies," *American Journal of International Law* 93 (1999): 860.

13. Reisman, "Kosovo's Antinomies," 860.

14. Reisman, "Kosovo's Antinomies," 862.

15. Tony Blair, "Doctrine of the International Community," speech given to the Economic Club of Chicago, Chicago, April 22, 1999.

16. Tony Blair, "Statement on the Suspension of NATO Air Strikes against Yugoslavia," London, June 10, 1999.

17. Jennifer L. Beard, *The Political Economy of Desire: International Law, Development and the Nation State* (London: Cavendish-Routledge, 2006), 2.

18. Beard, *Political Economy of Desire*, 3, 4, 11.

19. Independent International Commission on Kosovo, *The Kosovo Report* (Oxford: Oxford University Press, 2001).

20. See Gareth Evans, "From Humanitarian Intervention to the Responsibility to Protect," *Wisconsin Journal of International Law* 24 (2006): 708.

21. Francis M. Deng, Sadikiel Kimaro, Terrence Lyons, Donald Rothchild, and I. William Zartman, *Sovereignty as Responsibility: Conflict Management in Africa* (Washington DC: Brookings Institution Press, 1996), 1–2.

22. Evans, "From Humanitarian Intervention," 708.

23. Evans, "From Humanitarian Intervention," 708.

24. Evans, "From Humanitarian Intervention," 708.

25. ICISS, *Responsibility to Protect*, 11.

26. United Nations High-Level Panel on Threats, Challenges, and Change (2004), "A More Secure World: Our Shared Responsibility," synopsis.

27. UN Secretary-General, "In Larger Freedom," para. 135.

28. UN Secretary-General, "In Larger Freedom," para. 135.

29. UN Secretary-General, "In Larger Freedom," para. 135.

30. World Summit Outcome, para. 138–139.

31. Ramesh Thakur, *The United Nations, Peace and Security: From Collective Security to the Responsibility to Protect* (Cambridge: Cambridge University Press, 2006).

32. UN Secretary-General, *Address to the Summit of the Africa Union*, Addis Ababa, Ethiopia, January 31, 2008.

33. UN Secretary-General, "Implementing the Responsibility to Protect: Report of the Secretary-General," A/63/677, January 12, 2009.

34. UN Secretary-General, address at an event on *Responsible Sovereignty: International Cooperation for a Changed World*, SG/SM/11701, July 15, 2008.

35. Edward C. Luck, *The United Nations and the Responsibility to Protect* (Muscatine: Stanley Foundation, 2008).

36. See "The Responsibility to Protect," GA Resolution 63/308, A/RES/63/308, October 7, 2009; UN Security Council Resolution 1674, S/RES/1674, April 24, 2006 (thematic resolution on the protection of civilians in armed conflict); UN Security Council Resolution 1706, S/RES/1706, August 31, 2006: "*Recalling* also its previous resolutions . . . and 1674 (2006) on the protection of civilians in armed conflict, which reaffirms inter alia the provisions of paragraphs 138 and 139 of the 2005 United Nations World Summit outcome document . . . "and UN Security Council Resolution 1755, S/RES/1755, April 30, 2007 (authorizing the deployment of peacekeepers to Darfur).

37. For a discussion of state practice until 2010, see Anne Orford, *International* Authority, 17–22.

38. See, for example, African Union, "The Common African Position on the Proposed Reform of the United Nations: 'The Ezulwini Consensus,'" Ext/EX.CL/2 (VII), March 1–8, 2005 (adopting the principle of the responsibility to protect); African Commission on Human and Peoples' Rights, "Resolution on Strengthening the Responsibility to Protect in Africa," A.C.H.P.R./Res. 117 (XXXXII), November 28, 2007 (endorsing the 2007 Security Council decision to deploy an AU/UN Hybrid Operation in Darfur as an exercise of the responsibility to protect).

39. World Summit Outcome, para. 139.

40. UN Secretary-General, "Implementing the Responsibility to Protect."

41. UN Secretary-General, "Early Warning, Assessment and the Responsibility to Protect: Report of the Secretary-General," A/64/864, July 14, 2010, 1, 8.

42. UN Secretary-General, Address at *Responsible Sovereignty*.

43. UN Secretary-General, Address at *Responsible Sovereignty*.

44. See Council on Foreign Relations, "Preventing Mass Atrocities: Transcript of Interview with Louise Arbour, UN High Commissioner for Human Rights," June 12, 2007, where Louise Arbour argues that the "international community's obligations" are the "'real added value' of the responsibility to protect."

45. Carl Schmitt, *The* Nomos *of the Earth in the International Law of the Jus Publicum Europaeum*, trans. G. L. Ulmen (New York: Telos Press, [1950] 2003), 140.

46. Carl Schmitt, *The Leviathan in the State Theory of Thomas Hobbes: Meaning and Failure of a Political Symbol*, trans. George Schwab and Erna Hilfstein (Westport, Conn.: Greenwood Press, [1938] 1996), 5.

47. Thomas Hobbes, *Leviathan*, ed. J. C. A. Gaskin (Oxford: Oxford University Press, [1651] 1996).

48. Christopher Hill, *Puritanism and Revolution: Studies in Interpretation of the English Revolution of the 17th Century* (New York: St Martin's Press, 1997), 112.

49. See Richard Tuck, *Hobbes* (New York: Oxford University Press, 1989), 1–27; Noel Malcolm, *Aspects of Hobbes* (Oxford: Oxford University Press, 2002), 200–229.

50. Hobbes, *Leviathan*, 84.

51. Hobbes, *Leviathan*, 84–85.

52. Hobbes, *Leviathan*, 215 (equating the laws of nature and divine law).

53. Hobbes, *Leviathan*, 86.

54. Hobbes, *Leviathan*, 87.

55. Hobbes, *Leviathan*, 111.

56. Hobbes, *Leviathan*, 84.

57. Hobbes, *Leviathan*, 87.

58. Hobbes, *Leviathan*, 114.

59. Hobbes, *Leviathan*, 470.

60. Hobbes, *Leviathan*, 470.

61. Istvan Hont, *Jealousy of Trade: International Competition and the Nation-State in Historical Perspective* (Cambridge: Belknap Press, 2005).

62. Hobbes, *Leviathan*, 222.

63. David Dyzenhaus, "Hobbes' Constitutional Theory," in *Leviathan*, ed. Ian Shapiro (New Haven, Conn.: Yale University Press, 2009), 453, arguing that "Hobbes' view of sovereignty is a legalist one, by which I mean not that a sovereign is under a duty to rule both by law and in accordance with the rule of law, but that a sovereign in order to be recognized as such has so to rule."

64. J. G. A. Pocock, "" in James Harrington, *The Commonwealth of Oceana* and *A System of Politics* (Cambridge: Cambridge University Press, 1992), xiv.

65. Hobbes, *Leviathan*, 189.

66. Tracy B. Strong, "How to Write Scripture: Words, Authority and Politics in Thomas Hobbes," *Critical Inquiry* 20 (1993): 128, 157.

67. Dyzenhaus, "Hobbes' Constitutional Theory."

68. Hobbes, *Leviathan*, 111.

69. Strong, "How To Write Scripture," 131.

70. Hobbes, *Leviathan*, 222.

71. Dyzenhaus, "Hobbes' Constitutional Theory."

72. Hobbes, *Leviathan*, 144.

73. Herbert Marcuse, *A Study on Authority*, trans. Joris De Bres (London: Verso, [1936] 2008), 43.

74. Anne Orford, "International Law and the Making of the Modern State: Reflections on a Protestant Project," *In-Spire: Journal of Law, Politics and Societies* 3 (2008): 5, 6–7.

75. Marcuse, *Study on Authority*, 72.

76. Marcuse, *Study on Authority*, 55.

77. Eric D. Weitz, "Foreword to the English Edition" in Pierre Broué, *The German Revolution 1917–1923*, trans. John Archer, (Chicago: Haymarket Books, 2006), xi.

78. Vladimir Lenin, *The State And Revolution* (Moscow: Foreign Languages Publishing House, [1918] 1951). On the revolutionary situation in Weimar Germany, see generally Pierre Broué, *The German Revolution, 1917–1923*, trans. John Archer (Chicago: Haymarket Books, [1971] 2006).

79. Weitz, "Foreword," xii.

80. See generally Theo Balderston, *Economics and Politics in the Weimar Republic* (Cambridge: Cambridge University Press, 2002).

81. Schmitt, *State Theory of Thomas Hobbes*, 85.

82. Schmitt, *State Theory of Thomas Hobbes*, 96.

83. Schmitt, *State Theory of Thomas Hobbes*, 96.

84. Carl Schmitt, *The Concept of the Political*, trans. George Schwab (Chicago: University of Chicago Press, [1932] 1996), 52.

85. Schmitt, *State Theory of Thomas Hobbes*, 34.

86. Carl Schmitt, *Legality and Legitimacy*, trans. and ed. Jeffrey Seitzer (Durham, N.C.: Duke University Press, [1932] 2004), 20.

87. Schmitt, *Legality and Legitimacy*, 19.

88. Schmitt, *Legality and Legitimacy*, 24.

89. Schmitt, *Legality and Legitimacy*, 28.

90. Carl Schmitt, *Political Theology: Four Chapters on the Concept of Sovereignty*, 2nd ed., trans. and intro. by George Schwab (Chicago: University of Chicago Press, [1934] 2005), 5.

91. Schmitt, *Political Theology*, 34.

92. Schmitt, *Political Theology*, 26.

93. Schmitt, *Political Theology*, 33.

94. Jef Huysmans, "International Politics of Exception: Competing Visions of International Political Order between Law and Politics," *Alternatives* 31 (2006): 135, 148.

95. Thomas Hobbes, *On the Citizen* (Cambridge: Cambridge University Press, [1642] 1998), 12.

96. Schmitt, *Concept of the Political*, 39.

97. Schmitt, *Concept of the Political*, 52.

98. Reisman, "Kosovo's Antinomies," 862.

99. ICISS, *Responsibility to Protect*, 70.

100. For a critique of this tendency, see Alex de Waal, "Darfur and the Failure of the Responsibility to Protect," *International Affairs* 83 (2007): 1039.

101. Anne Orford, *Reading Humanitarian Intervention: Human Rights and the Use of Force in International Law* (Cambridge: Cambridge University Press, 2003), 126–143.

102. ICISS, *Responsibility to Protect*, 39.

103. ICISS, *Responsibility to Protect*, 39, 43, 65.

104. Martti Koskenniemi, "International Law as Political Theology: How to Read *Nomos der Erde*," *Constellations* 11 (2004): 492, 498.

105. Security Council Resolution 1625, S/RES/1625 (2005), adopted on September 14, 2005.

106. Security Council Resolution 1706, S/RES/1706 (2006), adopted on August 31, 2006; Security Council Resolution 1755, S/RES/1755 (2007), adopted on April 30, 2007.

107. *Report of the High-Level Mission on the Situation of Human Rights in Darfur Pursuant to Human Rights Council Decision S-4/101*, A/HRC/C/80 (2007), adopted on March 9, 2007. Cited as *Report of the High-Level Mission (Darfur).*

108. *Report of the High-Level Mission (Darfur)*, para. 73.

109. On the latter point, see Robert Cryer, "Sudan, Resolution 1593, and International Criminal Justice," *Leiden Journal of International Law* 19 (2006): 195.

110. United Nations Press Release, *Security Council, Following Day-Long Debate, Underscores Critical Role of International Law in Fostering Global Stability, Order*, June 22, 2006.

111. For an analysis of the development of the "zones of protection" concept in European refugee policy, see Gregor Noll, "Visions of the Exceptional: Legal and Theoretical Issues Raised by Transit Processing Centres and Protection Zones," working paper (2003), at http://www.ecre.org/eu_developments/debates/noll_response_rev.pdf.

112. Hobbes, *Leviathan*, 84.

113. Hobbes, *Leviathan*, 85.

114. Hobbes, *Leviathan*, 85.

115. Hobbes, *Leviathan*, 85.

116. Schmitt, Nomos *of the Earth.*

117. Schmitt, Nomos *of the Earth*, 96.

118. Schmitt, Nomos *of the Earth*, 97.

119. Schmitt, Nomos *of the Earth*, 98.

120. Schmitt, Nomos *of the Earth*, 97.

121. Schmitt, Nomos *of the Earth*, 98 (spelling standardized to American English).

122. Ken Macmillan, *Sovereignty and Possession in the English New World: Legal Foundations of Empire, 1576–1640* (Cambridge: Cambridge University Press, 2006), 33.

123. Janet McLean, "Problems of Translation: The State in Domestic and International Public Law and Beyond," in *The Fluid State: International Law and Domestic Legal Systems*, ed. Hilary Charlesworth, Madelaine Chiam, Devika Hovell, and George Williams (Sydney: Federation Press, 2005).

124. Nasser Hussain, *The Jurisprudence of Emergency: Colonialism and the Rule of Law* (Michigan: University of Michigan Press, 2003), 139–144.

125. Schmitt, Nomos *of the Earth*, 98.

126. Schmitt, Nomos *of the Earth*, 98.

127. Schmitt, Nomos *of the Earth*, 225.

128. Schmitt, Nomos *of the Earth*, 227.

129. Schmitt, Nomos *of the Earth*, 227.

130. Anne Orford, "The Gift of Formalism," *European Journal of International Law* 15 (2004): 179.

131. Alexander Somek, "Austrian Constitutional Doctrine 1933 to 1938," in *Darker Legacies of Law in Europe*, ed. Christian Joerges and Navraj Singh Ghaleigh (Oxford: Hart Publishing, 2003), 361.

132. See Orford, *Reading Humanitarian Intervention*, chapter 4; Anne Orford, "International Territorial Administration and the Management of Decolonization," *International and Comparative Law Quarterly* 59 (2010): 227.

133. Gillian Rose, *Mourning Becomes the Law: Philosophy and Representation* (Cambridge: Cambridge University Press, 1996), 19, discussing the general tendency to idealize the concept of community in this way.

134. Outi Korhonen, "The Problem of Representation and the Iraqi Elections," *Finnish Yearbook of International Law* 14 (2003): 35.

135. Orford, *Reading Humanitarian Intervention.*

136. Rose, *Mourning Becomes the Law*, 16.

137. David Dyzenhaus, *Legality and Legitimacy: Carl Schmitt, Hans Kelsen, and Hermann Heller in Weimar* (Oxford: Oxford University Press, 1997), 257.

10

The Legitimacy of Invading Religious Regimes

Mark Juergensmeyer

In contrast to Iraq, the US attack on Afghanistan in October 2001 is often regarded as the good war. Unlike the Iraq invasion in 2003, which is now seen by most Americans—and by most people around the world—as an unnecessary and unwarranted incursion into another country's sovereignty, Afghanistan is thought to be different. The reasons for the 2001 attack on Afghanistan seemed to most Americans at the time and since then as morally legitimate and politically expedient, though perhaps not legally sanctioned. The point of this essay is to raise the question of whether this was the case—whether the moral and political reasons were all that compelling—and to raise the larger question of whether the threat of terrorism and the draconian rule of religious regimes give legitimate sanction for acts to undermine them, including those deemed illegal in the international arena, such as toppling other nations' governments.

In the days after the tumultuous events of September 11, 2001, there seemed to be no question in the minds of most sensitive people around the world that the perpetrators of this hideous act needed to be caught and brought to justice. When it became clear that the Taliban regime in Afghanistan had played a role in harboring Osama bin Laden and other leaders of the global jihadi movement who had their base of operation in the country, it seemed obvious to many that the regime itself had to be confronted. Though no one had ever accused the Afghan leaders of being directly involved in the planning and conduct of the terrorist act, they were presumed to be guilty of willingly harboring terrorists. Moreover, the Taliban was a harsh extremist rule with very little international support. Only three countries in the world had extended it official recognition before 9/11—Saudi Arabia, the United Arab Emirates, and Pakistan—and after the attacks, even these few ties were severed. Thus, it seemed, no one was willing to come to Afghanistan's defense as the US military prepared to invade the country.

Yet the invasion of Afghanistan has raised some interesting questions. It may also have set some troubling precedents. For one thing, it raises the question of how far one can go in the pursuit of terrorists. In some ways, this question is not a new problem for international law—it is similar to ones raised in pursuit of international drugdealers or members of a mafia. Presumably the first overture would be to work with the country in which the criminal elements are hiding or using for their operations. The situation becomes problematic, however, when the regime that houses the criminal elements are in cahoots with them—worse still if that regime can be considered terrorist by its nature and ideologically opposed to the victims of the terrorist acts. Then the issue is whether another country is justified in working around that government to try to locate the criminal activists and bring them to justice. To some extent this was the issue in Afghanistan.

The Taliban and Terrorism

The Taliban was one of several contending Islamic parties in the aftermath of the fall of the Soviet-backed regime that had ruled the country since the Saur Revolution brought a socialist form of government to power in 1978.[1] After a long and debilitating struggle between the Soviet-backed Afghan socialist regime and the Islamic resistance forces—the *mujahadin* ("fighters")—the Soviet Union withdrew its support in 1989. The regime of Mohammad Najibullah was soon toppled. Fighters who had come to join the *mujahadin* from throughout the Islamic world returned to their own countries and to expatriate communities in Europe and the United States having been trained in guerrilla warfare and fired with rebellious zeal. Some of these became the terrorists of the new jihadi struggle against the secular governments backed by Europe and the United States, and changed the course of international relations in the post-Cold War world—including jihadi militants such as Khalid Sheikh Mohammad and Osama bin Laden.

Taliban literally means "student" and refers to the origins of the movement: young men who had attended *madrassas,* or Muslim schools, in the Pashtun-dominated areas of southern and eastern Afghanistan and of the Baluchistan and North-West Frontier provinces of Pakistan. One of the chief leaders of the movement, Mullah Mohammed Omar, came from a village near Kandahar, attended a religious school—a *madrassa*—and served as a mullah. He was missing one eye, which he lost in the resistance struggle against the Soviet occupation of Afghanistan. He is said to have never flown on a plane and was uneasy around foreigners.

Though the Taliban was best known outside of Afghanistan for its religious conservatism, the main differences between it and the other religiously conservative groups in the country, such as the Northern Alliance headed by Ahmed Shah Massoud, were ethnic. Massoud and most of his followers were Tajik, and Mullah Omar and his Taliban cadres were Pashtun (Pathan). Mullah Omar was also distinguished by his effective military strength, rumored to have been aided by elements of the Pakistan intelligence agency. By 1995, Taliban forces were able to capture the capital, Kabul. In 1997, Omar renamed the country the Islamic Emirate of Afghanistan. In August 1998, almost all of the last outposts of opposition in northern Afghanistan crumbled to his control, though the forces of the Northern Alliance led by Massoud fought on. Massoud's armies were at the forefront of the US-based military conquest of the Taliban in 2001, though Massoud himself had been killed, most likely by Osama bin Laden's cadres, days before the attack on the World Trade Center and the Pentagon.

Shortly after the Taliban had gained control of the country in 1996, bin Laden, along with his Egyptian colleague, Ayman al-Zawahiri, and some two hundred of their band of jihadi warriors returned to their old base in Afghanistan. Bin Laden had been abruptly asked to leave his headquarters in Sudan, and thought that the Taliban would provide a more hospitable field of operations. His hopes were fulfilled, and Afghanistan turned out to be a friendly platform for bin Laden and al-Zawahiri to launch a campaign of global jihadi warfare. Bin Laden soon ingratiated himself with the leader, Mullah Omar, showering him with gifts and more—some say that he arranged the marriage of one of his daughters to the Taliban leader. Bin Laden and al-Zawahiri provided training for their cadres in the old Tora Bora headquarters left over from the Afghan-Soviet war. They were able to communicate with their operatives and supporters over the world by utilizing new communication devices, through radio, telephone, and internet as they became available. One of bin Laden's first acts in 1996 was to release a statement, "A Declaration of Jihad Against the American Occupation of the Land of the Two Holy Sanctuaries." The land of the two holy places referred to Saudi Arabia, where both Mecca and Medina are located, and the presence of American military bases amounted to an occupation in bin Laden's frame of reference.

Two years later, in 1998, bin Laden and Zawahiri, along with Khalid Sheikh Mohammad and other militants from Pakistan, Bangladesh, and Egypt, proclaimed a World Islamic Front against the "Crusaders and Zionists"—the United States, Europe, and Israel. Though the *mujahadid* struggle in the Afghan-Soviet war in the 1980s was the origin of global jihad, the 1998 proclamation helped to launch an expanded international campaign of violence. The declaration was issued as a *fatwa*—a religious edict. It implored Muslims "to kill the Americans and their allies civilians and military" as "an individual duty" in any country "in which it is possible to do it," in order to liberate the Dome of the Rock and the al-Aqsa mosque in Jerusalem, to free the land of the holy places—Saudi Arabia—from foreign forces, and to remove the American military from all Islamic lands, "defeated and unable to threaten any Muslim." Hence this *fatwa* gave an ideological justification for an international network to respond to what it described as a global scheme of America and the West to control and denigrate Islamic society.

Within a few months of the proclamation, in August 1998, the al Qaeda network was able to carry out a spectacular pair of bombings almost simultaneously on US embassies in two African countries, Kenya and Tanzania. Over two hundred were killed and many more injured, many of them Africans speared by falling glass from high-rise buildings adjacent to the shattered embassies. Within days, US President Bill Clinton proclaimed that bin Laden and the "Islamic Army Organization" were responsible for the bombings. He ordered a military raid on an al Qaeda camp in Afghanistan, seeking but failing to kill bin Laden and his inner circle. In October 2000, bin Laden's network was associated with a brazen attack on the American navy vessel, the USS Cole, by a suicide squad of jihadi activists as the US Navy guided missile destroyer was docked in the Aden harbor in Yemen.

The attacks on September 11, 2001, constituted the high point in the coordinated jihadi campaign against the United States and a turning point in the global jihadi movement. Almost immediately, members of the jihadi movement in general and Osama bin Laden's al Qaeda network in particular were the prime suspects. Mohammad Attah, who was on the first plane to crash into the World Trade Center towers, was quickly identified as one of the leaders of the operation. Papers in his luggage, which did not make it on the transfer from his earlier flight from Portland, Oregon, to Logan Airport in Boston, identified all nineteen of the highjackers. Most were from Saudi Arabia. Attah, however, was an Egyptian who had studied in Germany. He is said to have come under the influence of radical Islam in Europe and to have met Osama bin Laden in 1999. He then received his mission to participate in what was called by jihadi leaders as the "Planes Project."

On September 20, 2001, President George W. Bush accused the Taliban of harboring al Qaeda terrorists. He delivered a nonnegotiable ultimatum demanding that the Taliban government do five things: hand over Osama bin Laden and other al Qaeda leaders to the United States for prosecution; release all foreign nationals, including Americans, "unjustly imprisoned" in Afghanistan; destroy bin Laden's terrorist training camps in the country; allow US inspectors into Afghanistan to make sure that the camps were destroyed; and "protect all journalists, diplomats, and aid workers" in Afghanistan, as well.

Interestingly, the ultimatum included two items (release of political prisoners and protection of journalists) that were not directly related to al Qaeda. But it is unlikely that the Taliban would have accepted the demands even if they were limited to what were regarded as terrorist operations. The Afghan government rejected Bush's demands, saying that they would hold a trial for bin Laden if the United States offered any evidence of his complicity in the attacks. At the same time, the Grand Islamic Council of Afghanistan—a convocation of the leading clerics in the country—met in response to the Taliban's request for their advice on how the Afghan government should respond. Perhaps to the Taliban leadership's surprise, they suggested that Osama bin Laden and his foreign militants immediately leave the country. News reports indicated that the Taliban leader, Mullah Omar, was considering the recommendation and would likely have accepted it if he had an indication from Washington that this would be sufficient to keep the United States from invading his country. The response from the White House was immediate and negative, however, saying that it would not be sufficient to allow bin Laden to leave Afghanistan only to slip into hiding in another country.

The Taliban government then offered another solution. It would remove bin Laden from Afghanistan under guard in order for him to stand trial in a neutral, third-party country (not specified) if the United States would provide evidence that Osama bin Laden was indeed implicated in the attacks. Although this proposal seems reasonable, by the time the Taliban leadership suggested it the matter was moot, since the United States military had already attacked the country and were attempting to destroy bin Laden's likely hideouts and forcibly remove the Taliban from office. The combined efforts of American military air strikes and the revived forces of the Northern Alliance caused the Taliban regime to crumble at the end of 2001. Though the resistance to the US invasion was strong at the outset, eventually few Afghanis remained to defend the Taliban government. When the regime fled from Kabul on November 12, 2001, even members of the Taliban's own ethnic community, the Pushtuns, celebrated as if the country had been liberated from an evil oppressive rule.

Clearly, the Bush government had been determined to topple the Taliban regime regardless of whether or not it banished bin Laden from the country or released him into the hands of a third-party nation for a trial. It was apparent that the Bush administration in the United States regarded the Taliban government not only as an accomplice of al Qaeda but also as a kind of terrorist movement in its own right. It was regarded as a terrorist regime not only because of its association with Osama bin Laden and his al Qaeda network (a connection that was never publicly proven and is still somewhat unclear), but also because it was itself an extremist religious state. In other words, regardless of whether it could be proven that the Taliban knowingly abetted in the attack on the World Trade Center and the Pentagon on September 11, 2001, it was guilty of association with those who were (or rather, who were presumed to have been) directly involved with it, even though evidence was never given at the time for bin Laden's complicity in the 9/11 attack. And in retrospect it appears that another jihadi miltant, Khalid Sheikh Mohammad, based in Pakistan, had much more to do with the direct planning of the operation than bin Laden. Nonetheless, the Taliban seemed to be implicated in the al Qaeda attack. The most important link in the minds of many who regarded the Afghan invasion as justified was a conceptual one: the notion that the Taliban and al Qaeda were essentially the same kind of thing.

Many in the Bush administration assumed that a radical Islamic regime like the Taliban was terrorist by its very nature. Their actions indicated that they thought that whether or not there was an al Qaeda link, they thought that toppling a radical religious regime such as the Taliban was politically legitimate and morally warranted. It is this perspective that I want to explore.

Are Attacks on Radical Religious Regimes Legitimate?

There are two ways to question the legitimacy of the US invasion of Afghanistan. One is to ask whether the circumstances in this particular case left no other option other than to topple the Afghan government. Since the facts of the case in the days after 9/11 have shown that other options might indeed have been available but were not fully explored, this leads us to the second question: did the United States assume that the Taliban regime was inherently despotic and incapable of internal rehabilitation, thereby giving the United States the political legitimacy to destroy it regardless of its ties to bin Laden and his al Qaeda network?

There is no doubt that Afghanistan was ruled by an unsavory band of leaders. What frightened many Americans and Europeans about the Taliban was not only its reliance on brutal exercises of violence as a way of controlling its citizenry but also the restrictions on civil liberties that gave the government the appearance of enslaving its populace. Even if the most dark assessments of the Taliban's harsh rule were true, however, the question remains as to whether *it was immoral by nature* and thereby an external invasion to topple the government would be recognized as legitimate by the international community even though the protection of a nation's sovereignty from outside intervention is a cardinal principle of international law. The fundamental underlying point of view in the Bush administration's position was that a religious regime of the Taliban sort is capable of internal change without the necessity for an invasion from outside.

This is an interesting perspective and is built on a complex set of considerations. The attitude that religious regimes are legitimate targets for invasion by their very nature contains several key assumptions:

- that religious regimes are unusually dogmatic by nature
- that religious regimes are inflexible and incapable of change
- that religious law is fundamentally opposed to secular law
- that religious regimes are undemocratic by nature
- that radical religion cannot protect minority rights
- that radical religion cannot support individual rights

Each of these points is worthy of discussion, not only in relation to the Taliban but to religious regimes in general, in order to ascertain whether there is an argument to be made that they characterize the sort of despotic rule that, by its very nature, legitimately warrants opposition and regime change.

ARE RELIGIOUS REGIMES UNUSUALLY DOGMATIC?

When it comes to moral issues, it is true that the positions of religious regimes are often rigid and inflexible. The arguments are often buttressed with the assertion that these principles are based on nonnegotiable divine mandates. A Muslim leader in Algiers underlined his opinion that the place of women is in the home with the statement, "It is not I who demand this, but God."[2] Having a strong religious vision often also means settling on a single figure as the authority for the entire movement. In India, for example, a member of the Hindu nationalist movement, the RSS, claimed that its "skilled and efficient leadership" should not only be obeyed but also revered, just as a guru in traditional Hinduism is lauded, even worshiped.[3] In Iran, some thought Khomeini led his country with divine providence. Even those who disagreed with Khomeini's ideology and religious point of view often appreciated his leadership abilities. Though the Palestinian Hamas leader, Sheik Ahmed Yassin, regarded the Iranian revolution as "an experiment that failed," he said that he "admired Khomeini."[4] From the opposite camp in Israel, the leader of an anti-Arab Jewish movement, Rabbi Meir Kahane, also professed an admiration for the Iranian leader and led his own movement in the way that Khomeini led his—autocratically, with virtually no rivals.[5] A Christian activist in the United States pointed to Khomeini as the sort of leader that he wished that conservative Christians could have in America. Religious activists from Egypt to Indonesia have admired in the Khomeini style a sense of order and certainty that came with a clear religious vision and unchallenged authority.

Yet, although religious movements are often dogmatic and authoritarian, the same is sometimes true of secular regimes. In some cases, the authoritarianism of secular ideologies has resulted in dictatorships as brutal as any that religious politics has produced; the Soviet Union's Stalin is one example; Germany's Hitler is another. Though one could argue that at times communism and Nazism took on the character of religion, there have been fascist tendencies in many secular states. In most secular societies, however, strong central authority has devolved to systems of authority involving an elected parliament of representatives and an independent judiciary. Most secular nationalists refer to this system when they speak of democracy. The question, then, is whether religious nationalism could ever follow a similar path and be capable of embracing democratic values.

ARE RELIGIOUS REGIMES INFLEXIBLE?

The diversity of political positions within the Islamic Republic of Iran gives an indication that even a rather rigid religious regime is indeed capable of flexibility and perhaps significant change on its own. Muslim militants in other parts of the world—including Sheik Ahmed Yassin in Palestine and Qazi Turadqhonqodz in Tajikistan—have disagreed with the Ayatollah Khomeini and rejected many of his positions. Other post-revolution leaders in Iran, including Mohammad Khatami and Akbar Hashemi Rafsanjani, have been considerably more moderate than the extremists. Despite the heavy-handed suppression of political dissent after the June 2009 elections, however, the regime went to some lengths to demonstrate its openness to opposition candidates and public dissent, at least for a limited period of time.

When the Hindu-based Bharatiya Janata Party (BLP) first ascended into power in India, many secular political observers were convinced that the country was at the point of political collapse as a result. Some claimed that the very reputation of India as a modern nation was at stake. One commentator asserted that "the separation of the State from all faiths" was a fundamental attribute of modernity and was characteristic of "a modern outlook anywhere."[6]

But when the BJP actually ascended to power from 1997 to 2004, it acted like any other political party in its organizational calculations, often to the frustration and disappointment of some of its more religious supporters. Though it angered many intellectuals by rewriting history textbooks in order to display the glories of India's Hindu past and downplay the role of Muslims, and though minority groups of Muslims, Christians, and Sikhs often regarded the BJP as biased against them, the BJP did not turn out to be a Hindu Taliban.

IS RADICAL RELIGION COMPATIBLE WITH DEMOCRACY?

The rhetoric of many religious nationalists suggests that they are remarkably enthusiastic about democracy. Even those activists most opposed to the secular state affirm the political importance of the democratic spirit. Sheik Yassin, for instance, told me that "Islam believes in democracy."[7] One of his Buddhist counterparts in Sri Lanka said that Buddhism also "is democratic by its nature."[8] A member of the Muslim Brotherhood in Egypt told me that "democracy was the only way" for an Islamic state.[9] A leader of Israel's Gush Emunim said that "we need democracy," even in "a religious society."[10]

Some of this enthusiasm for democracy is self-serving. If democracy simply means majority rule, then it means letting the people have what they want. If the people want a religious society rather than a secular one, then they should have it. "Since 80 percent of the people in Egypt are Muslims," one Muslim activist explained to me, "Egypt should have a Muslim state."[11]The same line of reasoning has been used in Sri Lanka and in Punjab, where Sinhalese and Sikh activists, respectively, think that democracy is the legitimization of rule by whichever camp has the preponderance of the population on its side. In these cases, democracy means simply the will of the majority. But even religious activists who interpret democracy solely as majority rule stress that this control should not come about by fiat. The decision to have an Islamic state, Sheik Yassin argued, "should come about through democratic vote."[12]

Ultimately, however, it is not the will of the people that matters in a religious frame of reference but the will of God. For that reason, religious nationalists often state that good leadership involves the ability to discern what is godly and truthful in a given situation. As Rabbi Kahane said, "you don't vote on truth."[13] Most religious activists agree; they regard the discernment of truth as ultimately beyond the democratic process. Thus the normal way of transacting politics in democratic states—through voting, political bartering, and the interplay of competing interest groups—is seen as irrelevant and perhaps even contrary to a higher morality. In an interesting moment in my conversations with a Buddhist *bhikkhu* in Sri Lanka, he cited as an example of the immorality of secular government its tendency to pander to the self-interests of contending parties. That, however, is precisely what democratic politics in the United States and elsewhere in the West is supposed to do: respond to competing interests. It is supposed to distribute the largess of the state as widely as possible and supply the greatest amount of happiness to the greatest number of people. But this is a morally insufficient notion of government from the *bhikkhu*'s point of view. He wanted the government to adopt a larger vision of ethical order and uphold *dhamma* (virtue).[14]

Many religious activists around the world agree with the *bhikkhu* and have an ambivalent attitude towards the democratic processes. Though they are eager to embrace the spirit of democracy—at least in the sense that governments should express the will of the people—they do not share the rationalists' faith that reason alone is sufficient for finding the truth, nor do they feel that unbridled self-interest is an adequate moral base for a political order. A similar discussion about the potential excesses of democracy—the fear that unbridled democratic engagement with government would amount to nothing less than the rule of the mob—is to be found in Plato's *Republic* and in the debates among the founding fathers of the French and American republics.[15]

IS THERE FLEXIBILITY IN RELIGIOUS LAW?

Religious nationalists have one advantage over Plato, however: they are more certain than he was about where truth may be found. For most religious activists, their tradition provides a framework of religious law that is considered normative for human activity. Because religious law is the only certain repository of social and ethical truth, they reason, it should be the basis of politics. According to some activists, the establishment of religious law is the primary goal—some would say the sole aim—of religiously political movements. Religious leaders in Egypt, for instance, explained that the main problem with the Sadat and Mubarak government was that it ignored *shari'a* and did not make it the law of the land. They resented the fact that the government preferred Western law instead. "Why should we obey Western laws when Muslim laws are better?" one of them asked me.[16] This question was again raised in the political turmoil following the collapse of Mubarak's regime in 2011.

A similar sentiment has been echoed in Israel, where Jewish nationalists felt that the Knesset gave more credence to Gentile laws than to Jewish ones, even though, as one of them put it, "Jewish law was formulated long ago when the Gentiles were still living in the bushes."[17] The same speaker, on another occasion, told me that Israel should strive for "Torahcracy" rather than democracy.[18] He developed a constitution for the State of Israel based entirely on Halakhic laws, but, significantly, except for the slightly archaic language, it looked much like a modern constitution based on Western secular law. The Torah constitution, for example, granted individuals freedom of expression. The main deviation from a Western secular constitution was its provision of an ultimate arbiter of what is good for society: the council of judges, the Sanhedrin.

The constitution of the Islamic Republic of Iran is also, to a remarkable extent, similar to the constitutions of most modern Western countries. It contains guarantees of civil rights and minority rights and prescribes three branches of government—executive, judicial, and legislative—and the balances of power among them. The president and the members of the legislature are to be elected by the people for fixed periods of time. The only unusual features of the constitution, from a secular Western point of view, are the insistence on Islamic law as the basis from which all principles of law are to be derived and the role of Islamic clergy in telling the lawmakers which laws are appropriate. The constitution also establishes an unusual role of "leader"; initially, this role was delegated specifically to the Ayatollah Khomeini and after his death Sayyed Ali Khamene. The leader appoints the council of clergy who pass judgment on Islamic law, selects the Supreme Court and the commanders of the army, leads the National Defense Council, and declares war and peace. Interestingly, the leader does not have the power to appoint the president of the country—the role played by elected officials such as Khatami and Ahmadinejad—but the leader can withhold signing the decree approving the election of the president if the leader chooses. The leader can also dismiss the president but only if the Supreme Court convicts the president of "failure to fulfill his legal duties," or the National Consultative Assembly testifies to "his political incompetence."[19] Similarly, the leader has the power to pardon convicts or reduce their sentences, but only after receiving a recommendation to that effect from the Supreme Court. Thus, the Iranian constitution has provided the country with an Islamic version of Plato's philosopher-king—but it has placed this religious monarch within a modern parliamentary system.[20]

In other movements of religiously inspired rebellion, the clergy has also played a limited role. The main leaders of al Qaeda have been a businessman, Osama bin Laden, and a medical doctor, Ayman al-Zawahi. In other movements, the leadership has included rabbis, sheikhs, and other religious figures, but they have not been the sole guardians of the movement. Sheik Yassin, for instance, claimed that the leadership of an Islamic political movement should be open to all and the clergy should not be forced into political activity if they were not interested in it.[21] In Buddhist and Christian movements, monks and priests have joined rebellious movements as active partners without being the primary leaders. A *bhikkhu* in Sri Lanka told me that it was not necessary to have monks in power as long as government officials are mindful of consulting with religious leaders: "They should seek their advice."[22] In Egypt and India, the religiously based political movements are generally not led by clergy. In Egypt, a Muslim activist said that the clergy should be teachers of religious principles rather than politicians.[23] In India, where large numbers of *sadhus* (religious ascetics) have worked to bring out the votes for the Hindu-nationalist BJP, the leaders of the party have given public assurances that the *sadhus* will not exert a significant influence on party policy. Although the party has allowed some *sadhus* to run for office under the BJP banner, they did not become a significant bloc within the party leadership. In virtually every movement for religious nationalism the idea of theocracy—rule by the clergy—has been rejected.

In fact, as long as religious law is affirmed as the basis for political action, the method for discerning that law and the procedure for choosing leaders who will carry it out can be democratic: the system can rely on ballots and elections. "These days we expect our governments to be democratically elected," a *bhikkhu* explained to me in Sri Lanka, indicating that democracy is consistent with Buddhist principles as long as the leaders are mindful of the fact that they are upholding *dhamma* (divine order).[24] In Egypt, some religious activists have thought that only through the democratic process will the legitimate religious parties succeed.[25]

Most movements of religious activism also follow democratic procedures within their own organizations. Even though Rabbi Kahane advocated an autocratic rule for Israel, he endorsed democratic procedures for the committee he set up to establish an independent state of Judea.[26] Radical religious committees from Sri Lanka to Algeria, and from Palestine to Montana, have been chosen internally by wide consultation if not by vote.

The implication is that the electoral process, as a means of choosing leaders and making decisions, has become well established throughout the world, including places where rebellious movements for religious politics are on the rise. If this process is the hallmark of democracy, religious activists are as democratic as any secular politician. Religious nationalists and transnationalists are concerned not with the process but with the purpose: from their point of view, the political system exists ultimately only for divine ends, to make certain that human activity is consonant with the fundamental moral order that undergirds it. Religious activists break with democratic theorists primarily over the issue of whether the democratic system can legitimate itself: religious politicians deny the possibility. A democratic gang of thieves, they argue, is still a gang of thieves. For the process to be morally valid it must be put to noble purposes, and that is why religious law must be the basis for any moral state.

CAN RADICAL RELIGION TOLERATE MINORITY RIGHTS?

In many parts of the world, minority communities have watched the rising tide of religious activism with great apprehension. Their misgivings, often exacerbated by the warnings of secularists, center around the concern that a society commanded by outspoken proponents of one religion will favor the majority religious community at the expense of the minorities.

This apprehension is warranted, for at the very least religious nationalists want the symbols and culture of their own religious communities to be glorified as part of the heritage of the nation. Most members of minority communities can live with reminders that they are residents of a nation dominated by another religion if it is simply a matter of putting up with the Sinhalese lion or the phrase *Allahu Akbar* ("God is Great") on their national flag, as they do in Sri Lanka and the Islamic Republic of Iran, or a matter of enduring a string of national holidays that celebrate someone else's faith, as Muslims and Jews do in the United States.

Minorities, however, are concerned about two, more problematic, possibilities: the potential for preferential treatment of majority community members in government hiring and policies, and the possibility that the minorities will be required to submit to religious laws that they do not respect. Beyond these concerns is a third, more apocalyptic, fear: that they will eventually be driven away from their own homelands, or persecuted or killed if they remain.

The problem of minority rights and the assertion of minority identities are not peculiar to religious regimes, however. They are fundamental problems in secular societies as well. In fact, secular nationalism is unable to deal easily with any kind of collective identity except those defined by geography. African Americans in the United States, for instance, constitute over 10% of the population but do not supply 10% of the representatives in the US Congress because not all of them reside in one place. A system that is set up to represent people on the basis of where they live almost invariably fails to represent equally the groups that people identify with, unless the groups happen to be coextensive with the geographical boundaries of a city or state.

In India, the British recognized this flaw in the Western system of democratic representation and tried to correct it with the device of "reserved constituencies"—a system that allowed only members of certain minority communities (people from formerly untouchable castes, for instance) to run as candidates in selected constituencies. In most cases, however, secular governments have dealt with the political representation of minority communities by denying that a problem exists—that is, they have held to the illusion propounded by democratic theory: that all people are equal, and for that reason discrimination should not occur among groups. The illusion is reinforced by law: if people are, in fact, found to be discriminating on the basis of communal distinctions, they will be punished. Thus the myth of equality is enforced.

Some religious activists have argued that this myth should be exposed, and that governments should deal with communal identities more honestly, especially in dealing with minority groups. In India, for example, the BJP claimed that tensions between the government and the unhappy Muslim and Sikh minorities were eased under BJP rule because government leaders appreciated communal identities. In Israel, similarly, Rabbi Kahane told me that when his group fought for its own religious rights, it became more sensitive than it had been to Muslim groups who were fighting for theirs.[27] (Nonetheless, Kahane said, the Arabs should leave what he regarded as Jewish sacred land.) In Iran, one of the early leaders of the revolution, Bani-Sadr, argued that every group should have rights—minority groups as well as majority ones. "Considering one's identity and rights as one's own and someone else's as his own is an Islamic idea," he claimed; "therefore, we have no quarrel with those who say: our rights belong to us."[28]

The question, however, is how religious regimes deal with the issue of minority rights if and when a religious state is established. In general, they have proposed two solutions. One is to provide a separate status (or even a separate state) for minority communities—similar to the British solution of providing reserved constituencies for minorities in India. The other solution is to accommodate the communities within the prevailing ideology—primarily by regarding the dominant religious ideology as a general cultural phenomenon to which a variety of religious communities are heir. This is the approach of the BJP in India, which claimed all of Indian tradition—including Sikhism, Buddhism, and Jainism—to be Hindu tradition and which allowed the religions from outside India, such as Christianity and Islam, to be affiliated with Hinduism as syncretic Christian-Hindu and Muslim-Hindu branches. In Sri Lanka, efforts were made to create a Buddhist "civil religion" that would incorporate various strands of the country's religious traditions.[29]

The first solution—separate status—is problematic in that it requires finding an appropriate status or place for the minority groups. Whereas the British could provide separate electoral positions in parliament, most religious nationalists have been required to come up with a much more substantial peace offering for minorities: land. The issue of land is significant because religious nationalism is often rooted in a particular place. Judaism is intimately connected with biblical locations, many of which are on the West Bank of the Jordan River in Palestine. The religious nationalists of Sri Lanka insist on the political integrity of the whole of the island, and the Hindu nationalism of the BJP glorifies all of India. There is not much room in these positions for granting separate territory to minority communities. For that reason, religious nationalists who want to solve the minority problem through separatism might be forced to return to the British solution of separate political representation after all.

The second solution—accommodation of cultural differences—also has its problems, but it provides a more flexible range of options. One of the more promising is an idea that I first heard discussed by Muslim activists in Egypt, and then again, in an entirely different context, among Muslim leaders in Gaza.[30] These Muslim leaders insisted that Egyptian and Palestinian nationalism should subscribe to Islamic *shari'a*, but they indicated that there are two kinds of *shari'a*, or rather two levels of it: at a general cultural level there are social mores that are incumbent on all residents of the nation, regardless of their religious affiliations. This general level of *shari'a* is much like what passes for law-abiding, civilized behavior everywhere. At a more particular level, however, are detailed personal and family codes of behavior that are required only of Muslims. This formulation is similar, they said, to patterns they had experienced while traveling abroad. When in England or North America, they were expected to obey the laws and standards of Western civilization in public, but privately they followed Muslim, rather than Western, customs.[31] They would expect Christians to return the favor when visiting, or living in, Muslim countries.

Could the accommodation approach work with secular minorities? Even in traditional religious cultures there are people who were raised in religious households but who, through travel, education, or association with modern urban culture, have lost interest in religion. Should there not be a safe cultural haven for such people in a religious society, just as the cultures of Copts and other minorities are maintained as islands in seas of religiosity? From most religious nationalists to whom I posed the question, the answer was a resounding no. They could accept the idea that other religious traditions provide valid alternatives to their own religious law but not secular culture: it has, in their eyes, no links with a higher truth. From their point of view, it is simply antireligion. Some religious nationalists found it difficult to accept secularism even in Europe and the United States, where, they felt, Christianity failed to keep its backsliders in line. Still, it seems to me that the logic of the two-level *shari'a* admits at least the possibility of islands of different cultures within a religious state.

WILL RADICAL RELIGION PROTECT INDIVIDUAL RIGHTS?

Behind the question of minority rights is a more fundamental issue: the protection of individuals. Terms such as *separate status* and *accommodation* ultimately are important only insofar as they define how persons are treated. If a separate status for minority groups leads to new political positions or a semiautonomous state through which individuals may express their needs and concerns, that is one matter. If it leads to oppression and ostracism, that is quite another.

The term that has evolved in the West to indicate resistance to oppression and respect for people is *human rights.* The minimum definition of human rights—the notion that people should be able to reside peacefully alongside each other in dignity and with personal security—is embraced by virtually every religion, albeit in its own terms. For example, one might find, as one Western scholar has, "deep and surprising parallels" between Islamic notions of religious tolerance and one's own.[32] The problem that Islam and many other religious traditions have is with the notion of individual rights: the idea that persons possess on their own some characteristics that do not come from the community or from God.

When rights are conceived as being held by individuals rather than groups, some religious activists feel this definition connotes the unacceptable idea that a society is made up of persons who are granted authority and independence—their rights—at the expense of the integrity of the communal whole. Rather than using the term *rights,* then, most religious activists would rather describe the relationship between the individual and society as one of moral responsibility. As one of them put it, "We have no rights, only duties and obligations."[33]

In a way the controversy over rights makes little difference as long as societies respect the personal security and dignity that is at the heart of both human rights and the moral values of all religious traditions. In Egypt, for instance, Muslim nationalists speak ardently about the "uplift of the oppressed."[34] In Sri Lanka, religious nationalists insist that one of the prime purposes of a nation is to uphold free expression and personal dignity—the sorts of "rights" listed in the United Nations' Universal Declaration of Human Rights—but they describe them as Buddhist values rather than as secular humanistic ideals.

The constitution of the Islamic Republic of Iran affirms that one of the purposes of an Islamic republic is to protect the "exalted dignity and value of man, and his freedom, joined to responsibilities, before God."[35] The constitution describes the protection of this dignity in terms that echo constitutions everywhere: the language of human rights. These are, however, the rights of "the people" rather than of individuals. The constitution contains a whole chapter—some twenty-one articles—devoted to the "rights of the people," including equal protection under the law, the equality of women, freedom to express opinions, freedom from torture or humiliation while in incarceration, and freedom to hold "public gatherings and marches," with the condition that "arms are not carried and that they are not detrimental to the fundamental principles of Islam." The constitution also goes beyond the usual list of human rights and includes the right to being provided with "basic necessities," including housing, food, clothing, healthcare, education, and employment.[36]

The only part of the Iranian constitution's list of rights that would give a Western advocate of human rights pause is the occasional use of the phrase "subject to the fundamental principles of Islam." This wording, for example, accompanies Article 24, freedom of the press. It also accompanies the last article of the constitution, regarding mass media: Article 175 guarantees that the media, especially radio and television, will be dedicated to "the free diffusion of information and views" but "in accordance with Islamic criteria."[37]

Is this caveat about Islamic principles the loophole through which massive violations of human rights can enter Iranian society? The answer to that question depends on how much one trusts the Iranian leaders to be true to their word and on how much one believes that the fundamental principles of Islam are consistent with human rights. A good many Muslims outside of Iran think that the Ayatollah Khomeini and his "Judge Blood" comrades took liberties in interpreting Islamic principles and gave Islam the image of being narrow and intolerant. Even Sheik Yassin, the Palestinian Muslim leader, disapproved of taking Americans hostage and said that Khomeini "went too far" in bridling freedom of speech.[38] Yassin and other Muslim leaders thought that Khomeini's actions contradicted his own constitution, which on the face of it seems as dedicated to human rights as any created by a secular state.

Is It Legitimate to Topple Religious Regimes?

If the legitimacy of a military intervention of a religious regime is based on the idea that religious regimes are "terrorist"—despotic and unworthy of existence—by their very nature, then the legitimacy argument cannot be sustained. Each of the assumptions that undergird the notion that religious regimes are illicit by their nature can be challenged. Though religious regimes tend to be autocratic, they are not necessarily dogmatic; they can be flexible and capable of change; divine law can be compatible with secular law; religious regimes are eager to be democratically validated; and they are sensitive to issues of minority and individual rights. This is not to say, though, that religious ideologies are fundamentally the same as secular ideologies.

The traditional Islamic—or Jewish, or Christian—version of human rights is ultimately not the same as the humanistic secular version. From the point of view of traditional religious cultures, stark individualism and a laissez-faire attitude toward personal expression run fundamentally counter to the collective loyalty and disciplined demeanor typically found in the religious life. It is unlikely, therefore, that radical religious nationalists will ever fully support a libertarian version of individual rights, even though in many other ways they may look and talk like human rights advocates anywhere in the world. The fact is that most religious activists would carry the values of communal life to an extreme that would be uncomfortable even for the most sympathetic Westerner. This difference between the role of an individual in Western "individualistic" countries and in non-Western "communitarian" societies is basic, and stands behind many of the controversies over the protection of human rights.

Whether this difference justifies military invasions and the removal of religious regimes in general is questionable, if only because the variety of political regimes among the world's nations is immense, and their differences over issues of minority and individual rights are considerable. The mere existence of a very parochial and narrow-minded religious regime would not usually be sufficient basis for military invasion and occupation. Still, there may be cases in which the threat to human life and the abuses of civil liberties by a regime are so palpable as to provide moral legitimacy for military intervention even when no legal authorization for such an act exists. Whether the Taliban was such a regime—and whether the United States was politically legitimate and morally justified in making that determination and then invading Afghanistan solely on its own prerogative—remains questionable in the court of world opinion.

Endnotes

1. For a useful overview of the rise of the Taliban in Afghanistan, see Ahmed Rashid, *Taliban: Militant Islam, Oil and Fundamentalism in Central Asia* (New Haven, Conn: Yale University Press, 2001).

2. Quoted in Kim Murphy, "Algerian Election to Test Strength of Radical Islam," *Los Angeles Times*, December 26, 1991, 244

3. Dina Nath Mishra, *RSS: Myth and Reality* (New Delhi: Vikas, 1980), 73; see also Embree, "Function of the Rashtriya Swayamsevak Sangh," 9–17.

4. Interview with Sheik Ahmed Yassin, founder and spiritual leader of Hamas, in Gaza City, Gaza, January 14, 1989.

5. Quoted in Mergui and Simonnot, *Israel's Ayatollahs*, 40–41.

6. Sarvepalli Gopal, "Introduction," in Gopal, *Anatomy of a Confrontation*, 13.

7. Interview with Yassin.

8. Interview with Uduwawala Chandananda Thero, February 2, 1988.

9. Interview with el-Arian.

10. Interview with Rabbi Levinger.

11. Interview with Shitta, January 10, 1989.

12. Interview with Yassin.

13. "The goal of democracy is to let people do what they want," Kahane claimed. "Judaism wants to make them better." Quoted in Mergui and Simonnot, *Israel's Ayatollahs*, 36.

14. Interview with Uduwawala Chandananda Thero, February 2, 1988.

15. Plato, *The Republic,* translated by B. Jowett (New York: Modern Library, n.d.), 312.

16. Interview with el-Geyoushi.

17. Speech by Yoel Lerner at the celebration to establish an independent state of Judea, Jerusalem, January 18, 1989. I appreciate the simultaneous translation of his speech at that occasion provided by Ehud Sprinzak and his students.

18. Interview with Lerner.

19. Hamid Algar, trans., *Constitution of the Islamic Republic of Iran* (Berkeley, Calif.: Mizan Press, 1980), 68.

20. The leader is leader for life, presumably, and when he dies, the constitution specifies that "experts elected by the people" will choose a new leader; if none is to be found, they will appoint from three to five members of a leadership council, which will perform the leader's functions. Algar, *Constitution,* 66. See also H. E. Chehabi, "Religion and Politics in Iran: How Theocratic Is the Islamic Republic?" *Daedalus* (Summer 1991): 69–92. For the clergy's ambivalence toward politics in the period immediately prior to the revolution, see Shahrough Akhavi, *Religion and Politics in Contemporary Iran: Clergy-State Relations in the Pahlavi Period* (Albany: State University of New York Press, 1980).

21. Interview with Yassin.

22. Interview with Uduwawala Chandananda Thero, February 2, 1988.

23. Interview with el-Arian.

24. Interview with Uduwawala Chandananda Thero, February 2, 1988.

25. Interview with Shitta, January 10, 1989.

26. Interview with Kahane. Michael ben Horin, a leader of the event for proclaiming a state of Judea, explained that all the delegates had been chosen from Judea and Sumaria, two elected from each settlement. Leaders of the founding congress were elected by a secret ballot. The list of people nominated for the executive committee was read out (and other names could be added); each candidate gave a little nominating speech. Interview with Michael ben Horin, manager, Kach office, in Jerusalem, January 15, 1989.

27. Interview with Kahane.

28. Bani-Sadr, *Fundamental Principles and Precepts of Islamic Government,* 40.

29. The International Centre for Ethnic Studies in Colombo produced a series of television programs describing the "unity through diversity" in Sri Lankan society. The Hindu god Vishnu, for instance, was shown to be frequently worshiped at Buddhist temples, and the distinctly Sri Lankan god Kataragama was seen to be venerated equally by Buddhists and Hindus.

30. Interviews with Shitta, January 10, 1989; el-Arian; el-Geyoushi; and Yassin. Their comments about a two-level *shari'a* were made without knowing that similar comments had been made by the others.

31. Interview with el-Geyoushi.

32. David Little, "The Development in the West of the Right to Freedom of Religion and Conscience: A Basis for Comparison with Islam," in *Human Rights and the Conflict of Cultures: Western and Islamic Perspectives on Religious Liberty*, David Little, John Kelsay, and Abdulaziz A. Sachedina, (Columbia: University of South Carolina Press, 1988), 30. For other 56. For other discussions of human rights in comparative perspective, see Max L. Stackhouse, *Creeds, Society, and Human Rights: A Study in Three Cultures* (Grand Rapids, Mich.: W. B. Eerdmans, 1984); Arlene Swidler, ed., *Human Rights in Religious Traditions* (New York: Pilgrim Press, 1982); Leroy S. Rouner, ed., *Human Rights and the World's Religions* (Notre Dame, Ind.: University of Notre Dame Press, 1988); Kenneth W. Thompson, ed., *Moral Imperative of Human Rights* (Washington, D.C.: University Press of America, 1980); and Irene Bloome, Paul Martin, and Wayne Proudfoot, eds., *Religion and Human Rights* (New York: Columbia University Press, 1995). For an exploration of the interesting thesis that human rights is itself a religious tradition, see Robert Traer, *Faith in Human Rights: Support in Religious Traditions for a Global Struggle* (Washington, D.C.: Georgetown University Press, 1991).

33. Speech given by Rabbi Meir Kahane, Jerusalem, January 18, 1989 (the English translation was supplied to me on that occasion by Ehud Sprinzak and his students). See also the transcript of an interview with Kahane in Mergui and Simonnot, *Israel's Ayatollahs*, 33–34.

34. Interview with el-Arian.

35. Algar, *Constitution*, 27.

36. Ibid., 38 and 43.

37. Ibid., 91.

38. Interview with Yassin.

11

Legality and Legitimacy in the Global Order

THE CHANGING LANDSCAPE OF NUCLEAR NON-PROLIFERATION

Aslı Ü. Bâli

Introduction

The Non-Proliferation regime is arguably one of the most important achievements of international law in the twentieth century. The significance of the regime derives from two basic conditions of the post-World War II period: first, the advent of nuclear weapons, with the attendant possibility of destruction on a previously unthinkable scale. Second, following decolonization, the enlargement of the international order to include a vast number of sovereign states, each with an equal claim to seek a nuclear deterrent and each capable of wreaking catastrophic destruction should they acquire and use a nuclear weapon.

The leveling effect of nuclear weapons—with the potential to confer a military deterrent capability on any country regardless of size—introduced a seemingly irreducible instability at the heart of the new international order emerging out of the two convulsive world wars of the twentieth century. The strategy to manage this new and destabilizing reality centered on a bargain struck between the existing nuclear-weapons states and the non-nuclear-weapons states to address the incentives for proliferation and stem the threat. The core of that bargain took the form of the Nuclear Non-Proliferation Treaty (NPT) regime, which was based on a tradeoff of access to civilian nuclear energy in exchange for forgoing the acquisition of nuclear weapons.

While all countries benefited from a stable Non-Proliferation regime, the principal beneficiaries of this bargain were the nuclear-weapons states that were able to enshrine in a consensual treaty regime a hierarchical ordering of the international security system. This framework enabled them to largely retain their nuclear arsenals while prohibiting others from acquiring nuclear weapons. It also radically reduced the cost of maintaining the security of an international order in which the recognized nuclear-weapons states—which, by the time the NPT came into force, were also the veto-wielding permanent members of the UN

Security Council—enjoyed a privileged position in the permissible distribution of military capabilities.

Recent developments impacting the global norm of Non-Proliferation may, however, have the cumulative effect of eroding the Non-Proliferation regime. On the one hand, there remain powerful disincentives to acquiring nuclear weapons. These include various considerations, from the financial cost and technical difficulty of developing nuclear weapons to the damage that would be done to collective security alliances by acquiring a nuclear arsenal. On the other hand, the emergence of new nuclear-weapons states, the violations of the reporting obligations of non-weapons states, and the apparent abandonment of disarmament commitments in the new nuclear posture of the United States may signal the arrival of a new nuclear age. Among the most damaging developments has been the shift in American policies away from multilateral treaty-based Non-Proliferation toward unilateral counter-proliferation and preemption policies. This shift has led some critics to call the legitimacy of the NPT regime—absent the compliance of the nuclear-weapons states with their disarmament obligations—into question. Moreover, these developments have arisen at a time when the basic prohibition of the use of force built into the international security order, centered on the United Nations, has also come under pressure.

This chapter examines the implications of the weakening of the international norm of nonintervention for the sustainability of the Non-Proliferation regime. In particular, I argue that the loosening of constraints on the use of force is especially dangerous should it be applied to justify arms control–b ased interventionism at a time when the core of the Non-Proliferation regime is already subject to erosion.[1] To build this argument, the essay first considers recent legal debates concerning humanitarian intervention, which have given rise to new exceptions on the strict prohibition on the use of force in the UN Charter framework. Debates about the doctrine of humanitarian intervention occasioned a rethinking of the institution of sovereignty under the UN Charter system. Where the equal sovereignty of all states was understood as an institutional property of the international system, mediating the appropriate boundaries in the relations between states, it has been reconceptualized as an individualized property of states conditional on the performance of particular responsibilities. These responsibilities are both internal (the responsibility of states to protect the welfare of their civilian populations) and external (the responsibility of states to observe international obligations). In extreme cases, where states fail to meet their internal responsibilities, the logic of conditional sovereignty suggests that intervention may be authorized on humanitarian grounds. By extension, determinations that external obligations of conditional sovereignty have been violated may also be seen as a new basis for justifiable intervention.

The perceived need to legitimate humanitarian intervention in the 1990)))s resulted in a rethinking of fundamental norms, such as sovereignty, with implications beyond the humanitarian context. The exception to the norm of nonintervention based on this conditional concept of sovereignty[2] represents a weakening of the UN Charter prohibition of non-defensive uses of force. Further, this weakening has emerged at a time when new arguments for intervention are being advanced in the international system in a completely different context. The coincidence of humanitarian-based legal arguments for permissible intervention with arguments concerning the right of states to engage in preemptive and even preventive uses of force may be conjunctural. This chapter argues, however, that these arguments share a common underlying logic that is profoundly destabilizing for the United Nations' collective security mechanism. In the area of arms control, that same logic undergirds the recent shift away from Non-Proliferation toward counter-proliferation and from multilateral treaty-based approaches to a preference for ad hoc and selective interdiction exercises.

The new interventionism discussed in this chapter has particularly adverse consequences for the viability of the Non-Proliferation regime. The Non-Proliferation regime is built on a bargain that provides non-nuclear-weapons states with incentives to refrain from proliferation in exchange for the concrete benefits of membership in the regime. These benefits include access to civilian nuclear technologies, negative security assurances that non-nuclear-weapons states will not be subject to nuclear attack, and a commitment by the nuclear-weapons states to work toward disarmament. The pillars of this arrangement have come under increasing pressure as a result of efforts on the part of the nuclear-weapons states, and particularly the United States, to unilaterally renegotiate the core bargain by restricting access to nuclear technologies while diluting disarmament commitments. With the Non-Proliferation regime already under pressure from these developments, the weakening of the prohibition of the use of force may irreparably damage the incentive structure and the crucial negative security assurances on which the NPT depends. Against this risk, this chapter offers an argument for reinforcing the traditional UN use-of-force regime and the current Non-Proliferation regime rather than resorting to new counter-proliferation measures or attempts at coercive enforcement actions.

Part I of this chapter sets out an interpretation of the international law narrative concerning the emergence of a doctrine of humanitarian intervention centered on the principle of a collective "responsibility to protect." It argues that the debates in international law and international relations scholarship concerning the relationship between legality and legitimacy have subjected foundational UN Charter principles to reinterpretation and renegotiation. Emerging from the experience of NATO's 1999 intervention in Kosovo, these debates respond to the challenge of an unauthorized use of force that may generate humanitarian benefits. The outcome of the debates gave rise to a new exception on the prohibition of non-defensive force, but one that legal scholars and institutions sought to confine to the domain of humanitarian objectives. Efforts to bridge the gap between legality and legitimacy are the subject of many of the chapters herein. This chapter considers, rather, the implications in the area of arms control of the weakened prohibition on non-defensive force.

In the context of the "Global War on Terror," the concepts that evolved out of the legality/legitimacy debate in the humanitarian context have migrated to other forms of intervention in the broader international security arena.[3] The emergence of a new interventionism based not on humanitarian considerations but on a broadened concept of defensive force extended to encompass preemption is traced through the chapter. The license to engage in preemptive uses of force, particularly on the basis of unilateral threat determinations, extends the logic underlying arguments for humanitarian intervention in directions that profoundly destabilize the authority and viability of the collective security mechanism of the UN system. The Iraq war is an example not only of the risk to the international security order of a conception of preemptive interventionism, but also of the potential convergence of humanitarian and preemption-based arguments for intervention.

Part II sets forth a detailed account of the significance of the Nuclear Non-Proliferation Treaty (NPT) and developments that have adversely impacted the Non-Proliferation regime in the last decade. This account provides the contemporary Non-Proliferation context against which to consider the potential implications of the new interventionism in the area of arms control. These implications are then taken up in part III. The chapter offers an assessment of the relationship between the erosion of the Non-Proliferation regime and the emergence of a strong counter-proliferation emphasis in American arms control policy. This counter-proliferation emphasis not only threatens to displace the priority of non-proliferation, but it also reinforces new and destabilizing policies including the uncoupling of Non-Proliferation from disarmament commitments, a strategy of selective nonproliferation, and an embrace of the preemptive use of force for arms control purposes.

All these developments fit into a broader trend of eschewing rule-bound order in favor of ad hoc enforcement actions. The doctrine of conditional sovereignty connects to such recent trends in Non-Proliferation insofar as the underlying logic of the doctrine may be extended to arguments for security-based preventive intervention. The possibility of preventive intervention on Non-Proliferation grounds is corrosive to the NPT bargain in a number of ways taken up in part III. The chapter concludes that the combination of the erosion of the Non-Proliferation norm and the emergence of new legal arguments for interventionism may have the unintended consequence of generating perverse proliferation incentives.

I. From Legality and Legitimacy to Interventionism

With the end of the Cold War in the 1990s, the international security order faced a new set of challenges unsettling the previous focus on the prevention of inter-state war. The problems of humanitarian crisis, civil war, and violence committed by non-state actors raised questions not easily addressed under the UN Charter framework for collective security and its prohibition of the non-defensive use of force.

Further, trends set in motion with the adoption of the UN Charter, but long repressed by the bipolar order of the Cold War period, gained greater salience. These trends included the growth of international civil society organizations and the prominence of human rights agendas advocated by non-governmental organizations (NGOs), concern with the prevention of humanitarian catastrophes, and the impact of increasing international political and economic interdependence on the sovereignty of states. Against this backdrop, the challenge of how and when to intervene in cases of humanitarian catastrophe became a focus of serious concern in international diplomacy and widespread debate in international law during the 1990s.[4]

The atrocities in the former Yugoslavia and the genocide in Rwanda posed the question of humanitarian intervention with considerable urgency. With the precedent of inaction in these earlier cases, the possibility of an ethnic cleansing campaign in Kosovo created an international legal crisis. The framing of the humanitarian intervention question in the Kosovo case gave rise to a debate about the relationship between legality and legitimacy. Specifically, if the legal mechanism for authorizing the use of force—namely Security Council action—were unavailable in the case of a humanitarian emergency, was there a legitimate basis to intervene anyway?

As Richard Falk makes clear in his chapter, the gap between law and legitimacy in any system, domestic or international, grows out of the aspiration to connect the authority of law to the dictates of a moral conception of justice. While the standard for legality defined by the rules set forth in the UN Charter is relatively objective—at least with respect to use of force—the definition of legitimacy depends on more subjective determinations.[5] The appeal to legitimacy has the benefit of introducing flexibility in the operation of international law in extraordinary circumstances. The risk, however, is that appeals to legitimacy loosen international legal constraints in ways that may invite opportunism by providing powerful states new resources to justify their circumvention of international law when expedient to fight wars of choice.[6]

The appeal to legitimacy to trump legal constraint is likelier to occur because of an absence of geopolitical consensus rather than the existence of an extraordinary circumstance.[7] Yet, the Security Council mechanism was explicitly designed to forbid recourse to non-defensive force absent consensus. The absence of consensus for intervention was not an unanticipated circumstance for which the charter failed to account, but very much the concern at the heart of the horse-trading mechanism that is the Security Council. To use force in the absence of consensus was deemed too destabilizing to the international security order by the drafters of the charter, predicated on tense cooperation among great powers. Arguments that the appeal to legitimacy should trump this prohibition bear the burden of demonstrating that the benefits attendant to intervention are greater than those safeguarded by the nonintervention principle. Yet in a post–Cold War context, the view that a veto should not prevent intervention deemed to have a humanitarian purposes gained considerable support.

The story of the NATO intervention in Kosovo absent Security Council authorization is by now a familiar one in international legal circles.[8] The subsequent finding by the independent International Commission on Kosovo that the intervention had been "illegal, but legitimate" brought into sharp focus the gap between law and legitimacy and suggested the emergence of new criteria to guide extralegal action as a last resort in the case of a humanitarian emergency.

Because the Kosovo intervention and the debates concerning its legality have been very widely studied, there is a clear international law narrative concerning the evolution from the Kosovo precedent to a broader principle of humanitarian intervention. The starting point of this narrative is the view that the Kosovo intervention identified the exact point at which the old norm of nonintervention had begun to fray, giving way to a new and more permissive norm. The perceived legitimacy of the Kosovo intervention suggested the need for a new norm that would permit the use of force in extreme circumstances on purely humanitarian, nondefensive grounds. For those convinced of the need for a new norm and an emerging consensus to buttress it, Kosovo represented a precedent that in retrospect might constitute the first application of the new norm of humanitarian intervention. The remaining steps in the international legal narrative concerning humanitarian intervention trace the emergence of this new norm beyond the first instance of state practice in Kosovo through the development of scholarly consensus and ultimately institutional recognition.

A. THE KOSOVO COMMISSION'S VERDICT: "ILLEGAL, BUT LEGITIMATE"

In the Kosovo case and the humanitarian intervention debates that ensued, the legality-legitimacy tension concerned contestation over norms and procedures for authorizing recourse to force. To the extent that concerns about legality were overridden in the Kosovo intervention, what followed was not the resolution of debates about legality and legitimacy but a whole new set of questions. Specifically, if legal constraints are to be loosened by introducing considerations of legitimacy, how then are the permitted departures from the law to be circumscribed? The independent International Commission on Kosovo (the "Kosovo Commission") represented an initial effort to respond to this question. However, the commission's solution of reconciling the illegality of the intervention with its potentially beneficial results by recourse to the language of legitimacy may have raised more questions than it answered.

The determination of legitimacy relied, in the commission's formulation, heavily on the post hoc assessment that the outcome of the intervention had been beneficial from a humanitarian perspective. Without debating the empirical validity of this claim, neither the net positive effect of the intervention nor the fact that the civilian Kosovar population offered its support once the intervention was underway could have been ascertained in advance.[9] Judging legitimacy on the basis of the outcome of an intervention is a problematic benchmark since it offers little guidance ex ante as to the potential legitimacy of subsequent undertakings. The question raised by the commission's formula was how one might delimit the precedent set by the Kosovo intervention.

The recommendation of the commission toward this end was the adoption of "a principled framework for humanitarian intervention which could be used to guide future responses to imminent humanitarian catastrophes."[10] An outstanding question raised by the commission's proposed guidelines is: who decides? Determinations about the application of the principles remain necessarily subjective, discretionary, and non-consensus-based if they are to be made outside of the United Nations' peace and security institutions. Despite the effort to constrain the precedent, its practical effect absent the specification of an agreed-upon procedure of authorization would enable the powerful to substitute their judgments for the collective security mechanism of the United Nations.

The Kosovo Commission wrote its recommendations to modify the prohibition on non-defensive uses of force in the context of humanitarian emergencies, arguing that the greatest danger to human rights was not too much intervention, but too little.[11] This perspective found little resonance among the states of the global South.[12] In light of their colonial history and Cold War experiences, much of the developing world took the view, rather, that interventionism, not its absence, represented the greater threat.

B. THE INTERNATIONAL COMMISSION ON INTERVENTION AND STATE SOVEREIGNTY: "RESPONSIBILITY TO PROTECT"

The unsettled status of humanitarian intervention after the Kosovo Commission led the UN secretary-general to call on the international community to forge consensus on the principal issues at stake: "when should intervention occur, under whose authority and how."[13] A reframing of the basis for international responses to humanitarian crises was in order.

In response to the secretary-general's challenge and the concerns of the global South in response to the *Kosovo Report*, a second international commission was convened. The title of the commission reflects a shift in the underlying debate. The independent "International Commission on Intervention and State Sovereignty" (the ICISS) was convened in 2000 and issued its report one year later.[14] The commission's approach shifted the debate away from intervention and toward sovereignty as the basis on which to build a framework to deal with humanitarian crisis.

Sovereignty is a foundational principle of the rule-based international order centered on the United Nations. While the definition of sovereignty is much contested in political theory, the international legal definition is based on the principle of nonintervention. The standard conception of sovereignty in the UN Charter system has been succinctly described by Ian Hurd as "the principles of nonintervention and mutual recognition that create the boundaries between nominally independent states."[15] While sovereignty is not an absolute shield against intervention, the UN Charter determines when intervention is permitted in the name of the collective security order. In this sense, sovereignty is more an institutional property of the collective security order than a right of statehood. Altering the rules of nonintervention or displacing the United Nations as the sole body authorized to make determinations concerning permissible uses of force necessarily affects the institution of sovereignty.

The approach of the ICISS was to reframe the debate, abandoning the language of intervention and adopting a new sovereignty-centered concept, which they called the "responsibility to protect."[16] This approach is grounded in a reinterpretation of the UN Charter's definition of sovereignty. According to the commission, in signing the charter states voluntarily accepted the responsibilities flowing from membership, which involved a "necessary re-characterization" of sovereignty: "from sovereignty as control to sovereignty as responsibility in both internal functions and external duties.[17] The "responsibility to protect" approach thus stems from a characterization of the institution of sovereignty as entailing particular responsibilities. The rights of the sovereign—understood as a shield from intervention—depend upon its capacity to fulfill these responsibilities.[18]

In the ICISS formulation, sovereignty entails a primary obligation of the state to protect its population from humanitarian emergencies such as those that arise from war crimes, ethnic cleansing, crimes against humanity, and genocide. The responsibilities of the international community, by contrast, are secondary in nature—the international community has an obligation to protect civilian populations only in the event that a state fails to meet its primary responsibilities. This subsidiary conception of the international responsibility to intervene in the event of humanitarian crises relocates the onus to act with the state, an allocation of obligations more congruent with the concern of developing countries to reinforce the institution of sovereignty. The principle of a "responsibility to protect" gained significantly more traction in international circles than the conceptualization of humanitarian intervention that arose from the recommendations of the Kosovo Commission.[19]

C. FROM RESPONSIBILITY TO PROTECT TO CONDITIONAL SOVEREIGNTY

The first significant institutional recognition of the responsibility to protect framework took the form of the 2004 Report of the United Nations High-Level Panel on Threats, Challenges and Change.[20] The High-Level Panel Report brought to the fore the language of shared responsibility and provided a more expansive concept of responsibility as a facet of sovereignty:

> In signing the Charter of the United Nations, states not only benefit from the privileges of sovereignty but also accept its responsibilities. Whatever perceptions may have prevailed when the Westphalian system first gave rise to the

> notion of state sovereignty, today it clearly carries with it the obligation of a state to protect the welfare of its own peoples and to meet its obligations to the wider international community.[21]

In this formulation, sovereignty under the UN Charter entails more than internal obligations regarding the welfare of civilian populations but also external obligations toward the international community. The High-Level Panel's description underscores the fact that the ICISS framing of sovereignty as responsibility introduced a new conception of *conditional* sovereignty, whereby a state must satisfy the obligations associated with sovereignty to enjoy its privileges. The High-Level Panel went on to argue that when a state fails to meet its obligations "to protect its own people and avoid harming its neighbors,"

> the principles of collective security mean that some portion of those responsibilities should be taken up by the international community, acting in accordance with the Charter of the United Nations and the Universal Declaration of Human Rights.[22]

By linking conditional sovereignty, shared responsibility, and the principles of collective security, the High-Level Panel emphasized two crucial aspects of the ICISS conception of a responsibility. First, the panel highlighted both internal and *external* responsibilities of sovereignty, where the ICISS focus had been almost exclusively on the former. Second, the panel explicitly connected the concept of a responsibility to protect to the collective security mechanism of the UN Charter. As is made clear elsewhere in the panel's report, the responsibility to protect embraced by the report returns the Security Council to a central role in determining when force may be authorized.[23]

Following the High-Level Panel's lead, the norm of collective responsibility was embraced in numerous UN documents.[24] The report presented by the UN secretary-general to the 2005 World Summit session of the UN General Assembly adopted the recommendations of the High-Level Panel, including the responsibility to protect.[25] Following the secretary-general's report, the UN General Assembly's World Summit Outcome Document explicitly embraced the responsibility to protect and linked it to the collective security mechanism of the Security Council.[26] It was next adopted by the UN Security Council, initially in a thematic resolution on the protection of civilians in armed conflict that affirmed the World Summit Outcome Document's endorsement of the responsibility to protect,[27] and then in an operative resolution deploying peacekeepers to Darfur.[28]

The trajectory from humanitarian intervention to the responsibility to protect and the attendant notion of conditional sovereignty provides a partial genealogy for the emergence of a new legal norm through all of the necessary elements, from state practice to *opinio juris* to institutional recognition.[29] The emergent norm of the "responsibility to protect" is not exactly analogous to an embrace of the broader notion of a right of humanitarian intervention independent of UN authorization.

Nonetheless, the responsibility to protect signals a shift in the international legal landscape in the direction of a weakening of the nonintervention norm or, at the very least, a more expansive concept of the circumstances under which the Security Council may authorize force.

D. THE NEW INTERVENTIONISM

The attempt to establish limiting criteria in the humanitarian intervention context has been fraught with two difficulties: first, the definition of the specific criteria to establish legal constraints on intervention; and second, the question of who will decide whether the specified criteria have been satisfied. The contested but emerging conditions for legitimate intervention that arose from the debates of the 1990s include the existence of a humanitarian emergency, the necessity of forcible intervention to prevent or end such an emergency, and the justification of force only as a last resort. By at least one definition, only two circumstances constitute a sufficient emergency to merit intervention: large-scale loss of life as a result of deliberate state action or mass ethnic cleansing.[30]

The potential transition from a humanitarian intervention posture to one of regime change is latent in the debates canvassed above. The principle of a responsibility to protect provides a guide for the obligations of the international community should a state fail to meet its *internal* obligations to safeguard the welfare of its civilian population. A second possibility, implicit in the notion of conditional sovereignty, is that a state's perceived failure to meet *external* obligations to the international community might also be deemed a legitimate basis to authorize non-defensive uses of force.[31]

Anne-Marie Slaughter offers a useful consideration of the arguments for a new, conditional conception of sovereignty. In her analysis, she argues for a redefined concept of sovereignty whereby states benefit from the protection of nonintervention only to the extent that they fulfill the twin responsibilities of advancing the best interest of their citizens and meeting their obligations to the wider international community.[32] In other words, her analysis picks up on and makes explicit the *external* responsibilities of sovereignty. Based on such a conception, it follows that should states fail in either of these responsibilities, they might become the legitimate object of collective intervention.

This conception of sovereignty as responsibility, in turn, may buttress arguments that different states are entitled to the benefits of the nonintervention rule to varying degrees. For instance, the argument that certain states have forgone the benefits of the nonintervention rule might result from an assessment that the state has failed to comply with significant external obligations to the international community.[33] Such arguments have been advanced, in some quarters, in response to suspicions of noncompliance with arms control obligations or as a framework for dealing with proliferators, as will be discussed below. Similarly, a state may be said to forgo some of the benefits of sovereignty because the nature of its internal regime is inconsistent with the criteria of advancing the best interests of its civilian population.[34] Cosmopolitan arguments that democratic states should occupy a privileged position in making legitimacy determinations at the international level suggest that internal regime-type may become a criterion for decision-making about intervention.[35] Logically, it follows that those excluded from determinations about the legitimacy of an intervention are also more likely to become the target of such an action.

The idea that states may be subject to forcible intervention as a result of their regime type or as part of an enforcement action for international obligations casts the original humanitarian intervention debate in a relatively different light, particularly in the post–September 11 context.[36] Clearly the extension from the principle of a responsibility to protect to a notion of conditional sovereignty that might countenance a significant additional loosening of the prohibition of non-defensive force was not in the minds of the international lawyers and diplomats debating the merits of humanitarian intervention. Yet when the politics of the current international security order are combined with the logic underlying the responsibility to protect norm, the extension of that logic with all the attendant destabilizing complications in the area of arms control and beyond are far from implausible.[37] This chapter is concerned with the implications of such a potential extension.

1. Legality and Legitimacy after Iraq

After Kosovo, arguments about the legality and legitimacy of military intervention have arisen primarily in the cases of Afghanistan and Iraq.[38] As argued above, the Kosovo intervention yielded a call to develop fixed legal criteria to determine when an intervention may be undertaken on humanitarian grounds. The drive for explicit criteria was in part due to a desire to constrain the Kosovo precedent. Despite concern that the precedent should be limited, there were those who invoked Kosovo as a precedent for an unauthorized intervention in Iraq.[39]

There were several legal rationales offered for the war in Iraq by the United States and the United Kingdom. The most radical of the American legal justifications was a doctrine of preemptive self-defense, whereby the United States argued that the legal authorization for defensive uses of force be extended to the prevention of future attacks from states that constitute “emerging threats” and may harbor aggressive intentions.[40] This widened conception of self-defense was plainly at odds with the UN Charter framework which defines defensive force as a response to an armed attack that has occurred or is imminent.[41]

The preemption doctrine developed by the United States, if broadly adopted, would undermine collective security mechanisms in favor of a self-help system dependent on unilateral threat determinations. The more limited definition of self-defense in the UN Charter was drafted, under post-WWII American leadership, precisely to avoid according individual states a broad license to use force subject only to their own threat perceptions.

A second argument presented to justify military intervention in Iraq was that an implied Security Council authorization for such force existed on the basis of previous resolutions passed by the council. This implicit authorization argument rested on a combined reading of the resolution that authorized force against Iraq in 1990, the ceasefire resolution of 1991 and the 2002 resolution threatening Iraq with serious consequences for failure to dispose of its stockpiled weapons of mass destruction.[42]

While it is difficult to make a credible legal case for implicit Security Council authorization of the Iraq intervention on the basis of the plain language of the resolutions,[43] the more interesting facet of the argument advanced here was the introduction of the novel rationale of an arms control basis for military intervention.[44] Perhaps the starkest statement of this rationale was the one offered by President Bush at a press conference in March 2003, just prior to the invasion of Iraq. In answering a question regarding the mission of an intervention in Iraq, the president provided the following response:

> Our mission is clear in Iraq. Should we have to go in, our mission is very clear: disarmament. And in order to disarm, it would mean regime change.[45]

Thus, the purpose of the intervention was disarmament, and the means by which that purpose was to be accomplished was regime change. Underlying the president's approach is the suggestion that disarmament is in and of itself a sufficient justification for the intervention and that regime change is a legitimate means to accomplish that justified end.[46] The implication that the mere presence of weapons stockpiles in Iraq might be a sufficient basis to justify a military intervention is an innovative facet of the Iraq intervention that risks contributing to the further weakening of the norm of nonintervention.[47]

The third legal rationale offered for the invasion of Iraq was the argument that there was an international duty to intervene in Iraq to liberate the Iraqi people from a brutal dictatorship. This rationale was only occasionally referenced in advance of the intervention, but the humanitarian justification became increasingly prevalent retroactively. The connection between the disarmament rationale and the requirement of regime change, implied in the statement by President Bush above, facilitated the post hoc transition from an arms control rationale for intervention to a regime change argument more focused on the welfare of the Iraqi civilian population. Without question, the Iraq war fails to meet any of the principled constraints on justifiable humanitarian intervention advanced by the ICISS, the General Assembly, or the Security Council in embracing the principle of a collective responsibility to protect. Had the humanitarian justification been the prin cipal argument for the intervention *ex ante* it would have likely occasioned widespread objection for this reason. Nonetheless, there were some proponents of the humanitarian intervention approach that favored the Iraq war on these grounds in 2003.[48]

The convergence of the preemption and arms control arguments heralded the emergence of a new doctrine of intervention. This doctrine was admittedly distinct from and arose on very different grounds than the earlier arguments rooted in humanitarianism. The arguments advanced prior to the Iraq war framed the action as necessary to disarm a dangerous dictator, not as a chance to liberate his people. Nonetheless, the latent *ex ante* presence of a humanitarian argument for the Iraq intervention among some of its proponents provided a valuable resource for bolstering legitimacy arguments, if not legality arguments, in the aftermath of the war, when the arguments based on preemption and arms control began to fail.

The rationale for intervention offered by the United States in the case of the 2003 Iraq war demonstrates the potential convergence of arguments from the Right and from the Left in the weakening of the norm of nonintervention. Despite efforts by the Kosovo Commission and others to delimit the Kosovo precedent, scholars have noted the invocation of the precedent by advocates of the Iraq war to justify intervention.[49] Efforts to legitimize the Iraq war through the discourse of humanitarianism illustrate the risks attendant to humanitarian rationales when pressed into the service of power.

2. CONDITIONAL SOVEREIGNTY AND ARMS CONTROL

In the previous sections, I have traced the ways in which recent debates in international law have led to a weakening of the nonintervention norm. In the remainder of this chapter, I am most concerned with drawing out the implications of these arguments for weakening prohibitions on the use of force in the context of arms control and more specifically in light of changes in the Non-Proliferation regime. I argue that the line of international legal reasoning that emerged out of the tensions between legality and legitimacy in the Kosovo context may now connect the humanitarian intervention debates of the 1990s to debates on the legitimate use of force in the post-September 11 period and current crises in the Non-Proliferation regime. Specifically, the transition from debates about humanitarian intervention to those concerning a "responsibility to protect" vulnerable populations, to new arguments about a "duty to prevent" catastrophic acts provides a legal and intellectual mapping of arguments that have anticipated the greater recourse to intervention in the new millennium.[50]

The relatively open-ended interventionist mandate asserted by the United States in the context of the "war on terror" provides a geopolitical context against which the evolution of arguments about the forcible enforcement of Non-Proliferation obligations in such cases as Iraq and now, arguably, Iran, may be understood.[51] In the next part, I will draw out the implications of the weakening of the nonintervention norm for the Non-Proliferation regime. First, however, it may be helpful to make explicit the connection between a conditional conception of sovereignty, drawing on the responsibility to protect, and arguments for intervention based on arms control considerations.

The principled effort to think through the logic of the Kosovo precedent and connect sovereignty as responsibility to arms control is exemplified in an argument advanced by Anne-Marie Slaughter, published the day after the 2003 invasion of Iraq. Slaughter, then the president of the American Society of International Law, cited the Kosovo precedent as a potential source of provisional legitimacy for the Iraq intervention, despite her assessment that the intervention itself was illegal. To meet the legitimacy requirements set by the Kosovo precedent on her reading, Slaughter argued that certain basic conditions would have to be met in an *ex post* assessment of the intervention. The three conditions she cited were: (1) if weapons of mass destruction (WMD) are found; (2) if the intervention enjoys the support of a majority of Iraqis; and (3) if the United Nations takes over the reconstruction of Iraq and the restoration of its sovereignty following the intervention.[52]

Slaughter's argument presents a revealing portrait of the post-Kosovo debate on intervention among international legal scholars. First, none of the conditions she cites require the presence of a humanitarian emergency as was originally suggested in the framework advocated by the Kosovo Commission and the ICISS to delimit the Kosovo precedent. Rather, the argument rests on an extended conception of conditional sovereignty according to which the presence of WMD would presumably furnish evidence of material breach on the part of the Iraqi regime of one of the external conditions on Iraq's sovereignty. The second and third of Slaughter's conditions follows from the emphasis in the humanitarian intervention and responsibility to protect literature on judging an intervention on the basis of its net outcome. If the intervention proved to enjoy popular support among the civilian population and gave way to immediate reconstruction efforts supervised by the UN, Slaughter's reasoning implies that there would be a presumption of a net positive outcome, which would strengthen claims that the intervention had been legitimate. The failure of Slaughter's conditions of being met, in the event, in Iraq, illustrates one danger of offering legitimacy criteria that can only be assessed post hoc while according powerful actors the discretion to determine *ex ante* whether an intervention is justified.

Ultimately, the judgment of almost all international lawyers is that the Iraq war was both illegal and illegitimate.[53] Thus, it cannot be said that a new legal rule exists that reconciles the emergent norm of responsibility to protect with the Bush administration's embrace of regime change. Nonetheless, the notion of conditional sovereignty, which is still very much present in the humanitarian intervention context, does provide a potential bridge. The power of arguments setting forth conditions on sovereignty has proven difficult to constrain to the specific circumstances that arose in Kosovo.

As developed by the Kosovo Commission and the ICISS, the criteria for constraining instances of force outside the usual authorizing mechanism of the Security Council required an emergency involving the potential for large-scale loss of life. The variety of circumstances that might arguably contribute to the occurrence of such an emergency may become subject to broad interpretation. If it is conceivable that possession of large stocks of conventional weapons might be a basis for legitimate intervention, then surely nuclear proliferation might equally constitute a basis for forcible intervention. The implications of the loosening of constraints on the use of force in one context—humanitarian intervention—clearly have the potential to buttress new arguments for intervention in other areas of international security, including that of nonproliferation. While there has been significant retrenching on assertive arguments in defense of intervention for regime change purposes since 2003, the ongoing debate about the legitimacy of a forcible intervention in Iran based on arms control considerations suggests that the underlying rationale for preventive intervention has not been entirely abandoned.

II. The Non-Proliferation Regime and the Risk of Erosion

The possibility of extending the conception of conditional sovereignty in support of arguments for intervention based on arms control considerations, discussed in the previous section, has troubling implications for the stability of the nuclear Non-Proliferation regime. This section first offers an overview of the origins and achievements of the Non-Proliferation regime centered on the NPT. Next, recent developments that have undermined the stability of the core bargain at the heart of the treaty are considered. Against this background, the section concludes with an assessment of the potentially damaging consequences of arguments for the coercive enforcement of Non-Proliferation obligations, and the more subtle shift from Non-Proliferation policies to an emphasis on counter-proliferation activities.

The Non-Proliferation regime is a rare example of a successful and near-universal arms control treaty in the international security system. Further, it arose in the least propitious context, from an international relations perspective, for the emergence of a cooperative regime. There is a strong assumption in international relations that regimes cannot be established and sustained in the area of security, much less the high stakes realm of nuclear proliferation. Despite this assumption, the Nuclear Non-Proliferation Treaty and the attendant Non-Proliferation regime not only came into existence, but succeeded in entrenching a nuclear taboo on the acquisition or use of nuclear arsenals.[54] Explanations for the emergence and stability of the regime center on great power cooperation, American leadership, and the perceived urgency of the need to stem nuclear proliferation.

The Non-Proliferation bargain itself was built on a tacit alliance between the powerful nuclear-weapons states and weak states that were unlikely to ever acquire nuclear weapons. Together these states colluded in establishing a stable regime to prevent major industrial states with a latent nuclear-weapons capability from exercising a break-out option and acquiring nuclear weapons. Identifying bases for cooperation and building an incentive scheme capable of drawing adherents from among states that might otherwise have exercised a proliferation operation remains an immense achievement driven to a significant extent by American leadership.

Moving from an anarchic international security system that generated powerful incentives to acquire a nuclear deterrent to a rule-based order capable of containing the spread of nuclear weapons was arguably the single most important arms control accomplishment of the twentieth century.

More than fifty years have passed since the beginning of the nuclear age, and the international system now has nine known nuclear powers. The first five nuclear states had all acquired their weapons within twenty years of Hiroshima: the USSR tested a nuclear device in 1949, the United Kingdom joined the nuclear club in 1952, France conducted a nuclear test in 1960, and finally China tested a nuclear device in 1961.[55] Despite widespread international concern that the pace of proliferation of nuclear weapons would produce a world with as many as thirty nuclear-weapons states by the end of the twentieth century, the following three decades did not witness such drastic increases. With US assistance in civilian nuclear technology and covert British and French assistance in acquiring necessary fissile materials and weapons technologies, Israel was known to have acquired a nuclear-weapons capability by the end of the 1960s.[56]

On May 18, 1974, India conducted a successful nuclear test, becoming the sixth declared nuclear power. This prompted several decades of work on a nuclear-weapons capability in Pakistan, which was believed by US intelligence estimates to have attained a nuclear bomb as early as 1990 but did not conduct its own nuclear tests until May 1998, following the first Indian nuclear tests since 1974.[57] Finally, on February 10, 2005, North Korea declared that it had obtained nuclear weapons following the collapse of its Non-Proliferation negotiations with the United States.[58] Over eighteen months later, North Korea claimed that it had performed a successful nuclear test, prompting the Security Council to adopt Resolution 1718 imposing sanctions on the DPRK.[59]

The number of nuclear-weapons states has not fulfilled the worst-case scenarios that were feared in the 1950s. In addition, there have been numerous developments that have positively impacted prospects for Non-Proliferation since the dark predictions of the initial post-WWII period. The end of the Cold War and the conclusion of arms control agreements between the United States and Russia to reduce their nuclear stockpiles generated renewed hopes of strengthening disarmament measures among existing nuclear powers. The break-up of the Soviet Union raised the specter of new entrants to the nuclear club, notably the newly independent states of Ukraine, Kazakhstan, and Belarus, each of which inherited significant quantities of Soviet nuclear weapons. Fortunately, by the mid-1990s, all three of these states had agreed to destroy or return the strategic nuclear warheads located in their territory and to accede to the NPT as non-nuclear-weapons states.[60]

There were additional Non-Proliferation successes in the mid-1990s, including the official renunciation by both Argentina and Brazil of nuclear-weapons programs coupled with their joint acceptance of the comprehensive International Atomic Energy Agency (IAEA) safeguards agreement.[61] South Africa admitted that it had assembled a small arsenal of nuclear weapons during the 1980s and proceeded to unilaterally dismantle its weapons and accede as a non-nuclear-weapons state to the NPT on July 10, 1991.[62] South Africa further took steps to act as a mediator between the nonaligned movement states and nuclear-weapons states, to strengthen the global Non-Proliferation regime. South Africa was also one of the early supporters of a nuclear-weapons-free zone in Africa, signing the African Nuclear Weapons Free Zone Treaty (the Treaty of Pelindaba) as soon as it opened for signature on April 11, 1996.[63] Finally, the indefinite extension of the NPT following intense negotiation at the 1995 NPT Review Conference (and thanks in part to South African mediation) was a significant accomplishment reinforcing the global Non-Proliferation regime and strengthening claims of an emerging customary international law norm of nonproliferation.

Since the 1990s, however, a number of key developments have raised concerns that the positive Non-Proliferation environment which followed the end of the Cold War may have given way to a new era of accelerated proliferation. As mentioned above, the emergence of two new declared nuclear powers—Pakistan and North Korea—since the end of the 1990s has impacted regional and international security balances and raised the specter of a chain reaction of states that might pursue arsenals of their own. Changes in the American approach to nonproliferation, shifting the emphasis away from the global Non-Proliferation norm and attendant multilateral regimes toward ad hoc and informal counter-proliferation networks, have also adversely impacted the international Non-Proliferation environment.[64]

When these developments are combined with the weakening of the nonintervention norm discussed above, the reemergence of strong incentives to acquire a virtual nuclear deterrent for some states in the international system may prove irresistible. In the following sections, I will review the legal framework of the nonproliferation regime, identify pressures on the regime that have may lead to erosion, and discuss the failure of the most recent NPT Review Conference. Against this backdrop, I argue that the convergence of new arguments for intervention in the international system and the growing American preference for ad hoc counter-proliferation over traditional Non-Proliferation poses a substantial risk to the sustainability of the Non-Proliferation regime.

A. THE LEGAL FRAMEWORK OF THE NON-PROLIFERATION REGIME

Global Non-Proliferation norms and multilateral Non-Proliferation initiatives are much broader than the Nuclear Non-Proliferation Treaty (NPT), but the treaty system remains the anchor at the center of the Non-Proliferation regime.[65] The NPT was opened for signature on July 1, 1968, and came into force on March 5, 1970, with the United States' ratification.[66] The terms of the treaty represent a fundamental bargain between the five acknowledged nuclear states at the time of the drafting of the treaty and the non-nuclear-weapons states: in exchange for agreeing not to develop nuclear weapons (Article II) and to allow the IAEA to inspect their nuclear facilities and materials to ensure that peaceful nuclear technology is not diverted to military uses (Article III and the Comprehensive Safeguards Agreement), the non-weapons states are guaranteed access to peaceful nuclear technologies (Article IV) and the weapons states agree to reduce and eventually eliminate their own nuclear arsenals (Article VI).[67] In other words, the three pillars of the Non-Proliferation regime codified by the NPT are nuclear non-proliferation, peaceful nuclear cooperation, and nuclear disarmament.[68] In addition, the nuclear powers also extended negative security assurances to the non-nuclear-weapons states in connection with the conclusion of the NPT and then its indefinite extension in 1995.[69] On the other hand, the Non-Proliferation obligation of the non-nuclear-weapons states is not absolute. Article X of the NPT recognizes that Non-Proliferation is not the only goal of the treaty regime and that considerations of national security, deterrence, and reciprocity may give rise to legitimate withdrawal.[70]

The approach of the NPT is to counter demand for nuclear weapons with a set of concrete benefits to forgo pursuit of an arsenal. The Non-Proliferation regime, centered on the NPT bargain, creates an incentive structure for non-nuclear-weapons states to make a verifiable commitment to forgo the development of a nuclear arsenal in exchange for access to civilian nuclear technologies, a commitment on the part of nuclear-weapons states to disarmament, and negative security assurances. With Cuba's accession to the NPT on November 4, 2002,[71] participation in the treaty rose to 188 state parties, bringing adherence to the NPT to near-universal levels.[72]

In accordance with the treaty's terms, an NPT Review and Extension Conference was convened in May 1995 to determine whether to extend the treaty and if so, under what conditions. The 1995 conference resulted in the indefinite extension of the treaty,[73] the adoption of guidelines for the continued implementation of treaty obligations,[74] and the development of an enhanced review process for future conferences.[75] The set of principles and objectives developed at the 1995 Review Conference included the principle of universality, namely that the treaty should be made universally applicable through the accession of all states.

The NPT is the principal legal and institutional framework for international Non-Proliferation policy, containing the legal obligation not to engage in nuclear-weapons proliferation as either a supplier or a producer, and establishing an agreement between the IAEA and the non-weapons states to permit routine inspections of their nuclear facilities. This monitoring system is set forth in the Comprehensive Safeguards Agreement that determines the specific verification protocols for the implementation of the Article III commitment by non-weapons states to facilitate the inspection of any facilities that contain declared fissionable materials.[76] While the IAEA does not have enforcement powers, any discrepancies revealed as a result of its inspections can result in referral to the UN Security Council for consideration under the council's Chapter VII enforcement powers. The inspections system is thus designed to deter clandestine proliferation activities by raising the possibility of detection and subsequent enforcement measures through Security Council referral.[77] To render deterrence through inspections effective, the monitoring and verification system has to carry a real threat of detection. As a result of revelations in the aftermath of the 1991 Persian Gulf War that Iraq had been able to partially reconstitute its nuclear-weapons program despite regular IAEA inspections, steps were taken to strengthen the safeguards system and to adopt an additional protocol to the NPT providing IAEA inspectors broader access to activities and facilities for inspection, and imposing additional reporting obligations on non-weapons states. The Model Additional Protocol was approved by the IAEA Board in May 1997.[78]

Where the 1995 Review Conference resulted in the indefinite extension of the NPT, and the adoption of the 1997 Model Additional Protocol strengthened the NPT inspections regime applicable to non-weapons states, the 2000 NPT Review Conference emphasized the obligations of the nuclear-weapons states to meet their Article VI commitment to disarmament. In particular, the state parties agreed to "Thirteen Practical Steps" toward the implementation of Article VI disarmament commitments at the 2000 Review Conference.[79] These steps included: a moratorium on nuclear testing, a conference on disarmament and the negotiation of a verifiable fissile material production cutoff treaty, a reaffirmation of the commitment of nuclear-weapons states to the elimination of their nuclear arsenals, the preservation and strengthening of the Anti-Ballistic Missile (ABM) Treaty and other US-Russian arms control agreements, the development of IAEA or international verification capabilities to ensure compliance with nuclear disarmament agreements, and regular state reporting on Article VI implementation.[80]

The 2000 NPT Review Conference was widely regarded as a resounding success, and much of this success was attributable to the role played by the United States in providing leadership in the preparatory phases of the conference and at the conference itself. Following the predominant role played by the Clinton administration in securing the indefinite extension of the NPT in 1995, in preparation for the 2000 Review Conference, the administration made clear that it would prioritize the disarmament components of the treaty.[81] Cognizant of skepticism regarding American commitments to the treaty regime's disarmament obligations, the Clinton administration took affirmative steps to build credibility, with public statements by President Clinton and engagement with key countries by Secretary of State Madeleine Albright.[82] Secretary Albright addressed the opening of the NPT Review Conference in person and emphasized that the review should focus on all three prongs of the bargain at the heart of the NPT, including "how the Treaty is working to prevent nuclear proliferation, to advance nuclear disarmament and to enhance cooperation in the peaceful uses of nuclear energy."[83] As a result, at least in part, of the Clinton administration's commitment to the NPT review process, the 2000 Review Conference produced a final consensus document that contributed to the strengthening of the Non-Proliferation regime.[84] Central to the final document was the stronger language on disarmament obligations set forth in the Thirteen Practical Steps as well as the emphasis on universal adherence.

Developments between the 2000 NPT Review Conference and the subsequent review conference held in 2005 saw few of the Thirteen Practical Steps implemented and significant pressure on the Non-Proliferation regime as a result both of developments in the nuclear programs of certain non-weapons states and policies and actions taken by nuclear-weapons states.

B. THE EROSION OF THE NONPROLIFERATION REGIME

A review of developments since 2000, including a consideration of the widely acknowledged failure of the 2005 NPT Review Conference, substantiates the argument that recent developments in the area of Non-Proliferation have had adverse consequences for the sustainability of the regime.

Several key steps were taken by the nuclear-weapons states in this period toward the weakening of the fundamental bargain underlying the Non-Proliferation regime, particularly by the United States. All three principal pillars of the Non-Proliferation regime are currently under assault. By calling into question its disarmament commitments, proposing new limitations on nuclear energy cooperation, and adopting policies suggesting the development of new "usable" low-yield nuclear weapons and a doctrine of potential use of nuclear weapons against non-nuclear-weapons states, the Bush administration in particular has significantly reduced the incentives for the non-nuclear-weapons states to abide by their end of the NPT bargain.[85]

The weakening of the bargain at the heart of the NPT was compounded by the emergence of new potential incentives for proliferation. In particular, to the extent that the 2003 Iraq war has come to be seen as an instance of the pretextual invocation of arms control concerns to engage in regime change, countries that fear an Iraq-style intervention may now have a strong additional incentive to pursue a nuclear deterrent. Though for much of the international community the Iraq war served as a decisive repudiation of counter-proliferation-based arguments for intervention, such arguments have persisted in the wake of the war in American legal and policy circles. The following sections assess the erosion of the NPT regime under the pressures of changes in the Non-Proliferation and disarmament policies of the nuclear-weapons states against the backdrop of the new interventionism detailed in this chapter.

1. Repudiation of Disarmament and Negative Security Assurances

In December 2001, Washington formally announced its decision to withdraw from the 1972 Anti-Ballistic Missile (ABM) Treaty in order to pursue missile defenses, which would have been prohibited under the treaty. Specifically, American efforts to develop missile defenses were perceived to contravene the Article VI commitment in the ABM Treaty to "pursue negotiations in good faith on effective measures relating to the cessation of the nuclear arms race."[86] The coalition of non-weapons states that effectively negotiated with the nuclear-weapons states to agree on the Thirteen Practical Steps were especially aggrieved by the US withdrawal from the ABM Treaty.[87] Together with the earlier failure to ratify the Comprehensive Test Ban Treaty, the American withdrawal from the ABM Treaty was widely seen as part of a broader pattern of maintaining strategic nuclear flexibility in violation of nuclear disarmament obligations.[88]

Following the ABM withdrawal, in his January 2002 State of the Union address, President George W. Bush suggested that the United States might be willing to pursue military approaches to counter-proliferation.[89] The speech was interpreted internationally as a deepening of American unilateralism, eschewing the existing Non-Proliferation regime in favor of a preemptive posture in tension with international law.[90] Further, the presidential speech raised serious concerns that such a preemptive doctrine might encourage defensive proliferation among potential target states, rather than deterring such proliferation. One analysis describes the response to the 2002 State of the Union speech as follows: "Critics, especially among America's European allies, viewed this muscular response as a unilateral impulse that overemphasized a military solution to the proliferation problem, violated international law, undermined the Non-Proliferation regime and could lead to more, not less, nuclear weapons states."[91] The release of the September 2002 United States National Security Strategy formalized the shift in American national security policy to a posture of military preemption.[92]

The US Nuclear Posture Review, made public in January 2002, added another element to American doctrine in tension with the commitments of nuclear-weapons states under the NPT.[93] A leaked version of the classified Nuclear Posture Review outlines circumstances under which the United States should be prepared to use nuclear weapons (including in response to or to prevent a non-nuclear biological or chemical weapons attack) and lists seven countries that might raise contingencies requiring nuclear strike capabilities.[94] Several of the countries listed as potential targets for a nuclear strike are non-nuclear-weapons states. The potential first use of nuclear weapons against non-nuclear states that are parties to the NPT would be a direct violation of the negative security assurances that are a core element of the Non-Proliferation regime's incentive structure. The report also calls for a revitalization of American nuclear-weapons infrastructure and discusses the development of new or modified nuclear weapons. The review makes no mention of the US commitment under Article VI to take concrete steps toward eliminating its nuclear arsenal, nor does it reference the Thirteen Practical Steps to which the United States committed itself at the 2000 NPT Review Conference. The position taken in the Nuclear Posture Review was further strengthened by the 2002 National Strategy to Combat Weapons of Mass Destruction (WMD) Proliferation, which continued the emphasis on counter-proliferation strategies including the possibility of responding to a biological or chemical attack on the United States with nuclear weapons.[95]

The disregard shown by the United States for disarmament commitments was badly compounded by the apparent repudiation of negative security assurances toward certain non-nuclear-weapons states. The negotiating history of the NPT makes clear the centrality of negative security assurances to the Non-Proliferation regime. The nations of the nonaligned movement demanded, in exchange for their NonProliferationobligations, "security assurances from the nuclear-weapon states that they would not attack countries whose decision to abjure from nuclear weapons might leave them vulnerable."[96] While negative security assurances were not incorporated into the text of the treaty, they were set forth in a Security Council resolution in 1968, coinciding with the opening of the NPT for signature.[97] The undertaking was updated and reaffirmed immediately in advance of the 1995 NPT Review and Extension Conference, underscoring the significance of the negative security assurances in securing acceptance by the non-nuclear-weapons states of an indefinite extension of their Non-Proliferation commitments.[98]

The structure of the Non-Proliferation regime is precisely designed to reduce the demand for nuclear weapons by providing both security-related and technology-related assurances that Non-Proliferation will not adversely impact the economic or military security of the non-nuclear-weapons states. The US 2002 Nuclear Posture Review runs directly counter to this logic, by embracing a strategy that *would* permit the use of nuclear weapons against a non-nuclear-weapons state in violation of American undertakings in Security Council Resolution 984. The French soon followed suit, declaring that France might respond to a conventional attack with a nuclear strike, irrespective of the NPT-status of the target.[99]

The combination of American withdrawal from existing disarmament agreements, willingness to pursue missile defense research, and the development of low-yield "usable" nuclear weapons (or "mini-nukes") significantly undermined American undertakings at the 2000 Review Conference and more generally American disarmament commitments under the NPT. Further, the aggressive policy of nuclear first-use, adopted by the United States and soon embraced by other nuclear-weapons states, not only rescinds the negative security assurances that undergird the NPT, but amounts to a nuclear threat against non-nuclear parties to the treaty.

2. Counter-proliferation versus Nonproliferation

The downgrading of disarmament commitments was not the only departure from the Non-Proliferation regime framework by the United States. The new approach to nuclear policy adopted by the Bush administration was also marked by the ascendance of counter-proliferation strategies over more traditional Non-Proliferation policy. Where Non-Proliferation approaches focused on reducing demand for nuclear weapons through an incentive structure built on the NPT bargain and monitored through the attendant inspections regime, counter-proliferation strategies were focused on supply-side access denial, often through direct interdiction efforts.

On May 31, 2003, President Bush announced the first major policy initiative designed to implement some of the recommendations of the December 2002 National Strategy to Combat Weapons of Mass Destruction (WMD) Proliferation, adopting an activist approach toward countering proliferation. The Proliferation Security Initiative (PSI)[100] entails a "new channel for interdiction cooperation outside of treaties and multilateral export control regimes," designed to "create a web of counter-proliferation partnerships through which proliferators will have difficulty carrying out their trade in WMD and missile-related technology."[101] The basic PSI approach, consistent with the Bush administration's preference for what it termed "à la carte multilateralism," is to adopt a cooperative agreement on interdiction principles without creating formal mechanisms for monitoring adherence to the principles or reporting instances of interdiction.[102] The goal of the PSI is to coordinate the efforts of participating states to adopt domestic legislation enabling interdiction, to enter into ship-boarding agreements with other states, and to use all available legal options to stop and inspect suspected transports of WMD.[103] The PSI has a specific emphasis on preventing proliferation to "states of concern" as well as non-state actors.[104]

The NPT system is one that embodies universal opposition to horizontal proliferation—that is, the NPT prohibits all forms of proliferation activity by all state parties. The PSI approach, by contrast, embodies the view that the degree of opposition to proliferation may vary depending on the identity of the states involved. On this view, certain potential proliferators are more worrisome and require more robust counter-proliferation efforts than others.[105] The US position is that the interdiction activities contemplated by the PSI are consistent with international law. This position has been questioned by a number of international law scholars concerned that such activities, particularly where they involve naval interdiction exercises, might be interpreted as acts of aggression.[106] One significant concern raised by the PSI approach is that if all countries were to take unilateral measures to interdict shipping that they deemed suspect, it might wreak havoc in the oceans and contravene the terms of the United Nations Convention on the Law of the Seas.[107]

Like the exceptionalism of new intervention doctrines discussed in earlier sections of this chapter, if the logic of interdiction were adopted universally, the international system would revert from rule-based order to anarchic self-help. The absence of an agreed international definition of what constitutes a "state of concern" lends further support to this objection. Although the PSI represents an effort to advance an important objective—that of restricting the transit of WMD to restrict proliferation—its success would depend on internationally accepted standards for interdiction and uniform application of the rules. As it stands, without coordination with the Security Council and organized on an ad hoc basis,[108] the PSI runs the risk of undermining international law governing the use of the high seas and setting the stage for potential confrontations over the authority to interdict shipping.[109]

3. Damage to Inspections Regimes

The Iraq war not only set a damaging precedent weakening the norm of nonintervention, but it also raised serious concerns from a Non-Proliferation standpoint. First, the attack was a repudiation of the comprehensive inspections regime that was in place on the ground in Iraq prior to the invasion. The UN Special Commission (UNSCOM) inspections throughout the 1990s followed by the UN Monitoring, Verification and Inspection Commission (UNMOVIC) inspections in 2003 were the most invasive and comprehensive weapons destruction, monitoring, and verification system ever undertaken.[110] The failure of the UNSCOM and UNMOVIC inspections to satisfy critics that Iraq had met its disarmament obligations raised the suggestion that no inspection or monitoring system would be adequate to verify compliance with disarmament or Non-Proliferation obligations should powerful states suspect the existence of a clandestine weapons program.[111] Second, the war had a powerful demonstration effect; the suspected presence of biological and chemical weapons in Iraq was apparently not a sufficient deterrent to an attack on the country. Yet, in the same year as the Iraq invasion, North Korea had withdrawn from the NPT and resumed unsafeguarded nuclear activities without incurring multilateral enforcement action against it through the UN Security Council.[112]

The conjunction of the Iraq war and the North Korean withdrawal from the NPT may impact the underlying incentive scheme that has long sustained the Non-Proliferation regime. Non-nuclear-weapons states might conclude from a comparison of the Iraqi and North Korean cases that the suspected acquisition of nuclear weapons is the only adequate deterrent to coercive enforcement action, including preemptive attack, against states perceived by the United States or other great powers as adversaries with WMD capabilities. Another potential demonstration effect of the war is the suggestion that Non-Proliferation concerns might be pretextually advanced in the service of a regime change agenda. This reading of the Iraq intervention is particularly worrisome given the avowed support for regime change in some quarters of the American government.[113] Personnel changes toward the end of the second term of the Bush administration, including the departure of John Bolton as the American ambassador to the United Nations, have somewhat eased concerns that US policy may pursue additional aggressive counter-proliferation measures, including regime change.[114] However, not only non-aligned movement countries, but also European allies of the United States have continued to express alarm concerning American counter-proliferation policies with respect to Iran.[115]

One less well-known but extremely serious blow to support for inspection regimes was American unwillingness to give IAEA inspectors access to Iraqi nuclear facilities, notably at al-Tuwaitha and al-Qaqaa, to secure nuclear materials after the invasion. The US curtailment of cooperation with the IAEA and apparent attempts to cover up the looting of Iraq's nuclear facilities hardly represent an endorsement of the inspection and reporting obligations of non-weapons states under the NPT. Department of Defense officials provided a briefing concerning IAEA access to nuclear sites in Iraq on June 5, 2003, indicating that "the United States has the resources to handle the disarmament and other tasks" in Iraq and does not require IAEA assistance or inspections other than on an extremely limited basis.[116] The subsequent discovery that 350 metric tons of explosive materials had disappeared from the al-Qaqaa facility led to an invitation to the IAEA to return to Iraq more than a year after the initial invasion.[117]

A final consequence of the Iraq war from a Non-Proliferation perspective was that it enabled inspectors to ultimately establish that Iraqi WMD disclosure to the United Nations and the results of the UNMOVIC/IAEA inspections were substantially complete. Despite the difficulties of "proving a negative"—that is, definitively confirming that a clandestine weapons program does *not* exist—the combination of Security Council sanctions and an intrusive inspections regime of unprecedented proportions had, in fact, led to the complete and ultimately verified disarmament of Iraq in advance of the war.[118] The effect of the confirmation that Iraqi weapons programs had either been destroyed or dismantled following the 1991 Gulf War and the subsequent UN weapons inspections is double-edged. On the one hand, the Iraqi case demonstrates that a strengthened inspections system is capable of producing reliable intelligence and verifying compliance with disarmament obligations. On the other hand, despite the fact that seven years of UN inspections yielded no evidence of a clandestine weapons program, Iraq was nonetheless the subject of an armed invasion justified chiefly on the basis of arms control concerns and the alleged threat of Iraqi weapons of mass destruction.

Reflecting on the intelligence failures that led to the Iraq intervention, the former CIA deputy director for arms control, Torrey Froscher, noted that the absence of concrete and specific information about countries' weapons programs makes it difficult to "dislodge strongly held preconceptions," which in turn lead to faulty analysis and poor policy decisions.[119] These comments only further highlight the Non-Proliferation lessons of the Iraq case: first, that strengthened inspections and verification mechanisms are the best way to check proliferation and obtain early, accurate information about the status of a country's nuclear and other programs. Second, the failure to prove a negative should not be a basis for confirming preconceptions based on subjective interpretations of intentions or assessments of regime type. Unfortunately, the precedent of regime change undertaken on arms control grounds in Iraq runs the risk that countries will view weapons inspections as either politicized or futile.

To counter this appearance and strengthen the role of monitoring and verification mechanisms in arms control, it is important that the ambivalence exhibited toward international agencies charged with inspections be corrected.[120] In the nuclear Non-Proliferation context, this would require reinforcing the IAEA's authority and supporting opportunities to strengthen inspections regimes. Further, countries should be given assurances by the nuclear-weapons states that cooperation with the IAEA and compliance with their Non-Proliferation obligations are a sufficient basis to enjoy their rights under the NPT, including access to nuclear energy and negative security assurances. By contrast, continuing failure to reinforce the bargain that incentivizes non-nuclear states to cooperate with the IAEA while simultaneously downgrading the significance of its inspections will cut the international community off from one of the most valuable benefits of the Non-Proliferation regime: the production of reliable and actionable intelligence on the nuclear programs of the non-nuclear states.

4. Restricting Access to Civilian Nuclear Technology

Rather than facilitating access to civilian nuclear technology and energy resources through the IAEA, President Bush has proposed restricting access to enrichment and reprocessing technologies for non-nuclear state parties to the NPT on a selective basis. First, he proposed encouraging states to renounce uranium enrichment and plutonium reprocessing by ensuring "reliable access at reasonable cost to fuel for civilian [nuclear] reactors."[121] Under this proposal, non-nuclear states would have to forgo their treaty right to develop an indigenous nuclear fuel supply capacity. Second, he proposed that the states in the Nuclear Suppliers' Group (NSG) only engage in enrichment and reprocessing nuclear exports to those states that have already acquired fully operational uranium enrichment and plutonium reprocessing facilities.[122]

In both cases, the president was willing to make exceptions for some non-nuclear states with advanced energy programs—all of which represent industrial powers with which the United States has positive relations—while imposing stricter restrictions on the developing world. By restricting enrichment and reprocessing to states that already have such facilities, the president's proposal would effectively create a new distinction between nuclear "haves" and "have-nots," arguably undermining the bargain underlying the NPT. Whereas non-nuclear-weapons states currently participate in the regime, renouncing the pursuit of a nuclear-weapons arsenal precisely to *facilitate* access to and transfer of permitted civilian nuclear energy technologies under IAEA supervision, this proposal would limit access to technology transfers to only those states already in possession of advanced civilian nuclear energy programs.

The NPT bargain already presents a distinction between states that have acquired nuclear weapons and those that are prohibited from doing so.[123] The added dimension of distinguishing between the rights of non-weapons states with advanced civilian nuclear energy programs and those that are not as advanced in terms of their entitlement to nuclear technology transfers under IAEA supervision is unlikely to be accepted by the nonaligned movement states and more generally by the non-weapons states.[124] It is worth noting that for the non-nuclear states of the developing world, the right to pursue nuclear energy is considered vital to the achievement of energy independence. In light of the tight international energy market and the significance of energy for economic development and subsistence, this right is deemed nonnegotiable in much of the global South.

Because the acquisition of uranium enrichment and plutonium reprocessing facilities is permissible for civilian nuclear energy programs under the NPT, proposals to restrict access to these technologies would require a renegotiation of the rights of the non-nuclear states under the NPT. Any attempt to affect a de facto alteration of these rights would be especially controversial. While the G-8 did endorse the president's proposal in principle in June 2004, this is best understood in light of the fact that all members of the G-8 already possess civilian nuclear energy programs that would entitle them to ongoing nuclear trade.[125] For states that are not already in possession of advanced nuclear energy programs, serious consideration of the president's proposal would likely trigger a proliferation race to the bottom as states would seek to acquire as much technology as possible to immediately establish their own nuclear energy programs, through open trade or black market networks, before potential restrictions came into effect.

The day after President Bush's speech, the director general of the IAEA, Mohamed ElBaradei, presented his own proposal to strengthen the Non-Proliferation regime in light of revelations concerning the activities of the AQ Khan network.[126] Specifically, he suggested universal adherence to the Additional Protocol, amendment of the NPT to restrict or eliminate the withdrawal provision in Article X, subjecting sensitive or dual-use aspects of the nuclear fuel cycle to multinational control, commencing negotiation of a Fissile Material Cutoff Treaty (FMCT),[127] bringing the Comprehensive Test Ban Treaty into force, and reviewing the nuclear-weapons states disarmament obligations.

While aspects of ElBaradei's proposals related to disarmament, the CTBT and the FMCT might be controversial among weapons states, his proposal for multinational control of sensitive aspects of the nuclear fuel cycle and his subsequent call for a five-year moratorium on all new enrichment and reprocessing plant construction may be no less problematic for non-weapons states than President Bush's proposals.[128] Unless ElBaradei's proposal were to be extended in a nondiscriminatory manner to the nuclear-weapons states as well—something that seems politically unlikely—it would amount to an additional restriction of the non-weapons states' rights, and further asymmetry in the commitments required by the NPT.

ElBaradei convened an experts' group to consider multilateral approaches for controlling "sensitive aspects of the nuclear fuel cycle," which issued its report recommending five options to the IAEA in February 2005.[129] No effort to implement the expert group's recommendations has been undertaken as yet, and the hope that some of these recommendations for multilateral controls on the nuclear fuel cycle would be discussed at the 2005 NPT Review Conference did not materialize. The importance of efforts to develop a proliferation-resistant fuel cycle through a combination of potential proposals including enhanced inspections, regional multinational fuel centers with black-boxed technologies, and other possible formulae goes without saying. However, it is also necessary to bear in mind that the Article

IV right of non-nuclear-weapons states to nuclear energy is not a "loophole" in the treaty but one of the three pillars of the core bargain between the parties to the NPT. Excessively restricting non-nuclear-weapons states' access to nuclear technology may unduly weaken the Non-Proliferation regime if care is not taken to preserve compliance incentives including in the area of nuclear cooperation.

5. The Failure of the 2005 NPT Review Conference

With the numerous assaults on the Non-Proliferation regime's basic structure between 2000 and 2005, it is perhaps small wonder that the 2005 NPT Review Conference was marked by deep divisions between the positions of the nuclear-weapons states and non-weapon states. The three preparatory committee meetings convened in 2002, 2003, and 2004 had already been marked by increasing division, specifically over the implementation of the Thirteen Practical Steps adopted at the 2000 Review Conference, on the one hand, and the right to peaceful development of nuclear energy and technical cooperation on the other. With the changes in US doctrine signaling a willingness to develop new weapons and adopt a policy of potential use of nuclear weapons in response to non-nuclear threats, the withdrawal of the United States from the ABM Treaty and the failure of the United States Senate to ratify the CTBT, the non-weapons states were not prepared, on the whole, to be sympathetic to American calls for additional restrictions on their access to the nuclear fuel cycle. Similarly, with the North Korean withdrawal from the NPT and revelations about Iran's clandestine nuclear research program, the United States was not prepared to shift the focus of the conference from the Non-Proliferation elements of the NPT to disarmament.

The Review Conference occurred from May 2–27, 2005, in New York and was marked by controversy. The non-nuclear-weapons states' priorities were twofold: first, insistence on the implementation of weapons states' disarmament commitments in keeping with the agreement reached at the 2000 Conference. Second, the non-nuclear-weapons states, and particularly the members of the nonaligned movement, placed emphasis on respect for the "inalienable right" of the parties to the NPT to develop, research, produce, and use nuclear energy for peaceful purposes without discrimination, in keeping with Article IV of the NPT. These priorities led to a deadlock between the US insistence on a focus on strengthening Non-Proliferation commitments and restricting access to the nuclear fuel cycle for non-weapons states and the insistence of non-weapons states on the verifiable implementation by the United States and the other weapons states of their disarmament obligations.[130] The Canadian representative to the conference, Paul Meyer, lamented that "we have let the pursuit of short-term, parochial interests override the collective, long-term interest in sustaining the treaty's authority and integrity."[131]

Vindicating the long-term interest in Non-Proliferation regime maintenance would have required the same American leadership in favor of substantive proposals at the 2005 Review Conference as was exhibited in the previous two conferences, resulting in the indefinite extension of the treaty regime in 1995 and the adoption of stronger disarmament commitments, including the Thirteen Practical Steps, in 2000. Instead, the United States role at the conference was obstructionist, prompting one respected American arms control expert to remark that:

> The arrogant and clumsy U.S. strategy has almost certainly reinforced the view of the majority of countries that the United States and the other nuclear-weapon states do not intend to live up to their NPT-related nuclear disarmament commitments. This not only scuttled the chance that this conference might have supported useful U.S. proposals on strengthening the Non-Proliferation elements of the treaty, but it will in the long-run erode the willingness of other states to fulfill their own treaty obligations.[132]

The failure of the 2005 Review Conference is, more than anything, a reminder that international regimes will erode where they lose the support of, or are unable to bind, their most powerful members.

6. Selective Proliferation

Following the failure of the 2005 Review Conference to produce progress on either the disarmament or the Non-Proliferation components of the NPT regime, a further development reinforced the standoff between nuclear "haves" and "have-nots" that was in evidence at the 2005 meetings. On July 18, 2005, in a joint declaration, the United States and India announced the establishment of a global strategic partnership, widely interpreted as part of Washington's effort to counter the growing influence of China as an Asian regional hegemon. Among the elements of this partnership was one that overturned decades of American Non-Proliferation policy. The United States pledged to end its moratorium on cooperation with India's nuclear program, despite the fact that India has not acceded to the NPT and continues to produce fissile materials for use in its nuclear-weapons program. As was noted in a report by the Congressional Research Service:

> If implemented, this cooperation would dramatically shift U.S. Non-Proliferation policy and practice towards India. Such cooperation would also contravene the multilateral export control guidelines of the Nuclear Suppliers Group (NSG), which was formed in response to India's proliferation. At a time when the United States has called for all states to strengthen their domestic export control laws and implementation and for tighter multilateral controls, U.S. nuclear cooperation with India would require loosening its own nuclear export legislation as well as creating an NSG exception . . . Observers note that the U.S.–India cooperation could have wide-ranging implications for the international nuclear Non-Proliferation regime, and could prompt other suppliers, like China, to justify their supplying other non-nuclear weapon states, like Pakistan.[133]

The United States had ended its nuclear cooperation with India following India's 1974 nuclear test and had adopted Non-Proliferation legislation specifically requiring that states not acknowledged as nuclear-weapon holders by the NPT place all of their nuclear activities under IAEA safeguards in order to receive nuclear cooperation from the United States.[134] The Nuclear Suppliers Group, to which the United States belongs, also requires full-scope safeguards to permit the export of any nuclear materials or technology to non-nuclear-weapons states. Under the agreement, India will allow IAEA inspectors to access its civilian nuclear facilities, but retains the right to designate which of its facilities are to be classified as civilian and to continue to operate, in parallel, its military nuclear program.

The United States marshaled several arguments in defense of cooperation with India including India's acceptance, under the terms of the deal, of safeguards on the facilities that it designates as civilian, its past record of preventing horizontal proliferation of its own nuclear technologies, and its voluntary adherence to nuclear export controls. In addition, the United States argued that India's continuation of a moratorium on nuclear-weapons testing since 1998 and its willingness to negotiate a fissile material cutoff with the United States were added benefits of the deal. On the basis of India's record, and despite India's refusal to accede to the NPT and its development and testing of nuclear weapons, President Bush referred to India "as a responsible state with advanced nuclear technology."[135]

Critics of the US-India nuclear cooperation deal, including many American arms control experts, note that the geostrategic objective of strengthening ties with India could have been accomplished through economic and security cooperation without compromising core Non-Proliferation principles. In particular, the agreement required few concessions from India in exchange for resumed nuclear cooperation with the United States. While the agreement does encourage India to submit the facilities it classifies as civilian to safeguards, the agreement would not cover fissile materials produced prior to the agreement, nor does it require that India limit its current fissile material production or restrict the number of nuclear weapons it produces.[136] In addition, some critics note that nuclear cooperation was not the most economically efficient way to improve India's energy sector.[137]

At a more general level, the US–India nuclear cooperation deal risks further altering and undermining the incentives built into the NPT regime, already weakened by the developments discussed above. The first article of the NPT requires that nuclear-weapons states will not enable non-nuclear-weapons states to acquire such weapons. But the provision of fungible nuclear materials by the United States to India may well enable India to enhance its nuclear weapons programs. Perhaps even more critically, the NPT represents an ultimatum to non-nuclear-weapons states: accede to the NPT or be cut off from all trade in nuclear materials and assistance in developing civilian nuclear energy. This principle is badly undermined by an agreement with India that would afford it enhanced civilian nuclear energy cooperation, beyond that enjoyed by most non-weapon state members of the NPT, without requiring it to accede to the NPT nor to adopt full-scope safeguards for all of its nuclear program.[138]

That a state which has refused to join the Non-Proliferation regime and has developed and tested nuclear weapons outside of the treaty regime should appear to be rewarded with a nuclear cooperation deal compromises many of the other Non-Proliferation objectives the Bush administration had sought, including restrictions on the fuel cycle for NPT members and strengthened export controls. The inconsistency in the enforcement of the rules of the NPT represented by the US–India nuclear deal sends mixed signals to other would-be nuclear-weapons states, suggesting that behavior inconsistent with the Non-Proliferation regime will not necessarily lead to reduced nuclear cooperation.[139] The Bush administration's view of India as a "responsible state with advanced nuclear technology" makes clear that the definition of "responsible" does not require adherence to the Non-Proliferation norm.[140]

The focus on characteristics of the Indian regime independent of its nuclear-weapons policy is consistent with the more general reorientation of American nonproliferation policy around strategic alliances based on the perceived identity of states rather than their behavior. The resulting Non-Proliferation policies are deeply undermining of the NPT regime insofar as they are indexed to regime type rather than compliance with the legal requirements of the treaty. Indexing Non-Proliferation policy to strategic alliance considerations or assessments of the regime type of a particular state is inherently unstable. Alliances shift and regimes change, but a state that acquires nuclear weapons will retain that stockpile whatever its regime or allies. One need only consider the nuclear cooperation provided by the United States to the Shah of Iran in the 1970s, then a strategic ally governed by a friendly regime, to grasp the risks associated with such selectivity.[141] In the words of one American arms control expert in his testimony to the US Senate Foreign Relations Committee, the "proposed US-India nuclear deal would destroy the international norm against nuclear proliferation embodied in the NPT."[142]

The selective proliferation policy evidenced by the change in American policy toward nuclear cooperation with India is part of a broader trend of displacing Non-Proliferation principles in favor of other security objectives. This has been especially pronounced in the post-September 11 period as the Bush administration has tended to conflate its antiterrorism priority with other aspects of its security strategy. In the area of arms control, the consequence of this reorientation has been a preference for proliferation deterrence through preemptive uses of force—either in counter-proliferation interdiction exercises or in straightforward arms control-based military intervention—over traditional nonproliferation. In addition, the antiterrorism priority has also led to the subordination of Non-Proliferation principles the establishment of strategic partnerships in pursuit of American objectives in the war on terror. As a result, American policy has selectively embraced proliferation in South Asia, offering nuclear cooperation to India, despite its acquisition of a nuclear arsenal and repudiation of the Non-Proliferation regime. At the same time, the American administration has also sought to selectively withhold nuclear cooperation from non-nuclear states party to the NPT. On balance, such a selective policy is corrosive to NPT compliance incentives for non-nuclear states.

7. Legality, Legitimacy and the NPT

As a result of the foregoing developments, both the legality and the legitimacy of the Non-Proliferation regime have been drawn into question in some quarters. Questions of legality and legitimacy take on a different meaning in the NPT context than the framing presented by the humanitarian intervention debate. Nonetheless, the basic challenge to the sustainability of the international legal order in the face of unilateral and discretionary exceptionalism remains the underlying question.

The Non-Proliferation Treaty has been plagued by legitimacy challenges from the outset.[143] Because the treaty perpetuates a hierarchical two-tier system of nuclear haves and have-nots, the Indian government has always objected to the treaty, arguing that it is an illegitimate form of "nuclear apartheid." In particular, Indian negotiators questioned the legitimacy of a treaty in the postcolonial period that places disproportionately higher burdens on the states with lesser endowments and greater vulnerabilities. Despite this fundamental unevenness, however, other states were eventually willing to participate in the treaty regime as a result of the linkage of disarmament and Non-Proliferation obligations, which offset the unusual asymmetry of the treaty.[144] The negotiating history of the treaty shows that significant middle power states, such as Brazil, Scandinavia, Canada, Egypt, and even Germany, insisted on the linkage to disarmament before they were willing to accept Non-Proliferation obligations under the NPT.[145] The concept at the heart of the regime was that *nuclear weapons* were the problem, rather than an exclusive focus on the danger of their spread or the identity of those who acquire them.

The post-2000 disarmament record of the nuclear-weapons states—and particularly the United States, the United Kingdom, and France—has been retrogressive. Far from taking concrete steps toward disarmament, each of these states has undertaken to renew and expand their nuclear arsenals. As discussed above, publicly available excerpts of the 2002 United States Nuclear Posture Review detail American plans to renew and restore the existing nuclear-weapons arsenal and infrastructure, including possible resumption of nuclear testing, and to expand the role of nuclear weapons in national security strategy from one of deterrence to possible first-use.[146] Similarly, the United Kingdom announced plans to develop a new generation of nuclear-armed submarines, with American assistance,[147] while France embraced a nuclear first-use policy.[148]

The contemporary attitude of the nuclear-weapons states lends new credence, in the eyes of some non-nuclear-weapons states, to the Indian position of the illegitimacy of the bargain, by exacerbating its asymmetry. By both repudiating, de facto, their disarmament obligations and placing heightened emphasis on the requirements of nonproliferation, the nuclear-weapons states are normalizing a situation in which states have unequal legal obligations to obey a treaty mechanism. Eschewing the elements of the treaty that curtail their potential future discretion, while simultaneously claiming the right to take coercive measures to enforce Non-Proliferation provisions, these states are exacerbating rather than offsetting the unevenness of the treaty. This is compounded by the suggestion that certain rights of the non-nuclear-weapons states under the NPT—including the Article X right of withdrawal and Article IV access to civilian nuclear technologies—may be curtailed in future.

Frustration with the nuclear-weapons states' non-adherence to disarmament obligations compounded with concerns about access to nuclear energy contribute to disenchantment with the NPT among the non-weapon states. Numerous non-nuclear-weapons states have expressed regret that they agreed to an indefinite extension of their Non-Proliferation commitments in 1995 because they now consider that they have lost what leverage they had to ensure compliance with disarmament obligations by the nuclear-weapons states.[149] Ironically, the Indian government, which always viewed the NPT as illegitimate, dealt another blow to the standing of the regime by undertaking nuclear cooperation with the US outside of the treaty framework. Not only the legitimacy but even the legality of the treaty has been questioned by some, who argue that the actions of the nuclear-weapons states amount to material breach of the terms of the NPT.

The question of whether the nuclear-weapons states are in material breach of their NPT obligations requires an assessment of the terms of Article VI. The authoritative interpretation of Article VI was set forth in the International Court of Justice's 1996 Advisory Opinion concerning nuclear weapons. In that opinion, the International Court of Justice established the binding and compulsory nature of the disarmament provisions of the NPT. Where the nuclear-weapons states had sought to characterize their Article VI obligations as requiring only that they engage in disarmament negotiations, the International Court of Justice held that the obligation extended to a requirement of bringing those disarmament negotiations to closure.[150] The undertakings of the nuclear-weapons states at the 2000 NPT Review Conference shed additional light on their obligations. The Final Document produced at that review conference included a list of practical steps for "systematic and progressive efforts to implement Article VI of the NPT."[151] The "Thirteen Practical Steps" adopted at the 2000 conference reaffirmed the binding nature of Article VI obligations and added specific proposals for the implementation of those obligations. While the Final Document of the conference does not have the legal character of a formal amendment to the NPT, outcome documents of NPT Review Conferences have been cited by the Security Council as having legal authority and were given weight by the ICJ.[152] At least one assessment of the question based on the negotiating history of Article VI and the 2000 Final Document concluded that the failure of the nuclear-weapons states to comply with their obligations under Article VI constitutes a material breach of the treaty.[153]

Even if the nuclear-weapons states are deemed to be in material breach of their obligations under the NPT, however, it does not necessarily follow that the legality of the treaty or the obligations of the non-nuclear-weapons states are thereby void. Under the Vienna Convention on the Law of Treaties, a determination of material breach in a multilateral treaty entitles the other parties to suspend the operation of the treaty or to terminate it by unanimous agreement, but these are not the only options and, from the perspective of the non-nuclear-weapons states, may not be attractive.[154] One alternative is to demand performance from the noncompliant states. While the non-nuclear-weapons states are not in a position to take coercive measures to require enforcement, the demand of performance may be made effective should those states threaten, in the alternative, to agree to suspend their obligations. Of course, attaining the unanimous agreement of the non-nuclear states (including many Western countries) to such a measure would be difficult. Nonetheless, the presence of such an option and the possibility that a sizeable number of nonaligned states might consider it, particularly should they face access restrictions in the civilian nuclear-energy market, should be a source of serious concern.

The analysis in this section puts the question of legality and legitimacy in the Non-Proliferation realm in stark terms. The legality of NPT is at stake due to nonreciprocity in the implementation of the Non-Proliferation and disarmament obligations under the treaty. The legitimacy of the treaty is at stake because the core bargain—designed to reduce demand for nuclear weapons by offering substantial benefits for nonproliferation—has been undermined. Some of the benefits are now on offer outside the treaty regime (such as the India–US nuclear cooperation), suggesting that compliance with Non-Proliferation obligations is immaterial to gaining access to relevant technology and materials. Other benefits have been rescinded, whether by acting to reduce access to trade in civilian nuclear energy for NPT members or by repudiating disarmament commitments and negative security assurances. To the extent that these developments are eroding the Non-Proliferation regime, the obvious corrective would be to reconnect Non-Proliferation to disarmament and return to the core bargain of the NPT. But even this solution might not be sufficient unless the new interventionism that has coincided with these adverse developments in Non-Proliferation is also addressed. The remainder of this chapter will turn to the question of arms control interventionism and its implications for exacerbating the erosion of the NPT.

III. Arms Control Interventionism and Dangers for the NPT

The nuclear Non-Proliferation regime has been badly destabilized by the developments discussed above. As we approach the end of the first decade of the new millennium, treaty-based multilateralism in the area of nuclear Non-Proliferation is giving way to a greater emphasis on unilateral or ad hoc counter-proliferation measures. The incentive structure at the heart of the NPT, designed to deter demand for nuclear weapons among non-nuclear-weapons states by affording security guarantees and access to civilian technologies, is being undermined in favor of coercive supply-side access denial through interdiction. Negative security guarantees that once assured non-nuclear-weapons states that they would not become the targets of nuclear attacks have been replaced by nuclear policies of first-use and the potential targeting of non-nuclear states. Horizontal opposition to proliferation has been replaced by selective forms of proliferation, whereby strategic allies are permitted to flout the Non-Proliferation norm while adversaries may be denied rights afforded by the NPT. Finally, the attempted decoupling of the Non-Proliferation and disarmament provisions of the treaty has exacerbated the asymmetry at the heart of the NPT in ways that may compromise perceptions of its legitimacy and even its legality. Against this backdrop, the possibility of an international security order in which the nonintervention norm is weakened and arms control objectives form a justified basis for coercive intervention may deal a fatal blow to the non-nuclear-weapons states' incentive to comply with Non-Proliferation obligations. The sections below will consider the risks of a posture of arms control interventionism to the sustainability of an already damaged Non-Proliferation regime.

A. SHIFTING INCENTIVES OF THE NON-NUCLEAR-WEAPONS STATES

The greatest risk of arms control interventionism in the Non-Proliferation context is that it may incentivize certain non-nuclear-weapons states to engage in proliferation for deterrence purposes. Generally speaking, there are two categories of states that may be deemed potential proliferators. One set of states may have regional incentives to proliferate due to the presence in their region of a nuclear-armed adversary. A second set are those for whom proliferation incentives result from their position with respect to the international balance of power. For the former states—like India–Pakistan, the two Koreas, Argentina–Brazil, and so on—the best mechanism for promoting Non-Proliferation is to encourage disarmament on both sides or to extend security assurances that reestablish balance between the sides if one side cannot be deterred from proliferating. In the case of Argentina and Brazil, both sides were induced to disarm or disavow nuclear ambitions through positive incentives; in the case of the Koreas, South Korean nuclear ambitions have been checked by a significant security assurance provided by the United States. In the case of India and Pakistan, both sides were effectively shielded from consequences for proliferation and as a result both acquired nuclear arsenals. Techniques for managing proliferation risks that arise from regional competition are well established and have a track record of success, where applied. The greatest difficulties in this context have arisen when the threat of serious consequences for proliferation has been attenuated or removed for strategic reasons. This has been the case for all three countries that have stayed outside of the NPT regime and engaged in proliferation with impunity: Israel, India, and Pakistan.[155] Because the established nuclear-weapons states chose to tolerate proliferation in these countries, there was no concerted international effort to reverse their nuclear-weapons programs.

By contrast, the case of countries that have an incentive to proliferate as a result of their position in the international balance of power is a more challenging question. These are countries that find themselves in adversarial relationships with one or more of the declared nuclear-weapons states and are unable to acquire security assurances that would counteract that threat. Examples of such states in the post–Cold War context include Syria, Iran, North Korea, Cuba, and until recently Libya. To the extent that these countries have the economic and technological means to acquire a nuclear capacity, they have every incentive to do so, notwithstanding their membership in the NPT. This is particularly true since the publication of the 2002 Nuclear Posture Review put them on notice that they could no longer rely on the negative security assurances from nuclear-weapons states to avoid becoming the target of a nuclear attack.

For countries like Cuba and arguably Syria, despite the incentive to proliferate, they lack the economic and technological means to make a nuclear arsenal a viable option for their security strategy. The larger or more economically powerful countries in this category lie on a spectrum from Libya to North Korea. Libya was invested in pursuing a nuclear weapon and had the economic ability to do so, but did not have the domestic resources to develop an indigenous nuclear program. As a result, when faced with the possibility of aggressive counter-proliferation intervention by the United States, the Libyan regime preferred the route of renouncing its still virtual nuclear ambitions and revealing the black market networks through which it had sought to acquire a capacity.[156] By contrast, in the case of North Korea, which had already developed an indigenous nuclear-energy program and had the technological capacity to acquire a nuclear weapon indigenously, the threat of arms control interventionism had the opposite effect. Following designation of the North Korean regime as a member of the "axis of evil" and in light of the listing of Pyongyang as one of the potential targets of an American first-use of nuclear weapons, it is perhaps unsurprising that the DPRK decided to invoke its right of withdrawal from the NPT in pursuit of a nuclear deterrent.

Between the cases of Libya, with no indigenous nuclear program, and North Korea, with a mature indigenous nuclear capacity, lie interim cases like that of Iran. Faced with similar risks as North Korea due to its inclusion in the "axis of evil" and on the list of potential targets of an American nuclear first strike, Iran arguably has a strong incentive to acquire a nuclear deterrent. Unlike North Korea, however, Iran does not have a sufficiently advanced indigenous nuclear program to produce a nuclear weapon in the near term. The case of Iran is perhaps the most telling example of the dangers of arms control interventionism.

Whereas the Iranian regime initially responded to the post-2001 international security environment by seeking an accommodation with the United States, when faced with aggressive American counter-proliferation and intervention policies, the country began to pursue a different path.[157] The demonstration effect of the Iraq war is an especially important element for Iranian security considerations. All three members of the so-called axis of evil were accused of nuclear proliferation as of 2002. Iraq, which was widely understood by the international community to have dismantled its nuclear program and to have been disarmed of most (if not all) of its WMD as a result of an invasive twelve-year inspection regime, became the subject of an invasion. North Korea, which declared itself a nuclear power and represented a far more significant proliferation threat, was not threatened with attack and was ultimately successful in conducting negotiations to attain security guarantees against any future American intervention. Faced with these precedents, the Iranian regime might conclude that its security would be better served by proliferation than by observing their Non-Proliferation obligations. In the event, the intelligence on the Iranian program currently available through the IAEA and the American National Intelligence Estimate of 2007 suggest that the Iranian regime is not currently pursuing a nuclear-weapons program.[158] Notwithstanding that determination, the Iranian nuclear-energy program is deemed a proliferation risk and thus a source of serious concern.[159] The extent to which a counter-proliferation posture of arms control interventionism contributes to that risk is a matter of some importance.[160]

B. INTERVENTIONISM AND THE EROSION OF THE NPT

The posture of coercive counter-proliferation adopted by the United States and accepted by other nuclear-weapons states, notably Britain and France, resonates with the post-Kosovo interventionism countenanced elsewhere in the international security order and outlined in the first part of this chapter. In the context of humanitarian emergencies, the view that international action to avert both natural and man(made atrocities was justified gave rise to a redefinition of sovereignty, more permissive of international intervention. As discussed in this chapter and elsewhere in this volume, sovereignty was reconceived around the doctrine of a "responsibility to protect." This doctrine evolved in response to a perceived gap in the UN Charter system between legality and legitimacy in the case of humanitarian emergencies. An analogous claim concerning the inadequacy of the international legal order to address the new challenges of terrorism and the proliferation of weapons of mass destruction has been asserted by some analysts and scholars.[161] This argument extends the logic underlying the "responsibility to protect" to argue that the prohibition of non-defensive force should be loosened to permit certain forms of preventive intervention. Distinct from the Bush administration's parochial justifications of its own unilateral right to use preventive force, this argument has been expounded by international legal scholars as a necessary and justifiable extension of the responsibility to protect doctrine. Although the arguments were ideologically independent, the Bush administration's pre-Iraq rationale for intervention and the post-Iraq arguments offered by international legal scholars to justify some instances of preventive force are congruent.

An early statement of the argument for revising the traditional conception of sovereignty to permit arms control interventions was offered by Richard Haass, then director of policy planning at the State Department. Haass argued in 2002) that sovereignty should be understood as limited in cases where a government fails to meet certain international obligations. In this vein, Haass stated that

> If a government fails to meet these obligations, then it forfeits some of the normal advantages of sovereignty, including the right to be left alone inside your own territory. Other governments, including the United States, gain the right to intervene.[162]

While this argument was initially stated by Haass in connection to American efforts to establish a justificatory framework for attacking Iraq, the logic was significantly broader than the narrow circumstances of the Iraqi case. Later, in early 2003), (Haass restated the argument, this time specifically identifying a continuum of exceptions to the norm of nonintervention extending from humanitarian intervention to arms-control-based intervention. It is worth excerpting his argument at some length:

> . . . sovereignty is not a blank check. Rather, sovereign status is contingent on the fulfillment by each state of certain fundamental obligations, both to its own citizens and to the international community. When a regime fails to live up to these responsibilities or abuses its prerogatives, it risks forfeiting its sovereign privileges—including, in extreme cases, its immunity from armed intervention. I believe that exceptions to the norm of non-intervention are warranted in at least three circumstances. . . . [genocide, failure to fight terrorism and w] hen certain regimes with a history of aggression and support for terrorism pursue weapons of mass destruction.[163]

Haass' argument is illustrative of the continuum between interventionist arguments based on humanitarian considerations and the logic of arms control interventionism. After leaving the State Department, Haass expanded on his reconceptualization of sovereignty, arguing that sovereignty should be understood as "contractual."[164] This variation on the theme of conditional sovereignty does not significantly alter the underlying notion that sovereignty represents a balance of rights and responsibilities where violations of the latter may lead to suspension of the former. What was distinctive about Haass's contributions through 2003), however, was that he made explicit the linkage between arms control interventionist arguments and those derived from the logic of humanitarianism. Also apparent in Haass's approach is the convergence (or, perhaps even conflation) of the post-September 11 antiterrorism agenda with arms control priorities. This elision between antiterrorism and arms control facilitates the shift from Non-Proliferation to counter-proliferation and even preventive intervention, by importing into the proliferation context the expansive sets of authority claimed by the powerful states in the international system in their global war on terror.

Articulating a strikingly similar linkage, Lee Feinstein and Anne-Marie Slaughter have advanced a new argument drawing explicitly on the "responsibility to protect" framework.[165] Slaughter and Feinstein specifically argue that the post-September 11 threat of WMD proliferation requires a new approach, modeled on the one adopted in the area of humanitarian intervention.[166] Their argument draws directly on the logic of a "responsibility to protect" for inspiration:

> We propose a corollary principle [to the responsibility to protect] in the field of global security: a collective "duty to prevent" nations run by rulers without internal checks on their power from acquiring or using WMD. . . . Like the responsibility to protect, the duty to prevent begins from the premise that the rules now governing the use of force, devised in 1945 and embedded in the UN Charter, are inadequate. . . . The duty to prevent has three critical features. First, it seeks to control not only the proliferation of WMD but also people who possess them. Second, it emphasizes prevention, calling on the international community to act early in order to be effective and develop a menu of potential measures aimed at particular governments—especially measures that can be taken well short of any use of force. Third, the duty to prevent should be exercised collectively through a global or regional organization.[167]

The argument elaborates on the external conditions on sovereignty implicit in the "responsibility to protect" doctrine, arguing that the loosening of the prohibition of non-defensive force for humanitarian purposes should be logically extended to the arms control context. Feinstein and Slaughter argue that distinctions between humanitarian intervention and intervention based on national security considerations are less tenable after September 11, in a global order where both humanitarian and security disasters require proactive response. The authors connect the work of the International Commission on Intervention and State Sovereignty—the source of the "responsibility to protect" concept—to their own proposed principle of a "duty to prevent." In this vein, they argue that:

> The commission's effort to redefine basic concepts of sovereignty and international community in the context of humanitarian law are highly relevant to international security, in particular to efforts to counter governments that both possess WMD and systematically abuse their own citizens. After all, the danger posed by WMD in the hands of governments with no internal checks on their power is the prospect of mass, indiscriminate murder. . . . The duty to prevent is the responsibility of states to work in concert to prevent governments that lack internal checks on their power from acquiring WMD or the means to deliver them.[168]

Feinstein and Slaughter's position crystallizes the convergence of arguments for humanitarian intervention and preventive intervention in their proposal for a new norm of prevention drawn out of the logic of the responsibility to protect. Further, their argument highlights the degree to which the basis for intervention, according to this logic, would depend on the regime type of the potential target state, and not only the regime's actions. In the words of the authors, the duty to prevent in the case of proliferation depends not on the possession of illegal weapons but on the identity of "the people who possess them." Moreover, their final phrase—authorizing intervention to prevent the acquisition of WMD *or the means to deliver them* on the basis of regime type—suggests that preventive intervention related to proliferation might be permissible on their reasoning in a wide array of contexts including circumstances where missile systems, not WMD, are at issue.

While Feinstein and Slaughter state explicitly in their article that they are "not trying to distinguish 'good' from 'bad' governments,"[169] the claim is hard to reconcile with the thrust of their argument. Gareth Evans, co-chair of the ICISS, responded to the "duty to prevent" principle advanced by the authors by seeking to distance the "responsibility to protect" concept from this extension. One of his principal concerns with the Feinstein-Slaughter argument was its "focus throughout on regimes rather than actual behavior in relation to WMD."[170] Feinstein and Slaughter's rationale for their focus on regime type is that the absence of domestic accountability mechanisms in a state makes its acquisition of WMD more dangerous. Putting aside the empirical validity of this claim,[171] this explanation does not provide a compelling reason to focus on imputed intentions based on regime-type rather than actual state *behavior* of both open and closed societies. Whatever dangerous intentions may be imputed to closed societies, the selective treatment of the acquisition of illicit arsenals as impermissible only in some cases introduces an inconsistency of enforcement that undermines the legal character of the Non-Proliferation norm.

The loosening of the norm of nonintervention introduces an asymmetry in the international institution of sovereignty, as acknowledged by Feinstein and Slaughter when they concede that for practical reasons, the duty to prevent would have to be limited to cases where it would be likely to produce a beneficial result. The example they provide to give content to this practical constraint is that the duty to prevent principle would apply against North Korea, but not China. The example illustrates the asymmetry in sovereignty introduced by the duty to prevent principle, whereby only small states are subject to the loosened prohibition on intervention.

This asymmetry is enhanced by the regime-type considerations introduced by Feinstein and Slaughter, linking threat determination not strictly to the behavior of potential target states but also imputed intentions based on regime type. By their reasoning, a small state in possession of missiles with a government that lacks internal checks might be a legitimate target of preventive intervention on that basis alone. Such a principle would introduce such a degree of nonreciprocity and inequality in the legal institution of sovereignty as to effectively replace international legal order with something closer to a balance of power system policed by the great powers. While the Security Council places balance of power concerns at the core of the international security order, the constraining function of the legal institution of sovereignty and the nonintervention rule currently distinguish the UN system, providing it a normative grounding that facilitates buy-in by all states despite the elements of great power rule. The legitimacy and sustainability of the current international legal order depends to some extent on this buy-in secured by the reciprocity of the rules on authorized force and the formal equality of the institution of sovereignty. The forms of preventive counter-proliferation envisioned by Feinstein and Slaughter risk making discretionary intervention the rule not the exception, resulting in a far less predictable, reliable, and stable structuring of international order.

When combined with the corrosive pressures on the Non-Proliferation norm discussed in the foregoing sections of this chapter, the arguments from within and without the American government supporting a counter-proliferation stance of preventive intervention is perhaps most destabilizing to the Non-Proliferation regime. To summarize, the trends that have weakened the NPT include the evolution away from treaty-based multilateralism in American nuclear policy, the retention and renewal of nuclear arsenals as part of strategic security doctrines and an effort to introduce new restrictions on the rights of non-nuclear states while loosening the obligations of the nuclear powers. Each of these developments, and particularly the increased emphasis on counter-proliferation, is related to a greater reliance on interventionism at the expense of collective security mechanisms and rule-based order. American security policies reflect not only a weakening of the prohibition of unauthorized uses of force but also a willingness to go outside of collective mechanisms based in international law whenever such mechanisms fail to issue decisions that coincide with unilateral preferences.

Indeed, the United States has come close to repudiating the legitimacy of the NPT regime by replacing the bargain at the heart of the treaty with an entirely security-oriented unilateral Non-Proliferation policy. This new policy is built on strengthening nuclear cooperation and security guarantees for strategic partners, weakening negative security assurances to non-nuclear NPT members and emphasizing coercive interdiction and intervention strategies to restrict access to nuclear technologies. Perhaps the clearest link between the new interventionism, under American leadership, in the international security order and the erosion of the traditional Non-Proliferation regime is apparent in the framework adopted by the 2002 US National Security Strategy.[172] By explicitly embracing arms control objectives or the proliferation of WMD as a legitimate basis for forcible intervention to preempt "emerging threats," US nuclear security doctrine replaces Non-Proliferation with counter-proliferation.[173] The logic at the heart of the NPT was to make the acquisition of a nuclear arsenal less attractive for the non-nuclear states by assuring them access to civilian technologies, providing negative security assurances and enshrining a disarmament commitment on the part of the nuclear states. The American emphasis on counter-proliferation reverses the NPT's demand-side approach to nonproliferation with a supply-side emphasis on cutting off access to nuclear materials and engaging in direct interdiction exercises and even intervention to limit the spread of nuclear weapons, among other WMD. In the process, US policy has the perverse effect of undermining the NPT.

The jettisoning of the demand-side approach taken by the NPT in favor of supply-side interdiction exercises is questionable when considered in light of the relative success of the treaty-based Non-Proliferation regime. First, the NPT together with the Safeguards Agreements and the work of the International Atomic Energy Agency affords the very real benefit of relative transparency in the nuclear programs of the non-nuclear states, the provision of objective information by a specialized agency with the technical capabilities and access to provide thorough inspections and accurate reporting, and thereby a considerable reduction in the costs of policing proliferation for the nuclear-weapons states. Even in the cases where information-provision and reporting under the NPT has been called into question, such as the case of the revelations concerning the Iranian nuclear program in 2002, the IAEA has proved itself to be the most reliable source of accurate information on known nuclear facilities. The most recent American National Intelligence Estimate concerning the Iranian nuclear program not only confirms the IAEA's findings over the last five years, but also relies in part on the intelligence provided by the agency.[174]

The NPT has an excellent record over nearly forty years of information gathering, and the widespread horizontal proliferation anticipated in the late 1960s when the treaty was signed has not materialized. The treaty's incentive scheme focused on limiting demand for nuclear weapons through the benefits of relative transparency, civilian nuclear-energy cooperation, disarmament commitments on the part of the nuclear-weapons states and negative security assurances for the non-nuclear-weapons states has a considerable empirical record of Non-Proliferation success. Against this record, the abandonment of treaty-based order in favor of a more ad hoc self-help system of counter-proliferation will likely raise the costs of stemming proliferation (particularly by sidestepping the benefits afforded by the IAEA) while potentially reducing the effectiveness of multilateral efforts.

The delinkage of American nuclear policy from the NPT regime deals a devastating blow to the sustainability of a regime dependent on aligning its incentive structure to the distribution of capabilities and threats in the international security order. The adoption of a first-use doctrine that might target non-nuclear states is not a departure from the incentive structure of the NPT, but its negation. Particularly for the non-nuclear states that are perceived as adversaries by the United States, a policy of first-use of nuclear weapons and preemption of emerging threats will likely generate new incentives to acquire a nuclear deterrent where possible. A counter-proliferation policy that incentivizes adversaries to proliferate while also selectively permitting proliferation among strategic partners will lead to proliferation among both friends and foes. The shift toward increasingly coercive forms of counter-proliferation is not only consistent with the new interventionism traced throughout this essay, but draws on arguments for exceptionalism in relaxing the prohibition on non-defensive force and shares in the basic logic rejecting the constraints of rule-based order on the powerful.

To avert further damage to the Non-Proliferation regime and to repair the damage already done would require immediate measures to reverse current trends in American nuclear policy. Though it may seem counterintuitive in light of arguments that the international security order has been irrevocably transformed by the attacks of September 11, the policies most likely to stabilize the international security order are the original pillars of the NPT bargain. To reinforce that bargain and realign the international security order with the incentive structure built into the treaty regime would require, at a minimum, the abandonment of ad hoc counter-proliferation policies in favor of a rule-based multilateral order to stem weapons transfers, the relinking of disarmament commitments with the Non-Proliferation goals of the NPT regime, serious negotiations concerning multilateral fuel cycle arrangements that would not restrict non-nuclear states' access to nuclear energy, and a binding commitment by the nuclear states to extending negative security assurances to the non-nuclear states party to the NPT. Such a return to traditional Non-Proliferation policy would also require a defense of the traditional institution of sovereignty, with its bright-line rules prohibiting non-defensive uses of force outside of the collective security mechanism of the United Nations, eschewing both the new interventionism and the preference for counter-proliferation attendant to it. Lest these proposals appear unattainable or undesirable from a realist perspective on international security, it is worth noting that they capture a recent bipartisan initiative taken by former US secretaries of state and defense, led by arch-realist Henry Kissinger, calling for a reversal of the reliance on nuclear weapons globally and an American recommitment to the goal of nuclear disarmament.[175]

Conclusion

Where humanitarian intervention and the more general weakening of the norm of nonintervention are presented by their proponents as the moral alternative to the injustices and threats countenanced by international law, it is important to keep sight of the other values that are diminished in the name of such interventions. Preserving the possibility of a rule-based international legal order at the beginning of the twenty-first century may demand that we err on the side of bright-line rules that constrain the discretion of the powerful and reinforce multilateral, consensus-based security mechanisms. The history of twentieth-century interventionism provides ample basis for entertaining the possibility that such a system of less, and not more intervention may better serve not only the interests of preserving peace and security, but also thereby may provide the greater humanitarian benefit.[176]

As with all legal systems, the power of international legal rules in the area of Non-Proliferation derives at least in part from the interest of states in their reciprocal application. The absence of reciprocity threatens the legitimacy of the rules and ultimately their enforceability as law. As the nuclear-weapons states downplay their disarmament obligations, going so far as to renew and possibly expand their nuclear arsenals,[177] the proposition embodied by the NPT that non-nuclear-weapons states do not require a nuclear deterrent is commensurately weakened. The loud trumpeting of threats of intervention in response to assessments of noncompliance with Non-Proliferation obligations, as is currently the case in Iran, only exacerbates this legitimacy crisis. It is precisely the absence of any threat of reciprocity that enables powerful states to advance theories of conditional sovereignty or to relax the rules for intervention. But it is also this absence of reciprocity—the effective reality that none of the nuclear-weapons states will ever face an enforcement action or threat of intervention for their own failure to meet their obligations under the treaty—that both weakens the legitimacy of interventionist practices and undermines the incentives of the non-weapons states to comply with the existing, lopsided, and inconsistently enforced rules.

Some of the issues raised concerning the rise of a new interventionism and the undermining of the Non-Proliferation regime require an assessment of the nature of a legitimate and mutually acceptable international legal order in light of the current unipolar distribution of power. This assessment in turn will likely depend on whether there are constraints available in the international system that might bind the hegemon to a rule-based order. At an earlier time, American statesmen chose to be bound under the architecture of an international security system of which they were the principal authors. This act of self-constraint was in no small measure due to a long-term interest in the viability of regimes that structured international hierarchy to secure American dominance. But when this posture of self-constraint gives way to increasing exceptionalism, the viability of those regimes may be compromised.

The chief question raised by the legality-legitimacy debates with which this chapter began and the arguments in favor of a norm of conditional sovereignty related to those debates is whether it is better to authorize "reasonable" departures from legality or whether it is more important to maintain constraints on geopolitical discretion. In this chapter, I have sought to argue that now more than ever, the constraints on the use of force imposed in the post-WWII international legal architecture are vital to the stability of the international security order. The weakening of the prohibition of the use of force in the international system, and particularly the precedent set by the discretionary interventions of choice waged by the United States and its allies in the last decade, have altered the incentive schemes of weaker states in ways that may have destabilizing consequences. Nowhere are these deleterious consequences more apparent than in the area of arms control, and more specifically the erosion of the Non-Proliferation regime. If the norm of nonintervention, the institution of sovereignty and the negative security assurances of the arms control architecture are diminished, weaker states in the international system will be left with incentives to acquire new deterrent capabilities. In the case of nonproliferation, this distortion of the incentive structure of the NPT under the pressure of the new interventionism, if unchecked, may introduce a new nuclear age with all its attendant dangers.

Endnotes

I am grateful, for helpful comments and suggestions, to Richard Falk, Owen Fiss, Heather Gerken, David Golove, Daniel Halberstam, Paul Kahn, Harold Koh, Tony Kronman, Maximo Langer, Darryl Li, Karuna Mantena, Aziz Rana, Kal Raustiala, Steven Ratner, Nisreen Salti, Reva Siegel, Anne-Marie Slaughter, Richard Steinberg, Jeremy Waldron, participants of the "Legality and Legitimacy in the International Order" workshop at the University of California–Santa Barbara, and participants at the numerous law school workshops at which I presented different versions of this chapter.

1. Note that the argument here is not merely against *unilateral* interventions without Security Council authorization. While encompassing opposition to unilateral intervention, the argument against intervention outside of the UN Charter framework presented in this chapter applies equally to multilateral interventions (say, by "coalitions of the willing") that lack Security Council mandate.

2. "Conditional sovereignty" is one way that this rethinking has been described. Another possible description, however, is "contractual sovereignty," emphasizing the degree to which the conditions on sovereignty are themselves a reflection of treaty obligations that were contracted by sovereign states. To the extent that the framers of the "responsibility to protect" principle (the International Commission on Intervention and State Sovereignty, discussed at length below) conceived of a contractual model of sovereignty, the treaty from which they derived the conditions on sovereignty is the UN Charter. See Charter of the United Nations, October 24, 1945, 1 UNTS XVI, Article 51. For a discussion of sovereignty as "contractual," see Richard Haass, *The Opportunity: America's Moment to Alter History's Course* (New York: PublicAffairs, 2005). The UN Charter obligations clearly entail some contractual obligations related to the prohibition on non-defensive uses of force. The logic of contractual sovereignty provides grounds to extend the conditions on sovereignty to other international obligations, beyond those found in the charter's prohibition on force. This extension, in turn, is the basis for arguments that the breach of such additional obligations, too, may provide new grounds for justifiable intervention. As will be discussed below, Haass is among those scholars who have proposed precisely such an extension

3. The concepts in question—conditional sovereignty and a more permissive norm of intervention—evolved out of the legality/legitimacy debate but were not a logically necessary corollary of the debate. Another way to close the gap between legality and legitimacy might have been a recommitment to the basic principles of the charter system coupled with a recommendation that permanent members of the Security Council refrain from exercising their veto powers in cases of humanitarian emergency. See, e.g., Thomas Franck, "Rethinking Humanitarian Intervention: The Case for Incremental Change" in *Humanitarian Intervention: Ethical and Legal Dilemmas*, ed. J. L. Holzgrefe and Robert O. Keohane (Cambridge: Cambridge University Press, 2003). Further, the doctrine of conditional sovereignty might have been restricted to the state's internal responsibility to protect the humanitarian welfare of its population. By observing that concepts have migrated from one context to another, or that debates have evolved in a particular direction, I do not mean to suggest a necessary (let alone *causal*) relationship between the claims of humanitarian intervention and a doctrine of preemptive intervention.

4. It is worth noting here that there are many ways in which a state or group of states may intervene in the domestic affairs of another state. Recently, in surveying pervasive

"external efforts to influence domestic authority structures in other states," Stephen Krasner identified the following spectrum of activites: hortatory influence (e.g., international condemnation or censure), symmetrical contracting, asymmetrical contracting and imposition. The last category—imposition—comprises forcible efforts by external actors to alter the domestic authority structures of a state. Recently, such coercive intervention has come to be defined as "regime change." In this chapter, I am concerned exclusively with the most coercive end of the spectrum of potential intervention—that involving the use of non-defensive force by external actors against another state. Krasner's spectrum—though concerned with intervention for democracy promotion, which is not necessarily the goal of the forms of intervention discussed in this chapter—is a useful reminder that a wide array of activities may contravene the rule of nonintervention without involving the use of force. The argument against intervention presented herein does not extend to such non-forcible forms of intervention. See Stephen Krasner, "Sovereignty and Democracy Promotion," paper prepared for presentation at the U.S.-Islamic World Forum, Doha, February 16–18, 2008.

5. There has been significant interest in the question of legitimacy in recent international law scholarship, not all of it concerned with the sense in which legality and legitimacy are used in the humanitarian intervention literature. For examples of other conceptions of legitimacy, see Thomas Franck, *The Power of Legitimacy among Nations* (Oxford: Oxford University Press, 1990); Brad Roth, *Governmental Illegitimacy in International Law* (Oxford: Oxford University Press, 1999); and Ian Clark, *Legitimacy in International Society* (Oxford: Oxford University Press, 2005).

6. The flexibility benefits of the appeal to legitimacy may well be overstated. Where there is consensus on the need for flexibility, the law itself is well suited to adapting either through formal revision or through an informal consensus around an innovative interpretation to buttress new practices. Such was the case with the interpretation of the UN Charter as authorizing peacekeeping operations through a combined reading of the provisions of Chapters VI and VII of the Charter. The view that peacekeeping is authorized under "chapter-six-and-a-half" captures the sense that the Charter had sufficient flexibility to adapt informally to enable the conduct of these operations.

7. Kosovo is a clear example of the appeal to legitimacy as a result of the absence of geopolitical consensus. By contrast, the presence of an extraordinary humanitarian emergency alone was not sufficient to yield intervention despite the presence of geopolitical consensus in the case of Rwanda and the availability of a clear legal basis for intervention in the guise of the requirements of the Genocide Convention. For a discussion of the uses of "legitimacy" in the Kosovo and Iraq contexts that is consistent with this view, see Nathaniel Berman, "Intervention in a Divided World: Axes of Legitimacy," *European Journal of International Law* 17, no. 4 (2006): 743–769.

8. In this volume, see the chapters by Richard Falk, Anne Orford, and Christine Chinkin for exhaustive discussions of these debates and their outcomes.

9. The empirical validity of the claim that the intervention had a positive net effect from a humanitarian perspective requires the following judgments: (1) a counterfactual assessment of the likely humanitarian outcome if no intervention had taken place or if diplomatic negotiations with the Serbian regime together with pressure through the Security Council mechanism on the Russian government had been pursued further in support of the Rambouillet accord; and (2) an assessment of the humanitarian costs of the intervention as it

occurred under NATO command (by aerial attack) as opposed to an intervention that might have occurred under different rules of engagement, particularly rules that might have limited appropriate tactics to those proportionate to the humanitarian goals of the mission. Because the claimed net positive effect rests on these two counterfactuals, it remains debatable.

10. Independent International Commission on Kosovo, "Executive Summary: The Future of Humanitarian Intervention," *The Kosovo Report: Conflict, International Response, Lessons Learned* (Oxford: Oxford University Press, 2000), 10. (Cited as *Kosovo Report.*)

11. In this regard, the commission argued that the "challenge for the future is certainly not that countries or groups of countries are too eager to intervene to stop serious abuse human rights, but rather the opposite. The pattern of the recent past suggests that states are eager to find excuses not to intervene." *Kosovo Report*, 195.

12. In this chapter, I use the terms "global South" and "developing world" interchangeably. The perspectives that I attribute to the states of the developing world or the global South are largely those articulated by the nonaligned movement or the Group of 77 (G-77). See "About the Group of 77," available at http://www.g77.org/doc/.

13. Kofi A. Annan, *We the Peoples: The Role of the United Nations in the 21st Century*, Report of the United Nations Secretary-General to the General Assembly (New York: United Nations, 2000), 48.

14. The only overlap in the membership of the two commissions was the presence of Michael Ignatieff on both. Like the Kosovo Commission, the ICISS strove for a measure of geographical diversity among the experts convened to address the issue. The composition of the ICISS, however, was more inclusive of experts drawn from the developing world than its predecessor. The twelve expert members of the Commission were: Gisele Cote-Harper (Canada), Gareth Evans (Australia), Lee Hamilton (U.S.), Michael Ignatieff (Canada), Vladimir Lukin (Russia), Klaus Naumann (Germany), Cyril Ramaphosa (South Africa), Fidel Ramos (Philippines), Cornelio Sommaruga (Switzerland), Eduardo Stein (Guatemala), Mohamed Sahnoun (Algeria) and Ramesh Thakur (India).

15. Ian Hurd, "Legitimacy and Authority in International Politics," *International Organization* 53, no. 2 (1999) 379–408, here 393. Hurd draws on international relations scholarship as well as international law in providing this definition.

16. The phrase "responsibility to protect" became the title of the report issued by the ICISS. International Commission on Intervention and State Sovereignty (ICISS), *The Responsibility to Protect* (December 2001). Available at http://www.iciss-ciise.gc.ca/menu-en.asp. The difference between the doctrine of humanitarian intervention and the concept of the responsibility to protect is described in detail by Gareth Evans, one of the two principal authors of the ICISS Final Report. See Gareth Evans, "From Humanitarian Intervention to Responsibility to Protect," *Wisconsin Journal of International Law* 24, no. 3 (2006): 703–723.

17. ICISS Final Report, p. 13, para. 2.14 (italics omitted). The Commission emphasized that the principle of sovereign equality enshrined in the charter (Article 2.1) and the norm of nonintervention (Article 2.7) do not entail unlimited powers for states, but rather imply a "dual responsibility—externally, to respect the sovereignty of other states, and internally, to respect the dignity and basic rights of all people within the state" (p. 8, para 1.35).

18. For a detailed discussion of the genealogy of the "responsibility to protect" norm, see the chapter by Anne Orford in this volume.

19. For instance, countries of the global South were more positively disposed toward the framing of the doctrine around the responsibilities of sovereignty rather than intervention.

The principle reportedly gained support among such "key representatives of the global south [as] Rwanda, South Africa, Mexico, Chile and Argentina." See William R. Pace and Nicole Deller, "R2P: The International Context—Recent Developments and Forthcoming Steps. A Civil Society Perspective," *Responsibility to Protect Engaging Civil Society*, a report prepared for the International Coalition for the Responsibility to Protect. Available at http://www.responsibilitytoprotect.org/index.php?module=uploads&func=download&fileId=327. Quotation found on p. 2.

20. United Nations High-Level Panel on Threats, Challenges and Change, *A More Secure World: Our Shared Responsibility* (New York: United Nations, 2004). Available at http://www.un.org/secureworld/. (Cited as *More Secure World.*)

21. *More Secure World*, part 1 at paragraph 29.

22. *More Secure World*, para. 29.

23. For instance, in its consideration of collective security and the use of force in part III of the report, the panel explicitly endorses "the emerging norm that there is a collective international responsibility to protect." However, the panel locates that responsibility squarely in the Security Council, writing that the responsibility to protect is "exercisable by the Security Council authorizing military intervention as a last resort, in the event of genocide and other largescale killing, ethnic cleansing or serious violations of international humanitarian law which sovereign Governments have proved powerless or unwilling to prevent." *More Secure World*, part III, chapter IX, para. 203.

24. Soon after the publication of the ICISS Report, an initiative entitled the "Responsibility to Protect–Engaging Civil Society Project" (R2PCS Project) was founded with funding from the Canadian and British governments in addition to private foundations. The R2PCS Project maintains a website that archives documents referencing the "responsibility to protect" principle that have been promulgated by governments, international organizations, civil society groups, and the media. The archive can be accessed at http://www.responsibilitytoprotect.org/index.php/united_nations/. For a detailed discussion of the trajectory of the concept of "responsibility to protect" from the ICISS report to its incorporation in the work of the United Nations and NGOs, see the chapter by Anne Orford in this volume.

25. Kofi Annan, *In Larger Freedom: Towards Development, Security and Human Rights For All*, A/59/2005 (New York: United Nations, 2005). Available at http://www.un.org/largerfreedom/. The report explicitly adopts the recommendations of the High-Level Panel Report at paragraphs 76–77, 126 and 135. Specifically, the Secretary-General noted that the High-Level Panel,

> endorsed what they described as "an emerging norm that there is a collective responsibility to protect." While I am well aware of the sensitivities involved in this issue, I strongly agree with this approach. I believe that we must embrace the responsibility to protect, and, when necessary, we must act on it. This responsibility lies, first and foremost, with each individual State, whose primary raison d'être and duty is to protect its population. But if national authorities are unable or unwilling to protect their citizens then the responsibility shifts to the international community . . . [and] the Security Council may out of necessity decide to take action under the Charter of the United Nations, including enforcement action, if so required." Para. 135.

26. United Nations General Assembly, *2005 World Summit Outcome Document*, GA Res. 60/1 UN Doc A/RES/60/1 (October 24, 2005), paras. 138–139. Available at http://daccessdds.un.org/doc/UNDOC/GEN/N05/487/60/PDF/N0548760.pdf?OpenElement. Proponents of the "responsibility to protect" principle were concerned until the last minute that no reference to the principle would be included in the Outcome Document. The R2PCS project notes in this regard that: "In the negotiations leading to the UN reform summit in 2005, few predicted that states would adopt an affirmation of the responsibility to protect. . . . [t]hroughout the debates many governments were dismissive of this new norm." Ultimately, according to the R2PCS account of the summit process, it was the deemphasis on the use of force and support among key governments of the global South that led to the inclusion of the principle in the final document. Pace and Deller, "R2P: The International Context."

27. United Nations Security Council Resolution 1674, UN Doc S/RES/1674 (April 24, 2006), at para. 4.

28. United Nations Security Council Resolution 1706, UN Doc S/RES/1706 (August 31, 2006), at second preambular para. and para. 12. In the preambular language of the resolution, the Security Council notes that it is authorizing peacekeepers in Darfur, recalling its previous resolutions, including "1674 (2006) on the protection of civilians in armed conflict, which reaffirms inter alia the provisions of paragraphs 138 and 139 of the 2005 World Summit outcome document." Subsequently, in operative paragraph 12(a), the resolution specifies that the Chapter VII authorization for the UN Mission in the Sudan (UNMIS) includes all necessary means inter alia to protect civilians.

29. I characterize this as a partial genealogy because it provides the necessary elements to identify an *emergent* norm and to lay a legal foundation upon which subsequent United Nations actions and national practices may build. The present crisis in Darfur provides precisely an occasion for such additional intergovernmental or state action guided by the "responsibility to protect," that may generate a more substantial record of state practice and *opinio juris* in support of the norm.

30. ICISS, "The Just Cause Threshold," *Responsibility to Protect*, at xii.

31. To be clear, the ICISS doctrine of responsibility to protect emphasized the *internal* obligations of sovereignty, though it did also recognize that sovereignty as responsibility entails some external duties. The only external duty referenced by the ICISS report was the duty of respecting the sovereignty of other states. The extension of the external duties of sovereignty to other international obligations, though easily extrapolated from the recharacterization of sovereignty as responsibility, was not offered by the ICISS but rather by the High-Level Panel as discussed above. While the narrower conception of responsibility to protect is the one embraced by the General Assembly and Security Council, the subsequent scholarly debate has laid the groundwork for an expansion of the concept. Conceptual slippage from the responsibility to protect to a wider interventionist mandate on the basis of alleged state violations of external responsibilities of sovereignty is present in some of the scholarly literature, as discussed below.

32. Anne-Marie Slaughter, "Security, Solidarity and Sovereignty: The Grand Themes of UN Reform," *American Journal of International Law* 99, no. 3 (July 2005): 619–631, here 628.

33. What is new in this conception is that the violations of obligations to the international community that might trigger justified intervention may exceed the grounds enumerated under Article 2(4) of the UN Charter. Such violations, which do not rise to the level of a threat or use of force against another state, may arguably arise, for example, in the area of arms control.

34. See, e.g., W. Michael Reisman, "Sovereignty and Human Rights in Contemporary International Law," *American Journal of International Law* 84, no. 4 (October 1990): 866–876. Reisman makes a broader argument that because sovereignty lies with the popular will and not with any particular government, intervention against a regime suppressing popular sovereignty may itself be sovereignty-enhancing. International law has "prescribed criteria for appraising the conformity of internal governance with international standards of democracy" (868). Where internal governance falls short of such criteria, Reisman argues that the norm of nonintervention is either weakened or may cease entirely to apply.

35. Allen Buchanan and Robert Keohane have recently developed an argument in defense of a cosmopolitan framework to justify preventive war. According to this framework, such preventive action must either by authorized by the Security Council, or failing such an authorization, should be brought before a *coalition of democratic states*, which would then apply its own institutionalized accountability mechanism for authorizing preventive action. This second body—convened specifically for the purpose of authorizing preventive uses of force—has a membership criteria based on internal regime-type (i.e., democratic pedigree). Specifically, the authors note that "[i]f preventive action were blocked by a majority vote of the Security Council or a veto by one of the permanent members, those seeking to engage in preventive action could then make the case in a different body—a coalition of democratic states—with its own institutionalized mechanisms of accountability." Allen Buchanan and Robert O. Keohane, "The Preventive Use of Force: A Cosmopolitan Institutional Proposal," *Ethics & International Affairs* 18, no. 1 (2004)(: 2.

36. A more specific link to the role of regime type in providing grounds for justified intervention, particularly where combined with arms control concerns, is offered by Anne-Marie Slaughter and Lee Feinstein in their article, considered at length below. See Anne-Marie Slaughter and Lee Feinstein, "A Duty to Prevent," *Foreign Affairs*, 83, no. 1 (January/February 2004)): 136–151.

37. In considering such implications, a note on the causal role of law may be in order here. One way to think about this question is as follows: if legal authority were extended to intervention for arms control purposes, would such authority lead to greater intervention? Does law have a causal role with respect to intervention (or lack thereof)? There is a tendency among scholars of international relations—particularly realists—to treat international law as epiphenomenal and thus to dismiss any causal role of international legal rules. The perspective reflected in this chapter, rather, is that legal authority has causal effect insofar as it would facilitate justification of intervention, thereby lowering the costs of such an action. The justificatory basis for an action plainly plays a role in any calculation of the costs and benefits of intervention, as evidenced by the lengths to which the United States was willing to go in seeking legal authority, ultimately in vain, for the Iraq intervention. Moreover, the authority of international law is too often considered from the perspective of hegemonic actors or great powers that are better able than most states to insulate themselves from the consequences of violating international legal rules as a result of their asymmetric power in the international order. Even such violations come at a price—namely, the destabilization of the wider use-of-force regime in ways that may adversely impact the interests of great powers in the long term. More importantly, the vast majority of states do not enjoy such asymmetric power and are much likelier to experience international law as a meaningful constraint.

38. For detailed discussions of the application of the humanitarian intervention/legality-legitimacy frameworks to the cases of Afghanistan and Iraq, see the contributions of Richard Falk and Christine Chinkin to this volume.

39. In building the case for an intervention in Iraq, British Prime Minister Tony Blair invoked the example of Kosovo while addressing the House of Commons in September 2002. Responding to critics of his argument for intervention in Iraq, with or without Security Council authorization, Blair argued "look at Kosovo and Afghanistan. We proceeded with care, with full debate in this House and when we took military action, did so as a last resort. We shall act in the same way now." Tony Blair, "Prime Minister's Statement to Parliament on Iraq and Weapons of Mass Destruction" (September 24, 2002). Available at http://www.number10.gov.uk/output/Page1727.asp. Nothing in this chapter is intended to suggest, however, that there is a causal link between the Kosovo precedent and the decision to intervene in Iraq. Notwithstanding efforts, like those of Blair, to suggest that an intervention in Iraq might be justified by reference to Kosovo, the decision itself was not motivated either by the "responsibility to protect" nor by any related principle underlying humanitarian intervention. For an account of the apparent motivations for the decision to intervene in Iraq, see generally Bob Woodward, *Plan of Attack* (New York: Simon & Schuster, 2004); and Thomas E. Ricks, *Fiasco: The American Military Adventure in Iraq* (New York: Penguin Press, 2008). Rather the relationship between responsibility to protect and the emergence of arguments for preemptive intervention, as in Iraq, has to do with the *logical* links between the two arguments, not a causal link between two different instances of actual intervention.

40. George W. Bush, "President Bush Delivers Graduation Speech at West Point" (June 1, 2002). Available at http://www.whitehouse.gov/news/releases/2002/06/20020601-3.html. The speech marked the introduction of the Bush administration's preemption doctrine. Bush states, inter alia, that "our security will require all Americans to be forward-looking and resolute, to be ready for preemptive action when necessary to defend our liberty and to defend our lives." The preemption doctrine was then elaborated by the National Security Council in September 2002. See National Security Council, "National Security Strategy of the United States of America 2002," September 17, 2002, available at http://www.whitehouse.gov/nsc/nss.html. United States National Security Council, *The 2002 National Security Strategy of the United States of America* (September 2002), available at http://www. white-house.gov/nsc/nss.pdf. It is worth noting here that the preemption argument was tied both to the threat that the Iraqi possession of WMD might pose to the United States and to the alleged links between the Iraqi regime and terrorist groups. The latter argument concerning an Iraqi link to al Qaeda was largely discredited prior to the war, and the focus shifted almost entirely to the claims concerning WMD. Nonetheless, the convergence between a counter-proliferation/disarmament argument and a counterterrorism agenda which emerged in the debates about the Iraq war has persisted and is an important element of the framing of recent arguments in favor of preemptive action against Iran.

41. UN Charter, Article 51.

42. These resolutions were Security Council Resolution 678 (1990), Security Council Resolution 687 (1991), and Security Council Resolution 1441 (2002): United Nations Security Council Resolution 678, UN Doc S/RES/678 (November 29, 1990), United Nations Security Council Resolution 687, UN Doc S/RES/687 (April 3, 1991), United Nations Security Council Resolution 1441, UN Doc S/RES/1441 (November 8, 2002).

43. For a detailed discussion of the international legal consensus that the resolutions did not provide an implied or continuing authorization of force, see Mary Ellen O'Connell, "Addendum to Armed Force in Iraq: Issues of Legality," *American Society of International Law Insights* (April 2003). Available at http://www.asil.org/insights/insigh99a1.htm.

44. From the American perspective, the arms control rationale was deemed sufficient in and of itself, independent of council authorization. Where the British government regarded a determination of legality as essential to the conduct of an intervention in Iraq, the United State. was less concerned with fitting their rationale for an intervention into the charter framework for authorized use of force. See, e.g., "White House: US doesn't need UN permission on Iraq," *CNN*, November 10, 2002: "if the council is unable to agree on a second resolution authorizing the use of force, the United States would not be restrained in its response, Powell told CNN's 'Late Edition With Wolf Blitzer.'" Available at http://archives.cnn.com/2002/US/11/10/iraq.policy/index.html.

45. George W. Bush, "President George Bush Discusses Iraq in National Press Conference," White House Office of the Press Secretary (March 6, 2003). Available at http://www.whitehouse.gov/news/releases/2003/03/20030306-8.html.

46. The specific legal rationale advanced by administration lawyers was that the presence of such weapons stockpiles would be evidence of a breach of the disarmament terms of previous resolutions and that such breach would warrant intervention. This legal rationale carried little weight internationally because the negotiating history of Resolution 1441 made clear that breach was not deemed to automatically give rise to authorization for intervention in the view of several of the permanent members of the council. As is evident in the president's broader statements, the legal rationale concerning stockpiles merged with a security-based rationale that suggested that the presence of weapon stockpiles itself, in light of the nature of the regime, constituted an intolerable threat. When the president stated that the purpose of the intervention was disarmament, the legal and security rationales blurred into a single, disarmament-based argument.

47. Another novel claim that was advanced with respect to Security Council authorization was that should the United States and United Kingdom table a second resolution for the authorization of force based on a finding that Iraq had not complied with Resolution 1441, that it would be "unreasonable" for any of the other permanent members to veto. While this claim is not directly pertinent to the argument presented herein, it is worth taking a moment to consider its implications. The doctrine of the "unreasonable veto" suggested that a failure to authorize force by the council mechanism would not be a definitive judgment of the legality of an attack against Iraq but rather would be evidence of the council's failing as a "reasonable" arbiter of appropriate uses of force. Thus, George Bush argued that a United Nations failure to authorize the Iraq war would consign the organization to "fade into history as an ineffective, irrelevant debating society." George W. Bush, "President Salutes Sailors at Naval Station Mayport in Jacksonville," (February 13, 2003). Available at http://www.whitehouse.gov/news/releases/2003/02/20030213-3.html. For an American international law argument suggesting that the Iraq war demonstrated the inadequacy of the United Nations' collective security mechanism, see Michael Glennon, "Why the Security Council Failed," *Foreign Affairs* 82, no. 3 (May/June 2003): 16–35. A more cynical reading of the "unreasonable veto" argument would be that it represented an effort by the United States and the United Kingdom to weaken the validity of vetoes cast against their preferences. Thus, a veto cast by China, Russia, and at times France, was deemed suspect while a veto

cast by the United States or the United Kingdom was presumptively reasonable. The attempted legal distinction between reasonable and unreasonable vetoes did not survive debates around the Iraq war, but the instinct to go outside of the council mechanism and adopt a coalition-of-the-willing approach when threatened with a veto persists, as is evident in the approach to sanctions against Iran. For an account of British and American uses of the "unreasonable veto" argument in the run-up to the Iraq war, see Peter Fray, "Blair Lays Down Law against Using Veto," *Sydney Morning Herald*, February 8, 2003, noting that "Britain warned France, China and Russia against using an 'unreasonable veto' in the United Nations against approving a United States-led invasion." Available at http://www.smh.com.au/articles/2003/02/07/1044579937638.html. The Bush administration also suggested in the run-up to the Iraq war that they might avoid a vote in the Security Council on the use of force against Iraq because of what they viewed as the potential use of "unreasonable" vetoes by certain permanent members of the council. White House Press Secretary Ari Fleischer, in a press briefing on the eve of the Iraq war, characterized a possible French veto on Security Council authorization of force in Iraq as an example of an "unreasonable veto" (Commenting on a French rejection of a draft resolution tabled by the British, Mr. Fleischer stated: "France also looked at the British proposal and they rejected it before Iraq rejected it. If that's not an unreasonable veto, what is?"). Ari Fleischer, "Press Briefing by White House Press Secretary" (March 13, 2003). Available at http://www.whitehouse.gov/news/releases/2003/03/20030313-13.html.

48. See, e.g., Michael Ignatieff, "I Am Iraq," *New York Times*, March 23, 2003, arguing in defense of the intervention; and Ignatieff, "The Year of Living Dangerously," *New York Times*, March 14, 2004, arguing a year into the war in defense of maintaining troop levels. For a more general account of advocates of humanitarianism who supported the war, see Michelle Goldberg, "The Crisis of the Pro-War Liberals," *Salon.com* (September 22, 2003). Available at http://dir.salon.com/story/news/feature/2003/09/22/pro_war_left/.

49. As we have seen above, Tony Blair cited Kosovo as precedent in arguing for the Iraq intervention before the House of Commons. Tony Blair, "Prime Minister's Statement to Parliament on Iraq and Weapons of Mass Destruction" (September 24, 2002). See also Robert W. Tucker and David C. Hendrickson, "Sources of American Legitimacy," *Foreign Affairs* 83, no. 6 (November/December 2004): 18–32, here 31–32 (noting that "[i]n the aftermath of Kosovo, NATO governments repeatedly claimed that the intervention 'would constitute the exception from the rule, not an attempt to create new international law,' in the words of former NATO Secretary-General Javier Solana. But this attempt to limit the reach of the Kosovo precedent did not prevent the advocates of the Iraq war from invoking it to justify toppling Saddam").

50. The principle of a "duty to prevent" will be taken up below in part II, section C.

51. The mandate I refer to here is the preemption doctrine first articulated in the Bush administration's 2002 National Security Strategy and then restated in modified form in the 2006 National Security Strategy. The modified version of the doctrine is set forth in the 2006 National Security Strategy as follows:

> [T]he first duty of the United States Government remains what it always has been: to protect the American people and American interests. It is an enduring American principle that this duty obligates the government to anticipate and counter threats, using all elements of national power, before the threats can do grave damage. The greater the

> threat, the greater is the risk of inaction—and the more compelling the case for taking *anticipatory action to defend ourselves*, even if uncertainty remains as to the time and place of the enemy's attack. . . . To forestall or prevent such hostile acts by our adversaries, the United States will, if necessary, *act preemptively* in exercising *our inherent right of self-defense*. The United States will not resort to force in all cases to preempt emerging threats. Our preference is that nonmilitary actions succeed.

United States National Security Council, *The 2006 National Security Strategy of the United States of America* (March 2006), Chapter VI (emphasis added). Available at http://www.whitehouse.gov/nsc/nss/2006/nss2006.pdf. In this reformulation, the right of preemption and anticipatory self-defense remains pronounced, but the doctrine also makes clear a preference for nonmilitary means and acknowledges that every "emerging threat" need not yield a resort to preemptive force. That said, no reference is made to the United Nations security architecture governing the use of force. Rather, the emphasis remains on an inherent right of self-defense subject, it would seem, only to discretionary determinations by the American government as to the need to resort to anticipatory action. Though more circumspect in the 2006 restatement, the doctrine of preemptive action remains open-ended as compared to the narrowly circumscribed permissible uses of defensive force under the UN Charter.

52. Anne-Marie Slaughter, "Good Reasons for Going Around the U.N," *New York Times*, March 18, 2003.

53. UN Secretary-General Kofi Annan acknowledged the illegality of the Iraq war in a statement as early as September 2004. "Iraq War Was Illegal, Says Annan," *BBC*, September 16, 2004, available at http://news.bbc.co.uk/2/hi/middle_east/3661134.stm. Anne-Marie Slaughter, who had acknowledged the illegality of the war from the outset, subsequently came to an *ex post* determination that the intervention had also been illegitimate. She discussed the illegitimacy of the intervention in her farewell address to the American Society of International Law in March 2004. Anne-Marie Slaughter, "The Use of Force in Iraq: Illegal and Illegitimate," *American Society of International Law Proceedings* (2004): 262–263. An exception to the general view concerning the illegality of the war can be found in the work of Ruth Wedgwood, "The Fall of Saddam Hussein: Security Council Mandates and Preemptive Self-Defense," *American Journal of International Law* 97 (2003): 576–585.

54. The international relations literature has been understandably interested in explaining the anomaly of the Non-Proliferation regime and attendant nuclear taboo. See, e.g., Richard Price and Nina Tannenwald, "Norms and Deterrence: The Nuclear and Chemical Weapons Taboos," in *The Culture of National Security: Norms and Identity in World Politics*, ed. Peter Katzenstein (New York: Columbia University Press, 1996).

55. For an overview of the global trends in proliferation since the middle of the twentieth century, see "Chapter 1: Global Trends," *in* Joseph Cirincione, *Deadly Arsenals: Tracking Weapons of Mass Destruction* (Washington, D.C.: Carnegie Endowment for International Peace, 2002).

56. See Warner D. Farr, *The Third Temple's Holy of Holies: Israel's Nuclear Weapons* (Alabama: United States Air Force Counterproliferation Center, Maxwell Air Force Base, 1999); Avner Cohen, *Israel and the Bomb* (New York: Columbia University Press, 1998); see also Hannah Strange, "How Britain Helped Israel Make the Bomb," *United Press International*, August 13, 2005, reporting on revelations based on official government papers released by the British National Archives forming the basis of a BBC inquiry in 2005.

57. Howard Diamond, "India Conducts Nuclear Tests; Pakistan Follows Suit," *Arms Control Today* 28, no. 4 (May 1998). Available at http://www.armscontrol.org/act/1998_05/hd1my98.asp.

58. By formally declaring its withdrawal from the NPT under Article X of the treaty and expelling IAEA inspectors from its territory in 2003, North Korea became the first state party to withdraw from the formal NonProliferationregime, setting what many feared would be a damaging precedent. The DPRK did not declare itself a nuclear power for more than a year after its initial NPT withdrawal. Anthony Faiola, "North Korea Declares Itself a Nuclear Power," *Washington Post*, February 10, 2005.

59. "North Korea Claims Nuclear Test," *CNN*, October 9, 2006, available at http://www.cnn.com/2006/WORLD/asiapcf/10/08/korea.nuclear.test/; "US Confirms N. Korea Nuclear Test," *BBC* October 16, 2006, available at http://news.bbc.co.uk/2/hi/asia-pacific/6056370.stm; and United Nations Department of Public Information, "Security Council Condemns Nuclear Test by Democratic People's Republic of Korea, Unanimously Adopting Resolution 1718 (2006)," (Press Release, October 14, 2006), available at http://www.un.org/News/Press/docs/2006/sc8853.doc.htm.

60. Office of the US Secretary of Defense, "Section I: The Former Soviet Union: Russia, Ukraine, Kazakhstan and Belarus," *Proliferation: Threat and Response* (Washington, D.C.: Department of Defense, April 1996), Available at http://fas.org/irp/threat/prolif96/fsu.html.

61. For detailed discussion of the Argentine and Brazilian cases, see Cirincione, *Deadly Arsenals*, 337–357 ("Chapter 20: Argentina" and "Chapter 21: Brazil").

62. On South Africa's nuclear-weapons program and the decision to dismantle it, see Waldo Stumpf, "South Africa's Nuclear Weapons Program: From Deterrence to Dismantlement," *Arms Control Today* 25, no. 8 (December 1995/January 1996). For an annotated chronology of South Africa's nuclear-weapons program, the decision beginning in 1989 to dismantle the program and the country's accession to the NPT as a non-nuclear-weapons state, see Center for Non-Proliferation Studies, "CNS Resources on South Africa's Nuclear Weapons Program." Available at http://cns.miis.edu/research/safrica/chron.htm.

63. For background on the trajectory of South Africa's Non-Proliferation efforts since it dismantled its weapons program and acceded to the NPT, see "South Africa Country Profile: Nuclear Overview," National Threat Initiative. The text of the Treaty of Pelindaba and information concerning the fifty state signatories is available at http://www.state.gov/t/ac/trt/4699.htm. Treaty of Pelindaba (1996) (African Nuclear-Weapon-Free-Zone Treaty), April 11, 1996, 35 I.L.M. 698, U.N. Doc. A/50/426 (1996).

64. One such example is the Proliferation Security Initiative (PSI), which will be discussed in greater detail below. Where Non-Proliferation policy relies on multilateral regimes, international law and enforcement in a collective security framework, counter-proliferation is defined by the United States office of the secretary of defense as "the full range of military preparations and activities to reduce, and protect against, the threat posed by nuclear, biological, and chemical weapons and their associated delivery means." Office of the U.S. Secretary of Defense, *Proliferation: Threat and Response* (2001).

65. Other components of the Non-Proliferation system include, for instance, Multilateral Export Control regimes, the Missile Technology Control Regime, the Biological and Chemical Weapons Conventions, the Comprehensive Test Ban Treaty (CTBT), more informal multilateral arrangements like the Proliferation Security Initiative, informal international groups including the Nuclear Suppliers Group and the Zangger Committee, and

various bilateral and multilateral disarmament agreements. In addition, the norm has also been stated in numerous United Nations Security Council resolutions, in the International Court of Justice's advisory opinion on the use of nuclear weapons, and in the broader non-proliferation- and disarmament-related branches of the United Nations system, including the United Nations Conference on Disarmament in Geneva.

66. The three depositary governments of the treaty are the Russian Federation, the United States, and the United Kingdom. China and France acceded to the treaty well after it came into force, with China acceding on March 9, 1992 and France acceding on August 3, 1992. With their accessions, the five acknowledged nuclear-weapons states as of the time of the drafting of the treaty became parties. For the current status of ratifications bringing into force the Comprehensive Safeguards Agreement enabling inspections by the IAEA of non-weapons states nuclear facilities, see "Overview of Status of NPT Comprehensive Safeguards Agreements," International Atomic Energy Association (October 18, 2005), available at http://www.iaea.org/Publications/Factsheets/English/nptstatus_overview.html.

67. The core agreement under which non-weapons states forgo nuclear weapons in exchange for access to technology and materials necessary for commercial nuclear power was first proposed by President Eisenhower in 1953 under his "Atoms for Peace" initiative. Dwight D. Eisenhower, "Atoms for Peace," Address by the U.S. President to the General Assembly, 470th Plenary Meeting of the United Nations General Assembly (December 8, 1953), available at http://www.iaea.org/About/history_speech.html.

68. Article I of the NPT further supports these pillars by requiring that none of the nuclear-weapons states provide any assistance or support that might enable a non-nuclear-weapons state to manufacture or acquire a weapon. As will be discussed elsewhere in this chapter, recent American efforts to engage in nuclear cooperation with India are very much in tension with the requirements of Article I.

69. United Nations Security Council Resolution 985 (1995) was the most recent occasion on which these negative security assurances not to use nuclear weapons against non-nuclear states were reaffirmed. In operative paragraph 1, the Council "takes note with appreciation of the statements made by each of the nuclear-weapon States in which they give security assurances against the use of nuclear weapons to non-nuclear weapon States that are Parties to the NPT." See United Nations Security Council Resolution 985 (1995), S/Res/985 (April 13, 1995). The negative security assurances are contingent only on the non-nuclear-weapons states continuing to act in accordance with their NPT obligations. Treaty on the Non-Proliferation of Nuclear Weapons, July 1, 1968 (entered into force on March 5, 1970), 21 U.S.T 483, 729 U.N.T.S. 169, http://disarmament.un.org/wmd/npt/.

70. The presence of Article X as part of the basic architecture of the regime is today lamented, primarily by the nuclear-weapons states, as a loophole. The right of withdrawal was not a loophole, however, but a recognition that the goal of Non-Proliferation was to be balanced with other values of the international security order, including the defensive rights of all states. Where negative security assurances cease to be a sufficient basis to meet the national security or deterrence concerns of a non-weapons state, the treaty's drafters provided for withdrawal with notice.

71. "Cuba Accedes to NPT, Joins Tlatelolco," *Arms Control Today* 32, no. 10 (December 2002), available at http://www.armscontrol.org/act/2002_12/briefs_dec02.asp.

72. As of 2007, the only non-parties to the NPT are India, Pakistan, Israel, and North Korea pursuant to its 2003 withdrawal from the treaty. There is reason to believe, however,

that following an accord reached with North Korea in the framework of the six-party talks in February 2007, North Korea may eventually rejoin the NPT. See "Text of the Joint Agreement on North Korea's Nuclear Disarmament as Released by the Chinese Foreign Ministry," *Associated Press*, February 13, 2006, available at http://www.iht.com/articles/ap/2007/02/13/asia/AS-GEN-Koreas-Nuclear-Text.php.

73. "Extension of the Treaty on the Non-Proliferation of Nuclear Weapons," Decision 3 of the 1995 NPT Review and Extension Conference (May 11, 1995), United Nations Document NPT/CONF.1995/32 (Part I) Annex, Decision 3. Available at http://disarmament.un.org/wmd/npt/1995dec3.htm.

74. "Principles and Objectives for Nuclear Non-Proliferation and Disarmament," Decision 2 of the 1995 NPT Review and Extension Conference (May 11, 1995), United Nations Document NPT/CONF.1995/32 (Part I) Annex, Decision 2. Available at http://disarmament.un.org/wmd/npt/1995dec2.htm.

75. "Strengthening the Review Process for the Treaty," Decision 1 of the 1995 NPT Review and Extension Conference (May 11, 1995), United Nations Document NPT/CONF.1995/32 (Part I) Annex, Decision 1. Available at http://disarmament.un.org/wmd/npt/1995dec1.htm. The new review process included the creation of preparatory committees to meet between review conferences to address substantive issues and prepare the next agenda.

76. Only 36 (of the 183) non-nuclear-weapons states parties to the NPT have not yet brought into force a comprehensive safeguards agreement with the Agency. None of these 36 countries is considered to represent a proliferation risk at present. For a list of the countries that do not have comprehensive safeguard agreements in force, see International Atomic Energy Association, "Overview of Status of NPT Comprehensive Safeguards Agreements" (October 18, 2005), available at http://www.iaea.org/Publications/Factsheets/English/nptstatus_overview.html.

77. The Security Council's authority pertaining to proliferation derives from its powers under the UN Charter to maintain international peace and security. However, none of the Non-Proliferation treaties or agreements specify when a violation must be referred to the council nor what course of action the council should take. The council's authority under Chapter VII of the UN Charter enables it to take enforcement action, but any determination of the appropriate course of action is left to a case-by-case determination based on its responsibility for the maintenance of international peace and security. The absence of an agreed set of enforcement measures in the event of noncompliance with the Non-Proliferation norm aggravates the inconsistencies in the enforcement of the norm. As a review of the council's role in confronting proliferation concluded in 1995, "the Council has no institutional expertise to monitor and analyze proliferation threats. It has addressed proliferation concerns only on an episodic and ad hoc basis. . . . A more consistent approach will be needed to meet the challenge of the future." The United Nations Association of the United States of America, *Confronting the Proliferation Danger: The Role of the Security Council* (New York: UNA-USA, 1995), 7.

78. As of the 2005 NPT Review Conference, 63 NPT States parties had ratified the Additional Protocols to their IAEA Safeguards Agreements, for the agency's application of strengthened safeguards. For the text of the protocol, see "Model Protocol Additional to the Agreement(s) Between State(s) and the International Atomic Energy Agency for the Application of Safeguards," IAEA INFCIRC/540 (September 1997). Available at http://www.iaea.org/Publications/Documents/Infcircs/1998/infcirc540corrected.pdf.

79. Final Document of the 2000 Review Conference of the Parties to the Treaty on the Non-Proliferation of Nuclear Weapons, "Part I: Review of the Operation of the Treaty," para. 15, subsections 1–13. United Nations Disarmament Department, "2000 Review Conference of the Parties to the Treaty on the Non-Proliferation of Nuclear Weapons, Final Document: Volume I," (New York 2000), http://disarmament.un.org/wmd/npt/2000FD.pdf.

80. For a detailed discussion of the Thirteen Practical Steps and the nuclear-weapons states' record of compliance with the 2000 NPT Review Conference commitments, see Lawrence Scheinman, "Disarmament: Have the Five Nuclear Powers Done Enough?" *Arms Control Today* 35, no. 1 (January/February 2005), available at http://www.armscontrol.org/act/2005_01-02/Scheinman.asp.

81. President Clinton's special representative for nuclear nonproliferation, Ambassador Norman Wulf, was responsible for the administration's preparations in advance of the conference. In a subsequent article, Wulf emphasized the advance public and private diplomacy undertaken by the administration to underscore its commitment to disarmament priorities despite the US Senate's failure to ratify the CTBT in 1999 and the strain on the ABM Treaty associated with American missile defense deployments. Ambassador Norman A. Wulf, "Observations from the 2000 NPT Review Conference," *Arms Control Today* 30, no. 9 (November 2000), available at http://www.armscontrol.org/act/2000_11/wulf.asp?print. Wulf notes that "as the conference approached, the nuclear-weapons states consulted frequently and sought to work together pragmatically." He credits these efforts with enabling the United States and Russia to find a compromise to achieve consensus on preserving the ABM Treaty in spite of American missile defense initiatives, removing a potential stumbling block to progress at the conference (3).

82. Wulf, "Observations from the 2000 NPT Review Conference."

83. Madeleine Albright, "Remarks to 2000 NPT Review Conference," (April 24, 2000), available at http://www.fas.org/nuke/control/npt/news/000424-npt-usia1.htm.

84. *Final Document of the 2000 Review Conference of the Parties to the Treaty on the Nonproliferation of Nuclear Weapons*, UN Document NPT/CONF.2000/28 (Vol. 1, Part I and II) (2000). Available at http://disarmament2.un.org/wmd/npt/finaldoc.html.

85. Of course, the non-nuclear-weapons states might still have significant disincentives from pursuing nuclear weapons; after all, the technology remains costly, the acquisition of such weapons may profoundly destabilize regional balances of power in ways that undermine the overall security of the proliferator, and the pursuit of nuclear weapons carries the risk of international counter-proliferation measures. However, these disincentives were not deemed sufficient by the United States at the time that the Atoms for Peace program was proposed and the NPT ultimately adopted. Indeed, as recently as 1995 and 2000, as indicated above, American administrations were willing to expend significant political capital in order to strengthen, universalize, and indefinitely extend the Non-Proliferation regime. Accordingly, it is reasonable to surmise that the bargain at the core of the treaty regime was believed to provide a significant Non-Proliferation benefit by past American administrations, beyond those disincentives that extend beyond the treaty framework.

86. Controversy in 2007 over proposed American plans to install missile defenses in Eastern Europe highlight the concern that new missile defense deployments by the United States might spark a new arms race with Russia in particular. See, e.g., "U.S. Denies Aiming Missile Defense at Russia," *Global Security Newswire*, January 23, 2007; "Missile Defense Diplomacy Escalates in Europe," *Global Security Newswire*, February 26, 2007; and "More

Missile Defense Talks Needed, Russia Says," *Global Security Newswire*, March 8, 2007. For an account of the strain on US-German relations related to American missile defense plans, see "Europe Divided Over US Missile Defense Plan," *Der Spiegel* (Germany), March 5, 2007, available at http://www.spiegel.de/international/spiegel/0,1518,469828,00.html.

87. That coalition, known as the "New Agenda Coalition," was formed in 1998 to give leadership and focus to calls by the non-weapons states for implementation of the NPT's disarmament provisions. The coalition, composed of the governments of Brazil, Egypt, Ireland, Mexico, New Zealand, South Africa, and Sweden, submitted a paper at the 2002 Preparatory Committee meeting noting specifically that the ABM withdrawal and the pursuit of ballistic missile defenses raise the prospect of a "new nuclear arms race on earth and in outer space" with "negative consequences on nuclear disarmament and nonproliferation." Preparatory Committee for the 2005 Review Conference of the Parties to the Treaty on the Non-Proliferation of Nuclear Weapons, "New Coalition Agenda Paper," April 5, 2002, United Nations Document NPT/CONF.2005/PC.I/9 (2005), para. 20.

88. For instance, the executive director of the Arms Control Association, Darryl Kimball, has argued that the Bush administration's policies suggest an expansion in the role of nuclear weapons in American security policy in violation of its disarmament commitments under the NPT. Kimball's remarks offer a revealing summary of developments in American nuclear policy since 2000 that suggest a rejection of disarmament in favor of renewed reliance on and expansion of nuclear arsenals. Darryl Kimball, "U.S. Nuclear Weapons Policy: Present and Future," Remarks Prepared for a Breakfast Briefing to Governmental Delegates (May 5, 2004), available at http://www.armscontrol.org/events/USNuclearweapons-policy_5_04.asp.

89. President Bush stated in the address that "I will not stand by as peril draws closer and closer. The United States of America will not permit the world's most dangerous regimes to threaten us with the world's most destructive weapons."

90. The international response to the 2002 State of the Union was canvassed in a *Newsweek* article excerpting coverage in the international press. The article cites British, French, Canadian, Australian, and Dutch editorials all characterizing the speech as alternately alarmist, unilateralist, and dangerous. The author of the article notes that "George W. Bush's first State of the Union Message may have played well domestically, but it has not won the same acclaim abroad. In France, the influential daily newspaper *Le Monde* described it as 'alarmist.' In Australia, the moderate *Sydney Morning Herald* described the U.S. president's worldview as 'worryingly simplistic and selective.'" Arlene Getz, "Cool and Cooler: Outside the US, Little Praise for Bush's State of the Union Speech," *Newsweek*, January 30, 2002.

91. Mitchell B. Reiss, "The Nuclear Tipping Point: Prospects for a World of Many Nuclear States," in *Nuclear Tipping Point: Why States Reconsider Their Nuclear Choices*, ed. Kurt M. Campbell (Washington, D.C.: Brookings Institution Press, 2004), 11.

92. The National Security Strategy of the United States of America 2002. The new doctrine set forth by the NSS moves away from traditional theories of deterrence, suggesting that the post-September 11 world requires a more aggressive, preemptive strategy to meet challenges as they emerge rather than deterring threats after they arise. The subsequent release of the 2006 National Security Strategy was interpreted as shifting the emphasis back somewhat to the need for "effective multinational efforts" to resolve international security challenges, though it also reaffirms the United States' option to wage preemptive war. Further, by stating that "we may face no greater challenge from a single country than from Iran," the

2006 NSS appeared to endorse the possibility that such a preemptive doctrine would be most applicable in the area of arms control.

93. Submitted to Congress on December 31, 2001, and publicly summarized in a Pentagon briefing on January 9, 2002, excerpts of the leaked Nuclear Posture Review Report are available at http://www.globalsecurity.org/wmd/library/policy/dod/npr.htm. United States Department of Defense, *The 2002 Nuclear Posture Review [Excerpts]*, (January 8, 2002).

94. This list included Iran, Iraq, Libya, North Korea, and Syria, as well as China and Russia. For a discussion of the implications of the Nuclear Posture Review for targeting and nuclear strike doctrine, see Philipp C. Bleek, "Nuclear Posture Review Leaks, Outlines Targets, Contingencies," *Arms Control Today* 32, no. 3 (April 2002), available at http://www.armscontrol.org/act/2002_04/nprapril02.asp.

95. The unclassified version of the 2002 National Strategy to Combat WMD Proliferation became available in December 2002. The *Washington Times* reported on January 31, 2003, the following sentence leaked from the classified version of the document: "The United States will continue to make clear that it reserves the right to respond with overwhelming force—including potentially nuclear weapons—to the use of [weapons of mass destruction] against the United States, our forces abroad, and friends and allies." See Nicholas Kralev, "White House Makes Option Explicit to Counter Biological, Chemical Attacks," *Washington Times*, January 31, 2003, available at http://www.nicholaskralev.com/WT-nuke-response.html.

96. Rebecca Johnson, "Is the NPT up to the Challenge of Proliferation?" *Disarmament Forum* 4 (2004): 9–19, here 12. Available at http://www.unidir.ch/pdf/articles/pdf-art2186.pdf.

97. United Nations Security Council Resolution 255, UN Doc S/RES/255 (June 19, 1968).

98. United Nations Security Council Resolution 984, UN Doc S/RES/984 (April 11, 1995).

99. On January 19, 2006, French President Jacques Chirac delivered a speech in which he set out a new French nuclear-deterrent doctrine, connecting deterrence to prevention and suggesting that states deemed to be sponsors of terrorism against France or that contemplate the use of WMD against France would be deemed legitimate targets of a conventional or nuclear response. The speech effectively signaled that France might use nuclear weapons against non-nuclear-weapons states in the face of a significant, conventional threat, thereby abandoning a no-first-use policy. Jacques Chirac, "Speech by the President of the French Republic, during his visit to the Strategic Air and Maritime Forces at Landivisau/L'Ile Longue" (January 19, 2006). Available at http://www.elysee.fr/elysee/elysee.fr/anglais/speeches_and_documents/2006/speech_by_jacques_chirac_president_of_the_french_republic_during_his_visit_to_the_strategic_forces.38447.html. See also Molly Moore, "Chirac: Nuclear Response to Terrorism Is Possible," *Washington Post*, January 20, 2006, A12.

100. PSI is formally set forth in a Statement of Interdiction Principles adopted in Paris on September 4, 2003. For a detailed discussion of the PSI and its participants, see Sharon Squassoni, "Proliferation Security Initiative," Congressional Research Service Report for Congress (September 14, 2006). Available at http://www.fas.org/sgp/crs/nuke/RS21881.pdf.

101. John R. Bolton, "The Bush Administration's Non-Proliferation Policy: Successes and Future Challenges," Testimony of the Under Secretary for Arms Control and International

Security before the U.S. Congress, House Committee on International Relations (March 30, 2004). Available at http://www.nti.org/e_research/official_docs/dos/dos03302004_bolton.pdf.

102. The phrase "à la carte multilateralism" to describe the Bush administration's approach to international cooperation was coined by Richard Haass when he was serving as director of policy planning at the State Department in 2001. Haass is quoted in an article in the *New York Times* as stating that "What you are going to get from this administration is 'à la carte multilateralism." Thom Shanker, "White House Says the U.S. Is Not a Loner, Just Choosy," *New York Times*, July 31, 2001.

103. The October 2003 interdiction of a shipment of uranium centrifuge enrichment parts from Malaysia to Libya on the German-owned ship, the *BBC China*, while passing through the Suez Canal is often cited as an example of a successful instance of multilateral cooperation for interdiction. There is some debate, however, as to whether this example of interdiction is related to the implementation of PSI or preexisting efforts to uncover the AQ Khan network. See, e.g., Wade Boese, "Key U.S. Interdiction Initiative Misrepresented," *Arms Control Today* 35, no. 6 (July/August 2005), available at http://www.armscontrol.org/act/2005_07-08/Interdiction_Misrepresented.asp.

104. According to one report, as of 2005 the PSI had expanded from its original 11 members "to include 60-plus supporters, a series of military and law enforcement exercises, enhanced information sharing, ongoing legal discussions, bilateral boarding agreements, and a public political commitment to stop proliferation to states and nonstate actors of concern." Andrew C. Winner, "The Proliferation Security Initiative: The New Face of Interdiction," *Washington Quarterly* 28, no. 2 (Spring 2005): 129–143, here 141.

105. The best argument in support of counter-proliferation efforts is to view them as a supplement to the Non-Proliferation regime, rather than a substitute. For instance, one might argue that the optimal institutional design to deter proliferation would be a hybrid arrangement including a multilateral regime, side arrangements between coalitions of actors and the occasional resort to coercive counter-proliferation actions. The constraints of this chapter do not permit of an exhaustive consideration of potential hybrid arrangements. However, the core difficulty presented by such an argument for "hybridity" is the irreconcilability of the underlying logic of the different approaches suggested. For the incentive scheme of the Non-Proliferation regime to function, compliance must yield the benefits promised under the regime. Should selective criteria based on regime-type or alliance structures introduce distinctions between states, as in the PSI approach, the incentive to comply with inspections under the NPT will be distorted. Designating some potential proliferators as "states of concern" liable to be face robust "counter-proliferation" efforts, while other states engaging in the same compliance behavior are treated more favorably undermines the principle of horizontal opposition to proliferation on which the NPT is based. The development of ad hoc side agreements intended to "supplement" the NPT through a hybrid approach runs the risk—absent multilateral coordination and the creation of a transparent institution with formal rules governing interdiction—of undermining the existing regime to the net detriment of arms control objectives.

106. See, e.g., Jofi Joseph, "The Proliferation Security Initiative: Can Interdiction Stop Proliferation?" *Arms Control Today* 34, no. 5 (June 2004), available at http://www.armscontrol.org/act/2004_06/Joseph.asp. While Joseph is generally positive about the PSI approach as an opportunity to enhance multilateral cooperation, he worries about the resistance to formalizing its terms and mandate by the United States and other core members. He notes, for instance, that

> PSI core members have also remained vague in describing the types of shipments they are targeting, speaking only in general terms of nuclear, chemical, or biological weapons and delivery systems and related materials. They have not offered definitions for these terms, even declining to reference specifically the international conventions governing the possession of nuclear, chemical, and biological weapons and the spread of missile technology. Perhaps most vexing of all is the lack of delineation of "related materials." Are the PSI members referring to only those components that are unambiguously destined for a nuclear, chemical, or biological program; or do they encompass dual-use materials? If the latter, how do PSI members reconcile that approach with the fact that the nuclear Non-Proliferation Treaty, the Chemical Weapons Convention, and the Biological Weapons Convention all expressly provide signatory states the right to possess and trade such dual-use materials?

Here the ambiguity of the legal basis for potentially far-reaching interdiction exercises is clear. Moreover, as Joseph also notes, the deliberate plan of the PSI members is to direct their interdiction efforts selectively, based on the identity of the suspected proliferator rather than the nature of its actions. So Joseph cites then-undersecretary of state for arms control and international security, John Bolton, one of the principal architects of PSI, as arguing that "[t]here are unquestionably states that are not within existing treaty regimes that possess weapons of mass destruction legitimately. We're not trying to have a policy that attempts to cover each and every one of those circumstances. What we're worried about are the rogue states and the terrorist groups that pose the most immediate threat." Thus PSI would not address the proliferation activities of states like Israel, India, and arguably Pakistan, by this reasoning. While they are outside of the NPT regime, in Bolton's estimation they have a legitimate right to possess WMD. The relevant criteria here is not the *legality* of the proliferation actions, but their *legitimacy* as seen by the members of the PSI. Characterizing the views of critics of PSI, Joseph asks "Is the initiative entitled to target only the states and nonstate actors on the 'bad guy' list, as interpreted by PSI core members?" Considerations like those raised in Joseph's otherwise-laudatory piece about PSI are indicative of some of the potential legal questions attendant to the selective invocation of international law and national legal authorities in territorial waters to engage in interdiction activities. On this point, see also Benjamin Friedman, "The Proliferation Security Initiative. The Legal Challenge," Policy Brief, Bipartian Security Group, Global Security Institute/Middle Powers Initiative (September 2003). Available at http://www.middlepowers.org/gsi/pubs/09_03_psi_brief.pdf.

107. At least one author has noted the irony that the United States led countries during the negotiation of the Law of the Seas in opposing the development of norms that would prohibit the unhindered military use of the oceans to transport WMD. Devon Chafee, "Freedom or Force on the High Seas? Arms Interdiction and International Law," Nuclear Age Peace Foundation (August 15, 2003). Available at http://www.wagingpeace.org/articles/2003/08/15_chaffee_freedom-of-force.htm.

108. In 2004, the Security Council did pass a resolution on combating proliferation of WMD—Resolution 1540—that incorporates some of the PSI logic. However, the resolution does not authorize third-party interdiction exercises. It calls on all states to take appropriate *domestic* measures to prevent trafficking of nuclear, biological, and chemical weapons. See United Nations Security Council Resolution 1540, UN Doc S/Res/1540 (April 28, 2004).

109. For an overview of arguments on this point, see Nigel Chamberlain, "Interdiction under the Proliferation Security Initiative: Counter-Proliferation or Counter-Productive?" British American Security Information Council (BASIC) Briefing (October 6, 2003). Available at http://www.basicint.org/nuclear/UK_Policy/psi20031006.htm.

110. UNSCOM was the United Nations Special Commission, mandated by the United Nations Security Council to disarm Iraq and to operate a system of verification and monitoring to ensure that no resumption of weapons programs could occur. It was replaced by the United Nations Monitoring, Verification and Inspections Commission (UNMOVIC) in 1999 through the adoption of Security Council resolution 1284 of December 17, 1999. UNMOVIC was led by Hans Blix, the former director-general of the IAEA, from March 1, 2000, to June 10, 2003. For more information on UNMOVIC, its mandate, and its inspections, see the official United Nations website of the commission at http://www.unmovic.org/.

111. Another way of putting this point is that arms control and Non-Proliferation inspections are susceptible to being structured to "prove a negative." That is, the absence of evidence of a clandestine weapons program might not be deemed sufficient to establish that no such program exists. But the exhaustive and intrusive degree of inspections necessary to prove that negative—that there are no clandestine weapons programs—may be infeasible. The intrusiveness of the UNSCOM and UNMOVIC inspections in Iraq were unprecedented and yet deemed inadequate by the United States and its allies. Under these circumstances, it is hard to imagine any inspections regime that would fully satisfy proliferation issues with respect to states deemed to be "of concern" as a result of their regime type or on the basis of suspicions regarding their intentions.

112. See notes 59–60 above and accompanying text on the North Korean withdrawal from the NPT.

113. For instance, as undersecretary of state for arms control and international security, John Bolton quipped that the American government does not engage with its adversaries, but rather that "We're in the business of changing regimes." An article describing Bolton's approach to arms control issues continued with the following: "When asked by reporters about whether he favored taking a carrot-and-stick approach toward North Korea, Bolton famously responded, 'I don't do carrots.' According to [former assistant secretary for non-proliferation, Bob] Einhorn, 'His view is that you don't deal with dictators—that the only reliable way of disarming tyrannical regimes is to get rid of the regimes.'" David Bosco, "The World According to Bolton," *Bulletin of the Atomic Scientist* 61, no. 4 (July/August 2005): 24–31, here 5. It is unsurprising, perhaps, that the accord reached with North Korea in 2007 occurred after Bolton had left the State Department and was interpreted as a victory of pragmatists over neoconservatives in the Bush administration. For accounts of the differing positions within the administration on the North Korea accord, see David E. Sanger and Thom Shanker, "Rice Is Said to Have Speeded North Korea Deal," *New York Times*, February 16, 2007, A1; and Helene Cooper, "Pragmatism in Diplomacy," *New York Times*, March 1, 2007, A3. Bolton, for his part, went on the record opposing the deal as did his colleague and successor as undersecretary, Robert Joseph, who announced his resignation from the position in January, reportedly in opposition to engagement with North Korea. On Bolton's criticisms, see Helene Cooper and Jim Yardley, "Pact With North Korea Draws Fire From a Wide Range of Critics in U.S," *New York Times*, February 14, 2007, A10. On Robert Joseph's resignation from the State Department and his criticisms of the North Korea accord, see

David E. Sanger, "Sensing Shift in Bush Policy, Another Hawk Joins Exodus," *New York Times*, March 21, 2007, A1.

114. Since leaving the administration, John Bolton has become a prominent critic of negotiations with the North Korean regime over its nuclear program and a vocal advocate of regime change in Iran. See, e.g., Steven Lee Myers, "Bush Loyalist Now Sees a White House Dangerously Soft on Iran and North Korea," *New York Times*, November 9, 2007.

115. See, e.g., Michael A. Fletcher and Keith B. Richburg, "Bush Tries To Allay E.U. Worry Over Iran," *Washington Post*, February 23, 2005, A1.

116. US Department of Defense, "Background Briefing on IAEA Nuclear Safeguards and the Tuwaitha Facility," (June 5, 2003). Available at http://www.dod.mil/transcripts/2003/tr20030605-0250.html.

117. See "High Explosives 'Missing in Iraq,'" *BBC*, October 26, 2004, available at http://news.bbc.co.uk/2/hi/middle_east/3950493.stm; and "Iraq Asks Nuclear Watchdog Back," *BBC*, October 12, 2004), available at http://news.bbc.co.uk/2/hi/middle_east/3737996.stm.

118. The Iraq Survey Group's Final Report concluded that Iraq did not retain stockpiles of WMD. Iraq Survey Group, "Comprehensive Report of the Special Advisor of the DCI on Iraq's WMD" (September 30, 2004). Available at http://www.globalsecurity.org/wmd/library/report/2004/isg-final-report/. In his Senate testimony, the head of the Iraq Survey Group, Charles Duelfer, testified that the United States was "almost all wrong" in its intelligence on Iraqi WMD stockpiles and that the United Nations' inspectors' findings that Iraq had not reconstituted its nuclear weapons or WMD programs had been substantiated. Dana Priest and Walter Pincus, "U.S. 'Almost All Wrong' on Weapons: Report on Iraq Contradicts Bush Administration Claims," *Washington Post*, October 7, 2004, A1. For an interview with the chief weapons inspector of the United States charged with surveying Iraq for stockpiles of WMD, following the publication of a final report that Iraq had no stockpiles, see Julian Borger, "The Inspector's Report: Interview with David Kay," *Guardian* (UK), March 3, 2004, available at http://www.guardian.co.uk/Iraq/Story/0,2763,1160916,00.html.

119. Froscher characterized the Iraq case as the "poster child" for the limitations of analysis based on inadequate amounts of good data. Jon Fox, "Intelligence Analysts Have Misjudged Nuclear Threats Since Day One, Ex-CIA Official Says," *Global Security Newswire* (March 14, 2007).

120. This ambivalence is not only exhibited by states subject to inspections, but also by powerful states that are skeptical of the results of inspections when they do not confirm their preconceptions concerning a country's proliferation record, as the Iraq case demonstrates.

121. George W. Bush, "Weapons of Mass Destruction and Proliferation," National Defense University (Fort Lesley J. McNair), Washington, D.C. (February 10, 2004). Available at http://www.whitehouse.gov/news/releases/2004/02/20040211-4.html.

122. As of the time of the president's speech, NSG member states had agreed to restrict such nuclear exports to only those states with comprehensive nuclear safeguards agreements concluded with the IAEA. For an overview of the export controls adopted by the Nuclear Suppliers Group, see Arms Control Association, "Fact Sheet: The Nuclear Suppliers Group (NSG) at a Glance" (June 2004). Available at http://www.armscontrol.org/factsheets/NSG.asp.

123. Itself a source of much criticism among the countries of the southern hemisphere, an objection traditionally represented in the position of the Indian government that a status quo of haves and have-nots in nuclear weaponry is an unfair double standard and so long

as the existing nuclear-weapons states do not renounce their own arsenals, they are not entitled to require that non-weapons states renounce their option to pursue the same capability.

124. There is also the logical risk that this proposal might actually encourage states to accelerate their efforts to acquire these technologies in advance of a cut-off that might designate them as "have-nots" should President Bush's proposal be adopted.

125. The Group of Eight adopted a plan at the Sea Island Summit stating: "we agree that it would be prudent not to inaugurate new initiatives involving transfer of enrichment and reprocessing equipment and technologies to additional states." Group of Eight, "G-8 Action Plan on Nonproliferation," Sea Island Summit, Georgia (June 9, 2004). Available at http://www.g8.utoronto.ca/summit/2004seaisland/nonproliferation.html.

126. Mohamed ElBaradei, "Saving Ourselves from Self-Destruction," *New York Times*, February 12, 2004.

127. The goal of an FMCT would be to end the production of fissile material—enriched uranium and plutonium—for use in nuclear weapons through an international commitment to existing constraints on weapons-usable fissile materials. For background on the FMCT proposal, see Federation of American Scientists, "Fissile Material Cutoff Treaty (FMCT)." Available at http://www.fas.org/nuke/control/fmct/. For a discussion of the Bush administration's reservations about verification mechanisms for the FMCT as of 2004, see Matthew Bunn, "Ending Further Production: Fissile Material Cutoff Treaty," Nuclear Threat Initiative (August 11, 2004). Available at http://www.nti.org/e_research/cnwm/ending/fmct.asp.

128. ElBaradei's proposal does not limit access to the nuclear fuel cycle exclusively to states with advanced nuclear-energy programs. This is likely because he is aware of the sensitivities of the G-77 states on this issue. Further, ElBaradei's proposed five-year moratorium on new construction of enrichment or reprocessing facilities would apply to all states, not only the non-nuclear states. While this feature makes the proposal less politically viable among the nuclear-weapons states, it avoids the new asymmetry introduced by President Bush's proposal and thus is less likely to alienate the non-nuclear-weapons states. Given that Non-Proliferation priorities focus on providing incentives to the non-nuclear-weapons states, ElBaradei's proposal may well be the more advantageous.

129. ElBaradei announced at the June 2004 meeting of the IAEA's board of governors that he had appointed an international group to consider multilateral approaches to the fuel cycle. The options proposed by the experts group included fuel leasing and take-back agreements, an international system of guaranteed nuclear fuel supply through the IAEA, the conversion of existing facilities to multilateral nuclear supply sources, creation of joint ownership agreements for new facilities, and stronger multilateral arrangements to govern, in coordination with the IAEA, the expansion of nuclear energy. International Atomic Energy Agency, "Multilateral Approaches to the Nuclear Fuel Cycle: Expert Group Report submitted to the Director General of the International Atomic Energy Agency," IAEA INFCIRC/640 (February 22, 2005).

130. For a comprehensive discussion of the causes and consequences of the failure of the 2005 NPT Review Conference, with a detailed examination of the positions taken by the United States, the other nuclear-weapons states, Egypt, Iran, and the nonaligned movement, see Harald Muller, "The 2005 NPT Review Conference: Reasons and Consequences of Failure and Options for Repair," The Weapons of Mass Destruction Commission, Paper No. 31, Sweden (2005).

131. Quoted in David E. Sanger, "Month of Talks Fails to Bolster Nuclear Treaty," *New York Times*, May 28, 2005, A1. For a detailed discussion of the procedural and other pretexts used to delay the adoption of an agenda at the conference and to avoid the numerous issues tabled by middle power states, see Rebecca Johnson, "Politics and Protection: Why the 2005 NPT Review Conference Failed," *Disarmament Diplomacy* 80 (August 2005), available at http://www.acronym.org.uk/dd/dd80/80npt.htm.

132. Kimball's comments were widely reported in the wake of the conference. See, e.g., Rebecca Johnson, "Spineless NPT Conference Papers Over Cracks and Ends with a Whimper," The Acronym Institute for Disarmament Diplomacy (UK) (May 27, 2005). Available at http://www.acronym.org.uk/npt/05rep12.htm. Kimball's comments were also picked up in an op-ed written by Richard Butler, the former chief United Nations weapons inspector and Australian ambassador to the United Nations. Richard Butler, "Nuclear Hegemony Will Blow the United Nations Apart," *Sydney Morning Herald*, June 8, 2005, available at http://www.smh.com.au/news/Opinion/Nuclear-hegemony-will-blow-the-United-Nations-apart/2005/06/07/1118123836066.html.

133. Sharon Squassoni, "U.S. Nuclear Cooperation with India: Issues for Congress," Congressional Research Service Reports for Congress (July 29, 2005), 2. Available at http://www.fas.org/sgp/crs/row/RL33016.pdf.

134. For an overview of the history of US-Indian nuclear cooperation, see Fred McGoldrick, Harold Bengelsdorf, and Lawrence Scheinman, "The U.S.-India Nuclear Deal: Taking Stock," *Arms Control Today* 35, no. 8 (October 2005), available at http://www.armscontrol.org/act/2005_10/OCT-Cover.asp.

135. For a description of the agreement, see George W. Bush and Manmohan Singh, "Joint Statement between President George W. Bush and Prime Minister Manmohan Singh," White House Office of the Press Secretary (July 18, 2005), available at http://www.whitehouse.gov/news/releases/2005/07/20050718-6.html; and "U.S.-India Joint Statement," White House Office of the Press Secretary (March 2, 2006), available at http://www.whitehouse.gov/news/releases/2006/03/20060302-5.html.

136. For an overview of these criticisms, see Esther Pan, "The U.S.-India Nuclear Deal: A Backgrounder," Council on Foreign Relations (February 24, 2006), 4. Available at http://www.cfr.org/publication/9663/.

137. For instance, the American arms control expert, former Pentagon official, and executive director of the Non-Proliferation Policy Education Center argued that rather than contributing to meeting India's energy needs the deal would be "sending, or allowing others to send, fresh fuel to India—including yellowcake and lightly enriched uranium—that will free up Indian domestic sources of fuel to be solely dedicated to making many more bombs than they would otherwise have been able to make." Henry Sokolski is quoted in Pan, "The U.S.-India Nuclear Deal."

138. For instance, on this point, Henry Sokolski remarked that the agreement "pretty much signaled the end to any benefit for following the rules [of the NPT]" while Daryl G. Kimball, executive director of the Washington-based Arms Control Association remarked that "for the president to say this is good for Non-Proliferation suggests he's being badly advised." Peter Baker, "Bush Signs India Nuclear Law: Critics Say Deal to Share Civilian Nuclear Technology Could Spark Arms Race," *Washington Post*, December 19, 2006, A3.

139. A letter to US Senators released by the Center for Arms Control and Non-Proliferation offers a compelling articulation of the argument that the US-India nuclear

deal would "significantly complicate" ongoing negotiations with Iran and North Korea to limit their nuclear programs. Among the signatories of the letter are Ambassador Thomas Graham, Jr., the lead American negotiator for the indefinite extension of the NPT in 1995, former Secretary of Defense Robert McNamara, and Ambassador Rolf Ekeus, former chief weapons inspector for the UN Special Commission on Iraq. The full text of the letter is available from the Center for Arms Control and Nonproliferation: "Letter Signed by 15 Former US Government Officials, Diplomats and Current International Legislators sent to US Senators on November 15, 2006," Center for Arms Control and Nonproliferation. Available at http://www.armscontrolcenter.org/nonproliferation/india/resources/documents/20061115_india_letter.pdf.

140. For a discussion of the Bush administration's characterization of India as a "responsible" nuclear state, see Miriam Rajkumar, "A Nuclear Triumph for India," Carnegie Endowment Proliferation Analysis (July 19, 2005). Available at http://www.carnegieendowment.org/npp/publications/index.cfm?fa=view&id=17215.

141. Declassified memoranda from US President Ford's administration make plain the intended scope of American cooperation with the development of an Iranian nuclear program. See, e.g., "U.S.-Iran Nuclear Cooperation," National Security Decision Memorandum 292 (April 22, 1975). Available at http://www.fordlibrarymuseum.gov/LIBRARY/document/nsdmnssm/nsdm292a.htm. The decision to provide extensive support to the Iranian nuclear-energy program was taken in 1975 despite American suspicions that the Iranian government might pursue a clandestine nuclear-weapons program. Dafna Linzer, "Past Arguments Don't Square With Current Iran Policy," *Washington Post*, March 27, 2005, A15. Similarly, many Non-Proliferation advocates in the United States are concerned that the sacrifice of Non-Proliferation priorities to other strategic considerations in the case of Pakistan will prove disastrous should the current Pakistani regime be overthrown. On the intermittent record of US sanctions on Pakistan for its proliferation record, see Robert M. Hathaway, "Confrontation and Retreat: The US Congress and the South Asian Nuclear Tests," *Arms Control Today* 30, no. 1 (January/February 2000), available at http://www.armscontrol.org/act/2000_01-02/rhjfoo. For a discussion of US and international concerns about the security of the Pakistani nuclear arsenal in light of the political instability of the Musharraf government, see Paul Kerr and Mary Beth Nikitin, "Pakistan's Nuclear Weapons: Proliferation and Security Issues," Congressional Research Service Reports for Congress (January 14, 2008), available at http://fas.org/sgp/crs/nuke/RL34248.pdf; see also, "Musharraf Assumes Nuclear Control," *BBC*, December 14, 2007, available at http://news.bbc.co.uk/2/hi/south_asia/7144710.stm; and "Pakistan Dismisses Reports about Nuclear Arms Security Concerns," *CNN*, August 11, 2007, available at http://www.cnn.com/2007/WORLD/asiapcf/08/11/pakistan.security/index.html.

142. Robert L. Gallucci, "The Proposed US-India Nuclear Deal," Testimony of Robert L. Gallucci, Dean of the Edmund A. Walsh School of Foreign Service, Georgetown University, before the Senate Foreign Relations Committee" (April 26, 2006), 2. Available at http://www.senate.gov/~foreign/testimony/2006/GullucciTestimony060426.pdf.

143. The critique of the NPT as illegitimate, however, employs a different conception of "legitimacy" than the one employed in the legality-legitimacy debate with which this chapter began. In that earlier context, legitimacy is invoked as a normative framework outside of the law by reference to which deficiencies in the law may be corrected and the law reformed. By contrast, in the case of the Indian critique of the legitimacy of the NPT, the criterion

being referenced is a property of the law itself. Legitimacy here is conceived as a necessary property of the law of treaties—that a treaty be characterized by symmetrical obligations and reciprocity—the absence of which is the source of its illegitimacy. What I wish to emphasize here is not the precise distinction between the two usages, but simply that the word legitimacy functions differently in the two cases. I thank Jeremy Waldron for a helpful conversation concerning this distinction.

144. In presenting an argument for a strengthened Non-Proliferation compact, the director-general of the IAEA emphasized that no such arrangement would be imaginable without retaining the link between Non-Proliferation and disarmament. Mohamed ElBaradei, "Preserving the Non-Proliferation Treaty," *Disarmament Forum* 4 (2004): 3–7, here 6. Available at http://www.unidir.ch/pdf/articles/pdf-art2185.pdf.

145. For a detailed account of the negotiating history of the treaty regime, see Rebecca Johnson, "Is the NPT up to the Challenge of Proliferation." On the significance of the disarmament provisions of the treaty, the author notes that "[i]t is apparent from the negotiating history that nuclear disarmament was considered an integral part of the NPT by contracting non-nuclear weapon states parties" (12).

146. Excerpts of the 2002 Nuclear Posture Review were posted to the website of GlobalSecurity.org in March 2002. Especially relevant sections include those headed: "Adaptive Planning" (29); "The Current U.S. Nuclear Warhead Infrastructure" (30); and "Restoring Production Infrastructure." *United States Nuclear Posture Review Report* (January 2002), Reliable Security Information. Available at http://www.globalsecurity.org/wmd/library/policy/dod/npr.htm.

147. Ian Davis, "The UK Trident Vote Explained," *BASIC Notes*, March 15, 2007, available at http://www.basicint.org/pubs/Notes/BN070315.htm.

148. David Yost, "France's New Nuclear Doctrine," *International Affairs* 82, no. 4 (July 2006): 701–721.

149. See, e.g., Ambassador Eineje Onobu, "Statement to the 2002 NPT Preparatory Committee" (April 9, 2002). Available at http://www.basicint.org/nuclear/NPT/2002prepcom/nigeria.htm. The ambassador noted in his statement that "it would be a mistaken view to equate the indefinite extension of the NPT with the indefinite extension of the possession of these weapons of mass destruction by the nuclear-weapons states. Regrettably, this is the unfortunate reality as we are witnessing the evolution of new strategic and defense doctrines that place reliance on nuclear weapons for security."

150. International Court of Justice, "Legality of the Threat or Use of Nuclear Weapons," 1996 *International Court of Justice Reports*, 226, Advisory Opinion of July 8, 1996, para. 1056(2)(f).

151. The "Thirteen Practical Steps" to implement the obligations contained in Article VI and preambular paragraphs 8–12 of the NPT are contained in paragraph 15 of the 2000 NPT Review Conference Final Document. *Final Document of the 2000 Review Conference of the Parties to the Treaty on the Nonproliferation of Nuclear Weapons* (2000), para. 15.

152. For instance, Security Council Resolution 1172 (1998) refers to the Principles and Objectives adopted in the Final Document of the NPT Review Conferences of 1995 as having legal authority. United Nations Security Council Resolution 1172, UN Doc S/RES/1172 (June 6, 1998).

153. Christine Chinkin and Rabinder Singh, "UK Trident Replacement a 'Material Breach' of the NPT," Joint Opinion on the Maintenance and Possible Replacement of the

Trident Nuclear Missile System (December 19, 2005), para. 80. Available at http://www.acronym.org.uk/docs/0512/doc06.htm.

154. Vienna Convention on the Law of Treaties, May 23, 1969, 1155 UNTS 331, Article 60(2)(a). Available at http://untreaty.un.org/ilc/texts/instruments/english/conventions/1_1_1969.pdf.

155. Israel has been entirely shielded from any scrutiny of its nuclear program as a consequence of its alliance with the United States, while India and Pakistan faced symbolic sanctions, as discussed above, after the 1998 nuclear tests. Even those mild measures were quickly terminated within four years of their imposition.

156. For a description of the dismantlement of Libya's incipient nuclear program, see Andrea Koppel, "ElBaradei: Libya Nuclear Program Dismantled," *CNN*, December 29, 2003, available at http://www.cnn.com/2003/WORLD/africa/12/29/libya.nuclear/index.html.

157. The Iranian regime's nuclear policy since the revelation of its clandestine nuclear program is examined in detail in Aslı Bâli, "Standing at the Nuclear Precipice: Iran," in *At the Nuclear Precipice: Catastrophe or Transformation?* ed. David Krieger and Richard Falk (New York: Palgrave Macmillan, 2008).

158. The most recent intelligence on the Iranian nuclear program is available in the November 2007 report of the IAEA and the U.S. National Intelligence Estimate on Iran, *Iran: Nuclear Intentions and Capabilities*. United States National Intelligence Council, *National Intelligence Estimate: Iran—Nuclear Intentions and Capabilities*, (November 2007). Available at http://www.dni.gov/press_releases/20071203_release.pdf.

159. The Iranian case is the most worrisome contemporary case in which a Non-Proliferation concern might undergird an argument for intervention. Proponents of intervention in Iran to destroy their nuclear facilities frequently use the heuristic device of a "ticking time bomb" to communicate their concern that an Iranian nuclear arsenal would represent an intolerable threat to the stability of the international security order generally, and the Middle East in particular. There are several difficulties with this argument. If there were international consensus that an Iranian nuclear weapon presents a clear and present danger to international peace and security, the basis *already exists* in the UN Charter to authorize coercive intervention to address such a threat. That is the very purpose of the collective security mechanism at the heart of the Security Council. In other words, in the presence of a real ticking-time-bomb scenario, the law of self-defense and collective security already applies and no new doctrine is necessary. Absent international consensus on the presence of such an imminent threat, however, an intervention against Iran would likely be more destabilizing to international security than an Iranian nuclear weapon. Such an intervention over the objections of Security Council permanent members like China and Russia—particularly in light of the Iraq precedent—may deal a fatal blow to the hope of collective security through the council. If it were established that great powers can circumvent one another's objections on the council through unilateral action, the international security order would revert to a purely self-help anarchic system with no mechanism to build consensus or avert drawing the great powers into war with one another. Moreover, as a practical matter, few analysts believe that coercive intervention would set the Iranian program back more than a decade in light of the dispersed and underground location of Iranian facilities. There is, however, every reason to believe that following a military attack on its facilities, any Iranian government would devote considerable

resources to reconstituting a nuclear program outside of any IAEA verification protocol, as happened in Iraq following the Israeli strike on Iraq's Osiraq nuclear facility. William W. Keller and Gordon R. Mitchell, "The Osiraq Illusion," *Pittsburgh Post-Gazette*, June 7, 2006, available at http://www.post-gazette.com/pg/06158/696160-109.stm (summarizing the conclusions of a working group convened by the Ridgway Center for International Security Studies at the University of Pittsburgh to study the Osiraq precedent, which determined that the strike likely provoked, rather than deterring, the development of a nuclear-weapons program in Iraq). As a result of these and other considerations, some American defense officials and analysts have concluded that living with a nuclear Iran would be considerably less dangerous than an attack on Iran's nuclear facilities. One prominent voice in this group is the former commander of U.S. Central Command, General John Abizaid, who oversaw American military operations in Iraq from July 2003 until his retirement in March 2007. See Robert Burns, "Abizaid: World Could Abide Nuclear Iran," *Associated Press*, September 17, 2007; and "Retired General: U.S. Can Live with a Nuclear Iran," *CNN*, September 18, 2007, available at http://www.cnn.com/2007/WORLD/europe/09/18/france.iran/index.html. Prominent national security and international relations scholars have also echoed this view. See, e.g., Barry R. Posen, "We Can Live With a Nuclear Iran," *New York Times*, February 27, 2006, available at http://www.nytimes.com/2006/02/27/opinion/27posen.html. Similarly, Israeli military historian Martin van Creveld of Hebrew University has argued that a nuclear Iran would be deterrable while a strike on Iran's nuclear facilities would be of questionable use. Martin van Creveld, "The World Can Live With a Nuclear Iran," *The Forward*, September 24, 2007, available at http://www.forward.com/articles/11673/.

160. It is worth noting in this regard that IAEA Director-General Mohamed ElBaradei recently stated in an interview that he would resign from his position should Iran be attacked for arms control purposes. ElBaradei noted in particular that the current Iranian program does not represent "a current, grave and urgent danger," but that a military strike against Iran would be the worst result, destabilizing the region and leaving the IAEA unable to continue its work. "ElBaradei: I'll Resign if Iran Attacked," *Jerusalem Post*, June 21, 2008, available at http://www.jpost.com/servlet/Satellite?cid=1213794292053&pagename=JPost%2FJPArticle%2FShowFull; "Strike on Iran Could Turn Mideast into Fireball, Official Says," *CNN*, June 21, 2008, available at http://www.cnn.com/2008/WORLD/meast/06/21/iran.israel.ap/.

161. Richard Haass, Anne-Marie Slaughter, and Lee Feinstein are among the scholars that have sought to extend the international law argument for intervention to address WMD or terrorist threats, as will be discussed below.

162. The interview with Richard Haass was reported by Nicholas Lemann in "The Next World Order: The Bush Administration May Have a Brand-New Doctrine of Power," *The New Yorker*, April 1, 2002, available at http://www.newyorker.com/archive/2002/04/01/020401fa_FACT1?currentPage=4.

163. Richard Haass, "Sovereignty: Existing Rights, Evolving Responsibilities," Remarks of the School of Foreign Service and the Mortara Center for International Studies, Georgetown University, January 14, 2003. Available at http://www.state.gov/s/p/rem/2003/16648.htm.

164. Haass, *Opportunity*.

165. Lee Feinstein and Anne-Marie Slaughter, "Duty to Prevent."

166. Indeed, they note that "in comparison to the changes that are taking place in the area of intervention for the purposes of humanitarian protection, the biggest problem with the Bush preemption strategy may be that it does not go far enough."

167. Feinstein and Slaughter, "Duty to Prevent," 137–138.

168. Feinstein and Slaughter, "Duty to Prevent," 143–144.

169. Feinstein and Slaughter, "Duty to Prevent," 142.

170. Gareth Evans, "Uneasy Bedfellows: 'The Responsibility to Protect' and Feinstein-Slaughter's 'Duty to Prevent,'" American Society of International Law Conference, Washington, D.C., April 1, 2004. Available at http://www.crisisgroup.org/home/index.cfm?id=2560&l=1.

171. Though open societies frequently exhibit an opacity comparable to that of closed societies with respect to their military capabilities and doctrines.

172. While the 2006 National Security Strategy struck a somewhat less aggressive note, it reprised the emphasis on preventive action, particularly in the area of nonproliferation. This is especially clear in Section V of the 2006 NSS.

173. There is significant slippage between the language of preemption and prevention in the current American conception of counter-proliferation intervention. At base, however, the preemption of an emerging, rather than an actual threat, is the equivalent of a broader *prevention* doctrine.

174. 2007 U.S. National Intelligence Estimate on Iran, *Iran: Nuclear Intentions and Capabilities.*

175. The bipartisan initiative was made public in an article published by the *Wall Street Journal.* Henry Kissinger, George P. Schultz, William J. Perry, and Sam Nunn, "Kissinger, Shultz, Perry & Nunn Call for A World Free of Nuclear Weapons," *Wall Street Journal*, January 4, 2007. For an analysis of this initiative, see Rebecca Johnson, "The Realist Message: Abolish Nuclear Weapons," *Disarmament Diplomacy* 83 (Winter 2006), available at http://www.acronym.org.uk/dd/dd83/83rej.htm.

176. A detailed discussion of this point is beyond the scope of this chapter. Briefly, though, it is worth noting that arguments that intervention will produce a net humanitarian benefit are rendered less plausible in the presence of two additional features: (1) where the intervenor(s) is(/are) external to the region in which the target state is located; and (2) where there are significant asymmetries of power between the intervenor(s) and the target state. In the first place, if intervention is undertaken by parties external to the region, there is a serious risk of underestimating the costs associated with regional destabilization. Such costs may result from refugee flows, the consequences of long-term positioning of foreign military forces in the region, the environmental impact of the war itself, or a host of other factors. Where intervenors are not neighbors that will bear some of these regional costs domestically, there may be a bias toward excessively discounting such costs in estimating the "net humanitarian benefit." Second, where there is a significant asymmetry of power and the external intervenor may rapidly overrun the target state, there may also be a distortion in estimating the actual long-term costs of intervention due to the projected ease of the initial military victory. A variant of this consideration is another form of asymmetry that arises when an intervention is undertaken through overwhelming aerial bombardment—here the asymmetry is between the minimization of military risk to the intervenor when compared to the massive destructive force unleashed against the putative beneficiaries of the action, the citizens of the target state. There is good reason to think that the

rules of proportionality in the case of any non-defensive use of force should prohibit aerial bombardment. In particular, bombardment of so-called "dual use" facilities (such as transportation, communication, and power networks) should be barred where force is allegedly being used for humanitarian ends.

177. For the comments of IAEA Director General Mohamed ElBaradei decrying the decisions of the United States and United Kingdom to revamp their nuclear arsenals while claiming to other countries that they do not require a nuclear deterrent, see Mohamed ElBaradei, "Transcript of the Director General's Interview on Iran and DPRK" (February 19, 2007). Available at http://www.iaea.org/NewsCenter/Transcripts/2007/ft190207.html.

PART THREE

12

Legality and Legitimacy: The Environmental Challenge

Lorraine Elliott

Introduction

The global politics of the environment is characterized by plenty of legality—defined as public international law—but much dispute over the legitimacy of that legal order, its institutions, the value-systems that it represents, and its outcomes. This chapter addresses these two connected themes of legality and legitimacy in the context of what is often referred to as a crisis in global environmental governance. Globally, the environment continues to worsen (as attested, for example, by the United Nations Environment Programme's (UNEP's) regular reports on the global environmental outlook). The institutions of global environmental governance are often poorly funded, and global spending on sustainable development comes nowhere close to the kinds of money spent on more traditional forms of security. Those who are already economically and socially vulnerable are those who suffer most from environmental degradation frequently not of their own making and the richest countries outstrip their ecological footprint by up to 80%. These conditions are sufficient to raise doubts about the legitimacy of the rule systems and institutions of global environmental governance. Rather than simply present a litany of environmental problems and failures, however, this chapter delves into the character of legitimacy and its assumptions about "right to rule," consent, and compliance to do two things: to explore how environmental challenges bring some of that character into sharp focus and to present a critique of the existing legal and political order, the assumptions about legitimacy that support it, and the environmental governance outcomes that are generated by it. This chapter begins with two brief overviews: first, of the crisis of legitimacy in global environmental governance and second, of the character of legitimacy. The body of the chapter examines three key themes that are central to any assessment of legitimacy *in* global environmental governance and the legitimacy *of* global environmental governance. Those themes are legality and sovereign authority, rightful membership and the global political community, and actual political practice.

This analysis is informed by a cosmopolitan sensibility. The measure for what counts as legitimate in global environmental governance should ultimately reflect cosmopolitan principles and seek to achieve cosmopolitan outcomes which not only protect the environment but do so in a way that is also congruent with human security. Cosmopolitan principles can be understood as those that acknowledge a global community of humankind based on a structure of mutual recognition, solidarity, and equal moral worth, and that recognize global justice among peoples as well as among states as a fundamental objective of international political practice. These demands illuminate the limits of a legalistic-statist approach to legitimacy, the limits of a notion of international community that relies on states as those who alone have the legitimate "right to rule" or who alone are the subjects of that rule, and the limits of rule systems and processes that are either unable or unwilling to take seriously the demands for justice in the global politics of the environment.

The use of the term "global" in this chapter, applied to environmental change (and therefore to governance) encompasses more than global commons problems such as the atmosphere and climate system. Environmental challenges are also global because they are so widespread as to be matters of common concern and/or because their causes and consequences are not defined or hindered by local practices or territorial boundaries. As Lipschutz and Conca point out, "phenomena such as soil erosion and land degradation that are depicted as 'local'—and thus relegated to a lesser sense of urgency—are . . . linked by economic, political and social institutions of much broader, and often global, extent."[1] The local causes of deforestation, for example, are also driven by a global political economy that demands export-led growth for developing countries and that sees timber resources extracted legally and illegally from one part of the world for consumption in other parts of the world. Demand for soy products in Europe and North America is one of the drivers of land clearance in the Amazon. Biodiversity loss in Columbia or in Indonesia or in Tibet is driven (among other things) by an illicit demand for endangered wildlife or wildlife products that are smuggled globally. Unequal structures of power and interest mean that some environmental problems are made more "global" than others. As Sachs asks, did Senegalese peasants "ever pretend to have a say in Europe's energy consumption, or did the people of Amazonia ever rush to North America to protect the forests in Canada and the North-West Pacific?"[2] The "global," then, is not simply a geographic term to describe increasing environmental interdependence, as it is most often used in a reformist governance tradition. It is also a political term and one which, according to scholars such as Shiva, provides the North with a new political space in which to control the South through what is often referred to as green imperialism.[3]

The Crisis of Legitimacy in Global Environmental Governance

Claims about crisis and disturbance in the international order have generally brought a sense of urgency to investigations about legitimacy and legality. The nature of contemporary global environmental degradation is no exception. Judgments about legitimacy and legality should be made of governance and governing arrangements in all situations. Nevertheless, it is the extent of global environmental degradation, the apparent failure of political institutions to respond adequately to those challenges, and the sense that those who are most affected by environmental degradation are most alienated from the institutions of global environmental governance that bring legitimacy concerns to the fore. These concerns weave themselves through the rest of this chapter and the "snapshot" provided here is therefore a brief one.

The challenges of global environmental degradation are the product of a complicated history of imperialism, the expansion of technology, industry and capital, and modernization models of development that have relied on the exploitation of living and non-living resources in a world assumed to have few limits to the capacity either to generate ecological capital or to absorb the wastes generated by human activity. The consequence is a global environment (understood, as suggested above, to include multiple local sites) that is under threat. In 1997, UNEP reported in its first *Global Environment Outlook* that the overall state of the global environment was continuing to deteriorate.[4] This message was repeated in UNEP's second global report in which it argued that "the global system of environmental management is moving . . . much too slowly."[5] The third *Outlook*, published in 2002 just before the World Summit on Sustainable Development, was hardly any more comforting, observing that "sustainable development remains largely theoretical for the majority of the world's population."[6] The fourth *Global Environment Outlook*, released in 2007, expressed again the concern that "real change has been slow" and that "environmental degradation continues to threaten human well-being, endangering health, physical security [and] social cohesion."[7] There have been some success stories. Depletion of the ozone layer, for example, is slowly being turned around; transboundary movements of hazardous waste are slowly being reduced under the Basel Convention on the Control of Transboundary Movements of Hazardous Wastes and their Disposal (although illegal dumping is hard to track); the Long Range Transboundary Air Pollution convention has reduced the incidence of acid rain in Europe; some species are now more effectively protected under the Convention on International Trade in Endangered Species (CITES). But the more general picture is not so encouraging. The loss of global forests has barely been slowed. Habitat of vulnerable and endangered species continues to be destroyed. The 2007 assessment report from the Intergovernmental Panel on Climate Change—the most recent at time of writing—is firm in its conclusion that human activity is influencing the climate system in negative and potentially irreversible ways.[8] Air pollution continues to be a major problem for many of the world's major cities and their people as well as for much smaller communities. Water scarcity and poor water quality are serious threats for over one-fifth of the world's population, and a similar proportion of the world's people are vulnerable to the impacts of desertification and land degradation. Many of the world's fisheries are close to exhaustion. Illegal environmental activity (transnational environmental crime) now ranks on a par with the illicit market in drugs and arms. Concerns about the state of global environmental governance are driven not only by the physical challenges of environmental degradation, but also by the apparent inadequacy of governance institutions and rule systems to manage these challenges successfully. The institutional terrain is cluttered with hundreds of legal agreements, commissions, conferences, and meetings of parties, working groups, panels, programs, forums, secretariats, subsidiary and advisory bodies, councils, compacts, networks, and partnerships in the public, private, and public-private space. A reasonable counterfactual argument suggests that without all this activity, the state of the environment would be worse. However, the apparent limitations to what has been, or perhaps even can be, achieved within the current institutional architecture is increasingly presented as a question of legitimacy as much as one of efficiency, effectiveness, or even capacity. These legitimacy questions are illuminated further by the influence on environmental outcomes of the policies pursued and enacted by agencies outside the "environmental" cordon—such as the World Bank, the World Trade Organization, or the International Monetary Fund—and the "democratic deficit" that distances or excludes much of civil society (and the multiplicity of public concerns) from the institutions of environmental governance.

Legitimacy: A Character Assessment

There is no one particular approach to what constitutes legitimate behavior or practice on which international relations scholars can agree.[9] It is possible, however, to make some general observations about the character of legitimacy, even if the interpretation of what that means in practice is in dispute. Suchman defines legitimacy as a "generalised perception or assumption that the actions of an entity are desirable, proper or appropriate within some socially constructed set of norms, values, beliefs and definitions."[10] Legitimacy, then, is not fixed or given. Rather it is a product of shifting norms about who should do what and how. This understanding weaves sociological approaches that focus on popular attitudes about whether institutions and rules are accepted as justified with normative ones about whether claims to authority are well founded.[11]

Investigating the character of legitimacy in global governance (and global environmental governance) and the basis upon which "entities" are judged legitimate is an important and useful exercise. As Buchanan and Keohane point out, judgments about institutional legitimacy "shape the character of our responses to the claims [such institutions] make on us and the form that our criticisms of it take."[12] In effect, judgments about who has the right to rule have consequences for compliance or otherwise on the part of those who are assumed to be "governed" or "ruled." Hall and Biersteker suggest that "having legitimacy implies some form of normative, uncoerced consent or recognition of authority on the part of the regulated or governed."[13] Legitimacy is also a "decisive yardstick for measuring change within international society."[14] Legitimacy therefore provides a critical purchase on the nature of consent, change, and resistance in global environmental governance.

Three specific themes in the "legitimacy debate" inform this chapter. The first is the challenge to the meaning and value of legality as a proxy for legitimacy. The most orthodox of International Relations theory approaches argue that the structures and practices of global governance derive their legitimacy from international law because this is law among states, made by states, and consented to by states who are the only authoritative members of international society. This authority derives, in turn, from mutual recognition and by virtue of states' (theoretical) status as representative of their peoples. The international legal order must therefore be recognized as legitimate *and* as a source of legitimacy. Legality, in this view, is the basis for the "right to rule." It not only demands compliance (the acceptance of "being ruled") but also authorizes sanctions. This conflating of legitimacy with international legality "understood as state consent" is, as Buchanan and Keohane point out, an "increasingly discredited conception of legitimacy."[15] The limits to the "legality as legitimacy" argument are exposed by at least two features of international law. The first is a political one—despite claims about uncoerced consent, contemporary international environmental law is very much a product of and reproductive of relations of power and powerlessness. The second objection is a more empirical one. As Claire Cutler observes, "state-based . . . international law and 'public' notions of authority are being combined with or, in some cases, superseded by nonstate law, informal normative structures and 'private' economic power and authority as a new transnational legal order takes shape."[16]

Rather than focusing on the conflation of legitimacy with legality, a more useful approach (and this is the second theme in the literature) has been to focus on the nature of political community, a focus that Ian Clark suggests is "essential to any meaningful engagement with legitimacy."[17] If legitimacy is based on consent, and consent in turn is assumed to reflect the general will (rather than arising from domination by the most powerful or from rational calculations of self-interest), it is important to investigate whose will this is and whose views about legitimacy should be taken seriously. In other words (and returning to Suchman's approach introduced earlier in this chapter), whose generalized perception or assumption about legitimacy should count? This concept of the *political community* refers to "equal citizens bound together in joint rule"[18] or a community of fate which defines not just the rule-makers or even the rule-followers. Rather it suggests that "rightful membership" belongs to all those who are *affected* by the rules. It is they, therefore, who can rightfully judge legitimacy and whose claims about legitimacy must be taken into account. When it comes to the global politics of the environment, there are good reasons for resisting claims that the "community of general will" is or must be the community of states, a proposition explored in greater depth later in this chapter.

The third theme in this chapter focuses on the normative or moral dimension of legitimacy—the judgment about what is desirable, proper, or appropriate and the socially constructed norms within which such judgments are embedded. This interest in legitimacy as a normative function has been motivated by the impact of globalization and the hegemony of a neoliberal political and economic paradigm, the growing condition of global injustice, and concerns about a global democratic deficit. These normative underpinnings of legitimacy (or what counts as legitimate) are intimately connected to ideas about the centrality or otherwise of the legality principle and about the bounds of the community of "rightful membership." This is an intersubjective relationship—legality and community constitute particular social norms, and social norms constitute views about legality, authority, and community. Three components that constitute this normative assessment are explored here (recognizing that they necessarily and unavoidably overlap in practice). The first is the procedural one, which assesses whether the *processes* by which rules are made are desirable or appropriate. In particular, this procedural concern focuses on the relevance for legitimacy (and therefore for "rule-following") of the norm of democratic or participatory governance. The second component is that of the moral acceptability of the objectives and modalities that result from global decision making. The assumption that providing global public goods and regulating global public bads[19] is or should be the primary purpose of the institutions and rule systems of global governance (including global environmental governance) is itself open to challenge as a particular social construct. At a fundamental level, this returns the legitimacy debate to a central theme in the theory and practice of international relations—that of the tension between order and justice as global public goods. The third normative component addresses the problem of substantive outcomes, which is often neglected in narratives of legitimacy. This can be posed as a question or even a series of questions rather than a proposition. To what extent do or should consequences feature in the legitimacy calculus? Is there a "competence" meter for legitimacy in global governance? Should institutions or social orders be evaluated on the basis only of their proximate objectives or tasks, or must they also contribute to the broader social objectives that inhere in a particular social order? If institutions or social orders are either unable or unwilling to deliver fundamental public goods (however defined), does this necessarily render them illegitimate or, at least, vulnerable to challenges regarding their legitimacy? As I suggest below, inability might be a function of limited capacity, but unwillingness—or what some prefer to characterize as a lack of political will—is directly linked to questions of legitimacy.

Legitimacy, Legality, and Sovereign Authority

The institutional and regulatory heart of global environmental governance has developed, in the first instance, in international environmental law made by states as sovereign actors and codified in formal, legally binding treaties and in soft-law declarations, programs for action and implementation, guidelines, and statements of principles. This legal order of statist public international environmental law is presented as legitimate through the claims made for it and through the ways in which it reinforces the expectation that states have the "right to rule." States are understood as the "*sole* legitimate source of public policy."[20] International environmental law is assumed to have at its heart the purpose of "elaborating [the] general rights and obligations of States,"[21] a formulation that also goes to the issue of "rightful membership" explored later in this chapter. States have presented themselves not just as the subjects of international environmental law and therefore those whose consent is crucial to legitimacy, but also as the legitimate authoritative authors or legislators of such a legal order, as the negotiators of and parties to multilateral environmental agreements (MEAs), and as the decision-makers of final resort under the Conferences and Meetings of the Parties (COPs/MOPs) established under the various conventions and protocols that have come into legal force.[22]

The rhetoric that reinforces the legality-as-legitimacy paradigm in the global politics of the environment is one of responsible states in an international society of states. This is embedded in expectations that states will ensure that activities "within their jurisdiction or control do not cause damage to the environment of other States or areas beyond the limits of national jurisdiction" (Principle 2 of the Rio Declaration); that they will notify other states of any "natural disasters or other emergencies that are likely to produce sudden harmful effects"; that they will "provide prior and timely notification . . . to potentially affected States on activities that may have a significant adverse transboundary environmental effect"; that they will "consult with [other] States at an early stage and in good faith" (Principles 18 and 19) and that they will fulfill their responsibilities for the further development of international environmental law. In other words, public international environmental law (legality) is presented as legitimate not only because states are the legitimate bearers of rights and responsibilities but because they have demonstrated that they take those responsibilities seriously in the pursuit of a better environment.

Claims that legality is both a necessary *and* sufficient condition for the legitimacy of global environmental governance based on states as rightful legislators in the international community warrant further scrutiny. Legitimacy claims will be stronger if the empirical reality of the exercise of authority matches the theoretical claims about the legal order and the right to rule. Legitimacy will also be stronger if the fundamental organizing principle of that legal order—sovereignty—can be shown to be capable of engendering a governance regime relevant to the policy task at hand. For global environmental governance, there are doubts that either of these assumptions are so.

STATE VERSUS PRIVATE AUTHORITY

The assumption that underpins legality—that states have the legitimate right to rule (and that those who are governed take this for granted)—is increasingly contingent and challenged. In practice, states are no longer (if they ever were) the only source of authority in global environmental governance. Governance is increasingly diffuse, located in the private as well as public spaces in what Karkkainen calls a "nascent polycentric substitute for the more familiar forms of sovereign authority"[23] or what Rosenau refers to as the "criss-crossing flow of transformed authority."[24] This is not about the visibility of other actors. It is about the recognition of other forms of agency and authority . . . and legitimacy.

Private authority, or private governance, is a prominent feature of the rule systems and institutions that seek to regulate the behavior of actors and agents in pursuit of environmental protection and conservation. Global environmental governance is, in effect, being "privatized." Examples of private global environmental governance schemes include the Forest Stewardship Council, the Marine Stewardship Council, the Global Reporting Initiative, the Global Compact, and the Global Forest and Trade Network. These initiatives show non-state actors—although private actors is often now the preferred term—functioning as regulatory authorities. The Forest Stewardship Council (FSC) established by the WorldWide Fund for Nature, for example, has elaborated stringent performance-based criteria against which it certifies forest owners and forestry companies who fulfill requirements for sustainable forest management practices. While compliance is voluntary, the FSC has become an authoritative certification program and the FSC "stamp of approval" is now considered an important vehicle for marketing timber-based products. Indeed, in some cases states have themselves committed to this private certification program in their capacity as forest owners.[25] The authority of such governance systems is not simply residual of state authority. As Cashore points out, "the state's traditional sovereign decision-making authority is not granted (or ceded) by the state to these new systems . . . and is not used to enforce compliance."[26] This casts doubt on two assumptions about legitimacy: first, that it is sufficient to define legality or a global legal order in inter-state terms and, second, that states are the only actors in whom the "right to rule"—or rule-making authority—could lie.

Global environmental governance is also complicated as a project of public international law by governance structures that are initially established through state action but which come to function independently or semi-autonomously in a way that places limits on what states can or cannot do as rule-makers. The Intergovernmental Panel on Climate Change (IPCC) provides one example.[27] It was established in 1988 by the United Nations Environment Programme and the World

Meteorological Organization (the former a program under the UN Economic and Social Council and the latter an intergovernmental organization). Yet the IPCC's legitimacy arises not because it was established by states, or by agencies that were themselves established by states, but because of its scientific credibility. Its assessment reports influence public debate on climate change but also demand, in effect, that state actors respond to those reports. Governments are increasingly constrained in how they manage their own roles in the IPCC—ignoring or seeking to influence the panel's findings brings claims that states are behaving illegitimately. This applies also to a range of other scientific and technical advisory bodies and processes that are established under the auspices of MEAs but which become increasingly important as authoritative and therefore legitimate sources of knowledge and rule-systems.

Private governance schemes such as the FSC do raise the question about whether private authority translates into some broader notion of legitimacy. Hall and Biersteker argue that it does: "to have authority," they suggest, "actors must be perceived as legitimate." Or, to put it another way, legitimacy arises when private actors "obtain some form of obligation from those subject to their authority."[28] The proposition that private actors are not legitimate as global legislators because they are not states (and therefore not representative) is thin. It assumes that legitimacy is based only on particular notions of representation and that the general will that is required to give consent to actors functioning as legislators in the international political community can come only through state practices that admit domestic accountability as a fundamental function of legitimacy. Not only is this a statist approach to legitimacy, but it overlooks the fact that many states (or governments) are neither the outcome of democratic, consent-based processes nor representative of or accountable to "their" people.

THE SOVEREIGNTY PRINCIPLE

The sovereignty principle is assumed to be the benchmark for legitimacy in global governance. Not only is it the defining criteria for membership of the international community of rule-makers but the legal order that results is argued to be legitimate when it recognizes and protects sovereignty. Yet the transboundary and global dimensions of environmental change, and the demands for effective political and institutional responses, have raised questions about the ability of state actors to manage problems that cross borders or affect areas beyond national jurisdiction and the relevance (and therefore the legitimacy) of sovereignty as a fundamental organizing principle of the world order of states. As Biermann and Dingwerth suggest, the mutual dependence that characterizes ecological interdependence "undermin[es] the idea of sovereignty as enshrined in the traditional Westphalian system."[29]

Under international law, states have the sovereign right to "possess and determine freely the use of natural resources."[30] The denial of such a right is considered to be contrary to the principles and spirit of the Charter of the United Nations. Internal sovereignty is therefore understood as a form of property rights, "with all that this entails in terms of exclusive use, disposition and control."[31] The concept of permanent sovereignty over natural resources was initially associated with the demands of anti-colonialism and self-determination, expressed through a series of UN General Assembly resolutions in the 1950s and 1960s.[32] Resolution 626 (VII) of December 1952 confirmed the "right of peoples freely to use and exploit their natural wealth and resources" and determined that this right was "inherent in *their* sovereignty."[33] While this could be interpreted as national rather than state sovereignty (a meaning that is used to support indigenous rights against and within sovereign states), in most multilateral environmental agreements permanent sovereignty is expressed in terms of a state's physical rights to resources and authority rights to determine how those resources will be used.[34] This self-regarding sovereign rationality inspires concerns about a tragedy of the commons. If each state pursues its national interests (and property rights) in using its territory and resources as it will, planetary resources are drawn down, and environmental integrity is compromised not simply within the state but across borders.

Two caveats are warranted here. The first is that there is no necessarily *inherent* tension between sovereignty and environmental protection. States could well exercise their sovereign rights individually or collectively in the *interests* of the environment, to implement domestic policy that seeks to protect the environment, and to do so in a way that is more stringent than any relevant multilateral agreement that might be in force. The number and scope of MEAs that are central to global environmental governance show that cooperation among states is a regular pattern of behavior although the principle that states cannot be bound to such agreements without their participation and consent remains central. The second caveat is that sovereign rights to resources and over environmental policy are also being constrained through the development of countervailing norms such as the precautionary principle, the polluter-pays principle and the principle of intergenerational equity, which appear to place restrictions on the exercise of sovereign rights—of both the physical and authority kind.[35]

Legitimacy: Rightful Membership and the (Global) Political Community

Assessing legitimacy requires some idea of both the general and particular aspects of its character. The first addresses the question "what do we measure to assess whether something is legitimate or not" and the second addresses the question "is *this* particular rule/institution/practice legitimate according to that broader measure." The question of "*whose* beliefs about legitimacy should count" is central to this analysis.[36] Identifying the relevant political community and the grounds for rightful membership in that community can tell us not only whose *views* count but also whose interests and needs should be reflected in rule systems. If the definition of a political community is that it "rightly governs itself and determines its future,"[37] this "rightful governing" should extend to beliefs about the legitimacy of rule systems of global environmental governance and the kinds of legitimate (environmental) duties and obligations that should be expected to inhere in such a community. This is important in assessing legitimacy because, as explored further below, rule systems of global environmental governance are not just regulatory rules. They are also ethical ones that carry with them implicit value judgments about the good life, about justice, and about the nature of rights and duties and to whom these are owed.

As suggested above, conventional views about legitimacy in the international order assume that it is the community of states that can and should generate beliefs about the character of legitimacy and about whether particular rule-systems are legitimate. As a consequence, duties are owed to other states as rightful members of that international political community rather than to some kind of global community of people. There is, in this view, no global polity and therefore no global moral community because there is no form of global citizenship by which the general will can be expressed. The only caveat to this is a residual one—where individual states act in a way contrary to the norms agreed by the community of states and enshrined in international law, such as committing genocide against their own peoples or invading another country in contravention of the laws of war, then their legitimacy and rightful membership of the community of states is called into question. States might then have a legitimate responsibility to protect those whom the renegade state has failed to protect.

The challenges of environmental change render problematic this claim that the international political community is and should be only a community of states. Those whose views count about what constitutes legitimacy and about whether any particular rule or rule system is legitimate must first include those who are most *directly* affected by those rules because they are required to implement them or conform to them. In the case of global environmental governance, this can include businesses, scientific bodies, other international agencies, local authorities, and so on. The community of governance and consent must also include those who are most affected by the *impact* of rules or rule systems, and this cannot be confined to states (or extended only to other rule-implementing agents). The globalization and deterritorialization of environment degradation fractures the link between people and the state as a bounded political community and ensures that the constituency of global environmental governance is not states but people.[38] The increasingly global, shared, and common character of environmental harm creates an ecological community of fate or what Beck calls a "world risk society" that has global reach.[39]

This global political community is constituted in two ways. The first arises through the connections that come from the displacement of environmental impacts onto distant others. Environmental harm of the kind noted in the introduction is displaced transnationally and globally through the dumping or dispersal of the pollutant and waste outputs of economic activity and through the global trade in resources whose extraction has local and at times global environmental consequences. Those who will be most immediately and severely affected in environmental, social, political, and economic terms by this displacement are the poor and marginalized, particularly in developing countries. The displacement of environmental harm means that the lives of others are then "shaped and determined in near or far-off lands without their participation, agreement or consent."[40] This is in great measure a function of the ecological shadow cast primarily by industrialized countries. Estimates suggest that the world's richest people, who constitute about 20% of the world's population, consume approximately 60% of the world's resources and produce a similar proportion of the world's waste. Wolfgang Sachs calculates that the OECD (Organisation for Economic Co-operation and Development) countries exceed their ecological footprint (in effect their local resource and biological capacity) by a magnitude of about 75–85%.[41] The political (ecological) community is constituted as global also because, in the long term, the consequences of climate change, deforestation, overfishing, or excessive demands on water resources will also be felt by those who, in the short term, are able to minimize their own experience of environmental harm. Indeed, Beck goes so far as to suggest that with ecological threat, which "eliminates all the protective zones and social differentiations within and between nation-states," comes "the 'end of the Other', the end of all our carefully cultivated opportunities for distancing ourselves."[42]

Legitimacy: Procedures, Norms, and Performance

Determining whose beliefs count provides some purchase on what is considered to be "desirable, proper, or appropriate" and how such views are to be reached by those who have rightful membership in the political community. This points to three important questions foreshadowed in the introduction. First, what judgments can be made about the procedures by which the rule systems of global environmental governance are made and, particularly, whether those procedures are democratic or participatory? Second, what judgments can be made about the normative consistency and moral acceptability of the objectives and modalities of the rule systems of global environmental governance and also about the procedures by which norms shift over time? Third, what judgments can be made about the outcomes of global environmental governance?[43]

PROCEDURES

The demand that global environmental governance be democratic and participatory arises from two, at times competing, expectations. The first is that global environmental governance will be more effective and more legitimate if the views of those who are likely to be the rule-followers are taken into account by those who are the rule-makers. This emphasis on democratic efficiency inspired, for example, the inclusion in Agenda 21 of several chapters on the important role in sustainable development of what are there called the "major groups" or the "independent sector" and the pursuit of more open forms of diplomacy at inter-governmental negotiations. The second expectation is that the voices, concerns, and interests of those who are most affected by environmental degradation and who will therefore benefit or lose from rule systems should be heard or accounted for in rule-making deliberations. This reflects the legal principle *quod omnes tangit ab omnibus comprobetur*—what touches all should be agreed to by all.[44] The task is to ensure that individuals are able to pursue and enact their rights in transnational and international structures of power and that those who are most vulnerable, powerless, and marginalized are empowered to refuse, renegotiate, and contest.[45] Consent lies at the heart of these demands for democratic participation. Henry Shue argues that the responsibility "not to introduce damaging or dangerous conditions into other people's lives . . . without their fully informed consent, is ordinarily taken . . . to be universal."[46] People, he continues, "are entitled to decide for themselves whether they wish to accept additional risks."[47] This goes to the heart of a democracy deficit in global environmental governance. Those who are expected to follow the rules or who are affected by them are often excluded from decision making. Rule-making deliberations are not always transparent, and there are limited opportunities for holding institutions and rule-makers accountable for their decisions and practices.

The institutions of global environmental governance have a mixed record when it comes to addressing this democracy deficit.[48] The practice of multi-stakeholder dialogue is now a regular feature of global public debate in bodies such as the Commission on Sustainable Development or fora convened by the various MEA secretariats. Formal inter-governmental negotiations include any number of "side-events" held by stakeholder groups. Non-governmental organizations ranging from environmental organizations to industry representatives have been more extensively included in the fora of inter-governmental negotiations (as formally accredited observers for example) since the Rio Conference (UNCED) of 1992 and some now have semiformal roles in the "day-to-day" processes of global environmental governance.[49] The Governing Council of UNEP convenes a Global Civil Society Forum. The Global Environment Facility (GEF) has responded to criticism of its decision-making and membership structures from both developing countries and from NGOs to the extent that at least one study has described it as now "perhaps the most inclusive and open international organization."[50] Private governance structures such as the Forest Stewardship Council have adopted "multi-chambered" approaches to decision making, reflecting a commitment to some form of participatory democracy that also seeks to prevent the domination of proceedings by corporate interests. The concept of (prior informed) consent has been codified formally in a number of conventions, most notably the Basel Convention on the Transboundary Movement of Hazardous Waste and the 1998 Rotterdam Convention on Prior Informed Consent. Some private governance arrangements have established their own form of accountability arrangements, through practices such as the Global Compact or the Equator Principles—partly to improve their own legitimacy—although compliance has been uneven. Multilateral environmental agreements and international environmental law now call for improved access to information, education, and decision making, official websites provide copies of formal documents, reports of meetings and deliberations and NGOs offer extensive and often daily reports of key diplomatic events on the environment.

This suggests that a focus on procedural democracy—access to decision making and information—is slowly giving way to more inclusive forms of deliberation. But this is hardly yet of the form of a substantive democracy based on consent and accountability. The reliance on state agencies to confirm consent—under the processes established in the Basel and Rotterdam conventions for example—makes some practical sense.[51] It makes normative sense, however, only if those agencies act in the interests of local communities and particularly those most vulnerable within the state. Frequently they do not. Sometimes this is a function of capacity, and conventions such as the Basel agreement include expectations that developing countries will be supported in their capacity-building efforts. But consenting agencies are also often captured by interests in the pursuit of profit rather than protection. The emphasis on "stakeholders" in preference to "rights-holders" can exacerbate this because it takes little account of the relations of power and powerlessness that mute local or marginal voices in global diplomacy.[52] The institutions of global environmental governance remain more accessible and comprehensible to those non-state actors (whether NGOs or corporate sector) that are well financed and well organized. Those who are most harmed by environmental degradation—such as the poor, women, and indigenous peoples—often remain defined as objects to be acted upon, to be empowered from above or from outside, or as a source of knowledge to be appropriated and incorporated into the discourse of "the global" as and when needed. Even within the political community of states, there is a pattern of participatory inequity with the foreign and environment ministries of small and poorer states often hard-pressed to cover the range of meetings and negotiations or to match the expertise accumulated in large delegations from the world's richer countries.

Problems arise also when the interests of rule-followers (the democratic efficiency argument) and those whose lives are most vulnerable to the impact of those rules come into contest. For example, those who are the substantive rule-followers of the Kyoto Protocol to the UN Framework Convention on Climate Change will include companies in the coal industry, the timber industry, and the transport industry whose views about what are the "best" rules might run counter to the interests of those, such as poor communities in the delta region of Bangladesh, who are most affected by climate change. Those who are the substantive rule-followers of the Convention on Biological Diversity and the Cartagena Protocol on Biosafety will include pharmaceutical companies whose interests are likely to conflict with those of indigenous communities whose territorial locations hold a considerable proportion of the world's biodiversity and who themselves hold knowledge about the medicinal use of those species.

This raises the difficult question of what is required for democratization to be more substantively legitimate. Two themes are important here. The first of these is that the institutions of global environmental governance need to be more accountable, not just to states but to a global political community. Accountability requires two things—transparency and the possibility of redress. As suggested above, transparency remains uneven in the global politics of the environment despite some useful steps. The opportunity for redress is almost nonexistent except in rather circuitous and informal ways.[53] This demand for better accountability applies not only to the institutions and procedures of MEAs, or bodies such as the Commission on Sustainable Development and the United Nations Environment Programme. It applies also to non-environmental institutions such as the World Trade Organization that have taken environment concerns onto their agenda and to the various global policy networks and private arrangements of the kind described above that are increasingly part of the terrain of global environmental governance.

The second theme that connects democratization with legitimacy is the demand for a "thicker form of public dialogue [that] goes beyond the thin 'proceduralism' of liberal democracy."[54] This points, as it does in much cosmopolitan literature, to the importance of a consciously dialogic or communicative ethics that gives equal weight to the views and voices of all those in the global political community. In practice, of course, this is not an easily achievable goal. However, dialogic or communicative processes do not require *actual* participation. Rather they require a structure of mutual recognition that demands that "all who are possibly affected *could* assent as participants in rational discourses."[55]

NORMS

This points to the importance of the normative consistency and the moral acceptability of the rule systems of global environmental governance. The legitimacy of states and the international or global legal order that they inspire "has come to rest as much on the justice of their rule as on their de facto hold on power."[56] Coicaud argues that authority and the right to rule must attend "in some explicit way [to] a dynamic of the common good."[57] The norms and principles of global governance rule systems need, therefore, to reflect a commitment to environmental stewardship, global justice, and the broader concept of global rights, which must be "actively affirmed as policy goals to be seriously pursued."[58] These themes now have a prominent place in the broad map of the global politics of the environment. The 1987 report of the World Commission on Environment and Development (the Brundtland Commission) called for a commitment to "social justice within and amongst nations,"[59] and spoke of a "moral obligation to other living beings and future generations."[60] Indeed, the whole concept of sustainable development articulated in the Brundtland Report and in subsequent environmental agreements and declarations appears to acknowledge and invoke obligations across both time and space. The 1992 Rio Declaration also called for a "new and equitable global partnership" for sustainable development, one to include people as well as states.

The principles of precaution, common but differentiated responsibilities, intergenerational equity, and the common heritage of humankind seem to reflect various versions of an ethic of common endeavor and stewardship in protecting both the environment and those who are most vulnerable to environmental harm. But in each case, implementation has been uneven across governments and private-sector actors with some demonstrating real commitment and others fulfilling the role of laggards. For example, even in the narrow sense of "precaution" (that lack of full scientific certainty is no excuse for taking no action), powerful governments and corporate actors have often resisted anything other than business-as-usual, preferring to be cautious about the likely economic costs rather than precautious about the likely environmental consequences. The kinds of financial and technological resources that might be expected as forthcoming to assist poorer countries under the principle of Common But Differentiated Responsibilities (CBDR) have not materialized in any meaningful way.[61] Burden sharing is often conditional or relies on high levels of supplementarity by which high-polluting industrialized countries buy their way out of their environmental responsibilities by demanding and sometimes funding mitigation programs in poorer countries while proving reluctant to adjust their own economic practices and policies. At the same time, the neoliberal norms and principles of the global economic order that are taken for granted within bodies such as the IMF and the World Trade Organization have legitimized forms of trade, investment, comparative advantage, and a global division of labor that is often at odds with the public-good objective of environmental protection and conservation. The rule systems of global environmental governance reflect this, demanding for example that trade and environment be made compatible (by which is meant that environmental rules be made compatible with trade rules) or exhibiting a preference for market-based mechanisms and the use of pricing signals over regulatory, command-and-control, or progressive global tax regimes.

PERFORMANCE

Oran Young has suggested that the final test of an "effective governance system" is that it must "channel behavior in such a way as to eliminate or substantially ameliorate the problem that led to its creation."[62] While some commentators prefer to separate performance and effectiveness from legitimacy, the more usual approach is to embed this in the idea of "output legitimacy."[63] The extent of output legitimacy that can be based on performance and effectiveness in global environmental governance is both uneven and contested. Output legitimacy requires that institutions and rule systems deliver what is expected of them. The section on the environmental crisis earlier in this chapter, whose details need not be repeated here, showed that the substantive purposes of institutions and rule systems are fulfilled only in part. Emphasizing expectations as the key to performance and effectiveness can run the risk of tying legitimacy to subjective assessments of success, on the one hand, or overlooking the extent of weak capacity for achieving compliance on the part of some states and 'rule-followers' on the other. A more nuanced approach to effectiveness can bring a degree of "analytical subtlety" to questions about willingness and capacity that connect specifically with assessments of legitimacy although, as Christoff points out, "which specific measures of effectiveness are emphasized and *how* is itself a highly political act."[64] It is also reasonable, however, to assess performance and therefore legitimacy on some more "objective" ground in terms of the effects of rule systems and whether institutions deliver the outcomes that are constitutionally or contractually promised. All multilateral environmental agreements include a statement about the objective of the convention or protocol, sometimes in rather general terms, sometimes in more specific terms. The constitutional arrangements that establish international organizations or transnational agencies function as mission statements against which some judgment about performance can be made. Thus output legitimacy should include the "problem-solving quality of [those] laws and rules,"[65] and achievement of the "substantive purposes" of those organizations or institutions.[66]

Output legitimacy in global environmental governance is also important as a key to arrangements of trust. Institutions, rule systems, and policy practices that fulfill their substantive purposes are more likely to be trusted by those who are most affected by those rules or the environmental problems being addressed, or by those for whom environmental protection is valued as an important public good. Trust, as the UN Millennium Report noted, is inspired by practical performance.[67] The extent of trust on the part of the "rightful community" is difficult to assess. It has proved easier to identify conditions of *distrust*. Many, for example, point to the fact that developing countries and marginalized groups are often distrustful of the existing institutions of global environmental governance.[68] Others identify the need to (re)inspire public trust in the science of environmental degradation.[69] Multi-stakeholder dialogues in the CSD, for example, have been characterized as important for building trust between participants.[70] The Forest Stewardship Council's system of accrediting independent bodies is presented as a strategy to ensure that certification and verification is done in a "trustworthy way."[71] Trust building has, therefore, also been an important factor in moves toward more transparent and accountable practices in global environmental governance, thus linking output legitimacy or performance with input legitimacy or procedure.

Some Concluding Thoughts

As an ethical vocabulary, legitimacy in the global politics of the environment is bound up as much with concepts of justice and acceptability as it is with authority and legality. In a global order of environmental governance in which states are no longer the only sites of regulatory or decision-making authority, when other actors can generate consent and compliance, when the ties that bind people cross state boundaries, and when states and intergovernmental institutions are either unable or unwilling to function as "local agents of the world common good" as Hedley Bull put it,[72] then it is not clear why legitimacy should continue to be "what states make of it."[73] Legality, then, cannot function as a proxy for legitimacy. Further, the rule systems, institutions, and practices of global environmental governance can be judged legitimate only if they acknowledge both the global nature of world risk society and the obligations and duties that arise from the environmental (and other) injustices in such a risk society.

The difficult issue is whether the problems and consequences explored in this chapter render the rule systems and institutions of global environmental governance illegitimate, or merely inadequate. The latter is certainly the case. The former may simply be too hard a call to make, despite the range of problems outlined above. More is certainly required of those who are the rule-makers and who claim the right to rule if they are to have surer grounds upon which to argue that the existing system of global governance is legitimate. This is a system that demands to be "legitimised not through abstract juridical principle but constituted with reference to a new normative framework . . . to accomplish . . . objectives deemed to be for the public good,"[74] notwithstanding that the definition of the "public good" is likely to be contested and changing. Legitimacy in the context of global environmental governance points to the relevance of both specific consent (that is, consent to a specific rule) and general consent to an ongoing system of governance.[75] The expectations over time of global environmental governance demonstrate that legitimacy and consent also need to be understood as a dynamic, ongoing process in which the right to rule, and the grounds on which such rule is claimed, can and should be under constant scrutiny.

Endnotes

1. Ronnie D. Lipschutz and Ken Conca, "The Implications of Ecological Global Interdependence," in *The State and Social Power in Global Environmental Politics*, ed. Ronnie D. Lipschutz and Ken Conca (New York: Columbia University Press, 1993), 331.

2. Wolfgang Sachs, "Introduction," in *Global Ecology: A New Arena of Political Conflict*, ed. Wolfgang Sachs (London: Zed Books, 1993), xvii.

3. Vandana Shiva, "The Greening of the Global Reach" in Sachs, ed., *Global Ecology*, 154.

4. United Nations Environment Programme [henceforth UNEP], *Global Environment Outlook: Executive Summary* (Nairobi: UNEP, 1997), http://www.uneorg/unep/eia/geo1/exsum/ex2.htm; accessed March 10, 1998.

5. UNEP, *Global Environment Outlook 2000* (London: Earthscan, 1999), xxiii.

6. UNEP, *Global Environment Outlook 3* (London: Earthscan, 2002), xx.

7. UNEP, *Global Environment Outlook 4: Environment for Development* (Nairobi: UNEP, 2007), 34.

8. See G. C. Hegerl et al., "Understanding and Attributing Climate Change," in *Climate Change 2007: The Physical Basis. Contribution of Working Group I to the Fourth Assessment Report of the Intergovernmental Panel on Climate Change* (Cambridge: Cambridge University Press), 2007.

9. For more on approaches to defining legitimacy in International Relations, see Ian Clark, "Legitimacy in a Global Order," *Review of International Studies* 29, no. 1 (2003): 75–95; Friedrich Kratochwil, "On Legitimacy," *International Relations* 20, no. 3 (2006): 302–308; and Christian Reus-Smit, "International Crises of Legitimacy," *International Politics* 44, no. 1 (2007): 157–174.

10. Mark C. Suchman, "Managing Legitimacy: Strategic and Institutional Approaches," *Academy of Management Review* 20, no. 3 (1995): 571–610, here 574.

11. See, for example, Daniel Bodansky, "The Legitimacy of International Governance: A Coming Challenge for International Environmental Law," *American Journal of International Law* 93, no. 3 (1999): 596–624.

12. Allen Buchanan and Robert O. Keohane, "The Legitimacy of Global Governance Institutions," *Ethics and International Affairs* 20, no. 4 (2006): 405–437, here 406.

13. Rodney Bruce Hall, and Thomas J. Biersteker, "The Emergence of Private Authority in the International System," in *The Emergence of Private Authority in Global Governance*, ed. Rodney Bruce Hall and Thomas J. Biersteker (Cambridge: Cambridge University Press, 2002), 4–5.

14. Clark, "Legitimacy in a Global Order," 82.

15. Buchanan and Keohane, "Legitimacy of Global Governance Institutions," 406

16. A. Claire Cutler, *Private Power and Global Authority: Transnational Merchant Law in the Global Political Economy* (Cambridge: Cambridge University Press, 2003), 1.

17. Clark, "Legitimacy in a Global Order," 76.

18. Andrew Linklater, *The Transformation of Political Community* (Cambridge: Polity Press, 1998), 1.

19. Shirin Rai, "Gendering Global Governance," *International Feminist Journal of Politics* 6, no. 4 (2004): 579–601.

20. Marc A. Levy, Peter M. Haas, and Robert O. Keohane, "Institutions for the Earth: Promoting International Environmental Protection," *Environment* 34, no. 4 (1992): 12–17, 29–36, here 36 (emphasis added).

21. United Nations General Assembly, *United Nations Conference on Environment and Development*, Resolution 44/228, 85th Plenary Meeting, December 22, 1989, Part 1, 15(d).

22. This is perhaps a more extensive version of legality than that suggested by Bodansky, for whom legal legitimacy is an internal process relating to states' consent to specific rules about the procedures for and restrictions on the exercise of authority; "Legitimacy of International Governance," 608. Brunnée counters this with an interactional and therefore dynamic account of lawmaking rather than one that is crystallized only in formal consent; Jutta Brunnée, "COPing with consent: Law-Making under Multilateral Environmental Agreements," *Leiden Journal of International Law* 15, no. 1 (2002): 1–52. It is worth noting that in issue areas such as forceful intervention and the laws of war, the norms and practices

of international law—legality—can provide protection for smaller states against unhindered exercise of force by the most powerful.

23. Bradley C. Karkkainen, "Post-sovereign Environmental Governance," *Global Environmental Politics* 4, no. 1 (2004): 72–96, here 74.

24. James Rosenau, "Governance and Democracy in a Globalising World," in *Re-imagining Political Community: Studies in Cosmopolitan Democracy*, ed. Daniele Archibugi, David Held, and Martin Köhler (Cambridge: Polity Press, 1998), 35.

25. It is notable that governments are expressly prohibited from being members of the FSC or voting in decision-making although they can show their support in other ways.

26. Benjamin Cashore, "Legitimacy and the Privatization of Environmental Governance: How Non-state Market-Driven (NSMD) Governance Systems Gain Rule Making Authority," *Governance: An International Journal of Policy, Administration and Institutions* 15, no. 4 (2002): 503–529, here 504.

27. Other examples of semi-autonomous bodies relevant to global environmental governance include the International Standards Organization and the Codex Alimentarius Commission.

28. Hall and Biersteker, "Emergence of Private Authority," 204.

29. Frank Biermann and Klaus Dingwerth, "Global Environmental Change and the Nation State," *Global Environmental Politics* 4, no. 1 (2004): 1–22, here 2.

30. United Nations Commission on Sustainable Development, *Report of the Expert Group Meeting on Identification of Principles of International Law for Sustainable Development*, Geneva, September 26–28, 1995, para 53.

31. Veronica Ward, "Sovereignty and Ecosystem Management: Clash of Concepts and Boundaries?" in *The Greening of Sovereignty in World Politics*, ed. Karen Litfin (Cambridge, Mass.: MIT Press, 1998), 79.

32. See for a detailed history Nico Schrijver, *Sovereignty over Natural Resources: Balancing Rights and Duties in an Interdependent World*, (Cambridge: Cambridge University Press, 1997).

33. United Nations General Assembly, *Implications, under International Law, of the United Nations Resolutions on Permanent Sovereignty over Natural Resources, on the Occupied Palestinian and Other Arab Territories and on the Obligations of Israel Concerning Its Conduct in These Territories: Report of the Secretary-General*, A/38/265; E/1983/85, June 21, 1983, para I.3 (emphasis added).

34. See the working paper prepared by Erica-Irene A Daes, chairperson-rapporteur of the Working Group on Indigenous Populations, as an example of how the idea of permanent sovereignty over resources has been used to support indigenous claims; United Nations Commission on Human Rights, *Indigenous Peoples' Sovereignty over Natural Resources*, E/CN.4/Sub/2002/2, July 30, 2002. United Nations reports have attempted to show that the principle of sovereignty over resources is a "right of both States and peoples," United Nations General Assembly, *Implications*, para 15(b).

35. For a more detailed discussion of these countervailing norms, see Lorraine Elliott, "Cosmopolitan Environmental Harm Conventions," *Global Society* 20, no. 3 (2006): 345–363.

36. Clark, "Legitimacy," 88 (emphasis added).

37. David Held, "Cosmopolitan Democracy and the Global Order: A New Agenda," in *Perpetual Peace: Essays on Kant's Cosmopolitan Ideal*, ed. James Bohman and Matthias Lutz-Backmann (Cambridge, Mass.: MIT Press, 1997), 239.

38. Although it is beyond the scope of this chapter, the issue of rightful membership or legitimate constituency can be problematic for environmental concerns. For example, does this also include other sentient species, non-human nature, or posterity (future generations) and how can the views of such "others" about what constitutes legitimacy and what is legitimate be accounted for. For a discussion of this in the context of the development of cosmopolitan harm conventions, see Elliott, "Cosmopolitan Environmental Harm Conventions."

39. Ulrich Beck, *World Risk Society* (Cambridge: Polity Press, 1999). Risk society defines the ecological crisis in part as a product of the institutional practices associated with the technological advances of industrial modernity. As Marshall summarizes it, "the risk society becomes gripped by the hazards and potential threats unleashed by the exponentially growing productive forces in the modernisation process," Brent K. Marshall, "Globalisation, Environmental Degradation and Ulrich Beck's Risk Society," *Environmental Values* 8, no. 2 (1999): 253–275, here 264. In turn, the risks associated with modern society impel the transformation of that society.

40. Held, "Cosmopolitan Democracy," 244.

41. Wolfgang Sachs, "Fairness in a Fragile World: The Johannesburg Agenda," *Development* 45 (2002): 12–17, here14.

42. Beck, *World Risk Society*, 62.

43. Drawing on Fritz Scharpf's work, procedure and performance are sometimes referred to as the input and output forms of legitimacy (see, inter alia, Steven Bernstein, "Legitimacy in Global Environmental Governance," *Journal of International Law and International Relations* 1, no. 1–2 [2005]: 139–164, here 157 and Friedrich Kratochwil, "On Legitimacy").

44. See Nicholas Low and Brendan Gleeson, "Global Governance for Environmental Justice," *Pacifica Review* 11, no. 2 (1999): 177–193, here 189.

45. See Held, "Cosmopolitan Democracy," 246 and Onora O'Neill, cited in Charles Jones, *Global Justice: Defending Cosmopolitanism* (Oxford: Oxford University Press, 1999), 92.

46. Henry Shue, "Exporting Hazards," *Ethics* 91, no. 4 (1981): 579–606, here 588.

47. Shue, "Exporting Hazards," 593.

48. It is perhaps worth noting that bodies such as the Commission on Sustainable Development and the United Nations Environment Programme do not have "universal" membership in terms of their governing body arrangements, in part because of their derivative status under the UN system and in part because to do so is usually assumed to have unwieldy decision-making consequences. The question of universal membership for UNEP in particular has, however, been prominent in debates on the reform of international environmental governance in advance of the 2012 UN Conference on Sustainable Development. This points to the problems of trade-offs between consent (in statist terms) and efficiency.

49. The role of TRAFFIC or the hybrid-NGO IUCN in CITES is a case in point.

50. Payne and Sambat, cited in Bernstein, "Legitimacy," 150.

51. The Basel Convention on the Control of Transboundary Movements of Hazardous Wastes and their Disposal (1989) and the Rotterdam Convention on the Prior Informed Consent Procedure for certain hazardous Chemicals and Pesticides in International Trade (1998).

52. Underhill refers to this as the distinction between representation and voice; see Geoffrey R. D.Underhill, "Voice, Representation and Legitimacy: Governance and the IMF," presentation to a conference on The International Monetary Fund in Transition: Rediscovering Its Monetary role, Cape Town, May 29–30, 2006, http://www.rbwf.org/2006/Capetown/Underhill.doc.

53. For example, those who might suffer the environmental or other consequences of projects funded by the World Bank have been supported by NGOs in encouraging the bank to place more stringent controls on governments or to withdraw project or program funding.

54. Ian Barns, "Environment, Democracy and Community," *Environmental Politics* 4, no. 4 (1995): 101–133, here 103.

55. Cited in Robert J. Brulle, "Habermas and Green Political Thought: Two Roads Converging," *Environmental Politics* 11, no. 4 (2002): 1–20, here 4.

56. Richard Bellamy and Dario Castiglione, "Between Cosmopolis and Community: Three Modes of Rights and Democracy," in Archibugi, Held and Köhler, eds., *Re-imagining Political Community* (Cambridge: Polity Press, 1998), 156.

57. Jean-Marc Coicaud, *Legitimacy and Politics: A Contribution to the Study of Political Right and Political Responsibility* (Cambridge: Cambridge University Press, 2002), 33.

58. Richard Falk, "Humane Governance and the Environment: Overcoming Neo-liberalism," in *Governing for the Environment: Global Problems, Ethics and Democracy*, ed. Brendan Gleeson and Nicholas Low (Basingstoke: Palgrave Macmillan, 2001), 222.

59. World Commission on Environment and Development [henceforth, WCED], *Our Common Future* (Oxford: Oxford University Press, 1987), 47.

60. WCED, *Our Common Future*, 37.

61. The CBDR principle was articulated in Principle 7 of the Rio Declaration adopted at the 1992 United Nations Conference on Environment and Development and codified in a number of multilateral environmental agreements including the UN Framework Convention on Climate Change (UNFCCC). In brief, it reflects a political bargain between developed and developed countries by which, in the words of the Rio Declaration, "developed countries acknowledge the responsibility that they bear in the international pursuit of sustainable development in view of the pressures their societies place on the global environment and of the technologies and financial resources they command."

62. Oran Young, *International Governance: Protecting the Environment in a Stateless Society*. Ithaca, N.Y.: Cornell University, 1994, 30.

63. On the separation of performance and legitimacy, see for example Gørild Heggelund, Steinar Andresen, and Sun Ying, "Performance of the Global Environment Facility (GEF) in China: Achievements and Challenges as Seen by the Chinese," *International Environmental Agreements* 5, no. 3 (2005): 323–348. On "output legitimacy," see for example Bernstein, "Legitimacy," 157–164.

64. Peter Christoff, "Post-Kyoto? Post-Bush? Towards an Effective 'Climate Coalition of the Willing,'" *International Affairs*, 82, no. 5 (2006): 831–860, here 832–833 (emphasis in original).

65. Thomas Risse, "Transnational Governance and Legitimacy," unpublished paper, February 2004, http://web.fu-berlin.de/atasp/texte/tn_governance_benz.pdf, 7–8.

66. Robert O. Keohane, "The Contingent Legitimacy of Multilateralism," GARNET Working Paper 09/06, University of Warwick, Centre for the Study of Globalization and Regionalization, 2006, 3.

67. United Nations Secretary-General, *We the Peoples: The Role of the United Nations in the 21st Century, Executive Summary*. New York: United Nations General Assembly, 2000, http://www.un.org/millennium/sg/report/summ.htm.

68. See Adil Najam, Mihaela Papa, and Nadaa Taiyab, *Global Environmental Governance: A Reform Agenda* (Winnipeg: International Institute for Sustainable Development, 2006), 24.

69. Karin Bäckstrand, "Civil Science for Sustainability: Reframing the Role of Experts, Policy-Makers and Citizens in Environmental Governance," *Global Environmental Politics* 3, no. 4 (2003): 24–41.

70. Shona E. H. Dodds, W. Bradnee Chambers, and Norichika Kanie, *International Environmental Governance: The Question of Reform—Key Issues and Proposals* (Tokyo: UNU Institute of Advanced Studies, 2002), 26.

71. Bas Arts, "Non-state Actors in Global Environmental Governance: New Arrangements beyond the State," in *New Modes of Governance in the Global System: Exploring Publicness, Delegation and Inclusiveness*, ed. Mathias Koenig-Archibugi and Michael Zürn (Basingstoke: Palgrave Macmillan, 2006).

72. Cited in Andrew Linklater, "The Evolving Spheres of International Justice," *International Affairs* 75, no. 3 (1999): 473–482, here 478.

73. Clark, "Legitimacy," 81.

74. Duncan A. French, "The Role of the State and International Organisations in Reconciling Sustainable Development and Globalization," *International Environmental Agreements* 2, no. 2 (2002): 135–150, here 141.

75. See Bodansky, "Legitimacy of International Governance," 604.

13

Legality and Legitimacy of International Criminal Tribunals

Vesselin Popovski

Legitimacy can have a dual role toward legality—it can empower legality; but also it can challenge legality, play a corrective role, and trigger developments in international law. The recent evolution of international criminal law provides solid material for analysis of the relationship between legality and legitimacy. The establishment of international criminal tribunals have often been legally challenged, no matter whether established by victorious states after war, by the UN Security Council, or by an international treaty. The legitimacy of the international criminal tribunals also has often been questioned, particularly when their work has political implications. This chapter presents the dialectic relationship between legality and legitimacy, illustrates how in the lack of legal rules the common perceptions of humanity and legitimacy can serve as substitute, and analyzes the legality and legitimacy of the international criminal tribunals—Nuremburg, Tokyo, International Criminal Tribunal for former Yugoslavia (ICTY), International Criminal Tribunal for Rwanda (ICTR), and International Criminal Court (ICC).

Legality and Legitimacy: Dialectic Relationship

The legality-legitimacy debate stems from two competing visions of law: legal positivism and the natural-law school. Legal positivism[1] regards law as a firm set of rules to be always followed, regardless of consequences. Positivists separate law from ethics; they regard international law as strictly rule oriented and conceptually derived from domestic law. They reject policy-oriented jurisprudence and accuse the natural-law school of turning international law into a tool of political expediency.[2]

The natural-law school regards international law as a gradual result of political, legal, and ethical evolutionary processes of authoritative decisions. International law does not only adjudicate: it also plays a societal role; it is functional. It exists in a social context and is developed through international treaties and institutions.[3] Natural lawyers accuse positivists of moral ignorance; they argue that when laws are harmful (slavery laws, segregation laws) or obsolete, they should be challenged and corrected.[4] The positivists simply equate legitimacy with legality. The natural lawyers argue that legality, as a black-and-white choice, is not able to address real world situations.

Legality and legitimacy are interconnected categories, and the positivists are correct to claim that, ideally, they should match. However, in reality they often do not, and there is a need for corrective adjustments. International law is "uncertain" law, or at least less certain than domestic law, and there are situations when challenging the law is preferable to preserving the law. And this uncertainty necessitates the introduction of legitimacy—a softer category between firm law (*lex lata*) and firm politics (*lex ferenda*). The legality judgments are made by lawyers, whereas the category of legitimacy engages all people as bearers of public morality and social constructivism.

The legitimacy of an action is derived from a combination of initial consent and acceptance by affected people and states. It depends on compliance with formal legal rules and can be explicit as well as implicit. The concept of legitimacy is connected to legality, or lawfulness, to conformity to standards, which, apart from being legal, could also be ethical, religious, rational, or even subconscious. Legitimacy refers to actions, undertaken by political agents, regarded as correct, proper, and shared by many. One problem is that actions may be considered legitimate by one group and not by another. Legitimacy, in contrast with legality, is not a black-and-white category—it is highly subjective, built up by a sufficient degree of common agreement, and can change over time.

Compliance with legal rules helps to confer legitimacy, but the effect is conditioned by the perceived legitimacy of these rules in the circumstances of the time. There are controversial laws—such as gun possession in United States, or mild drug use in Holland—that are constantly challenged by a large and representative part of the population. There are examples of legality-legitimacy disconnection not only with regard to specific laws, but also with regard to entire governmental regimes—the juntas in Latin America, the communist parties in Eastern Europe, the apartheid rule in South Africa—which were constitutionally legal, but unpopular and illegitimate for the majority of people in these countries and for the international community. Such regimes could not survive long and, undermined by lack of legitimacy, they collapsed under domestic and international pressures. The revolutions and coup d'état are stricto sensu constitutional violations; however, some political parties, after coming to power through force, may nevertheless gain legitimacy and acceptance by people, particularly if they produce progressive changes. Some revolutions, such as those in Eastern Europe in 1989, were perceived as legitimate and popular, and were rapidly accepted. Others, such as the Russian Bolshevik Revolution in 1917, required decades of totalitarianism and state terror to survive. One tool of legitimating a regime, which has come to power in a legally uncertain way, is through diplomatic recognition by the international community.

The legality and legitimacy can match, but they can also differ in terms of timing and means of assessment. While legality is a view from the beginning of a process, legitimacy is a view from the end of the process. The legality of an action is usually assessed by its conformity with legal texts—constitutions, charters, courts' decisions, precedents, judges' statements, legal opinions. Legality is estimated and judged through an adjudicative process with a clear final answer in favor or against. There can be dissenting opinions, challenges, and appeals against legality judgments, but these can also be seen as part of the process of deliberation. Legitimacy needs more time to develop; it can build up or slip down, gain or lose support. Legitimacy needs to be sustained by continuous efforts and could be linked to effectiveness. It is a more result-dependent category than legality. Legitimacy can be lost, for example, if a policy, adopted in a legally perfect way, has made people's life worse or has no prospect of achievement. The sanctions against Iraq (1991–2003) were legally perfect, imposed by UN Security Council (UNSC) resolutions, but their legitimacy was questionable due to the humanitarian suffering of millions of Iraqi civilians. This example reveals the imperfection of laws—international humanitarian law protects civilians in war, but does not protect civilians from "economic warfare," like sanctions. Legitimacy could be instrumental in manifesting examples of legal gaps.

States sometimes challenge and ignore international law, driven from narrow and selfish definition of national interests. Some even withdraw from previously signed legal treaties—President Kim Chen Il (North Korea) withdrew from the Non-proliferation Treaty and ex-president George W. Bush (USA) unsigned the Rome Statute for the ICC and imposed bilateral sanctions on states-parties to the ICC. Such negative legality challenges exist in the anarchical international society, in the lack of a global parliament (legislative organ), global government (executive organ) or global court (judicial organ) to impose and consistently enforce international rules.

States can also positively challenge existing laws when there is a higher legitimate rationale—for example saving human life in emergency situations. Such actions would be legally problematic, but legitimate. When repeated, they can accumulate and produce changes in the law. International intervention in domestic affairs of sovereign states to protect human life, no matter how urgent and necessary, has been historically resisted because of the legal prohibition of use of force and the vision of sovereignty as an absolute and unlimited state power. The gap between legality and legitimacy of such intervention has gradually widened. On one hand, the legitimate concern of people at risk of massive death has moved toward the recognition of sovereignty as a responsibility,[5] but on another, international law still prevents the international community from intervening to halt genocide and other mass atrocities. After NATO intervention in Serbia over Kosovo in 1999, the International Commission on Kosovo judged the intervention to have been "illegal but legitimate," effectively demonstrating the legality–legitimacy disconnection, but remaining neutral as to whether the gap should be left open or confronted.[6] The concept of the "Responsibility to Protect" (R2P)[7] was developed after Kosovo, representing an attempt to close the gap between legality and legitimacy. However, the R2P concept can also be abused—the 2003 invasion of Iraq was not triggered by humanitarian purposes, but attempts were made to employ such terminology. The time to intervene in Iraq—if it was to protect people—was not in 2003, but in 1988 when massive crimes against humanity against the Kurdish minority in Northern Iraq were committed. The 2003 invasion in Iraq revealed how far the illegal invasion was also illegitimate. Russia, similarly, attempted to utilize R2P language when invading Georgia in August 2008.

Legitimacy can strengthen legality and add authoritative power to norms that exist in treaties and customary rules. But legitimacy can also challenge legality. The legal positivists would accept only the first role, whereas the natural-law scholars would emphasize the second. Ideally, what is legal should be legitimate and what is legitimate should be legal. However, such unity does not always exist—when laws are paralyzing, obsolete, or discriminatory, legitimacy can be the corrective force, invoked to address claims for global justice, human dignity, emergency protection, or environmental security. State sovereignty as an absolute unlimited power has been gradually challenged by legally uncertain, but legitimate, international actions. The Nuremberg and Tokyo tribunals, established after the Second World War, were manifestations of such legally innovative bodies. The legality–legitimacy gap can be progressively resolved by development of international norms and laws—the 1948 Genocide Convention and the 1949 Geneva Conventions are such instrumental developments of law, closing the legality gaps experienced by the Nuremberg and Tokyo tribunals.

The complex relationship between legality and legitimacy can be demonstrated by the historical evolution and practice of international criminal tribunals. In 1474, the first known such tribunal, in Breisach, prosecuted Peter von Hagenbach, the military officer in charge of the troops that had committed appalling acts of murder, torture, rape, and looting. Twenty-eight judges from various nationalities denied the defense of supreme command orders and sentenced von Hagenbach to death.[8] Four centuries later, Gustav Monnier proposed the establishment of a permanent international criminal court for violations of the 1864 Geneva Convention (amelioration of the condition of the wounded in armies in the field), but the idea did not receive support from any state—this was too progressive a proposal, very much ahead of its time, to challenge the legality of the existing international order.

"Martens Clause": Filling a Legality Gap

At the first Hague Peace Conference in 1899, a debate erupted between the delegates on how to treat civilians who take arms against occupiers—are they lawful or are they unlawful combatants, with the former status affording protection and the latter allowing execution on capture. The Russian delegation came up with a proposal, read at the conference by Professor von Martens: “Until a more complete code of the laws of war is issued . . . the populations and belligerents remain under the protection and empire of the principles of international law, as they result from the usages established between civilized nations, from the laws of humanity and the requirements of the public conscience.”[9]

This text is a significant precedent for how a legitimate concern with human life, belonging to unlawful combatants, produces a consideration that became central for the legality of international treaties. The Martens proposal was approved and entered into the preamble of the 1899 Hague II Convention, repeated again in the preamble of the 1907 Hague IV Convention, “Laws and Customs of War on Land,” restated in 1949 Geneva Conventions for the Protection of Victims of War and their 1977 Additional Protocols, when it was moved from the preamble and made a substantive provision of the First Protocol. It became famously known as “Martens Clause” and was repeated hundreds of times in various conventions, legal texts, and judges’ opinions,[10] immortalizing the Russian jurist who had been little known prior to 1899.

The Martens Clause is a good example of emphasizing legitimacy alongside legality—it requires that the lack of codified written law does not remove states’ obligations to humanitarianism based on common perceptions of legitimacy. It asserts that customs continue to be relevant after the adoption of legal norms. The Advisory Opinion of the International Court of Justice (ICJ) on the Legality of the Threat or Use of Nuclear Weapons (July 8, 1996) made considerable references to Martens Clause, for example, in saying that the absence of a specific treaty prohibition on the use of nuclear weapons does not in itself mean that the weapons are capable of lawful use.[11] The clause did not itself establish the illegality of nuclear weapons; rather, it made recommendations to indicate a rule of customary international law for such a prohibition. One of the judges—Koroma—in his dissent opinion challenged the whole notion of searching for specific ban on the use of weapons, stating that “the futile quest for specific legal prohibition can be attributable to an extreme form of positivism.”[12] Judge Shahabuddeen went even further and stated that the Martens Clause is not simply a reminder of the existence of other norms of international law not contained in a specific treaty, but it has a normative status in its own right and works independently of other norms. He stated that the principles of international law allow looking beyond treaty law and custom to judge states’ behavior as legitimate: “the Martens Clause provided authority for treating the principles of humanity and the dictates of public conscience as principles of international law, leaving the precise content of the standard implied by these principles of international law to be ascertained in the light of changing conditions . . . The principles would remain constant, but their practical effect would vary from time to time: they could justify a method of warfare in one age and prohibit it in another.”[13]

The Martens Clause, in this interpretation, provided an opportunity for legitimacy to complement legality, but also to put the legality to the test of the conditions of the time. Principles, constantly put to test in real life situations, need preservation, as they are the carriers of what humanity believes is proper and correct. But also the principles need to be challenged over time, too, in order to see how they endure these challenges. The legitimacy is effectively the radar that constantly puts the legal rules under the screen of what would be regarded as acceptable and legitimate. And when the disconnect between what is legal but what might be unacceptable is widened, the legality becomes the corrector. The developing concept of prosecuting individual leaders—perpetrators of aggression and crimes against humanity in international law, is a good illustration how difficult it might be, and how long time it might take, to reach a globally accepted consensus on the norms and practice of international criminal tribunals. After World War I, the Versailles Peace Conference set up a Commission on the Responsibility of the Authors of War, which recommended creating an international tribunal to prosecute war criminals, including Kaiser Wilhelm II for "supreme offence against international morality and sanctity of treaties."[14] The victorious states, however, opposed such a tribunal, regarding the prosecution of a head of state in an international court as "unprecedented in national and international law—contrary to the basic concept of national sovereignty."[15] The kaiser found refuge in the Netherlands, which refused demands for his extradition, legalistically arguing that such a "supreme offence" does not exist as a crime in Dutch law.[16] The missed opportunity to establish international tribunals for the kaiser's crimes during World War I, and also for the Turkish political and military leaders, responsible for the Armenian genocide, effectively extended the culture of impunity and failed to restrict Nazi leaders of repeating crimes against humanity later. There was an attempt to institute an international criminal court within the framework of the League of Nations: in 1937, a text of a Convention establishing such a court was drafted, but it failed to attract enough votes for ratification to enter into force before the start of World War II. When the victorious states established the Nuremberg and Tokyo military tribunals after World War II, the Martens Clause became the best way of legitimating the tribunals and countering their legality problems of introducing law and jurisdiction against the principle of *nullum crimen sine lege*.

Legality and Legitimacy of the International Military Tribunals (IMTs)

The legality of international criminal tribunals is determined by the constitutionality of their establishment and statutes, and by judgments and legal opinions when the legality was challenged by a defendant. To judge the legitimacy of a tribunal is more of a complex and historical process—one must assess fairness, independence from political pressure, achievements, timing, balance of indictments, equality of arms, impact on victims' expectations, and so on. The legality of Nuremberg and Tokyo has serious problems—for example, their establishment by the victorious states, their procedures, the applicable laws, the prosecution of only

Germans and Japanese. Nevertheless, the two tribunals were largely accepted by future generations as a legitimate way of dealing with the horrendous war crimes, genocide, and crimes against humanity, introducing individual criminal accountability for international crimes and contributing to long-term peace in Germany and Japan.[17] To recall the opening remarks at Nuremberg, US Chief Prosecutor Robert Jackson recognized that, if "these men are the first war leaders of a defeated nation to be prosecuted in the name of law, they are also the first to be given a chance to plead for their lives in the name of the law."[18] The post–Second World War tribunals can be seen as a good example of legitimacy coming into support of missing legality, and they played an important role in the subsequent development of international humanitarian law and international criminal law.

From the legality point of view, the IMTs had serious deficiencies—all prosecutors and judges were from victorious states, and all the accused from defeated states. The IMTs relied entirely on their own investigation to produce evidence and no separate investigative bodies were set up.[19] Substantive law was used selectively and "new" law was introduced where necessary. In addition to the general problems of victor's justice and jurisdiction, there were fundamental flaws in procedure—no right of appeal was provided, some defendants were tried in abstentia, and due process was sacrificed to speed up guilty sentences. The Tokyo tribunal was established by the personal executive order of US Supreme Commander General MacArthur, whose authority was extended not only to nominate the president of the tribunal and appoint the judges, but he could even "reduce or otherwise alter the sentences" (Art.17). At one point the joint defense counsel in Tokyo had to approach MacArthur to highlight the fact that the tribunal accepted "the prosecution 'evidence' in the form of newspapers reports, second-hand findings . . . but ignored all defense evidence in its verdict, saying that the evidence of the Japanese witnesses (although not those who testified for the prosecution) was unsatisfactory and unreliable."[20] All these failings left a general suspicion that the trials were aimed at revenge, rather than at justice. Indeed, many of the victors were themselves uncomfortable with these issues at the time, leading General Willoughby, the head of intelligence operations in Japan, to confide to one of the eleven judges who had sat on the Tokyo tribunal that the "trial was the worst hypocrisy in recorded history."[21]

The trial in Nuremburg was also beset by ironies: the Soviet prosecutor listed as one of the war crimes the execution of thousands of Polish officers in Katyn Forest—but later it was found that this massacre was actually perpetrated by the Soviet Army, not by the accused Nazis. The French prosecutor charged the Nazis for mistreatment of prisoners of war, but some German prisoners of war were in fact subjected to worse treatment when captured by the French. The Nazi Admiral Donitz was accused of inhumane submarine fighting—sinking of enemy merchant ships—but this charge was later dropped after one witness, a US admiral, disclosed that such tactics were regarded as normal and regularly applied by the US Navy in the Pacific, in fact, sinking a much higher number of Japanese civilian ships than the Nazis did against all the Allies. The bombing of cities was prosecuted as a war crime by countries that had themselves bombed and destroyed Dresden, Hamburg, Hiroshima, and Nagasaki. In fact, the number of German civilian casualties of Allied forces' air bombing was up to ten times higher than the number of British casualties from Nazi air bombing. The use of incendiary bombs against Japan by the US Air Force in March 1945 resulted in the deaths of over 100,000 civilians in Tokyo over two days, and a further 150,000 in other cities over the following nine days. Germany and Japan were accused of "subverting the League of Nations"—the accusation came from the United States, which had never ratified the covenant and joined the League, as well as from the Soviet Union, expelled from the League because of its invasion (or "crime against peace," to use Nuremburg's language) of Finland and Baltic states. The most serious Nazi crime against peace—the 1939 invasion of Poland—had been agreed with by the Soviet Union and signed in the Ribbentrop–Molotov Pact.

The two IMTs were exceptional measures without prior historical precedent. They will remain known as retroactive victor's justice, tainted by serious legal problems; however, no matter how imperfect they were, the alternatives—extrajudicial execution or pardon—would have been even less legitimate. The IMTs were the first to establish the principles of individual responsibility for international crimes and the accountability of officials, up to and including heads of state, in international law for both crimes of commission and crimes of omission. The prosecutions of individual war criminals helped to expunge the collective guilt (more evident in Germany than in Japan) and heal the wounds of the war. The IMTs, although legally problematic, gradually gained legitimacy and enjoyed international and domestic support. Furthermore, they made significant contributions to the development of international humanitarian law and human rights law. The defense lawyers in Nuremburg argued that international law should deal only with actions of sovereign states, not of individuals, and therefore the defendants should not be liable for international crimes. The judges rejected this defense, and in a landmark advance against the ancient state-centric tradition, they made individuals directly accountable in international law. But if individuals are bound by international law and can be prosecuted in an international court, then it must logically follow that individuals must be equally protected in international law. The recognition of individuals as subjects of international duties led to the recognition of individuals as beneficiaries of international human rights. The individualization of the accountability of the perpetrators has been paralleled with the individualization of the protection of the victims. The Nuremburg and Tokyo tribunals played a corrective role, challenging the gaps in international law, and influenced the codification of international humanitarian law, developed significantly with the adoption of the 1948 Genocide Convention and the four 1949 Geneva Conventions. The gap between legality and legitimacy has narrowed. Another attempt to establish a permanent international criminal court in 1951 failed because of the iron curtain dropping between the East and West. Accordingly, despite the rapid codification of international humanitarian law after Nuremburg and Tokyo, its implementation in international tribunals had to wait for half of a century until the establishment of the ad hoc ICTs in the 1990s.

Legality and Legitimacy of the ad hoc International Criminal Tribunals (ICTs)

The ICTY and ICTR were established by the UNSC under Chapter VII with Resolutions 808 and 827 (ICTY) and 855 (ICTR). The resolutions established the tribunals with great legal care. First, they explicitly determined that the two situations constituted threats to the peace, a necessary legal precondition to invoke Chapter VII. Second, they expressed serious and firm commitments to put an end to the crimes by taking effective measures to bring to justice the individuals responsible for them. Finally, they emphasized that the measures would be taken exclusively and specifically to address the particular circumstances in the former Yugoslavia or Rwanda, in order to avoid some states' fears of setting precedents.[22]

ISSUES OF LEGALITY

The legality of both ICTs, however, was challenged in the very first trials—*The Prosecutor v. Tadic* (ICTY) and *The Prosecutor v. Kanyabashi* (ICTR).[23] Later, other defendants, Milosevic in particular, refined these challenges and continued to question the legality of the tribunals. The main objection against the legality of the ad hoc ICTs is that they were established neither through an international treaty nor by the UN General Assembly, but as subsidiary organs of the UNSC (Art. 29) within its powers under Chapter VII to eliminate threats to the peace. Both the Trial and the Appeals chambers in the *Tadic* case defended the legality of the ICTY, although in different ways. The Trial Chamber simply rejected that it had the competence to pronounce whether the ICTY was legally established. The Appeals Chamber, by contrast, argued that the ICTs were "self-contained systems" that could respond to a challenge to their lawful constitution, otherwise they would be at the mercy of their creator—the UNSC—which would undermine their judicial character. With this view, the Appeals Chamber in *Tadic* effectively granted the ICTY the power to deliberate on the legality of its own establishment.

The defense lawyers in *The Prosecutor v. Kanyabashi* challenged the legality of ICTR using similar objections: that the tribunal was established not by the General Assembly or through a treaty; that the sovereignty of states was being violated; that the UNSC lacked competence; that the primacy of the ICTR over domestic jurisdiction violated the principle of *jus de non evocando* (the right to be prosecuted by a domestic court established by law); that the tribunal cannot be impartial and independent; and so on. These legal challenges occurred within broader debates already developing in international law regarding the constitutionality and possible judicial review of other UNSC measures, after the International

Court of Justice (ICJ) engaged in deliberating in the *Lockerbie* case whether UNSC Resolution 748 (imposing sanctions on Libya), and in a separate *Bosnia* case whether Resolution 713 (imposing an arms embargo on Bosnia-Herzegovina as part of former Yugoslavia), may have been *ultra vires* or outside the original constitutional powers of the UNSC.[24]

The legality of the establishment of the ad hoc ICTs by the UNSC has been questioned on the following grounds:

(1) The UNSC is a political organ, empowered exclusively to restore and maintain international peace. There was no precedent for creating a judicial body in the history of the United Nations, prior to 1993. If the UNSC can establish a criminal court, it can practically do anything. What if the UNSC demands to dissolve a state's constitution, dismiss an elected government, framing this as "maintenance of international peace"? Can a judicial body be independent, if it is established by (and terminated by) such a powerful political organ as UNSC?

(2) The logic of peace that drives UNSC actions may be different than the logic of criminal justice. Peace is a forward-looking goal; it may try to reconcile, rather than punish. Criminal justice is backward-looking—it is retributive and confronts rather than reconciles.[25] Article 29 of the Charter states that subsidiary organs are supposed to exercise the same functions as the UNSC; these organs normally come into being when the UNSC is overburdened and are composed by the same member-states (sanctions committees, for example). The ICTs exercise judicial functions, different in nature from the peace efforts of the UNSC.

(3) The logic of Article 41 of the charter is to impose sanctions against non-cooperative states, in order to urge them to change policies and to comply with previous resolutions. A criminal tribunal is a measure against individuals; it does not address states and urge them to make policy changes to restore peace (Chapter VII's raison d'être).

(4) The UNSC has its own legitimacy deficit—it is not a fully representative body, having only ten elected members and five non-elected. It is often seen as an anachronistic remnant of the post–Cold War status quo.

In *Tadic*, these four legal challenges were simply avoided by the Trial Chamber, declaring that it did not have the competence to deliberate on whether the UNSC may have exceeded its constitutional power under Chapter VII. In principle, however, the chamber could have argued that because the investigations, indictments, and prosecutions isolate former political and military leaders from exercising political influence, they can both deter future atrocities and play a role for peace, which is UNSC's prima facie responsibility. The Appeals Chamber in *Tadic* referred to the *Effect of Awards Case* in which the International Court of Justice ruled that the General Assembly had a precedent of legally establishing a tribunal to hear cases regulating UN staff personnel relations. However, this legality argument is somewhat weak, as the General Assembly dealt with a matter that could not have been dealt with in a domestic equivalent; in contrast, the UNSC created ICTY as an alternative to a national court's jurisdiction.

Another challenge, presented in *Tadic*—that the ICTY was not established strictly by law—is more difficult to contest. The right to be prosecuted by a tribunal established by law is unequivocally recognized as a basic human right (Art. 14, para. 1 of the ICCPR; Art. 6, para. 1 of the European Convention on HR; Art. 8, para. 1 of the American Convention on Human Rights). The Appeals Chamber's reply to this legality challenge was not very persuasive—it said that this rule can apply to domestic, but not to international tribunals in the absence of a legislature in international society. It also stated that the tribunal was grounded in the rule of law as it offered the defendants all human rights guarantees. No matter whether true in practice, such argumentation confuses two issues—whether the ICTY has been established *by law*, and whether the ICTY is operating *in accordance with the law*. Even if the second position is satisfied, one must still prove the first. The Appeals Chamber could have at least said that the ICTY was established under a legally binding instrument—the UN Charter—as a way of approaching this challenge.

There is always an inherent danger in the creation of a court through political force and through a stretch of interpretation of constitutional powers, and even more so when such a court does not simply adjudicate disputes, but is a criminal court that can sentence people to prison for life. The criminal law will only be efficacious if the body that determines criminality is viewed as legitimate. It is simply not acceptable for a tribunal to say to a defendant that s/he is subject to the decision of the UNSC, instead of to the rule of law. Also, how can a court whose existence was challenged act as a final judge of its own legality? Can a panel of judges rule that their own court is illegally established and walk themselves out of their jobs? Even if so, how will such a decision, made by an "illegal" body, have a meaningful force? Any court of law should not be taken for granted, and its existence and jurisdiction can normally be challenged. But the legality of the two ad hoc ICTs was judged by their own judges, who either referred to the powers of the UNSC—in itself a non-reviewable and non-challengeable organ—or simply repeated that they assume that they act within the law.

ISSUES OF LEGITIMACY

The ad hoc ICTs' legitimacy and independence is grounded in their statutes. Although created by a political organ—the UNSC—the tribunals have been left free to pronounce on matters of jurisdiction, competence, and procedures. The judges decide when to grant arrest warrants evaluating independently the accumulated evidence of crimes, as presented by the prosecution.[26] The ICTs have no obligations to take political advice or to report back to the UNSC or any other organ. Still, the legitimacy of the ICTs has been questioned with some controversies regarding the objectivity, impartiality, and the timing of issuing indictments. Also the reluctance of the ICTY to investigate evidence of possible war crimes committed by NATO in Kosovo in 1999 raised voices of discontent. The first cases in the ICTY (*Tadic, Erdemovic*) dealt with soldiers low in the chain of command and had little relevance to the major political motive of the tribunal, namely restoring international peace and security. The number of indictments of the ICTY has been weighted against Bosnian Serbs and not equally against criminal activities lead by Croats, Muslims, or Albanians.[27] There were very few indictments and prosecutions against Bosnian Muslims; only two senior Croat military leaders (*Blaskic, Gotovina*) were prosecuted; and only few charges were issued against Kosovo Albanians, and they ended with either very lenient sentences or acquittals.

Similarly, the ICTR prosecuted mostly Hutus, but not many crimes committed by Tutsies, even if there was enough evidence that Tutsies also committed crimes against humanity prima facie within the Tribunal's jurisdiction. The ICTR had legitimacy difficulties in addition to initial legal and technical difficulties. It faced problems of independence, impartiality, and distance from the victims, equally serious as those faced by the ICTY. The establishment of ICTR was initially strongly opposed by the Government of Rwanda due to the absence of the death penalty, and its subsequent work may have been accordingly adjusted to prevent frustration with the authorities in Kigali, raising doubts of its impartiality.

The legitimacy has been also affected by the ICTs being seen as slow and inefficient. In almost two decades since their establishment the ICTs—very well-funded bodies—have together been able to prosecute just over two hundred individuals. The time factor needs to be nuanced—"quick justice" would be the worst justice—otherwise the Stalinist criminal justice system would be most "efficient," as it incarcerated a maximum number of people in the minimum amount of time. Certainly, alternative bodies, such as the truth and reconciliation commissions, can be more efficient—they can deal with thousands of perpetrators in a non-protracted and less adversarial way. They can also reveal the genuine truth of what exactly has happened—whereas the truth in the practice of the tribunals is usually divided between one "truth," presented by the prosecution, and another "truth," presented by the defense.

Another major legitimacy problem of the ICTs is that they are located far away from the countries where the victims of crimes and survivors still reside, and these victims do not have the opportunity to see justice being done.[28] Legitimacy, in comparison with legality, is a very variable category: it depends on who regards what are the main purposes of the ICTs. If someone considers that the main purpose of the ICTs was strictly the prosecution of a limited number of war criminals in a neutral country, then the ICTs are fully legitimate. However, the ICTs were initially created by the UNSC under Chapter VII as measures to restore international peace and security, and the expectations therefore were raised too high. Normally the effectiveness of other UNSC measures to restore international peace and security—such as arms embargos or diplomatic and economic sanctions—is measured by the maximum effect in the immediate time period after their imposition.

The ICTs, by contrast, require longer time to show effective results, to establish all the criminal evidence, formulate the indictments, allow equivalent time for the defense team to prepare their arguments, for the judges to hear all the testimonies and debates in the courtroom, for parties to file appeals, for the appeals to be challenged and the judges to deliberate the final sentences, and so on. While such processes may be consistent with international criminal standards, detaining a suspect for many years may provoke human rights concerns based on delay.

The illness or death of a defendant before a verdict is reached may result in public dissatisfaction and a perceived lack of justice. Particularly when high-profile defendants die in custody, this may affect the tribunal's legitimacy. Milosevic repeatedly tried in his defense to diminish the ICTY's legality and legitimacy by politicized speeches, but ironically, it was his death that produced a severe blow to the ICTY, as both sides remained unsatisfied—the victims could not see him being pronounced as "guilty" by the judges, whereas his advocates accused the detention conditions in The Hague as contributive to his death. The Cambodian criminal tribunal is experiencing similar problems of dealing with crimes a long time after they are committed, because there are only very few and very old defendants left, whereas many others—Pol Pot included—died even before the prosecutions started. This disappoints the remaining survivors and relatives of victims, whereas the younger generation, not directly affected by the crimes, regard the prosecution of old, ailing men with dissatisfaction. Therefore, the time factor is an important element of the legitimacy of tribunals, and questions still remain as to what is a reasonable period of time for a case at the ICTs to be completed; how to achieve a more delicate balance between a fair trial for the perpetrators and remedies for the victims; how to make sure that the justice served thousands of miles away from the victims is exercising its retributive and restorative role.

COMPARING THE LEGITIMACY OF THE AD HOC ICTS WITH IMTS

As suggested earlier, if legality can be judged from the outset of a process, legitimacy is best evaluated at the end. While it might be early to give a final assessment of the legitimacy of the ad hoc ICTs as their work is still under way, it would be possible to look at their legitimacy in a comparative perspective with the IMTs in Nuremberg and Tokyo. In contrast with the IMTs, the two ad hoc ICTs are global and comprised of prosecutors and judges from many countries. This multinational composition is in itself a measure of legitimacy and independence—no single government (like the United States in the Tokyo Tribunal) can exercise political influence over the decisions of the judges who come from all parts of the world—South and North, East and West. Therefore the ad hoc ICTs do not have the legitimacy problem of victors' justice experienced by the IMTs.

The ad hoc ICTs have similar goals to their predecessors: to dispense individual justice by naming and punishing individual war criminals, to prevent acts of personal revenge, to efface the collective guilt from communities, and to deter future war crimes. The environment and conditions to implement these aims, however, were very different from the time of Nuremburg and Tokyo. Firstly, the war crimes were not committed in a declared war between states, and no victorious or defeated sides can be identified. Second, the hostilities were still continuing at the time of establishment—the ad hoc ICTs were intended to have an immediate deterrent effect on the parties in conflict. Third, at the outset neither local nor international control existed on the territory where the war criminals remained at large, requiring additional deliberations over how to arrest and bring those indicted to justice. Fourth, the mandate included the prosecution of not only the main leaders and architects of war, but a larger number of war criminals.[29] All these different circumstances made the work of the ad hoc ICTs more complicated, but also made them more acceptable.

Although the legality of the ad hoc ICTs was frequently challenged in the courtroom, the unanimous adoption of dozens of UNSC resolutions over the last two decades is indicative of widespread international support and expectations of the international community that by prosecuting individual criminals, the tribunals would help to maintain the peace and security while avoiding personal revenge and repetition of crimes. The jurisdiction of the ad hoc ICTs, in contrast with Nuremburg and Tokyo, allows defendants to appeal sentences (in fact all cases go through appeals!) with all extra-legal opportunities for them to challenge the prosecutorial evidence. The ICTs established a high threshold of proof beyond reasonable doubt, somewhat higher than in many domestic courts because of the mixture of common and civil law standards. Despite their legality and legitimacy difficulties, the ad hoc ICTs are certainly a significant step forward compared with their two predecessors in Nuremburg and Tokyo. They were created as manifestations of the world's adherence to a minimum standard, relating to the life and dignity of human beings, and preparedness to provide the machinery to enforce those standards. The national courts might have been a more effective and feasible way to achieve this enforcement, but in the absence of such courts in the former Yugoslavia and Rwanda in the 1990s, their establishment by the UNSC remained the best way forward.

In summary, the two ad hoc ICTs avoided some of the legality and legitimacy deficiencies of Nuremburg and Tokyo, but experienced their own problems, rooted in the fact that they were established by a political organ, the UNSC—in itself a questionably legitimate and representative body.[30] Some blame remains that the ICTs came in existence because the UNSC could not prevent the massacres in Croatia, Bosnia, and Rwanda as expression of post facto guilt. Also, the UNSC resolutions gave the tribunals an overly ambitious task—to maintain international peace and security, a role certainly beyond the limited capacity and authority of purely judicial bodies. It would be inappropriate to blame the ICTY, if, for example, the peace in Kosovo is still fragile—other institutions are authoritative, have capacity, and should be accountable. Without their own police force, the two ad hoc ICTs could only rely on states to arrest and extradite suspects, and this explains why some senior suspects, like Karadjic and Mladic, came before the dock so late.

Similarly to Nuremburg, the ICTs were better than any alternatives. They contributed to the individualization of the crimes and removed the stigma of collective guilt, they filled a gap in the international system in the early 1990s, when neither a permanent international criminal court was in place, nor could domestic courts have taken the task of investigation and prosecution effectively. The final judgment on the legitimacy of the ICTs will come when the remaining cases are transferred to Rwanda, Serbia, and the other independent states that emerged from the former Yugoslavia, and the two ad hoc ICTs will have fulfilled their historical missions.

Legality and Legitimacy of the International Criminal Court

In a radical development of international criminal law, in July 1998 the Rome Statute for the International Criminal Court was adopted. It entered into force four years later when the ratification documents of sixty states were presented to the UN Secretary-General.[31] The rapid acceptance of the Rome Statute demonstrates the desire of the majority of states in the world to enhance the application of, and the respect for, international humanitarian law and see the perpetrators of international crimes judicially punished.

ISSUES OF LEGALITY

The legality of the ICC is difficult to contest: unlike the ad hoc ICTs, the ICC was established as an international treaty in accordance with international law, in respect of the Vienna Convention on the Law of Treaties. Some scholars attempted to challenge the legality of the ICC by arguing that it is an organ that can reduce the UNSC's primary role in the maintenance of international peace and security.[32] As I argued in an article back in 2000, the ICC does not limit the powers of the UNSC; it rather provides the UNSC with a pre-established, permanently funded body to refer all those situations that would otherwise require establishment of ad hoc Chapter VII measures.[33] Furthermore, under Article 16 of the ICC Statute, the UNSC can compel the ICC to postpone an investigation and prosecution for a period of twelve months, if international peace is threatened. The ICC cannot and would not injure the powers of the UNSC, because even if a legal collision occurs, Article 103 of the UN Charter ensures that the obligations under the UN Charter prevail over obligations from other treaties, including the Rome Statute for ICC.

In contrast with the ad hoc ICTs, which override domestic jurisdiction, Article 17 of the ICC Statute preserves the primacy of the national courts. The ICC can only exercise jurisdiction when it demonstrates that states are unable or unwilling to genuinely investigate or prosecute. The ICC complements national courts and does not intrude into well-established legal systems, and this complementarity effectively expresses the major significance of the ICC in provoking states to develop laws and legal capacities, incorporate them, and apply the Statute's jurisdiction in the national legal systems as to avoid their citizens being tried in The Hague. This standard-setting role of the ICC might be a greater achievement than the direct application of international criminal jurisdiction against indicted persons.

Another legal challenge, raised by some opponents to the ICC, was that the ICC prosecutor is too powerful and not subject to the usual domestic constitutional restraints. The fear was that such a prosecutor could undertake proceedings against nationals of any state, including non-party states. The statute indeed provides broad discretion for the prosecutor; however, it also clearly ensures (Art. 15) that the prosecutor cannot begin an investigation without the approval of a pretrial chamber of judges, which has to confirm all charges. The decision of whether to issue an indictment or arrest warrant is always made by a collective panel of judges, not by an individual prosecutor. During the negotiations prior to the adoption of the Rome Statue, the issue of independence and guarantees against the politicization of the prosecutor was raised by the US delegation, which made crystal clear that the statute should contain all adequate safeguards against political abuse and ensuring respect for a high level of due process. As a result, the ICC's guarantees for fair trial are probably the most extensive ever employed in any civil or common law system. For example, the statute provides narrow jurisdictional opportunities, limited to only the most horrific atrocities—genocide, crimes against humanity, and war crimes. The ICC will not investigate allegations of isolated single crimes; rather, the prosecutor must prove a high threshold of evidence beyond reasonable doubt that the suspect had a specific intention and planned to commit large-scale crimes. The statute also provides one of the most extensive lists of defendant's rights.[34] Ironically, when the US administration turned its back on the ICC, a possible politicization of the prosecutor was blamed as a key problem, despite the fact that the final text of the statute incorporated absolutely all the proposals initiated by the US team before Rome. In a statement during the discussion on Resolution 1487, the European Union reiterated "its belief that the concerns expressed by the US about politically motivated prosecutions are unfounded, since those concerns have been met and sufficient safeguards against such prosecutions have been built into the Statute. Indeed, the latter contains substantive safeguards and fair trial guarantees to ensure that such a situation will never arise."[35]

ISSUES OF LEGITIMACY

The Rome Statute is still not signed and ratified by many countries, including three of the five permanent members of the UNSC. The US opposition to the ICC created perhaps the greatest ever divide in the international community over a legal regime in the recent history. This is a split not only over the practical implications of participation or nonparticipation in a treaty, or a disagreement on certain political actions, but also a deep gap in comprehension of the role and functions of international law and politics. In the initial stage of the ICC, the disputes were presented as ideological rifts, questioning fundamental concepts such as the legality of international judicial decisions, the accountability of individuals and of states, and the subjection of citizens to judgment by an international court, all of which were seen as confrontational to well-established democratic procedures and checks and balances. The US position on the ICC has de-escalated from a proactive engagement at the beginning of the negotiations on the statute, through growing hesitance and dissatisfaction during the process of drafting,[36] toward a final and total rejection. The George W. Bush administration threatened termination of economic aid, withdrawal of military assistance, and other measures against states parties to the ICC. In one of the most extraordinary steps in the history of international law, on May 6, 2002, the then–undersecretary of state, John Bolton, sent to the UN Secretary-General a letter seeking to unsign former President Clinton's signature to the ICC. William Schabas assesses that this negative turn of events came as a result of the deviation from the original US vision of the ICC, elaborated in the first draft by the International Law Commission as a mechanism triggered only by UNSC resolutions.[37] The United States would have supported a version of the ICC limited to referrals only by the UNSC as a potential prospect to have a permanent mechanism to which to refer future genocidal situations. The adoption of UNSC Resolution 1593, referring to the atrocities in Darfur, is confirmation that the United States will not oppose the ICC absolutely, and may even cooperate in some situations.

Another part of the US antagonism toward the ICC—that it may be an obstacle to the interventionism of the US military abroad—has been a bluff: only months after the ICC came into existence, the United States invaded Iraq, and never since the Vietnam wars have so many US troops been actively engaged abroad. Another irony is evident in the fact that the former Yugoslavia in 1999 was the only country in the world where foreign military engagement fell within the territorial jurisdiction of an existing international criminal court—the ICTY, with full authority to prosecute any citizen of any country for war crimes on all the territory of former Yugoslavia. This never impeded the US Air Force during the bombing campaign against Serbia over Kosovo in 1999. Another paradox: the United States strongly urged Serbia to extradite Karadjic and Mladic and cooperate with the ICTY, which Serbia eventually did, but at the same time the United States requested Serbia to ignore the neighboring tribunal in The Hague—the ICC.

The ICC regime has been antagonized further by the bilateral immunity treaties agreements (BITs) that the United States has concluded with parties to the ICC, an additional measure to prevent the surrender of US citizens to the court. These agreements originate in Article 98 of the Rome Statute, which states that "the Court may not proceed with a request for surrender, which would require the requested State to act inconsistently with its obligations under international agreements pursuant to which the consent of a sending State is required to surrender a person of that State to the Court."[38] The EU reacted to the BITs negatively:

in September 2002, it issued "General Affairs Conclusions" with annexed EU Guiding Principles,[39] stressing that the proposed BIAs were inconsistent with the ICC statute as well as with obligations arising from other international treaties. No EU member state has entered into a BIA; only Romania, an EU candidate member at that time, signed such an agreement in August 2002. However, the Romanian parliament did not ratify the agreement despite the US pressure. Two other European countries—Albania and Bosnia-Herzegovina—signed BIAs with the United States in May 2003 and later ratified them. The European Union on both occasions expressed dissatisfaction (stronger regarding Albania) and urged the two states to reconsider their choices, bearing in mind the European Union's common position on the issue. Bosnia-Herzegovina was compelled to sign the BIA after the US administration presented the agreement as a follow-up obligation from the 1995 Dayton Peace Accord. This was a misinterpretation—there is no need for a separate BIA, as the Dayton Accord in itself guards possible extradition of peacekeeping personnel to international tribunals.

The ICC has provoked a fundamental legal rift between Europe and the United States, never experienced in the last century. On December 7, 2004, the US Congress adopted the "Nethercutt Amendment" as part of the Appropriations Bill 2005, aimed to cut the economic support aid to all countries that have ratified the ICC treaty, but have not signed a BIA with the United States. This huge $2.5 billion dollar budget included funding for a wide range of programs such as counterterrorism, drug traffic combat, peace-building, truth and reconciliation commissions, and HIV education. Countries threatened under the amendment initially were Jordan, Peru, Ecuador, Venezuela, South Africa, but also some EU members such as Ireland and Cyprus. On December 10, 2004, the European Union issued a declaration regretting the act, reiterating that any BIAs should preserve the integrity of the Rome Statute, and urging the US president to make full use of the waiver powers he has under the amendment.[40] The European Union expressed particular concerns that apart from refusing significant amounts of US economic aid to vulnerable countries in Latin America, Africa, or the Middle East, this law further antagonizes relations with countries whose cooperation is necessary in the fight against terrorism. Nevertheless, George W. Bush signed the amendment into law on November 14, 2005.[41]

The legitimacy of the ICC arises from its complementarity to domestic jurisdiction; I have argued that the ICC will in fact be instrumental not so much in bringing criminals from around the world to The Hague, but rather in the opposite direction—in spreading international standards from The Hague to the rest of the world.[42] The ICC can be a solution to the "international-domestic tribunal dilemma," as the ICC only steps in when the domestic courts fail. The ICC, by its mere existence, helps domestic courts to adopt higher international standards of due process, fair trial, victim protection, independence from political pressures, and so on. The Special Court for Sierra Leone became a pioneer hybrid of such a domestic–international model. Also, a truth and reconciliation commission was established in Sierra Leone, and the synergy between the court and the commission exemplifies a solution to yet another dilemma over which is a better mechanism for transitional justice—ideally they should coexist. A recent positive sign has been Japan's ratification of the Rome Statute, channeling more funds to the ICC. Nevertheless, major countries—China, India, the United States, Indonesia, Pakistan, Russia (the most populous in the world) at the time of writing still remain outside the ICC regime.

The ICC is currently engaged mostly in Africa, with all indicted and prosecuted persons so far coming from there. However, this is not an imperialist imposition of a "Court for Africa"—it should be noted that the African countries themselves welcomed the establishment of the court most enthusiastically, and regarded it as beneficial for them, rather than as legitimacy-destructive. The first cases of the ICC were referred by states—Uganda, DR Congo—requesting the ICC to investigate and prosecute leaders and members of rebel armed forces for crimes against humanity, including the forceful recruitment of child soldiers, a new crime listed for the first time in the scope of crimes in the Rome Statute. In a controversial development, the government of Uganda, which initially referred leaders and members of the Lord Resistance Army (LRA), including Joseph Kony, later expressed willingness to withhold the indictments in order to allow these leaders an opportunity to enter into peace negotiations.

The referral of the Darfur situation by the UNSC with Resolution 1593 was the first test of the opportunity to trigger ICC jurisdiction against non-cooperative states through the UNSC, and it signaled that the United States, China, and Russia, although not states parties to the Rome Statute, may not jeopardize the ICC through their veto in the UNSC. The indictment and the arrest warrant against Omar Al-Bashir, president of Sudan, in early 2009 raised a lot of debates. The Rome Statute allows investigations and prosecutions of everyone, including current heads of state. Also, the arrest warrant was confirmed by a panel of judges coming from various countries; it was not an individual decision by an individual prosecutor, and there cannot be any problems with the legality of the action. At the Summit of the League of Arab States in Doha on March 30–31, 2009, there were statements that the ICC arrest warrant is politicized, aimed at dividing Sudan, and should be categorically rejected (not surprisingly one such statement was made by Bashar al-Assad, a possible future "candidate" himself for an arrest warrant). Certainly, it is not the arrest warrant, but exactly such statements by politicians, that politicize international criminal justice. Omar Al-Bashir does not need to travel to many capitals and defy the Court; he may rather decide to travel to only one capital—The Hague—to prove he is innocent.

On February 26, 2011, the UNSC adopted Resolution 1970, referring the situation in Libya to the ICC, and on June 27, 2011, the ICC issued an arrest warrant against Colonel Muammar Gaddafi, the second time a Head of State was indicted while still in office. On August 18, 2011, the UN High Commissioner for Human

Rights, addressing the UNSC in a closed meeting, suggested a referral of the situation in Syria to the ICC.

Problems with the legitimacy of the ICC may appear, if the UNSC, often regarded as a nonrepresentative, obsolete body with a legitimacy deficit, employs double standards and selectiveness, referring some situations but failing to refer other, similar situations, based on the narrow national interests of its permanent members, rather than the interest of international criminal justice. The legitimacy of the ICC can also suffer, if states refer cases as part of their strategies to fight rebellions, "employing" the ICC to indict rebels. The ICC should not be utilized for political purposes—neither by the UNSC members, nor by individual states. The legitimacy of the ICC could be at risk also from the Office of the Prosecutor, if it demonstrates bias, inefficiency, or poor management. Julie Flint and Alex de Waal summarized some charges against the Office and personally against the Chief Prosecutor Moreno-Ocampo[43] that need to be taken seriously.

The legitimacy of the ICC can also be in jeopardy in terms of cost-effectiveness—some may ask why time and money should be spent on an enterprise that might have little work to do. If the main role of the ICC is standard setting, why is there a need to pay huge salaries to permanent judges in a court without many cases to take on? While it is still early to evaluate the ICC's effectiveness, having a preventive deterrent organ may always preferable to paying a much higher cost later, when in the absence of such deterrence, crimes against humanity intensify. If the ICC had been established in the early 1950s (when the International Law Commission produced a first draft statute), in all likelihood many human lives could have been saved in Cambodia, Bosnia, Rwanda, Guatemala, Sudan, Libya, Syria and elsewhere.

Legality–Legitimacy Analysis

Legitimacy strengthens legality when laws meet and reflect public expectations and are largely accepted. Legality and legitimacy should be, and often are, in a harmony. However, when the existing laws are seen as paralyzing the progress, states can undertake legally uncertain actions, while claiming legitimacy and challenging the existing status of law. Such occasional challenges can result in adjustments or developments in law, therefore closing the gaps and reharmonizing legality and legitimacy. Legitimacy often supports legality, but can also challenge legality and lead to progressive developments in international law.

The two IMTs—Nuremburg and Tokyo—had serious legal deficiencies, but their alternatives would have been even less legitimate. Their legitimacy increased over the years, particularly with the acceptance of their legacy by the people of Germany and Japan. The two ad hoc ICTs—the former Yugoslavia and Rwanda—were legally unique and precedent setting, plus their judicial work followed high international standards of due process, but they were initially rejected by the people in the former Yugoslavia and Rwanda. The analysis of the legality and legitimacy of the ad hoc ICTs suggests that there are still significant questions to answer before the international criminal justice system becomes a consolidated and smooth global process. The legality of the establishment of the ICTs by the UNSC was questioned by the defendants, but refuted by the judges as falling outside of their competence. The ad hoc tribunals may leave a mixed legacy; it is as yet uncertain whether the people of the former Yugoslavia or Rwanda will appreciate the role of these tribunals in the process of peaceful reconciliation, or will regard them with continuous dissatisfaction. The legitimacy of the ICTs will also depend on the domestication of international criminal justice; as subsidiary organs of the UNSC, their life is limited and once they terminate their activities, Serbian and Rwandan courts will take over the remaining cases. A good example of the domestication of criminal justice was the setting of a war crimes court in Belgrade in 2003. When in 2007 this court prosecuted and sentenced four members of the notorious Bosnian Serb assassination group "Scorpions" for the murder of six young Bosnians, including an underage boy, near Srebrenica in July 1995, the people in Serbia accepted the sentences with relief.

Legality is usually judged by looking at strict adherence to laws; it is normally a clear black-or-white, yes-or-no judgment, exercised by people from the legal profession aware of complex criminal law issues, such as the selection of defendants, the prosecutorial strategy, and the severity of penalties. Legitimacy has various actors and sources of judgment: international NGOs, governments, local communities, groups of people, victims of crimes, their relatives, and the society as a whole—each of whom may have different measures of assessment. Therefore, legitimacy might not be a single and final judgment, but rather a mosaic of opinions—some coming from the victims in need of closure, justice, and compensation, and others from a wider society in need of reconciliation. Obviously, there needs to be a balance between the demands of the victims for harsh treatment of all perpetrators and the demands of societies for restoration of intercommunal relationships. This process is not quick, not cheap, and not easy.

The legitimacy of the ICTs suffered as a result of the courts being exploited for publicity purposes. In some high-profile cases, like Milosevic or Karadjic, inevitably the defense floor was often abused to make political speeches. The move toward transparency and visibility of the court's proceedings has been recognized, but also one has to recognize the danger of distorting and politicizing the judicial process. Too much media publicity surrounding a criminal case may jeopardize its fairness.

Purpose of Peace vs. Purpose of Justice

The ICTs, although created by the UNSC as measures to "maintain international peace and security," may not play this role well. There are more powerful military, political, economic, and other players to execute the purposes of peace.

One should not blame the ICTY—a purely legal body—if, for example, the peace in Kosovo is in jeopardy. Or blame the ICC, if the peace in Uganda, Sudan, or Libya, is in jeopardy. Peace is not the task of Moreno-Ocampo, it is the task of mediators, negotiators, peacekeepers, peacemakers and all the rest of the peace machinery of the UN and regional organizations. Similarly, it is a mistake to ask peacemakers to appear in criminal courts and give testimony, as done with Lord Owen and Cyrus Vance in the ICTY. The purpose of peace should not be confused with the purpose of justice, and also the agents of peace should be clearly differentiated from the agents of justice.

The formula "peace through justice" is a nice slogan, but it has to be understood within its own natural limits. Also the notion of justice is much broader than the mere prosecution of war crimes. Effective criminal justice should be complemented by social justice, and this demands a larger societal effort. One example is Iraq: the Iraqi Special Court, a domestic court with some legal assistance offered by the United States, but which the UN refused to assist, left a shameful record of disregard of due process and of abuse of the judiciary for political purposes.[44] When approaching the legality and legitimacy of criminal tribunals, one needs to remember that mere compliance with law does not automatically make criminal justice effective—as there are gaps between law and justice. States may passively comply with the rule of law, but do little to satisfy the social, economic, political, and other indicators of justice.

Regarding the ICC, its legality does not raise doubts, but the assessment of legitimacy needs still to be made. Its legitimacy may well be harmed by its relationship with the UNSC, as the latter is being seen as less and less legitimate due to the lack of UN reform. By contrast, its closer relations with NGOs and national courts may enhance its legitimacy. It would be challenging to see whether the ICC may lose legitimacy by indicting political actors if later it was to waive these indictments to allow the accused to participate in peace negotiations. It is important to segregate the purpose of peace from the purpose of justice and not demand the same organ to pursue both purposes.

I would also argue that the indictments as such do not jeopardize peace. Quite the opposite—they may coerce indicted leaders to beg for amnesty and negotiate. When Pinochet was arrested, some argued that this may send the wrong signal and make dictators less likely to relinquish their power to maintain their immunity against threats of prosecution. The same was said about Milosevic and Charles Taylor. However, the truth is that dictators and warlords cannot hold onto power forever. Once they face the reality of prosecution, their choice is either to hide forever (becoming prisoners in their bunkers) or to beg for amnesty.

The skeptical voices that suggest prosecutions will result in re-escalations of conflict and jeopardize the peace have often been proven wrong. Indictments of leaders, among other factors, have pushed them out of power, or made them eager to negotiate and beg for amnesty. International criminal justice has never been a straightforward and easy process, and in fact it does not need to be.

Faced with genocide and crimes against humanity, the world does not need to reach a harmony and consensus. Let the process of justice be confrontational, accusatory, and divisive; in contrast and in balance with the process of peace, that can reconcile, harmonize and pacify—both processes are equally necessary and valuable, but they should be kept separate, pursued in parallel by different actors.

I would even argue that if the peace in a country has to be temporarily sacrificed to bring justice for the victims, so be it! All 120 states that met in Rome in July 1998 and signed the Rome Statute for the ICC were aware that such a situation might arise, and they decided that preventing future atrocity crimes by prosecuting recent crimes is a worthy exercise, even if this may create discomfort and tensions.

Such discomfort and tensions are not as dangerous as impunity for past crimes might be. When Pinochet, Milosevic, or Charles Taylor were indicted, the same panicking voices were heard, that this may bring chaos. But there is no evidence at all—if we ask today people in Santiago, Belgrade, or Monrovia whether they still regret the arrests of Pinochet, Milosevic, or Charles Taylor, we can find the answer.

The same voices shouted when the indictment of Sudanese President Al-Bashir was issued, warning that this may jeopardize the peace. This has not been the case; on the contrary, the United Nations reported that "Sudan has been working to speed up the deployment of the UN-AU force," and that the government's attitude has been one of "working with us and helping us."[45] Al-Bashir indeed expelled a dozen nonpolitical, humanitarian NGOs as a reaction to the arrest warrant, but this could only show his true face.

Conclusion

There will be tribunals in need of future legality-legitimacy assessment—at the time of writing, the Extraordinary Chambers in the Courts of Cambodia advances with the prosecution of Khmer Rouge leaders, and so does the work of the Special Tribunal for Lebanon into the assassination of the former Lebanese prime minister Rafik Hariri, which has recently issued indictments. The legality-legitimacy debate will continue to be a central element of assessment for various international legal regimes, and international criminal law in particular.

Endnotes

1. A. Rubin, *Ethics and Authority in International Law* (Cambridge: Cambridge University Press, 1997).

2. Sir Gerald Fitzmaurice, "Vae Victis or Woe to Negotiators! Your Treaty or Our Interpretation of It," *American Journal of International Law* 65 (1971).

3. Rosalyn Higgins, *The Development of International Law through the Political Organs of the United Nations* (London: Oxford University Press, 1963); and *Problems and Process: International Law and How We Use It* (London: Oxford University Press, 1994).

4. M. S. McDougal and W. M. Reisman, "The Changing Structure of International Law," *Columbia Law Review* 65 (1965).

5. Francis Deng et al., *Sovereignty as Responsibility: Conflict Management in Africa*" (Washington, D.C.: Brookings Institutions 1996).

6. *The Kosovo Report: Conflict, International Response, Lessons Learned* (The Independent International Commission on Kosovo) (Oxford: Oxford University Press, 2000).

7. "The Responsibility to Protect," Report of the International Commission on Intervention and State Sovereignty (2001). For a recent assessment, see Gareth Evans, *The Responsibility to Protect: Ending Mass Atrocity Crimes Once and for All* (Washington, D.C.: Brookings Institution Press, 2008).

8. More details on the Breisach trial are available in Georg Schwarzengerger, *International Law as Applied by International Courts and Tribunals: The Law of Armed Conflict*, vol. 2 (London: Stevens & Sons, 1968), 462–464.

9. Preamble "Convention (II) with Respect to the Laws and Customs of War on Land," The Hague, July 29, 1899.

10. For full list of these and analysis, see Theodor Meron, "The Martens Clause, Principles of Humanity, and Dictates of Public Conscience," *American Journal of International Law* 94, no. 1 (January 2000): 78–89. Also R. Ticehurst, "The Advisory Opinion of the International Court of Justice on the Legality of the Threat or Use of Nuclear Weapons," *War Studies Journal* 2, no. 1 (Autumn 1996): 107–118.

11. International Court of Justice, "Legality of the Threat or Use of Nuclear Weapons," July 8, 1996, Advisory Opinion, 1996 ICJ Report, 226-406, available at http://www.icj-cij.org/docket/files/95/7495.pdf.

12. Ibid., p. 236.

13. Ibid., p. 243.

14. Article. 227, Part VII "Penalties," The Treaty of Peace between the Allied and Associated Powers and Germany (Signed at Versailles, June 28, 1919).

15. Lyal Sunga, *Individual Responsibility in International Law for Serious Human Rights Violations* (Dordrecht: Martinus Nijhoff, 1992), 23.

16. It is ironic that the Netherlands today is the country where the prosecution of former heads of states is most common, with Radovan Karadjic following Slobodan Milosevic in the dock of the ICTY and Charles Taylor under prosecution by the Special Court for Sierra Leone. But back in 1919, the Netherlands protected the German ex-kaiser, using the legality principle that no one can be prosecuted for crimes that have not been written in law at the time of committing these crimes (*nullum crimen sine lege*).

17. Telford Taylor, *The Anatomy of Nuremberg Trials: A Personal Memoir* (New York: Knopf,1992); George Ginsburgs and V. Kudriavtsev (eds.), *Nuremberg Trial and International Law* (Dordrecht: Martinus Nijhoff, 1990).

18. See Joe Heydecker and Johannes Leeb, *The Nuremberg Trial: A History of Nazi Germany as Revealed through the Testimony at Nuremberg*, (London: Heinemann, 1962).

19. This criticism was raised by Mohamed Cherif Bassiouni, "Former Yugoslavia: Investigating Violations of International Humanitarian Law and Establishing an International Court of Justice," *Security Dialogue* 25(December 4, 1994): 409–425.

20. From Richard Minear, *Victors' Justice: The Tokyo War Crimes Trial* (Princeton, N.J.: Princeton University Press, 1971), 96–97.

21. John W. Dower, *Embracing Defeat: Japan in the wake of World War II*, (New York: W. W. Norton & Company, 1999) 451.

22. Virginia Morris and Michael Scharf, *An Insider's Guide to the International Criminal Tribunal for the Former Yugoslavia: A Documentary History and Analysis* (Hotei Publishing, 1995), Michael Scharf, *Balkan Justice* (Durham, N.C.: Carolina Academic Press, 1997) Rachel Kerr, *The International Criminal Tribunal for the Former Yugoslavia: An Exercise in Law, Politics and Diplomacy* (Oxford: Oxford University Press, 2004); William Schabas, *The UN International Criminal Tribunals: The Former Yugoslavia, Rwanda and Sierra Leone* (Cambridge: Cambridge University Press, 2006).

23. All documents from the tribunals' cases are available on the websites: www.icty.org and www.ictr.org.

24. See Jose Alvarez, "Judging the Security Council," *American Journal of International Law* 90, no. 1 (1996).

25. This shortcoming has been recognized (though a bit late), and the ICTs have developed outreach programs to fill this gap and make sure that justice is not only done, but is also seen to be done. Alternative forums for truth and reconciliation, such as the Gacaca in Rwanda, were proposed as a better way to deal with the thousands of perpetrators, to push for confessions, and to satisfy victims' rights to discover the truth and receive compensation.

26. There were some speculations regarding the timing of Milosevic's indictment being dictated by Western powers to happen during the NATO bombing of Serbia in 1999 over Kosovo; however, these speculations were never confirmed. Rather the opposite—observers in several of the Western capitals expressed discomfort and surprise from the indictment, regarding this as a barrier for possible negotiations to end the bombing. Louise Arbour, at the time ICTY chief prosecutor, always stressed that the indictment had nothing to do with the NATO bombing of Yugoslavia in 1999.

27. See Aleksandar Fatic, "The Need for a Politically Balanced Works of The Hague International War Crimes Tribunal," *Review of International Affairs* 47 (May 1996): 8–11. Fatic recently told me that there is a paradoxical unity among Serbs, Croats, and Bosnian Muslims against ICTY, with all three groups similarly critical against the ICTY for its distant work, mostly irrelevant to the victims of crimes.

28. See Ramesh Thakur, "Conclusions," in *From Sovereign Impunity to International Accountability: The Search for Justice in a World of States*, ed. Ramesh Thakur and Peter Malcontent (Tokyo: UNU Press, 2004).

29. Bassiouni, "Former Yugoslavia," 416.

30. The chapters by Ramesh Thakur and Christine Chinkin in this volume address this.

31. See further William Schabas, *An Introduction to the International Criminal Court* (Cambridge: Cambridge University Press, 2011); Leila Nadya Sadat, *The International Criminal Court and the Transformation of International Law: Justice for the New Millenium* (Ardsley, N.Y.: Transnational Publishers, 2002).

32. Ruth Wedgwood, "The International Criminal Court: An American View," *European Journal of International Law* 10, no. 2 (1999): 93–107 and "Fiddling in Rome," *Foreign Affairs* 77, no. 6 (November–December 1998): 20–24; John Bolton, "The Global Prosecutors: Hunting War Criminals in the Name of Utopia," *Foreign Affairs* 78, no.1 (January–February 1999): 157–164 and "Why an International Criminal Court Won't Work," *Wall Street Journal*, March 30, 1998.

33. Vesselin Popovski, "ICC: A Necessary Step Towards Global Justice," *Security Dialogue* 31, no. 4 (December 2000): 405–419.

34. These rights include: presumption of innocence (Art. 66); right to counsel (67.1.b & d); right to disclose exculpatory evidence (67.2); right to compulsory process to obtain witnesses and to cross-examine them (67.1.e); privilege against self-incrimination (54.1.a, 67.1.g); right to remain silent (67.1.g); exclusion of illegally obtained evidence (69.7); right to be tried without undue delay (67.1.c); prohibition against ex–post facto crimes (22); protection from double jeopardy (20); right to a written statement of charges (61.3); freedom from arrest and search without warrant (57 bis. 3, 58); right to be present at trial (63, 67.1.d).

35. Statement by H.E. Ambassador Adamantios Vassilakis, Permanent Representative of Greece to the UN on behalf of the European Union, New York, June 12, 2003 before the SC Meeting 4772, UN Document S/PV.4772, June 12, 2003, p. 9. Available at www.amicc.org/docs/EUGreece1422Stmt12June03.pdf (accessed 25 August 2011).

36. See David J. Scheffer "The United States and the International Criminal Court," *American Journal of International Law* 93, no. 1 (January 1999): 12.

37. William Schabas, "US Hostility to the International Criminal Court: It's All About the Security Council," *European Journal of International Law* 15, no. 4 (2004): 701–720.

38. Rome Statute of the International Criminal Court on http://untreaty.un.org/cod/icc/statute/romefra.htm (access day 25 August 2011).

39. Draft Council conclusions on the International Criminal Court http://www.amicc.org/docs/EC9_30_02.pdf (access day 25 August 2011).

40. Council of the EU, 15864/1/04 REV 1 (Presse 353) P 136/04.

41. Limitation on economic support fund assistance for certain foreign governments that are parties to the International Criminal Court, http://www.amicc.org/docs/Nethercutt%202006.pdf (access day 25 August 2011).

42. Popovski, "ICC: A Necessary Step."

43. Julie Flint and Alex de Waal, "Case Closed: A Prosecutor without Borders," *World Affairs: Journal of Ideas and Debate* (Heldref Publications), (Spring 2009).

44. "The Iraqi Special Court: Corruption of Justice," report by Ramsey Clark and Curtis Doebbler at http://www.justiceonline.org/site/PageServer?pagename=IST.

45. "Sudan Cooperating," *Daily Yomiuri*, August 23, 2008, p. 7.

14

Legality and Legitimacy of Exporting Democracy

Daniele Archibugi and Mariano Croce[1]

1. Introduction

As already recalled by Richard Falk in this volume, the distinction between legality and legitimacy in international affairs reemerged after the 1999 NATO-led war in Kosovo. The war was sanctioned by several multilateral institutions including NATO and the European Union, but lacked UN Security Council approval, due to the opposition of Russia and China. The motivation of the war was supposedly humanitarian, in other words, to prevent an ethnic cleansing of the Albanian Kosovars akin to that experienced by Bosnian Muslims in 1992–1995. The intervention was an anomaly compared to the previous state of international wars, since NATO countries, and the militarily dominant United States, did not have a clear stake in the Balkans. As a result, an authoritative independent commission was established to assess whether the intervention, as well as the methods used, were justified.[2]

The commission turned out to reach a general consensus on the basic distinction between legality and legitimacy. Actually, the NATO intervention was considered to be illegal under current international law since what happened in Kosovo was under the jurisdiction of a sovereign state, but legitimate in terms of its aim to prevent an imminent humanitarian calamity.[3] The difference was somehow associated to two different disciplines: within positive international law, there was nothing that could justify the Kosovo intervention. But inasmuch as international politics was concerned, what can or cannot be considered legitimate is much more subjective.

In a few short years, the international climate changed considerably; President Bill Clinton vacated the White House to George Bush, Jr. The change of incumbent implied a shift away from the philosophy of multilateralism to that of a "coalition of the willing." The main outcome was the Iraq war, justified with a mixture of arguments including the supposed presence of weapons of mass destruction, humanitarian willingness to remove a despot from power—even the declared intention to impose a regime change—and finally, to facilitate the building of democratic institutions. Similar arguments were used to justify the invasion of Afghanistan.

As we know, the Iraq invasion was not authorized by the UN Security Council. But in comparison with the Kosovo case, the number of countries opposed to the invasion was considerably higher, including not only China and Russia, but also France, Germany, and several other SC elected members. Neither NATO nor the European Union provided authorization to the coalition of the willing assembled by George Bush and Tony Blair. The front of democratic countries was much more divided than in the Kosovo case. It was therefore very difficult to claim any legality for such an operation, which in fact implied a return in international relations to the state of nature. And, unsurprisingly, the distinction between legality and legitimacy was not used again to defend that war, nor an independent commission established to assess its validity.

But in spite of these basic differences, it is worth investigating whether the distinction between legality and legitimacy can be of any use in assessing the project to export democracy. Western democratic countries dominate today's world politically, economically, and also militarily. And for the first time since the end of World War II, some of their leaders explicitly declare their aim to spread democracy, albeit militarily, in all countries of the world. Is such an intention legal under current international law, norms, and institutions? If these intentions should be considered illegal since they clearly contradict one of the main pillars of the UN Charter—noninterference—is it useful to again use the category of legitimacy or should we stick to sole concept of legality? These are the issues to be addressed in this chapter. We address these issues with the tools of political theory and, although we take for granted the current state of international law, we also try to investigate if there any room for a different interpretation or any need to reform international law.

In the next section, we sketch some paradigmatic views of the concepts of legality and legitimacy, mainly developed for the internal context. We then discuss some of the characteristics of the "good" that is intended to be exported, namely democracy. The fourth section addresses the crucial issue, namely the methods used for such an adventure; in fact, we argue that the issue of legality and legitimacy cannot be assessed without discussing the means employed. Finally, we focus on different ways for exporting democracy and draw conclusions.

2. Preliminary Considerations on the Legitimacy/Legality Issue

2.1 THE CONCEPT OF LEGALITY

The concept of legality recalls that of law: an action or a decision is considered legal when it complies with a positive rule belonging to a legal system. Within domestic organizations, a legal system is composed of different general types of rule: rules regulating private conduct, rules imposing duties, rules conferring powers, rules of judgment, rules for changing the rules. Owing to the complexity of modern legal systems and to the intricate logic of regulations themselves, the endeavors to reduce these different types of rule to a single one (e.g., a sovereign's command) have generally tended to underestimate decisive features of law, which are highly relevant for grasping how the legal machinery works. Therefore, in the wake of the failure of such attempts to catch the "real" essence of law, jurists and legal philosophers resolved to recognize that the central government is neither the sole nor the ultimate source of law. But, when focusing on the international legal system, most of them are still inclined to depict it as primitive and rudimentary, as a *law-like* system, that is, a weak mechanism of control which reveals only few analogies with the domestic ones. In this view, H. L. A. Hart warned: "International law lacks a legislature, states cannot be brought before international courts without their prior consent, and there is no centrally organized effective system of sanctions." It is perfectly clear to everyone that it is this deviation of international and primitive legal orders "from the standard case which makes their classification appear questionable. There is no mystery about this."[4]

Nonetheless, in the last decades these formalist tenets have been brought into question by virtue of both theoretical developments (such as the rediscovery of legal pluralism) and factual reasons (the rise of the international legal regime). On the one hand, the difficulties in outlining precisely and unquestionably the main features of the legal system compels us to recognize, as Raz underlines, that the

> general traits which mark a system as a legal one are several and each of them admits, in principle, of various degrees. In typical instances of legal systems all these traits are manifested to a very high degree. But it is possible to find systems in which all or some are present only to a lesser degree or in which one or two are absent altogether. It would be arbitrary and pointless to try and fix a precise borderline between normative systems which are legal systems and those which are not. When faced with borderline cases it is best to admit their problematic credentials, to enumerate their similarities and dissimilarities to typical cases, and leave it at that.[5]

In addition, many interesting studies on legal pluralism have proven under several aspects the fallacies and the abstractness of the monist and state-centered conceptions of law and legality.[6] On the other hand, the progressions of international political and legal bodies make the international charters no longer dead papers but the body of a positive (i.e., gradually but increasingly adopted by international courts as bases for their deliberations) though embryonic suprastatal statute.[7]

Comparing the international normative system to a state of nature has served more often than not as an excuse for patently illegal behaviors and acts of mere force. Nowadays such behaviors may no longer lurk in the folds of uncertainty, since precise standards of legality are being outlined for assessing the actions of states and individuals.

2.2 THE CONCEPT OF LEGITIMACY

We turn now to the question of legitimacy, which immediately appears as even more complicated. There is no general definition for it, nor does it necessarily refer to positive law. Legitimacy is intertwined with morality and ethics, since it is often seen as a justification for political and legal power. As Falk points out, "there exists a bewilderingly diverse set of uses of legitimacy in contemporary commentary on world order that marks the historical moment as one of contested conceptual and normative boundaries."[8] In our opinion, the confusion about legitimacy is an inescapable characteristic of the whole of modern political theory and practice. In order to account as tidily as possible for the multifaceted and controversial meanings of legitimacy, we can single out four general understandings of it and of its connections with legality.

(a) Legitimacy *after* legality: an act or a decision is legitimate when it complies with a legal procedure; there is no legitimacy without positive laws defining procedures.
(b) Legitimacy *along with* legality: the substance of the legal system is to be consistent with the diffused conceptions of the social parties; that is, law/legality has to adapt itself to the key values and to the basic ideals of the political community.
(c) Legitimacy *before* legality: constitutions and/or governments have to embody the *interest* of the majority, to such an extent that law is what the majority considers to be legitimate; legality is a by-product.
(d) The elucidation of the previous approaches allows us to outline a fourth conception, which attempts to embed the good points of the first two and, in addition, to underline the indispensable connection between legitimacy and democratic participation.

The first approach reduces legitimacy to legality: *the former comes from the latter, in that there is no legitimacy before legal criteria on whose basis acts or decisions can be declared as legitimate.* An easy example is that of *Leviathan*: in the state of nature it is to be considered as legitimate everything that enables human beings to save their lives. There is no previous *ius* but the one which allows individuals to do anything which, in their own judgment and reason, they will conceive to be the aptest means for preserving their lives. Only the establishment of a sovereign—which is entrusted by all with the task to create the law—fixes those criteria of legality which allow people to understand whether something is legitimate or not.

The second approach considers both legitimacy to be the source of legality and legality to be the cradle of legitimacy within a bordered community. They come to be complementary concepts. On the one hand, *a stable legal framework enables a citizenry to display and highlight its basic values, needs, requirements, wills, interests*: political power is legitimately exercised insofar as it creates the legal conditions in which people can freely elaborate and express those instances which public institutions have to pursue. On the other hand, *the legitimate will of the citizenry cannot override those basic legal principles and rights which permit each individual to remain free and to escape from the dominance of majority*. This is the notion that has generally inspired the enactment of the twentieth century's constitutions.

The difference between the first and the second approach lies in the *degree of formality*: while the first is interested in the mere form of law—to the extent that whichever legal form is able to design criteria of legitimacy (as some paradoxes of legal positivism show) and that legal criteria may sometimes assess as fully legitimate highly immoral laws[9]—the second pretends law to reflect the key values of the parties within civil society. Such a difference is radicalized in the third approach, according to which *legality is nothing but the product of a communitarian form of life*. To make a graspable example, in Carl Schmitt's view, the legitimate regent embodies the idea of national unity and reproduces it through a concrete homologation of the people, which can be attained by means of a decision, or rather, by the actual exercise of its power to distinguish the enemy from the friend and to unify the friend against the enemy.[10] Here legitimacy stems from the action of a sovereign who establishes conditions of legality. As a consequence, the form of law always needs a concrete decision along with a concrete order, which reflect the basic unit of people.

Although these different conceptions have been advocated by several eminent scholars in the last centuries, we maintain that they all are more or less flawed. In particular, they disregard a fruitful link with the notion of *democratic participation*, which allows us to outline a fourth concept of legitimacy. Such a notion is able to integrate the first's concern about formality with the second's reference to the substance of people's interests and needs.[11] Briefly and in Habermasian terms,[12] we could say that just those rules are to be considered legitimate that are the result of discourses in which every affected person has had the possibility to take part and have a say.[13]

With respect to the legal form, the fourth conception follows the first approach, inasmuch as it does not consider material matters (i.e., values, beliefs, history, culture, ethnicity, religion) as an inescapable basis for the validity of the law; in other words, legitimacy is linked only to a free, open, and inclusive participation, and such a participation demands no prerequisite except for the responsibility to accept the consequences of the discourses along with the willingness to contribute by providing the indispensable resources for implementing their outcomes. Radical and exclusive positivists are right in stating that the effectiveness of the legal form does not depend on its material substance (to put it otherwise, it may be as attractive as untrue as Augustine's saying, *pour cause* quoted by Aquinas, "Non videtur esse lex, quae iusta non fuerit"); at the same time, they cannot pretend legitimacy to be reduced to a mere consequence of its effectiveness. Legitimacy is an *external standpoint* that is not connected to a private or transient moral point of view—which may vary (and actually does) throughout history—but is tied to a process, or better, to an activity engaged in by those who are affected by the consequences of the norms of the legal system. To put it otherwise, if we want law to be not only effective but also legitimate, law must reject the ultrapositivist Hobbesean principle "Auctoritas non veritas facit legem" (authority, not truth, makes law) along with the Ulpianian "Quod principi placuit, legis habet vigorem," (what pleases the prince has the force of law) no matter who is the *auctoritas* or the *princeps*).

With respect to the substance of legislation, the conception we advocate follows the second approach, since the activity of political institutions can be deemed legitimate only insofar as it takes into due account the outcomes of the *discourses among citizens*. Nevertheless, legality places some legal constraints to the effective power of discursive exchanges: they are not a Rousseauian general will with the unlimited constituting power to write again and again the rules of the game. Some rules are inherently tied to the concept of legitimacy itself, that is, the possibility for every affected person to take part and have a say: rules that open indisputable spaces of liberties, which only allow individuals to remain (and to understand themselves) as qualified and autonomous authors of laws.

In sum, we realize that legality and legitimacy are highly intertwined as soon as we understand that they are structurally connected to democratic participation, which only establishes criteria of legitimacy and ultimately justifies the enforcement of laws.

2.3 LEGALITY/LEGITIMACY AT THE INTERNATIONAL LEVEL

So far we have mainly focused on domestic politics. It would be quite naive to use the domestic analogy and to apply the above mentioned concepts to international politics. Yet, the account of the legality/legitimacy issue within territorially bounded communities highlights the general difference between the two concepts. We wanted to show that, regardless of the sphere of application, legality is a stable (although variable over time and space) criterion for assessing the conduct of social actors, while legitimacy is a highly contested concept; in particular, when separated from democratic participation, the concept of legitimacy risks being totally exposed to ideological and self-concerned manipulation. This is the reason why we assess that, while international legality is a fruitful (although fallible and always improvable) criterion for assessing the conduct of international actors, international legitimacy is hardly usable in the field of suprastatal relations. This does not mean that international legitimacy is a vacuum or nonsense; this merely emphasizes that the current situation cannot assure suitable conditions for defining criteria of international legitimacy, or rather, that democratic legitimacy imposes some specific requirements which the present suprastatal politics cannot fulfill. Therefore, from a suprastatal standpoint, while the assessment of the act of an international player as legal or illegal rests on a reasonable degree of certainty, the assessment of the same action as legitimate or illegitimate could be quite ambiguous and raise many doubts. In fact, such an act could be understood as legitimate or not in relation to the concept of legitimate one holds, or rather, it could be differently described and evaluated according to the various concepts of legitimacy we singled out above. For instance, a military action could be presented as legitimate because it is aimed at defending international legality (*sub a.*), or because it is meant to safeguard the internal sovereignty of a self-determining community against the undue pressures of an external actor (*sub b.*), or because it is part of a broader clash of civilizations in which a deadly enemy is about to colonize our territories and annihilate our Western way of life (*sub c.*). In sum, each one of the three conceptions of legitimacy may be, in principle, used for justifying a military action.

On the contrary, by referring to the current international regulations we would be able to judge such an action as legal or illegal, regardless the actor's good or bad intentions. Therefore, we must commit ourselves to clarify and reinforce, following precise standards, the international regulations.

Needless to say, the present focus on legitimacy and legality is strictly related to the specific problem of exporting democracy. In fact, although we will defend here the reliability of international legality *contra* the pliable legitimacy claims, sometimes the limits imposed by the criterion of legality may be justifiably brought into question or even suspended—such as, for instance, in case of genocide, war crimes, ethnic cleansing, and crimes against humanity, which may be legally justified by the law of those who undertake such criminal activities. Thus, the conclusion that adherence to legality is preferable to some questionable appeal to legitimacy does not imply that legality is an indisputable criterion no matter what its application may bring about. This conclusion, on the contrary, implies that legitimacy is an ambiguous notion, which can hardly justify the forcible export of democracy.

In the next pages, we will take up the case of exporting democracy by showing that it is completely meaningless to pretend an act of force, even if aimed at exporting democracy, to be legitimate: not only and not just because it is an act of force, but because it is represents an *inconsistent concept*. In the light of our account of legality/legitimacy issue, we will show that the increasingly popular concept of exporting democracy is highly deficient and that it is thoroughly meaningless to assess that a military action is aimed at exporting democracy.

3. What Are Exporters Exporting?

Before proceeding, it is worth clarifying what in the discussion about exporting democracy is usually taken for granted, that is, the nature and the meaning of the matter of exportation. Democracy is not just a regime; it is also a political process requiring sociohistorical developments and human efforts. Following Beetham and Bobbio, we describe democracy as a *nonviolent* regime in which *equal citizens* regularly *control* (or have the theoretical possibility to control) the activities of their governments; therefore, the main features of democracy appear to be *nonviolence, popular control*, and *political equality*.[14]

Nonviolence expresses the *preexisting will* of the political parties to take turns at governing without the need for violence. Political parties must be interpreted in the broad sense and may be made up of social, ethnic, and religious groups that live side by side in the same political community. Even more than a requirement, nonviolence is therefore a prerequisite. It is the rule of law that regulates the procedures of political interchange between decision-makers and citizens.

In addition, democracy is characterized by the fact that governmental actions are constantly under public scrutiny. The actions undertaken are subjected to the people's control both at the time of decision making and throughout the administrative action. In other words, both decisions and decision-makers are under control. This means that political action must be authorized and accountable and, in order to allow popular control, it must be shaped by transparent rules. This obliges the administration to *respond to people's needs, wants, requirements, and interests*. In this way, at least to some extent, decision-makers' actions can be ideally considered to be coincident with the interests of citizenry: accountability of and control over governmental actions are basic foundations for the principle of representation.

Finally, the principle of equality demands that all members of the community have the same rights, foremost among them the right to participate in political life. All members must be able to contribute, directly or indirectly, to the process of making appointments to public office and to be appointees. For this to be possible the political community must guarantee equal chances for everyone to satisfy those basic requirements that are the precondition for participating in political activities.

Obviously, democracy has not yet attained its goals, nor can it, as it is on an interminable journey shrouded in uncertainty. Democracy's great vitality lies precisely in its ability to set itself new goals and critically evaluate what has been achieved. A democracy that does not progress by virtue of the work performed by its institutions is already defunct. Democracy is essentially progressive, while different political systems, such as autocracy, oligarchy, or anarchy all relegate the task of innovating to outside the dialogical debate.

This "political-process definition" is preferable to others owing to its emphasizing two main features of democracy: the ongoing activity of self-criticism undertaken by each sincerely democratic organization and the link between people's self-commitment and democratization (social awareness, political struggles, willingness to participate, mutual solidarity, fair competition, etc.). These basic features make us aware of two facts: on the one hand, that democracy has to entail inherently an unquenchable tendency to self-suspicion, that is, it has to remain permanently willing to unmask the "false consciousness" that induces ancient democracies to judge themselves as perfect democracies (where the adjective "perfect," according to its Latin root, comes to mean both excellent and thoroughly accomplished); on the other hand, that democracy depends on the *political dispositions of individuals*. And actually, while it is only to be expected that all individuals wish to survive, it cannot be taken for granted that they wish to participate in the management of public affairs or even that, if asked, they would spontaneously choose a democratic organization.

Let us briefly analyze these two kinds of problems, which can be rendered into two basic questions concerning the exporter and the importer:

1. Who is legitimate to judge the exporter's degree of democracy?
2. Is the exporter going to meet the real requirements of the importer? That is to say, will the importer have the real freedom to choose its form of government?

The first question refers to the *way of assessing* the political regime not only of the importer, but also of the exporter. In fact, it would be necessary to perform at least an independent assessment to establish whether the former actually needs a change of regime and whether the latter is in a position to propose an alternative regime. Notoriously, the criteria for assessing democratic regimes are highly controversial, and consolidated democracies are reluctant to accept external assessments. At the international level, the would-be exporter of democracy should rely on the opinion expressed by existing institutions or third-party organizations.

The second question is related to the willingness to sound out the intentions of the affected community with regard to a democratic regime. A democracy-exporting agent acting in good faith should in other words give priority to the importer's reasons rather than her/his own. Otherwise, one of those typical cases arises that, in Robespierre's words, reflects the "mania to make peoples happy against their will." As a matter of fact, a democratic regime inescapably needs a civil humus on which and along with which democratic institutions can grow and thrive: if we want to prevent regime change from being perceived as a mere shift from an authoritarian regime to another, the new institutions should adapt themselves to the citizens' theoretical and practical conceptions and, at the same time, the citizens' theoretical and practical conceptions should at least to some extent shape the new political institutions.

It should be borne in mind that societies undergoing democratic exportation are seldom composed of a despotic monarch and an oppressed people. Each action of exporting democracy at least involves many parties, such as: parties holding political power; parties that benefit from the political state of things; parties that have little or no political influence but are not interested in regime change; excluded and/or oppressed parties that are able to put up some resistance; excluded and/or oppressed parties that are not able to put up any resistance; and other governments and/or trans- and inter-national organizations that are interested in regime change. Although this list does not pretend to be exhaustive, it reminds us that each society is multifaceted and that it is necessary not only to assess the intentions of outside agents carrying out an intervention, but also those of the parties that compose the whole political community where it is intended to intervene and the possible interference of outside supporters of the status quo. This problem is strictly related to the intention to give the population *freedom of choice* regarding their form of government.

Paradoxically, it is anti-democratic to want to export democracy without allowing the affected people to decide which organizational form they prefer. Exporting democracy actually means giving people the chance to decide which organizational form to apply. This may sound like a typical communitarian stance, according to which any single society has to produce its own institutions, given that the different moral doctrines underpinning the different societies are reciprocally incommensurable. Even though we are very far from endorsing such a tenet, it is necessary to underscore two undeniable facts: the need for historical developments and the fruitfulness of pluralism. Among the political developments of Western societies, it was the distinction between the *foro interno* and the *foro externo* that paved the way for democracy: the modern secular governments only required the external behavior of citizens to comply with statal positive norms, and it left them to maintain privately their inner beliefs. That represented an enabling condition for pluralism to spread, so as to sanction definitely the separation between the internal beliefs and the external behavior of democratic citizens.[15]

4. Means, Ends, and the Path for Democracy

After sketching the general difficulties that affect the concept of exporting democracy, we are now ready to analyze the different export strategies according to the chosen means and to declared ends. As already stressed in the introductory section, there is nothing in the current corpus of international law that allows using coercive means to export democracy.[16] But from the perspective of political theory, it is equally important to compare the consistency of the current status of international law with the aims of democratization. Basically, we can distinguish between coercive and persuasive strategies, which we name the "stick" and the "carrot."

4.1 THE STICK STRATEGY

The means of coercion par excellence for exporting democracy is war, as in Afghanistan and in Iraq. In this case, the means (war) is clearly in conflict with the end (democracy). The violent means represented by war does not involve despots alone but inevitably ends up by affecting also the individuals who are expected to benefit from the regime change. The use of such means is the least suitable for effectively promoting a regime based on nonviolence and for protecting their interests. Rather than establishing a ruling class alternative to the one in power, a war of aggression creates a vacuum and only aggravates local conflicts. Also in the case in which an explicit will is expressed by public opinion to have a democratic government, this does not mean that the same public opinion will be willing to accept a military invasion. Let us take the case of Panama in May 1989 when, after losing the elections, Manuel Noriega and his regime refused to hand over power. Although the Panama citizens had expressed their desire to have a different government, they feared the risks of an armed intervention by the United States to overthrow Noriega.[17] This was a classic case in which the population would have preferred external help of the nonviolent kind, for instance, a naval blockade.

But as well as representing a clear-cut contradiction between means and ends, historical experience shows that only in rare cases can a democratic regime be set up using external military means. What happened in Germany, Japan, and Italy in 1945 represents a unique experience that is unlikely to be repeated—and, besides, we must reckon that in these countries liberal and social-democratic traditions were at work long before the establishment of totalitarian regimes. A survey by the Carnegie Endowment for International Peace dedicated to US involvement in military operations abroad in the twentieth century indicates that only rarely was the result obtained the exportation of democracy.[18] In the first half of the twentieth century, these failures involved countries that were neighbors of the United States and apparently easy to control, such as Panama (1903–1936), Nicaragua (1909–1933), Haiti (1915–1934), the Dominican Republic (1916–1924), and a good three times Cuba (1898–1902, 1906–1909, and 1917–1922).

Other military occupations, such as in Korea in the 1950s and South Vietnam and Cambodia in the 1960s and 1970s, were dictated mainly by the intention to block communist expansion, and the strategy of democratization was not even attempted. Since the end of the Cold War, the US administration has not achieved any lasting success even in Haiti. After World War II, the only cases of clear-cut success have been Panama (1989) and Grenada (1983), two small states closely linked to the US economy and society and, in the case of Panama, a heavy price was paid.[19]

Even more discouraging is the record of the two old European colonial powers, France and Great Britain. In their case, military interventions abroad were almost never dictated by the explicit intention of favoring democratic forces, but followed the traditional power logic. According to Peceny and Pickering,[20] French and British interventions after World War II almost always led to a reduced political liberalization and to the support of the existing regimes, even when they were oppressive. The current failures in Afghanistan and in Iraq actually have numerous precedents. How can such disappointing results be accounted for?

One of the first ingredients that seem to be missing in the attempt to export democracy militarily is the determination of the exporters, who are more often inclined to promote reliable and faithful regimes than to allow the self-organization of peoples.

But the strongest reasons for concluding that military exportation cannot be successful rely on the nature of democracy itself. Exporters might at least accomplish two different operations, which both are hardly able to establish a process of democratization. On the one hand, the exporter could succeed in stabilizing a legal system, or rather, in enacting a series of compulsory norms enforceable by an administrative apparatus. That would be a condition of legality similar to the first approach we sketched above. Yet, in this case we will have no guarantee that the underpinning concept of legality will really correspond to the political conceptions diffused among individuals and groups; therefore, such a legal system could be perceived as an unwelcome imposition from above, just like the pervious regime. The imposed legal institutions, probably mimicking the exporter's domestic ones, would be considered by the importers as totally unrelated to their inner convictions, needs, requirements, and interests.[21] On the other hand, the exporter could succeed in creating the condition for self-determination of people. Nonetheless, more often than not self-determination fails to promote democracy and turns out to facilitate the affirmation of the powerful groups and elites. Hence, exporter always runs the risk of realizing the conditions for the third kind of legitimacy, in which new actors replace the old ones and establish a new form of despotism, even under the "legitimizing" aegis of the exporter.

In conclusion, the stick strategy is likely to be:

- illegal as regards international law, since, as recent occurrences have shown, it is difficult to provide dependable reasons for waging "democratic" war;
- illegitimate as regards international consensus and practices, since it is always questioned and contrasted by the other actors of the international arena;
- illegal as regards domestic law—that is, the functioning law of the challenged regime—since it is an attempt to change the system by using means that do not belong to it;
- illegitimate as regards domestic consensus and practices, since it is not the result of internal struggles and commitments and it hardly reflects the political view of people.

In addition, it should be noted that the external threats are often capable of unifying the threatened internal parties, which could perceive the exporter as a mere self-interested aggressor, with the end result of decreasing the internal pluralism that is, as we said above, one of the few successful paths to democracy.

Finally, the stick strategy exerts negative consequences on the exporter's internal situation. In war, each state is compelled to forego some of its own freedom. The citizens are sent to war, civil freedoms are reduced, the relative weight of the strong powers (army, secret service, security apparatus) increases at the expense of transparency and control. Democracies that are perpetually at war develop chronic diseases. The United States and Great Britain, which have been involved in a never-ending series of high- and low-intensity conflicts since the end of World War II, have so far resisted incredibly well in preserving their own democratic system at home. But not even these two states have been able to avoid sacrificing part of their own democratic institutions on the altar of national interest. In the state of necessity produced by war, acts of torture and the killing of unarmed prisoners have been committed and justified, which are all acts that would never have been tolerated by public opinion in peacetime conditions. As a matter of fact, exporting democracy by military means also signifies reducing it on the home front.

4.2 THE CARROT STRATEGY

Must it therefore be concluded that nothing can be done to export democracy outside one's borders, and the only useful thing that democratic countries can do is to perfect their own political system so much so that other people will want to imitate them? There is no reason to be so skeptical. If democratic states contributed to the creation and expansion of institutional avenues in which individuals can freely elaborate and express (autonomously and cooperatively) their requirements and needs, they would concretely help the latter develop suitable and feasible conditions for influencing governmental activities and for increasing the spaces of liberty. In fact, the error implicit in the mania to export democracy refers both to choice of the means and to the design of the end. Means and ends should be consistent as far as possible with the intimate *ratio* of exporting democracy, namely, as we argued above, to start or facilitate a twofold process. On the one hand, this process involves a *top–down* change, that means a progressive amendment of governmental institutions toward general standards of nonviolence, accountability, and political equality, by virtue of which political establishment would or at least should go forward to a much clearer distinction between the control of lives and the regulation of behaviors. On the other hand, this process also involves a *bottom-up* transformation, that is, an indispensable diffusion and stabilization of ideas such as equality, freedom, reciprocity, and likewise, within the general political culture and the inner conceptions of individuals.

If the end is exporting this kind of democracy—thought of as an ongoing and incessant process—what instruments are therefore available to the democratic states?

The first and most obvious instrument is linked to economic, social, political, and cultural incentives. The present-day domination of the West is so widespread that, if their priority is truly to expand democracy, they ought to commit more resources to it. But we are far from moving in this direction: in 2005, the United States defense appropriation amounted to more than 4% of the Gross Domestic Product, and that of the European Union countries to more than 2%. In view of this military expenditure, considering the present international scenario, it is quite euphemistic to call it "defense" expenditure, since only the small change is dedicated to official development aid: currently only 0.1% of the US GDP and 0.3% of that of the European Union.[22] And only a small proportion of these funds are explicitly earmarked for encouraging democracy.

But the carrot does not consist solely of economic aid. Economic aid can be effective, but may also be perceived as a form of imposition by a rich and powerful state on a small and weak one. Logically, the most convincing way of exporting democracy is to have it transmitted by the citizens of the democratic countries: opening up direct channels between themselves and the citizens of the authoritarian countries.[23]

The difference between the "stick" and the "carrot" approaches also concerns the players involved. In the case of the stick strategy, the promoters are mainly the governments, which use the coercive instruments of the state against the despotic government but also against the civilian population. Since war does not allow singling out among the population, both the supporters and the opponents of the despotic government are likely to suffer the consequences of the war. The carrot strategy, on the contrary, requires that both the government and the public opinion of democratic countries take an active role, while the (limited) damages inflicted to the nation run by a despotic government might be much better tuned in order to target the policies and the actions which violate human rights.

Professional and cultural associations and other forms of transnational organization play an important role in connecting citizens. During the years of the Cold War, these channels proved fundamental in supporting the opposition in the eastern bloc countries and in forming an alternative ruling class.[24] The incumbent regimes have often difficulties in isolating entirely their society from international economic, social, cultural, and technological exchanges. If there is a widespread support for a regime change, this will also be played by non-governmental actors which, in turn, may provide financial, political, and social support to opposition. The existence of non-governmental channels may itself be considered an excellent indicator of the feasibility of exporting democracy: the civil society in the democratic countries had numerous contacts with the Eastern European countries during the years of the Iron Curtain despite control and repression. Nothing comparable exists today between Afghan and Iraqi citizens and those of the occupying countries.

The political power of global civil society is often politically weak and easy to counter: the leaders of the opposition that maintain personal contacts are often placed under surveillance and are the first to be subjected to repression. The governments in power are capable of brushing off for decades all requests for political liberalization, as we learn from the case of Myanmar and the persecution suffered by the opposition leader Aung San Suu Kyi, even in the face of a pressing international solidarity campaign. And yet, one must not discount the political importance of these channels. At least they demonstrate to the oppressed inhabitants of authoritarian regimes the existence of political societies that express solidarity for their aspirations. Without them, it would never have been possible for Vaclav Havel, Nelson Mandela, and Lech Wałęsa to be transformed from political prisoners to heads of state.

An alliance among progressive civil societies is certainly not easy to achieve. Both in democratic and non-democratic states, civil society is often a mixture of progressive and conservative tendencies.[25] But it is reasonable to expect that the citizens of democratic states have a larger degree of fidelity to their own institutions than the citizens of non-democratic states. In such conditions, which may exist today in Myanmar, it is possible that an alliance between internal civil society and external civil society, also fostered by state diplomacy, may effectively obtain a regime change and lead to democratic governance. But not in all countries of the world is there a uniform civil society predisposed to democratize. Take the case of a theocratic regime with neither pluralism nor rule of law, but which nonetheless is vastly supported by the majority of the population. The civil society of democratic states can usefully ally with the few democratic tendencies repressed by the theocratic regime, but it is unlikely, at least in the short run, that this internal-external alliance will be in the position to generate a peaceful and stable regime change.

We wish also to stress that using persuasive means has also the positive effect of reinforcing, rather than weakening, democracy in the exporting countries. Involving civil society in the foreign policy choices, for example by directing trade, tourism, and economic aid flows toward countries that respect human rights and where self-government prevails, helps the populations of democratic countries to pursue the values underlying their own social contract. If the citizens themselves become ambassadors for their own political system and plead its cause abroad, they themselves become defenders of the democratic values.

It is equally important to offer countries that might choose democracy the chance of joining the club of democratic states on equal terms, rather than establish a clear-cut hierarchy in which a state deems it can export its own system instead of allowing different states to participate in a political union in which the various systems are compared and reinforced. If democracy can be defined as a journey, some peoples could benefit from travelling together. Such a conviction mirrors two specific and differing approaches which we will explain in the next section.

In conclusion, the carrot strategy is likely to be:

- legal as regards international law, as it does not infringe any international prescription about the use of aggressive means;[26]
- legitimate as regards international consensus and practices, since it is ideally aimed a creating an open, free, and inclusive international environment;
- legal as regards domestic law—that is, the functioning law of the challenged regime—since it tries to make it change from within;
- legitimate as regards domestic consensus and practices, since it endeavors to create the conditions for people to elaborate their need and requirements and induce them to claim an increasing involvement in the political organization of their society.

4.3 IN BETWEEN THE STICK AND THE CARROT: ECONOMIC SANCTIONS

There is a third category to be considered, namely economic sanctions. On the one hand, sanctions use an amount of violence much more limited than war. On the other hand, sanctions do not provide an incentive but rather a punishment. In this sense, economic sanctions can be considered genuinely in the middle between the stick and the carrot strategies.

Within the UN Charter, sanctions are included in Chapter VII, Article 41, and therefore they are recognized as a coercive measure. There is, therefore, a basic distinction between sanctions that are authorized by the Security Council (SC) and have a collective nature (such as the sanctions against South Africa during apartheid) from unauthorized and unilateral sanctions (such as those of the United States against Cuba, which have been repeatedly condemned by the UN General Assembly). While the first conform to international law and can be imposed also through coercive methods, the second have no legal status. In the case of economic sanctions, considerations about their legitimacy and legality are generally less significant than those about their effectiveness.

Of course, there is a basic difference between "sanctions," as defined for example in Chapter VII of the UN Charter, which could be applied only when there are threats to international peace and security, and the polices that can be inscribed in the term "isolation," which could be defined as policies adopted to discourage contacts with the leadership of selected countries. Under the current international law, sanctions could not be applied under Chapter VII to promote democracy unless the promotion of democracy is functional to prevent threats to peace and security. A case could be represented when a country is risking a civil war among ethnic countries and a neighboring country may be also involved in terms of refugee flows or military participation. In such a case, sanctions might be used to induce the leaders of the country to share power among the various ethnic groups, in other words to employ democratic methods. Cases of use of sanctions as methods to foster democracy have seldom been used. The application of "isolation" policies is much more flexible. No country is required to exchange cultural, social, or sport visits with other countries if they feel that their internal regime is unlawful. These policies of isolation are not regulated by international law.

With the lens of political theory, there is another basic difference to be made: sanctions can be divided between those that are strongly supported by the population and those which, on the contrary, are promoted by the governments but not by the people. The support received by the population seems to be the crucial element to assess their effect in terms of democracy promotion. Sanctions generally tend to create a strong divide among peoples: on the one hand, the coalition of nations that apply them and, on the other hand, the "culprit" nation. Very often, the effect of the sanctions is to reinforce the popular support for the undemocratic government since they generate the "rally round the flag" effect. As Thakur underscores, "in contrast to war, sanctions shift the burden of harm solely to civilians. They inflict pain on ordinary citizens while imposing questionable costs on leaders who are often enriched and strengthened on the back of their impoverished and oppressed people by law of perverse consequences."[27] Paradoxically, sanctions might make the people with a despotic government less willing to struggle for democracy.

It would be useful to refine new forms of sanctions, making them "smarter" in order to target the individuals or collective groups that most oppose to the development of democracy.[28] An important attempt in this direction in the way the international community, led by the United States and the European Union, is handling the political case in Myanmar, a country where a government has been removed through unlawful means. In this case, the international community can rightly assume that the population is willing to be ruled democratically and has even expressed a preference for a specific political party. In spite of this, smart sanctions have not yet proven to be particularly effective in restoring the elected government into power.

5. Different Approaches, Different Results

Our argument that democracy cannot be exported militarily does not imply that democracy is a form of government specific to a few enlightened populations. On the contrary, we agree with those that argue that all people of the earth can grasp benefits of democracy and that democracy can be built from scratch even in countries with low economic and social resources. In particular, we are persuaded that democracy helps achieve a better quality of life and that economic and social backwardness should not be considered an insurmountable obstacle to its development. Nonetheless, we endeavored to show that democracy building requires an endogenous social fabric that nurtures democratic values and procedures. This is why the above mentioned "carrot strategy" requires a multiple approach involving economic and cultural cooperation, not only with governments but above all with the societal parties, in other words, with the real persons and groups which compose the peculiar *humus* of a country.

The European Union is a champion in this kind of operations. In the last decades, it played a pivotal role in Eastern Europe by enhancing the vitality of many active social and political movements. So far, the European Union has included countries relatively likely to embrace democratic faith and institutions. European countries in the South and in the East already had a high level of social capital and good political infrastructures. The specific traits of the EU approach are the following. On the one hand, it employs not a *military* but a *civilian* power.[29] People would laugh if anybody in Brussels threatened to "shock and awe." Actually, the fact that the European Union has so many different voices also implies that no single nation can fully dominate the others. On the other hand, what makes the European Union so appealing for those living in non-democratic countries is *political dignity*. As soon as a new member is accepted, it enjoys all the privileges of the oldest members of the club. For instance, if Turkey ever joins the European Union, it will get a number of parliamentarians equal to France, Italy, and the United Kingdom. Therefore, a basic principle of European ensemble is that each member has equal dignity.

Moreover, the process of European integration requires interactions at a variety of institutional and social levels. It is not just an inter-governmental process, but it involves citizens, companies, professionals, students, and so on. The top-down process manages to be effective only because it is matched by a net of bottom-to-bottom relationships.

The invasion of Iraq has made the Bush administration (along with the Blair administration) the champion of democratization through military force. The rhetoric used is also the opposite from that of Brussels. Rather than discuss, negotiate, and reconcile, American leaders have spoken in messianic terms. The top members of the US administration have praised liberty and democracy much more than any EU bureaucrat has ever done—and at the same time contributed to the killing of an unknown number of civilians. It is surprising how effective the power of rhetoric is, and there is no doubt that many of those who voted to reelect Bush in 2004 were influenced by his words rather than his actions.

Let us mention the attempt to address Iraqi civil conflict through free elections. Since the different religious communities do not trust each other, fair and free elections simply replicate the statistics of religious and ethnic division. But the different communities trust the occupation troops even less. They have very good reasons to be suspicious about the intentions of the invaders, given the long history of misconduct by Western powers. Iraq is a colonial creation; in the 1980s, it was used as a tool to contain Iran in one of the dirtiest wars of the twentieth century. One million Iraqis died in this war, while the West was silent. Thanks to Western support, Saddam Hussein managed to reinforce his domestic power. After Saddam invaded Kuwait, most civilian infrastructure in Iraq was destroyed by Western bombing; the only institution that managed to survive almost untouched was the Republican Guard, which immediately was used to repress internal opposition. Twelve years of Western sanctions kept the Iraqi people hostage to their own tyrant without any possibility of rebellion. How could be expected that ordinary Iraqi citizens would trust an Anglo-American army to build a regime able to serve their interests? Here we can draw a pragmatic lesson on exporting democracy: the population of the target country should have a prior trusting relationship with the invaders. If it has none, the outcome is more likely to be insurgency or civil war than democratic development.

6. Conclusions: Institutional Reforms, Democratic Ideals and the Human Rights System.

The analysis made in the present chapter has revealed that the specific form of democratic government can only be imported, that is, it needs to be formed starting from a suitable *endogenous political framework*. This not only highlights the unfeasibility of military exportation of democracy, but also shows the inconsistency of the concept itself. A serious conceptual analysis, along with a review of the main historical experiences, confirms that the cases of successful spreading of democracy were carried out by means of persuasion, incentives, and international collaboration. This is one of those cases in which there is no dilemma regarding the choice of means and ends: the end of democracy is attained only when coherent means are adopted.

This is the reason why it is meaningless to claim a military attempt of exporting democracy (even granting that democracy is the real purpose and not a mere cover for private aims) to be legal or legitimate. Chapters VI–VIII of the United Nations Charter definitively rule out the possibility of waging war (whether for establishing democracy or not) without a Security Council resolution. In addition, no sound concept of legitimacy can be evoked for justifying a unilateral use of violence.

Yet, it seems equally meaningless to pretend a peaceful attempt to export democracy is legal or legitimate. In fact, peacefully exporting democracy is not a single action or a well-defined strategy. It is an ongoing endeavor to involve individuals, groups, and communities in the process of outlining and revising international regulations, to cooperate with them, to persuade their governments to align with international human rights standards—in a word, to create suitable conditions in which citizenries may develop democratic ideals, dispositions, and practices. It does not bring about any problem with either legality (since it infringes no rule) or legitimacy (since it needs to advance no particular conception of legitimacy other than that of inclusive participation).

If so, it may be wondered why we are dwelling upon the legality/legitimacy issue in relation to the case of exporting democracy. By following the thread of our argument, the conceptual scheme of legality/legitimacy seems to have nothing significant to say about exporting democracy: the use of force turns out to be both illegal and illegitimate, while peaceful activities cannot be defined as either illegal or illegitimate. However, such a conclusion would be at best naïve and unsatisfactory. On the contrary, the case of exporting democracy sheds light on the dangerous fact that, nowadays, democracy and the defense of its values are being increasingly used as a rationale for breaching international laws.

As we showed above, the vocabulary of legitimacy is overexploited for justifying military actions of *preemptive defense*, with the result of weakening international legality and democratic governance; the word "democracy," associated with unilateral actions of *regime change*, is often used to cover violence (whether military or symbolic) with a self-legitimizing aura; the shadow of terrorism is bandied about in attempts to reshape the norms regulating international power and the use of force. Such challenges to international legal rules on war and military intervention, as Bartholomew underlines, pursue the aim of reshaping international regulations and to "*constitute* rule/law unilaterally and 'mono-logically'; in this view, affected persons, groups, and communities are treated as mere "addressees of legal obligation,"[30] and not as qualified authors of it.

Still, if our arguments are aimed at showing that it is highly misleading and even dangerous to claim the strategy of preemptive defense and regime change to be legitimate, it is worth addressing some considerations about the precise content of what we named the "carrot strategy." Such a method of spreading democracy cannot merely rely on the endogenous forces of a society (as if it sufficed to finance and encourage the groups of civil society in order to reach a democratic regime). What it is required above all is the *peaceful enhancement and revision of international regulations*, that is, what we consider as the only way to settle conflicts and to make suprastatal democracy thrive. In fact, our theses do not aim to make a defense for the principle of nonintervention: peacefully spreading democracy suggests the proper pathway both for *amending international legality* (conceived of as a cooperative process of fixing legal standards, equally binding on individuals, peoples, and states) and for *defining sound criteria of international legitimacy* (conceived of as a procedural and cooperative corrective to international legality, since it invites to understand that legal standards are to be fixed by way of cooperation between their addressees).

To explain what ought to be achieved in making the international legal regime more effective and for fixing dependable criteria of international legitimacy, let us distinguish two levels:

1. the lofty level of institutions; and
2. the grassroots level of consciousness.

The first level is related to the possible and necessary revision of the international legal regime. Just to mention two examples, think of the management of humanitarian intervention and the uneven use of sanctions, either of which are likely to have contradictory and undemocratic consequences. On the one hand, the politics of humanitarian intervention, which today tend to be interpreted as "responsibility to protect," increasingly risks recalling the Schmittian deciding sovereign: "International administrations—Orford writes—adopt an authoritarian model of governance in which democratic participation is suspended until political order and economic integration are secured. They oversee the implementation of corporatist model in which the economy is liberalised and protection of the rights and investments of corporations are given priority in the new political order."[31] On the other hand, the use of sanctions, originally thought of as a way to prevent war and its tragic outcomes, sometimes not only fails to achieve its aims—namely, a progressive weakening of despots—but paradoxically reinforces despots and damages their citizenries. More generally, international law still embodies undemocratic features, such as the executive's comprehensive power in international affairs, the scarce or null popular mediation for the enactment of treaties, the asymmetrical application of the principle of nonintervention, and the strategic application or misapplication of the principle of self-determination.[32]

Exporting democracy with arms reveals itself as a way of weakening legality at both the domestic and the international level. The recent cases of unilateral adoption of war with the aim of international security and pacification did not meet with a satisfactory reinforcement of legal definitions of the new forms of war, self-defense, terrorism, and so on. As a consequence, the idea of legitimacy, associated to it and dissociated from legality, turns out to represent a battering ram for destabilizing and altering the international legal regime. The way suggested by a careful analysis of legitimacy and democracy is that of cooperating in order to revise the international order and make it more effective. This lesson is fully compliant with the cosmopolitan view, according to which conflicts end up reinforcing authoritarian regimes, while an international system based on peace and collaboration makes life difficult for dictators and encourages the internal opposition required for an effective political democratization. The basic guidelines for doing this within cosmopolitan projects are the following: both individuals and states should have their own representatives in the global sphere; together with their citizenship of the state, individuals should also acquire a cosmopolitan citizenship; this envisages a minimal list of rights and duties vis-à-vis constituting cosmopolitan institutions; internal state sovereignty would be limited by global constitutional rules; external state sovereignty would be replaced by a global constitutionalism; member states should accept the compulsory jurisdiction of the international courts; and cosmopolitan institutions could resolve to accept citizens also representing states that do not intend to participate.[33] All of these reforms would be able to link the revision of international legal parameters to a sound condition of legitimacy, in other words, a situation in which all the addressees of laws are involved in order to deliberate about those rules that will impinge on them.

Yet, such goals cannot be attained unless the addressees of reforms are convinced of their desirability and fairness: we have to go down to the grassroots level of consciousness. As Susan Marks stresses, "proposals for institutional reform become ideological if they are not accompanied by moves to ground the reform at the level of consciousness."[34] Exporting democracy, *pace* its fierce advocates, causes democracy to be seen as a product of exportation, as something which comes from outside and does not fit with either the convictions or the needs of the importer. In contrast with that, what we name the "carrot strategy" is precisely aimed at making citizens feel an active part of a broad process. The cosmopolitan democratic project is not only directed toward institutional reform; it is primarily interested in popular participation and rights protection. It is designed to overcome progressively the conditions of political, social, and economic marginalization that prevent people from being authors of the laws to which they are subject.

Today the international legal regime is still far from assuring concrete opportunities and effective protection for individuals and groups. What is more, it is menaced by its own structural inability to face urgent problems, which Chinkin portrays as follows: "The difficulties in securing agreement on change to the legal regime—as epitomised in the failure to secure reform of the SC, failure to agree on a definition of terrorist acts, ambiguous and equivocal SC decision-making—all undermine the legitimacy of the international system. Legitimacy is also undermined by the manipulation of international law in pursuit of an imperialist, neoliberal agenda."[35] The tendency to return to an international *state* of nature dismisses as worthless the coincidence between authors and addressees of laws—with the end result of "privatizing" the concept of legitimacy—while the rhetoric of protection and preemptive defense is emptying out the real meaning of human rights.

The veracity of this frame is proven not only by the misleading use of exporting democracy, but also by the limited progression of human rights as a system of effective and enforceable rights. More than half a century after its enactment, the human rights regime still suffers from the burdens highlighted by Hannah Arendt,[36] whose sharp (and explicitly Burkean) observations induce us to believe that such rights should progressively provide their bearers with *actionable instruments of self-defense along with the ability/possibility to design their own destiny.* They must not remain the rights of those who have no right, rights which are actionable by well-intentioned third parties only in case of oppression of right-bearers. The human rights regime has to become part of a stronger legal regime, a cosmopolitan rule of law capable of creating the status of *homo juridicus*, according to which human beings are equal as long as they share a common legal framework. This framework should embody some enforceable means of coercion, with the task of ensuring the respect of human rights *before* their violation. Nonetheless, this top-down process, as we have often recalled, requires a bottom-up diffusion of democratic ideals and practices among populations, whose voice should become more and more pressing.

No legitimacy exists without participation, and no legal system (whether effective or not) is legitimate without legitimacy: therefore, spreading democracy, in the way we addressed above, also means contributing to enlarging the basis for legitimating the international legal system and to enhance its functioning in order to establish a condition of legitimate legality for each single human being.

Endnotes

1. We wish to thank Richard Falk, Vesselin Popovski, the other participants of the conference and the referees for their comments on previous drafts. This article is the fruit of a common project. Daniele Archibugi wrote sections 1, 4, 5, while Mariano Croce wrote sections 2, 3, 6.

2. Independent International Commission on Kosovo, *The Kosovo Report. Conflict, International Response, Lessons Learned* (Oxford: Oxford University Press, 2001).

3. See Richard Falk, "Legality and Legitimacy: The Quest for Principled Flexibility and Restraint," in *Force and Legitimacy in World Politics*, ed. David Armstrong, Theo Farrell, and Bice Maiguashca (Cambridge: Cambridge University Press, 2005).

4. Herbert L. A. Hart, *The Concept of Law* (Oxford: Clarendon Press, 1961), 3–4.

5. Joseph Raz, *Practical Norms and Reasons*, 3rd ed. (Oxford: Oxford University Press, 2002), 150.

6. For an analysis about the fruitfulness of the noble tradition of *legal pluralism* in domestic and international affairs, see Mariano Croce, *Sfere di dominio. Democrazia e potere nell'era globale* (Roma: Meltemi, 2008), chap. 3.

7. As Allen Buchanan argues against the positivistic skepticism:

> There is a complex, highly normativized conception of what counts as customary international law, including not only the requirement of *opinio juris* (that to count as custom state behavior in conformity with a norm must be thought to be legally required or legally permissible), but also the idea of peremptory norms (*jus cogens*), which have a status similar to that of constitutional law in determining the validity of other norms. The international legal system also includes norms governing the interpretation and validity of treaties (in part codified in the Vienna Convention on Treaties). Once these complexities are appreciated, the assertion that international law is a primitive legal system or a proto-legal system looks rather dubious.

Allen Buchanan, *Justice, Legitimacy, and Self-Determination: Moral Foundations for International Law* (New York: Oxford University Press, 2004), 31.

8. Richard Falk, "Legality and Legitimacy: Creative Tension and/or Geopolitical Gambit," in this volume.

9. In advocating the coherence of positivist analysis of law, the Danish jurist Alf Ross incisively affirms that, according to the scientific nature of legal theory, law is to be studied in its objective features and not in relation to moral standards; as a consequence, it makes no sense to judge Nazi racial laws or laws on polygamy as immoral; accordingly, they are part of an effective legal order and that comes to prove that law can take whichever form without losing its effectiveness.

10. On Schmitt's idea of legitimacy, see the sharp observations in Anne Orford, see chapter XX, p. XX.

11. Obviously, the third approach represents a dangerous degeneration of the second, in that it considers legality as strictly dependent upon the affirmation of a peculiar worldview. As we will show below, this is precisely the risk connected to exporting democracy.

12. See, for instance, Jürgen Habermas, "Remarks on Legitimation through Human Rights," in *The Postnational Constellation* (Cambridge, Mass.: MIT Press, 2001).

13. As Amy Bartholomew rightly shows, the core tenet of Habermas's political proposal is the coincidence between authors and addressees of laws: "The key insight of a Habermasian conception of deliberative democratic legitimating is that those who are the addressees of law must also be able to understand themselves, in some sense, as its authors." Amy Bartholomew, see chapter XX, p. XX. Indeed, Habermas's stress on this coincidence explains why legitimacy and legality are to be seen as two coins of the same political-deliberative process.

14. See David Beetham, *Democracy and Human Rights* (Cambridge: Polity Press, 1999), chap. 1; Norberto Bobbio, *The Future of Democracy*, trans. Roger Griffin. (Minneapolis: University of Minnesota Press, 1987), chap. 1. For a discussion, see Daniele Archibugi, *The Global Commonwealth of Citizens. Toward Cosmopolitan Democracy* (Princeton, N.J.: Princeton University Press, 2008), chap. 2.

15. As a matter of fact, the distinction between "private" and "public" is essential to the development of democracy and to the mitigation of governmental power: as Orford shows about Schmitt's conception of state power, the German jurist traces back the being "soulless"

of the modern state precisely to Hobbes's distinction between *foro interno* and *foro externo*: "Schmitt argued that the state could not retain its legitimacy if private interests were able to develop in the civil real and eventually oppose to state" (Orford, see chapter XX, p. XX).

16. Franck has argued in favor of a right to democratic governance, but this does not imply that other states have the faculty to use force to impose this right. Thomas M. Franck, "The Emerging Right to Democratic Governance," *American Journal of International Law* 1, no. 86 (1992): 46–91. For contrasting opinions, see the essays in Gregory H. Fox and Brad R. Roth, eds., *Democratic Governance and International Law* (Cambridge: Cambridge University Press, 2000).

17. Cf. Eytan Gilboa, "The Panama Invasion Revisited: Lessons for the Use of Force in the Post Cold War Era," *Political Science Quarterly* 4, no. 110 (1995): 539–562. It is estimated that the United States intervention cost the lives of 500 to 5000 Panama inhabitants and 23 US soldiers.

18. Minxin Pei and Sara Kasper, *Lessons from the Past: The American Record on Nation Building* (Washington, D.C.: Carnegie Endowment for International Peace, 2003).

19. Cf. Pei and Kasper, *Lessons from the Past*. See also the following studies, which all confirm the negative outcome regarding democratization of the majority of US military interventions: James Meernik, "United States Military Intervention and the Promotion of Democracy," *Journal of Peace Research* 4, no. 33 (1996): 391–402; Margaret G. Hermann and Charles Kegley, "The U.S. Use of Military Intervention to Promote Democracy: Evaluating the Record," *International Interactions* 2, no. 24 (1998): 91–114; and Karin von Hippel, *Democracy by Force: U.S. Military Intervention in the Post–Cold War World* (Cambridge: Cambridge University Press, 2000).

20. Jeffrey Pickering and Mark Peceny, "Forging Democracy at Gunpoint," *International Studies Quarterly* 3, no. 50 (2006): 539–560.

21. And, at any rate, convictions cannot be induced with the force, in spite of what Virgil Starkwell's father in *Take the Money and Run* seems to believe when he proudly keeps on saying he "tried to beat God" into his son.

22. World Bank, *World Development Indicators* (Washington, D.C.: World Bank, 2005).

23. See Nadia Urbinati, *I confini della democrazia. Opportunità e rischi dell'universalismo democratico* (Roma: Donzelli, 2007).

24. See, for instance, Mary Kaldor, ed., *Europe from Below: An East-West Dialogue* (London: Verso, 1991).

25. For a disenchanted analysis, see Mary Kaldor and Denisa Kostovicova, "Global Civil Society and Illiberal Regimes" and Armine Ishkanian, "Democracy Promotion and Civil Society," both in *Global Civil Society 2006/7*, ed. Mary Kaldor, Helmut K. Anheier, Marlies Glasius, 86–113 and 58–85 respectively (London: Sage, 2007).

26. It may also help revise or even overcome some excessive limit imposed by the principle of noninterference, which recently some countries still embracing death penalty have evoked against external pressure to start considering human life as an unquestionable and untouchable good.

27. Ramesh Thakur, "Law, Legitimacy and United Nations," see chapter XX, p. XX.

28. For a review, see Arne Tostensen and Beate Bull, "Are Smart Sanctions Feasible?" *World Politics* 2, no. 54 (2002): 373–403, esp. 399–403.

29. See Mario Telò, *Europe: A Civilian Power: European Union, Global Governance, World Order* (Houndsmill: Palgrave, 2005).

30. Bartholomew, "Legality/Legitimacy," chapter XX, p. XX.

31. Orford, "Responsibility to Protect," chapter XX, p. XX."

32. James Crawford, "Democracy and International Law," *The British Yearbook of International Law* (1993): 113–133, here 117–119.

33. To understand the cosmopolitan project beyond this concise sketch, see Archibugi, *Global Commonwealth of Citizens*; David Held, *Global Covenant: The Social Democratic Alternative to the Washington Consensus* (Cambridge: Polity Press, 2004).

34. Susan Marks, *The Riddle of All Constitutions: International Law, Democracy and the Critique of Ideology* (Oxford: Oxford University Press, 2000), 106.

35. Christine Chinkin, "Rethinking Legality/Legitimacy after the Iraq War," chapter XX, p. XX.

36. See the chapter entitled "The Decline of the Nation-State and the End of Human Rights," in Hannah Arendt, *The Origins of Totalitarianism* (London: Trinity Press, 1950).

15

Conclusion: Legitimacy as Complement and Corrective to Legality

Vesselin Popovski and Nicholas Turner

Assessments of acceptable state behavior can be based on a variety of criteria. In international order, such assessments are primarily made with reference to the system of recognized standards and agreements among states; international law can define a certain act as legal or illegal. However, other criteria—humanitarian, ethical, and political—can clearly play a significant role in judging state behavior in modern international relations. These often find expression as assessments of the legitimacy of certain regimes and acts. While legitimacy considerations would complement international legality in most circumstances, there are situations when legality could be challenged by the ethical, humanitarian, or political demands of legitimacy. This is most evident in situations where strict adherence to international law would lead to considerable harm, and questions are raised of whether it would be appropriate or beneficial to seek alternatives. In extreme cases, such alternatives are sought in the form of direct challenges to legality, rejecting its constraints, advocating and even undertaking illegal actions.

The development of the legitimacy narrative has drawn more attention to questions of appropriate authority to act coercively in contested situations, when the basis for assessment does not belong to the primacy or relevance of international law. This narrative breaks free from the straitjacket of legalism and evaluates state behavior with sensitive reflection on ethical and political considerations, loosening the constraints of legality and embracing humanitarian and moral discourse to justify controversial policy. Undoubtedly, legitimacy enters into consideration in particular when the issues at stake are highest and international law is most rigid, such as the global distribution of power, the norms of recourse to force, the interplay between states and within states in times of violence, postwar arrangements, the nature of power leadership, and geopolitics, among others.

Indeed, it was in such a situation that the "illegal but legitimate" argument rose to prominence—the 1999 NATO intervention over Kosovo was conducted on the claimed basis of humanitarian necessity, but it violated the international legal prohibition on the use of force, Article 2/4 of the UN Charter. International lawyers and statesmen were divided between those who supported the intervention, and those upholding the strict UN Charter prohibition on the use of force. The debate further reflected the opposing concerns of those who saw this as an example of legitimizing an act which otherwise was legally dubious, but necessary for a higher humanitarian purpose—saving human life; and those more concerned with not creating loopholes in the regime of prohibiting unauthorized intervention.

Thus the Kosovo intervention, as well as the Nuremberg tribunal and other circumstances explored within this volume, highlights a perceived disconnection between international legality and legitimacy. This is also evident in situations where actions are undertaken with a clear legal mandate, but are nevertheless seen as illegitimate. A revealing example would be the sanctions imposed on Iraq for over a decade by the United Nations Security Council (UNSC), from 1991 to 2003. Under international law, the sanctions were perfectly authorized by the UNSC's powers under Chapter VII, but their legitimacy was highly questionable as they led to widespread suffering among civilians. These cases also reveal that discords between legality- and legitimacy-based assessments of behavior are not confined to the context of military intervention, even if it is here where they have drawn most debate and concern. The deep and polarized nature of these tensions even suggests that these cases could be merely symptomatic of a wider discord in international order.

Explaining such tensions relies not only upon examining past, present, or potential future cases, but also on an appreciation of the exact qualities of the relationship between legality and legitimacy. This theoretical understanding itself rests on how the two concepts are defined and applied. The preceding chapters have offered a variety of interpretations of and insights on these questions, whether tackling them in general terms or informed by the context and specifics of particular issue-areas, from nuclear nonproliferation to international criminal tribunals and environmental governance. They have shown that, if anything, legitimacy is a more contested and subjective concept than legality, including elements of morality, public support, and participation in decision-making processes. Accounts of legitimacy clearly vary in their consideration of how it is constituted, who or what is the source of legitimacy, and who can make such judgments. But there is general agreement that legitimacy constitutes a more variable category of norms, and can be built up, or lost, over time, whereas legality judgments are more clearly deterministic and binary.

Under the natural law conception of legality, it exists in a social context where it may be challenged on moral grounds. By this understanding, legitimacy justifications can be invoked as a necessary corrective to laws that sanction harm, or are detached from human aspirations or actual circumstances. This conception would suggest that the relationship between legality and legitimacy can take on a different character—harmonious, contradictory, or progressive. Legitimacy does not necessarily replace or transcend legality—as long as laws reflect public expectations, legitimacy supports and strengthens legality, adding more authoritative power to treaty-based or customary rules. But when laws are seen as harmful or obstructing progress, legitimate actions are sometimes conducted outside the law, challenging legality. The resulting discord can then produce adjustments and corrections to law, thereby closing gaps between legality and legitimacy and regaining harmony.

Conversely, the existence of any discord between legality and legitimacy would be denied by legal positivism, which equates the two and sees laws as rules to be followed regardless of circumstances. Legal positivists would maintain that only legal actions can be legitimate, and warn of the dangers of allowing any departure from legal constraints.

States can and do ignore international law, and disregard even their own previously signed treaties. President Kim Jong Il withdrew North Korea from the Nuclear Non-Proliferation Treaty (NPT) in order to develop a nuclear capacity. President George W. Bush "un-signed" the Rome Statute of the International Criminal Court and imposed bilateral sanctions on states that were signatories to this statute. The lack of a global parliament (legislature), a global government (executive), and a global police force already allows states to manipulate and violate laws, and so any weakening or undermining of legal constraints invites further abuse. But the law does not become irrelevant because it is violated by individual, self-interested states.

Whether or not claims of legitimacy can trump legality in any particular case, there is a clear need to understand the nature and implications of the relationship between the two, and to ascertain the existence of a gap. If a gap does exist, this raises the inevitable question of how it could be reconciled, and if indeed this would be beneficial. It is such difficulties that formed the subject of this enquiry—the proper framing of the relationship between legality and legitimacy, the nature of the two concepts, and the implications for international order.

Below we briefly highlight the principal contributions of each chapter, both in terms of substance and methodology. It is our hope that the cumulative impact of the volume becomes clearer, as well as that doing so gives a broad overview of the various approaches taken to the legality/legitimacy distinction by the authors with an eye to overall coherence despite considerable diversity of approach and assessment.

In the opening chapter, Richard Falk outlines the key tensions in the relationship between legality and legitimacy, to highlight both the potential dangers and the benefits of vindicating legitimacy as an alternative to legality. He warns that disregarding international law risks setting precedents, as evident with the invocation of the Kosovo precedent during the build-up to the 2003 Iraq war. Falk acknowledges that allowing flexibility outside the law could create further opportunities for the perpetuation of the prevailing geopolitical primacy. However, international law itself is inherently vulnerable to manipulation by powerful states, in the absence of international legislative agency. Legitimacy, being based more in the wider domain of society and public morality, has potential as a less power-driven corrective to legality's narrow concern with state action. In this sense, invoking legitimacy arguments in exceptional circumstances can be seen either as introducing necessary flexibility or as creating space for geopolitical opportunism.

Falk addresses the Kosovo Commission's attempts to reconcile and explain that the NATO intervention, while a violation of international law, nevertheless had a net positive outcome. In the context of the subsequent development of the responsibility to protect (R2P), he highlights the question of whether to encourage an explicit framework for exceptional cases or to leave such decisions to the interplay of opinions in each instance. In raising the possibility of a renewed appetite for the authority of legal texts as a backlash against contempt for international law, Falk sees the fixed nature of law combined with rapidly changing conditions as likely to reinvigorate the legality-legitimacy discourse in areas other than the use of force. His argument suggests that the flexibility provided by legitimacy is indeed beneficial, but that clearly if there was greater legitimacy of law itself, and of the processes by which it is made, there would be less need to invoke such alternatives.

Ramesh Thakur's chapter examines both the symbolic and the practical implications of the underestimated gulf between lawful and legitimate behavior, at and by the United Nations. He cites the use of comprehensive trade sanctions as an example of legal but discredited measures which have eroded the UN's legitimacy. Despite their solid legal basis in the UN Charter, sanctions inflict harm mainly on the general population and are usually ineffective—if not actively counterproductive by strengthening repressive regimes. Thakur also questions the legitimacy of the global nuclear order, whereby the permanent members of the UNSC are neglecting their disarmament obligations while at the same time aggressively enforcing the nonproliferation elements of the NPT. The United Nations remains a channel between legal authority and political legitimacy, but while the UNSC is the core enforcement mechanism for international law, its numerous representative and legitimacy deficits have resulted in states increasingly willing to defy its authority.

Thakur stresses that in order for the United Nations to effectively promote values such as accountability and good governance, it must exemplify those values in its own behavior, calling upon examples where they have been lacking to various degrees, including those of the North-South divide evident within the United Nations, the selection process for the position of secretary-general, and the problem of abuses committed by UN peacekeepers. His analysis suggests that the category of legitimacy should serve to close the gap between power and justice in international affairs. Thakur also highlights the impunity for violations of law by powerful states and draws attention to the dangers of the language of human rights being appropriated in the service of power and geopolitical interests, further exacerbating the divergence of legality and legitimacy.

The following chapter by Andrew Loomis explores the processes and means by which legitimacy considerations impact upon international politics. He casts the tension between legality and legitimacy as one between stability and transformation, which is ultimately resolved through the political process. Loomis observes that the rigidity of legal structures normally impedes the capacity of norms to influence political outcomes. When norms evolve beyond law, the two are in tension and legitimacy leads the way as a catalyst for incremental change in legal regimes. Loomis advances the idea that the people are the right constituency to initiate such change in international politics, and therefore to take a central role in making legitimacy assessments.

Public demands for legitimacy involve different criteria than those of the political elites who design and implement policy. Such elites are accountable for policy success, and thus make judgments in mainly utilitarian terms, while the public is both more able and more inclined to evaluate policy in normative terms. Loomis suggests that while legal norms are vital in judgments by policy elites, moral and societal standards of legitimacy hold greater value to the wider public. He sees the sensitivity of policy elites to public legitimacy claims, and their strategic use of legitimacy norms, as evidence that such norms constrain policy choices—and thereby insists that any comprehensive account of legitimacy in international politics must include a thorough examination of the public voice.

Amy Bartholomew's chapter offers a sophisticated and nuanced response to arguments (epitomized in many Bush administration policies) that marginalize international law. In recent years, such arguments have been evident both in the contempt in which international law has been held and in the reactionary urge to reject law as an "instrument of empire." Bartholomew asserts that American empire depends on law, and more alarmingly, it threatens to produce what she terms "empire's law," characterized by a state treating others as the addressees of law while exempting itself from legal obligations. Bartholomew contrasts this empire's law—law made by arbitrary sovereign decision—with legitimate law, to suggest that the question of whether a certain law is legitimate or not depends both upon law's internal legitimacy and upon its relation to external democratic processes of legitimization.

Empire's law threatens both the internal legitimacy of law and the possibilities for its external democratic legitimization. In this sense, the Bush administration's manipulations of law to reflect the empire's goals were worse than merely lawless acts and had much more ominous implications. Thus, Bartholomew emphasizes the importance of not only developing and defending legitimate legality, but of doing so as part of a wider politics that rejects the legitimacy of empire.

Friedrich Kratochwil examines the changing notion of sovereignty—a concept established by, and central to, international law—which has been seriously challenged by the legitimacy debate. He suggests that in its dependence upon empirical methods, the conventional analysis of the theory of sovereignty has been flawed and argues that the meaning of sovereignty is rather established by its use and by its connections with other concepts such as legitimacy that authorize or reject certain practices. In his casting of sovereignty, it serves to link decisions with the notion of legitimacy—that they should have authority and be respected by its subjects. Sovereignty plays a crucial legitimizing role in domestic politics, but in its external dimension it has been transformed from the politics of nationalism and identity, to international recognition by states now dependent upon participation in international organizations, revealing the communal character of such judgments.

Kratochwil maintains that real situations cannot be reduced to universalist principles; principles cannot prescribe their own application, rather, they must always be interpreted, developed, sustained—or legitimized. He questions the sustainability of the continued global emphasis on consumption and free trade as one example, given the role the people have assumed as providers of sources of law. His analysis suggests that when individuals are participants in, and not simply subjects of, sovereignty, it must be regarded as vital for the political project of humanity.

In his chapter, Yasuaki Onuma discusses the dynamic correlation of law and power and the problems of legitimacy in international society. He notes that law is needed by powerful states to legitimize their dominance, to instrumentally decrease the political costs of hegemony by securing voluntary submissions to their authority. Yet law also provides opportunities for the weak to challenge the powerful, and this is respected—if reluctantly—by the latter, in pragmatic recognition of the costs of ignoring the law.

Onuma offers a nuanced understanding of the relationship between law and power and examines the constructive, constitutive function of international law. He finds that normative ideas can constitute power, even though they require power in order to be disseminated and exercise influence. The power of international law depends upon its legitimacy—if norms of law are perceived as illegitimate, doubts will be raised as to whether they should be obeyed. Onuma advances a trans-civilizational perspective on international law, supplementing and modifying the prevalent, West-centric perspectives of the international and the transnational. He asserts that existing international and transnational perspectives neglect the aspirations, expectations, and frustrations of over 80% of the global population, and therefore it is necessary to rectify this imbalance, to achieve a greater global legitimacy and relevance to the expected realities of power in the twenty-first century. Onuma's argument suggests that strengthening the legitimacy of international law through the adoption of a trans-civilizational perspective, with greater attention to culture, religion, and history, is vital for today's global system.

Similarly, Giles Gunn's chapter further examines how the normative basis of legitimacy is constituted. Gunn suggests that it may be difficult to think in "trans-civilizational" terms in today's increasingly fragmented world. He observes a form of opposition between the global and the local and highlights the difficulties involved in finding elements within various civilizations that could constitute common or shared values. New forms of the "clash of civilizations" thesis—those of a clash *within* civilizations—are evident in terms of secularism and extremism, between various forms of geopolitical organization, and between integration and separatism. However, in Gunn's analysis, the divide between the global North and the global South constitutes the clash with the most powerful argument for an inter-civilizational perspective rather than a transnational one.

Gunn calls for a reconceptualization of what is perceived to be human, as a process rather than a condition—in that the human is dependent upon learning from its exposure to otherness. By this understanding, all human experiences are potentially instructive, yielding insights not only for the individual, but also for cultures and civilizations. In advocating his concept of the intercivilizational over Onuma's of the trans-civilizational, Gunn suggests that it avoids the pitfalls of reductionism and universalism, while allowing us to see the other as a potential collaborator for our mutual benefit. He maintains that this conception of the intercivilizational, supported by a re-conceived notion of the human, provides a better account of the normative basis of legitimacy. Gunn asserts that it is through otherness that individuals, cultures, and civilizations become instruments for self-formation—and that if the normative can transform this otherness, it can indeed transcend the legal.

The volume's second part addresses more specific settings or international regimes wherein the legality/legitimacy distinction offers either opportunities for analysis and policy, or presents divergences. The first such area is the legality and legitimacy of military interventions by Western powers, examined by Christine Chinkin in her chapter by tracing their evolution from the end of the Cold War until the 2003 Iraq war. In the 1990s, the UNSC understood—and applied—the notion of a threat to international peace and security in an expanded range of circumstances. Powerful states have also intervened without explicit UNSC approval, instead either claiming legality outside the charter, or asserting legitimacy in its absence. Chinkin draws attention to the difficulty in assessing legality and legitimacy, and in particular to when and how such judgments should be made. Legality relies on compliance with binding rules, while legitimacy is based in subjective, changing perceptions. Indeed, legitimacy can expose gaps between such perceptions and law. Therefore actions seen as "illegal but legitimate" or "legal but illegitimate" raise serious questions regarding the legitimacy of law itself—and of the institutions and processes by which it is made.

The military interventions in Kosovo, Afghanistan, and Iraq have all contributed to a legitimacy deficit of the international legal system in the post–Cold War period. Chinkin suggests, similarly to Falk, that the Kosovo intervention may have directly influenced further unauthorized actions, including the Iraq war. Following the 2003 invasion of Iraq, the coalition desperately sought symbolic legitimacy, while the United Nations tried to repair the damage that this unauthorized action had done to its reputation. Chinkin argues that the UNSC continues to be instrumentalized by permanent members in furtherance of their national interests. She cautions against the continuing displacement of international legality by powerful states' assertions of legitimacy, but highlights and advocates the balancing effect of civil society, media, legal activism, and scholarship.

Anne Orford also tackles the legality and legitimacy of intervention, but concentrates in particular on the shift from the concept of humanitarian intervention to that of R2P. She asserts that the legitimacy arguments invoked in support of Kosovo intervention were based in a metaphysical conception of law, whereby universal values transcend particular laws. Suggesting that humanitarian intervention's appeal to universal values shielded it from discussion and distanced it from politics, Orford welcomes R2P as a shift away from abstract universal notions, bringing a conception of law closer to the practicalities of international relations. She acknowledges the long history of international legal obligations for states to protect their citizens against atrocity crimes, but suggests that the value of R2P is in its idea of an international duty, of attendant obligations for the international community. As R2P brings not only the responsibility to react to crises, but also to prevent harm and to rebuild, the protection role of international governance is expanded, raising further questions such as how the international community's authority can be legal and legitimate. The shift from humanitarian intervention to R2P reveals such questions to be fundamentally political, to be answered in political terms.

The responsibility to protect provides a focus on how to guarantee security and protection for vulnerable people, which Orford suggests is much better suited to political analysis than are metaphysical questions such as how to ensure the universal values of humanity. She notes that much of the pro-humanitarian-intervention literature simply sees the international community as a benevolent actor and fails to acknowledge that intervention could create new exploitative relations and grievances. Orford concludes that such risks further underline the value of R2P in raising issues of legitimacy and political authority which should be central to any intervention.

Mark Juergensmeyer's chapter examines the legality and legitimacy of regime change, taking the war in Afghanistan in 2001 as a point of departure. At the time, forceful arguments were put forward advocating the removal of the Taliban regime purely on the basis of its nature as an extreme religious regime, in addition to its alleged links to al Qaeda. It is toward this controversy that Juergensmeyer directs his analysis, examining the possibility for such moral justifications for toppling regimes that base their political legitimacy in religion. He suggests that religious regimes can be relatively flexible and produce change from within, as evident in the diversity of political positions in the Islamic Republic of Iran. But religious positions—especially when supported by assertions of divine mandate—can also be rigid and authoritarian, particularly concerning matters of morality. While the same can be true of secular regimes, these have overwhelmingly progressed from systems of central authority to those of democracy, with elected representatives and independent judiciaries.

Religions ultimately place greater value on the will of God than on the will of people; and indeed, religious figures often criticize democracy as a system of pandering to the self-interests of various groups. But almost every religious nationalist movement has rejected theocracy—rule by the clergy. While democratic theorists would argue that the system legitimates itself, religious politicians hold that it must be put to higher purposes—and thereby achieve moral validity. Juergensmeyer claims that while most religious regimes would not identify and protect *rights* as such, they mostly uphold some fairly equivalent concept of human dignity and personal security. Although there remain fundamental cultural differences between individualistic and collectivistic societies, Juergensmeyer maintains that it is highly questionable whether these differences can justify the removal of religious regimes. Nevertheless, he suggests that there may be cases of widespread human rights abuses in which at least moral legitimacy, if not legal authority, for intervention exists.

Aslı Bâli's chapter draws attention to the negative implications of undermining legality through legitimacy justifications in the context of the arms control regime. Bâli warns that the logic underlying humanitarian intervention has recently been stretched to provide a new basis for interventionism involving unilateral preemptive and even preventive use of force to destroy potential weapons-producing facilities. Extending intervention arguments, particularly on the basis of unilateral threat determinations, undermines and destabilizes the collective security mechanism of the UN system. This is particularly dangerous in the context of the nuclear nonproliferation regime, at a time when its core bargain is already under intense pressure.

Bâli observes that the disarmament commitments of the Nuclear Non-Proliferation Treaty (NPT) have been ignored or disregarded by nuclear states, which have also restricted access to nuclear technologies. Of most concern is the emergence of strong unilateral approaches to counter-proliferation, which raise the alarming possibility of preventive military intervention in the name of nonproliferation. These tendencies in their totality threaten to incentivize weak states to acquire new deterrent capabilities—a distortion of the nuclear nonproliferation regime's incentive structure that Bâli cautions could even bring about a new nuclear age. On the central question related to the norm of conditional sovereignty—whether to permit "legitimate" departures from legality, or whether to maintain constraints on geopolitical discretion—Bâli argues that such constraints are vital to the stability of the international security order.

In her chapter, Lorraine Elliot explores legality and legitimacy issues in the context of global environmental governance. Legitimacy concerns are relevant in this area primarily due to the widely acknowledged failure of political institutions to respond adequately to climate change, as well as the exclusion of much of civil society from representation within such governance. Elliot suggests that the nature of environmental change, transcending national borders and demanding effective political responses that states alone cannot provide, questions the very relevance of sovereignty. She criticizes the statist concept of international environmental law, which sees states as both the authors of legal order and subjects of law, and therefore those whose consent is required for legitimacy. Authority in environmental governance is no longer held exclusively by states, because private actors, functioning independently, are increasingly taking on regulatory roles, deriving legitimacy from their scientific credibility, rather than by being established by states.

In making assessments of legitimacy, Elliot maintains that we must consider whose needs count, as well as what criteria apply. Environmental challenges highlight the problem of conceiving legitimacy in international order as constituted by a community of states without a proper notion of global citizenship—those directly affected by policies have little say in their formation or application. Environmental harms, with their associated social, political, and economic implications, are inflicted transnationally, often against those most vulnerable. In the long term, all citizens will eventually suffer from the effects of environmental change, and so global citizens should be the constituency of global environmental governance. Therefore, Elliot suggests, legality is not sufficient for governance to be legitimate; rather, it depends upon recognition of the global nature of its constituency and the duties arising from environmental injustices within this constituency. Furthermore, the institutions and rules of environmental governance must be accountable to their constituents and perform effectively to build trust. Elliot concludes with an appeal for continuous scrutiny of consent and legitimacy, not only that of specific rules and decisions, but that of the entire system of global environmental governance.

Vesselin Popovski's chapter considers the legality and legitimacy of international criminal tribunals, from Nuremburg to the International Criminal Court (ICC). He traces arguments supporting and objecting to these tribunals from both legality and legitimacy perspectives and reflects on the implications for the relationship between the two concepts. Popovski sees the Nuremberg and Tokyo trials as good examples of a disconnection between legitimacy and legality, which later forced international law to address the gaps they highlighted. The trials were exceptional, unprecedented measures, replete with legal shortages, but were nevertheless accepted as a best choice against the alternatives of extrajudicial executions or amnesty. They suffered from numerous legal failings related to their establishment and flaws in legal procedure, but despite these shortcomings, they gradually gained widespread legitimacy by contributing to sustained peace in Germany and Japan, and implementing the concept of individual criminal accountability in international law.

This implementation progressed with the ad hoc International Criminal Tribunals for the former Yugoslavia and for Rwanda (ICTY and ICTR). Their legality was also challenged by defense lawyers on several grounds, such as their establishment by a political organ—the UNSC—rather than by law. But in terms of process, ICTY and ICTR provided very robust guarantees of proof beyond reasonable doubt that were in fact even higher than those of domestic courts. Popovski suggests that the ad hoc tribunals served to fill a gap in the international system, in the absence of an international criminal court or the necessary domestic capacity. The creation of the ICC aimed to address this gap permanently, demonstrating the desire of the international community to enhance the enforcement of international humanitarian law and human rights law. While acknowledging the persisting uncertainties and legitimacy problems of the ICC, along with strong opposition from powerful states, Popovski suggests that it benefits from its complementarity to domestic jurisdiction, stringent legal procedures, and close relations with civil society. Popovski concludes that assessments of legitimacy will naturally vary between victims seeking justice and compensation on the one hand, and the needs of societal reconciliation on the other. In this sense, legitimacy is essential in considering the need to balance demands for justice with considerations of communal cohesiveness. To achieve greater legitimacy, a wider conception of justice that follows the spirit as well as the letter of the law would be preferable and accordingly criminal justice must be complemented by social justice.

The final chapter by Daniele Archibugi and Mariano Croce provides an assessment of the concept of exporting democracy, informed by distinctions between legality and legitimacy. They suggest that the notion of democratic participation constitutes the relationship between the two, by both constructing criteria for legitimacy and providing a rationale for the enforcement of laws. Indeed, when legitimacy is separated from democratic participation, it is vulnerable to manipulation and self-serving instrumentalization. Archibugi and Croce see exporting democracy as an inconsistent concept, paradoxically denying the affected people the opportunity to democratically decide on their form of government. Using force as the means to promote democracy is ineffective historically, and is both illegal and illegitimate—not least because democracy is a nonviolent regime. Violence will inevitably harm the individuals who are supposed to benefit from, and be protected by, democracy.

Using persuasive rather than coercive means to export democracy avoids many of these difficulties. Democracy can be promoted through a combination of top-down economic and political incentives offered by democratic states, as well as bottom-up progress with improved links and cooperation between citizens. Archibugi and Croce suggest that as far as peaceful means are used to pursue an internal process of democracy, rather than an externally imposed change in the system, they can be seen as both legal and legitimate. Conversely, invoking democracy as a justification for acting illegally both weakens international legality and appropriates legitimacy. The authors highlight a deficit of democratic participation in international legitimacy and advocate peacefully spreading democracy as a way forward. This would enlarge the basis for legitimization of the international legal system and encourage cooperation for necessary reform of international regulations, by both modifying international legality and agreeing on criteria for corrective legitimacy.

As we hope this brief overview has shown, all the chapters of the volume, through their diverse array of approaches, illustrations, and interpretations, provide numerous significant conclusions that will serve to further the ongoing debates on these issues. In both its conceptual and its practical dimensions, the relationship between legality and legitimacy will undoubtedly remain a major theme to address in future academic research and policy.

INDEX